# ANCIENT PAINTING

Plate I. Naples. National Museum. "Flora," from Stabiæ. First Century A.D.

# ANCIENT PAINTING

## FROM THE EARLIEST TIMES TO THE PERIOD OF CHRISTIAN ART

BY MARY HAMILTON SWINDLER, Ph.D.

ASSOCIATE PROFESSOR OF LATIN AND CLASSICAL ARCHÆOLOGY
IN BRYN MAWR COLLEGE

NEW HAVEN · YALE UNIVERSITY PRESS

LONDON · HUMPHREY MILFORD · OXFORD UNIVERSITY PRESS

1929

TO

CAROLINE RANSOM WILLIAMS

*IN APPRECIATION OF HER QUALITIES AS*

*SCHOLAR, TEACHER, AND FRIEND*

# PREFACE

THERE exists today no monumental work on Ancient Painting which is concerned with material antedating the period of Christian art. German archæologists may have in mind such a publication in *Denkmäler der Malerei,* which is being edited by Herrmann and which up to the present has dealt with Pompeian wall-paintings and a few mosaics. There is no handbook treating the subject except the one by P. Girard, *La Peinture antique,* dating from the year 1892. Most of the research in this field has been confined to single investigations, covering some one branch of the subject, such as Etruscan painting, Greek vases, or Egyptian tomb-decoration. On the other hand, a history of Ancient Painting cannot be written until many more investigations have been made, notably in Egypt, Etruria, and the East.

It is hoped that this book will fill the very definite need which exists for a work on Ancient Painting. The discovery of many new monuments, such as the wall-paintings from Crete and Rome, the painted stelæ from Pagasæ, and wall-decorations as far afield as Southern Russia and Palestine, calls for a discussion of new material; increased research, which has advanced our knowledge of various fields, demands a revision of our information about many phases of the subject. Such a consideration must of necessity enrich our knowledge of painting in general and of Greek painting in particular.

This book is designed primarily for students of Classical Archæology, and for students of Art in general. The survey of ancient civilizations which is presented will also, we believe, prove useful to students of History. Last of all, it is hoped that it may interest the general reader and that he may find in the pages which follow something of the achievement of the painter in ancient times and of his influence on the art of later ages.

The plan of the book is relatively simple: beginning with the earliest attempts at painting in prehistoric times, the chapters follow in chronological order the development of Egyptian, Oriental, Cretan, and Greek work, and range in time down through Etruscan, Pompeian, Græco-Roman, and Roman painting. In beginning the book some years ago, I was primarily interested in bringing together available material for a survey of Greek painting, but it becomes increasingly evident that Greek art cannot be treated as an isolated phenomenon. Its prehistory and early stages must be examined and this examination involves a consideration of Egyptian and Oriental art. I have prefixed the chapter on prehistoric painting in order to show how the primitive artist functioned; primitive peoples after him, arriving at the same stage of development, have met his problems in a similar way. We may later have more knowledge of this Magdalenian artist and of his relation to the culture of the ages following his appearance. Finally, I have allowed myself to digress at several points to discuss technical problems, drawing, and other topics of interest.

For the benefit of those who wish to pursue the various chapters beyond the limits of the text, I have added detailed bibliographies at the end of the book. It is not claimed that these are exhaustive but the standard works have, I believe, been cited, and those of most importance to the student and to the general reader. I have also included a general bibliography of books and articles which summarize the entire field of Ancient Painting.

I am indebted to many scholars who have been generous enough to read the manuscript and to offer suggestions and criticisms, but who are in no way responsible for the opinions expressed. I wish to express my gratitude to those who have read the entire book: Professor George H. Chase, Professor and Dean of the Graduate School of Arts and Sciences of Harvard University; Professor D. M. Robinson, Vickers Professor of Archæology, Johns Hopkins University; Miss Gisela M. A. Richter, Curator of Classical Art in the Metropolitan Museum, New York; Professor Rhys Carpenter, Director of the American School for Classical Studies in Athens; and Professor Alfred Mansfield Brooks, Professor of Art in Swarthmore College. Professor George Grant MacCurdy of Yale University and Mrs. MacCurdy very kindly read and criticized the chapter on the Cave-Paintings; Professor George A. Barton of the University of Pennsylvania, Mr. John Maynard, formerly of Bryn Mawr College, and M. Léon Legrain, Curator of the Babylonian Section of the Museum of the University of Pennsylvania, the chapter on the Orient. Dr. Edith Hall Dohan read the Ægean material, and Professor Carl Blegen of the University of Cincinnati offered some helpful suggestions where this chapter touched the mainland of Greece. Mr. Prentice Duell, Lecturer in Classical Archæology at Bryn Mawr College, aided me in the chapter on Etruria, and Professor Rostovtzeff of Yale University kindly read the Hellenistic chapter. I am very grateful to Mr. J. D. Beazley, Lincoln Professor of Classical Archæology in the University of Oxford, for criticizing the chronological table of vase-painters. The late Professor Joseph Clark Hoppin, Research Professor in the American School at Athens, had read the Greek chapters which deal especially with vases. I am indebted to Dr. Alice Walton, Professor of Latin in Wellesley College, for notes on the stelæ from Pagasæ. I wish to acknowledge my gratitude to Miss Helen Fernald, Assistant Curator of the Section of Far Eastern Art in the Museum of the University of Pennsylvania, who made several maps and drawings in the book. She has also been good enough to help me with her criticism of the text. My former student, Dr. Marjorie Milne, now Assistant in the Classical Department of the Metropolitan Museum, New York, has been of the greatest assistance to me. She has read the manuscript critically and verified the material in some of the Greek chapters. She has made many valuable additions and has saved me from many inaccuracies. Another one of my students, Miss Mary Wyckoff, drew the head- and tailpieces in the book and much merits my appreciation.

I am under great obligations to many friends who have made possible some of the things indispensable in this book: to Mr. H. M. Pierce of Wilmington, Delaware, who gave the colored plates; to Mrs. Joseph Clark Hoppin of New York; Mr. Stephen B. Luce of Boston; Mr. George Parmly Day of the Yale University Press, Mr. Albert Gallatin of New York, and Miss Frances Browne of Bryn Mawr. My sincere thanks are due for what they have done.

I wish to thank those who have helped in making the book, especially Mr. Charles R. Pancoast of Germantown who produced most of the photographs for the plates and Mr. Richard Deats of Philadelphia, his successor, who also furnished some of the photographic material; to Miss Rose Bruckner, who prepared the manuscript, I am also under obligations. The color plates are the work of Zeese-Wilkinson Co., Inc., Long Island City, N. Y.

Finally, Dr. Caroline Ransom Williams, formerly Associate Professor of Classical Archæology at Bryn Mawr College and Assistant Curator in the Egyptian Department of the Metropolitan Museum of Art, and now Honorary Curator of the New York Historical Society, has aided me in countless ways with the chapter on Egypt. I take pleasure in dedicating to her this book, which owes its origin to work done as a student in her courses.

I have tried to acknowledge in detail my indebtedness to the various scholars who have worked in Ancient Painting. The Germans have been the pioneers in this field and their names form a brilliant galaxy. The English, French, and Italian scholars follow, with many famous signatures in the field of vase-painting, methods of painting, and research in Egypt and Etruria. The Greeks have had not a few scholars of note, especially in the Cretan and Northern Greek fields, and Denmark has also furnished its quota. America has produced some well-known names in vase-painting. To all of these I am indebted. Finally, to the many scholars and publishers who have been kind enough to allow me to reproduce material belonging to them, I am most grateful and tender my thanks. A list of these acknowledgments will be found in the opening pages. To publishers, who, like Macmillan & Co., Ltd., London, have aided me in procuring permissions for reproductions, additional thanks are due. I take this opportunity here to thank for unusual courtesy, Paul Geuthner, Henri Laurens, and Ernest Leroux of Paris; Max Niemeyer, Halle; Walter de Gruyter & Co., Berlin; the Alfred Kröner Verlag, Leipzig; and F. Bruckmann A.-G., München. The latter firm has allowed me to reproduce large numbers of plates from Furtwängler, Reichhold, *Griechische Vasenmalerei*. These are referred to in the list of illustrations as *F.R. Griechische Vasenmalerei*. The trustees of the British Museum, the Reale Accademia dei Lincei, the École Française d'Athènes, the Académie des Inscriptions et Belles-Lettres, the Council of the Hellenic Society, the German Archæological Institute, the Metropolitan and Boston Museums and the Faculty of the British School in Rome all merit additional mention for their kindness. Finally, I must thank Dr. Rodenwaldt, Sir Arthur Evans, the Abbé Breuil, Sir W. M. F. Petrie, M. Morin-Jean and Dr. B. Nogara for their generosity in allowing me to use material published by them. I am also greatly indebted to Alinari, Ltd., Rome, for permission to reproduce photographs.

Lastly, I wish to thank the Yale University Press for its interest in the production of the book and for its unvarying courtesy and consideration. Warm thanks are due to Mr. George Parmly Day, its President; to Mr. Norman V. Donaldson of the Educational Department, and especially to Mr. George T. Bailey, Manager of the Manufacturing Department, for making the book what it is.

Some fifteen years have been spent in the preparation of the manuscript, with various summers in Italy, Egypt, Greece, the Caves of France, and the Museums of Europe. The shortcomings of the book are obvious to no one so much as the author; another ten years could be spent in working over the material, especially with the constantly increasing discoveries. It is hoped that the work will be useful. It has been difficult to cover all of the material and keep a proper balance. Some will doubtless prefer to emphasize points which I have neglected. The less significant things are oftentimes passed over with nothing more than bibliography. This is true of some of the paintings in the provinces, such as those of France, Britain, and Hungary. No attempt has been made to touch upon Greek influence in the paintings of the Caves at Ajanta. The Far East has not been included. Those monuments have been chosen for discussion which seemed most significant for the student of Classical Archæology and most important for their influence on the development of painting.

In the matter of spelling, I have tried to follow the Greek forms except where the word has become so well established in the Latin form by usage that it would be pedantry to employ the Greek. This system naturally leads to inconsistencies which will trouble the reader less, I hope, than they have troubled the writer. Some hybrid spellings have been included, such as Polykleitan and Sikyonian, which cannot be justified, but which have seemed more in harmony with the Greek spelling. The matter of consistency is a difficult one to compass in a book of this size. How much time may be spent upon it the reader may gather by looking into the problem of stags, goats, does, gazelles, antelopes, oryxes, chamois—or whatever they may be—on Greek vases. Stele and stelæ are written as the more usual forms.

The writer wishes to emphasize the fact that every known painting and mosaic from ancient times is not discussed in the volume in hand. An attempt has been made to treat examples characteristic of each age and in this selection it is believed that fairly representative material has been secured.

To those who would wish to have the book different, we can only say in the words of Apollodoros: It is easier to criticize than to imitate.

M. H. S.

*Bryn Mawr College,*
   *August* 29, 1929.

# CONTENTS

# ABBREVIATIONS

| | |
|---|---|
| *A.J.A.* | American Journal of Archæology |
| *Annali* | Annali dell'Instituto archeologico |
| *Ant. Denk.* | Antike Denkmäler |
| *Arch. Anz.* | Archäologischer Anzeiger, in Jahrbuch des Deutschen archäologischen Instituts |
| *Ath. Mitth.* | Mittheilungen des kaiserlich deutschen archäologischen Instituts, Athenische Abtheilung |
| *A.Z.* | Archäologische Zeitung |
| *B.C.H.* | Bulletin de correspondance hellénique |
| *B.P.W.* | Berliner philologische Wochenschrift |
| *B.S.A.* | Annual of the British School at Athens |
| *B.S.R.* | Papers of the British School at Rome |
| *C.A.H.* | Cambridge Ancient History |
| *C.R.* | Compte-rendu de la commission impériale archéologique, St.-Pétersbourg |
| *C.V.* | Corpus Vasorum Antiquorum |
| *Eph. Arch.* | Archaiologike Ephemeris |
| *F.R.* | Furtwängler-Reichhold, Griechische Vasenmalerei |
| *Gaz. Arch.* | Gazette archéologique |
| *Gaz. des Beaux-Arts* | Gazette des Beaux-Arts |
| *Gött. Gelehrt. Anz.* | Göttingische gelehrte Anzeigen |
| *I.P.E.K.* | Jahrbuch für prähistorische und ethnographische Kunst. |
| *Jahr.* | Jahrbuch des deutschen archäologischen Instituts |
| *J.E.A.* | Journal of Egyptian Archæology |
| *J.H.S.* | Journal of Hellenic Studies |
| *J.R.S.* | Journal of Roman Studies |
| *Mon.* | Monumenti inediti dell'Instituto archeologico |
| *Mon. Ant.* | Monumenti antichi pubblicati per cura della Reale Accademia dei Lincei |
| *Mon. Piot* | Monuments et mémoires, Fondation Eugène Piot |
| *N.J.* | Neue Jahrbücher für das klassiche Altertum |
| *Not. d. Sc.* | Notizie degli scavi |
| *Oest. Jahr.* | Jahreshefte des oesterreichischen archäologischen Institutes |
| *P.W.* | Real-Encyclopädie der classischen Altertumswissenschaft |
| *Rev. arch.* | Revue archéologique |
| *Rev. des ét. anc.* | Revue des études anciennes |
| *Rev. des ét. grecques* | Revue des études grecques |
| *Rh. Mus.* | Rheinisches Museum für Philologie |
| *Röm. Mitth.* | Mittheilungen des kaiserlich deutschen archäologischen Instituts, Römische Abtheilung |
| *Sitz. Berl. Akad.* | Sitzungsberichte der Berliner Akademie der Wissenschaften. Philol.-hist. Kl. |
| *W.V.* | Wiener Vorlegeblätter |

# ADDENDA AND CORRIGENDA

## LIST OF ILLUSTRATIONS

Fig. 81. *Read* Zadamonefonukhu.
Fig. 282. *After* Xenotimos, *add* Painter.
Fig. 384. *Read* Iphigeneia.
Fig. 394. *Read* Scene.
Fig. 397. *Read* Lionesses.
Fig. 434. *Read* Leipzig *for* Berlin.
Fig. 464. *Read* mirror *for* mirror-cover.
Figs. 612-614. *Read* Lévy, Neurdein reunis *for* Neurdein Frères.

## CAPTIONS OF ILLUSTRATIONS

Fig. 81. *Read* Zadamonefonukhu.
Fig. 229. *Delete* Painter.
Fig. 245. *Read* krater *for* cup.
Fig. 282. *Add* Painter *after* Xenotimos.
Figs. 294, 301. *Add* Painter *after* Andokides.
Figs. 310, 315. *Add* Painter *after* Sosias.
Fig. 393. *Read* Augurs.
Fig. 464. *Read* mirror *for* mirror-cover.
Fig. 510. *Read* Scene.

## TEXT

Page 76. Second paragraph, line 8, *read* high *for* long; *read* long *for* wide.
Page 95. Note 30*b*, *read* adapting *for* adopting.
Page 192. *Delete* Syriskos *and* Copenhagen Painters *under* 490-480; *add them under* 470-460.
Page 289, line 25, *read* mirror *for* mirror-cover.
Page 356, note 85, *read* Apulien.
Page 370, line 12, *read* Tablinum.
Page 374, line 9, *read* two *for* pair.

## NEW BIBLIOGRAPHY

Antiken Freskenfaksimiles nach römisch. Fresken im Vatikan und in Museen von Neapel, München, 1922.
Beazley, J. D. Jacobsthal, P., Bilder griechischer Vasen, 1929.
Bicknell, C. D., Hutchinson, R. W., Greek Vases (Methuen).
Bieber, M., Der Mysteriensaal der Villa Item, Jahr. 43 (1928), pp. 298 ff.
Brusin, Not. d. Sc. 1927, 263-277 (Aquileia).
Dawkins, R. M., The Excavations at the Sanctuary of Artemis Orthia at Sparta, British School, Athens, 1906-1910.
Evans, Sir Arthur, The Shaft Graves and Their Interrelations, London, 1929.
Gadd, C. J., History and Monuments of Ur, New York, 1929.
Hall, H. R., A Handbook of Egyptian Archæology (Methuen).
Payne, H. G. G., Necrocorinthia (Announced).
Sartiaux, Les Civilisations de l'Asie Mineure, Paris, 1928.
Smith, Sidney, A Handbook Mesopotamian Archæology (Methuen).
Toynbee, J., J. R. S. 1929 (Villa Item).

# ILLUSTRATIONS

## *DAWN OF ART*

## EGYPT

## THE ORIENT—MESOPOTAMIA

## CRETE

*Fig.*

163. Candia Museum. Sarcophagus from Hagia Triada. *Mon. Ant.*, XIX (1908), Pl. I (R. Paribeni), Ulrico Hoepli, Milano.
With the permission of the R. Accademia dei Lincei.

164. Cretan Vases:

*a.* Candia Museum. Polychrome vase from Phæstos, *Mon. Ant.*, 14 (1905), Pl. 35b (color), (L. Pernier), Ulrico Hoepli, Milano.
With the permission of the R. Accademia dei Lincei.

*b,* Candia Museum. Polychrome vase from Knossos. *J.H.S.*, 23 (1903), Pl. VI, 3 (color), Macmillan & Co., Limited, London.
Published with the permission of the Council of the Hellenic Society and the courtesy of Mr. George Macmillan.

*c,* Candia Museum. Polychrome vase from Knossos. *B.S.A.*, IX (1902-1903), Fig. 75, p. 120, Macmillan & Co., Limited, London. *Cf.* Evans, *Palace of Minos*, I, Pl. III (color), oppos. p. 247.
Published with the permission of the Committee of the British School in Athens and the courtesy of Mr. George Macmillan.

*d,* Candia Museum. Polychrome vase with lilies, Knossos. *J.H.S.*, 21 (1901), Pl. VI, *b* (color), oppos. p. 78, Macmillan & Co., Limited, London.
Published with the permission of the Council of the Hellenic Society and the courtesy of Mr. George Macmillan.

*e,* Candia Museum. Vase with lily pattern, *B.S.A.*, X (1903-1904), Fig. I, p. 7, Macmillan & Co., Limited, London.
Published with the permission of the Council of the Hellenic Society and the courtesy of Mr. George Macmillan.

*f,* Candia Museum. Vase from Zakro. Marine life. *J.H.S.*, 22 (1902), Pl. 12 (color), Macmillan & Co., Limited, London.
Published with the permission of the Council of the Hellenic Society and the courtesy of Mr. George Macmillan.

*g,* Athens, National Museum. Crocus vase, Melos. *J.H.S.*, Suppl. IV (1904), Pl. 23, 5. Macmillan & Co., Limited, London.
Published with the permission of the Council of the Hellenic Society and the courtesy of Mr. George Macmillan.

*h,* Athens, National Museum. Vase from Pylos. *Ath. Mitth.*, 34 (1909), Pl. XXII (L. M., I-II), Beck und Barth, Athen.
With the permission of the German Archæological Institute and of Director Rodenwaldt.

*i,* Athens, National Museum. Vase from Pylos. *Ath. Mitth.*, 34 (1909), Pl. XVII (L. M., I-II), Beck und Barth, Athen.
With the permission of the German Archæological Institute and of Director Rodenwaldt.

*Fig.*

*j,* Restoration of a Melian vase, Athens, National Museum. Bossert, *Alt Kreta*, Pl. 185, Verlag Ernst Wasmuth, Berlin, 1921. *Cf. J.H.S.*, Suppl. IV, Pl. 21, 4.

*k,* Candia. Vase with *Nymphœa cœrulea* (L. M., I). *J.H.S.*, 22 (1902), Pl. XII, 2 (color), Macmillan & Co., Limited, London.
Published with the permission of the Council of the Hellenic Society and the courtesy of Mr. George Macmillan.

*l,* Marseilles. Vase, L. M., I. Evans, *Palace of Minos*, II, 2, Fig. 312, p. 509, Macmillan & Co., Limited, London, 1928.
Published with the permission of Macmillan & Co., Limited, London, and of Sir Arthur Evans.

165. Cretan-Mycenæan Pottery:

*a.* Candia. Octopus vase from Gournia. Hawes, *Gournia*, Pl. H, The American Exploration Society, Free Museum of Art and Science, Philadelphia, 1908.
With the permission of Harriet Boyd Hawes.

*b,* Athens, National Museum. "Palace" style vase from Mycenæ. *J.H.S.*, 24 (1904), Pl. 13, Macmillan & Co., Limited, London.
With the permission of the Council of the Hellenic Society and the courtesy of Mr. George Macmillan.

*c,* Candia. Vase from Isopata. Plant designs. Evans, *Prehistoric Tombs of Knossos*, Fig. 142a. *Archæologia*, LIX, Pl. CI, Society of Antiquaries, London.

*d,* Candia. Vase from Isopata. Architectural motives. Evans, *Prehistoric Tombs of Knossos*, Fig. 144, p. 159. *Archæologia*, LIX, Fig. 144, Society of Antiquaries, London.

*e,* Candia. Painted jar with papyrus. Royal Villa. *B.S.A.*, IX (1902-1903), Fig. 88, p. 139, Macmillan & Co., Limited, London.
Published with the permission of the Committee of the British School in Athens and the courtesy of Mr. George Macmillan.

*f,* London, British Museum. Mycenæan kylix with octopus. H. B. Cotterill, *Ancient Greece*, Color Plate II, New York, 1913. Frederick A. Stokes Co.

*g,* Paris, Louvre. Mycenæan octopus. Morin-Jean, *Le dessin des animaux en Grèce*, Fig. 21, Librairie Renouard, H. Laurens, Éditeur.

*h,* Paris, Louvre. Mycenæan octopus. Morin-Jean, *Le dessin des animaux en Grèce*, Fig. 22, Librairie Renouard, H. Laurens, Éditeur, Paris, 1911.

166. Athens, National Museum. Fresco from Mycenæ. Siege of a city. Restored. Rodenwaldt,

*Fig.*

Hackl, *Tiryns II*, Pl. 21, 1 (color), Eleutheroudakis und Barth, Athen, 1912.
Reproduced with the permission of the German Archæological Institute and of Director Rodenwaldt.

192. Tiryns. Floor-decoration. Dolphins, octopods. Hackl, *Tiryns II*, Pl. 21, 3, 4 (color), Eleutheroudakis und Barth, Athen, 1912.
Reproduced with the permission of the German Archæological Institute and of Director Rodenwaldt.

193. Athens, National Museum. Warrior vase from Mycenæ (photo). *Cf.* Furtwängler-Loeschcke, *Mykenische Vasen*, Pl. XLII, detail, Verlag von A. Asher & Co., Berlin, 1886.

194. Athens, National Museum. Vase fragment from Tiryns. Hunt. Schliemann, *Tiryns*, Pl. XIV (color), Charles Scribner's Sons, New York, 1885.

*Fig.*

195. Athens, National Museum. Fisherman lampstand from Melos. *J.H.S.*, Suppl. IV, Phylakopi, Pl. 22, Macmillan & Co., Limited, London.
With the permission of the Council of the Hellenic Society.

196. Candia. Vase from Muliana, Crete. *Eph. Arch.*, 1904, Pl. III (Xanthoudides), Sakellarios, Athens.

197. New York, Metropolitan Museum. Mycenæan vase from Cyprus. Perrot and Chipiez, *Histoire de l'art*, III, Fig. 525, p. 714, Librairie Hachette et Cie, Paris, 1885.

198. Vase from Cyprus. Chariot. Women. Perrot and Chipiez, *Histoire de l'art*, III, Fig. 526, p. 715, Librairie Hachette et Cie, Paris, 1885.

## GREECE

*Fig.*

199. Athens, National Museum. Dipylon vase. *Mon.*, IX, Pl. 40, Pubblicati dall' Instituto di Corrispondenza Archeologica, Roma MDCCCLXIX-LXXIII.

200. Athens, National Museum. Bœotian geometric vase. Mistress of the Wild Things. *Eph. Arch.*, 1892, Pl. X (P. Wolters).

201. Paris, Louvre. Bœotian bowl. Perrot and Chipiez, *Histoire de l'art*, X, Pl. I (color), oppos. p. 30, Librairie Hachette et Cie, Paris, 1914 (drawing by Mlle. Evrard).

202. Boston Museum. Corinthian vases. (a) Animal frieze; (b) Warriors in combat; sirens; (c) Panthers and birds; (d) Aryballos with bird. Photo.
With the permission of Mr. L. D. Caskey, and of the Boston Museum.

203. Paris, Louvre. Corinthian vase. Herakles at the house of Eurytios. *Mon.*, VI, Pl. 33, Pubblicati dall' Instituto di Corrispondenza Archeologica, 1857-1863. *Cf.* Perrot and Chipiez, *Histoire de l'art*, IX (1911), Fig. 344.

204. Paris, Louvre. Corinthian vase. Suicide of Ajax. Detail of Fig. 203. Longpérier, *Musée Napoléon III*, Pl. XXXVI (color).

205. Berlin Museum. Clay plaques from Corinth. *Ant. Denk.*, I, Pl. 7 (Fraenkel), Verlag von Georg Reimer, Berlin, 1887.
With the permission of the German Archæological Institute and of Director Rodenwaldt.

206. Berlin Museum. Clay plaques from Corinth. *Ant. Denk.*, I, Pl. 8 (Fraenkel), Verlag von Georg Reimer, Berlin, 1887.
With the permission of the German Archæological Institute and of Director Rodenwaldt.

*Fig.*

207. Athens, National Museum. Clay antefixes and water-spouts, Thermos. *Ant. Denk.*, II, Pl. 53 (Sotiriades), Verlag von Georg Reimer, Berlin, 1908.
With the permission of the German Archæological Institute and of Director Rodenwaldt.

208. Thermos. Restoration of entablature, Temple of Apollo, Thermos. *Ant. Denk.*, II, Pl. 49 (G. Kawerau), Verlag von Georg Reimer, Berlin, 1908.
With the permission of the German Archæological Institute and of Director Rodenwaldt.

209. Athens, National Museum. Metope from Temple of Apollo, Thermos. Hunter with game. *Ant. Denk.*, II, Pl. 51, 2 (Sotiriades), Verlag von Georg Reimer, Berlin, 1908.
With the permission of the German Archæological Institute and of Director Rodenwaldt.

210. Rome, Palazzo dei Conservatori. Aristonothos Krater. Naval battle; Odysseus blinding the Cyclops. *Mon.*, IX, Pl. IV, Pubblicati dall' Instituto di Corrispondenza Archeologica, 1869-1873. *Cf.* Buschor, *Greek Vase-Painting*, Fig. 30.

211. Paris, Louvre. Rhodian oinochoë. Longpérier, *Musée Napoléon III*, Pl. XXVII.

212. London, British Museum. Euphorbos pinax. Photo.
With the permission of the Trustees of the British Museum.

213. Athens, National Museum. "Melian" vase. Artemis, Apollo, and goddesses. Conze, *Melische Thongefässe*, Pl. IV, Verlag von Breitkopf und Härtel, Leipzig, 1863.

214. Vienna. Busiris vase, Cære. Furtwängler, Reichhold, *Griechische Vasenmalerei*, Pl. 51

*Fig.*

(Furtwängler), F. Bruckmann A.-G., München, 1904.

215. Würzburg. Blind Phineus and Harpies. F. R., *Griechische Vasenmalerei*, Pl. 41 (Furtwängler), F. Bruckmann A.-G., München, 1903.

216. Munich. Labor of Herakles. Disemboweling the Erymanthian boar. Gerhard, *Aus. Vasenbilder*, Pls. 132-133. *Cf.* Heinemann, *Landschaftliche Elemente*, Fig. 8, Verlag von Friedrich Cohen, Bonn, 1910.

217. Paris, Louvre. Vintage scene. Perrot and Chipiez, *Histoire de l'art*, X, Fig. 91, p. 127, Librairie Hachette et C$^{ie}$, Paris, 1914 (drawing of Mlle. Evrard).

218. Paris, Louvre. Vineyard scene. Perrot and Chipiez, *Histoire de l'art*, X, Fig. 149, p. 232, Librairie Hachette et C$^{ie}$, Paris, 1914 (drawing of Mlle. Evrard).

219. Athens, National Museum. Odysseus and sirens. *J.H.S.*, XIII (1892-1893), pp. 1 ff., Pl. I (color), (E. Sellers), Macmillan & Co., Limited, London.
With the permission of the Council of the Hellenic Society.

220. Berlin. Sarcophagus from Klazomenai. *Ant. Denk.*, II, Pl. 26 (F. Winter), Verlag von Georg Reimer, Berlin, 1898.
With the permission of the German Archæological Institute and of Director Rodenwaldt.

221. Berlin. Sarcophagus from Klazomenai. *Ant. Denk.*, II, Pl. 58 (R. Zahn), Verlag von Georg Reimer, Berlin, 1908.
With the permission of the German Archæological Institute and of Director Rodenwaldt.

222. Berlin. Sarcophagus from Klazomenai. *Ant. Denk.*, II, Pl. 25 (F. Winter), Verlag von Georg Reimer, Berlin, 1898.
With the permission of the German Archæological Institute and of Director Rodenwaldt.

223. London, British Museum. Sarcophagus from Klazomenai. Cover. Chariot races. Battle scenes. Murray, *Terracotta Sarcophagi, Greek and Etruscan in the British Museum*, Pl. I, London, 1898, British Museum.
With the permission of the Trustees of the British Museum.

224. London, British Museum. Sarcophagus from Klazomenai. Funeral games. Murray, *Terracotta Sarcophagi*, Pl. II, London, 1898, British Museum.
With the permission of the Trustees of the British Museum.

225. Berlin. Krater from Capua. Palæstra scenes. Style of Euphronios. A.Z., 37 (1879), Pl. IV (Klein). *Cf.* F. R., *Griechische Vasenmalerei*, Pl. 157.
With the permission of the German Archæological Institute and of Director Rodenwaldt.

226a. Athens, National Museum. Proto-Attic vase.

*Fig.*

*Jahr.*, II (1887), (J. Boehlau, *Frühattische Vasen*, Pl. IV).
With the permission of the German Archæological Institute and of Director Rodenwaldt.

226b. Athens, National Museum. Proto-Attic vase. Dance; decorative patterns. *Jahr.*, II (1887), (J. Boehlau, *Frühattische Vasen*, Pl. III).
With the permission of the German Archæological Institute and of Director Rodenwaldt.

227a. Athens, National Museum. Herakles and Nessos. *Ant. Denk.*, I, Pl. 57 (V. Staïs, P. Wolters), Verlag von Georg Reimer, Berlin, 1891.
With the permission of the German Archæological Institute and of Director Rodenwaldt.

227b. Athens, National Museum. Slain Medusa with sisters fleeing. *Ant. Denk.*, I, Pl. 57 (V. Staïs, P. Wolters), Verlag von Georg Reimer, Berlin, 1891.
With the permission of the German Archæological Institute and of Director Rodenwaldt.

228. Florence, Archæological Museum. François vase. F. R., *Griechische Vasenmalerei*, Pl. 3, 10 (Furtwängler), F. Bruckmann, München, 1900.

229. London. British Museum. Amphora by Nikosthenes. Satyrs and Mænads dancing. Walters, *The Art of the Greeks*,[2] Pl. LXXIV, The Macmillan Co., New York, 1922.

230a. Paris, Cabinet des Médailles. Amphora by Amasis. Athena and Poseidon. Wiener Vorlegeblätter, 1889, Pl. III, 2c, d (O. Benndorf), Alfred Hölder, Wien, 1890.

230b. Paris, Cabinet des Médailles. Detail of 230a, Warriors. Wiener Vorlegeblätter, 1889, Pl. III, 2c (O. Benndorf), Alfred Hölder, Wien, 1890.

231. Paris, Cabinet des Médailles. Amphora by Amasis. Detail. Dionysos and Mænads, *W.V.*, 1889, Pl. III, 2 (O. Benndorf), Alfred Hölder, Wien, 1890.

232. Munich. Dionysos sailing over the sea. Exekias. Furtwängler and Reichhold, *Griechische Vasenmalerei*, Pl. 42 (Furtwängler), F. Bruckmann A.-G., München, 1903.

233. London, British Museum. Burgon amphora. Athena. *Mon.*, X, Pl. 48i, Pubblicati dall' Instituto di Corrispondenza Archeologica, 1874-1878. Von Brauchitsch, *Die panathenäischen Preisamphoren*, No. 1, pp. 6 ff., Fig. 5, B. G. Teubner, Leipzig, 1910.

234. Leyden. Panathenaic vase. Athena. *Mon.*, X, 48 N, Pubblicati dall' Instituto di Corrispondenza Archeologica, 1874-1878. Von Brauchitsch, *Die panathenäischen Preisamphoren*, No. 13, pp. 18 f., Fig. 8, B. G. Teubner, Leipzig, 1910.

## DRAWING AND DESIGN ON GREEK VASES

*Fig.*

Renouard, Henri Laurens, Éditeur, Paris, 1911.

257. Vienna. Busiris vase. Negroes on the run. F. R., *Griechische Vasenmalerei*, Pl. 51 (Furtwängler), F. Bruckmann, München, 1904.

258. Paris, Collignon Coll. Corinthian vase. Rayet et Collignon, *Histoire de la céramique grecque*, Pl. V (color), Georges Decaux, Paris, 1888.

259. Paris, Louvre. Corinthian vase. Detail, lion. Morin-Jean, *Le Dessin des animaux en Grèce*, Fig. 81, p. 75, Librairie Renouard, Henri Laurens, Éditeur, Paris, 1911.

260. Paris, Louvre. Corinthian vase. Detail, fantastic animal. Morin-Jean, *Le Dessin des animaux en Grèce*, Fig. 100, p. 86, Librairie Renouard, Henri Laurens, Éditeur, Paris, 1911.

261. Paris, Louvre. Corinthian vase. Detail, sphinx. Morin-Jean, *Le Dessin des animaux en Grèce*, Fig. 87, p. 79, Librairie Renouard, Henri Laurens, Éditeur, Paris, 1911.

262. Paris, Louvre. Corinthian vase. Detail, heraldic lions. Morin-Jean, *Le Dessin des animaux en Grèce*, Fig. 97, p. 85, Librairie Renouard, Henri Laurens, Éditeur, Paris, 1911.

263. Paris, Louvre. Corinthian vase. Detail, rider leading another horse. Morin-Jean, *Le Dessin des animaux en Grèce*, Fig. 63, p. 64, Librairie Renouard, Henri Laurens, Éditeur, Paris, 1911.

264. Paris, Louvre. Corinthian vase. Detail. Herd of oxen. Morin-Jean, *Le Dessin des animaux en Grèce*, Fig. 55, p. 58, Librairie Renouard, Henri Laurens, Éditeur, Paris, 1911.

265. Paris, Louvre. Attic vase with some Corinthian details. Morin-Jean, *Le Dessin des animaux en Grèce*, Fig. 232, p. 201, Librairie Renouard, Henri Laurens, Éditeur, Paris, 1911.

266. Paris, Louvre. Cup by Exekias. "Kleinmeister" type. Doe. Perrot and Chipiez, *Histoire de l'art*, X, Fig. 127, p. 197, Librairie Hachette et Cie, Paris, 1914.

267. Bryn Mawr College. Fragment of "Kleinmeister" cup. Head of a woman (photo).

268. Rome, Vatican. The Dioscuri at home. Exekias. F. R., *Griechische Vasenmalerei*, Pl. 132 (Hauser), F. Bruckmann, München, 1912.

269. Paris, Louvre. Horsemen. Morin-Jean, *Le Dessin des animaux en Grèce*, Fig. 246, p. 215, Librairie Renouard, Henri Laurens, Éditeur, Paris, 1911.

270. London, British Museum. Cheiron receiving

*Fig.*

the child Achilles from Peleus. *J.H.S.*, Plates. Pl. II (color), Macmillan & Co., London. With the permission of the Council of the Hellenic Society.

271. Florence, Archæological Museum. François vase: Calydonian Boar Hunt; Theseus landing from Crete. F. R., *Griechische Vasenmalerei*, Pl. 13 (Furtwängler), F. Bruckmann, München, 1901.

272. Munich. Panathenaic vase. Runners. *Mon.*, X, Pl. 48, m, Pubblicati dall' Instituto di Corrispondenza Archeologica, Roma, 1874-1878.

273. London, British Museum. Cup signed by Pamphaios. Running Warriors. Photo. *Cf.* Hoppin, *Handbook of Attic R.-F. Vases*, II, p. 297. With the permission of the Trustees of the British Museum.

274. London, British Museum. Hydria. Scene at a fountain. *Ant. Denk.*, II, Pl. 19 (Wiegand), Verlag von Georg Reimer, Berlin, 1895. With the permission of the German Archæological Institute and of Director Rodenwaldt.

275. New York, Metropolitan Museum. B.-F. Amphora (photo). With the permission of Miss G. M. A. Richter, Curator of Classical Art, and of the Metropolitan Museum.

276. Paris, Louvre. R.-F. Amphora. Oltos. Photo. *Cf.* Pottier, *Vases antiques*, Album, II, Pl. 88, Librairie Hachette et Cie., Paris.

277. London, British Museum. Cup by Epiktetos. Young rider. *J.H.S.*, 29 (1909), Pl. XII (Walters), Macmillan & Co., Limited, London. With the permission of the Council of the Hellenic Society.

278. Panathenaic vases. *Mon.*, I, Pl. 22, Pubblicati dall' Instituto di Corrispondenza Archeologica, Roma, 1829-1833.

279. London, British Museum. Stamnos by Oltos. Herakles and Acheloös. Photo. *Cf.* Hoppin, *Handbook of R.-F. Vases*, II, p. 293. With the permission of the Trustees of the British Museum.

280. Paris, Louvre. Stamnos by Hermonax. Revel. Photo. *Cf.* Hoppin, *Handbook of R.-F. Vases*, II, 25.

281. Rome, Villa Giulia. Labors of Theseus. Skythes. *Mon. Piot*, XX (1913), Pl. VI (Rizzo), Ernest Leroux, Éditeur, Paris. With the permission of the Académie des Inscriptions et Belles-Lettres and of M. René Cagnat, Secretary.

282. Boston. Birth of Helen. Cup by Xenotimos. Photo. *Cf.* Hoppin, *Handbook of R.-F. Vases*, II, p. 477. With the permission of Mr. L. D. Caskey and the Boston Museum of Fine Arts.

# ILLUSTRATIONS

*Fig.*

Pls. I, II (A. Philadelpheus), E. de Boccard, Paris.
With the permission of the École Française d'Athènes.

309. The drawing of the eye on Greek vases. Pottier, *Catalogue des vases antiques*, III (1906), Fig. 3, p. 855 (Pottier), Librairies-Imprimeries réunies, Paris, 1906. L'administration du Musée du Louvre.

310. Berlin. Achilles binding up the wound of Patroklos, Sosias Painter. F. R., *Griechische Vasenmalerei*, Pl. 123 (Hauser), F. Bruckmann, München, 1910.

311. Paris, Louvre. The Sack of Troy, Brygos Painter. F. R., *Griechische Vasenmalerei*, Pl. 25 (Furtwängler), F. Bruckmann, München, 1902.

312. Vienna. Contest between Ajax and Odysseus for the armor of Achilles, Douris. F. R., *Griechische Vasenmalerei*, Pl. 54 (Furtwängler), F. Bruckmann, München, 1904.

313. Berlin. Revel of Mænads, Makron. Gerhard, *Trinkschalen und Gefässe*, Pls. 4-5 (color), Verlag von G. Reimer, Berlin, 1848.

314. Paris, Louvre. Antaios krater by Euphronios. Heads of Antaios and Herakles. Pottier, *Corpus Vasorum, France, Musée du Louvre*, Fasc. I, III, 1, c, Pl. V, 1, Édouard Champion, Paris.

315. Berlin. Patroklos wounded, Sosias Painter. Reichhold, *Skizzenbuch griech. Meister*, Pl. 75, F. Bruckmann, München, 1919.

316. Munich. Raging Mænad, Kleophrades Painter. F. R., *Griechische Vasenmalerei*, Pl. 45 (Furtwängler), F. Bruckmann, München, 1903.

317. Munich. Head of Priam, Euthymides. F. R., *Griechische Vasenmalerei*, Pl. 14 (Furtwängler), F. Bruckmann, München, 1901.

318. New York, Metropolitan Museum. Head of a warrior, Achilles Master. F. R., *Griechische Vasenmalerei*, II, Fig. 94A (Hauser), F. Bruckmann, München, 1909.

319. Paris, Louvre. Orvieto krater. Bearded man. F. R., *Griechische Vasenmalerei*, Pl. 108 (Hauser), F. Bruckmann, München, 1908.

320. Schwerin. Herakles and old woman, Pistoxenos Painter. *Jahr.*, 27 (1912), Pl. 8 (Maybaum), Verlag von Georg Reimer, Berlin. *Cf.* F. R., *Griechische Vasenmalerei*, Pl. 163, 1.
With the permission of the German Archæological Institute and of Director Rodenwaldt.

321. Munich. White-ground lekythos. Hermes bringing a woman to Charon. Riezler, *Weissgrundige attische Lekythen*, Pl. 26, F. Bruckmann, München, 1914.

*Fig.*

322. Athens, National Museum. Loutrophoros with mourning scene. Perrot and Chipiez, *Histoire de l'art*, X, Pl. XVIII, Librairie Hachette et Cie, Paris, 1914 (design by E. Laurent).

323. Rome, Vatican. Æsop and the fox. Baumgarten-Poland-Wagner, *Die Hellenische Kultur*, Fig. 244, p. 236, Verlag von B. G. Teubner, Leipzig, 1913.

324. Rome, Villa Giulia. Psykter with centaur battle, Harrow Painter. F. R., *Griechische Vasenmalerei*, Pl. 15 (Furtwängler), F. Bruckmann, München, 1901.

325. New York, Metropolitan Museum. Amazon Krater. Photo. "Apparently by the Painter of the Berlin Hydria."
With the permission of Miss G. M. A. Richter, Curator of Classical Art, and of the Metropolitan Museum.

326. New York, Metropolitan Museum. Amazon Krater. F. R., *Griechische Vasenmalerei*, Pl. 118 (Hauser). "Apparently by the Painter of the Berlin Hydria," F. Bruckmann, München, 1909.

327. Naples. Aryballos. Amazonomachy. Aison, *Mon. Ant.*, XXII (1914), Pl. LXXXVI, a, (Gabrici), Ulrico Hoepli, Milano.
With the permission of the R. Accademia dei Lincei.

328. Paris, Louvre. Apollo slaying Tityos and Ge. Photo, Giraudon. *Cf.* F. R., *Griechische Vasenmalerei*, Pl. 164.

329. Paris, Louvre. Apollo attacking Tityos and Ge. Detail, Tityos. Pottier, *Corpus Vasorum Antiquorum, France, Musée du Louvre*, Fasc. I, III, 1, c, Pl. 10, 1, Édouard Champion, Paris.

330. Paris, Cabinet des Médailles. Mænads, Achilles Master. F. R., *Griechische Vasenmalerei*, Pl. 77, 1 (Furtwängler), F. Bruckmann, München, 1906.

331. Oxford. Ashmolean Museum. Lekythos. Herakles and Deianeira, with Hyllos. P. Gardner, *Greek Vases in the Ashmolean Museum*, Pl. 18, Oxford Press, 1893.

332. Naples. Dionysiac celebration. Painter of the Berlin Deinos. F. R., *Griechische Vasenmalerei*, Pl. 36 (Furtwängler), F. Bruckmann, München, 1902.

333. Athens. National Museum. White-ground vase. Warrior at home. Riezler, *Weissgrundige attische Lekythen*, Pl. 36, F. Bruckmann, München, 1914.

334. Boston. White-ground lekythos. Youth beside tomb. Photo.
With the permission of Mr. L. D. Caskey, and of the Boston Museum of Fine Arts.

## POLYGNOTOS AND THE PAINTING OF THE FIFTH CENTURY

*Fig.*

26-27 (Furtwängler), F. Bruckmann, München, 1902.

359. Palermo. Amazon vase from Gela, Niobid Painter. F. R., *Griechische Vasenmalerei*, I, pp. 128-129 (Furtwängler), F. Bruckmann, München, 1904.

360. Palermo. Krater from Gela. Greek staying hand of Amazon, Niobid Painter. F. R., *Griechische Vasenmalerei*, I, p. 125 (Furtwängler), F. Bruckmann, München, 1904.

361. London, British Museum. Achilles and Penthesileia, Polygnotos. *Mon.*, X, Pl. 9, Pubblicati dall' Instituto di Corrispondenza Archeologica, Roma, 1874-1878.

362. Battle of Marathon. Reconstruction, left half. Robert, *Die Marathonschlacht in der Poikile, Hall. Winckelmannsprogr.*, XVIII (1895), Max Niemeyer, Halle.

363. Munich. Odysseus and Nausikaa. Nausikaa Painter. F. R., *Griechische Vasenmalerei*, Pl. 138, 1 (Hauser), F. Bruckmann, München, 1912.

364. Boston, Museum of Fine Arts. Pyxis. Odysseus and Nausikaa. Photo.
With the permission of Mr. L. D. Caskey, and of the Boston Museum. *Cf.* Hauser, Oest. Jahr., VIII (1905), Pl. 1 (color).

365. Berlin. Skyphos. Odysseus slaying the suitors, Penelope Painter. F. R., *Griechische Vasenmalerei*, Pl. 138, 2 (Hauser), F. Bruckmann. München, 1912.

366. Vienna. Reliefs from the Heroon, Gjölbaschi-Trysa. Benndorf-Niemann, *Das Heroon von Gjölbaschi*, Pls. 7-8, Verlag von Adolf Holzhausen's Nachfolger, Wien, 1889. *Cf.* F. R., *Griechische Vasenmalerei*, III, Figs. 48-49, pp. 102-103.

367. Underworld. Reconstruction by C. Robert, *Die Nekyia des Polygnot. Hall. Winckelmannsprogr.*, XVI (1892), Max Niemeyer, Halle.

368. Paris, Bibliothèque Nationale. Mad Ajax with Shepherds (?). S. I. Vase. F. R., *Griechische Vasenmalerei*, Pl. 60, 1 (Furtwängler), F. Bruckmann, München, 1904.

369. Berlin. Orpheus among the Thracians. *Berlin. Winckelmannsprogr.*, 50, Pl. 2 (Furtwängler), Georg Reimer, Berlin, 1890. *Cf.* F. R., *Griechische Vasenmalerei*, III, Fig. 52, p. 109 (Hauser).
With the permission of the German Archæological Institute and Director Rodenwaldt.

370. Oxford. Ashmolean. Hydria. Blind Thamyris. *J.H.S.*, XXV (1905), Pl. I (P. Gardner), Macmillan & Co., Limited, London.
With the permission of the Council of the Hellenic Society.

*Fig.*

371. Naples. Knucklebone-players of Alexandros. Alinari, 34122. *Cf.* Robert, *Hall. Winckelmannsprogr.*, XXI (1897), Max Niemeyer, Halle.

372. Rome, Villa Giulia. Ficoroni cista. Argonauts among the Bebrykes. F. Winter, *Kunstgeschichte in Bildern*, I (1900), Pl. 90, 3, Leipzig, Alfred Kröner Verlag.

373. Munich. Achilles and Penthesileia, Penthesileia Master. Reichhold, *Skizzenbuch griech. Meister*, Frontispiece, F. Bruckmann, München, 1919.

374. Geneva, Musée Fol. Combat of Greeks and Amazons. F. R., *Griechische Vasenmalerei*, II, oppos. p. 314, Fig. 105 (Hauser), F. Bruckmann, München, 1909.

375. Berlin. White-ground lekythos. Mourning scene. Winter, *Berlin. Winckelmannsprogr.*, 55 (1895).
With the permission of the German Archæological Institute and Director Rodenwaldt.

376. Ruvo. Death of the giant, Talos. F. R., *Griechische Vasenmalerei*, Pls. 38-39 (Furtwängler), F. Bruckmann, München, 1902.

377. Berlin. Mosaic from Hadrian's villa. Centaur slaying a tiger. Springer-Michaelis-Wolters, *Kunstgeschichte*,[12] I, Fig. 754, Alfred Kröner Verlag, Leipzig, 1923.

378. Naples. Painting on marble from Herculaneum, Peirithoos, Eurytion, Hippodameia (Alinari, 34125). *Cf.* Robert, *Hall. Winckelmannsprogr.*, XXII (1898), Max Niemeyer, Halle.

379. Naples. Painting on marble from Herculaneum. Greek *Apobates*. Robert, *Hall. Winckelmannsprogr.*, XIX (1895), Max Niemeyer, Halle.

380. London. British Museum. Dolon surprised by Odysseus and Diomede. F. R., *Griechische Vasenmalerei*, Pl. 110, 4a (Hauser), F. Bruckmann, München, 1908.

381. Boston Museum. Centauress. Vase fragment. F. R., *Griechische Vasenmalerei*, II, Fig. 94b, oppos. p. 264 (Hauser), F. Bruckmann, München, 1909.

382. Pompeii, House of the Vettii. Herakles strangling the serpents. Herrmann, *Denkmäler der Malerei*, Pl. 41, F. Bruckmann, München, 1907.

383. Athens, National Museum. Zeus enthroned. Painting from Eleusis. *Eph. Arch.*, 1888, Pl. V.

384. Naples, National Museum. Sacrifice of Iphigenia. Herrmann, *Denkmäler der Malerei*, Pl. 15, F. Bruckmann, München, 1907.

## ETRURIA AND SOUTHERN ITALY

*Fig.*

young girl). Symposium. *Ant. Denk.*, II, Pl. 43 (color), (Körte), Verlag von Georg Reimer, Berlin, 1901.
With the permission of the German Archæological Institute and of Director Rodenwaldt.

413. Chiusi. Tomba della Scimmia (Tomb of the Monkey). Funeral games. *Mon.*. V, Pl. XV, Pubblicati dall' Instituto di Corrispondenza Archeologica, Roma, 1849-1853.

414. Chiusi. Tomba del Colle Casuccini (Tomb of the Casuccini Hill). Symposium. *Mon.*, V, Pl. XXXIV, Pubblicati dall' Instituto di Corrispondenza Archeologica, Roma, 1849-1853.

415. Chiusi. Tomba del Colle Casuccini (Tomb of the Casuccini Hill). Funeral games. *Mon.*, V, Pl. XXXIII, Pubblicati dall' Instituto di Corrispondenza Archeologica, Roma, 1849-1853.

416. Chiusi. Tomba della Scimmia (Tomb of the Monkey). Dwarf and giant. *Mon.*, V, Pl. XVI, Pubblicati dall' Instituto di Corrispondenza Archeologica, Roma, 1849-1853.

417. Corneto. Tomba dell' Orco (Tomb of Hades). Underworld scene; Theseus in Hades; Odysseus blinding the Cyclops. *Mon.*, IX, Pl. 15, Pubblicati dall' Instituto di Corrispondenza Archeologica, Roma, 1869-1873.

418. Corneto. Tomba dell' Orco (Tomb of Hades). Heroes and demons. *Mon.*, XI, Pl. 15, Pubblicati dall' Instituto di Corrispondenza Archeologica, Roma, 1869-1873.

419. Corneto. Tomba dell' Orco (Tomb of Hades). Charon; head of a young woman, Velia. *Mon.*, IX, Pl. 14, 4, 5, Pubblicati dall' Instituto di Corrispondenza Archeologica, Roma, 1869-1873.

420. Corneto. Tomba dell' Orco (Tomb of Hades). Head of Hades. *Mon.*, IX, Pl. 15*a*, Pubblicati dall' Instituto di Corrispondenza Archeologica, Roma, 1869-1873.

421. Corneto. Tomba dell' Orco (Tomb of

*Fig.*

Hades). Head of Velia, wife of Arnth Velchas. Weege, *Etruskische Malerei*, Frontispiece, Halle, 1921. Max Niemeyer Verlag.

422. Corneto. Tomba del Cardinale (Tomb of the Cardinal). The underworld. Weege, *Etruskische Malerei*, Figs. 29, 30, 31. Max Niemeyer, Halle.

423. Orvieto. Tomba Golini. Banquet in Hades. Springer-Michaelis-Wolters, *Kunstgeschichte*,[12] Fig. 870, p. 454 (after Conestabile). Alfred Kröner Verlag, Leipzig.

424. Orvieto. Tomba Golini. Larder and kitchen scenes. Springer-Michaelis-Wolters, *Kunstgeschichte*,[12] Figs. 871-872, p. 455 (after Conestabile). Alfred Kröner Verlag, Leipzig.

425. Corneto. Tomba degli Scudi (Tomb of the Shields). Symposium. Alinari, 26098.

426. Rome. Torlonia Collection. Servius Tullius (Mastarna) freeing Cæles Vibenna. *Jahr.*, XII (1897), Fig. 2, p. 70 (Körte), Verlag von Georg Reimer, Berlin.
Reproduced with the permission of the German Archæological Institute and of Director Rodenwaldt.

427. Corneto. Tomba del Tifone (Tomb of Typhon). Demon. Moscioni, 24083.

428. Corneto. Tomba del Tifone (Tomb of Typhon). Decorative patterns. Moscioni, 24085.

429. Florence, Archæological Museum. Etruscan painted sarcophagus. Battle of Greeks with Amazons. *J.H.S.*, Plates, Pl. 36 (color), Macmillan & Co., Limited, London.
With the permission of the Council of the Hellenic Society.

430. Florence, Archæological Museum. Etruscan painted sarcophagus. Battle of Greeks with Amazons. Alinari, 17068.

431. Orvieto. Painted sarcophagus from Torre San Severo. Sacrifice of Polyxena. *Mon. Ant.*, XXIV (1916), Pl. II (E. Galli). Ulrico Hoepli, Milano.
With the permission of the R. Accademia dei Lincei.

## OSCAN AND SOUTH ITALIAN PAINTING

*Fig.*

432. Map of Italy showing Oscan sites.

433. Berlin. Tomb-Painting from Nola. Woman seated on a throne. *Jahr.*, XXIV (1909), Pl. VII (Weege), Verlag von Georg Reimer, Berlin.
With the permission of the German Archæological Institute and Director Rodenwaldt.

434. Naples. National Museum. Women engaged in a dance. Winter, *Kunstgeschichte in Bil-*

*Fig.*

*dern*, I (1900), Pl. 92, No. 4, Berlin, Alfred Kröner Verlag.

435. Lost painting from Pæstum. Rider bringing home a fallen comrade. *Gaz. Arch.*, VIII (1883), p. 335. Pls. 46-48 (color), Villefosse, A. Lévy, Éditeur, Paris.

436. Naples, National Museum. Painting from Pæstum. Returning warriors. *Mon.*, VIII (1865), Pl. 21, 1 (Helbig), Pubblicati dall'

## THE FOURTH CENTURY

## HELLENISTIC, POMPEIAN, ROMAN

*Fig.*

Zeichnung der Griechen, III, Fig. 658, F. Bruckmann, München, 1923.

488. Rome, Lateran Museum. Mosaic of the "Unswept dining-room." After B. Nogara, *I Mosaici Antichi . . . del Vaticano et del Laterano*, Pl. V, Ulrico Hoepli, Milano, 1910.

489. Rome, Capitoline Museum. Drinking doves. Mosaic. Photo.

490. Rome, Vatican. Mosaic. Basket of flowers. Nogara, *I Mosaici Antichi . . . del Vaticano et del Laterano*, Pl. XXVII, 2, Ulrico Hoepli, Milano, 1910.

491. Naples, National Museum. Still life, fruit, glass jar. Pfuhl, *Malerei und Zeichnung der Griechen*, III, Fig. 703, F. Bruckmann, München, 1923.

492. Naples, National Museum. Medea meditating the murder of her children. Herrmann, *Denkmäler der Malerei*, Pl. 7, F. Bruckmann, München, 1906.

493. Naples, National Museum. Medea meditating the murder of her children. Casa dei Dioscuri. Herrmann, *Denkmäler der Malerei*, Pl. 130, F. Bruckmann, München, 1915.

494. Naples, National Museum. Orestes and Pylades among the Taurians. Herrmann, *Denkmäler der Malerei*, Pl. 115, F. Bruckmann, München, 1913.

495. Naples, National Museum. Orestes and Pylades. Detail of Fig. 494. Herrmann, *Denkmäler der Malerei*, Pl. 116, F. Bruckmann, München, 1913.

496. Naples, National Museum. Herakles and Nessos. Herrmann, *Denkmäler der Malerei*, Pl. 147. *Cf.* Farbendruck, Pl. V, F. Bruckmann, München, 1927.

497. Naples, National Museum. Detail from Herakles and Omphale. Herrmann, *Denkmäler der Malerei*, Pl. 60, F. Bruckmann, München, 1909.

498. Naples, National Museum. Tired Silenus. *Hallisches Winckelmannsprogr.*, 23 (1899), Max Niemeyer, Halle.

499. Naples, National Museum. Ares and Aphrodite. Herrmann, *Denkmäler der Malerei*, Pl. 4, F. Bruckmann, München, 1906.

500. Pompeii, House of the Vettii. Wrestling-match between Pan and Eros. Herrmann, *Denkmäler der Malerei*, Pl. 44, F. Bruckmann, München, 1907.

501. Naples, National Museum. Mosaic. Lion rending a panther. Herrmann, *Denkmäler der Malerei*, Pl. 9, F. Bruckmann, München, 1906.

502. Naples, National Museum. African landscape with animals. Keller, *Antike Tierwelt,*

*Fig.*

I, 293, Fig. 96, Verlag von Wilhelm Engelmann, Leipzig, 1909.

503. Naples, National Museum. Mosaic with Nile animals (photo).

504. Naples, National Museum. Mosaic with cat, ducks, still-life (photo).

505. Naples, National Museum. Mosaic, sea animals (photo).

506. Rome, Vatican. Mosaic. Lion rending a bull in a rocky landscape. After B. Nogara, *I Mosaici Antichi . . . del Vaticano et del Laterano*, Pl. XXXIV, Ulrico Hoepli, Milano, 1910.

507. Rome, Vatican. Mosaic. Goats pasturing. After B. Nogara, *I Mosaici Antichi . . . del Vaticano et del Laterano*, Pl. 31.

508. Naples, National Museum. Pigmy landscape (photo). Alinari, 12027.

509. Palestrina. Palazzo Barberini. Nile mosaic. R. Engelmann, *Antike Bilder aus römischen Handschriften*, p. 29, 4, A. W. Sijthoff, Leyden, 1909.

510. Palestrina. Palazzo Barberini. Nile mosaic. Detail, photo. Alinari.

511. New York, Metropolitan Museum. Mummy-case with portrait (photo).
With the permission of Mr. Albert M. Lythgoe, Curator of the Egyptian Department, and of the Metropolitan Museum.

512. New York, Metropolitan Museum. Head of a woman (photo).
With the permission of Mr. Albert M. Lythgoe, Curator of the Egyptian Department, and of the Metropolitan Museum.

513. New York, Metropolitan Museum. Head of a Greek youth (photo).
With the permission of Mr. Albert M. Lythgoe, Curator of the Egyptian Department, and of the Metropolitan Museum.

514. Carlsbad. Portrait of a Greek youth. Petrie, *Roman Portraits and Memphis* (IV), Pl. IV (color), British School of Archæology in Egypt, London, 1911.
With the permission of Sir W. M. F. Petrie.

515. Strassburg University. Portrait of a Greek girl. Springer-Michaelis-Wolters, *Kunstgeschichte*,[12] Pl. XVI (color), Alfred Kröner Verlag, Leipzig, 1923.

516. Vienna, Graf Collection. Portrait of a man. *Katalog zu Th. Graf's Galerie antiker Porträts*, Wien, 1903, No. 21.

517. London, National Gallery. Portrait of a woman. Petrie, *The Hawara Portfolio*, Pl. 16 (color), British School of Archæology in Egypt, University College, London, 1913.
With the permission of Sir W. M. F. Petrie.

518. Vienna, Graf Collection. Portrait of a young

*Fig.*

596. London, British Museum. Rape of Persephone from Tomb of the Nasonii. *Röm. Mitth.*, 32 (1917), Fig. 1 (Rodenwaldt), W. Regenberg, Berlin.
With the permission of the German Archæological Institute and of Director Rodenwaldt.

597. London, British Museum. Eros, from Tomb of the Nasonii. *Röm. Mitth.*, 32 (1917), Fig. 6 (Rodenwaldt), W. Regenberg, Berlin.
With the permission of the German Archæological Institute and of Director Rodenwaldt.

598. Rome, Via Latina. Tomb of the Valerii. Detail of stucco vault (Moscioni). *Cf. Memoirs of the American Academy in Rome*, IV (1924), Pl. XXIII (Wadsworth).

599. Rome, Via Latina. Tomb of the Pancratii. Vault-decoration. *Memoirs of the American Academy in Rome*, IV (1924), Pl. 30 (Wadsworth), Instituto Italiano di arti grafiche, Bergamo.
With the permission of Director Gorham P. Stevens of the American Academy in Rome.

600. Rome. House in the Via de' Cerchi. Wall-decoration. *Papers of the British School at Rome*, VIII (1916), Pl. III (color), (Mrs. Strong), Macmillan & Co., Limited, London.
With the permission of the Faculty of the British School in Rome and of the Secretary, Mr. Roger Hincks.

601. Kertch. Vault discovered in 1895. Floral decoration. *J.H.S.*, 39 (1919), p. 151, Fig. 2 (Rostovtzeff), Macmillan & Co., Limited, London.
With the permission of the Council of the Hellenic Society and of Professor Rostovtzeff.

602. Kertch. Vault discovered in 1895. Ceiling-decoration. Demeter, flowers, birds. *J.H.S.*, 39 (1919), Pl. VII, 2 (Rostovtzeff), Macmillan & Co., Limited, London.
With the permission of the Council of the Hellenic Society and of Professor Rostovtzeff.

603. Kertch. Vault discovered in 1872. Wall-decoration. Incrustation, figure, and floral decoration. *J.H.S.*, 39 (1919), Pl. VIII (Rostovtzeff), Macmillan & Co., Limited, London.
With the permission of the Council of the Hellenic Society and of Professor Rostovtzeff.

604. Kertch. Catacomb of Anthesterios. *C. R.*, 1878, Pl. I (color), Imprimerie de l'Académie Impériale des Sciences.

605. Palmyra. Tomb-paintings. Strzygowski, *Orient oder Rom*, Leipzig, 1901, Pl. 1. J. C. Hinrichs'sche Buchhandlung.

606. Dura-Salihiyeh. Wall with religious rites. *Syria*, III (1922), Pl. XLI (Breasted), Paul Geuthner, Paris.
With the permission of Professor Breasted, and of the publisher, M. Paul Geuthner.

*Fig.*

607. Dura-Salihiyeh. Wall of Bithnanaia. Priests at the left. *Syria*, III (1922), Pl. XXXIX (Breasted), Paul Geuthner, Paris.
With the permission of Professor Breasted, and of the publisher, M. Paul Geuthner.

608. Dura-Salihiyeh. Wall of Bithnanaia. Head of chief priest. *Syria*, III (1922), Pl. XL (Breasted), Paul Geuthner, Paris.
With the permission of Professor Breasted, and of the publisher, M. Paul Geuthner.

609. Rome, Corsini codex. Tombs ornamented with floral designs. Engelmann, *Antike Bilder aus römischen Handschriften*, 1909, Pl. X, A. W. Sijthoff, Leyden.

610. Uthina (Oudna). Mosaic. Villa of the Laberii. Vintage scenes. *Mon. Piot*, III (1896), Pl. XXI (P. Gauckler), Ernest Leroux, Éditeur, Paris.
With the permission of the Académie des Inscriptions et Belles-Lettres and of the Secretary, M. René Cagnat.

611. Uthina (Oudna). Mosaic. Scene on a farm. *Mon. Piot*, III (1896), Pl. XXII (P. Gauckler), Ernest Leroux, Éditeur, Paris.
With the permission of the Académie des Inscriptions et Belles-Lettres and of the Secretary, M. René Cagnat.

612. Timgad, Museum. Mosaic in carpet style from the House of Sertius. Ballu, *Guide illustré de Timgad*, p. 84, Neurdein Frères, Paris.

613. Timgad, Museum. Mosaic from House in the S. E. Quarter. Carpet style. Ballu, *Les Ruines de Timgad*, oppos. p. 92, Neurdein Frères, Paris, 1911.

614. Timgad, Museum. Mosaic from the Baths of the Filadelfi. Apollo and Daphne (?). Ballu, *Les Ruines de Timgad*, oppos. p. 108, Neurdein Frères, Paris, 1911.

615. Rome, Catacomb of Domitilla. Wall-decoration. Cupid and Psyche. Marucchi, *Roma sotterranea*, cristiana, Pl. XI (color), Libreria Spithoever, Roma, 1909. Commissione di archeologia sacra.

616. Rome, S. Costanza. Ring vault. Decoration. Photo. *Cf.* Wilpert, *Die römischen Mosaiken und Malereien*, III, Pl. VII (color), Herdersche Verlagshandlung, Freiburg, 1917.

617. Rome, S. Costanza. Ring vault. Decoration. Vintage scene (photo). *Cf.* Wilpert, *Die römischen Mosaiken und Malereien*, Pl. VI (color), Herdersche Verlagshandlung, Freiburg, 1917.

618. Rome, S. Costanza. Ceiling-decoration. Floating figures (photo).

619. Pompeii, Stabian Baths. Ceiling-decoration (photo).

*Plate*

VII. Proto-Corinthian, Chalkidian and Laconian Pottery.

a. London. British Museum. Macmillan Lekythos. Warriors; hunt. *J.H.S.*, XI (1890), Pl. I (color), (C. Smith), Macmillan & Co., Limited, London.
With the permission of the Council of the Hellenic Society.

b. Boston, Museum. Bellerophon Slaying the Chimæra. Sphinxes. *A.J.A.*, IV (1900), Pl. IV (color), (J. C. Hoppin), The Norwood Press, Norwood, Mass.
With the permission of the Archæological Institute of America and of President Magoffin.

c. Boston, Museum. Hybrid lion; warrior; panther; winged male figure. *A.J.A.*, IV (1900), Pl. V (J. C. Hoppin), The Norwood Press, Norwood, Mass.
With the permission of the Archæological Institute of America and of President Magoffin.

d. Naples, Museum. Flat-bottomed jug. Stag. *Mon. Ant.*, 22 (1913), Pl. 39 (Gabrici), Ulrico Hoepli, Milano.
With the permission of the R. Accademia dei Lincei.

e. Berlin. Lekythos. Fighting warriors; chariot-race; hunt. *Jahr.*, 21 (1906), Pl. 2 (color), (Washburn), Verlag von Georg Reimer, Berlin.
With the permission of the German Archæological Institute and of Director Rodenwaldt.

f. Paris, Cabinet des Médailles. Chalkidian amphora. Herakles and Geryon; quadriga. *F. R., Griechische Vasenmalerei*, Pl. 152 (color), (Buschor), F. Bruckmann, München, 1925.

g. Paris, Cabinet des Médailles. Arkesilas cup. Weighing silphium. *F. R., Griechische Vasenmalerei*, Pl. 151 (color), (Buschor), F. Bruckmann, München, 1925.

VIII. Ionic Pottery.

a. London, British Museum. Sphinx. Naukratis. *J.H.S.*, VIII (1887), Pl. 79 (E. A. Gardner), Macmillan & Co., London.
With the permission of the Council of the Hellenic Society.

b. London, British Museum. Lions and stag. Naukratis. *J.H.S.*, VIII (1887), Pl. 79 (E. A. Gardner), Macmillan & Co., London.
With the permission of the Council of the Hellenic Society.

c. London, British Museum. Hybrid monster. Daphnæ. Walters, *History of Ancient Pottery*, I, Fig. 95, p. 351, John Murray, London, 1905.

d. London, British Museum. Woman

*Plate*

mounting a chariot. Daphnæ. *Ant. Denk.*, II, Pl. 21, 1 (Dümmler), Verlag von Georg Reimer, Berlin, 1895.
With the permission of the German Archæological Institute and of Director Rodenwaldt.

e. London, British Museum. Woman on horse. Man with dog. Daphnæ. *Ant. Denk.*, II, Pl. 21, 2 (Dümmler), Verlag von Georg Reimer, Berlin, 1895.
With the permission of the German Archæological Institute and of Director Rodenwaldt.

f. Munich. Women dancing around an altar. Klazomenai. Sieveking and Hackl, *Die Kgl. Vasensammlung zu München*, I, Pl. 20, J. B. Obernetter, München, 1912.
With the permission of Dr. J. Sieveking, Konservator der Kgl. Vasensammlung.

g. London, British Museum. Bird. Altenburg, Revelers. "Fikellura ware." Walters, *History of Ancient Pottery*, I, Fig. 91, p. 337, John Murray, London, 1905.

IX. Paris, Louvre. Theseus visits Amphitrite. Panaitios Master. *F. R., Griechische Vasenmalerei*, Pl. 5 (Furtwängler), F. Bruckmann, München, 1900.

X. a. New York, Collection of Albert Gallatin. Mænad. Hermonax. Photo.
With the permission of Mr. Albert Gallatin.

b, c. New York, Metropolitan. White-ground lekythoi; toilet scene; farewell. Photo.
With the permission of Miss G. M. A. Richter and of the Metropolitan Museum.

XI. Munich. Achilles and Penthesileia. *F. R., Griechische Vasenmalerei*, Pl. 6 (Furtwängler), F. Bruckmann, München, 1900.

XII. Boston, Museum. Amazon on horse. Sotades. Photo.
With the permission of Mr. L. D. Caskey and the Boston Museum of Fine Arts.

XIII. White-ground vases.

a. London, British Museum. White-ground alabastron. Purification of a house. Pasiades. *J.H.S.*, VIII (1887), Pl. 82 (color), (Murray), Macmillan & Co., Limited, London.
With the permission of the Council of the the Hellenic Society.

b. London, British Museum. *Prothesis* scene. Murray and Smith, *White Athenian Vases*, Pl. 7, British Museum, London, 1896.
With the permission of the Trustees of the British Museum.

c. London, British Museum. *Depositio.* Dead warrior borne by Sleep and Death. Murray and Smith, *White Athenian*

# ANCIENT PAINTING

## I

## THE DAWN OF ART

HUNDREDS of centuries before our era—between twenty and fifty thousand years ago—while there were still gigantic glaciers in the valleys of Europe, in an age when men sought refuge in caves and lived by hunting, we may trace the beginnings of art among mankind. The first artist belonged to the Palæolithic, or Old Stone Age. His weapons and implements were mostly of stone; metals such as copper and iron had not yet been discovered and utilized.

Life at this early time was a strenuous affair and art was apparently made to serve the needs of daily subsistence, to help provide food and to make life possible. In other words, the art which the "Dawn Artist"[1] created in this primitive period was not produced for æsthetic ends, but it was an art with a magical purpose,[2] designed to bring within the hunter's power and to multiply for him the animals which he needed for his daily existence; the stag which he engraved upon his tools of horn and bone, the wild game which he painted on the ceiling and walls of his dark cavern, were drawn in the belief that he could thus gain a "magical hold" over the animals, attract them to him, and capture them as his prey.

That the cave artist did not indulge an artistic instinct and compose merely for the love of art seems evident from the fact that the paintings are almost invisible, often far removed from the entrances and living centers of the caves, hidden away in

[1] I have employed the term used by Professor MacCurdy, *Art and Archæology,* 4 (1916), p. 71, to designate the earliest artist known to us at the dawn of civilization.

[2] S. Reinach, *Cultes, mythes et religions,*[2] Paris, I, 1908, p. 133; A. Della Seta, *Religion and Art,* 1914, p. 58 (tr. by M. C. Harrison); *vs.* this view, M. Hoernes, *Urgeschichte der bildenden Kunst in Europa,*[2] Wien, 1915, pp. 184 ff.; H. Kühn, *Die Malerei der Eiszeit,*[2] 1922, pp. 9 ff.

deep recesses. Furthermore, it seems scarcely probable that he would have blotted out the work of earlier artists to make a place for his own if the drawings had been intended primarily for decoration.

The magical origin of these works, although incapable of absolute proof, is accepted by most of the leading scholars in the prehistoric field. It has received confirmation by recent discoveries at Montespan, in southern France. The animals which are modeled or depicted there are often wounded by axes or javelins. It would thus appear that the remote recesses were centers for ritualistic ceremonies; that, before an important hunting expedition, the tribe gathered about its "witch doctor" and then and there stabbed and maimed the animals which they feared or wished to catch.[2a] But granting that the main motive of the "Dawn Artist" was utilitarian, it does not follow that all æsthetic criteria were nonexistent; it will be seen that in the execution of his work there was spontaneity, freedom, and pleasure. If the primary motive was magical, the artist's delight in his work shows that æsthetic considerations played an important part as well.[3]

The subject matter of these works was thus determined by grim necessity. Looking out upon an animal world more wonderful than any artist has since seen, the hunter of the reindeer period became one of the greatest "Animal Painters" of all times. In the wide panorama that passes before our eyes on the walls of the various caverns, the bison, horse, and mammoth are most often pictured, but the stag, reindeer, goat, wild boar, rhinoceros, and elephant are also represented. Lions and bears, wild oxen and the ibex, fish and birds are not wanting. These animals are all drawn with extraordinary truth to nature, because the trained eye and hand of the hunter reproduced vividly the images which a highly developed visual memory recorded. The kind of existence which he led thus determined in great measure the kind of art which he produced; an agricultural people striving ever so hard would probably have fallen short of the goal.[4] Be that as it may, the painter of the reindeer epoch

---

[2a] In favor of a magical origin for these paintings are: (a) their inaccessibility; (b) their subject matter, which mainly includes useful animals eaten for food; (c) the indications of arrows and wounds on the animals; (d) the superposition of the paintings; (e) the representation of masked figures, such as the "Sorcerer" of the tailpiece, Ch. I; (f) the practices among primitive peoples of later times; (g) the mere fact of their survival, which points to a religious significance. The purpose of the magic is unknown. It may have been a charm to get food; to promote fertility among the animals; to placate the spirit of the dead animal; to make the animal live again or to get rid of animals not wanted. On the other hand, the paintings may have been purely commemorative, recording the hunter's exploits, or they may have been executed to while away his idle moments.

[3] G. Baldwin Brown, *Burlington Magazine*, 29 (1916), pp. 66 ff.; "The Origin and Early History of the Arts in Relation to Æsthetic Theory in General," 41 (1922), pp. 91 ff.; *ib.*, pp. 134 ff.; *The Art of the Cave Dweller*, London, 1928; Franz Boas, *Primitive Art*, Oslo, 1927.

[4] E. Grosse, *Anfänge der Kunst*, 1894, pp. 156, 187, 190, tr. in English, *The Beginnings*

has rarely been surpassed in his drawings of animals; only the Assyrians and the Japanese, in more modern times, have approached the men of that period in their swift, almost intuitive impressions of animal life. We have to deal, then, with the art of the cave man painting animals of the chase, because by so doing he could gain a "magical hold" on the game that supplied his food; a realist in art because of the hunter's life which he led and because he must duplicate the original animal to have it most effective magically.

The centers which today reveal something of this fascinating period are to be found mainly in southern France and northern Spain (Figs. 1 and 2).[5] The finest known caverns with paintings are at Altamira in Spain, and at Font-de-Gaume (Les Eyzies), in France.

It was a Spaniard, Don Marcelino de Sautuola, who first recognized the significance of the paintings at Altamira. Inspired by records of the achievements of primitive man which he had seen at the Paris Exposition in 1878, he was searching in a cavern for traces of prehistoric work, when he was rewarded by frescoes of bisons, pointed out on the ceiling by his small daughter. He published an account of these paintings in 1880,[6] but great scepticism prevailed in regard to their genuineness. In fact it was not until fifteen years later, with the discovery of similar works in France,[7] that the importance of Sautuola's work was recognized, unfortunately after his death. The confirmation of the fact that the cave "frescoes" are of prehistoric date puts back the beginnings of painting more than ten thousand years; in comparison with these works, the paintings of the Egyptians are young in age.

In our discussion of the work of the Quaternary[8] artist, we shall consider mainly the "frescoes," with occasional mention of a few engravings on horn or bone, which show interesting features in adaptation and drawing. If we enter one of the great caverns, such as Altamira, the imagination is struck with amazement that the artist could have produced such works in the depths of dark caverns, with so many difficulties in the way of lighting, execution, and tools; hardly less surprising is it that

of Art, New York, 1897; A. Della Seta, La Genesi dello scorcio, 1907, p. 27, and n. 3; W. Deonna, L'Archéologie, II, 1912, p. 51.

[5] For a list of the caves, S. Reinach, Répertoire de l'art quaternaire, Paris, 1913; J. Déchelette, Manuel d'archéologie préhistorique, I (1908), p. 241; pp. 631-648; others known to Breuil are as yet unpublished. The leading centers are: (France) Pair-non-Pair, Font-de-Gaume, La Mouthe, Combarelles, Teyjat, Bernifal, Marsoulas, Mas d'Azil, Niaux; (Spain) Castillo, Hornos de la Peña, Alpera, Cogul, Altamira. G. G. MacCurdy, Human Origins, New York, II, 1924, p. 419, lists more than eighty caverns with mural decorations.

[6] Don Marcelino de Sautuola, Breves apuntes sobre algunos objetos prehistoricos de la provincia de Santander, Santander, 1880.

[7] La Mouthe by Emile Rivière and Pair-non-Pair by M. Daleau.

[8] The name given to the fourth or last of the geological periods, including the era from the last Great Ice Age.

the eyes of scholars should have ferreted out his work.[9] Apart from the wonder of
the achievement, the thing which most claims our attention is the palimpsestic character of the paintings; they are often superimposed one upon the other, sometimes
three or four deep. The cave artist has had no regard for the work of his predecessor.
Last of all, the marvelous realism of the work must impress everyone—a realism not
studied from nature and improved upon by observation, but a realism that is almost
instinctive, arising from close contact with the animals depicted, so that their essential characteristics are held in memory.

Turning to a consideration of the technique of the paintings, we shall see that they
follow a definite line of progress and development, passing through four different
phases. Abbé Breuil—to whom so much is owed because of his research into the
work of the Quaternary Age, and from whose paintings of the "frescoes" so many of
our reproductions have been copied—has studied the superimposed paintings and
arranged a chronological classification. First of all, we can distinguish a period of
archaic art in which the figures are in simple outlines, deeply engraved with a pointed
flint, or they are drawn in red or black ocher or manganese. The elephant in broad
red line, from Castillo, Spain, is a good example of this phase (Fig. 3). The animal
is represented in absolute profile and only one front and one hind leg are pictured.
With all its crudeness, the lines suggesting an elephant are there—the peculiar structure of the skull with the trunk attached, and the general lumpiness of the legs and
the whole figure. Further characteristics of this early work are seen in the bison from
La Grèze, Dordogne (Fig. 4). In this case, the horns are shown in full-face view,
though the bison itself is in profile. This inconsistency is due to the fact that the
artist of this period created his picture from memory, and in this "memory picture"
objects were usually seen in their broadest and most characteristic aspects. The outlines of the figure are deeply engraved. These drawings belong to the Aurignacian
linear style as contrasted with the later Magdalenian fashion. The latter style was
pictorial and the figures were modeled in a polychrome technique.[9a]

The manner of painting described above is found in the oldest caverns. It is used
in such caves as Pair-non-Pair, La Mouthe, Combarelles, Bernifal, La Grèze, and the
earliest "frescoes" of Altamira and Font-de-Gaume. The proportions are not always
true; the outlines of the figures are often deeply incised. In the second stage these
faults are in part corrected; the lines surrounding the figure become finer, details of
hair and hoofs are more often attempted and a suggestion of modeling is arrived at
by the use of patches of color and incision. This practice tends to make the figure
stand out in relief. The black bison from Altamira (Fig. 5) shows the advance made.

[9] Pierre Paris, *Promenades archéologiques en Espagne*, Paris, 1910, p. 16.
[9a] H. Kühn, *Ursprung und Entwickelung der paläol. Kunst, Mannus*, 17 (1925), pp. 271-
278.

But the promise given in this stage of great progress was not immediately fulfilled and Quaternary art suffered a retrogression in the third period when monochrome silhouettes became common, and the art of modeling was entirely lost. The animals belonging to the third phase are usually executed in solid black, red, or brown; the color is put on in flat tones, like "Chinese shadows," and the drawing loses its old-time vigor and truth. Some of the paintings at Font-de-Gaume, especially the one of the ancestral ox, done in black, show the inferiority of the mural work of this period (Fig. 6). There is also the peculiar technique found at Marsoulas, where the head of the bison is painted in red, the contours are black, and the body is covered with red dots regularly placed in parallel lines. It is interesting to compare this technique with that employed by the Bushmen, especially the example shown in the ostrich painting of Figure 25.

The culmination of the artistic efforts of the cave man is reached in the fourth period, the great Magdalenian Epoch, so called from the station, La Madeleine, in France. It is the well-known period of polychrome art and represents the highest development in Quaternary painting, attained probably as early as sixteen thousand years before Christ. Here belong most of the splendid "frescoes" of Altamira and Font-de-Gaume. The paintings found on the ceiling of the cavern at Altamira are shown in outline in the sketch reproduced in Figure 7. Numbers of wild animals are seen juxtaposed over the surface of the rock for about forty-five feet, sometimes one upon the other, and without any apparent attempt at arrangement or subordination. They appear much as the artist must have seen them in nature. They stand or lie in attitudes of repose, with the exception of the boar, which is shown in rapid motion at the right. If we examine the figures more closely, we see that the painter has again registered with remarkable accuracy the essential details that characterize each animal, as was the case in the earlier outline drawings. But instead of the cruder outlines, we now find the pigment covering the entire surface and so employed as to give the effect of relief, as in the black bison of Figure 8. This animal is about three feet in length and is carefully drawn. The outlines are broken up and the legs are drawn with a real attempt to indicate their anatomical structure; details such as hoofs and horns are rendered with greater care than in the earlier examples. But the striking thing is the use of pigment for modeling,[10] a feat in which the cave man surpassed more civilized artists living many centuries later. In this period, the painter drew the outlines in black and modeled the body by smearing on it various tints obtained by mixing red and black.

An additional element of beauty in these "frescoes" is the polychrome coloring. The

---

[10] E. Loewy, *The Rendering of Nature in Early Greek Art*, tr. by John Fothergill, London, 1907, p. 33, n. 40, does not consider the variations in the color of the animals as shaded modeling.

roe of Figure 9 has a soft tannish-red coat, though the outlines and minor details are black. The proportions are a bit faulty, but, aside from that, the artist has succeeded well in rendering the delicate grace of the animal and the beautiful texture of its hide. It may be, as Hoernes implies,[11] that the cave artist was more at home with his subject when he had masses of flesh to depict and that he reveled in the execution of the lumpy figures of bison, mammoth, and even women.[12] In arguing that these paintings have been overestimated, Hoernes suggests that the ideas of the cave man—to judge from his paintings—probably ran something like this: "Bison, large bison, strong bison! Woman, fat woman, beautiful woman!" However that may be, the bison is among the most successful creations of the cave man, whether seen at rest as in Figure 10, or with its huge frame drawn up, bellowing (Fig. 11). In both of the cases cited, the animals are done in polychrome; the first is perhaps the best preserved of all the figures at Altamira. The colors, still very vivid, are orange-red, black, and brown. Many of the details, such as horns, ears, eyes, nose, and mouth, are engraved. The bellowing bison shows very few traces of red, the color being rather a kind of sepia and darker brown with a mixture of white.

Among the most striking figures at Altamira are the wild boar (Fig. 12), and the recumbent bison (Fig. 13). The wild boar is one of the few animals seen in rapid motion, and the motive of the "flying gallop" is a primitive formula for rapid movement which we shall meet again in Ægean art. It is a question of spontaneous form, arising in quite independent centers, when the primitive artist wishes to express vivid motion. An orange-red color occurs on the legs and belly; elsewhere, perhaps following nature, black and brown are used. The bristles of the back and snout are rendered in great broad brush-strokes; the eye is almost a fleck. The "fresco" is a fine impressionistic painting of a momentary action. The recumbent bison is placed on a rocky projection of the ceiling and is interesting both because of its adaptation to the surface to be decorated and because of its apparent mannerism. Line no longer rules the painting but the power is taken from the outlines and the earlier flatness conquered. The large surfaces are broken up by shading, and light playing over the body raises the lighted parts, thus deepening the shadows.

At Font-de-Gaume, there are also excellent specimens of the fourth phase of the hunter's art, for example, the mammoth engraved on the rock (Fig. 14), and a bison (Fig. 15), which is a decided variant on any of those yet seen. One of the finest figures, however, is the reindeer, which, like the red roe at Altamira, gives evidence of the cave man's skill in depicting the lighter-footed, more delicate animals

[11] M. Hoernes, *op. cit.*,[2] pp. 117, 124. For a later edition, see, Hoernes, revised by O. Menghin, *op. cit.*,[3] Wien, 1925.

[12] *Cf.* Hoernes, *op. cit.*, p. 121, Fig. 1, woman from Willendorf, and p. 163—all sculptures in the round.

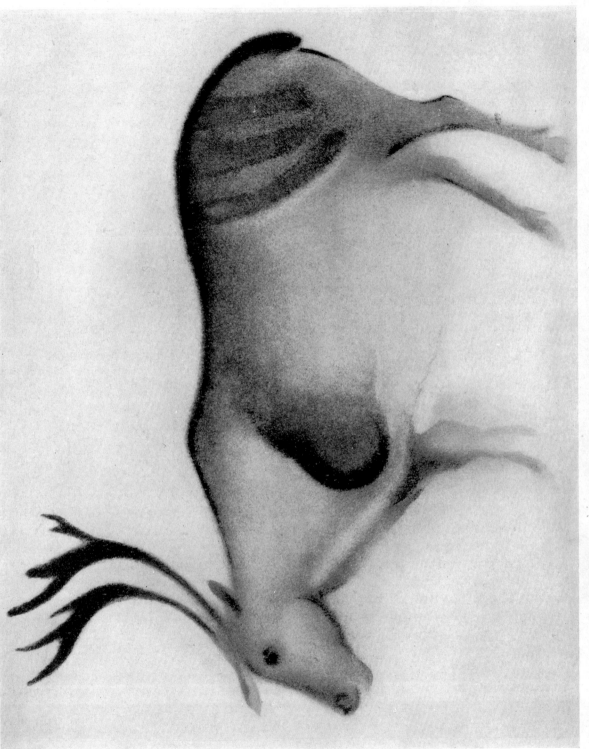

Plate II. Font-de-Gaume. Polychrome reindeer.

of the chase (Plate II). It is a real work of art, the combination of lines and colors arousing æsthetic emotion. Figure 16 is also an interesting example of the cave man's impressionistic painting. In this instance, he has smeared the background with red ocher and against this he has outlined a wolf's body in black. The color has been rubbed on the neck to suggest the thickness of the animal's coat. The hindquarters are covered with a layer of incrustation.

The technique of the polychrome paintings is interesting. The important parts of the outline were first incised or painted and the surface to be decorated was scraped clean. Then the red, brown, and yellow pigments were put on, sometimes as paste, sometimes as liquid. These layers of color were then toned down by scraping and washing and rubbing. Last of all, the hoofs and horns and some minor details were put in in black. In preparing the colors, earth ochers and oxide of manganese were ground into a fine powder. This powder was probably mixed with some grease or animal fat on an improvised palette, perhaps made from stone or from the shoulder blade of some animal. The paintings therefore are not true frescoes, though they are often loosely so called. The pigments were kept in mussel shells or in tubes fashioned of hollowed bone. No brushes have been found; they may have been made of bone, finely frayed at the ends. Traces of the brush are evident in the frescoes. In many cases, color was applied by means of crayons whittled from chunks of ocher or oxide of manganese, a mineral found in the beds of streams. Crayons of this nature have been discovered at Les Eyzies. Pointed flints were used for the incision.[12a]

From the examples of painting mentioned from the reindeer age, and in particular from the painted ceiling at Altamira, we are able to form an idea of the achievement of this era in art. The monuments which we have discussed are extremely interesting because they are some of our earliest human documents. But is it genuine art that we have here? Truth to nature and mere imitation do not constitute art, but rather representation. Furthermore, there is little thought of arrangement or design, no subordination of one figure to another, no interrelation of figures in groups. The figures are strewn over the ceiling at Altamira with no consideration of a ground line and no apparent idea of connection between the various animals.

On the other hand, in contrast to the weaknesses described, there seem to be the beginnings of art. There is selection. With a few strokes of his brush, the cave painter gives a remarkably fine impressionistic painting of a horse's head (Fig. 17), showing an unusual power of seizing upon the really significant features of a subject. The sketch of a herd of reindeer incised on the wing bone of an eagle is a notable example of such skill (Fig. 20). It is also a good exhibition of primitive shorthand

---

[12a] For further technical details, see Ch. XI. On the prevalence of red and yellow, *cf.* L. Franchet, *Les Couleurs employées aux époques préhistoriques*, Prag, 1924, Paris, 1926.

and we shall return to these primitive devices later in the case of similar independent attempts in Crete.

There is adaptation. The cave artist, seeing a protuberance of rock in the cavern at Altamira, adapts the figure of a recumbent bison to the projection (Fig. 13). In other words, he is beginning to attack the problem of the relation of design to space. There also seems to be here and there a suggestion of interrelation of figures, as in the rude engravings of Pair-non-Pair (Fig. 18), where one horse turns his head backward, or in the more famous group of reindeer facing one another, at Font-de-Gaume (Fig. 22). It may be that these groups are quite accidental. The hunter must often have seen two animals grazing face to face or following one another. This heraldic type of composition may even have arisen from an impulse on the part of the designer to represent both sides of the animal;[13] in keeping with such a primitive desire, might be mentioned the multiplication of legs of various animals, to represent different stages of their motion. We know that a fifth leg occurs in Chaldæan art.[14]

It is true that the notion of the group is unknown to primitive people and only gradually arises with technical progress. Even in the case of a group of red deer incised on a bone found at Lorthet (Fig. 21), where fish are swimming about among the legs of the animals, the effect is quite unintentional on the artist's part.[15] He wishes to represent deer crossing a stream and gives us a curious composite "memory picture" of it. But there does occasionally seem to be "group feeling," arising probably from the association of animals as seen in nature; the reindeer facing each other, or the herd of deer mentioned, where the artist multiplies the striking feature —the horns—and gives us a shorthand representation of the group, are examples of this.

In the art of the cave man, we have skilled technique, and, in this respect, advance is made. We have fine observation and selection, adaptation, and chance

---

[13] A. S. Murray, *J.H.S.*, II (1881), p. 319.

[14] The wild boar from Altamira, Cartailhac and Breuil, *La Caverne d'Altamira*, Pl. XIV, may be an example of an attempt to represent the boar in rest and motion. Eight legs occur here. At least this interpretation is accepted by Prof. G. Baldwin Brown, *Encyclop. Britannica*, 11th ed., *s.v. Painting*. It is interesting that attempts to represent motion in this way are deliberately made today by some artists of the futurist school, for instance, by Balla in his, "Person and Dog in Motion." A. J. Eddy, *Cubists and Post-Impressionism*, Chicago, 1914, p. 164. I owe the reference to Miss Fernald.

The desire in Chaldæan art was to give the animal the requisite number of legs in both front and side views. *Cf.* Perrot and Chipiez, *Histoire de l'art*, II, 1884, Figs. 216, 217 and C. Frank, *Kunstgeschichte in Bildern*, I, 2, *Babylonisch-assyrische Kunst*, 58, 1, 2. See M. Faure, "La représentation du mouvement dans l'art Magdalénien," *Rev. anthropol.*, XXIV (1914), p. 201.

[15] W. Deonna, *op. cit.*, II, 1912, p. 184, n. 3. One cannot take seriously an English suggestion that the artist wished to provide a fish course for his family before the venison!

grouping. But some qualities which we are accustomed to consider important in art
—such as design and imagination, are mostly absent. Yet it cannot be denied that the
artistic impulse has played a part in most of these paintings and that they deserve
to rank as genuine works of art. We can believe that the artist was an alert worker
taking pleasure in his task, striving to render nature impressionistically, and boldly
experimenting with new problems.

No mention has been made of the cave artist's attempt to paint human beings.
Some efforts exist, but they are of the crudest character, such as the infantile
sketches from Marsoulas (Fig. 19). It is a well-known fact that the representation
of the human form is much more difficult for the primitive painter than animal
forms; the structure of animals is less complicated and more uniform than is the
case with man.[16] "Perfection in the rendering of animal forms is in direct proportion
to the simplicity of their construction, that is, to the ease with which they are committed to memory."[17] This being the case, since the animal is easier to reproduce
than the human form, perfection in the representation of animals is to be expected
at an earlier stage of civilization. It is interesting also to note that as the execution
of human figures improves, that of animals declines. The "Dawn Artist" seems to
have evolved little more than caricatures in most of his efforts to depict human
figures, although somewhat better examples than those in France are found on the
painted rock surfaces at Cogul and Alpera in Spain. These latter paintings are
attempts at compositions representing hunts and ceremonial dances. The painting
at Cogul (Fig. 23) shows a large number of women, dressed in black or red, grouped
around a nude man, with a hunting scene above. The painting may belong to the
Palæolithic Age but seems later, both because of the attempt at grouping and because
of the human figures.[17a] The scene is probably ritualistic in character and concerned
with fertility. The hunting scene from Alpera is interesting on account of the interrelation of figures and the introduction of the bow, which is not found in earlier cave-
paintings (Fig. 24). These efforts, however, strike us as being decidedly more
primitive work than the earlier paintings of animals. The hunter did not need to
observe the human form. On the other hand, his life was closely bound up with the
pursuit of animals and he must have had a very vivid idea of their appearance both
in his waking hours and when dreaming of his encounters. When he ceased to follow
the chase, he lost his skill in drawing animals.

It is worth while to compare the artistic efforts of the Magdalenian Epoch with

[16] J. Lange, *Darstellung des Menschen in der älteren griechischen Kunst*, tr. by M. Mann,
Strassburg, 1899, p. 111.

[17] E. Loewy, *op. cit.*, p. 27, n. 30.

[17a] H. Obermaier, *Fossil Man in Spain*, New Haven, 1924, pp. 254 ff., assigns these paintings to the Palæolithic Age.

attempts of savages living in more modern times under conditions not dissimilar. Not a little light is thrown on ancient practices by the customs of these later races. Foremost among them are the Bushmen of southern Africa, whose paintings go back to a very remote antiquity.[17b] They often show less technical perfection and less formal artistic power than the Magdalenian painters, but a greater ability to express life, movement, and the composition of groups. Their skill is readily seen from paintings such as Figure 25, which shows an attempt to decoy ostriches, with a man impersonating an ostrich. Some of their paintings rival the best polychrome work at Altamira, as, for example, the antelope of Figure 26. The Bushmen have forgotten the significance of these paintings and have invented legendary explanations for them, but they have retained the memory of their connection with superstitious ceremonies. The civilization and mentality of the cave man seem to live again in these primitive peoples. They show art conditioned by the environment of the hunter's life. Similar paintings occur among the Eskimo, Australians, and American Indians.

The age in which the "Dawn Artist" lived cannot have left him much leisure for the contemplation of beauty! The works which we have discussed range in time from the Aurignacian Epoch through the Magdalenian period—anywhere from thirty to sixteen thousand years ago. While the climate was not rigorous, the difficulties attendant upon pursuing a livelihood must have been enormous. The mere fashioning of tools from bone, horn, and stone, the continual struggle against wild beasts, the hunting of game and other food, and the handling of the game when it was killed, were no trivial labors. The works which he created arouse our admiration because of their facility, beauty of line, and realism; as works of scientific and historic importance, they have an almost inestimable value. The artist who made them had a feeling for color and proportion; he possessed an appreciation of the beauty of animal forms and an ability to render them which later centuries, without his handicaps, have found it difficult to equal. This "Dawn Artist" probably belonged to the Cro-Magnon race—a tall, long-headed people, who may have come from Africa, as some believe, or from Central Asia. The thickness of the deposits in the caves proves a long period of culture, and their art seems to be autochthonous, as we can apparently trace it from its rude beginnings to the height of its development. In these people, a sense of proportion and beauty was instinct from the beginning and some writers have for this reason called them the "Palæolithic Greeks."[18] Their art

[17b] Cf. Neville Jones, *The Stone Age in Rhodesia*, London, 1926; H. Breuil, *Gravures rupestres du désert libyque identiques à celles des anciens Bushmen*, L'Anthropol., 36 (1926), pp. 125-127; M. C. Burkitt, *South Africa's Past in Stone and Paint*, Cambridge, 1928.

[18] H. Osborn, *Men of the Old Stone Age*, 1922, p. 316.

disappears from history with its creators, leaving no traces and no after-result, whether because of some catastrophe or the natural process of decay, we are unable to say. Their efforts form the first attempts at art in the history of mankind and we are at present not able to follow them any later in time than the Magdalenian Epoch.[19]

[19] Interesting theories as to the probable origin and affinities of the Magdalenians and their predecessors are given by R. A. S. Macalister, *A Text-book of European Archæology*, I, 1921, pp. 576 ff. These theories can in no way be proved because "our knowledge of the early peopling of Asia and Africa is practically *nil*," but they are extremely suggestive. Macalister also holds that Palæolithic man probably remained in Europe and formed the substratum of the population in the succeeding stages of the history of the continent. *Cf.* Osborn, *op. cit.*, p. 451. Most scholars now derive the Aurignacians and Magdalenians from the East, some by way of Africa.

# II

# EGYPT

WE turn from Europe to the valley of the Nile to discover the next attempts of man in the art of painting (Fig. 27). Here in the predynastic period, as early as 4000 or 5000 B.C., we find traces of a prehistoric civilization. In centers such as Abydos, Nagada, and Hierakonpolis, in Upper Egypt, recent excavations have revealed a primitive art belonging to the outgoing Neolithic Age when copper began to be used. Of the Old Stone Age there are practically no traces in Egypt with the exception of flints.[1]

The houses of this remote age have almost entirely perished because of their primitive construction, situation, and usage, but from the cemeteries and tombs we can gain some idea of this early stage of Egyptian progress. Buried with the dead in his grave have been found weapons of flint, beautifully wrought, articles of adornment, and clay vases for food and drink. They show us that the primitive Egyptian modeled pottery by hand, had a knowledge of weaving, and made clothes and baskets; they prove that he had invented glazes for beads and understood the working of metals such as gold for beads and bracelets, and copper for implements. Most

---

[1] J. H. Breasted, *Scientific Monthly* (1919), p. 301—carvings of boats, giraffes, ostriches, and other animals on rocks and cliffs, may date from the Palæolithic Age. In the lower alluvium of the Nile, there are fragments of pottery which go back 15,000 or 18,000 years. Then follows a gap until the predynastic age of metals. W. M. F. Petrie denies a Neolithic Age in Egypt, *Journal Manchester Egyptian and Oriental Soc.* (1918-1919), pp. 10 ff., *Diospolis Parva*, London, 1901, p. 28; J. H. Breasted, *Oriental Institute Communications, No. 3. First Report of the Prehistoric Survey Expedition* (K. S. Sandford, W. J. Arkell), Chicago, 1928.

of his weapons and tools were of stone. All of these objects were placed in the tomb to provide the necessities for the soul and "double" in the life beyond the grave. These men were among the earliest cultivators of the soil and breeders of cattle and sheep known anywhere and their settlements reached along the valley from lower Nubia to the sea.[2]

An examination of the predynastic pottery gives us a glimpse into the work of the early Egyptian painter. The oldest class of painted vases shows designs in white on a ground of hand-burnished red (Fig. 28). Sometimes these are linear or floral, or imitate basketwork; at times they have representations of animals, men, and ships. It is interesting to note schematization in form from the very beginning. A vase in the Petrie Collection, with a design of two warriors fighting, shows the triangular form employed for the human body (Fig. 29). We shall have occasion later to discuss the problem of schematization and realism in art.

In the second stage, the figures are painted in a reddish brown against a light, buff ground. They are filled in with solid color in contrast to those of the first class, which are cross-hatched. In some of the earlier examples, there is imitation of marble, basketwork, or cordage (Fig. 30). Zigzag lines, figures of men and women, goats, antelopes, ships, and aloe trees are common patterns. A good example of this second or later phase is a vase in the Museum at Cairo (Fig. 31), showing ships in the foreground and men, women, and animals in the background. In the center is a woman who seems to be in an attitude characteristic of dancing. On either side of her is a male figure, while some antelopes are seen at the right and left. From these early vases we find that a feeling for balance and rhythm is present from the very beginning in Egyptian design.[2a]

Last of all, as typical of this age, the paintings from a tomb at Hierakonpolis may be mentioned—the earliest wall-paintings known to us.[2b] This tomb, constructed entirely of bricks, was plastered over with mud mortar and the walls were then covered with a yellow wash, perhaps to represent the desert. Against this, in the foreground, human beings, animals, and a trapping scene are represented. In the middle, six boats with cabins are depicted. The background contains a hunting scene. In the section shown here (Fig. 32), in the upper right-hand corner, a man is seated in the stern of a boat and there are men above the cabins. In the space

[2] G. Reisner, *Archæological Survey of Nubia*, I. Objects made of ivory were common in this period, especially combs, hairpins, bracelets, rings, and harpoons. Slate palettes for face- and eye-paints were also found.

[2a] W. M. F. Petrie, *Prehistoric Egypt*, London, 1920, Chs. V, VI, Pls. X-XXII; *Corpus of Prehistoric Pottery and Palettes*, London, 1921, Pls. XX-XXV; XXXI-XXXVII. The combination of a rich hæmatite red with a highly reflecting black is the first satisfying use of color in Egypt.

[2b] J. E. Quibell, F. W. Green, *Hierakonpolis*, II (1902), Pls. 76-78 (color).

Plate III. Thebes. Amenhotep II on the knees of his nurse.

unoccupied by the boat, a gazelle and three goats are seen. The figures, crudely drawn as on the early vases, were colored a reddish brown and the boats with one exception were painted white with a wash of green malachite above. Black was employed for one boat and white for garments and various details. The scene is probably religious and funereal, with a magical significance, designed to ensure the hunter's happiness in Elysium. Below there are interesting sections representing crouching captives threatened by a man with a mace, lassoed antelopes, and, in one case, a man holding a lion by the neck with either hand. Such were the primitive attempts at tomb-decoration, consisting of childish figures awkwardly drawn in red ocher, some of the designs being linear in character, others solid silhouettes in red—perhaps an attempt to imitate nature. It is interesting to note that the wall in this early period is divided into two distinct parts. Below the decoration ran a dado of blue-black, ten and a half inches in height, with a red ocher line above.

The originators of these works were a people who pursued game in the desert and captured the hippopotamus from their boats. They lived in a tribal state and engaged in agriculture, hunting, fishing, and herding. They may even have been traders, their boat-standards indicating the place from which they came (*cf*. Fig. 31). From the very beginning, we discover a rather extraordinary development of their artistic sense; their works of art show a greater feeling for adapting designs to surfaces than was the case with the cave man (Fig. 33). The artist possessed a crude knowledge of the arrangement of figures in groups, though perspective is still so little understood that the problem of levels seems rather vaguely handled; the painting from Hierakonpolis has the same diffused composition and primitive treatment of depth found in the paintings from Cogul and Alpera in Spain.

In general, the skill and facility of the predynastic Egyptian are not comparable to that of the cave man of the reindeer age. The interesting development in early Egypt is the schematization of the figure, a phenomenon which we have seen occurring at the end of the Palæolithic Age in Spain. Does it indicate merely a degenerate stage of realism in which the artist degrades and simplifies natural forms in order to economize his efforts?[3] Looking out upon the world of nature with her many forms, does he create for himself a world of forms of his own, in order to free himself from the more complicated patterns of nature? In such a case, instead of imitating nature, he would thus proceed to dominate and rule her, actuated by motives of economy of labor and at times probably by the desire for rhythm and symmetry in his design. The probable truth is that the primitive artist was unable to reproduce nature better at this time, had he desired. In any case, he was working merely from a "memory picture" which was quite independent of the real appearance of the object and at times

[3] H. G. Spearing, *Childhood of Art*, pp. 119, 125 f.; A. Conze, *Sitz. der Berl. Akad.*, 1897, pp. 98 ff.

opposed to it. The graphic expression of this was a scheme of lines and planes approaching geometric form.[4] It is interesting to note that this turning from realism to schematization seems to come with the transition from the hunter's life to the agricultural stage. When the struggle for existence no longer demanded that the roving hunter sharpen his eye and develop aptitude of hand and keen visual memory, we find the more settled Neolithic farmer producing in his art a visible expression of *ideas,* no longer images of objects done in realistic fashion. Stylization appears to herald the downfall of Palæolithic art, although Loewy would have us believe that we do not have primitive art in the work of the reindeer period, but probably an advanced and developed production. He argues that the material of that age as presented to us is disconnected historically.[5]

A real change in the physical character of the people of Upper Egypt and in their art took place at the beginning of the dynastic period, about 3400 B.C.— owing perhaps to a fusion of the population of Upper and Lower Egypt. In this mingling, an Asiatic race may have been involved, as the slate palettes from Hierakonpolis with their Chaldæan affiliations seem to indicate.[6] It is unfortunate that there are so few remains of painting from this period, but the reliefs, a kindred art of the time, tell us something of the drawing. For the early Egyptian, no essential difference existed between painting and relief; both were often treated as outlines filled in with color. Furthermore, in relief the effect of modeling was frequently lost by the practice of using strong colors, such as red for outlines, without regard for light and shade. In origin, reliefs were merely flat drawings raised above the back-

[4] E. Loewy, *op. cit.,* p. 10.                     [5] E. Loewy, *op. cit.,* p. 31.

[6] G. Bénédite, *Le Couteau de Gebel el-'Arak, Mon. Piot,* 1916; J. Capart, *Primitive Art in Egypt,* pp. 248, 287; L. Heuzey, *Égypte ou Chaldée,* 1899; H. R. Hall, *J.E.A.,* VIII (1922), pp. 241-257, "Syria may be the home of the Armenoid race that so profoundly modified the ethnography of the Nile valley in the late predynastic and early dynastic period." Petrie, *Prehistoric Egypt,* London, 1920, finds Algerian (Berber-Lybian) influence in pottery at one time in Egypt, Elamite at another. I owe the reference to Prof. George A. Barton. L. W. King and H. R. Hall, *Egypt and Western Asia,* 1907, pp. 34 ff. *Cf.* L. W. King, *Sumer and Akkad,* pp. 325 ff. J. de Morgan, *L'Anthropologie,* XXXI, 185-238, 425-468; XXXII, 39-65, "De l'influence asiatique sur l'Afrique à l'origine de la civilisation égyptienne." See Ch. III, n. 10. *Cf. Cambridge Ancient History,* I, 1924, pp. 254 ff., 261 ff., 580. S. Langdon, "The Early Chronology of Sumer and Egypt and the Similarities in Their Culture," *J.E.A.,* VII (1921), pp. 133 ff.; H. Peake, H. J. Fleure, *Priests and Kings* ("The Corridors of Time," Vol. IV), New Haven, 1927, pp. 63 ff.

Thirty-four hundred is probably a minimum date for the First Dynasty. Professor Breasted has found the names of ten kings of the North who ruled over a united Egypt before the time of Menes. According to Professor Breasted, the calendar of Egypt was formed in a period of stability under these kings and the dating of Menes is probably not therefore to be pushed back beyond 3400, despite Borchardt's theories about the calendar. I owe the information to Mrs. C. Ransom Williams, co-author of *The Tomb of Perneb.*

ground which was cut away from the painted outline. The earliest reliefs have representations of animals, oftentimes shown in procession,[6a] but it is in the more elaborate slate palettes, such as the one of King Narmer, of the First Dynasty, that we begin to see what great strides art had made in the intervening period (Fig. 34). The king is represented seizing a prisoner by the hair with one hand and brandishing a mace with the other, a motive which we find in the predynastic painting from Hierakonpolis. Above the prisoner is a human head, a bunch of six papyrus stems, and a falcon, signifying that Horus has vanquished or seized 6,000 foes; that the people of the North have been overthrown.[7] Already in this early age, many of the conventions which characterize later Egyptian art were fixed, especially the composite "memory picture" of the human form with the eye in front view in the profile face, the shoulders *de face*, with the limbs again in profile by a strange twist at the waistline. In the lower panel, the running figures show the action which had come into art, while the marvelous advance in the treatment of anatomy and the power of imagination in the design of the long-necked animals must impress everyone. The tendency toward composition in registers, or divisions one above another, is also observable at this time—a practice which began, as we saw, in the prehistoric age.

Following the prehistoric and early dynastic stage, usually termed the Thinite Age, from This, near Abydos, the art of Egypt passes through three great epochs—that of the Old Kingdom or Memphite period, and the periods of the Middle Kingdom and the Empire, with the center of power at Thebes. During the Old Kingdom, roughly speaking, from 3000 to 2500 B.C., some of the finest works of Egyptian art were created. This is the period when the distinctive characteristics which afterward stamped Egyptian art with its national character were developed.[8] We know these works mainly from the tombs; most of the houses and palaces have perished.

Some of the earliest examples of flat painting from dynastic times are those from the Third Dynasty tomb of Hesi-Re at Sakkara. This tomb was made of crude brick

[6a] G. Bénédite, "The Carnarvon Ivory," *J.E.A.*, V (1918), pp. 1-15; 225-241.

[7] The falcon is taken by some to be the king: J. H. Breasted, *Ancient Times*, Fig. 28; L. Keimer, *Ægyptus*, VII (1926), pp. 169 ff.; by others, to be the god: L. Borchardt, *Grabdenkmal des Königs Sahu-re*, II, 18; A. H. Gardiner, *J.E.A.*, II (1915), pp. 72-73; *Egyptian Grammar*, Oxford, 1927, § 5; A. Erman, *Grammatik*, 4th ed., 1928, § 16; I owe the information to Mrs. C. Ransom Williams.

[8] H. Schäfer, *Einiges über Entstehung und Art der ägyptischen Kunst, Zeitschr. für ägypt. Sprache*, 52, 1915, pp. 9 ff. These included a loss of the tendency to express the purely animal strength of men and animals so often seen in Mesopotamian art and a turning away from barbarian to more human elements in representation:—the "poetry of battle" is given rather than the gruesomeness of it, which we see on the Stele of the Vultures. It means a gain in harmony and symmetry in composition, ability to express inner greatness and a charm added to relief because of technical innovations. Æsthetic considerations played a very important part in Egyptian art from the beginning.

and consisted of a long corridor with piers and recesses on one side in a complicated design. These piers and recesses were adorned with rectangular niches which were painted with geometrical patterns in a simple color scheme of black, red, yellow, green, and white. The artistic importance of the paintings is not great; the significant thing is the simple color scheme, which is the same one that was found at Hierakonpolis. The paintings copy in a realistic fashion, wall hangings. Even the rope loops at the bottom and the wooden pole which was fastened to the loops to weigh down the curtain were faithfully rendered. On the opposite wall were pictured many objects such as ointment jars, tools, games, and a large human figure, perhaps the deceased. Æsthetically, the paintings are not very significant but they may be regarded as an important landmark in the history of Egyptian painting. They represent a great advance over the paintings of Hierakonpolis in composition and in ability to depict the human figure. Crudity of form has disappeared. The originals are no longer available, having been reburied.[8a]

The composition of the geese from the mastaba of Nefermat at Mêdum, belonging to the Fourth Dynasty, forms one of the few remaining paintings from the great pyramid age (Fig. 35). At the left, three geese proceed to the left in contrast to those going to the right. The sincerity of observation met with in the earliest art of the hunter's age is seen in this flock of geese stalking among some green plants. The blue, green, and brownish coloring used for the plumage is true to nature and the artist has caught well the heavy gait, the serpentine bend of the neck, and the complacency of these birds. Clumps of growing plants added here and there to suggest landscape take away from the baldness of the background, which is gray, a color very commonly used for backgrounds in the painting of the Old Kingdom.

But a stray painting here and there gives us little conception of the vast use of polychromy which must have been prevalent in this period, not only for wall-paintings but to decorate the sculpture and the reliefs on the walls of the tombs. The portrait of the Princess Nefert from the Fourth Dynasty has been so often pictured that it seems superfluous to present it once more, but it reveals more clearly than most statues the Egyptian's love for vivid color (Fig. 36). The eyes are animated and show an eyeball of white set in a metal capsule which forms the eyelids. A ball of crystal gives the luminous look to the eye and a stud of metal constitutes the pupil. In addition to this, there is the blue-black coloring for the hair, the yellow of the skin, and the rich red, white, green, gray-blue, and black of the collar and headband. These masses of color were outlined in red and black.[9] The gray-blue is probably an original blue, the surface of which has changed somewhat in color.

[8a] J. E. Quibell, *Excavations at Saqqara* (1911-1912), Le Caire, 1913.

[9] L. Borchardt, *Statuen und Statuetten von Königen u. Privatleuten, Teil I*, 1911, Catalogue du Caire, No. 4.

Painting was also an auxiliary art in the service of architecture. The paintings in the temples are mostly lost. On the ceiling of the temple of Ne-user-Re, of the Fifth Dynasty, we see the commonly used decoration of stars of gold against a ground of midnight blue. This was characteristic of other sites than Abusir; in fact, it is often found on the ceiling, which corresponded to the Egyptian conception of the sky. For the most part, however, we must judge the painting of this period by reliefs, especially those from the royal and mastaba tombs (Fig. 37). In the mastaba, or "bench-like" tombs, figures were usually carved in low relief, especially in the chapel where the relatives and friends met to pay homage to the dead. Here were represented servants bringing offerings to the dead, tending cattle, carving meats, and following the chase—all for the sustenance of their master in the life beyond the grave. The statuettes scattered in the rooms and the scenes pictured on the walls lessened the danger of starvation and second death for the deceased. The Egyptian had the walls of his tomb covered with many scenes providing for his future maintenance, since he believed so firmly that the more his funereal supplies were multiplied the less likely he was to want. Crowds of servants revealed the master's wealth in lands; fields were ploughed for him to produce his bread, grain was cut for him, corn winnowed, ground, baked, and prepared for his food.[10] No detail providing for his support and happiness was spared. In the beginning, a very small amount of wall space was devoted to these reliefs; but, with time, the designs were piled up in registers one above another until the walls presented the appearance of veritable tapestries. The painter was interested merely in decorating the wall with the necessary scenes and seems to have felt no regard for the structure of the wall as a wall. Good examples of reliefs of this kind are found in the mastaba of Ptahhotep at Sakkara, a tomb belonging to the Fifth Dynasty (Fig. 38). The scenes from the south wall show Ptahhotep "contemplating the pleasant diversions that take place throughout the country." Animal life and hunting scenes in the desert are represented in the upper rows and, below, men are cleaning fish and making ropes and papyrus boats. The lowest panels show fowlers and peasants in Nile boats, fighting or busied with work of various kinds.

The Egyptian artist frequently conceived landscape in a conventional fashion, painting everything between himself and the horizon as it appeared to some one standing beside the Nile and looking inland, but placing the various levels on top of one another. At the bottom of the painting was the Nile; and, from that point, the marshlands—with people engaged in fishing, fowling, boat building, and the like— stretched away toward the top of the picture where the desert was represented. In the earlier examples, the different planes were sharply indicated by straight lines

[10] Cf. Luise Klebs, *Die Reliefs des alten Reiches*, 1915 (*Abh. der Heidelberg. Akad. d. Wiss., Ph.-hist. Kl.*), for a catalogue of the subjects represented.

which marked the field off into registers. The colors, red, black, white, green, blue, and yellow, were also used in a conventional scheme. The whole painting was merely outline drawing filled in with washes of solid color.[10a]

The achievement of the Egyptian artist at the very beginning of the Old Kingdom in drawing and modeling the human figure is perhaps best seen in the famous wooden panels from the tomb of Hesi-Re at Sakkara, mentioned above. They decorated the ends of niches opening on a long corridor and were originally painted in color. Figure 39 contains a splendid portrait of Hesi-Re, who was a secretary of importance and a favorite of the king. The modeling of the figure shows a strong feeling for the bony structure of the body. The flesh is solid with no suggestion of softness. There is a certain strength and vigor about the work which is heightened by the tightly closed, thin lips, the firmness of the muscles, and the rigidity of pose. The features show a fine aquiline nose and a thin, sensitive face. For sheer excellence of technique and resultant achievement, there are few superior monuments from the Old Kingdom.[11]

Characteristic also of the period under discussion are the reliefs from the tomb of Ti. In Figure 40, Ti and his wife are seen seated against a background formed by a mat of reeds and rushes in yellow and green. The colors employed for the figures are a terra cotta red for the flesh of Ti, yellow for the skin of his wife, black for hair and details, white for garments, and green, blue, and yellow for necklaces and armlets. One convention occurring here which becomes traditional in Egyptian painting is the colossal size given to the dead master of the house in contrast to that of his wife and servants.

A survey of some of the royal tombs should also be made in order to complete our ideas of the art of this period, but we shall merely indicate briefly some of the achievements found here. Two of the best known tombs at Abusir, those of King Sahu-Re and King Ne-User-Re, furnish excellent evidence for our purpose.[12] In Figure 41, we see some typical reliefs from the tomb of King Sahu-Re, depicting captive prisoners, realistically drawn. The modeling of the faces is done with great skill. The king is often seen vigorously trampling down his enemies. Other reliefs show trading ships and various subjects that are new.

The art of the Old Kingdom is much more advanced than the art of the predynastic age. Balance, rhythm, and action become more prominent. The work is sincere and forcible, even though bound by rigorous conventions. It is marked always by a certain archaic severity and attention to essentials. With the progress of time, we

[10a] For a different view in regard to the landscape convention, see H. Schäfer, *Von ägyptischer Kunst*, 2d ed., Leipzig, 1922, pp. 168-169.

[11] J. E. Quibell, *The Tomb of Hesy*, Cairo, 1913. Pls. VIII, IX (color), for matting; Pls. XXIX-XXXII, for panels of Hesi-Re.

[12] L. Borchardt, *Das Grabdenkmal des Königs Ne-user-re*, Leipzig, 1907; *Das Grabdenkmal des Königs Sahu-re*, II, Leipzig, 1913, *Die Wandbilder*, p. 5.

find greater intricacy of composition, greater beauty of line and increased wealth in motives. It is evident that the Egyptian of this period had a genius for decorative art. It is not difficult to see that painting was subordinated for the most part to the demands of architecture and sculpture and that Egyptian art was an art under the influence of magic, its main reason for existence being the cult of the dead and the necessity to provide for the life beyond.[13] This school had its center at Memphis, and Memphite art, which was but a continuation and outgrowth of Thinite, reveals a unity of tradition throughout. Compared with predynastic painting the work is highly developed, possessing assurance and even sophistication in the Fifth Dynasty.

At the end of the Sixth Dynasty, the monarchy fell and civil strife broke out. The political power was finally seized by Theban princes and it is in the Twelfth Dynasty, about 2000 B.C., that we witness the next great efflorescence of Egyptian art. Probably the growing power of the landed nobles accomplished the change. In their tombs at Beni Hasan, large numbers of wall-paintings are found in addition to reliefs. The subjects include not only scenes from the daily life of the people, noted in the Sixth Dynasty, but battle scenes, war dances, and sieges of cities, recalling the revolutions which resulted in the feudal age. Landscape also begins to play a more prominent rôle. During this period, the so-called Middle Kingdom, the duality of Egyptian art is more evident than usual.[14] There are two main trends in the art. First of all, there is the popular, or profane and realistic, tendency. This contrasts strongly with the second class of works which exemplify the more formal and classic art of official Egypt, the art which emanated from the rulers, princes, and priests. In general, the court style dominated at this time.

Maspero attempts to show that the school at Hermopolis was responsible for some of this realistic tendency,[15] but it was probably a much more widespread thing, as Kees has pointed out,[16] and cannot be assigned to one center. The school at Meir is, however, an interesting example of this movement. This school was characterized by a fondness for intensity and variety of movement and by a love of humor. It developed the types of the lean and the fat man which were done with not a little truth to nature (Fig. 42). It is questionable, however, whether this school can be credited with the influence on Beni Hasan and el-Bersheh which Maspero would assign to it. The lean herdsman is a type that could hardly be improved upon for

[13] The magical character of Egyptian art seems the more probable in view of the multiplication of portrait statues, the various rites performed, and the later ushabtis and papyri. Gardiner is, however, probably correct in emphasizing the fact that pride in the possession of a beautiful monument also had weight with the owner. Nina de Garis Davies, A. H. Gardiner, *The Tomb of Amenemhēt*, London, 1915, p. 19.

[14] W. Spiegelberg, *Geschichte der ägyptischen Kunst*, Leipzig, 1903, p. 22.

[15] G. Maspero, *Art in Egypt*, New York, 1912, p. 106.

[16] Hermann Kees, *Studien zur aegyptischen Provinzialkunst*, Leipzig, 1921, pp. 15-16.

sheer realism. The famished body with many ribs showing, the scraggy neck and thin face lined with wrinkles prove the artist to be a keen observer. This figure is the most remarkable one in the tomb and illustrates better than any other the naturalism of the school. The man is evidently a Hamite because of his long nose, scanty tuft of beard, lack of a mustache, and shaggy growth of hair. The body is actually in profile, not twisted around full face on profile legs.[17]

The fragile character of painting made it less desirable than sculptured relief for use in connection with the cult of the dead, where permanency was essential. Probably in early times flat painting was employed on mud brick walls or on stone walls that were too poor in quality to be sculptured. Perhaps the reason why we find a return to flat painting in the Middle Kingdom is the inferiority of the stone. There were no even surfaces in most of the rock tombs of this age as there were in the earlier mastabas of limestone. On the other hand, paintings were quickly and cheaply made and must have recommended themselves to people of moderate means. From the thirty-nine decorated tombs at Beni Hasan—an important source for our study—we shall select paintings from the tomb of Khnemhotep II (No. 3), and from that of Ameni (No. 2), to illustrate the art of this period (Fig. 43). The tombs are hollowed out of the rock and often have "Proto-Doric" columns in front or within the main hall, and elaborate painted patterns on the walls and ceilings.

Among the scenes most commonly found are those of fowling and fishing in the marshes (Fig. 44). In the one depicted here, we have a balanced composition in which Khnemhotep, accompanied by his wife and son, pursues game in the lowlands in a boat. Khnemhotep is shown at the left, hurling a throw stick at the birds in the papyrus reeds, while butterflies and birds dart about in confusion. This scene is reversed at the right where he is pictured spearing fish. In the center, seated behind a screen, he traps birds in a clapnet. Below the main panels, servants fish and enjoy sports in boats. The water, where fish and hippopotami abound, is conventionally represented by wavy lines of black against a blue ground. In the scene where Khnemhotep is spearing fish, the water, by a curious convention, is raised almost to the level of the eye in the midst of the papyrus. The decorative character of the whole composition is evident at a glance. The careful symmetry observed in repeating the figure of Khnemhotep at the right and left is emphasized by the distribution of the field into panels. The hieroglyphs form another element of decoration, filling in the upper parts of the panels and the spaces around the door. The entire composition is a splendid specimen of symmetry and beautiful spacing. It is also a good example of the golden mediocrity of Egyptian painting, much of which was probably prepared in advance for commercial purposes, as tombstones today. One of the most satisfying features is the manner in which the masses of color are spread out against

[17] A. M. Blackman, *The Rock Tombs of Meir*, II, London, 1915, pp. 17-18.

the background, although the patterns are overcrowded and the addition of the hieroglyphs gives an overloaded effect. The painting is entirely flat in character. Terra cotta red, yellow, green, brown, and white are the leading colors employed.

A detailed study of some of the animals living among the papyrus reeds discloses the same skill in depicting animal life which was found among the Egyptians of an earlier period—a skill which we have already observed as apparently concomitant with the hunter's life, and seemingly a result of his trained eye and hand. One of the finest of these animals is a cat sitting on a papyrus stem in search of prey (Fig. 45). It was probably being used to startle and catch birds, as falcons were employed, and seems to be seized in an attitude of recoil, ready to spring. The colors are green for the papyrus, which forms a very graceful background for the design, with red at the base of the umbel, and black outlining the green edges of the stems. Black, yellow, and brown are the colors employed for the cat, with touches of white and red here and there. The various kinds of birds are painted with the same cleverness (Fig. 46). On the water, below and at the left, are blue ducks with red wings and heads. There is a rich display of color in the plumage of the various birds—red, blue, yellow, white, and black prevailing. The base line is red, the background greenish in color, with a brownish yellow for the bush. These colors have probably altered with age. The wings of the flying shrike are outspread in the conventional Egyptian fashion.

The same fondness for truth to nature is apparent in the characterization of a caravan of Canaanites who come to trade in Egypt and who are represented on the walls as they must have appeared on the estate of this feudal baron (Fig. 47). According to Professor Breasted, the heavy figures, with large noses, reveal the Semite with an admixture of Hittite blood. They come armed with long bows and spears and bring their families and animals in their train.

In tomb No. 3, is a painting which shows a break with the old traditions of drawing (Fig. 48). In the main, the artists of the Twelfth Dynasty carried on the methods of the Old Kingdom in commonly pictured themes, with the exception that they sometimes introduced innovations in perspective.[18] A scene in a farmyard, where servants are feeding oryxes, is a good example of this practice. One peasant is about to seat himself on the back of an oryx, in order to force it to crouch down. The foreshortening of the shoulder and back is managed with a noteworthy skill, not to mention the disappearing shoulder blades and the correctly drawn action of the arms. In the painting of the Canaanites, there is also attempted foreshortening, where first one shoulder is advanced, then the other, and where an attempt is made to render a profile view more in accord with nature, however unsuccessful the result.

[18] Luise Klebs, "Die Tiefendimension in der Zeichnung des alten Reiches," *Zeitschr. für ägyptische Sprache*, 52 (1915), p. 31; N. de Garis Davies, *J.E.A.*, XII (1926), pp. 110 ff.

Greater freedom in drawing and a desire to suggest truth are evident in some of the wrestling scenes from the tomb of Ameni (Fig. 49). In variety of pose and delight in action, these paintings are comparable to designs found on Greek vases. The suppleness of line is at times amazing. The designs show an acquaintance with wrestling that probably came from close contact with the athletic exercises in which military recruits were trained. As a study in light and dark, the figures are interesting because the artist has painted one of the contestants in a clear red, and the other in a reddish-brown silhouette, in order to make the movements comprehensible. It is a primitive device but gives a vivid picture of the action. The besieging of a fortress below is doubtless a reminiscence of the hostile conditions between Hierakonpolis and Thebes which resulted in the feudal age. The rhythm is very pronounced, arising in part from the repetition of similar attitudes and lines.

Yet another example of vivid realism combined with a strangely primitive method of expression is found in some hippopotami modeled in faïence. The one pictured from the Metropolitan Museum in New York (Fig. 50) shows that the artist is familiar with the "good points in a hippopotamus." Combined with this gift of observation is a curiously naïve device for presenting a memory picture of the animal among the lotuses; the artist has painted the lotus buds, flowers, and leaves in black line on the blue faïence before the application of the glaze, to express his memory of the animal hunted among the reeds along the lowlands of the Nile.[19] Sometimes butterflies are incongruously added to the design as in the case of a similar specimen in the Cairo Museum. These formed a part of the tomb furniture and were evidently supposed to ensure the pleasure of the hippopotamus hunt in the life to come.

We gain some slight idea of the painting of private houses from extant remains belonging to the Middle Kingdom. At Kahun a whole provincial town of the Twelfth Dynasty has been found. The walls were sometimes whitewashed, sometimes painted in gay colors such as red and yellow, or adorned with figure scenes, occasionally domestic in character. A wall-painting from a house at Kahun pictures the exterior of a house in the lower section, with a view of the interior above.[20] The tradition found here is carried on in later times in the Eighteenth Dynasty. We may follow it in remains of houses at el-Amarna and in the palaces of Amenhotep III and IV.

The painters of the Twelfth Dynasty, though resisting fixed conventions, were

[19] A. M. Lythgoe, *Bull. of the Metropolitan Museum of Art*, N. Y., 12 (1917), p. 78 and cover. *Cf.* F. W. von Bissing, "Altägyptische Gefässe im Museum zu Gise," *Zeitschr. für ägyptische Sprache*, 36 (1898), p. 123; H. R. Hall, *J.E.A.*, XIII (1927), pp. 57 ff.; Henry Wallis, *Egyptian Ceramic Art*, 1898, Pl. I (color); L. Borchardt, G. Reisner, *Works of Art from the Egyptian Museum at Cairo*, Cairo, Pl. 34.

[20] W. M. F. Petrie, *Illahun, Kahun, and Gurob*, London, 1891, Pl. 16, painting on stairs. G. Maspero, *Manual of Egyptian Archæology*, 1914, p. 12, Fig. 9. For a new edition, see G. Maspero, *op. cit.*, N. Y., 1926.

strongly subject to them. The paintings of the time lacked the dignity of earlier work and the vivacity of the age to come.[21] Old motives were elaborately developed and new ones enriched the painter's field. The reliefs show the result of much training rather than adherence to nature. The sunken relief which began to be used as early as the Fourth Dynasty and which was a distinctly Egyptian invention never adopted elsewhere except as an imitation, goes out of favor and the new style is low, with sharp contours above the field and elaborated lines used for hair and ornaments. The art was in the main scholastic. This was partly due to demands placed upon it by the priests, who helped to control the traditions in matters relating to the dead.[22] Furthermore, the formulæ imposed upon the artist by preceding generations were not readily altered, so that there was little room for growth and much opportunity for stagnation. In the face of this conservatism, it is amazing to find the great variety which does exist in subject matter and treatment in the paintings and reliefs of the period.

After a dark age of more than one hundred and fifty years, when Egypt suffered under the Hyksos, or Shepherd Kings, Egyptian art once again burst forth in its last great period of splendor, the Eighteenth and Nineteenth Dynasties. This was a period of world empire,[23] when Egypt reached out in its influence to northern Syria, Babylon, Palestine, and the islands, and many new factors came into politics and life. The art of this age was at once so advanced technically, so free and delicate, that it has always met with appreciation. The characteristics of the painting and relief are a certain vivacity and romanticism of style, combined with great charm of outline.

There are innumerable reliefs and wall-paintings from this age, from tombs, temples, and palaces. Most of the wall-paintings were found in the necropolis at Thebes, where the nobles were buried. Paintings seem often to have been used instead of reliefs because of the unsuitability of the stone for carving. The intimate relation of the two must, however, always be borne in mind. It is well illustrated in a relief now in Berlin, coming from the Temple of Hatshepsut at Dêr el-Bahari, and dating from about 1500 B.C. (Fig. 51). The scene represents rowers in a barge and the ones in the foreground are carved out in relief, whereas those in the rear are sometimes painted on the flat to facilitate the perspective.

In the Eighteenth Dynasty, the tomb usually had a transverse hall and a forecourt, often adorned with columns and equipped with a narrow corridor leading back to a square recess, where statues of the dead and his relatives were set up (Fig. 52).

[21] W. M. F. Petrie, *Encyclop. Britannica, s.v. Egypt: Art and Archæology.*

[22] H. Schäfer argues that the priests influenced Egyptian art very little. Political changes vitally affected it and all of the great movements in art were intimately bound up with the political ascendency of the time, *Zeitschr. für ägyptische Sprache,* 52 (1915), pp. 1-18.

[23] J. H. Breasted, *History of Egypt,*[2] 1916, pp. 305 ff.

Paintings have been found on the walls of the vestibule, in the corridor, or in the rear chapel—or in all of these places. Not only was the choice of subjects rather limited in the decoration of Egyptian tombs but the place where certain subjects might be painted was also fixed, especially in the case of the earlier tombs. The rooms nearer the entrance often showed the connection of the dead with the world outside, his occupations, and amusements. The corridor, as a place of transit, was decorated with the burial procession and the rites which took place before the lowering of the mummy. In the funerary chamber the intimate life of the dead was depicted—repasts with members of his family, worship of sepulchral deities, and the like. This appropriateness of position was later disregarded.

In the tomb of Nakht, at Abd el-Kurna where many high dignitaries were buried, the paintings are still very brilliant (Fig. 53), and thoroughly reminiscent of life during the Empire. The old domestic scenes and those of agriculture, which were vital for the life beyond, are retained (Fig. 54), but they are not treated in quite the same way. In the use of registers, there is far greater freedom; they are not always superposed upon one another with horizontal separating lines, but an attempt is occasionally made at perspective. A division of the register is cut off, as here, by a dark brown, curving line, indicating muddy soil and the point to which cultivation was being carried. The inundation has retreated and pools and rich deposits have been left behind, where the peasants sink down to their ankles while at work. The servants are represented cutting down mimosa trees and digging the soil with mattocks, while the processes are observed by Nakht. Below, on the same wall, men prepare the ground with hoes, sow the grain, and plow. At the left a servant is seen drinking from a water-skin. Sometimes there are no lines to mark the registers.

On yet another wall, Nakht and his wife, seated in a booth, rejoice in the bounty from the papyrus-swamps piled up before them. At the end of the panel is a representation of a vintage and a fowling scene (Fig. 55). Men gather grapes under an arched arbor and others trample them in a vat, holding on to straps above to prevent themselves from slipping. They are screened from the heat by branches of foliage. In the fowling scene, richly colored birds are caught in a trap net. A second operation follows where they have been summarily handled and are being plucked and dried in the sun, to be salted down in the jars near by. Men carrying poles laden with birds and with fish complete the scene illustrated.

In the colors, flat tones are the rule; terra cotta red for the flesh and black for the hair are the colors which predominate, with white for the garments. The Nile is a muddy brown; the trees and pools, green and blue; yellow occurs for various objects, such as the mattocks, plows, and baskets; and green is the main color used for the booth in which Nakht sits. Some of the cattle are red, some white with brownish spots. The vintage and fowling scenes are richer in color. The grapes are done in blue clusters with black dots; the birds against the blue water are green and yellow and iridescent shades, with green papyrus in the background. In the drawing of animals, naturalism is still found. Another example to illustrate this is the pet cat of Nakht, seated under his chair, devouring a fish (Fig. 56). It is not a wild type trained for hunting, like the cat from Beni Hasan, but a house cat.[24] It has a coat of reddish yellow with black stripes, and yellow and white on its belly. The litheness of the feline species is well caught, especially in the sweep of line of the back.

Finally, attempts at faithful characterization are seen in the banquet for the dead, at which women guests and an old blind harper are gathered (Fig. 57). The harper is seated on his foot, playing the lyre. His blindness is marked by two long, black lines forming a mere slit-like opening for the eye. He is rather obese and the rolls of fat across his stomach are carefully marked out. The foreshortened left leg is cleverly managed; the artist has merely painted the bottom of a foot against the harper's white garment. Another striking feature of the painting is the nude slave girl who is arranging the earrings of the guests. She may be a dancer, but in any case, as Davies has shown, the nude female figure is not common[25] and the proportions prove that the artist had some difficulties with his task. He is more successful in the case of a second dancer from the same tomb. As a composition, the painting shows not a little skill. All of these paintings occur in the very small tomb of the burgher Nakht.

The problem of perspective was a difficult one for the Egyptian painter. He at least recognized that it existed and tried to meet it in various ways. In the case of the three seated women of Figure 57, in order to represent the two women who are farther away from us, he has merely projected the outline of their two forms beyond the overlapping figure of the first. In the scenes depicted in Figure 58, herds of cattle are being brought forward by slaves for inspection. The artist has handled the problem of perspective by multiplying the outline of the first bull and by varying the color. In the rear of the upper panel, he has merely repeated the outline of the head and legs of the bull in front. The impression of a herd is thus obtained. The design is executed in a kind of shorthand and is comparable to the primitive method used for representing herds of reindeer in the hunter's age, where only the horns are multiplied. When the Egyptian represented bands of marching warriors he superimposed the battle lines one above the other; he merely juxtaposed the figures in the same plane, transforming depth into height. In no field was he less successful in the treatment of perspective than in the case of landscape (Fig. 59). In the scene of a garden planted with trees and containing a pond in the center teeming with fish

[24] On Egyptian cats, see O. Keller, *Die antike Tierwelt*, Leipzig, 1909, I, 67 ff.

[25] N. de Garis Davies, *The Tomb of Nakht at Thebes*, New York, 1917, p. 58 ("Robb de Peyster Tytus Memorial Series," Vol. I, edited by Albert M. Lythgoe).

and ducks, he has merely made a map-like plan of the whole. The trees are laid down on all four sides of the pool and the fish swim about as if in an aquarium seen in elevation. The composition, in spite of these defects, is æsthetically significant; the pattern employed is very beautiful and calls to mind designs found today in Oriental tapestries. Soft greens and browns prevail.

Freedom in drawing the human figure increases in the Eighteenth Dynasty over the work of the Twelfth and earlier epochs (Fig. 60). The artist is not entirely successful at all times, but he is trying to draw the front and three-quarter view of the face and is attempting new poses. The figure of the nude girl in the tomb of Nakht approaches much nearer to a correct profile view than earlier attempts. The drawing of a girl somersaulting found on an ostrakon, or flake of limestone, now in Turin (Fig. 61), is an attempt of the boldest kind, executed with a sureness that could hardly be surpassed today. The Eighteenth Dynasty represents the height of achievement in Egyptian drawing and representation of space. These advances together with the refinement and elegance of many of the works are perhaps the greatest attainments of the age, although some fine examples of uncompromising realism deserve to be mentioned.

Under the Empire, the subjects employed for decoration were much the same as those found earlier but with notable additions and changed emphasis. Prominence is now given to the ritual connected with the dead—the funerary procession, the double taking possession of his tomb, the mummy receiving farewells, sacrifices, weeping mourners, and the like. A system of rewards and punishments for the soul begins to arise, which had no place in the mind of the youthful and vigorous Egyptian of the Old Kingdom. We shall see a similar thing happening later in Etruria where the early artist has little thought for the miseries of the other world in contrast to his late successors who are almost entirely absorbed with the theme.

Akhenaten, or Amenhotep IV, brought to an end the glories of the Eighteenth Dynasty. Whether he was a dreamer, or a religious fanatic, a tool in the hands of the priests of Heliopolis, who wished to discredit the dominant gods of Thebes, or a shrewd politician who saw the priests throttling the monarchy and attempted to break their hold, history has yet to show.[26] In any case, as Breasted has pointed out, he was the first monotheist and one of the first individuals in history.[27] Either by the weakness or the strength of his character, he effected the first great break in the

[26] J. H. Breasted, *op. cit.*, p. 356; H. Schäfer, "Altes und Neues zur Kunst und Religion von Tell el-Amarna," *Zeitschr. für ägyptische Sprache*, 55 (1918), pp. 1-43; *Die Religion und Kunst von El-Amarna*, Berlin, 1923; B. Gunn, "Notes on the Aten and his Names," *J.E.A.*, IX (1923), pp. 168 ff.—the best discussions of the subject.

[27] J. H. Breasted, *op. cit.*, p. 356; *Cambridge Ancient History*, II, 1924, 109 ff., against this view, see H. R. Hall, *Ancient History of the Near East*, pp. 298, 305, n. 1; *cf. J.E.A.*, VII (1921), pp. 39 ff.; James Baikie, *The Amarna Age*, N. Y., 1926; L. Borchardt,

religious and artistic traditions of Egypt. He sought to replace the old religion of Egypt by the worship of the sun. This god, Aten by name, meaning "disc," Akhenaten represented in art as the orb of the sun, with descending rays ending in outstretched hands. The worship was not an entirely new one; it was in all probability an outgrowth of the old sun-worship at Heliopolis. What was new was the exclusion of all other gods and the exaltation of sun-worship to monotheism. The king proceeded to change his own name, Amenhotep, to Akhenaten, "Aten is pleased." He transferred his capital from Thebes, the city of Amon, to el-Amarna, where he built his city, Akhetaten, "Horizon of Aten." For the worship of the sun, he composed hymns which are among the first poetic documents of the world and in these hymns there is a continual emphasis on "truth." This doctrine had its effect on art, needless to say, for whatever was natural to Akhenaten was true, and art was made as nearly as possible to tell what the eye saw. The main result was that some of the formality of earlier Egyptian art was definitely discarded and the work of the artist was vividly instinct with life. It is true, however, that, as a result of his newly found freedom, the artist sometimes fell into extravagance, for example, in rendering the lean figure of the king. Nature seems at times a very deformed thing in this art, as it may indeed have been where the family of the king was concerned. But certainly the entire court of Akhenaten did not look alike. There are some writers who see the influence of Crete and of Syria in the monuments of this period,[28] especially in painting, and there are close analogies to Ægean decoration, which we shall have occasion to mention later. But it was a period of mutual influence and it is difficult to know which side contributed most—probably Egypt. In turn, the things which she took from Crete and Syria were always transformed into new and individual creations. Spiegelberg regards the movement as a return to the popular style in art;[29] Petrie looks upon the period as "the death of Egyptian art in a fever of novelty and vociferation," a view which is certainly disproved by recent discoveries in the tomb of Tutankhamen, if it had not been disproved earlier.

Inasmuch as the ancient religion of Amon was once more followed after the death of Akhenaten, and the court returned to Thebes, his palace was deserted. It has been recently excavated and the plan of it is readily traceable today. Among the most striking remains found earlier was a stucco pavement, made by laying on the soil mud bricks, covered with a coat of mortar faced with fine plaster. On this plaster,

M.D.O.G., 57 (1917). Schäfer's article, Zeitschr., 55, is written to disprove many of Borchardt's statements. See Nora Griffith, J.E.A., IX (1923), pp. 78-79.

[28] H. R. Hall, Ancient History of the Near East, p. 304; cf. Springer-Michaelis-Wolters, Kunstgeschichte,[10] 1915, p. 47. Cf. 12th ed., p. 42.

[29] W. Spiegelberg, op. cit., p. 63; W. M. F. Petrie, Arts and Crafts of Ancient Egypt, pp. 20, 53. For a very sound statement of the situation, see H. Schäfer, Die Religion und Kunst von El-Amarna, 1923, pp. 3-5, 42 ff.

colored designs were painted of birds and animals among papyrus plants and flowers. Petrie seems to imply that the paintings were in the pure fresco technique but the recently discovered fragments were put on *al secco*. It therefore seems unlikely that the method used at the northern end of the site was different. We shall return to the problem of technique later. This pattern formed the floor of the "Harem" of the palace. The roof was upheld by twelve columns breaking the stucco patterns at regular intervals. The landscape was divided into two parts by a border of subject peoples on whom the king trod when entering. In each part was pictured an oblong pool, where fish were represented swimming about. In a swampy thicket along the shore, animals were depicted, all in lively action (Fig. 62). The details of the landscape are worked out with great freedom and truth to nature. In one of these scenes, a black and white bull is seen bounding through papyrus and some reedy plants with henna-colored blossoms (Fig. 63). The design is exceedingly graceful, because of the use of delicately curved lines. Rich shades of brownish red and green predominate, with touches of black, white, and yellow in the painting of the foliage and birds. In another part a young calf, characteristically drawn, is seen in the midst of long marsh grass and gracefully bending plants, while a startled bird flies up from the thicket (Fig. 64). The pavement seems to have been executed by more than one hand because the work is uneven and is not always equally successful. In one scene, where two calves are running with their heads turned backward (Fig. 65), we have a touch of mannerism and less success in the rendering of the birds, which have heavier wings and lack lightness. The background, however, reveals greater variety in plant life, with the introduction of insects such as the locust and the dragon fly. The colors for the flowers are the same as in the other sections. One calf is a brownish red with white spots, the other black and white. Last of all, for a scene of vivid action, there is a fine rendering of a calf bounding past some thistle-like plants into a clump of papyrus (Fig. 66). The instantaneousness of the action is marvelously grasped and held. The motive of the "flying gallop" seen here is not found in Egyptian art until this period and probably came in at this time under Cretan influence. The whole design shows freedom and a fondness for overlapping patterns impossible to conceive in an earlier epoch. The fish in the water at the right belongs to a part of the pavement that was broken and repaired later. A genuine appreciation of nature and an attempt to render it naturalistically are the dominant features in these paintings. Recent excavations have brought to light more art of this stamp from the palaces of Amenhotep III and IV. In one case pigeons with outspread wings formed the ceiling decoration—an interesting substitute for the vulture of earlier times. Some domestic scenes are found, others of outdoor life similar to those described.[30]

[30] R. de Peyster Tytus, *Re-excavation of the Palace of Amenhetep III*, New York, 1903.

A fresco from el-Amarna of the two daughters of Akhenaten, now in the Ashmolean Museum at Oxford (Fig. 67), reveals interesting advances toward freedom and attempts at truthful representation of the human form. The two princesses are seated on cushions, fondling each other. They formed part of a larger composition in which the King and Queen and their children were included. The proportions are rather extraordinary—especially the long head and thin neck and arms which apparently belonged to the royal house. But the artist has tried a background of cushions and has attempted to break away from traditional methods of representation. The unconventionality of pose is striking in the extreme and the nudity of the figures is a decided contrast to earlier representations of Egyptian princesses. Petrie argues that the artist has also abandoned the use of flat tones by introducing shading and that high lights have been employed in several instances, but this has not been proved.[31] The painting was placed on a uniform layer of mud, rarely more than one-eighth of an inch in thickness. The color of the ground is an orange-red with yellow and blue diamonds; the flesh is a yellowish red. Black and white are also used for eyes, nostrils, pupils, eyebrows, and toe nails.

The reliefs of the period show the same delightful liberation from the trammels fixed by earlier conventions—even though at times they fall into idiosyncracies almost as absurd. There develops a kind of genre relief where the ruler is seen in the intimacy of his family life, caressing his wife and children—much as any one of his subjects might be depicted (Fig. 68). The art of the time must have astounded the Egyptian populace who were accustomed to view the Pharaoh in much more rigid poses and more formal surroundings. Sometimes the Queen is shown presenting the King with flowers, as in the charming relief in Berlin (Fig. 69), where the lounging attitude of the King contrasts strongly with the stiff positions of earlier Pharaohs;[31a] or, in company, they worship the Aten (Fig. 70). In this last instance,

*Bull. Metrop. Mus. Suppl.*, March, 1918. C. L. Woolley, *J.E.A.*, VIII (1922), p. 78, Pl. XIII; F. W. von Bissing, Reach, *Annales du service*, VII, 65; T. E. Peet, C. L. Woolley, *The City of Akhenaten*, London, I, 1923; *The Mural Painting of Tell el-'Amarneh*, Egypt. Explor. Soc., 1929; H. Frankfort, *J.E.A.*, XIII (1927), pp. 216 ff., Pls. LI, LIV; J. A. Hammerton, *Wonders of the Past*, IV, 1052, Pl. (color). See also *Bull. Metrop. Mus.*, VII (1912), Figs. 2, 3, pp. 185-186; *A Handbook of the Egyptian Rooms*, Fig. 42, p. 97.

[31] The use of high lights and shading is denied by N. de Garis Davies, *J.E.A.*, VII (1921), p. 4 and Pl. I. He states that the bright yellow is due to degradation of the pigment. The innovation of shading seems, however, to be found on the bodies of birds on a ceiling in the palace of Amenhotep III. Nina de Garis Davies denies that the practice became known before the Nineteenth Dynasty, *Facsimiles of Theban Wall-Paintings*, 1923, p. 5. *Cf.* also, N. de Garis Davies, *Bulletin of the Metrop. Mus. of Art*, Part II, *The Egyptian Expedition* (December, 1922), p. 52.

[31a] P. Newberry, *J.E.A.*, XIV (1928), p. 117, argues that the figures are not Amenophis IV and Nefertiti, but probably Semenkhkarē and Merytaten. The Queen offers a lotus bud

the ludicrous exaggeration of the shape of the head, the narrow neck and waist and thick hips become grotesque. These characteristics came to be imposed upon all of Akhenaten's subjects by the sculptors of the time, as we see from the tombs at Tell el-Amarna.[32] Some of the older conventions were also retained, such as the doubling of the outline to represent two figures in similar attitudes (Fig. 71). In this example, Akhenaten and the Queen are pictured with hands clasped, seated on their throne, receiving the gifts of the South. On the whole, the freedom in drawing is very marked and the results bear witness to a strong naturalistic tendency in art. In the course of striving after realism of pose and form, the dignity and severity of an earlier age were, however, sacrificed.

The school of el-Amarna with its attempts at representing truth vanished as swiftly as it came into being, although its influence seems to be felt in the work of later times. The palace stood for some years, after which Thebes once more gained the ascendency. Maspero derives the impetus of the realistic movement from Hermopolis,[33] but its manifestations are unique and unparalleled. Undoubtedly the way for this art was being prepared earlier. Even under the Hyksos kings, there is evidence of acquaintance with Cretan art, and a greater bent toward realism was probably at work in this period. With the reign of Thutmose III, art received a stronger naturalistic impetus and this tendency was continued under his successors.[34] The increased freedom was partly due to changed conditions, but partly, we may believe, to the general influence of Cretan-Mycenæan work, coming directly from Crete and from Crete *via* Syria during the period of extensive intercourse. But we must not forget that the realistic tendency was widespread in Egyptian popular art and it may have needed only the personality of an Akhenaten to produce the Amarna movement.

For many years after the death of Akhenaten efforts were spent in destroying the works which he had created and in restoring the religion of Amon. Tutankhamen and Seti I were especially vigorous in their persistence and few undamaged reliefs survive from the earlier period. The Nineteenth Dynasty witnessed tremendous struggles against the Libyans, Syrians, and Hittites under the leadership of Seti I (1313-1292), and his son, Rameses II. Vast building operations were carried on at this time at Karnak, Luxor, Abydos, and Memphis. It is an age filled with architectural monuments. Much of our knowledge of the art of the epoch comes from

and two mandrake fruits, or "love apples," to the King, who is represented as a delicate youth.

[32] N. de Garis Davies, *The Rock Tombs of El Amarna*, London, 1903-1908, especially Pts. I, II. *Cf.* F. W. von Bissing, *Denkmäler zur Geschichte der Kunst Amenophis IV, Sitzungsber. der Kgl. Bayer. Akad. der Wiss.*, 1914, Pls. I-VIII.

[33] G. Maspero, *Art in Egypt*, New York, 1912, pp. 181 ff.

[34] Springer-Michaelis-Wolters, *op. cit.*,[12] pp. 42 ff.; Sir Arthur Evans, *The Palace of Minos*, II, 2, 1928, pp. 654 ff., 658.

reliefs, some of the finest of which are those from the tomb of Seti I at Thebes.[34a]
The tomb, which is 470 feet deep, consists of fourteen rooms—corridors, pillar
rooms, halls, and recesses, following one another and adorned with scenes of the
journey of the dead in the underworld. The reliefs illustrate the "Book of Him who
is in the Underworld" and "The Book of the Gates." The boat of the sun is often
seen, preceded by spirits with coiled snakes, and animal-headed gods (Fig. 72). In
the upper row of the scenes pictured here from room No. 5 are men with a coiled
rope, while below are genii with a snake on which stand the hieroglyphs for "time."
In antechamber IX, the king appears before Osiris, Isis, Anubis, and other gods for
judgment. In this period, emphasis is placed upon the difficulties through which the
soul must  pass in its journey through the lower regions. Reliefs of triumphal battle
scenes also begin to assume great prominence on the pylons and walls of monuments
of this age. They show dexterity in technique and great boldness in composition. The
walls are covered with designs which represent the king, sometimes riding over his
enemies, or dispatching them with his spear. These reliefs had their influence on the
historical reliefs of later peoples. They are truly pictorial compositions and form
one of the chief contributions to the art of this period. The scenes at Karnak, where
Seti I sacks a Palestinian fortress, remind one of later Assyrian reliefs in the way in
which the slain figures are strewn over the field up to the height (Fig. 73). This
motive is found on one of the newly discovered chests from the tomb of Tutankhamen.

How very delicate and refined the drawing of this age could be is readily seen
from a sketch in black on one of the unfinished piers in the tomb of Seti at Thebes
(Fig. 74). Great vigor and beauty of line are combined here with exquisite grace and
elasticity. In fact, the importance of the tomb lies largely in its unfinished decoration. We are able to trace in detail the processes of the Egyptian draughtsman and
to see the marvel of his contour lines, drawn often from head to foot without lifting
his brush. The scene represents Seti making an offering before Osiris.[34b] Another
example of the workmanship of this age may be found in Figure 75, a relief of Seti
making an offering before the symbol of Abydos and the god Osiris.[34c] This relief is
one of the treasures of the Metropolitan Museum and shows the power possessed by
the sculptors of the Nineteenth Dynasty. They sought after grace and elegance
rather than grandeur and energy. The beauty of the reliefs lies first of all in the
sinuous lines, drawn with a single bold sweep and in the charm of the transparent
draperies revealing the form beneath. The composition, which is balanced by a

[34a] For the astronomical scenes on the ceiling, see L. S. Bull, *Bulletin of the Metropolitan
Museum of Art*, N. Y., 18 (1923), pp. 283-286, Figs. 1-7.

[34b] Somers Clarke, *Archæologia*, 55 (1896); Pt. I, Pls. II-III, pp. 21 ff.

[34c] *Cf.* J. Capart, *Le Temple de Séti I<sup>er</sup>*, Bruxelles, 1912.

similar scene at the right where Rameses I is shown in worship, is one of great
excellence. The art of the time shows a certain dependence on that of the age of
Akhenaten.

Among the most successful achievements of the Eighteenth and Nineteenth Dynasties were the rich ornamental patterns which adorned the ceilings. They show
that a long period of skill must have preceded in order to produce such perfection.[35]
The earlier patterns consist of zigzag lines, checkers, and lozenges—patterns probably taken from textile fabrics (Fig. 76a). The ceiling in the tomb of Nakht (Fig.
53) indicates how these patterns, which were derived from mats hung on the walls,
were taken over into painting. The spiral appears to make its début in painting in
the Twelfth Dynasty, doubtless under Cretan influence (Fig. 76b), and was developed under Senusert I into a chain of coils. In the Eighteenth Dynasty the quadruple spiral, the glory of Egyptian decorative art, is found (Fig. 76c). It often
employs various patterns in the open spaces, for example, the rosette, or the bull's
head, perhaps under Cretan influence (Fig. 76e). Sometimes this design is even
elaborated into a quintuple pattern (Fig. 76d). Closely akin to the spiral is the fret
(Fig. 76f) used with manifold variations (Fig. 76g). Natural forms, strangely
enough, are not the earliest employed, but among the patterns used when they come
into vogue, the lotus holds one of the first places. By the Eighteenth Dynasty, it was
used as a border pattern and the bud was so conventionalized that something similar
to the Greek palmette was evolved. In Ptolemaic times, the lower part of the wall
was paneled in a design of lotus flowers and lilies on long stems (Fig. 76i). In the
same way, papyrus was often employed in decorative patterns (Figs. 76h, j), for
example, on the pavement at el-Amarna. Sometimes, in the Eighteenth Dynasty, the
ceilings were painted yellow and vine leaves and branches were designed as if hung
from a trellis. A similar pattern seems to be affected in Etruscan art in the Tomba
del Triclinio.

Captives were occasionally strewn among the ornamental flower patterns, as we
see from the Amarna pavement. Animals were also used, especially the ibex, falcon,
duck, and vulture. The last noted was very popular for ceiling patterns; with its
outstretched wings, it was employed as a symbol of the divine protection of Nekhbet,
tutelary goddess of the South (Fig. 76l). The upper design is one of the Eighteenth
Dynasty from Memphis and the lower shows a refinement of the type in the late
period of Egyptian art. From early days the natural decoration of the ceiling consisted of golden stars on a ground of deep night blue. Against this, the vulture was
often seen. It is found on the ceilings in the corridors of the tomb of Seti I. There
were many other symbolic designs, such as the uræus, the Hathor head, the lion, and

[35] W. M. F. Petrie, *Egyptian Decorative Art*, London, 1895; G. Jéquier, *Décoration
égyptienne*, Paris, 1911. *Cf.* also the Robb de Peyster Tytus Memorial Volumes.

the scarab. In Figure 76k, the scarab is shown with the disc of the sun between its claws, the whole design filling in the open spaces of a quintuple spiral. All of these patterns bear witness to the consummate skill of the Egyptian in decorative design and show his love for rhythm, balance, and harmony. Practically all ornamental patterns of later times hark back to some of the designs that we have discussed. Figure 76m gives an example from the Eighteenth Dynasty of the use of the shell pattern combined with the spiral. The design in Figure 76n is interesting because it recurs later in Crete on the garment of the Lady from Hagia Triada. Occasionally floor patterns were treated as naturalistically as in Figure 76o.

We have followed the course of Egyptian painting from its crude beginnings in rough memory pictures, through its *floruit* from the Fourth to the Sixth Dynasties; we have seen it suffering from the bonds imposed upon it by religion in the Twelfth Dynasty,—a period when direct copies were made of Old Kingdom reliefs for use in Middle Kingdom temples,—and finally attempting to free itself at the end of the Eighteenth. At that time, it attained great technical perfection, only to lose much of its former vigor and grandeur. The epoch after the Eighteenth Dynasty was, in general, one of decline and though there were some brief outbursts of magnificence, such as those under Seti I and Rameses II and III, they could not hide the declining power of Egypt or ward off the incessant hordes of barbarians thundering down upon the Nile. Reliefs such as the one of Rameses III at Medinet Habu, show apparent renascence in the midst of decline (Fig. 77). The scene represents Rameses hunting wild bulls in the marshes. It has a suggestion of Cretan influence in the rendering of the trapped animals. They are not far removed from figures like those on the Vaphio cups and the feathery marsh grass reveals a real appreciation of nature.

Some time after the Eighteenth and Nineteenth Dynasties, the Empire fell a prey to Libyans, then, in the Twenty-fifth, to the Ethiopians and Assyrians, and finally, to the Persians and Greeks. Most of the remnants of drawing and painting left today from this era are found on papyri, stelæ, coffins, and mummy-cases. The papyri are really miniatures of great beauty of line and freshness of color (Fig. 78). They show the weighing of the heart by Anubis, the jackal god, while the ibis-headed Thoth notes the results; they depict the burial of the dead and the judgment before Osiris. In the funerary papyrus of Queen Makare of Figure 78, we see the wife of one of the king-priests of the Twenty-first Dynasty present before Osiris at the ritual of the weighing the heart against the symbol for "Truth." The drawing is delicate; the colors mainly red, yellow, green, white, and black. The composition is one of unusual charm.

Most of the painted miniatures and pen drawings which we possess are copies of the Book of the Dead dating from the Eighteenth Dynasty or later, or of the Book

of Him who is in the Underworld, from the Twentieth Dynasty on. The papyri of
Hunefer and Ani in the British Museum give us an adequate idea of these paintings.[35a]
In Figure 79, the ceremony of opening the mouth of the mummy is represented. The
priest and his assistants perform the rite on the mummy of Hunefer before his tomb.
Anubis supports the mummy while the center of the design is occupied by the
weeping wife and daughter of the dead man. Sometimes the vignettes formed a line at
the top of the page; at other times, they were like letters in illuminated manuscripts,
or they occupied almost the entire page. The burial scene was placed at the beginning of the papyrus roll, the judging of the dead toward the middle, the arrival of
the dead in the fields of Yaru at the end. Copies of the Book of the Dead are so
numerous that from this source alone, as Maspero states, a history of miniature
painting in Egypt might be compiled.

Contemporary with these drawings on papyri is a series of interesting sketches on
flakes of limestone, known as ostraka.[36] They are whimsical drawings by Egyptian
artists living in communities near the Theban cemetery, often done to pass the
time or to give expression to a momentary impulse. They sometimes satirize the
weaknesses and foibles of the great. In Figure 80 we see the Egyptian love for
satire in the sketch of a mouse of distinction seated on a throne and being served
with food by a cringing tomcat. The work has been hastily executed with a brush
made of frayed reeds, but it is a masterly bit of drawing and humor. The scenes
pictured are often from the world of fable. Animals and birds are humorously shown
carrying on the activities of men. Frequently they are engaged in musical pastimes.
"Tales in which human life and relationships are shifted into the animal world for
purpose of caricature or instructive moralizing are of enormous age in the Orient. A
cycle of such tales with delightful illustrations existed as far back as the Empire."[37]

[35a] E. A. W. Budge, *The Book of the Dead*, British Museum, London, 1922, for a short account. Colored facsimiles of the papyri have been published by the Museum. See Bibliography.

[36] Mrs. C. Ransom Williams, *Quarterly Bull. of the N. Y. Hist. Soc.*, IV, No. 4 (January,
1921). Mrs. Williams considers the seated animal of Fig. 80 a mouse, *l.c.* p. 93; Maspero
calls it a cat, *Manual of Egypt. Arch.*,[6] 1914, pp. 196-197; *cf. Art in Egypt*, 1912, Figs. 282-
286, pp. 162-163; *Bull. Metrop. Mus. of Art, The Egyptian Expedition*, 1922-1923, p. 34,
Fig. 29; p. 21, Fig. 16; G. Daressy, *Ostraca, Cat. gén. des ant. égypt. du Caire*, 1901; H.
Schäfer, *Jahr. der Kgl. Preuss. Kunstsamml.*, 37 (1916), pp. 23-51.

[37] J. H. Breasted, *Communications of the Oriental Institute of the University of Chicago*,
I (1922), pp. 82 ff. I owe the reference to Mrs. Williams. That these tales may go back to a
remote antiquity in the Orient is indicated by the engraved shell plaques recently discovered
by Woolley at Ur. They decorated the front of the Royal Harp. In the upper row, Gilgamesh
is seen protecting two man-headed bison; below, a dog in the rôle of a priest with a sacrificial knife at his belt is carrying an altar on which are the heads of a bear and calf and a joint
of meat. Behind him follows a lion holding a lamp in one hand and a vase in the other. The

The texts are lost, however, and it is now proposed to collect the illustrations properly. Other drawings on limestone were often made as trial sketches for large wall compositions, or they were copies of something which interested the artist. The flakes were analogous to our note paper—a cheap writing material always at hand.

The stelæ usually have designs of the dead adoring Amon, Mut, or Harmachis. They often rival the miniatures in beauty. That of Zadamonefonukhu may perhaps be cited in illustration of the class, though it is unique because of the landscape which it introduces. In the upper register, the priestess stands in a reverent attitude before Harmachis, whereas the lower section is concerned with an earthly scene in which the mourning figure of a relative occupies the center of attention (Fig. 81). On a sandy mountainside of yellow streaked with red are three tombs, a group of trees, and an offering table. The style indicates a certain rejection of stereotyped forms in favor of more original conceptions. The background is a grayish blue, which is characteristic of a great many early paintings. Against this, the charming figure of the priestess is drawn with much grace. But in the end it is not so much the beautifully balanced design of the main scene which interests us as the attempt at a funerary landscape. We might well expect such innovations as these when art turned from less formal expression to the rendering of everyday events.

The Saïte period, 663-525, witnessed some ineffectual attempts to revive the Golden Age of the Old Kingdom. Psametik brought an epoch of archaizing and a short-lived renaissance. Close contact with the Greeks followed; Naukratis was settled at the instigation of Amasis, and finally, after independence was gained from the Persians, came the Græco-Roman period, 332 B.C.-640 A.D. Reliefs of temples such as Edfu, Dendera, Dêr el-Medineh, and Philæ, tell us of the approaching end. Restorations of the interior of the temple at Dendera with its Hathor columns, furnish an idea of the extensive decoration of columns and walls under the Ptolemies and reveal the sad lack of structural feeling, evident in the riot of carved reliefs on the columns. The interior of Dêr el-Medineh discloses the profusion and the monotony of painted and carved detail, which covered every available space (Fig. 82). The color must have compensated for much of the bad taste.

The Egyptian mummy cartonnages reproduce not only the masks, but often the greater part or all of the body. Painted coffins of wood are found in the Old Kingdom, but they are usually simple in character and adorned with funerary texts. During the Middle Kingdom, the decoration assumes greater proportions and by

scenes below contain even more interesting material. A seated donkey is playing on a lyre which is held by a bear at the right, while a jackal seated between them is playing a sistrum. In the lowest panel, a scorpion man walks along elegantly followed by a chamois bearing two goblets in his hands. These plaques are dated in the Fourth Millennium. See C. L. Woolley, *The Antiquaries Journal*, VIII (1928), Pl. LXIV, 2; Leon Legrain, *The Museum Journal*, Univ. of Penna., 1928, p. 233.

the Eighteenth Dynasty the square coffins and anthropoid mummy-cases, which came in during the Twelfth Dynasty, are oftentimes quite elaborate.[37a] Examples from the Eighteenth Dynasty are seen in Figs. 83a and b, two wooden coffins in the possession of the New York Historical Society. The exteriors are decorated with funerary texts and with figures of Thoth, Anubis, and the four sons of Horus. At the head of the coffin, where the dead looked out from his underground abode, the eye of Horus is painted. Across the breast of Figure 83b is the vulture with outspread wings. This coffin enclosed the mummy of Teti. The coffin of Figure 83a contained the mummy of Kami, and the end is adorned with a beautiful figure of Isis. The more elaborate examples of Figure 84 are the anthropoid cases of Khonsu of the Twentieth Dynasty, a priest of the Necropolis of Thebes, or "The Place of Truth," as the inscription tells us. The body was placed in the smaller coffin which was then put into the larger and buried. These coffins, which were commonly three in number, were of wood, painted with a white coat of paint.[37b] Against this, the figures were laid on in colors and then covered with a varnish. The white coat of paint has, however, turned yellow in most instances and gives much the effect of a yellow stucco. On the coffin of Khonsu at the left, beneath his hands which hold amulets, is the goddess Nut with her wings outspread. Below are figures of Isis and Nephthys and, still lower, the deceased in the presence of Osiris. These various figures are painted in red, black, and white with an occasional touch of green, but the dominant color is the yellow ground which was originally white.

The interiors of the cases were on occasion even more profusely adorned than the exterior. Very often they were covered with funerary texts which had a magical significance. These texts date from an early period. The Metropolitan Museum has in its possession a coffin of a priest of the Twentieth Dynasty, the interior of which is very beautifully preserved (Fig. 85). It is adorned with animal-headed gods and spirits, and the colors are almost as vivid as when they were laid on. The white ground has retained its original condition. The most prominent colors employed against this are blue, red, and black, with some green and yellow. The various animal-headed gods and genii of the dead have given the artist rare play for his

[37a] E. A. W. Budge, *A Guide to the First, Second and Third Egyptian Rooms*,[3] British Museum, London, 1924 (Coffins and Mummy-Cases). For a fine example of a polychrome coffin from the Middle Kingdom, see *Museum of Fine Arts Bulletin*, Boston Museum, XIX (1921), Aug.

[37b] A. P. Laurie, *Materials of the Painter's Craft*, London & Edinburgh, 1910, p. 26, says that they were covered with a thin coat of *gesso*, consisting of chalk mixed with glue. In order to attach the *gesso*, the surface of the wood had to be torn or scraped and then laid over with a mixture of sand and glue. On this bed of sand, the fine *gesso* was spread. The varnish might be made from resins, such as pine resin, mastic, or sandarac. All of these had to be obtained outside Egypt in Syria or Africa.

imagination. Many of the mummy-cases and masks were made of plaster and carton-nage, especially in the Roman period. They oftentimes show a profusion of gold and red and, in general, a very wide range of colors. The flesh of the gods is sometimes painted green or blue.

In the oases, mural paintings have also been found in many of the hypogæa. The Fayûm portraits belonging to the Græco-Roman period are more properly Greek and we shall reserve them for a later chapter. They seem to have owed their origin to the portraits on painted cartonnage and to the mummy-cases.

Nothing has been said of the technical methods employed by the Egyptian painter. No artist has ever used color more lavishly than the Egyptian but he did not employ it as the modern painter so often does, to gain illusionistic effects; he used color mainly to satisfy his taste for polychromy. His art almost always consisted in placing flat tones beside one another to produce harmony of color; in this achievement, the Egyptian was a "past master." But such work can scarcely be called painting in our sense of the word; it is rather illumination.

It was a common practice in decorating tombs, houses, or palaces to plaster the rough faces of the walls with Nile mud, on which the painting was executed. In the Old Kingdom, the designs were most often placed against a background of gray, which seems to recall this practice. Many of the better tombs show a very fine coat of highly polished plaster, sometimes two coats, placed above a rough layer of coarsely ground limestone, varying from one-half to one inch in thickness.[37c] Against this as a ground, the figures were sketched in with red or black paint and it is in these sketches that the really artistic temper of the Egyptian manifested itself. They were boldly drawn with long, swinging lines so that if mistakes were made, they were likely to be splendid ones. But only the contours were drawn and these outlines, usually red in color, were later filled in with flat tones—employed in a strictly con-ventional scheme. After the flat colors had been put in, another scribe or even the same one went over the outlines with a narrow red line and later ran a brush of white along the red. The lines of the figures are almost always free and strong, but the compositions fail in many instances to win our admiration because of the monotony induced by the representation of figures in similar attitudes. The best work of the masters consisted of stock designs adopted by their pupils and appar-ently used as types, but never as exact models. Such stereotyping of designs, how-ever, gave little scope for individuality and it was only in minor details that the artist was able to show his creativeness. There was always opportunity, however, for the true artist to express himself.

[37c] Gypsum was used as a ground in the earlier examples, *cf.* A. Eibner, *Entwicklung und Werkstoffe der Wandmalerei*, München, 1926, pp. 37 ff.; Nina de Garis Davies, *Facsimiles of Theban Wall-Paintings*, Victoria and Albert Museum, 1923, pp. 4 ff.; A. P. Laurie, *op. cit.*, pp. 16 ff.

We know something of the Egyptian painter's kit from the color, brushes, mortars, pestles, mixing jars, and palettes found in the tombs and from pictures on the walls of painters at work. The Egyptian used a brush of palm or reed fibers frayed at the end. Very often his mixing jars and saucers were of pottery. Mortars and pestles were used for grinding dry color. Palettes have also been found, such as were used by scribes, with places for red and black ink, for decorating the vignettes of papyri. The pigments employed as early as the Fifth Dynasty were red, yellow, brown, blue, green, white, and black. Later, the number of shades was greatly increased—to about sixteen or more. Blue is not found in the earliest paintings and seems to have been used later as an alternative for black; it was employed especially for hair and wigs. It is very common in the Fifth Dynasty but was sparingly used in the Fourth and in the still earlier tomb of Hesi-Re, the few instances cited of it seem a bit doubtful.[38] The colors were probably mixed with gum arabic or a binding medium such as the white of an egg, size, or honey. The process is known as *tempera*, that is, a process which involves "mixing" the colors with some material to hold them fast and applying them to the dry plaster. The fresco method, in contrast, has to do with painting "on the fresh" plaster, where no binding is necessary because the colors adhere to the plaster on which they are placed while it is still fresh and wet. This is due to the action of the lime in the plaster. The fresco method appears not to have been used in Egypt.[38a] The question of mediums and methods has not, however, been sufficiently investigated in Egypt. Gum arabic, which exudes from the acacia tree was certainly available and glue was also known from an early date. Wax may have been used at times as a medium.

The colors employed were earth colors and mineral pigments. Black was made from charcoal; white was a lime-white; blues and greens were oxides of copper; yellows, reds, and browns were ochers. Blue was an artificial product, the color of which varied greatly from light green to purplish tones. In making it, white quartz was ground to a coarse powder, mixed with alkali, lime and copper ore, then heated so as to combine without actually melting. The color depended upon the amount of

[38] Mrs. C. Ransom Williams, *The Tomb of Perneb,* New York, p. 79. Mrs. Williams informs me that "almost simultaneously with the use of blue for black, there is the use of blue for objects approximately blue, as the bluish tips of the *Nymphœa cœrulea* and bunches of grapes, but many hieroglyphs were now black, now blue, as those representing metal blades of weapons and implements, or plans of mud brick structures; the same is true of hair. This observation is interesting in connection with conventions in archaic Greek art, *e.g.,* the famous 'Blue Beard' of the Acropolis Museum." On Egyptian blue, see A. P. Laurie, W. F. McLintock, F. D. Miles, *Proc. Roy. Soc.,* Vol. 89, pp. 418-429. *Cf.* W. M. F. Petrie, *Ancient Egypt,* I, 1914, p. 186. On the preparation of the tomb, *cf.* Ernest Mackay, *J.E.A.,* VII (1921), pp. 154 ff.

[38a] See Ch. XI, p. 422.

copper employed, the degree of heat used, the amount of lime and the presence of iron. Red sand, for example, gives a greenish blue. Brown is usually an ocher un-burnt, a thin wash of hæmatite red over impure black. Gray is a pale yellowish earth with a little lampblack. In the Twelfth Dynasty violet was often used as a back-ground. Some Eighteenth Dynasty colors are illustrated in Plate III.

We also know something of the way in which the Egyptian painter worked, often with a definite system of guiding lines to keep his rows of figures in alignment and to regulate their proportions according to a canon understood from early times. In the Memphite period the figures were stocky in build but with the Empire they be-came taller and more elegant in proportions. In the Eighteenth Dynasty the height of a standing man was apportioned into nineteen equal parts; that of a seated man into sixteen: that is, the figure of a standing man was bounded by two lines above and below which were parallel; then it was cut by eighteen horizontals, the seated man by fifteen. A system of dropped verticals and horizontals cutting the field to be used into squares was thus the result (Fig. 86). These were made with a string which was dipped in ruddle and held taut and snapped. Such a string has been found in one of the Theban tombs wrapped about the sticks which were employed for paintbrushes. The use of these aids is especially evident in reliefs of various periods. Relief is a thing midway between painting and sculpture in the round and shows relation now with the one, now with the other. The Egyptian probably turned to relief in an attempt to gain shading and plasticity. This was unattainable with his usual system of flat colors, and relief gave somewhat more the effect of life that he desired. In later times, we find these reliefs clearly aiming at pictorial effects.

The Egyptian sculptor was versatile in relief cutting. For the most part his reliefs were low and differed little from paintings except for the modeling. Sometimes they were simply engraved with the point; or the background was cut away, permitting the figures to stand out and forming bas-reliefs (Fig. 51); at times they were incised and sunk, the background being left untouched, thus making reliefs *en creux* (Figs. 68-70). In the latter case, a unique method found only in Egypt, or in imitations, the sculptor drew his design on a flat surface with a fairly deep, incised outline. Then within this contour, he carved the form, leaving the original surface standing above the carved sunken relief. For the ordinary bas-relief, the sculptor usually drew a preliminary sketch in red paint. When many figures were to be represented, he very often used a system of guiding lines to mark out the various parts of the figure. With these as aids, the relief was cut. First, a furrow was made as an outline of the design, then the background was lowered and the figures modeled. Sometimes they were also covered over with a layer of fine plaster and a layer of gypsum before the color was applied in washes of flat tones, the preliminary sketch being repeated by a second sketch. In the Third Dynasty, the thickness of the reliefs was about that of one's finger; by the Fifth, they were almost as thin as paper.

The canon of proportions for the human figure seems to have been handed down from generation to generation, from master to apprentice, in the training given and in the sketchbooks which were also inherited from age to age. Whether or not they knew the secret of dynamic symmetry in art,[39] they had a feeling for proportion and balance that is evident to the most casual observer. Some of the beauty of their art lies there. But symmetry with them was sometimes carried to a point of rigidity. This was due in great measure to the repetition of traditional types and to adherence to fixed canons. It was also due somewhat to the utilitarian character of the art which led the poorer artists to copy rather than to create something new. Furthermore, the colored silhouette was a difficult medium of expression, as the Greeks found in later times, but in this mode of outlines and flat tones, undisturbed by considerations of chiaroscuro and perspective, the Egyptian achieved many wonderful paintings. This is the same mode of art which was later practiced with very definite outlines by the Greek vase-painters and which we may admire in Persian and Indian miniatures and in the early Buddhist paintings of China and Japan. Not to appreciate it means that one cannot appreciate good drawing or good design.

The Egyptian painter sought after truth of contour and he achieved it. His art is a two-dimensional art, suggesting form by well-drawn outlines. His success in the truthful rendering of nature as expressed in the contours of figures and objects is remarkable. He reduced the graphic delineation of objects to a system, carried out with certain fixed conventions. The human form was always conventionalized to the required flatness. The paintings and reliefs were perfectly adapted to the architectural surfaces which they were to decorate; there was great beauty of line, nobility of conception, and charm and simplicity of pattern. Even the small hieroglyphs are lively little pictures in themselves and show that the Egyptians knew how to use their writing decoratively as the Japanese, Chinese, Arabs, and few other peoples have done. These merits can counteract the unnatural drawing of the body, where the various parts are drawn from different points of view, and the uniformity of pose, to which we become accustomed. The Egyptian, it must be remembered, faced art with no precedents to guide him and no inheritance of artistic traditions. If the artist, drawing on a "memory picture," fixed upon a scheme that seemed lucid for the representation of the human figure, conservatism retained it, although many artists tried to escape and turned to nature as a guide. The achievement of the Egyptian painter lay largely in good designing which resulted from a fine decorative sense, in beauty of line and in charm of color.

However much we may criticize Egyptian art, there still remains much more to praise. It is idle to deny that the work of the Pyramid Age was splendid; it possessed a soundness and freshness such as belong to a young art in its vigor when no breath

[39] J. Hambidge, *Dynamic Symmetry*, Yale University Press, New Haven, 1920, pp. 25 ff.

of decadence or affectation has come near it. And we must grant as well in looking at the majority of Egyptian works that æsthetic considerations played a major part in their artistic creation. After the campaigns of Sesostris in the Twelfth Dynasty, when Egypt broke away from her isolation of the Old Kingdom, art began to be revivified by contact with outside influences. In the Eighteenth Dynasty under Thutmose III and his successors, when the whole Orient lay at the doors of Egypt, the imagination was stirred, foreign works furnished inspiration and conservatism became less and less the mentor of art. Many of the designs of this period show that the artist was genuinely inspired by his theme. With Amenhotep IV, we find that pictorial composition beginning which was to develop later into the grandiose scenes on the pylon of Rameses at Medinet Habu. In reliefs such as those at the Rameseum, the entire scene is one vast composition not separated into planes by ground lines.[40] The importance of this movement was very great and had its effect on the pictorial character of later historical relief. In turn, foreign influences were readily taken over into Egyptian art, as we know from scenes on the walls of Amenhotep's palace at Thebes.[41]

Undoubtedly the Egyptian passed on to Crete and the Orient many motives that were to live again in the art of later times—the ornamental patterns discussed stand out among the first contributions. Many motives, such as the cow licking her calf, and the fowler hunting with a cat in the marshes belong in the repertoire of Egypt. Figures looking out of a window, which Poulsen calls "Phœnician," may hark back to reliefs of the age of Akhenaten, where this motive occurs frequently. Many conventions, such as the use of red for the flesh of men, and yellow for women, passed on to Greece *via* Crete and Ionia. Possibly one of Egypt's contributions to the art of later times was her sense of symmetry, balance, and proportion, likewise one of the greatest assets in the art of Greece, whether it was derived from some outside source or was innate.[42]

[40] Maspero, *Art in Egypt,* N. Y., 1912, p. 165.

[41] R. de Peyster Tytus, *Re-excavation of the Palace of Amenhetep III,* New York, 1903; *Bull. Metrop. Mus. Suppl.,* March, 1918.

[42] For Egypt's contribution to later times, see F. W. von Bissing, *Die Bedeutung der orientalischen Kunstgeschichte für die allgemeine Kunstgesch.,* Utrecht, 1922; *Der Anteil der ägyptischen Kunst am Kunstleben der Völker,* München, 1912.

# CHRONOLOGICAL TABLE

| ORIENT (E. Meyer)* | EGYPT (Schäfer)* | B.C. | CRETE (Evans)* | MAINLAND (Blegen)* |
|---|---|---|---|---|
| 3500 (Woolley) or 3300 (Hall, Gadd) Predynastic Rulers of Ur: Mes-kalam-dug, Queen Shubad, etc. | Dyn. I, 3400 | 3400 | | |
| Ur-Nina, 2875 | | 3000 | E.M. I 3400-2800 | |
| Entemena | Old Kingdom Dyn. III-VI 3000-2500 | 2800 | | |
| Sargon I, 2652-2597 | | | | |
| Naram-Sin 2572-2517 | | | E.M. II 2800-2400 | |
| Gudea, 2450 | Dyn. VII-X | 2500 2400 | | E.H. Before 2500-2000 |
| | | 2200 | E.M. III 2400-2100 | |
| | | 2100 | | |
| Hammurabi, 1947-1905 | Middle Kingdom Dyn. XI-XII 2100-1800 | | M.M. I 2100-1900 | |
| Sack of Babylon 1750 (Hittites) | | 1900 1800 | M.M. II 1900-1700 | M.H. 2000-1600 |
| | XIII-XVII Hyksos | 1700 1600 | M.M. III 1700-1580 | |
| Kassite Period 1749-1173 | | 1580 1500 | L.M. I 1580-1450 | L.H. I 1600-1500 |
| | | 1450 | L.M. II 1450-1370 | L.H. II 1500-1400 |
| | New Kingdom Dyn. XVIII-XXII 1580-750 | 1400 1350 1200 | L.M. III 1370-1200 | L.H. III 1400-1100 |
| Assurnasirpal 884-859 | | 1100 | | |
| Sargon, II, 722-705 Assurbanipal 669-626 | | 750 | | |
| Nebuchadnezzar 605-562 | Late Period Dyn. XXIII-XXXI 750-332 | | | |
| Darius the Great 522-486 | | | | |

*E. Meyer, *Die ältere Chronologie Babyloniens, Assyriens und Ägyptens,* Berlin, 1925. Meyer's dates end with the Kassite Dynasty. Some may prefer the dates of Fotheringham.

*Schäfer, *Zeitschrift für ägyptische Sprache,* 52 (1915), pp. 2-4. Schäfer does not follow this in his book, *Von ägyptischer Kunst.*[2]

*Palace of Minos, I, II.

*Korakou, Boston, 1921, p. 123; A.J.A., 32 (1928), p. 153; Zygouries, Cambridge, 1928, p. 219.

# III

# THE ORIENT

IN Mesopotamia, the land of the two rivers, a civilization existed believed
by many to be older than the one by the Nile (Fig. 87). When it first meets
our eyes it is already well advanced; there are few traces of Palæolithic and
Neolithic remains. This is due, not to the fact that such an early civilization
did not exist, but to the alluvial character of the country which caused the former
settlements built of sun-dried brick to be washed away. Before 3000 B.C., perhaps
as early as 4000 or 5000 B.C., the Sumerian culture arose in the southern part of the
country later known as Babylonia, and with this group of Orientals we now know
that Babylonian civilization, in great part, originated. The Sumerians were a non-
Semitic people and most of their early history is concerned with the racial conflict
between themselves and the Semites who finally worsted them and gained the power.
These Semite nomads probably came into Sumeria from Arabia, attracted by the
fertility and wealth of the country.[1] They settled sites such as Kish and Akkad, in
the region that was later known as northern Babylonia.

It is not certain in spite of much new evidence who were the first inhabitants of

[1] G. A. Barton, *Sketch of Semitic Origins*, New York, 1902, Ch. I; *cf.* G. Contenau, *Manuel d'archéologie orientale*, Paris, 1927, I, 122 ff. (The Semites came from the region south
of the Taurus, from the country of the Amurru).

ancient Babylonia. Recent discoveries by Langdon at Kish prove that they were not Sumerians. Their pictographic system of writing is very closely related to the Sumerian, but their painted ware is clearly akin to that of early Elam. Some of their pictographs are strikingly like those on seals found in the Indus Valley at Harappa and Mohenjo-Daro, where remains of the culture of the founders of Indian civilization have now been brought to light. On the basis of these discoveries, Langdon argues that "a great prehistoric civilization spread from Central Asia to the plateau of Iran and to Syria and Egypt long before 4000 B.C. and that the Sumerian people, who are a somewhat later branch of this Central Asian people, entered Mesopotamia before 5000 B.C."[1a] This Pre-Sumerian culture had perished at Kish by 3500 B.C., as tablets in early Sumerian script are found at levels above this stratum, no less than seals and engraved wall plaques.[1b] For the moment, until further evidence is forthcoming it will be necessary to suspend judgment on the origin of the Sumerians and the earlier peoples of Central Mesopotamia. There appear to be three distinct cultures. First, we find the people who made the fine pottery in the earliest settlement at Susa, the Proto-Elamites (Figs. 100-102). This culture "extended from Anau in Turkestan, to Bushire on the Persian Gulf and to the south of Sumer at Eridu."[1c] It is traced by means of painted pottery and seals. They were followed by the people who made the polychrome ware of Susa II, who wore pigtails and who may have come from northern Syria. The Sumerians developed the next civilization of importance.[1d] Whatever the history and the relations of these various cultures may have been, we find that by 2650 B.C. the entire country from north to south was under Akkadian, i.e., Semitic, control.

The objects of art created by the Sumerians range in time from about 3500 to

[1a] *Cambridge Ancient History*, 1924, I², 362.

[1b] S. Langdon, *Excavations at Kish*, Paris, 1925, I. *Cf.* G. Contenau, *op. cit.*, 1927, I, 113 ff. (Origin of the Sumerians in Central Asia); G. Fougères, G. Contenau, R. Grousset, P. Jouguet, J. Lesquier, *Les Premières civilisations*, Paris, 1926, pp. 73 ff.; M. Rostovtzeff, *The Sumerian Treasure of Astrabad*, J.E.A., VI (1920), pp. 4-27; C. L. Woolley, *The Sumerians*, Oxford, 1928. V. Gordon Childe, *The Most Ancient East*, London, 1928 (Prehistory of the Nile Valley, Mesopotamia and the Indus Valley to 3000 B.C.).

[1c] Leon Legrain, *Culture of the Babylonians*, Philadelphia, University Museum, 1925, p. 11; *cf. Empreintes de cachets élamites*, *Mém. de la mission archéol. de Perse*, 16 (1921). Further traces of the culture have been recently found in China. *Geological Survey of China*, Pekin, I, 1923, *The Cave-deposit at Sha Kuo T'un in Fengtien*, J. G. Andersson; II, 1925, *Painted Stone Age Pottery from the Province of Honan, China*, T. J. Arne; *Memoirs of the Geological Survey in China*. Series A, No. 5, *Preliminary Report on Archæological Researches in Kansu*, J. G. Andersson, Pekin, 1925. *Cf.* V. Gordon Childe, *op. cit.*, Chs. VI, VII; H. Peake, H. J. Fleure, *The Steppe and the Sown*, New Haven, 1928, pp. 40 ff.

[1d] H. Frankfort, *Studies in Early Pottery of the Near East*, London, 1924, I; H. Peake and H. J. Fleure, *Peasants and Potters* (Corridors of Time, Vol. III), New Haven, 1927, pp. 91-96. (The Sumerians came from the Persian Gulf.)

2500 B.C. Most of our knowledge about them has been gained from excavations at Erech, Ur, Nippur, and Tello—the ancient Lagash.[2] They include sculptured reliefs, tablets and seals, statues in the round, pottery,[3] and metal work. The paintings of this time have of course perished, along with the mud brick buildings which they ornamented, but we are able to learn something about drawing and composition among these people from reliefs and objects of decorative art. From about 2875 B.C.,[3a] the time of Ur-Nina, King of Lagash, there are reliefs such as the one representing

[2] E. de Sarzec and L. Heuzey, *Découvertes en Chaldée*, Paris, 1884-1912. L. Heuzey, *Catalogue des antiquités chaldéennes*, Paris, 1902; L. Heuzey, E. de Sarzec, *Une Villa royale chaldéenne, vers l'an 4000 avant notre ère*, Paris, 1900; G. Cros, L. Heuzey, and F. Thureau-Dangin, *Nouvelles fouilles de Tello*, Paris, 1910; H. R. Hall, *J.E.A.*, VIII (1922), pp. 241-257.

[3] E. Banks, *Bismya*, New York, 1912, pp. 345 ff. Almost all of the pottery is undecorated. One black vase (p. 347) has two rows of pressed circles with one of squares between. Only one or two fragments show color. Painted Elamite ware is not included under Sumerian pottery, since the vases of Proto-Elamite I, at least, seem the work of a different race. C. L. Woolley apparently thinks that Langdon has found at Kish wares which furnish a connecting link between the earlier and the later Elamite pottery: H. R. Hall, C. L. Woolley, *Ur Excavations, I, Al 'Ubaid*, Oxford, 1927, pp. 155 ff. In his latest work, Woolley argues that the two styles, Susa I and II, are contemporary and posterior to the prehistoric wares of Sumer. The prehistoric painted pottery and the civilization it represents thus spread from Sumer to the highlands and not *vice versa*. C. L. Woolley, *The Painted Pottery of Susa, Journ. Royal Asiatic Society*, 1928, pp. 35-50. It is doubtful whether the contemporaneity of Susa I and II can be accepted. In *The Antiquaries Journal*, VIII (1928), pp. 417 ff., Woolley suggests that the painted pottery is Akkadian and that these Akkadians who lived in the lowlands were drowned by the Biblical Flood. This allowed the Sumerians to assume greater importance. F. Thureau-Dangin, *Rev. assyriologique*, XXIV (1927), pp. 206-209, suggests five periods (I-V), from Sargon of Akkad back to the first copper age. The Sumerians are connected with I, II, III. Their appearance in IV, which is the period of Susa I in painted pottery, is doubted. The inhabitants of the plain were, then, according to Hall and Thompson, "Præ-Sumerian," I owe the reference to M. Leon Legrain. *Centenary Suppl. to the Journal of the Royal Asiatic Society*, Oct., 1924, pp. 110 ff.

The latest discoveries unearthed by E. Herzfeld in a neolithic settlement near Persepolis indicate that he has found the prototype of the pottery of Susa I and the source of the first civilization at Susa. The oldest culture in Elam was, in his opinion, created on the Iranian plateau and was brought to Susa in an advanced stage of development. On the pottery are found eagles with wings outspread in frontal view—the forerunners of the heraldic eagles of the coats of arms of Sumerian and Elamite towns. The pottery shows relations in its designs with that of Samarra and of Honan, China. Herzfeld considers this neolithic civilization of Persepolis prior to anything so far known in the Near East (*Illustrated London News*, May 25, 1929, pp. 892 ff., June 1, 1929, pp. 942 ff.).

[3a] Most scholars give 3100 or 3000 for the date of Ur-Nina. I have followed E. Meyer's dating throughout, but the whole question of chronology is still very much unsettled, as is the case in Egypt. Fotheringham's dates are one hundred twenty years earlier, from Ur-Nina to the sack of Babylon.

the king and his family preparing to begin the construction of a temple to Ningirsu, the chief god of the city. They are of more interest archæologically for the pictures which they give of royal personages and great officials of the age with their large noses, shaven heads, and flounced skirts, than they are artistically. The relief of Ur-Nina is low and the figures crudely cut (Fig. 88). At either end Ur-Nina is represented, gigantic in stature, in fact twice the size of his sons. They advance toward him in processional array, in the upper register. In the lower register, a high official and members of the family are seen. The king bears on his head a basket containing material for the proposed temple. Below, he is seated offering a libation to the god, probably on the completion of the temple. The composition is well balanced and adapted to the space, and the execution is vigorous; but, on the whole, the work is crude and far below the level of Egyptian monuments of the same age. The style, while distinctive, has about it an almost barbaric character. It contains the germs of antithetic composition. A curious convention, apart from that found in Egypt of colossal size to represent power, is the one which makes the sons in the upper panel larger as they recede from the king, whether to suggest age or not we cannot say. In the lower panel, they are smaller. The king's faithful butler, Anita, appears in each scene offering him his cup.

The Stele of the Vultures, a relief from the reign of Eannatum, *patesi* of Lagash and a grandson of Ur-Nina, shows similar characteristics. It represents Eannatum leading his troops into battle against the neighboring city of Umma (Fig. 89). The name is given to the relief from the vultures sculptured in the upper portion, in a fragment not illustrated here. They are pictured swooping off with the heads and limbs of the slain in their beaks and claws. In the section shown here, Eannatum leads his men into the contest. They are protected by shields which entirely cover their bodies, and by pointed, cap-like helmets. Each soldier carries a long spear. Probably the artist has sought to represent a file of soldiers abreast, a feat for which his knowledge of perspective was not quite adequate; they seem to be drawn up in wedge formation. Below, the king in a chariot charges the enemy in advance of his bodyguard. The same convention found in Egypt of transforming depth into height is employed here in the ranks of soldiers. The results were arrived at quite independently. The gruesomeness of battle in scenes such as the trampling of the corpses of the enemy and the carrying off by vultures of the decaying bodies of the fallen, are the things that attracted the artist. They show that the originators of these works gave more attention to military pursuits than to the creation of art. The scenes are in part historical and commemorative, in part mythological and religious. They exhibit quite a little freedom in draughtsmanship and some ideas of composition.

These monuments are not so interesting artistically as the engraved silver vase of Entemena, great-grandson of Ur-Nina who ruled at Lagash about 2700 B.C. This vase, a dedicatory offering to the god Ningirsu, is very beautiful in shape[3b] and the engravings, executed with great skill, show the artistic power of the Sumerians at its best (Fig. 90). The design represents lion-headed eagles with outstretched wings, clutching with their claws, goats, lions, and stags in antithetic composition. The device of the eagle and lions presents the coat of arms of the city of Lagash. On the shoulder of the vase are seven heifers, all turned to the left and on the point of rising (Fig. 90). They are faithfully drawn, with truth to nature, in contrast to the animals below, which show much conventionalization (Fig. 91). The motive of one animal biting another is typically Sumerian and from there penetrated further west, especially into Ionia. The vase of Entemena is significant not only because of the beauty of the composition and drawing, but also because of the motives employed. The two-headed eagle of more modern times is probably descended from this eagle of Lagash. Beginning with early examples from Tello, such as a representation on the Vulture stele, where it is seen in the hand of the god Ningirsu, this eagle has a long history in art.[4] It is also found on a dedicatory tablet of the age of Entemena (Fig. 92). The composition here is similar to the design on the silver vase. It is interesting further for the introduction of the guilloche pattern, an ornamental design not used in Egypt and native to Sumeria. The history of the guilloche can be followed later in Oriental, Ionic, and Greek art. By the time of Gudea, 2450 B.C., the double-headed eagle appears. Its next stage of development can apparently be traced in Syria, in the rock-cut reliefs of Cappadocia[5] where we find an eagle with two heads, each turned outward toward the animal which it holds in its claws. This design is generally characteristic of Hittite art. The same fabulous monster appears in Persian art, then in Byzantine, and has been used in modern times in the coats of arms of Russia and the Hapsburg house.[6]

It is probably from this region that many of the fantastic and hybrid monsters which we usually associate with the Orient must have come into later art, and from Sumeria they were spread all over the Mediterranean area by means of tapestries and objects in metal and clay. From Mesopotamia came the gryphon, the centaur,[7]

[3b] The form resembles that of certain early Chinese vases.

[4] E. de Sarzec and L. Heuzey, *op. cit.*, p. 90. "The spread eagle may have a double lion's head . . . a favorite device in the time of Gudea and on a few ancient Elamite seals." L. Legrain, *The Museum Journal*, University of Pennsylvania, 1928, p. 234.

[5] E. de Sarzec and L. Heuzey, *op. cit.*, p. 91; G. Perrot, E. Guillaume, J. Delbet, *Exploration archéologique de la Galatie*, 1861, Pl. 51; *cf.* Pl. 38G.

[6] E. de Sarzec and L. Heuzey, *op. cit.*, p. 90; F. Poulsen, *Die dekorative Kunst des Altertums*, Leipzig, 1914, p. 29.

[7] L. W. King, *Babylonian Boundary-Stones in the British Museum*, London, 1912, Pl. XXIX, winged and wingless centaurs.

and the chimæra. The steatite vase of Gudea (2450 B.C.), Priest-King of Lagash, is a fine example of early Oriental art employing the gryphon in decoration (Fig. 93). Here, two heraldically posed gryphons, winged and wearing crowns, are placed on either side of two entwined serpents, symbol of the god of healing. Their bodies were originally inlaid with shell.[7a] These designs betoken a people richly imaginative and artistic in instinct. The gryphon probably originated and developed in Mesopotamia as Poulsen believes.[8] It occurs on early Babylonian seals as well as on this vase. From the early Sumerian period also come reliefs with representations of one animal following another and biting it. In Figure 94 we have an example of this motive from a shell cup of the period of Ur-Nina. The animals are shown in a landscape and the design once formed part of a larger composition. These are old Chaldæan motives which are very important in the art of later times. They occur only on reliefs but we must remember that relief developed out of drawing and that the first thing the artist of the relief had to do was to draw his design. Undoubtedly the same patterns and types of composition occurred wherever painting or enamels were employed.

Sumerian reliefs are thus seen to be significant in their drawing and composition and in the motives which appear on them. Probably one of their most interesting contributions is the heraldic and antithetic group which goes back to the beginning of time in Sumeria and which played such a vital part in Oriental art and, through the Orient, in the art history of later times. Professor Breasted believes that heraldically balanced figures occur in the Nile Valley not far from 4000 B.C., more than 800 years before they occur in Babylonian culture.[9] The prehistoric stages of Babylonian civilization are lost and it is a great question whether a type of composition which was so organic in Oriental art as the heraldic and antithetic group, could have been derived in the East from contact with early Egypt. Recent excavations tend to show that Babylonia influenced Egypt in this period rather than the reverse.[10]

[7a] This technique is Oriental. *Cf. The Museum Journal*, University of Pennsylvania, 15 (1924), oppos. p. 5; H. R. Hall, *The Civilization of Greece in the Bronze Age*, London, 1928, pp. 123 ff.; Sir Arthur Evans, *The Palace of Minos*, II, 1, 1928, pp. 262 ff.; V. Gordon Childe, *The Most Ancient East*, London, 1928, Pl. XXIII.

[8] F. Poulsen, *Der Orient und die frühgriechische Kunst*, Leipzig, 1912, p. 15. See W. H. Ward, *The Seal Cylinders of Western Asia*, Washington, D. C., 1910.

[9] J. H. Breasted, "Origins of Civilization," *Scientific Monthly* (1919); *cf.* L. W. King, *Sumer and Akkad*, p. 330. Many examples of heraldic design have been found recently by Woolley in his remarkable discoveries at Ur, dating probably as early as 3500 B.C. *The Antiquaries Journal*, VIII (1928), Pls. LV, LXII, LXIV.

[10] H. R. Hall, "The discoveries at Tell el-'Obeid in Southern Babylonia and some Egyptian comparisons," *J.E.A.*, VIII (1922), pp. 241-257: "In Egypt it is precisely those things that are most Babylonian in appearance that do not persist but were abandoned during the Old Kingdom or by the end of the Middle," *e.g.*, the paneled wall, cylinder seal, mace head,

Another feature of Sumerian art was the invention of the composite animal. The Sumerians and Elamites were the authors of Babylonian demonology and of the later "beast art" of Europe. In addition to the hybrid monsters which we have mentioned, their brains conceived the human-headed bull which was taken over by the Assyrians as a colossal guardian for their gateways. Furthermore, a tendency to indicate landscape is present in their monuments from the beginning (Fig. 95). Here, a mountainous height is represented by a scale pattern; above this a goddess is seated on her throne receiving worship. We should expect to find all of these motives in the repertoire of Oriental painting.

An idea of the patterns and colors employed in tapestry and in architectural decoration in this period may be gained from some remains found at Warka, the ancient Erech, and from stray ruins of buildings here and there in old Babylonia. Probably the walls of the interiors were in many cases merely left in the crude color of the brick and were hung with tapestries and mats. Crude brick houses excavated at Eridu show horizontal bands of red and white, or red, black, and white paint. The bricks had been covered with a thick lime plaster, or stucco, and date before 2300 B.C.[10a] The primitive three-color scheme of red, white, and black seems to be characteristic of early Sumerian art. A wall made of terra cotta cones, discovered by Loftus at Warka, showed a kind of mosaic decoration[11] (Fig. 96). The ends of the cones had been dipped in red or black color and were arranged to form geometric designs of various patterns, such as zigzags, diamonds, triangles, and lozenges. The wall was thirty feet in length and was composed of these small yellow terra cotta cones, three and a half inches long,[11a] set in a mixture of mud and chopped straw. The date of the construction is uncertain. Remains of glazed bricks similar to those which played such an important part in the decoration of Neo-Babylonia have also been found in this early period.

grinning lion, etc. "The Babylonian-looking element in archaic Egyptian art and culture then gives an exotic impression, as if due to some temporary impress which afterwards faded away. If these persisted in Babylonia it would look as if they came from Babylonia to Egypt rather than *vice versa*, or at any rate from a common source which impressed Babylonia more than Egypt." L. Curtius, *Studien zur Gesch. d. altoriental. Kunst, Sitz. der Bayer. Akad. der Wiss.*, 1912, pp. 1-70; A. Jolles, *Die antithetische Gruppe, Jahr.*, 19 (1904), pp. 27 ff.; *cf.* M. Rostovtzeff, *Iranians and Greeks in South Russia*, Oxford Press, 1922, pp. 191 ff.; H. Prinz, *Altorientalische Symbolik*, Berlin, 1915; H. R. Hall, *Cambridge Ancient History*, I, 580; Ziegler, *P.W. s.v. Gryps*.

[10a] This is Hall's dating. The reign of King Bur-Sin 1 is placed by Meyer at 2222-2214.

[11] W. K. Loftus, *Travels and Researches in Chaldæa and Susiana*, London, 1857, pp. 174, 188.

[11a] Similar cones have been found by C. L. Woolley at Al 'Ubaid: H. R. Hall, C. L. Woolley, *op. cit.*, pp. 48-50. They have also come to light in Egypt in the XIth and XVIIIth Dynasties. *Bull. of the Metropolitan Museum of Art, Egyptian Expedition*, 1925-1927, pp. 6 ff., Figs. 1, 4, 5.

A closer union of the southern Sumer and the northern Akkad took place after the Akkadian, Sargon I, came to the throne (2652 B.C.). Semitic influence now began to make itself felt in art. The finest monument of the period is the stele of Naram-Sin, son of Sargon of Agade. The king is represented armed with bow and arrow, battle-axe, and horned helmet. He is ascending a mountain to receive the submission of his enemies (Fig. 97). He tramples them down in his course. Behind him his men advance up the mountain in two columns rhythmically arranged. At the top of the monument are eight-pointed stars, insignia of the goddess Ishtar. The relief shows great animation and action. The artist has given a schematic treatment of the scene, vividly colored by his imagination. The feeling for landscape which is characteristic of later Babylonian art is seen here in its early development. The style of this monument represents the apogee of old Babylonian art.

The seal cylinders of the epoch in question are more delicate and beautiful than at any period before or after. Figures 98 and 99 show Gilgamesh in combat, in one case with a fabulous monster, and, in the other, with a lion. The beauty of the composition lies in the symmetry of the heraldic and antithetic groups. The figures are rendered with great fineness and yet with a minute attention to muscular detail which helps to produce the impression of strength and power.

We do not know how early Babylon was founded. Flint implements on the site carry the date back beyond historic times. By 2000 B.C. the name appears in the history of the First Dynasty.[11b] Under Hammurabi, the great lawgiver, 1947 B.C., it became independent and the chief city of Babylonia. Unfortunately, no remains of painting exist from this period, which was a brilliant one artistically. As the city was built of brick and suffered many sieges, it probably fell into decay. In fact, the old Babylonian culture greatly declined after the capture of Babylon by the Hittites and its later sack in 1750 B.C. by the Kassites. We may trace the artistic temper of the old Babylonian epoch in the sealstones, boundary stones, and reliefs and in the later monuments of Assyria and Neo-Babylonia. From the age of Hammurabi there are many good reliefs, the most famous of which is the one in the Louvre which represents Hammurabi standing before the sun god receiving the law.[12] The art is incomparably inferior to that of the age of Sargon. Both the relief of Hammurabi and the stele of Naram-Sin mentioned above were found in Elam, beyond the Tigris, where they had been carried as trophies by the Elamites during an incursion into Babylonia in the Thirteenth Century.

The region of Elam was the home of a very early culture akin in many of its aspects to the Sumerian, though beyond the limits of Babylonia. The Elamites made invasions into Sumerian territory and were in their turn conquered and ruled

[11b] There is an earlier mention of Babylon in records of Sargon, *C.A.H.*, I², 1924, p. 407.
[12] V. Scheil, *Délégation en Perse*, IV.

by the Sumerians. The material excavated at Susa, in Elam, goes back in time beyond the third millennium and offers us some of the earliest artistic efforts of man.[13] The pottery which was found at Susa by the De Morgan expedition is remarkable for its beauty and the character of its decoration, far advanced for so remote a period. It is divided roughly into two classes, the later of which, according to Pottier, does not date after 2500 B.C.[14] It represents an age later than the Neolithic, but with stone weapons still lingering on. This Proto-Elamite pottery, as Pottier calls the earlier class, at first sight seems to have employed only geometric ornament, but, on closer examination, we find that the decoration consists also of natural forms that have been stylized. Some of the vases show rectilinear patterns like those of the Dipylon ware of Greece (Fig. 100)—zigzags, lozenges, conventionalized birds, plants, and dogs. There is greater refinement in color, shape, and technique, however, than is found in the geometric ware of Greece. The vases often have a buff ground with patterns in a purplish red, black, brown, or yellow—colors probably produced in firing the black monochrome paint which was used in decorating the earlier class. The shapes include the cup, truncated cone, bowls, spherical goblets, and jugs with a broad neck. The bird is very commonly used in decoration; sometimes it is highly conventionalized, as at the top of the goblet in Figure 101, where the pattern has almost lost its original character because of the artist's love for fine, long lines. The bird's neck is elongated here to suit the space to be decorated and it is only on close examination that the origin of the pattern is seen. The running or seated dog is also conventionalized into very charming designs, as on the bowls in Figure 100, and below the band of birds in Figure 101. There is the greatest delicacy in pattern arising from the combination of curvilinear and straight lines, and there is very clever adaptation of design to space. In Figure 100, four dogs, one above the other, are used skilfully to decorate the circle in the bottom of the bowl. The long-horned goat, with body conventionalized into two triangles, joined end to end, and the horns done into a graceful curvilinear pattern is one of the most interesting motives employed, as we see from the vase in Figure 100 or the goblet, Figure 101. Later, the horns alone occur as a pattern. Occasionally, the geometrized human figure is used, as in the interior of the bowl, Figure 102. The later vases of the second

[13] *Vs.* De Morgan's early dating, *cf.* J. H. Breasted, "Origins of Civilization," *Scientific Monthly* (1919), pp. 573 ff. On an early dating, *cf.* H. R. Hall, *Cambridge Ancient History,* I², 1924, p. 579, who "sees no reason to date any of the Susian pottery earlier than the Fifth Millennium." Langdon also favors this date, *C.A.H.,* 1924, I², 361 ff. See J. de Morgan, *La préhistoire orientale,* Paris, 1927, III, 48 ff., Pls. I-III (color).

[14] J. de Morgan, *Mémoires de la Délégation en Perse,* XIII, *Céramique peinte de Suse,* Paris, 1912 (Pottier). *Cf.* E. Pottier, *Corpus Vasorum,* France, *Fasc.* I, 1923, I, *C a,* Pls. I-XII.

period, none of which are pictured here, show the degradation of pattern produced through successive copying.

This pottery, on the whole, displays an astonishing medley of inexperience and skill, as if the artist's power of conception had outstripped his ability and hand. The vases were made on a primitive wheel and the colors were applied directly to the clay, with a brush probably made from an ox's tail. The walls are oftentimes extremely thin and delicate. Pottier divides the vases into two classes, the black monochrome type found 20 to 25 meters below the soil in the necropoles, and the coarser fabrics of different shapes, with polychrome decoration, which were found 10 to 20 meters down. They were produced by different people.[14a] The designs include stylization of plants and animals, and geometric forms. They are very cleverly adapted to suit the shapes of the vases and the spaces in which they were to be used. In Figure 101, the triangles are employed to accentuate the height of the vase, and the long-necked birds are used on vases of this shape for the same purpose. On the bowls, the circle is often found and the patterns within the circle are employed artistically. The vases reveal a long past in decorative art and are remarkably beautiful objects. The animal repertoire shows a people advanced beyond the hunter's stage, with domesticated animals. Several rules of composition seem to be established by early Elamite art: the same subject may be repeated several times to form a frieze; the same subject may be repeated but reversed and opposed, upside down, to the preceding portion; or a heraldic composition may place symmetrical figures on either side of a central one.

It is Pottier's theory that the artist began with nature in these designs, then degenerated into conventionalized forms; that, in the first stage, we have pictographic formation of motives used with a magical or symbolic value; in the second stage, the utilitarian idea breaks down and we find the motives stylized; in the third, the artistic sense develops and symmetry and harmony overwhelm and destroy the original idea.

Not much pottery akin to the red ware of Susa II has been found. On the other hand, the vases resembling those of Susa I (Figs. 100-102), which have come to light on many sites, give evidence of a widespread culture.[15] Fairly close analogies have been found at Tepe Mussian north of Susa, under the Hittite site at Sakjegeuzi in northern Syria, in the low levels at Boghazkeui, and on the surface of early mounds in Cappadocia.[15a] Similar pottery occurs at Anau in Turkestan and on the Persian Gulf.

[14a] Some scholars hold that the same people produced the two classes. V. Gordon Childe, *op. cit.*, pp. 164 ff.

[15] *Cf.* pp. 53 ff. and note 3, Ch. III.

[15a] L. W. King, *History of Sumer and Akkad*, p. 341; J. L. Myres, *The Dawn of History*, p. 120; A. E. Cowley, *The Hittites*, 1920, pp. 24 ff. Similar pottery has recently been found

The Hittites must rank beside the Elamites, Sumerians, and Semite Babylonians as another great creative power which helped to develop the civilization of eastern Asia Minor and northern Syria and Mesopotamia. The name is used here as a cultural rather than an ethnical term, embracing a number of peoples with common cultural, linguistic, and artistic possessions. The leading people in the group were the Hatti. Hittite monuments extend from the Euphrates to Sardis. This nation formed a bulwark against Semitic power (see Map, Fig. 87), and thus allowed western Asia Minor and the Ionian states to develop independently. In so doing, they made a very important contribution to the development of the early Orient.

The Hittites occupied a cardinal point in the ancient world—the junction between Europe and Asia. They became a commercial group and dominated the trade routes in this area from the Fifteenth to the Thirteenth Century B.C.[15b] Among their most important centers as evidenced by discoveries were Boghazkeui and Euyuk in the north, Sindjerli and Carchemish in the south. On many of their sites, they built great palaces, sometimes approached by roadways lined with sphinxes. These buildings were entered through a broad propylon, flanked by towers. Huge lions or sphinxes adorned the entrance. These features were copied later in Assyrian and Persian architecture and are probably the characteristic elements referred to when Assyrian rulers boast that they "built in the Hittite style." The lower walls of the palaces were orthostates of stone carved with elaborate reliefs; the upper parts were of crude brick. These sculptured reliefs the Assyrians also adopted and developed into works of great beauty. In both regions the reliefs were painted in color. That there were any flat paintings on Hittite sites there is not the slightest evidence. There may have been, but one of the main reasons why the Hittites interest us here is because they handed down to later times through Assyria, Lydia, Syria, and Phrygia significant art motives. Their position in the history of Oriental art is not yet thoroughly understood and their influence was probably greater than is often conceded. Hogarth has published one of the best accounts of Hittite art and has arranged a chronological classification. The oldest works were found at Euyuk in Cappadocia; a second stage is represented by another class of monuments at Euyuk and by the sculptures of Yasili Kaia; and the third group, by the gateway at Boghazkeui. These monuments date from the beginning of the Fourteenth Century down to the late

in the excavations at Tell el-'Obeid near Ur and is on exhibition in the British and the University of Pennsylvania Museums. *Cf.* notes 1c, 1d, 3. For the pottery of Tepe Mussian, see *Délégation en Perse*, VIII (1906), Gautier, Lampre; for Bender Bushire, *Délégation en Perse*, XV (1914), Pézard; see R. Campbell Thompson, *Archæologia*, 70 (1918-1920), pp. 101-144; R. Pumpelly, *Explorations in Turkestan*, I, 1908.

[15b] I understand that the results obtained by the Oriental Institute of Chicago in Hittite territory will be published later by H. H. von Der Osten, in *Oriental Institute Communications*, No. 5; *cf.* No. 2.

Thirteenth. The southern ones do not show Cappadocian parentage. The art at Sindjerli and Carchemish is late and reveals Babylonian and Assyrian influence.[16] But the earliest sculptures of all these sites betray the same parents—"Sumerian art and an art of inner Asia." The oldest Sindjerli sculptures are not earlier than 1000 B.C.

The Hittite was more skilful in executing animal forms than he was in his attempts to depict human beings. The types, poses, and movements of men are confined to a few schemes which are repeated again and again and the forms are rather rigidly conventionalized. Among his best creations are fantastic genii and hybrid beings. Good examples of this tendency may be seen in the sculptures at Carchemish which date after 1000 B.C.[16] Heraldic bird-headed demons, which remind us of Sumerian and Kassite achievement, are seen holding up the roof of Heaven (Fig. 103). It is true that Hittite art borrowed often from its neighbors, especially in the later period. In the earlier epoch it is independent[17] though it soon acquires a Babylonian impress, introducing motives such as Gilgamesh, the tamer of animals. The sphinx, if derived from Egypt, bears none of the earmarks of Egyptian art. It is winged and has the forepart of a lion beneath the human head. The composite figures of Hittite art are fantastic creations of the imagination, probably picturing protecting genii who in the service of gods cared for men, but the human element has an all too realistic and sinister air and being. Even when the work shows evidence of borrowing, however, it always bears a vigorous and often barbarous native stamp.

Hittite art is thus seen to be an individualized art deriving many of its elements from neighboring peoples. Similarities in the representation of hybrid and demoniac forms shared with the Kassites may be due to ethnical relationship or to a common Sumerian borrowing. Other resemblances to the art of Elam have been discovered, especially in the pottery. Some scholars believe that the Hittites may have introduced the Susian pottery seeing that they invaded Babylonia at an early date. Some suggest that the similarities may be racial. The later Hittite period is at times strongly influenced by Egyptian and Assyrian art but it usually remoulds its material into new forms. In turn, the Hittites gave much to other tribes of Asia Minor —probably most to the Assyrians, Phrygians[18] (Moschoi), and Lydians. They, in

[16] A. E. Cowley, op. cit., pp. 30 ff.; D. G. Hogarth, Carchemish, London, 1914, I, plates; C. L. Woolley, Carchemish, London, 1921, II. The best account of the chronology of Hittite monuments is that of D. G. Hogarth, Cambridge Ancient History, 1924, II, 252, and especially 270 ff.; 1925, III, 132, and especially 148 ff., 156 ff. For a later account see the excellent articles of E. Pottier, L'Art hittite, Syria, I (1920), pp. 167 ff., 264 ff.; II (1921), pp. 6 ff., 96 ff.

[17] F. v. Reber, Die Stellung der Hethiter in der Kunstgeschichte, Sitzungsber. der Königl. Bayer. Akad. d. Wiss., 1910, pp. 4-112.

[18] A. E. Cowley, op. cit., pp. 27 ff.

their turn, passed on the heritage to the Etruscans and Ionian Greeks. The likeness of the word *Tarku* found so frequently in Hittite names to Tarquinius of the Etruscans cannot be accidental and the profiles of the two peoples are at times strikingly similar, to say nothing of details of costume and other minor points.

Shortly after the sack of Babylon by the Hittites in 1750[18a] B.C., there follows the domination of the Kassites, a warlike race who ruled Babylon and possibly Elam for several hundred years (1749-1173). They were apparently a barbarous people about whose origins and connections we know little. They seem to have been closely allied with the Hittites who, at any rate, found their rule beneficial to Hittite interests. They contributed little that we can name to the civilization of the East. Their art shows a close connection with early Sumerian and Elamite work. Most of our knowledge about it is derived from certain reliefs which are usually termed "boundary stones," but which the Babylonians called "Kudurru."[19] They were really deeds or titles to land granted to the god or to individuals, and they may have been set up in the temple of the god or on the owner's estate to prove his claim to the territory. Our interest in them lies largely in the fact that they show the old Sumerian composite and fantastic forms of animals in the symbols of the gods invoked to preserve the boundaries against encroachment or seizure. A stone belonging to the Third Dynasty of Babylon, marking a grant of land by a Kassite King to his son, is divided into registers, in each of which are represented various strange animals, the emblems of the gods whose protection is desired. Prominent among these monsters are the winged gryphon, the winged lion, the serpent with snail-like head, and a goat-headed animal with a fish body. Another of these monuments has a representation of a winged centaur drawing a bow (Fig. 104). Lion-headed demons and the possible prototype of the minotaur occur. The art of the Sumerians, Hittites, and Kassites exhibits a certain kinship, evincing the same fondness for fantastic and hybrid animals. Some of these animals are also found on Proto-Elamite tablets. From the Sumerian-Elamite circle demonology and fantastic animals came into Babylonian art and we shall trace their influence later in Assyria, Ionia, Corinth, and other centers.

After the end of the Kassite Dynasty about 1200 B.C., the art and power of Babylonia did not again rise to importance until the days of Nebuchadnezzar II (605-562). In the interim we hear of wars and the names of shadowy rulers. Meanwhile the Assyrian civilization in the north had arisen.

[18a] This event is dated by most scholars in 1926. The chronology of the text is that of E. Meyer.

[19] L. W. King, *Babylonian Boundary-Stones in the British Museum*, London, 1912; Wm. J. Hinke, *A New Boundary Stone of Nebuchadrezzar I from Nippur. Babylon. Exped. of Univ. of Pennsylvania*, IV (1907); V. Scheil, *Délégation en Perse*, IV; *cf.* Vols. II, VI.

The city of Assur, the leading power of the Assyrian empire, was early founded by Semitic nomads. It is possible to trace the names of Assyrian rulers by 2200 B.C., but the kingdom did not become independent until shortly before 1400. There is little artistic material from its earlier period. It was influenced by the Babylonians, and by the Aramæans of Syria. The first outstanding reign for the history of art is that of Assurnasirpal II (884-859). Before him, we read of the wars of Salmaneser I and Tiglathpileser I, but no reign possesses the vividness that belongs to the domination of this ruthless conqueror. Monuments preserved from his palace, such as the colossal, man-headed bulls and the historic bas-reliefs, also make his age more real to us.

The Assyrian builder, in addition to the employment of brick, made use of limestone and alabaster, which were mostly denied to the Babylonian. The walls of the palaces, which in their gateways and guardian animals imitated the Hittite, were also, in Hittite fashion, adorned with dadoes of sculptured reliefs. These reliefs were painted in color, in part at least. Many of them still show traces of paint today, especially for the hair, eyes, beards, and sandals of the figures. Red and black are the tones which predominate for these details, as we should naturally expect. The ground-color and the color for the undecorated parts appears to have been a yellow ocher.

Painting as an independent art never existed in Assyria. Some few wall-paintings are known from the Thirteenth Century. These have been admirably published by Andrae.[19a] They were found at Kar-Tukulti-Enurta, opposite Assur, on the left bank of the Tigris. They decorated the walls of the Temple of Assur and the Palace of Tukulti-Enurta, King of Assyria. As Andrae considers him the first of the name, the wall-decorations must be placed somewhere between 1260 and 1238 B.C., during his reign. They show squares with red or blue grounds and designs of "flower stars" composed of leaves, circles, and branches in black and white. The patterns were probably drawn from weaving. Red, black, and white rosettes are found at the corners of the squares; red and blue rosettes and lotuses above them. Sometimes figure decoration occurs, as in the case of two gazelles heraldically posed on either side of a conventionalized palm tree, with palmettos flanking. The colors are a red between vermilion and Indian; blue, which is probably a clay; white and black. The gazelles are a faded pink. Andrae also publishes some enamel paintings. The art goes back to the Thirteenth Century on this site, but was used more after 1100 B.C. because of the discovery of tin glaze. The walls were covered with the ruler's wars, camps, victories, and sacrifices (cf. op. cit., Pl. 6, color). One example, dating from the reign of Tiglathpileser I (1115-1103), was re-used later, in the Ninth Century.

[19a] W. Andrae, *Coloured Ceramics from Ashur*, London, 1925 (36 Plates, many in color).

It shows the King on horse, leading his army over a mountainous region. The ground is blue, the horses and garments mostly yellow, and the scale pattern, rising at intervals in mounds, is yellow with brown borders. Some of the excellent glazed pottery from the age of Sargon is decorated with leaping goats, trees, and scaly mountains which recall patterns on Elamite seals. The colors are often blues which bring to mind Persian pottery and tiles.

A few stucco paintings, some of which unfortunately disappeared shortly after excavation, are known from the palace of Assurnasirpal at Nimrud.[20] They seem to have been ornamental patterns in which reds and blues were mainly used. In Nimrud, frescoes have also been found portraying winged bulls facing one another heraldically (Fig. 105). Their bodies are in a dark blue, heavily outlined with black against a yellow ground. Ornamental patterns in white and blue are found above and below the main design and the battlement band-pattern makes its appearance. Frescoes were also employed on the walls in an ornamental fashion above the relief scenes, but it is from reliefs that we can gain much of our knowledge of drawing, composition, and painting among the Assyrians.

The history of Assyrian bas-relief really begins with the dynasty of Assurnasirpal. These reliefs must, in large part, have taken the place occupied by painting in Babylonia and the southern countries of Mesopotamia. For the most part, they are commemorative, recording the king's hunts, battle triumphs, and worship of the gods. The sculptors were, for this reason, somewhat handicapped by the necessity to glorify the royal household. But with all this, when they turned to scenes of hunting, they often produced some of the most brilliant reliefs known from any period. The lack of æsthetic feeling is seen, however, in the way in which the artist frequently covered his figures with cuneiform inscriptions.

A few examples of reliefs from the reign of Assurnasirpal will show the aims of the sculptors of the time. In Figure 106 the king in his chariot is hunting lions. The majesty of the ruler with his drawn bow, the onrush of the horses, the might of the attacking lion, and the agony of the beast which has been brought low, are well combined into a unified composition. But it is not stirring or inevitable as the later scenes of the days of Assurbanipal. There is the same exaggeration of muscles to show power and strength which we find among the primitive Egyptians and Sumerians. On the whole, the work lacks something, which, for want of a better word, we will call inspiration.

The Assyrian of this period was not unambitious. If he wished to render a landscape he attacked it boldly. In Figure 107 we have a scene of an assault by Assyrian archers on a walled town near a stream. The hilly ground is marked by scale-like eminences along which conventionalized trees are growing and the water is indicated

[20] A. H. Layard, *Nineveh,* II (1852), pp. 17, 238.

by wavy lines and by fugitives swimming toward a fortress on skins filled with air.[20a] The composition is one of extreme daring but can hardly be said to be successful. In most cases where a hilly landscape was intended, the ground was covered with this scale pattern (*cf.* Fig. 108). The convention began in early Elamite art: it appears on the Sumerian relief of a goddess seated on her mountain throne, probably from the time of Eannatum (Fig. 95). It became very common in Assyrian art and is later found on "Phœnician" bowls. In Figure 108 we have a typical landscape of this kind with a very clear indication of planes and depth. Two hunters are seen netting deer in a rocky, wooded region. The reliefs of this period also continued to make use of the traditional composite animals and demons. Eagle-headed, winged genii are common and exhibit heavy Assyrian proportions, with massive muscles and cumbersome conventionalized wings. Sometimes they are represented with human heads. Other forms occurring are lion-headed monsters with the claws of a bird of prey (Fig. 109) and the man-headed lion.

Glazed bricks are also to be found from the days of Assurnasirpal. They were known in Babylonia and their origin may go back to Egypt where glazes were early spread on the walls for the protection and adornment of houses. An example from the palace of Assurnasirpal at Nimrud is seen in Figure 110. The ground is a deep lapis blue, far richer than the later blues that we shall meet. In the center runs a guilloche pattern in red and blue with center circles of black and white. This band is ornamented on both sides by palmettes and lotus buds, in some cases conventionalized into a kind of pine cone. The colors are red, yellow, and blue, with black and white introduced here and there. Both the coloring and the pattern are effective. Entire figure compositions existed in this glaze technique. Perhaps our best idea of an ancient Assyrian painting may be gained from a specimen now in the British Museum coming from the central palace at Nimrud. It is a small glazed tile dating from the time of Salmaneser III, the son of Assurnasirpal (859-824). Against a yellow ground a procession is represented consisting of the king followed by his chief eunuch and his spear-bearer (Fig. 111). They advance toward an officer. The king is preparing to pour a libation. Above the group hangs a fringed curtain, and below, a guilloche pattern is painted. The colors are: yellow for the garments, with brown borders and stripes; white for the king's crown; white and brown for decorative patterns; black for hair, sandals, and bows. The garment of the spear-bearer is in part green. The processional character which belongs to a large proportion of Assyrian reliefs is evident in this work. The painting possesses dignity, but also a certain monotony and an almost wooden character. It lacks the vitality that we should like, but the absence of this quality may be due in part to the ceremonial nature of the scene.

[20a] The skins may have been filled with hay, *cf.* Xen., *Anab.*, I, 5, 10. I owe the reference to Miss Milne.

Plate IV. Khorsabad. Colored lion. Enameled tiles.

Assyria's foremost ruler was Sargon, a usurper (722-705 B.C.), though probably he was of royal birth. He found time in the midst of his wars to become one of the country's greatest builders. At Khorsabad, north of Nineveh, he built Dur-Sharrukin (Sargonsburg), a vast palace covering about twenty-five acres. It was modeled in part on earlier Babylonian palaces, in part on Hittite plans. It contained a ziggurat, or "Tower of Babel," more than 200 rooms built around several courts, and thirty corridors. To this were added terraces and an enclosing wall (Fig. 112). The decoration of this palace consisted in large measure of glazed brick tiles which protected and adorned the walls, and in reliefs of alabaster which formed a kind of dado on the interior. As one approached the palace of Sargon, one probably saw first the ziggurat painted in gay colors—the lowest story, white; the second, black; the third, red; the fourth, blue.[20b] After the ziggurat, one probably noted the crenelated towers and flat roofs and the glazed bricks with figures in yellow and creamy white against a sky-blue ground—the Oriental combination so familiar today in eastern mosques and in Persian pottery. Above the triple entrance flanked by massive towers and adorned with colossal, man-headed bulls were archways decorated with these glazed tiles (Fig. 113). In contrast to Babylonian tiles, they are not in relief but the flat edges of the bricks, which were about three and a half inches long, have been covered with a vitreous glaze. The ground color was blue and against this were posed genii in yellow, heraldically placed on either side of a white rosette. A line of green color has been added, running along the lower part of the headdresses. The figure shown here, which is engaged in some religious ceremony, was one decorating the springer of the arch. Glazed tiles also adorned the front of the palace below the crenelated battlements. Other well-preserved examples have been found in the "Harem" of the palace, covering the lower part of the walls on either side of the doorway (Fig. 114). They represented the king, followed by a lion, a raven, a bull, a tree, and a plough. The significance of the design does not seem to be very clear; it is perhaps symbolic. The upright slabs which it adorns are about three feet high and twenty-three feet long. The ground color is again a bright blue and the figures are yellow. Green, which is rare in Mesopotamian painting, occurs for the leaves of the trees. Above and below the design runs a band of white rosettes with yellow centers. The lion (Plate IV), which strides majestically along, is modeled after Babylonian examples, but we shall see that he hardly compares in power and rage with the lions from the "Procession Street" at Babylon. He is much more rigidly conventionalized and heavy in proportions. The beauty of the panel lies largely in the color, the rhythmic spacing and the element of conventionalization.

[20b] Since the discovery of the ziggurat at Ur, the color scheme of white, black, red, and blue seems established. It is now impossible to maintain that they were painted in seven colors emblematic of the seven planets. C. L. Woolley, *The Antiquaries Journal*, V (1925), p. 14 and note 1 (C. J. Gadd).

These tiles furnish some idea of the decoration of the more important rooms of Assyrian palaces. Probably many of the lesser ones were adorned with stucco, painted with figure designs and patterns of an ornamental nature. The tiles show characteristics not unlike the reliefs of the time—figures of stocky proportions rather rigidly conventionalized, marching in processional array, or heraldically posed in some ritualistic scene. They give but a faint idea of the rich coloring and splendid ornament which covered the walls of Sargon's great palace.

We shall not pause over the reign of Sennacherib, the son of Sargon, except to point out that he was the destroyer of Babylon in 689 B.C. Reliefs in his reign grew more pictorial and attempted elaborate landscape scenes representing figures and trees scattered over the field at different levels, without any accurate knowledge of perspective. The scale pattern was extensively employed to indicate rocky landscape.

Under Assurbanipal, Assyrian relief reached its zenith (669-626). The famous scenes of hunts in which the king participated have never been surpassed in their sympathetic portrayal of animal life and in fidelity of observation. As compositions they are not always skilful. The figures of slain lions are oftentimes strewn over the field in a purposeless way, though the single examples are always well executed. The reliefs of this period have just that life and spirit, lacking in the works of Assurnasir-pal, which raise them to the plane of great art. Most remarkable is the scene of the chase in which wild horses are represented[20c] (Fig. 115). The breathless swiftness of the pursuit is wonderfully suggested by the long straight lines carried on from one animal to the next in parallel courses. We share in the tragedy of the wounded and the anxiety of the mare turning backward to see whether her foal will escape. The reliefs are characterized by absolute knowledge of anatomy, sincere observation of nature, and truth of expression. Added to this is the imaginative element which seizes upon the dramatic or tragic and helps to excite our emotion. In the wounded lioness so often pictured, dragging her limbs on the ground, we have the acme of the sculptor's achievement in animal suffering. It is this appeal to human sympathy which adds so much to these reliefs, wonderful as they are in execution. A certain *ethos* is given to the animals and we feel the immense gulf which separates the work of the cave artist from specimens such as these. Comparing the composition of the chase in which wild horses are hunted with the boar fresco from Tiryns (Fig. 177), we observe again the great superiority of Assyrian work. Although the theme is similarly treated in the two instances, the Mycenæan artist fails to engage our emotions in the outcome of the contest, whereas, with the Assyrian masterpiece, we are all concerned that the flight may be successful.

[20c] These are usually called asses but the wild ass of antiquity was wrongly called by this name and was in reality a wild horse. *Cf.* O. Keller, *Die antike Tierwelt*, Leipzig, 1909, I, 271; A. W. Seaby, *Art in the Life of Mankind*, London, 1928, II, 39-40.

On the whole, Assyrian art with human figures is less intimate than Egyptian and, for this reason, less engaging. The pompous figures of Assyrian potentates attract us little. The artist seems to have felt the same way about it, which accounts for our attitude. He probably had little interest in studying the human form because it offered him small artistic opportunity, swathed in heavy draperies as he saw it. He seems to have turned with elation from the thickly set figures of men to the lithe, swift figures of animals in action or in quiet rest. Assyrian relief, better than Egyptian, combined landscape and figures into a successful composition; it had, in general, more of a feeling for perspective, without any scientific knowledge of it. It went further than Egypt in observation of nature and realized by means of color a system of decoration appropriate to the material.

The ornamental patterns employed seem not to have reached a stage comparable to the Egyptian. We have mentioned previously the fact that the guilloche pattern was invented in Mesopotamia but in many cases the Orient merely adapted traditional material, such as the lotus and palmette. The alabaster threshold from the palace of Assurbanipal, a slab decorated with lotus flowers, palmettes, rosettes, and stars in circles (Fig. 116), is one of the best examples known of ornamental design. It is carried out with the fineness of embroidery work and the patterns may indeed have been borrowed from tapestry.

Assurbanipal's was the last great Assyrian reign, brilliant in its culture and showing relations with Syria, Lydia, and Egypt. The city of Nineveh was sacked by the Medes in 612 and the power passed into the hands of the Neo-Babylonian Dynasty under Nabopolassar and his son Nebuchadnezzar (605-562). Diodorus describes Nebuchadnezzar's marvelous palace at Babylon with its great walls which were one of the seven wonders of the ancient world.[21] It was adorned with hanging gardens, a "Tower of Babel," temples, and a hundred gates of bronze. The ruins today are the most important still standing in Babylon. It was modeled after Assyrian palaces, such as Sargon's.

The site, excavated by the Germans, especially Koldewey,[22] was a mound, called today the "Kasr." Hundreds of rooms were laid bare, forming in the main the palace of Nabopolassar, enlarged by his son. The discovery of greatest importance, however, was that of the sacred "Procession Street," high above the houses of the city, leading up to the Ishtar Gate. Along this way, the images of Babylon's many deities were borne in procession on festivals such as New Year's Day. The walls facing the street were covered with glazed tiles representing a series of lions striding along in

[21] Hdt. I, 178-181: *cf.* Diodorus II, 8, 4; Edgar J. Banks, *The Seven Wonders of the Ancient World*, New York, 1916, pp. 39 ff. The account of Diodorus goes back to Ktesias.

[22] R. Koldewey, *Das wieder erstehende Babylon*, Leipzig, 1913, trans. by A. Johns, *The Excavations at Babylon*, London, 1914; R. Campbell Thompson, *Cambridge Ancient History*, 1924, I,[2] 506 ff.

majestic attitude (Fig. 117). They are modeled in relief and stand out in creamy white with tawny manes, or in yellow with red manes, against a ground of blue. This street formed a magnificent approach to the Temple of the Goddess.

The Ishtar Gate with the splendor of its lofty towers and the rich color of its enameled decoration must have been one of the most impressive sights in Babylon. Even today its ruins impress the spectator by their majesty (Fig. 118). The walls are still standing to a height of thirty-nine feet. The gateway is double, formed by an inner and an outer entrance close together, one behind the other. The lower parts of the walls are of crude brick and are decorated with lines of bulls in relief, unenameled (Fig. 119). The upper parts were enameled and ornamented with figures in relief (Fig. 120). Each tower contained figures of bulls in procession, alternating with rows of dragons in file. The figures, in height, occupied thirteen brick courses and the various rows were separated from one another by eleven plain courses of unenameled brick. Dragons and bulls were never mixed in the same horizontal row. Nine sections of these animals in relief are visible today and there were forty animals in the lower rows, fifty-one in the upper, making over 575 in all. One of the most interesting figures is the dragon or "sirrush" (Fig. 121), which stands out in creamy white against a lapis ground. Details such as claws, mane, hair, and tongue were done in a golden brown. It is the far-famed animal of Babylon and embodies some of the imaginative genius of Old Babylonia, from which it was perhaps derived. The clay relief of Figure 122 suggests that it was a common motive in this region.[23] It was a walking serpent with a viper's head, a forked tongue, scaly body, forefeet of a feline animal and rear legs of a bird of prey. It was sacred to the God, Marduk. The lion, on the other hand, was the sacred animal of Ishtar. As it strides along in hieratic gait, it gives an impression of tremendous dignity and power (Fig. 117). It is far finer in conception than the Assyrian lion of Plate IV which is directly modeled after it. The third animal pictured, the bull, was the sacred animal of Adad. It was rendered either in brown with blue details on the body and green horns and hoofs, or in white and blue with yellow hoofs and horns (Fig. 123).

The exterior of the palace of Nebuchadnezzar was adorned with glazed tiles. Remains from the court off the Throne room show ornamental patterns. Most of these have been destroyed, but enameled tiles from a Persian building of the time of Darius on the same site, have designs which are almost identical. Figure 124 reproduces a bit of this colored decoration. The designs include yellow columns with blue capitals united by a lotus pattern against a lapis ground. Above, runs a frieze of white double palmettos with yellow centers. The colors are again yellow, blue, white, and black.

[23] A. T. Clay, "Art of the Akkadians," *Art and Arch.*, V (1917), p. 82, derives it from the West.

The technique of the glazed tile is interesting. When the figures were to be in relief, a frame of the desired size was set up and a mould was fastened to the edge of the frame. The figures were then fashioned by these moulds. The moulds themselves must have been made from models obtained by building a temporary wall the size of one of the animals in bricks of plastic clay. With the help of these models, moulds could be made for each separate brick. When the separate bricks had been fashioned by means of moulds, then the contours were applied in a black vitreous glaze on each brick. Later, these outlines were filled in with colored enamels which were fused in a gentle fire. The bricks were then united in a picture.[24] The colors used were mineral: blue of copper and blue of lapis lazuli; dark brown of manganese, white of tin; yellow-orange of antimony; and red, a suboxide of copper. We are able to follow the development of this art in the fabulous monsters from the Palace of Darius at Susa.

It will be seen from the survey of eastern painting up to this point that the Sumerians, Babylonians, and Assyrians did not have painting in the sense in which we understand the word. They colored figures and reliefs and ornaments but did not use the art to create illusion. The architect covered his walls to conceal the poverty of the material and to protect it against the elements. The art was a purely decorative one in the service of architecture. In the interior, he at times used plaster, painted black by a distemper process, to protect the walls; this technique has been found in the palace of Sargon.[25] But the interior decoration was usually a dado or baseboard of stone and the figures, when figure decoration was employed, touched the ground with their feet. The artist seems to have sought after harmony and opposition of color, and after rhythm produced by traditional forms which succeeded one another or reappeared in almost the same order. The chief colors employed were yellow, blue, red, black, and white, with occasional green. Blue was almost always used as a background in the tiles; yellow often in stucco painting. The colors were flat. There was no blending, light or shadow, or modeling. All faces of animal figures were identical, and the same was often true of men. The fabulous monsters which occur so frequently would seem to indicate that greater play was given to the imagination than in Egypt but this is doubtful because the traditional forms are repeated from time immemorial with little variation, as the dragon type proves. Art has here passed beyond the utilitarian and magical to the commemorative and symbolic stage. It was used in the service of the rulers instead of being associated with the cult of the dead.

The next inheritors of the country of Babylonia and Assyria were the Persians. They conquered Babylon in 538 B.C.; Asia Minor in 546 to 544. By the middle of the

[24] R. Koldewey, *Excavations at Babylon*, pp. 28 ff.
[25] Perrot and Chipiez, *op. cit.*, II (1884), pp. 287 f.

Sixth Century they had made their power felt throughout the East. Like their predecessors, they built great palaces. After Cyrus founded his empire, he placed his capital at Pasargadæ and erected a palace there. But it was really under Darius the Great that the Persian Empire rose to its fullest splendor (522-486 B.C.). He built a palace at Persepolis, forty miles to the south of the capital of Cyrus, and another at Susa. It is from these structures that we form our ideas of Persian magnificence in the days when these conquerors were seeking to create a world empire and to include within it the little country of Greece.

The Persians drew most of their decorative forms from Oriental sources and not many elements in their art are original. They borrowed chiefly from Assyria. Like the Assyrians, they had inherited from Elam and Chaldæa the fashion of covering their walls with enameled bricks. This art was known to the inhabitants of Susa centuries before it reached Persia proper or became universal there. Although enameled tiles have been found only at Susa, they were probably employed at Persepolis and other cities because the palaces were all used by the same Persian prince. These reliefs and winged bulls are often poorly copied from Assyria and we shall see that their enameled friezes are really inferior to those of Babylonia which served as prototypes.[26]

The ruin of the palace at Susa, built by Darius in the days of Marathon, and reconstructed by Artaxerxes II, Mnemon, is a structure of 110 rooms—small and large—with six rectangular courts and three long corridors.[26a] It is harmonious in plan, both compact and symmetrical in its masses, and amply aired by great courts. It was fortified with formidable defenses consisting of a great deep ditch and triple fortifications with towers about the citadel. The throne room, or *apadana,* an immense hypostyle hall for audiences, was surrounded by hanging gardens, an attraction borrowed from Chaldæan palaces. So beautiful were their parks that the Bible borrowed the Persian word *Paradise* to designate the spot of Adam and Eve's fall.[27] The bases of the columns of this structure are still in place on the leveled ruins of the throne room of Darius I. To the ancient throne room of Darius probably belonged the enameled frieze of Persian Bowmen, so often pictured, and now in the Louvre (Fig. 125). It was discovered below the foundations of a gate of Artaxerxes' palace. Some of the archers are going to the right, others in the opposite direction; a part of them are dark; others, fair. Those pictured here are black skinned, with black hair and beards. They belonged to a race closely akin to the negroid and one

---

[26] F. Sarre, E. Herzfeld, *Iranische Felsreliefs,* Berlin, 1910, argue for the superiority of Persian reliefs over their Assyrian prototypes. I owe the reference to Professor Carpenter.

[26a] M. L. Pillet, *Le Palais de Darius I$^{er}$ à Suse,* Paris, 1914.

[27] M. Dieulafoy, *Les Antiquités de Suse,* Paris, 1913, p. 4. The word, *Paradise,* means a park stocked with game, or a garden.

that inhabited the Susian plain from a remote antiquity. They undoubtedly represent a part of the Persian army, in which there were also Aryan archers, recognizable by their white skins. These archers were the "Immortals" of Herodotus.[28] They proceed in stately procession, garbed in rich, long-sleeved garments of citron yellow and purple, or white and purple, embroidered with rosettes and symbols of the Susian citadel. They carry spears, but the large bow over the left shoulder and the enormous quivers indicate that they were primarily bowmen. The spear is the symbol of their service in the bodyguard of the ruler. The ground upon which the figures are painted is a turquoise blue with a decorative frieze above and below consisting of yellow and white triangles and palmettes against a field of blue. Some idea of the luxury of the Persian court is comprehensible from this frieze of richly equipped soldiers, wearing earrings, bracelets, and headbands, together with soft leather shoes and sumptuously embroidered robes. Just where the frieze belonged, it is difficult to say. The restoration by Pillet of the Tribune of the Court of Columns at Susa furnishes an idea of the way in which such friezes may have been employed as a sort of screen in the halls (Fig. 126). Friezes of this character added not a little splendor to the cedar roofs and the elaborately painted capitals of the columns.

The Persian introduced into his designs the fabulous monsters of the East. The enameled sphinx of Figure 127 is typical of his borrowing. These man-headed monsters, with the bodies of lions, have Assyrian heads with high tiaras and formal beards and curled hair. They are heraldically posed with the winged disc above them, symbol of Ahouramazda. The rich colors used are the same as those on the frieze of archers. The superb wings of the sphinxes, with six rows of feathers, are alternately citron yellow, orange, cobalt blue, yellow, cobalt blue, orange. The bodies are enameled in white, the hair was a greenish blue, and the heads, brown.

Other fabulous monsters probably decorated the approaches of interior gates and were designed to ward off evil genii. Such were the winged bull of Figure 128, much more stylized than Babylonian animals of this character, and the enameled gryphon of Figure 129. The latter has the body and head of a lion; the forefeet of a lion and the hindfeet of a bird of prey. Its horns are those of an antelope. The bodies are in white enamel with blue, green, and yellow for details. In this respect they resemble in many ways the technique of the Persian frieze of enameled lions, which from its position was obviously later than the frieze of Bowmen and which probably belongs to the period of Artaxerxes. The lions may have decorated a propylon. They are strongly conventionalized, the faces being literally tattooed with blue lines. Blue and yellow retouches mark prominent muscles and bones and give to the design a patchwork character. The archers, in contrast, are more true to nature. The same pale turquoise ground is used in both cases.

[28] Hdt. VII, 41, 83, 211; Athen. XII, 514b; Paus. VI, 5, 7, and note (Frazer).

Just how conventional the art of Persia is as opposed to that of Babylon may be seen from the relief coming from the *apadana* of Xerxes at Persepolis, representing a lion rending a bull (Fig. 130). The lines which were used by the enamelers to mark the hair on the back and other details have been made into a stereotyped pattern, the origin of which is still very evident. The same is true of the lion which harks back to old Sumerian patterns.

The art of Mesopotamia may be said to have ended with Persia. She accepted the traditions handed down to her and added to them elements which she borrowed from Ionia. This probably accounts for the folds on the drapery of the Persian Bowmen. Like her neighbors, she was fond of polychromy and carried the use of colors into an even wider range, usually separating the various fields of the glazed tile by spinning threads of vitreous glaze about them, making a kind of cloison in each case. She adhered to the old motives native in the East and added little that may be called original, although the reliefs are often splendid.

We have not spoken of the Phœnicians or Cypriotes who played their part in the civilization of the East sometime after the fall of Crete in 1200 B.C. It is becoming more and more a question who these Phœnicians were and what kind of art belonged to them.[28a] They are usually credited with a mixed art embodying Egyptian and Mesopotamian motives. Like their neighbors, they probably cared for polychromy too and painted objects in gay colors. Their oldest tombs show no trace of decoration but we may probably assume from the later ones that they had it. From Græco-Roman times, a few tombs with painted decoration of a very simple character are found. Their statues were probably, like Cypriote statues, painted in color; that is, significant details were marked—red for lips, hair, and beard, and sometimes for the pupil of the eye; red or blue for borders of garments. Probably the same red, blue, black, and white of Mesopotamian painting were used by the Phœnicians, not only on their statues but on stelæ and sarcophagi. The sarcophagi discovered show an even greater range of color. They have been found in numbers, often unpainted and in anthropoid form, but sometimes showing extensive coloring. We have mentioned the fact that the hilly landscape with the scale convention is found on their "Phœnician" bowls.

The painting of Mesopotamia was, like that of Egypt, "flat painting." The enameled technique seems to have been preferred to stucco painting, particularly on the exterior, where it was especially used at gateways. But much has been lost and we cannot therefore judge finally of this point. Whether the painting that did exist made use of a wider range of color than the enamel technique, we cannot say. What we possess on the whole is far more meager than what has been found in Egypt and

---

[28a] G. Contenau, *La Civilisation phénicienne*, Paris, 1926; F. von Bissing, *Die Kunst der Phoiniker*, Leyden, 1925.

is less subtle in character and more stereotyped in its use of color. It adhered to a limited number of types of compositions—the processional and heraldic being prominent. The Orient gave to the world a "beast art" which has had a tremendously wide influence on later times; many of the motives which were introduced have been current material for later ages.[28b] The importance of the glazed technique in the Orient has also been very great. The painting of Mesopotamia reveals a true interest in landscape art. The mountainous type which was introduced takes its place in later Ionic art and may even be followed in designs of animals running up mounds, on Cæretan vases. On the whole the art of Mesopotamia was a decorative one in the service of architecture, enhancing greatly the surfaces which it adorned, but it was not created for itself and very rarely did it express sheer joy on the part of the artist. It is dignified, majestic, even pompous at times. These qualities arise in great measure from the hieratic gait employed, especially in the case of striding animals, such as lions and gryphons. The Assyrian had a preference for mass, for the heavy and cumbrous, as opposed to the more delicate and refined work often found in Egypt. Color was much needed in this country where all colors are dull and the landscape dusty. It is surprising, with this call for color, that blue was used so extensively on the Oriental palette, together with yellow and white, and red so seldom.

[28b] M. Rostovtzeff, *Iranians and Greeks in South Russia*, Oxford, 1922, pp. 191 ff.

# IV

# CRETE AND THE AEGEAN

THE island of Crete, the stepping-stone from Egypt to Greece, was, like the Nile Valley, the home of a very early civilization (Fig. 131). Perhaps the Libyans wandering over from northern Africa founded its earliest settlements. In any case, a flourishing culture existed there from the fourth to the second millennium—from Neolithic times down to the Iron Age, when the oncoming hordes of northerners must have dealt the final deathblow.

The civilization of Crete is a unique phenomenon, appearing almost unheralded and passing from the world's stage without leaving as strong an impress on the history and art of later ages as its vitality would seem to promise. Because of its outward splendor and the wonder of its legends, it excites our imagination; because of the independence and beauty of its artistic manifestations it arouses our æsthetic emotion. In its art, Crete was absolutely individual, influenced occasionally in choice of subject matter by Egypt but always transforming the material into an entirely new and original creation.

We are transported back in time to the reign of King "Minos," who ruled the sea as well as the island, in the days of his greatest power. His capital was at Knossos on the northern coast, and there he built his vast palace which is standing in part today—the labyrinth through which Ariadne threaded Theseus and the home of the fabled Minotaur (Fig. 132). The civilization at its height used bronze and understood well the art of building great palaces with elaborate systems of drainage, of fashioning beautiful objects from clay, bronze, and hard stones. It knew how to heighten the beauty of the palace walls with gay paintings in fresco and relief. Workers in gold and carvers of ivory, makers of faïence and gems had a part in its life. In short, the Cretans surrounded themselves with every luxury that could add to a life of pleasure and give enjoyment to the eye.

In addition to the kingdom at Knossos, there were also centers of power at Phæstos and Hagia Triada on the southern coast of the island, less imposing in their magnificence and perhaps ruled over in the beginning by princes subject to Knossos.

The whole civilization, however, is a homogeneous one, developed and carried to its greatest height by one people. But the dominating figure in this land of a hundred cities[1] was King Minos. Sir Arthur Evans shows that the name "Minos" may be a title like "Pharaoh," belonging to a race of "Priest-Kings" who had in their power the political and religious life of the island. With this name the various chronological periods are today associated by scholars—the Early Minoan, Middle, and Late Minoan Ages. If we equate these with the Egyptian Dynasties, the Early Minoan period extending from about 3400 to 2100 B.C., is contemporary in E.M. II with the Fourth, Fifth, and Sixth Egyptian Dynasties; Middle Minoan, from about 2100 to 1580 B.C., with the Eleventh, Twelfth, and Thirteenth Dynasties; Late Minoan, from 1580 to 1200 B.C., with the Eighteenth and Nineteenth Dynasties.[1a] These agreements are confirmed by Cretan objects found in Egypt and Egyptian monuments discovered in Crete. We shall take as typical of the work of the reign of "Minos" and as exemplifying the life of the Cretans, the great palace at Knossos which was the center of Ægean power. Although many readers are familiar with this building which has only been revealed to the world since 1901, we shall try to give an idea of it as it was during the Middle Minoan Era, some time after 2000 B.C.

One saw, on approaching the site, a structure covering possibly five acres. The building was topped by a flat roof and rose in several stories from terraced basement structures. The foundations were of gypsum, the walls of rubble and sun-dried brick, the outside was probably stuccoed with colored plaster. On coming nearer and passing into the palace by the ceremonial entrance on the north[2] (Fig. 133), it was evident to the visitor that the plastered walls were broken here and there by wooden beams which formed an integral part of the architectural decoration. The palace itself was arranged around a central, paved court. On the west lay the reception rooms, where King Minos, seated on his ancient throne (Fig. 134), exercised his royal and religious authority. There were, in addition, great magazines for stores; rooms where tablets were kept which recorded gifts and tribute and the possessions of the palace; rooms for religious ceremonies. There were long corridors lined with

---

[1] *Iliad* II, 649; cf. *Odyssey* 19, 172.

[1a] The chronology is that established by Sir Arthur Evans. We may roughly equate E.M. II (2500 B.C.) with the Sixth Dynasty; M.M. II (1800 B.C.) with the Twelfth Dynasty; L.M. II (*ca.* 1450 B.C.) with the Eighteenth Dynasty. E. Meyer, *Gesch. des Alt.* II, 1, 1928, p. 165, note 1, protests against the use of this system of chronology and prefers to treat M.M. III, L.M. I and II, as a unit. He makes three great periods—that of the Kamares culture, M.M. II; the period of the new palaces, M.M. III, L.M. I-II; the Mycenæan Age, L.M. III. *Cf. ib.*, I, 504A.

[2] This is taken by many to be a theater but it was extremely uncomfortable if used for such a purpose, as the seats are so shallow that one's knees touch one's chin. Sir Arthur Evans, *Palace of Minos*, London, 1921, I, 207, states that "it was mainly used, perhaps, for ceremonial receptions."

frescoes of rich colors, gardens, porticoes, and courts. If we continue our visit to the eastern side of the palace, we shall find ourselves in the more private part of the structure. Passing by the quadruple stairway with its marvelous ashlar masonry (Fig. 135), we come to the Queen's Megaron with walls brightly embellished with frescoes; we shall see the small palace shrine and visit the quarters where the sculptors worked and other rooms connected with the more intimate daily life of the court.

The Cretans were instinctively an artistic race—perhaps the first people known to us who created works of art for the sheer joy of expressing the beauty which they felt in their restless, active lives. With the sea-wind always in their nostrils, they knew a spur to action which the Egyptian, baked and beaten by the blinding sun, never could have felt. And so most of Cretan art shows a passion for movement and action—a passion as restless as the waves which washed their shores or the winds which continually fanned their valleys. And along with the love of rhythmic motion and action must have been born a love for vivid color. The Cretan constantly had the sea before him, was seldom out of sight of it—"wine-dark" as Homer says, green, or deep azure; he saw meadows filled with flowers of every hue; even the rocks beside the shore were striped and veined with many colors. Color, motion, and the pulse of the sea must always have played their part in the lives of the Cretans. They "lived hard"—lives of pleasure and intensity of performance. Their art is a reflection of the vigorous and healthy joy which they knew as a result of this environment and because of the seafaring blood which ran in their veins.

What was more natural, when Minos, the ruler of the sea, built his palace, than that he should wish it adorned with vivid scenes from the teeming life of the court? And what was more to be expected than that these scenes should be painted in contrasting colors, blue and red, yellow, black and white?

Probably from Neolithic days when the Cretans lived in huts made of clay and reeds, they had plastered their houses for the sake of protection. At any rate, some of the earliest buildings of rubble and sun-dried bricks, such as those of Early Minoan I and II from Vasiliki, show a tendency to employ lime stucco as a facing. The thickness was about five centimeters, the upper coat being about one and one-half centimeters. It was backed by coarser material such as pebbles, pottery, and straw. The Cretan decorator seems to have constructed the walls that were to be ornamented with great care. He made a putty of lime, which had been prepared from burnt limestone slaked in water. In the earlier plaster, about forty per cent of the material is lime, the rest clay; later on, it became practically a pure lime stucco, ninety-four per cent of the composition being lime. This plaster of lime was usually put on in two layers and in the best examples the upper layer was often fine and white. When the stucco was placed on gypsum, it was usually thinner, from one-sixteenth to one-half inch in thickness, amounting in some cases to a stucco wash.

While the layers were still wet (and it must be borne in mind that the plaster was probably put on in sections in order that the surface might be kept moist while the painter was at work), the decorator drew his patterns—often with aids of various kinds. In the earliest period, the decoration would consist merely of a red wash of color. This has been found both on pavements and walls of the Early Minoan Age. Later on, we find the use of horizontal lines and stripes of red and white, marked out in the wet plaster with a taut string. By the close of Middle Minoan I, there are ornamental designs apparently stenciled on the plaster, in red, black, and white (Fig. 136). Next in order, probably, arose the friezes of conventional rosettes, spirals, and bands of flowers. Figure 137 shows a spiraliform design from Middle Minoan III with a color scheme of deep blue, black, and white. In Figure 138, the body color of the wall was red, the interlaced spirals blue, the ground white. To this was added black for outlines and spurs. Sometimes, rosettes were drawn with the help of a disc; more often, they were put in by free-hand. On occasion, incision with a compass was resorted to.

When, in the Middle Minoan period, the painter finally attained to the dignity of figure composition, he made a preliminary sketch. The outlines and the most important inner lines were sketched in in a dark red, though the painters of Hagia Triada and those later at Tiryns, employed yellow as well. These sketches were usually completely covered by the final work which was executed in haste, the colors, mixed with water, being put on the moist plaster. The action of the lime bound them to this without the aid of any binding medium. Incision was occasionally used for the contours, as we shall see in the Fresco of the Procession. At a late date, heavy black contour lines are commonly found. After the application of color and before the plaster was dry, the surface was smoothed with a knife-like instrument, in order to produce a brilliant finish. In the case of the earliest washes of red, it was later burnished by hand.

Among the various pigments employed was white from carbonate of lime. Often this was merely left in the color of the ground, but, at times, it was painted over a second color, or it helped to modify various shades. Black was obtained from shale, slate, or impure carbon containing mineral material. It was very destructible; with other pigments it made brown and gray. Yellow and red were earth colors, deep red containing about ninety per cent oxide of iron. The fusing of sand with copper and soda gave an "Egyptian blue" and the green with a bluish tinge was an Egyptian green. The green used for foliage was prepared by mixing yellow and blue.

The earliest figure painting in Knossos probably dates from Middle Minoan II, and was found in the northern part of the palace.[3] It is an archaic fresco of a boy

[3] I have followed Sir Arthur Evans, *Palace of Minos*, London, 1921, I, 266, in his dating. G. Rodenwaldt, *Der Fries des Megarons von Mykenai*, Halle, 1921, p. 9, places it in Late Minoan I because of the naturalistic treatment of plant life.

gathering saffron in a meadow filled with crocuses (Fig. 139). In spite of the lavish spreading of yellow and white against the red ground-color, and the extraordinary anatomy of the boy with his flesh painted in blue, the fresco has its charm. It is full of life and action. The artist has caught sight of a Cretan bending over a vase and filling it with blossoms, and he has put down in a few essential lines the characteristic features of the scene. There is a certain sketchiness about the work which is found in much of Cretan art. A momentary impression has fastened itself in the mind of the painter. This he has fixed in wet plaster—an operation apparently involving as much agility of hand as the design seems to have embodied quickness of mind. The painting of the Cretans almost always presents swift, intuitive impressions. The drawing is by no means correct; traces of the primitive triangle remain in the rendering of the torso, though the waists of the Cretans seem to have been narrow, whether because they laced or because it was a racial characteristic, we cannot say. Probably in Crete the narrow waist became a mark of elegance in drawing, and was often pushed to exaggeration. The artist has worked with a certain dash and assurance and the result gives one a feeling of freshness and spontaneity of execution. The unevenness of Cretan painting arises from an irresistible impulse on the part of the artist to express with his brush the many sensations which brought him pleasure. Untrammeled by tradition, he was set free in the world of nature to record his impressions and this he did with unbounded enthusiasm. But his knowledge and ability often failed him and he was unable to present adequately the material which his brain supplied him. Strange and bizarre effects, such as this "Blue Boy," therefore sometimes resulted—simply because we have art in an embryonic and experimental stage. The composition in the fresco of the saffrongatherer is not unpleasing. The formalism in rendering the rocky ground by a series of irregular scalloped hillocks—outlined in white, with veins of red or black, and looking more like burrs than landscape—is not so appealing. Obviously, the main thing which has interested the artist is the use of vivid and contrasting color. This may account for the blue flesh of the nude boy—if it is a boy, for male figures were usually shown in red—with his red armlets, bracelets, girdle, and pectoral band. Another thing is a certain impressionism of form.

The Cretan artist was at his best when he turned to nature for his inspiration, as he so often did. His most charming paintings are those which depict plant and animal life and the life of the sea—marine designs of octopods, flying fish, and dolphins. With these he was at home, his eye had observed these things with untiring pleasure and his memory retained an image of them which his mind and hand transformed into something lovelier far than anything seen in life. Some of the best examples of Middle Minoan paintings of the naturalistic group have been found in the palace at Hagia Triada on the southern coast of Crete. One fresco in particular shows a brown cat hiding behind some rocks overgrown with ivy, and preparing to spring upon a red pheasant (Fig. 140). The landscape breathes the out-of-doors. The crouching cat, ready to capture its prey, significantly expresses feline stealth. At the left, a startled roe leaps up and dashes away at full speed. But the painter has expended most of his care on the growing and blossoming plants and they are rendered with a charm which betrays an innate love for nature. Most of the flowers are painted in henna, sepia brown, and yellow against a neutral buff ground, but these tones have undoubtedly been changed by burning. We may therefore think of the colors as true to nature.[4] The leaves were certainly green, the blossoms gay and bright. We are not concerned to ascertain the various species of flowers depicted, and when we examine them, we find that the blossoms and foliage do not always belong together. But the artist understands how to picture plant life—if not with absolute botanical fidelity, at least with artistic charm. Even where the subject has probably been borrowed from Egypt, as in the case of the cat stalking a pheasant, there is no similarity of treatment. The Cretan flowers grow naturally and in profusion and there are no formal clumps of bushes repeated again and again. The Cretan knew a certain freedom in his art which was foreign to the Egyptian even at the time of Akhenaten, when Cretan artists may well have worked in Egypt. Yet another fragment from Hagia Triada portrays blossoming shrubs with ivy and henna-colored flowers (Fig. 141). Probably all of the Hagia Triada frescoes belong in Middle Minoan III.

Comparable to these in charm is the lily fresco from Knossos, in which white lilies with orange anthers and green foliage are seen against a red ground (Fig. 142). Blown white petals are found at the bottom of the picture in the colored restoration of Sir Arthur Evans. A cat and pheasant fresco has also been discovered at Knossos. But the most beautiful painting of this period is probably the Flying Fish Fresco found on the island of Melos at Phylakopi, and doubtless the work of a Cretan painter of the Middle Minoan III period (Pl. V). It formed a very small frieze twenty-three centimeters long and at least eighty centimeters wide. Just what part it played on the wall it is difficult to see—whether it was an isolated panel or whether it originally took in the breadth of the wall. As a composition it leaves nothing to be desired. The sweepingly curved bodies of the flying fishes, with wings outspread for flight or closed for a "nose dive," are satisfyingly spaced against a neutral creamy ground. Brown rocks and sponges dotted with black, and bubbles and spray of blue, help to complete the color scheme. The color is again arbitrarily used; the backs of the fishes are blue, their bellies yellow or white, and the wings are usually blue with some white or yellow added. The painter's brush, in rendering

[4] G. Rodenwaldt, *Tiryns*, II, Athen, 1912, p. 193.

Plate V. Athens. National Museum. Flying fish from Phylakopi, Melos.

the lines, glides along with the smoothness and facility of the skimming fishes. The Cretans were fond of this motive and have repeated it in their faïence (Fig. 143).

Closely akin to the Flying Fish Fresco in subject matter and in spirit is the Dolphin Fresco from the Queen's Megaron at Knossos. It decorated a light-well and was meant to give the impression of a stretch of sea. Only, in this case, it is much more like looking into an aquarium—which the Cretans may well have possessed[5] (Fig. 144). The coloring is very lively. Below, runs a dado of Venetian red and above this was evidently a series of rocks, sponges, and coral growths, to denote the floor of the sea. The coloring here was a sooty brown. The artist's real flair for contrasts, however, is revealed in the painting of the dolphins, which are a rich blue with pale orange stripes along their sides and creamy white bellies. They are shown against a neutral ground of creamy white. Some of the smaller fishes are a delightful pink, or yellow with rose markings. The composition is not so satisfying nor the drawing so vivacious and facile as in the case of the flying fish, but we have only a fragment of the painting. The artist again shows a decided fondness for and acquaintance with the finny tribe which he has chosen to represent. Frescoes such as these had a pronounced influence on the decoration employed in the minor arts. Examples of this trend are seen in the faïence objects noted above and in the dolphin vases from Pachyammos[6] with their pebbled shores, tossing sea, and white spray (Fig. 145). The naturalistic tendency has its full fruition in this period. There are no more charming creations in Cretan art than the lily vases and frescoes[7] (cf. Fig. 146). The artist begins with nature and uses only the very slight element of conventionalization which his design demands. The lily vases show how well the tall stalks of the growing plants were adapted to the upward expansion of the vase. Similar patterns were adopted on some of the inlaid daggers from Mycenæ (Fig. 147). The decoration on the votive robes of faïence—which were doubtless symbolic of robes presented to the goddess at intervals, as the peplos later in the case of Athena—proves again how delightfully this conventional element could be employed (Fig. 148). Here, crocuses are used in a clump and for a border, and the painter has had an opportunity to show his artistic power, especially in the border. The flowers are not stiffly erect as an Egyptian might have drawn them, but bend as if blown by the wind.

At the end of Middle Minoan III, the beautiful, naturalistic style, cultivated by

[5] Sir Arthur Evans, B.S.A., VI, 39; G. Rodenwaldt, Der Fries des Megarons von Mykenai, Halle, 1921, p. 12; M. Heinemann, Landschaftliche Elemente in der griech. Kunst, Bonn, 1910, p. 10.

[6] R. B. Seager, The Cemetery of Pachyammos, Crete (Anthropological Publications of the University of Pennsylvania, Vol. VII, 1), Philadelphia, 1916, Pl. XIV.

[7] Sir Arthur Evans, Palace of Minos, London, 1921, I, 604, Fig. 444 (Hagia Triada); 576, Fig. 420; 577, Fig. 421; 603, Fig. 443.

painters such as the Master of the Hagia Triada frescoes, begins to go out of favor—almost as mysteriously as it came. Writers are at a loss to explain its origin; its end is conventionalization. Some scholars feel that it was being prepared for in Middle Minoan II and point out the patterns on pottery which reflected the designs now lost that once adorned the earlier palace walls.[8] Rodenwaldt refers to it as the bursting forth of a naturalistic gift long latent. At the end of Middle Minoan II, the Knossian palace was destroyed and most of the frescoes of Knossos, Phæstos, and Hagia Triada date after this time, between Middle Minoan III and Late Minoan II—a relatively short epoch of grandeur. The rebuilding of the palace may have brought forth new genius in art, but it is evident that the naturalistic tendency was sporadic before it burst forth into its consummate glory.

Painted stucco relief also had its origin in the Middle Minoan III period, as the "Jewel Relief" proves (Fig. 149). This relief presents the hand of a man (dark red with white nails), toying with a necklace of gold beads. The necklace is attached to some blue material and, at the left, a black strand of hair partly conceals one of the negroid heads, employed as pendants. The rather fragmentary scene is interpreted as a wedding ceremony, a kind of ἱερὸς γάμος.[9] Perhaps the figures of women from the island of Pseira are also to be placed here.[9a] The use of stucco relief may have arisen to satisfy the desire for plasticity. The Cretan artist with his love for things true to nature, at least in semblance, must have sought to escape at times from the flatness of painting by means of relief. Stucco relief is, however, merely a sister art of Cretan painting and the artist seems never to have been lured from this to attempt work in the round on a monumental scale. His genius was, after all, more pictorial than plastic, as Rodenwaldt has shown.[10]

In this period we also find the forerunners of the class of frescoes termed "miniature." They are executed in a kind of shorthand and show crowds of spectators whose heads are outlined in black against waved zones of yellow and blue. A fragment of a bull's head found with some of them indicates that the people were attending games in the circus. Here belong too the earliest examples of architectural frescoes which picture the palace shrines or altars (Fig. 150). They are less good in execution than the later "Pillar Shrine" fresco, which is a direct descendant of

[8] Sir Arthur Evans, *Palace of Minos*, London, 1921, I, 253-256; 263-264. *Cf.* pp. 180-181; p. 42; G. Rodenwaldt, *Der Fries des Megarons von Mykenai*, Halle, 1921, p. 16; E. Reisinger, *Kretische Vasenmalerei*, Leipzig, 1911, p. 17. E. Meyer, *Gesch. des Alt.* I, 2,[2] p. 717, thinks the influence came from Melos. *Cf. ib.*, II, 1, 1928, pp. 162-302.

[9] Sir Arthur Evans, *Palace of Minos*, London, 1921, I, 526. This relief was "pulverized" in the earthquake of 1926.

[9a] R. Dussaud, *Les Civilisations préhelléniques*,[2] Paris, 1914, Pl. V; G. Rodenwaldt, *Arch. Anz.*, 38-39 (1923-1924), pp. 268-276, Figs. 1, 2 (Reconstruction). See K. Müller, "Frühmykenische Reliefs," *Jahr.*, 30 (1915), pp. 269 ff.

[10] G. Rodenwaldt, *Der Fries des Megarons von Mykenai*, Halle, 1921, pp. 14 ff.

the type, but show the same architectural façades, this time, against a greenish blue ground. The wooden columns are reddish brown with white double axes attached, and white "horns of consecration" occur between the columns (*cf*. Fig. 151). Below, runs a frieze of rosettes of green, black, red, and white, with bands of green and yellow and lines of black forming a kind of tooth pattern. Artistically, the "architectural" frescoes interest us little although they are of great importance for their bearing on the architectural history of the period. The "shorthand" method found in the other class of frescoes described is even less artistic but is interesting as a primitive device. It produces a very bizarre effect. We shall return to these classes of frescoes later.

The Late Minoan period is the age when fresco painting and work in *gesso duro* were at their height in Crete. The recent discoveries by Evans of an entire house of frescoes from the end of Middle Minoan III*b* may greatly increase our knowledge of the paintings of this period. The fragments found belong to a limited number of small rooms so that it has been possible to put together the principal elements of three or four whole scenes beside a number of detailed features. The pieces of painted stucco are very fragile being only about one centimeter in thickness. The designs executed on them show the strong naturalistic trend found earlier in the frescoes of Hagia Triada. The scenes are placed among rocks with flowering plants or marine growths. The rocks are striped and veined to imitate stones such as agate or sardonyx. Many kinds of flowers are represented, the colors of which are excellently preserved. They include clumps of crocuses, rose and blue in color, on orange and white wavy zones. These are executed in stencil and the details have been touched up later. Madonna lilies, iris, ivy, peas, olive, and flowering sedges occur, together with plants bearing red and yellow plums. In one instance a blue bird is rising from some rocks overgrown with peas and spiky plants. On the other side is a rose bush in full bloom. A fountain with falling spray occurs in one section. Monkeys of a type not found nearer than the Sudan are seen on one fragment among rocks and plants flowering in papyrus-like tufts. The main colors here are blue, yellow, red, and green. The subject matter suggests interesting African connections as does a second and somewhat later fresco which depicts a Cretan chieftain leading his men on the run. The soldiers are blacks, from which Evans concludes that Minos employed negro mercenaries. This fresco is a small frieze placed on a ground alternately blue and white. The marine scenes show seaweed, sponges, and coral growth, fine golden sand, argonauts, and some kind of a medusa. Inscriptions belonging to linear class A, with letters some five inches in height, were discovered from one wall. Some were painted in orange against a buff ground; others were black on a rose field. The publication of these frescoes will be awaited with great interest.[11]

[11] Sir Arthur Evans, *The Times*, London (August 28, 29, 1923). These frescoes have now been published by Sir Arthur Evans, *Palace of Minos*, II, 2, pp. 431 ff., Pls. X, XI (color);

The "House of Frescoes" belonged to a petty burgher and gives us some conception of the extensive use of fresco decoration and of Cretan love for landscape. It is supplemented by another important group of paintings found recently in a pavilion belonging to the "Caravanserai" or Rest House for travelers, south of the Palace. The upper part of the wall here was decorated by a frieze of partridges in a landscape of brightly colored rocks, striped and veined in blue, yellow, rose, and white. The russet birds are placed against changing backgrounds which are sometimes black, sometimes gray-blue, or white. Sir Arthur Evans thinks that the room which they decorated was a refectory. As the partridge was a particular food delicacy, the subject matter was very suitable. The paintings call to mind the fowls and still-life of Dutch dining-rooms.[11a] They belong at the end of Middle Minoan III.[11]

It is very likely that the majority of reliefs and paintings from Late Minoan I were mainly concerned with religious themes. Processions are found which are probably ritualistic in character. The bull-grappling scenes represented were doubtless religious in origin, whatever their import in the later days of the kingdom. Even the charming young girl with the "ox-eyes" and ruby lips, wears a "sacral knot" on the back of her dress. "Pillar shrines" appear in the paintings, and groves that probably formed a part of the *temenos* of the goddess. The gryphon so often pictured is a sacred animal and the "Chieftain" Relief may represent one of the great "Priest-Kings" of Knossos. Probably religious inspiration played a greater part in the origin of the Cretan frescoes than is usually conceded.

The layman is primarily attracted by two things in these paintings: the vivid, clear colors employed and the types of individuals represented. From these interests he will probably turn to a study of the compositions, the boldness and precociousness of the artist, the impressionism of form and the vital animation of the scenes. We shall consider first of all a group of frescoes of the Late Minoan I period which are taken from one of the processions. We may assume from the prominence given to such scenes that Crete passed on to Greece some of her love for sacred processions.

Just off the Western Court at its southern entrance, there opens a narrow passage termed the "Corridor of the Procession" (*cf.* Fig. 132, No. 13). On the left wall were remains of a fresco which originally exhibited a procession of distinguished men and women—four male figures in long, embroidered robes preceded by a woman in a flounced garment and, after a break, by a second woman in a robe covered with rich embroidery.[12] Evans suggests that the second woman may have been a queen

Figs. 264, 266; II, 2, pp. 755 ff., Pl. XIII (color). For the Partridge Fresco, see II, 1, pp. 109 ff., Figs. 51-54, Frontispiece (color). Evans dates these frescoes in M.M. III*b*.

[11a] Sir Arthur Evans, *op. cit.*, II, 1, p. 114.

[12] Sir Arthur Evans, *B.S.A.*, VI (1899-1900), pp. 13 ff. *Cf. Palace of Minos*, II, 2, pp. 719

and that the three male figures who face her were attendants. Only the lower parts of the figures are preserved—the feet of the men done in red, those of the women in white. We can gain a clearer idea of the character of this fresco from a restoration of another part of it by Gilliéron (Fig. 152). Before a background of yellow with a wavy band of blue in the center, two youths advance in stately fashion, bearing vases in their hands. They wear gaily decorated loin cloths—yellow with blue bands, or *vice versa*. From this garment, a net-like object hangs down in front. Around their waists are tight gold and silver belts with patterns of running spirals and rosettes. The flesh of these figures is a dark red and the outlines are incised. They are probably engaged in some sacrificial task and bear in their hands marble vases with silver bases. All the upper parts of the figures are lost but we have another fresco similar in character which is a fairly safe guide for the restorer. The "Cup-bearer," the most famous figure of this class, furnishes us with a real Cretan portrait (Fig. 153). It is almost classic in type. From his bearing we might well conclude that this youth belonged to the kingly caste of Knossos, but he may be only one of the priestly attendants who had learned to carry out his service with a certain pride and decorum. In any case, he seems to be taking part in some religious rite held in the palace. At least, this explanation seems more plausible than the theory that these figures represent tributaries from across the sea, or from another part of the island bearing offerings to the thalassocrats of Crete.[13]

The remains of this fresco were found in the "Corridor of the Cup-bearer," a passageway further east than the "Corridor of the Procession" and almost in line with the "Corridor of the Magazines" (Fig. 132, No. 13a). The background, like that of the "Corridor of the Procession," is in wave-like zones of yellow and blue. Against this wealth of contrasting color stands the erect and dignified figure of the Cup-bearer, holding a silver "filler" vase in his hands. The reddish brown of the flesh adds its emphasis to the color scheme and above his head is an inexplicable wave-like pattern of stripes of blue, black, red, and yellow—inexplicable unless we consider that the Minoan painter was bold enough to try to represent the sky or clouds as a background. The artist was not concerned so much with details as with the total impression which he wished to convey—the pride and quiet dignity of a distinguished race engaged in a ceremonial of lofty import. We are not, therefore, troubled because the chest is rendered after the "Egyptian" fashion, or because the right arm

ff. and restorations by Gilliéron in Fig. 450. Three groups are restored. In the first are two long-robed youths bearing the sistrum and one playing the pipes preceded by a woman with a male companion. The center of group B is occupied by a goddess with the double axe. She is approached from either side by pairs of youths. Group C is reproduced in our Fig. 152. Sir Arthur Evans believes that there were two rows of figures, one above the other. He thinks that more than 500 figures were represented.

[13] G. Rodenwaldt, *Der Fries des Megarons von Mykenai*, Halle, 1921, pp. 17 ff.

emerges very awkwardly from the breast, that proportions seem not always correct, or that the eye is in front view in the profile face. The fresco is of life size and is interesting not only from the artistic standpoint but because it tells us how the Cretans looked and dressed. The Cup-bearer has dark, wavy hair, dark eyes, a sun-burned skin, and an alert, wiry figure. His loin cloth is richly embroidered in red and blue patterns on a reddish ground; his belt is of silver and gold. He wears an agate, lentoid seal on his wrist, silver armlets and anklets, a necklace, and earrings. These frescoes formed an integral part of the architectural decoration, acting as a frieze above a narrow dado.

Another splendid representative of the old Mediterranean stock is recognizable in the portrait of a young girl with glossy black hair, large eyes, and lips of bright red (Fig. 154). She wears a blue and white dress with black and red stripes, and at her back a large knot plainly shows that she is a votary of the Cretan goddess. The portrait head seems to bear signs of the exaggeration which belongs to primitive art, especially in the large eye, and prominent nose, but it may be only a part of the sketchiness of the Minoan painter's work. The lips are a daub of color, the ear is only summarily indicated by a reserved space, and the curls are rendered with great carelessness. But the young lady is very much alive and we can believe that she would be a vivacious companion. The head is a fragment from a group of votaries—men and women seated on camp stools—some holding goblets made of precious metals. The figures were set on blue and yellow fields and were bordered above by bands of black, red, and white. They were arranged in two small friezes, one above the other. The painting is later than the Cup-bearer or the youths of the Procession Fresco and is to be dated probably in L.M. II.[13a]

From the "Queen's Apartments" at Knossos comes yet a third portrait, no more flattering than the last (Fig. 155). The figure is often called "Ariadne" and it is quite likely that she is a dancer, because of the movement of the arms and the treat-ment of the hair. We see at once that the artist's means are primitive and that he suggests energetic action largely by the aid of the strands of hair which fly out stiffly in opposite directions. The figure wears a jacket of yellow with a border of red and blue, and a transparent garment beneath. The work has been hastily exe-cuted as was the case with the preceding fresco and the conventions employed in rendering the hair are very far from pleasing. These frescoes show how uneven the work of the Cretan painter could be, but they also prove that the paintings were always done with spirit, no matter how primitive the means or how careless the tech-nique. We do not know whether the dance, if that is the subject represented, is reli-gious in character or executed for the joy of the rhythm. In some frescoes of "Minia-

---

[13a] B.S.A., VII (1900-1901), Fig. 17, p. 57; for "Ariadne," see B.S.A., VIII (1901-1902), Fig. 28, pp. 55, 58.

ture" type from Knossos, we see women in a similar attitude. They appear on the border of a sacred *temenos*, dressed in flounced garments of gay colors, performing some rhythmic action which is perhaps to be interpreted as a dance in honor of the Great Goddess (Fig. 156). The spatial composition is interestingly handled with the figures placed in rows above one another without ground lines and without reduction in size for those higher up. We shall return to this method of spatial arrangement later. The ground for these figures is blue. The most interesting part of this fresco, however, is the bizarre technique employed in the upper portion. Beneath and around pale blue, olive-like trees, are seated groups of women, indicated merely in black outline against a light ground. In some cases, the entire figure is given but in many instances only the heads are represented. Near by, against a ground of red, heads of men are shown in the same way. This "shorthand" process is undoubtedly a primitive method; we saw the cave man employing something similar in the case of a herd of reindeer. The Cretan artist, however, has added the device of color to the scheme, to indicate sex. The total effect, though not artistic, does give a vivid impression of crowds of spectators gathered together. The scene also shows that the Cretan artist was on the way toward solving the problem of the third dimension.

• Other examples of "miniature" work are found in the restored fresco of the "Pillar Shrine" (Fig. 158). Such shrines, or altars, must have been common in the palace. We see how tiny their proportions were when we observe the size of the women seated in the balcony. Undoubtedly the structures were of wood, with panels of bright-colored plaster set between beams. Round beam-ends painted red, white, and blue also contributed to the gaiety of the architectural decoration. The spectator must have been impressed on approaching the altar by the flashes of red, yellow, and blue; by the black and white checkerboard patterns at the top and the white "horns of consecration."

In the gay orgy of color found in this fresco, Figure 158, red is the predominating shade. The entire upper field of the painting is a Venetian red and against this innumerable heads of men are sketched in black outline. Immediately below this follows a zone of yellow on which crowds of women are represented in a kind of loggia, some standing, others seated, but all engaged in animated conversation. They usually wear dresses of blue with stripes of black, white, and yellow, but sometimes the garments are red. The center of the design is occupied by the representation of a small shrine topped by "horns of consecration" (Fig. 157). This building is partly supported on either side by a black column seen against a ground of red. The central part of the structure, which is higher, has two red columns which stand out distinctly against a field of blue, perhaps intended to denote the sky. The fresco as a whole, Figure 158, is divided into three parts by yellow piers and red columns. Below the "Pillar Shrine" occurs another zone of male spectators represented in "shorthand" fashion against a ground of red, with an irregular pointed section in white which was reserved "for ladies only."

The scenes are animated and give very cleverly the impression of dense crowds gathered together for a festival, but the work is, on the whole, inartistic and the fresco interests us largely for the light which it sheds on Minoan customs and architecture. As a cross section from Minoan life, it is a very important document for us. Perhaps the women standing on the high piers are priestesses engaged in some ritual in honor of the goddess. It may even be a bullfight that is being observed because fragments of frescoes of pillar shrines have been found in conjunction with parts of a bull fresco.

The "Toreador" or "Cowboy" Fresco doubtless also had its religious significance —for, although it may merely represent one of the sports in which the Cretans delighted at this period, its origin was in all probability a rite in honor of the bull god. Perhaps captives were dedicated to the sport, or tribute exacted from other countries, as the legend of Theseus and the Minotaur seems to indicate. But there may also have been trained toreadors who engaged in the sport for its excitement. This scene would then become merely a film from a Minoan circus.

The "Toreador" Fresco is one of the boldest compositions in Minoan art (Fig. 159). It deserves to rank with the scenes on the Vaphio cups or the little bronze recently published by Sir Arthur Evans[14] for its clever representation of swift and violent action. The ground of the painting is a clear blue. Across the center of this field a brown and white dappled bull charges, with legs outspread in the "flying gallop" fashion. On his back a male acrobat has just landed with his feet high in the air and his black locks flying out stiffly in different directions. He is nude except for a yellow loin cloth and his flesh is painted a deep red. He is preparing to bound from the bull's back and be caught by a young girl at the right who stands with arms outstretched to receive him. She is naked except for a yellow loin cloth and her black hair hangs in wavy strands down her back. A second toreador like her is seen at the left, resting on the bull's horns and about to make a leap similar to the one which the male acrobat is just completing. It is interesting to see that women played such a prominent part in these games.

The composition is beautifully balanced and the drawing extremely bold. We see that the women toreadors are own cousins to "Ariadne," executed in the same summary fashion. But the excitement of the bull ring is vividly conveyed and the artist is no less daring than are the intrepid performers whom he chose to depict in their rash feats. The fresco is framed by a colored border intended to represent variegated stones. The colors especially used are blue, yellow, and red with contrasting dots, circles, and wavy lines. Rodenwaldt considers this fresco a copy of an earlier and better one.

[14] Sir Arthur Evans, *J.H.S.*, 41 (1921), pp. 247 ff.

In Sir Arthur Evans' opinion, the bull frescoes grew out of the stucco reliefs of agonistic scenes which go back to Middle Minoan III; the reverse seems to me more probable. One of the finest Late Minoan reliefs of this class is a bull's head in reddish brown against a ground half red and half blue (Fig. 160). The only other colors added are the yellowish gray of the horns, the red of the iris, and a bluish white spot on the nose. The relief is a masterpiece of modeling and shows the genius of the Minoans for this kind of work. The sculptor has observed these animals closely and gives a very naturalistic representation of them. The bull probably formed part of a large landscape depicting sports in the Minoan circus.[15]

, The *chef d'œuvre* in Cretan relief is the portrait of a "Chieftain" (Fig. 161). Against a ground of red and yellow, a male figure wearing a crown adorned with lilies and peacock plumes strides majestically to the left through a field of lilies. He has a slender, sinewy form and a very narrow waist. He is clad only in a loin cloth and wears a necklace of red lilies and a broad bracelet. The background is divided in wave-like fashion into two zones of color. Against the lower yellow portion are charmingly conventionalized red lilies with blue stems and leaves. The color scheme, which is almost wholly red, blue, and yellow, is repeated again in the feather head-dress. Touches of white and black are also found. In the red upper field a conventionalized blue and white butterfly is also seen. We doubtless have before us, in this fresco, one of the great "Priest-Kings" of Knossos. He moves like a king and one feels in him a certain irresistible power. The lily, which was sacred to the Cretan goddess, may also mark him out as her minister. No more significant figure has come to light in Ægean excavation and no modeling has been found superior to this (Fig. 162). Not only are the muscular details subtly executed but even the veins are indicated. Some parts of the painting are given only in color; for example, the chain of lilies, the loin cloth, and the background of lilies and butterflies. The relief is therefore a thing midway between painting and relief, but, on the whole, it is much nearer to monumental painting.[16]

Religious also in character are the frescoes of gryphons, found in the Throne Room (*cf.* Fig. 134). Sir Arthur Evans is probably correct in considering that the Throne Room was used for religious functions and that the tank was a "lustral basin" for ritualistic purposes.[17] In other words, it was employed for rites of initiation and purification and the "Priest-King" sat on the throne as a representative on earth of the Great Goddess. The frescoes belong to the latest period of the palace, at the earliest to some time in Late Minoan II. This is shown by the large element of

---

[15] *Cf.* K. Müller, *Jahr.*, 30 (1915), p. 271, relief landscape; *B.S.A.*, VI, 52, Fig. 10.

[16] K. Müller, *Jahr.*, 30 (1915), pp. 271 ff.; see Sir Arthur Evans, *Palace of Minos*, II, 2, frontispiece (color), pp. 774 ff.; *cf.* I, p. 531.

[17] Sir Arthur Evans, *Palace of Minos*, London, 1921, I, 5; *cf. B.S.A.*, VI (1899-1900), p. 39.

conventionalization which enters into the flowers in the background and by the gryphon which is a later type without wings and with peacock's plumes issuing from the head. The earlier type usually shows the hawk or eagle head. The body of the animal is leonine in character and bears a red, white, and blue spiral on the shoulder with a rosette center. The background is again divided into vivid waves of red and yellow color which set off picturesquely the couchant gryphons facing the throne on either side in a conventional landscape. Similar frescoes occurred on both sides of the doorway leading from the Throne Room into the inner shrine. The gryphon would thus seem to be a guardian animal sacred to the goddess. Examples from the early Late Minoan I period were discovered above the northwest portico at Knossos. Sir Arthur Evans publishes a winged gryphon with notched plumes, coming from a miniature fresco found in this quarter.[18]

We can see clearly from this painting the tendencies in the later fresco painting of Late Minoan I and II. Formalism is becoming more pronounced and the charming naturalistic plants of Middle Minoan III are disappearing. The artist loves heraldic designs which involve a nicety of balance; he is more diverted by details such as the drawing of spirals and curls on the gryphon's mane. A certain element of strength gives way to a fondness for prettiness or exotic decoration. Frescoes of this character, however, with their gay colors and unusual patterns, must have greatly enlivened the walls of the palace. It is not surprising that the Greeks were struck at seeing the "Toreador" frescoes and reliefs—as they must have done on their arrival —and out of this and earlier practices in the palace they may have built up their myths of the Minotaur and the deeds of King "Minos." Probably they saw the portrait of one of these kings as pictured in the "Chieftain" Fresco. Sir Arthur Evans believes that he was represented leading a sacred gryphon in his train.

Just how the Cretan frescoes were placed on the walls, we are able to judge from the Gryphon Fresco in the Throne Room, from remains in the "Corridor of the Procession," from frescoes found at Hagia Triada and Thebes, and especially from those at Mycenæ. Usually the main design was a frieze of figures of approximately life size. This was broken here and there by doors and windows but continued around the corners. It was bordered above and sometimes below by parallel bands of color, and ornamental patterns, which were often rosettes. In fact, the ornamental friezes formed a kind of frame for the main design. The structure of the painted wall was not altered essentially from Cretan times until the end of the classic period. Its main divisions were: socle, frieze, ornamental bands. The system of painting remained practically the same,[19] but the Cretan-Mycenæan artists emphasized more strongly

---

[18] Sir Arthur Evans, *op. cit.*, I, 549, Fig. 400. *Cf.* pp. 709 ff.

[19] G. Rodenwaldt, *Tiryns*, Athen, 1912, II, 217 ff.; R. Pagenstecher, *Nekropolis*, Leipzig, 1919, pp. 171 ff.; G. Rodenwaldt, *Der Fries des Megarons von Mykenai*, Halle, 1921, p. 23.

the architectonic divisions of the wall. There was usually in Cretan and Mycenæan buildings a socle or series of high orthostates at the bottom of the wall, of gypsum or some other material, eighty centimeters or so in height. Above this was a horizontal wooden beam, probably about thirty centimeters in height. The Mycenæan artists have taken great pains to paint all this in their frescoes, not only the plinths, but the beam, on which, at Tiryns, a procession of women moves as on a stage. Above this wooden beam, the figure frieze was placed. The total height of the various divisions when closed by a second ornamental band at the top, was probably somewhere between 1.63 and two meters, allowing forty or fifty centimeters or more for the figure frieze. Above this, there was doubtless another wooden beam, running horizontally and sometimes acting as a kind of cornice. There are examples of panels surrounded by ornamental designs, arranged in two frieze-like rows, one above another, and at Mycenæ a narrow frieze is found, but the general practice was probably not unlike what we have described above, taking the frieze from the megaron at Mycenæ as typical.[20] The Partridge Fresco from the Pavilion of the Caravanserai formed a small frieze at the top of the wall.

Before turning to the contemporary art of mainland Greece, mention should be made of the sarcophagus found at Hagia Triada, a painted monument of limestone. It bears some decoration, belonging to Late Minoan II or III. It is primarily important for the interest which it arouses in Minoan funeral rites but it is a gaily decorated object which also concerns the student of painting. One remembers vividly the red, blue, and yellow employed against a creamy ground. It has been pointed out that the striped bands of color at the bottom of the panels seem much like a fringe and that the effect of the whole is rather that of a tapestry covering the bier of the dead. And so it is. The main patterns are framed along the sides by red, white, and blue spirals, and above and below by bands of rosettes of the same colors with yellow and blue vertical stripes. The background of the figure composition is in zones of color, as so often in Crete—blue and creamy white. On one of the long sides at the right, a stiffly erect figure—probably the form of the heroized dead—stands before his tomb (Fig. 163). Three male figures approach him with offerings —a ship and sacrificial bulls. The animals are rendered in the "flying gallop" pose, so familiar in Cretan art and so inappropriate here. Near the center, the composition divides and the remaining figures face sharply in the opposite direction. Here, a priestess is pouring a libation into a great krater placed between two green, cone-shaped trees. This rite is probably intended to conciliate the favor of the Earth Goddess, as the double axes and the birds which surmount them are connected with her cult. But the two parts are closely related and we are perhaps to understand that the good will of the goddess is being obtained in an evocation of the dead, who here

---

[20] G. Rodenwaldt, *Der Fries des Megarons von Mykenai*, Halle, 1921, p. 23.

appears before his friends in the upper world. The priestess is followed by a woman who wears a long blue robe and crown and carries two baskets on a pole. The last figure in the procession on this half is a man playing the seven-stringed lyre. The Egyptian character of the scene at the right has been noted by scholars.[20a]

On the opposite side of the sarcophagus, a scene of sacrifice occurs. In front of an altar, a priestess is engaged in a ritual of some kind. Behind her a bull dripping with blood lies bound upon a sacrificial table; beneath, other sacrificial animals are seen. A procession of three long-robed women approaches, led by a male flute-player wearing a stole. The ends, in each case, have representations of two figures in a chariot, drawn in one instance by winged gryphons, in the other, by a pair of horses.

Whatever the interpretation of the scene, the whole painting is permeated with the life and movement that belong to all Cretan art. Everyone is very actively engaged in the task before him. This eagerness to make the life about him live in color was certainly the dominating desire of the Cretan painter and we feel ourselves a part of the scene which he depicts, bustling along with the events. Cretan religion was evidently a "busy" religion with emphasis on ritual.

If we pause for a moment to follow the achievement of the Minoan painter, judged from the earliest works of Middle Minoan II or III, through the following epochs down to Late Minoan III, we shall see that the art appears to come to birth "full blown." There is no very definitely archaic period, though the "Blue Boy" and "The Girl with the Ruby Lips" seem to suggest such a stage. Neither is there any great improvement and progress in the art. It begins at its full fruition and then declines. It is not in any sense similar to the work of the Greek, who, by centuries of untiring endeavor, at last achieved the perfect product, building always on the past. The Cretan artist boldly crashes into the field of art, not seeking for the basic laws which govern it; not trying to improve upon his early attempts. He is satisfied to try to represent as well as he can what the eye sees. If this involves an attempt at spatial composition, the Cretan plunges *in medias res*. The perspective which he achieves, though crude, is about as successful as the work of the Greek after a long period of experiment. But in the end, the Greek arrived at something other than pseudo-perspective. Rodenwaldt suggests that the landscape views which the Cretan attempted were probably the natural result of the life which he lived. Spending much of his time in the upper storeys of the palace, he looked down upon episodes such as festivals in the sacred *temenos,* or bull-baiting scenes, and saw the façade of the palace with its loggias filled with spectators and with crowds grouped about below. He was thus accustomed to a bird's-eye view of the landscape, and the vistas

[20a] H. R. Hall, *Ægean Archæology*, London, 1915, pp. 172 ff.; R. Paribeni, *Mon. Ant.*, XIX (1908), pp. 6 ff., Pls. I-III (color). *Cf.* H. R. Hall, *The Civilization of Greece in the Bronze Age*, London, 1928, pp. 25-27.

of crowds about the miniature shrines are merely realistic scenes of what actually took place on the eastern side of the palace where the ground slopes abruptly away and where the region was probably planted with olive trees belonging to the grove of the Goddess. Cretan painting thus begins with a naïvely simple but truthful representation of actual localities, whereas Greek art usually gave only a typical landscape.[21] This may possibly be true but we know that until the discovery of lines converging toward a vanishing point and the beginnings of true perspective, the primitive artist, in order to show what was behind and further away, was forced to place it higher in the background. Cretan vistas were more probably primitive than realistic.

Cretan art had no knowledge of chiaroscuro. At times the color seems to have been put on heavily to obtain some such effect, but we may safely assert that the painting is entirely flat and that there is no attempt to model figures in light and shade. The Cretan painter used types almost from the beginning. When faced with the representation of the standing human figure, he treated it in one of two ways— (1) the entire figure in profile, or (2) the head in profile, the chest in front view and the legs in profile, as so often in Egypt. An example of this latter treatment is the "Chieftain" Relief. An attempt to approach nature more nearly is evident in the Cup-bearer. Here the chest is partially shown in side view but the arm emerges very awkwardly from the breast.

In certain respects, the Cretan artist was always primitive. He never learned to draw the human eye correctly but always gave the full front view in the profile face; he retained the primitive convention of red for representing the flesh of men and white for that of women. He seems to have represented animals impressionistically as far as form was concerned but not in color. For swift motion, he adhered to certain crude media of expression such as the "flying gallop" for animals and the streaming hair for human beings. In drawing, he preferred not to outline the face of human figures and reserved the eyes and ears usually in the ground color. His subjects are always represented in their surroundings and usually in energetic action. Motion, however, is never rendered in terms of muscular play but always by means of line. This is especially seen in the dagger blades from Mycenæ where there is a clean bright sweep along the blade to represent motion. It is always the effect of the whole which interests the artist and thus arise his apparent disregard for form and a certain lack of organic structure in his work. Practically all of his compositions are in the form of friezes placed above dadoes.

One of the most eccentric practices of the Minoan painter was the arrangement of the background in wave-like zones of blue and yellow, red and yellow, red and blue, or the like. We do not know why he did this, unless it was merely that he

[21] G. Rodenwaldt, *Der Fries des Megarons von Mykenai*, Halle, 1921, pp. 10 ff.

loved strongly contrasting colors in juxtaposition. Some writers suggest that the figures were intended to be painted standing against a marbled wall or that the artist wished to indicate that he was painting on marble panels. It is probably a kind of primitive scheme to produce an effective background of color—and may be compared with the marbling of rocks in the Hagia Triada frescoes or the conventional elements in the rocky landscape of the "Blue Boy."

In spite of its many peculiarities and numerous defects, the artistic importance of Cretan art is enormous. The Ægeans were, as Poulsen has shown,[22] the only people who attempted to break the yoke of Egypt's formalism in art. Their observance of nature gave something unexpected, fresh and unforeseen to their decorative style and though the Greeks turned back later to Egypt's formalism, and gave schematization to European art, some slight breath of Cretan inspiration was blown through later ages across Ionian seas. In the Ionians, the direct heirs of Crete, was instilled some of that taste for nature and picturesque detail once inherent in Crete. We shall see this later in the naturalistic character of their art, in the vividness of its movement and in the landscape motives which appear.[23]

We have not spoken of the ceramic art of the Cretans which reveals the same decorative sense we have seen in their frescoes. They achieved in this field great technical perfection and gave to Greece numberless motives and the black glaze varnish which was so important in later wares. Their clay was a buff color and was found in the vicinity. It remained much the same from early times until the end. The wheel was in use among them from Early Minoan days.[23a] They took their patterns from stone, weaving, and especially from the world of nature. The flora and fauna of Crete were used in a simplified, stylized form—without a trace of severe system or the abstraction of Greek geometric art. They renounced the human figure as a motive in ceramic decoration, probably considering it unsuitable. It appears, however, in late Mycenæan times, and may have influenced designs on early Greek vases.

The first artistic painted pottery of Crete is the polychrome ware.[24] Scholars point out that it was beginning even in Early Minoan III, and not a little of it was known in Middle Minoan I. But the great age of polychrome pottery is Middle Minoan II. In general, the designs are abstract. Figure 164a has linked spirals and lunate pat-

---

[22] F. Poulsen, *Der Orient und die frühgriechische Kunst*, Leipzig, 1912, pp. 76 ff.

[23] W. Deonna, *L'Archéologie*, Paris, 1912, II, 38; cf. III, 70 ff.

[23a] Sir Arthur Evans, *The Palace of Minos*, London, 1921, I, 259, 264, 589, places the introduction of the potter's wheel in the M.M. period. *Cf.* H. R. Hall, *The Civilization of Greece in the Bronze Age*, London, 1928, p. 47, note 4. See, *Essays in Ægean Archæology*, Oxford, 1927, pp. 111-128 (Xanthoudídes).

[24] Sir Arthur Evans, *The Palace of Minos*, I, Color Pls. II, III; *J.H.S.*, 21 (1901), Pl. VI (color); *Mon. Ant.*, 14 (1905), Pl. XXXV; *J.H.S.*, 23 (1903), Pls. V-VII (color).

terns combined into an effective composition. Here and there are floral motives in open spaces created by the divergent spirals.[24a] The colors are cherry red, orange, yellow, and white against a buff ground. Figure 164b shows the conventionalization of the calyx of a water lily with outer leaves of black, a central vein of orange, and inner petals of white. Against the dark ground, the petals seem to float as on a stream. The double axe motive in scarlet and white completes the design, which is eminently suited to the surface to be covered. The most elaborate example of polychrome ware is reproduced in Figure 164c. It is covered with scrollwork and curving sprays, with a sort of fleur-de-lis pattern under the handles. The decoration is in yellowish white, crimson, and orange on a lustrous dark ground. The design is not entirely symmetrical and von Salis criticizes it as an example of Cretan anarchy in art. He says that the pattern resembles a firework sparkler in the form of a revolving wheel with stars thrown off.[25]

At the time when these more abstract elements were being extensively used, naturalistic patterns were also coming into greater vogue. In Figure 164d, we have an example of this naturalistic movement. The jug has a lustrous black ground, against which lilies are painted in white with white leafy stalks, whereas the anthers are in bright red. The consummation of this tendency is seen in the lily vases of Middle Minoan III (Fig. 164e), which were directly influenced by wall-painting but which relinquish polychromy for a somewhat more effective monochrome style. In the lily vases the ground is usually a dark violet and the flowers and stems are painted in a chalky white. These vases are masterpieces of the decorator's craft. The pattern spreads out as the vase expands upward until at the top it covers the space between the handles with a varied design that gives very much the effect of the growing plant and satisfies entirely the eye of the observer. The artist understood that good designs are grasped as a whole at one glance of the eye and that the pattern should not disappear behind the handles, so that it cannot be comprehended from one point of view.

Certainly it is impossible to consider that the naturalistic style grew out of the abstract polychrome system of decoration but it should be pointed out that the two tendencies were long co-existent, although the abstract style was dominant until Middle Minoan III. The decoration of the new palace after the catastrophe of Middle Minoan II may have brought forth some great mural artists whose influence was at once felt in the ceramic field. Sir Arthur Evans believes that the beginnings of naturalistic decoration may go back to Neolithic days when branches were crudely indicated on the pottery of the time. Out of this was later to grow the decoration with crocuses, lilies, and ferns.

[24a] Sir Arthur Evans, *op. cit.*, II, 1, pp. 204 ff.
[25] A. von Salis, *Die Kunst der Griechen*, Leipzig, 1919, pp. 9-10.

Late Minoan I revealed a fondness for marine designs, of which the famous vase from Gournia (Fig. 165a), and the filler vase from Zakro, are typical.[26] In Figure 164f, the buff surface is adorned with shellfish, seaweed, and perhaps starfishes, rendered in a brownish red varnish. During the earlier part of this period the design tends to cover the entire vase, whereas in the later "Palace Style," the arrangement is in zones. Traces of the naturalistic tendency are still very evident. The jug from Melos (Fig. 164g) gives one an idea how this influence spread and how much more delicate the work at Knossos usually was. The crocuses on the Melos vase, for all their naturalism, have not the delicacy of many Cretan examples but are notably heavier. Figure 164j shows another splendid example of this tendency from Melos while in Figure 164k, we have a Late Minoan vase adorned with *Nymphæa cœrulea* in which the blossoms appear to be bent low by the wind.[26a]

The Octopus Vase from Gournia, dating about 1500 B.C., shows Cretan design at its best (Fig. 165a). The artist has so cleverly chosen his pattern to suit the stirrup vase that it is difficult to think of any other shape where the design would be suitable. Against this as a background he has painted a marine composition consisting of two octopods, with sea anemones, urchins, and seaweed floating about among the tentacles. The joy of the artist who created the vase was not less keen than ours, as the eye winds in and out among the rhythmic lines and is diverted by the repetitions of dots and circles and by the variety in unity. The painter has known well how to represent the cuttlefish in movement; we see the long arms close and open, and the drifting seaweed floating by. There is about the design something of the change and restlessness of the sea.[27] It would be easy to multiply adjectives in discussing the charm of the work, its grace and beauty—but the essential thing is that the elements of good design have been admirably chosen out by the artist; the shapes and lines are successfully adapted to the form of the vase, and this effect is heightened by the rhythmic movement of the writhing arms. The dark brown color of the paint against the light buff ground completes the harmony of the whole.[28]

It is interesting to trace this pattern in later times, especially on the mainland during the Mycenæan Age. It appears on the delicately shaped, high-stemmed kylikes, conventionalized into a pattern much less rich and imaginative, but still admirably adapted to the surface to be decorated and still capable of giving pleasure

[26] *J.H.S.*, 22 (1902), Color Pl. XII.

[26a] Sir Arthur Evans, *op. cit.*, II, 2, p. 472, calls the flower the star anemone. It grows abundantly in Crete.

[27] F. Poulsen, *Die dekorative Kunst des Altertums*, Leipzig, 1914, pp. 38 ff.

[28] Von Salis emphasizes the freedom and untectonic quality of Cretan art, *Die Kunst der Griechen*, 1919, pp. 9 ff. The Octopus design cuts across the body of the vase; the lily vase lacks absolute correspondence of parts; in the Kamares vase of Fig. 164c the absence of entire symmetry would have troubled a Greek; in Fig. 164a we have anarchy of design.

to the eye (Fig. 165f). The degeneration from successive copying is, however, recognizable in many other examples where the artist contents himself with more rigidly formal and often fantastic conventionalization (Fig. 165g, h).

The vases found at Pylos bridge over the gap in the development between Late Minoan I and II.[29] In shape, they go back to the great Middle Minoan painted *pithoi*, with their many handles. Figure 164h shows the blending of the naturalistic and conventionalizing tendencies. Palm trees are represented slightly conventionalized, but growing from their stems very strongly conventionalized leaves and blossoms. The design covers almost the entire vase wandering up on the shoulder in a free fashion characteristic of the period of Late Minoan I. In Figure 164i, a design of running spirals is similarly arranged over the whole vase. Amphoræ of this type were shortly to be succeeded in Late Minoan II by the grandiose "Palace Style," in which the vase was sharply marked off and decorated according to architectonic divisions. These originated in Crete but are also found on the mainland. In Figure 165b, we have a frieze-like pattern of stiffly stylized lilies running around the center of the vase like a cornice, with the shoulder and lower divisions carefully marked off and decorated with patterns drawn from plant life. Late Minoan II brought a profusion of these "Palace Style" vases decorated in the Mycenæan technique with brownish glaze on a buff ground. In Figure 165c, we see floral patterns adorning the shoulder, conventionalized flowers the body, and a wave pattern the neck, while the base is kept in dark varnish. The flowers probably began as stylized lilies but they have become more like columns with fan-like capitals in their final state.[29a] In Figure 165d, architectural motives are used—the elongated, divided rosette of Cretan and Mycenæan building and the well-known checkerboard pattern. In this instance, the vase is also marked off into horizontal divisions by foliate patterns. In Figure 165e, the main body of the vase is adorned with papyrus and conventional designs.

We thus see that the Cretans had a genius for decorating vases; that from Middle Minoan II until Late Minoan II both stylized naturalistic and more abstract ornamental patterns were employed, but the Middle Minoan II period tended rather toward abstract decoration, Middle Minoan III toward naturalistic. In Late Minoan I both styles survived but polychromy was largely a thing of the past. Finally the floral patterns become more and more stylized and decadent, until by the end of Late Minoan II, we often cannot trace the pattern back to its origin. The fate of the lily pattern illustrates well this evolution of Cretan design. In Figure 164e, the design is naturalistic. In the Palace vase of Figure 165b, the lily is used convention-

---

[29] K. Müller, *Alt-Pylos, Ath. Mitth.*, 34 (1909), p. 319, Pls. XII-XXIV.

[29a] They are really hybrid plants, combining elements from the papyrus blossom and the lily.

ally in a frieze arrangement. Its origin is recognizable in Figure 165c, if one compares the pattern with the lilies in the "Chieftain" Relief. Here it is combined with the papyrus motive. The architectonic decoration of vases became the paramount fashion in Late Minoan II. This greatly influenced Greek vase-decoration in the use of frieze- and metope-like zones. We may follow this process of conventionalization on Mycenæan kylikes and vases (cf. Figs. 165f, h).

When the Cretan civilization was at its height, there rose to prominence on the mainland of Greece a kindred culture, many of whose elements were distinctly Cretan. Its source is not certainly known. Some writers hold that it was essentially of northern origin and argue that the house form, costumes, armor, language, and certain themes and forms in art were distinctly different from what existed in Crete.[30] That more than one race resided in these mainland centers is evident from many proofs, notably the pottery, the death-masks, and objects of art. The origin and relations of these various stocks form a complicated problem which is only gradually becoming clarified.[30a] According to the opinion of Blegen, the "racial strata" in Greece were as follows: "I, Neolithic Age: Mediterranean race, from undatable beginnings to shortly after 3000 B.C.; II, Early Helladic: Anatolian, non-Indo-European race. They overran and absorbed the remnants of I, continuing in power until 2000 B.C.; III, Middle Helladic: first of many successive waves of Greeks. They arrived about 2000 B.C. and were gradually merged with a fusion of I and II." We might follow the various peoples, tracing them by their pottery, but we will begin with the mural decorations, neglecting the pottery somewhat, but pointing out that the lustrous varnish paint found on the mainland was brought there by the southern invaders from the Cyclades and Crete. The theory which we will sup-

---

[30] M. P. Nilsson, *The Minoan-Mycenæan Religion and its Survival in Greek Religion*, Lund, 1927, pp. 11 ff.; cf. E. Meyer, *Gesch. des Alt.*, II, 1, 1928, pp. 234 ff. G. Rodenwaldt, *Der Fries des Megarons von Mykenai*, Halle, 1921, pp. 46 ff.; *Die Kunst der Antike*, Berlin, 1927, pp. 16 ff. *Vs.* this Sir Arthur Evans, *The Palace of Minos*, I, 24. *Cf.* C. W. Blegen, *A.J.A.*, 27 (1923), 157, for the new dating and the use of "Late Helladic" for Mycenæan; *A.J.A.*, 32 (1928), pp. 146 ff.

[30a] H. Frankfort, *Studies in Early Pottery of the Near East*, II (*Asia, Europe and the Ægean and Their Interrelations*), London, 1927; H. R. Hall, *The Civilization of Greece in the Bronze Age*, London, 1928; D. Fimmen, *Die kretisch-mykenische Kultur²*, Leipzig, 1924; C. W. Blegen, *Korakou*, Boston, 1921; *A.J.A.*, XXXII (1928), pp. 146 ff.; E. J. Forsdyke, *Prehistoric Ægean Pottery*, London, British Museum, 1925, Vol. I, Part I. V. Gordon Childe, *The Dawn of European Civilization*, New York, 1925. On the Thessalian culture, see A. J. B. Wace, M. S. Thompson, *Prehistoric Thessaly*, Cambridge, 1912; on Minyan ware, E. J. Forsdyke, "The Pottery Called Minyan Ware," *J.H.S.*, XXXIV (1914), pp. 126 ff. J. P. Harland, "The Peloponnesos in the Bronze Age," *Harvard Studies in Classical Philology*, 34 (1923). L. B. Holland, "The Danaoi," *Harvard Studies in Classical Philology*, 39 (1928), pp. 59 ff.

port with reference to the mainland civilization of the Late Helladic I period is that it was essentially Cretan and non-Greek. The mainland rulers of the L.H. I period were Minoans, *i.e.*, Cretan princes, who, like the Norman overlords, imposed their sovereignty on a less civilized people. Mycenæ and Tiryns were thus tributary cities subject to Cretan sovereigns. This view is borne out by religious cults and rites, by their sports, their ideas of life and death, and their objects of art. Upon this civilization, certain features which were distinctly northern were imposed by the invading Greek peoples. The southern penetration may have been a gradual and peaceful one in the form of a colony, or it may have been an actual conquest by force. In Middle Minoan III, with the period of rebuilding in Crete, came the mainland expansion and by Late Minoan II, at least by the Fifteenth Century, the center of power had shifted to Mycenæ, after the overthrow of the Cretan palaces at Phæstos and Knossos. Late Minoan I is the "Golden Age" of Mycenæ—the period of the shaft graves; in Late Minoan II the tradition is continued, the apogee reached and passed and by Late Minoan III the "Silver Age" appears.[30b] In Late Helladic I, Cretans established trading posts on the mainland and gradually dominated it. Later the mainland inhabitants arose and sacked the southern sites. The Tholos Tomb Dynasty of L.M. II is a group of invaders from the north, perhaps Phrygians of the house of Pelops. This theory of a Cretan origin for the Mycenæan civilization is opposed by many leading authorities such as Wace, Blegen, E. Meyer, Nilsson, and others. There is doubtless much to be said for the Pre-Mycenæan civilization of the mainland and later excavations may reveal its significance. Either theory has its inexplicable difficulties. The most difficult thing to explain, if the Mycenæan civilization was Helladic, is the sudden acquisition of wealth by a people, who, up to L.H. I, are conspicuously poor.

The mural art of the mainland is fundamentally Cretan. In the subject matter there is the greatest difference between it and decadent Ægean work. It is more than likely that the majority of the paintings were executed by Cretans and that differences are to be accounted for by the fact that the artists employed at Mycenæ were working to satisfy the demands of mainland patrons. The age of the frescoes of Tiryns and Mycenæ is parallel to the work of Late Minoan I to III in Crete, but on the mainland we shall call these periods by the term "Helladic" rather than Minoan. The Helladic civilization really begins to be important in the Late Minoan age. The dates current for this epoch are: Early Helladic, 2500-2000; Middle Helladic, 2000-1600; Late Helladic I, 1600-1500; Late Helladic II, 1500 to shortly before 1400; Late Helladic III, 1400-1100. Late Helladic III is synonymous with Mycenæan.

Rodenwaldt considers that the paintings at Mycenæ are probably older and superior in execution to those at Tiryns but that on both sites there are frescoes dating

---

[30b] *Cf.* Blegen, *A.J.A.*, 27 (1923). Blegen's latest discoveries at the Argive Heræum show mainland pottery adopting Cretan designs.

from Late Minoan I-II. The excavators of the British school, on the other hand, feel that the dating of the Tiryns frescoes is uncertain and that the older palace may belong either in Late Helladic I or II. The paintings at Mycenæ for the most part picture hunts and battle scenes and are mainly epic in character. Though the fragments are not extensive, they form some of the best preserved examples known.[31] One of the most important paintings extant represents the siege of a city, in a fashion not unlike the method employed on the silver "Siege" cup from Mycenæ (Fig. 166). The recent reconstruction of the "Siege" cup would seem to indicate that the artist of that work also made use of the scale pattern found earlier in Sumeria to denote hilly ground.[32] This occurs on certain Cretan seals where a goddess stands on a mountain height, and was employed later in Assyria. The artist of the fresco uses the sort of spatial composition found on Cretan frescoes. He boldly places his city high in the frieze and strews the background with fighting figures, all of the same size—standing, running, and lying in several rows above one another. No ground lines are employed. One falling warrior is closely analogous in type to representations on Egyptian reliefs of the Nineteenth and Twentieth Dynasties— but the similarity is probably only a parallel phenomenon and, if derivative, its home was Crete (Fig. 167). Rodenwaldt insists upon the greater excellence of the paintings of Mycenæ in contrast to those from Tiryns in line drawing, in the slenderer proportions of the figures, and in the greater vividness of action conveyed. The colors are muddier and less pure than they were in Crete. The background still changes, but this time it is a brownish yellow in part, in part a gray-blue. On frescoes of the latest period it is usually a uniform blue. The long frieze probably depicted a continuous narrative, starting with a representation of a military camp, within which chariots were being harnessed for warriors departing for battle. Then followed scenes of combat, the besieged city, and many related events. This narrative composition had not been found in Crete until the discoveries of 1923 which seem to forecast similar subject matter and treatment of it. We do not know whether or not such scenes as occur at Mycenæ were arranged chronologically as the events happened or according to interest, but these fragments from the "Megaron of Agamemnon" at Mycenæ may well be pictures of events in the heroic age.[33] Rodenwaldt would date these frescoes in Late Helladic I because of the free arrangement of figures in the composition, the changing background, and absence of contour lines,

[31] G. Rodenwaldt, *Der Fries des Megarons von Mykenai*, Halle, 1921; *Ath. Mitth.*, 36 (1911), pp. 221 ff., Pls. IX-XII; *Jahr.*, 34 (1919), pp. 87-106; C. Tsountas, *Eph. Arch.*, 1887, Pls. 10-12.

[32] V. Staïs, *Ath. Mitth.*, XL (1915), Pls. VII-VIII.

[33] G. Rodenwaldt, *Der Fries des Megarons von Mykenai*, Halle, 1921, pp. 59 ff. *Cf. Eph. Arch.*, 1887, Pls. 11, 12.

together with their similarity to those of the early palace at Tiryns. According to
the British excavators, the frescoes of the megaron frieze, in spite of Rodenwaldt's
arguments, cannot belong to so early a period, because the megaron in which they
occur was not built until Late Helladic III. Further, the dating of the early palace at
Tiryns is not certainly to be placed in Late Helladic I.[34]

Paintings of women in the loggia of a shrine at Mycenæ show how very inferior
mainland work was to similar work in Crete (Fig. 168). This fresco needs only to
be compared with the "Pillar Shrine" frescoes of Knossos which treat a similar
theme, to understand the gulf which separates the two. The fresco in question gives
an opportunity for a study of the technical details.[35] On the moist stucco, the blue
of the ground, the ocher yellow on the right, and the red of other architectural parts
were first put on *al fresco;* in the white layer above, the stucco remained without
color. Everything else was painted over the colored ground. First, the contours of
the figures were outlined in dark red. Then this outline was filled in with a white
silhouette and the same white was used for double axes and wreaths. After that, the
sleeves were painted in yellow over the white of the arms. Finally, all black details
were added. Black, the most perishable color in Cretan-Mycenæan painting, is
almost everywhere found in a state of disintegration. Layers of color placed above
one another four or five deep in the fresco method must have required great skill and
haste in working. Contours and silhouettes were added with a binding medium.

The Mycenæan fragment discovered by Schliemann, with ass-headed demons
bearing a long pole, is also to be dated in the earlier period, probably in Late Helladic II. Against a greenish-gray ground remains of three demons are seen, their
bodies painted in yellow with reddish-brown details and contours in black (Fig.
169).[35a] Probably a cult scene is depicted. Demons of this character are found on a
gold ring from Mycenæ, watering a sacred tree and we are familiar with votaries in
Cretan art who bear poles and baskets in ritualistic scenes. Contemporary with this
is a painted pinax representing two women in worship before the Cretan sky god.
He is pictured with his figure-eight shield in the center of the design.[36] The ground
is blue; the border is made up of bands of red, blue, yellow, and black. The colors
used on the figures are yellow, blue, and white. Inner details are incised, the only
known example of incising of details in Mycenæan art.

One of the later painted monuments at Mycenæ, aside from vases, is the Warrior
Stele. Rodenwaldt thinks it may be dated in the Late Helladic III period and would

---

[34] W. Lamb, "School Excavations at Mycenæ," *B.S.A.*, XXV (1921-1923), pp. 254-255.
*Cf.* G. Rodenwaldt, *Gnomon*, 2 (1926), pp. 244 ff. I understand from Professor Blegen that
in the forthcoming book by K. Müller on the walls, etc., of Mycenæ, the earlier palace is
dated in L.H. III.

[35] G. Rodenwaldt, *Ath. Mitth.*, 36 (1911), pp. 223 ff., Pl. IX.

[35a] *Cf.* M. P. Nilsson, *op. cit.*, pp. 324 ff.        [36] *Eph. Arch.*, 1887, Pl. 10, 2.

assign it to the artist of the Warrior Vase (cf. Fig. 193).[37] The relief was used as a stele in the period of the shaft graves and the painting which now covers it was not the original decoration. It received a stucco coating and color and was used as a painted grave marker later. The decoration is arranged in three zones and shows a return to primitive art in many aspects (Fig. 170). In the upper row, we see a personage seated on a large chair, while most of the remainder of the design is lost. Below, follows a line of warriors—own brothers to the men on the Warrior Vase—armed with shields and brandishing spears in their right hands. The color scheme is very crude, yellow and greenish-blue alternating on the shields; red, yellow, and blue on the short fringed tunics. In the lowest zone are four long-necked stags and a porcupine. The stag at the left is blue except for the right hind leg which is red; the second one is yellow with one blue and three red legs—a zoning arrangement of color which is a primitive scheme and which we shall meet in the earliest Etruscan tombs in the painting of animals. The color is heightened by wave patterns in red, white, and brown, which surround the stele and mark off the various zones. The work is crude and naïve and does not really belong in the field of monumental painting.

Finer in quality than the Mycenæan paintings is a group of fragments discovered by Keramopoullos in the so-called house of Kadmos at Thebes.[38] Put together, they represent a group of women belonging to a procession similar to the ones found in Crete, but here made up of women only. They furnish interesting material for comparison with the Knossian frescoes and with one from Hagia Triada consisting also of women, but they are especially to be contrasted with the later frieze from Tiryns. Many details place the fresco in the older mainland period, Late Helladic I,—among these, the changing background of yellow, white, and blue, against which a frieze of women moving in different directions was represented. In Figure 171, one woman from this group is reproduced. She wears a bodiced type of dress with colored flounces—blue, red, yellow, black, and white being the leading colors. In her left hand, she carries a polychrome vase. The subject, therefore, is probably a cult scene. The care in technical execution, the good surface and color, the drawing, and the rendering of various details—such as hair—all help to prove that these life-size figures belonged in a period earlier than the frieze from the megaron at Mycenæ (Figs. 166-167). Below the Theban design ran a baseboard of yellow, gray-blue, and bright red, imitating marble paneling. The figure is a restoration.

Somewhat earlier than the paintings from Mycenæ is a series of fragments from the older palace at Tiryns,[39] most of which were found in the forecourt of the

---

[37] G. Rodenwaldt, *Tiryns*, II, 186-187; C. Tsountas, *Eph. Arch.*, 1896, Pl. I.

[38] A. Keramopoullos, *Eph.*, 1909, p. 90, Pls. 1-3; S. Reinach, *Gazette des Beaux-Arts*, I (1920), pp. 296 ff.

[39] G. Rodenwaldt, *Tiryns*, II, Pl. I.

megaron, or great hall. Although the earlier palace is traceable only in spots, it probably was of the same type as the later example and different from what was erected earlier in Crete.[40] But the walls were stuccoed in the same way and covered with paintings. An example of the work discovered there is seen in Figure 172. Two men, clad in short tunics with "kimono" sleeves, are starting on an expedition. They may be departing for a hunt, because they wear no helmets and carry in each case two spears across their right shoulders. The flesh of the figures in terra cotta red forms a pronounced contrast to the midnight blue of the ground. The man at the left wears a bluish white tunic with a black border; the other, a yellow one. Black is used for details such as hair and eyelids; white for the eyeball.

The technique of the fragment is interesting. In some places there are four layers of color placed above one another—the blue of the ground, with terra cotta for the flesh above; black over this for the hair, and red upon the black for the spears. The faces have no contour lines but an outline in black runs from the chin to the neckband along the neck. The figures are very similar and the composition was probably rather monotonous in its original state as the poses are repeated in almost identical fashion. The left hand extends rather awkwardly in front of the chest and the necks seem thick and heavy. But the old Cretan "sway-back" pose, and the narrow waist are there, and we are able to recognize the models from which the figures were derived despite differences in costume and a certain woodenness of movement. In some examples the background still changes in color. To this group belong fragments of chariots and horses, and ornamental patterns which we shall discuss later. The paintings may be placed in Late Helladic I or II, depending on the date of the earlier palace.

To the palace of Late Helladic III, a large number of important frescoes may be assigned (Fig. 175). The ruins of the later palace at Tiryns lie today within a mass of gray walls which rise from the midst of the green Argive plain. The palace belongs to the "mainland" type which has a megaron and central hearth as typical features (Fig. 174). The palaces of Crete, in contrast, mostly lacked these characteristics, at least until a late period, when they penetrated south under northern influence. The site of Tiryns was strongly fortified whereas walls seem to have played little part in the defense of Cretan buildings, though the northern entrance at Knossos shows a defensive front (Fig. 173). We no longer have in Tiryns, as in Crete, a great central court from which long corridors open with complexes of rooms, but we find instead a forecourt and propylon in front of an isolated living room, or "megaron." This room contained a hearth which the northern climate demanded, while the fore-

---

[40] The character of the earlier mainland palaces cannot be said to be finally established. A. J. B. Wace, *The Times, Literary Supplement,* London (October 26, 1922), p. 684; *B.S.A.,* XXV (1921-1923), pp. 266, 269, points out many Cretan connections.

court acted as a sort of light-well. The remains of friezes around the lower part of the walls, the stuccoed floors, the fragments of plaster found, sometimes on the walls—mostly fallen—show that the walls and floors of the mainland were decorated in much the same fashion as they were in Crete. Probably the practice was ultimately derived from Egypt where the painting of stuccoed walls and floors was of immemorial antiquity. These later mainland palaces were the homes of the Pelopid Dynasty—of the Achæan princes, Agamemnon and Menelaus.

One of the most interesting frescoes from the later palace depicts a boar hunt— probably the forerunner of the popular Calydonian Boar Hunt of Greek times. The frieze, bordered by a white band above and below, ran around the four walls, and measured about forty centimeters in height. The fragments narrate a story in which hunters are seen setting out for the chase, followed by guests in chariots. As the action advances, we observe the animals pursued through marshland and finally netted and pierced through the head by hunting spears. They appear against a grayish-blue ground which is often muddied and impure.

We may begin with a chariot group at the left (Fig. 175). The color here is used wholly for contrast and is rarely true to nature. The forest through which the chariot passes is represented by strongly conventionalized trees spread out like fans, terra cotta, blue, or gray in color, with a yellow border in each case. Against these uniform grounds, ivy-like leaves outlined in black represent the foliage of trees— much the technique used in the miniature frescoes of Crete. The crimson chariot, with blue- and black-rimmed wheels and yellow axles, is drawn by one red and one white horse. The white horse in the rear is indicated merely by outlining in white the red one in the foreground. In the chariot box stand two stiffly erect figures who may be women or young boys. The flesh of men is usually red in Cretan-Mycenæan art; that of women, white. Hall suggests that we may have here cloistered princes of the palace court,[41] but it is more probable that they are women taking part in the chase. They wear long garments with black borders—one blue, the other violet. Details of hair and features are in black. The poses, treatment of hair, the left hand projecting from the chest, and many details in technique are familiar to us. The fresco, bounded above and below by white bands, is bordered by a blue and a yellow tooth pattern and finally by an ornamental leaf pattern of yellow, white, blue, and red.

Next in order, perhaps, came the attendants with dogs on leashes (Fig. 176). The type of figure is similar to that of the hunters described from the earlier palace (Fig. 172). The groom shown here, clad in leggings and a yellow belted tunic, guides a large hound on a leash. Behind him follows a chariot group—at least, we have a fragment of a horse's head with the mane tied in several knots.

[41] H. R. Hall, *Ægean Archæology*, London, 1915, p. 190.

The next fragment (Fig. 177) presents the hunt in full progress with a wild boar fleeing through marsh grass and hotly pursued by dogs. The crisis of the hunt has arrived, for we see the hand of a male figure ramming his spear into the boar's neck. The scene is laid in swampy land and the artist has a chance to suggest a landscape, for which he always had a predilection. White, marsh-like plants, outlined in red, cover the background in profusion. But the *élan* of the scene is in the charging boar, pursued to his doom. The old motive of the "flying gallop" is employed for violent action and we feel the hounds hot upon their victim. The composition is very successful. The color scheme, on the other hand, is quite arbitrary. The boar is brown with yellow and black stripes; the dogs white with blue, pink, or black spots. The artist has probably engaged in the chase which he depicts—at least he seems familiar at first hand with the details of hunting the wild boar. The painting calls to mind the description in Xenophon of how the animal was driven into the net and killed.[41a] Other game were stirred up in the chase, among them hares and deer. In Figure 178, we have fragments of another important hunting frieze where the game consists of deer. The first deer is a uniform yellow, the second violet, the third blue. In each case there are black crosses on the body with stripes of white on the neck and back in two instances, yellow in the third. Friezes such as this greatly influenced the patterns on vases. That this was not a part of the larger frieze is evident from the technique. The outlines have now become heavy black bands. These compositions, together with the one from the megaron at Mycenæ, give us a vivid idea of the narrative friezes which ran around the walls of Mycenæan palaces. In spite of their fragmentary character, they are instinct with life and action. The Mycenæan liked about him the sports in which he indulged, the battles in which he fought, and his life, to judge from the frescoes, was one of stirring action.

Another famous fresco from the later palace at Tiryns depicted a procession of women engaged in a religious ritual. From some 600 fragments, typical figures have been reconstructed. The frieze was similar to the well-known but superior one from Thebes (*cf.* Fig. 171), to one from Hagia Triada, and remotely to the ones from Knossos which, however, included men.

In the reconstruction by Gilliéron (Fig. 179), we see a woman bearing a pyxis and advancing to the right. She is painted against a uniform field of blue and moves upon a horizontal, grained beam of wood which was intended to represent the wall structure of a shrine or some sacred part of the palace. Below this beam are orthostates alternately blue and red, so that the color scheme is far from sober. This part of the fresco is interesting for the light which it sheds on the structure and decoration of the palace walls. To this color scheme is added the brilliant red of the woman's jacket with a border of blue and white, a skirt of yellow, blue, red, and

---

[41a] Xen. *Kyn.*, X, 1 ff.

white, the black of her hair and the contrasted white of her flesh. A floral pattern above with its ornamental bands also lends color to the scene. The woman is probably a votary of the Cretan goddess and the cult may well have been continued in later times in that of Hera at Argos. This woman is only one of a series of similar priestesses.

In contrasting these figures with those from Crete, we see that the motives are essentially the same—but the mainland figure belongs to the decadent period of which "Ariadne" and "The Girl with the Ruby Lips" were predecessors. Movement is more wooden, the treatment of details, such as hair, less pleasing. The costume is Cretan with slight variations, so also the profile. The source, in fact, is everywhere clearly recognizable but the finished product gives little pleasure. The figures are almost life size.

Other examples of frescoes from Tiryns prove the dependence of the art on Crete and the deterioration which that art has undergone. The well-known "Bull Fresco" is typical (Fig. 180). It presents the same theme as the "Toreador" fresco from Knossos—but how different the treatment! The bull charges across the field in the "flying gallop" fashion, but it is no such spirited animal as the Cretan bull. The head is too small for the lumpy body and this, with the thick legs and hoofs, show how little the artist knew of correct proportions. He has meticulously tried to alter his design—a very difficult thing to do in the fresco technique—with the result that the bull has four front legs and three tails! A woman acrobat is seen performing in the field above the bull's back. The fresco dates from the later palace period and is almost a caricature of the favorite Cretan theme. The ground is a muddy blue, the bull yellow with brown patches.

The frescoes which we have been describing from the later palace belong to the Mycenæan age, Late Helladic III, to the time when frescoes are mostly lacking in Crete. We are able, however, to follow with some precision the history of Cretan-Mycenæan painting from Middle Minoan II down to Late Minoan III. In Crete it begins in Middle Minoan II-III and is at its height in Middle Minoan III-Late Minoan I. The next period is represented by mainland frescoes from Thebes and the earlier palace at Tiryns—Late Helladic I-II; lastly, come the paintings that belong to the later palaces at Tiryns and Mycenæ which are also supplemented by remains at Orchomenos on the mainland.[42] The difference between the frescoes of

---

[42] For the successive palaces at Mycenæ, see A. J. B. Wace, *B.S.A.*, XXV (1921-1922; 1922-1923), pp. 269 ff. In L.H. I under the Shaft Grave Dynasty the first palace was erected on the top of the Acropolis. This apparently served as the home of the earlier kings of the Tholos Tomb Dynasty in L.H. II. In L.H. III a second palace was built by the wealthiest kings of the Tholos Tomb Dynasty. This structure lasted until the fall of Mycenæ, and seems to have been the home of the Atreidai. H. Bulle, *Orchomenos*, München, 1907, pp. 71 ff., Pls. 28-30 (*Abh. der Kgl. Bayer. Akad. der Wiss., Philos.-phil. Kl.* 24). *Cf.* p. 97, n. 34.

Crete and the mainland sites is one of technical excellence and of artistic power. The island frescoes have an almost porcelain-like character, showing wonderfully fine preparation and finish in the case of the stucco. The frescoes on the mainland, especially the later ones, are much rougher and the plaster is very uneven. In both groups, the technique is similar—fresco work executed with the brush. But the drawing in Crete is far finer as a rule, although Rodenwaldt claims very superior drawing for the frieze at Mycenæ. The colors in Crete are more brilliant and warm. We find rich reds, blues, and warm yellows used as primary colors in the earlier period, with black and white. To these were added brown, gray, and violet. Green was rarely used, but, instead, blue seems to have been often employed for plants. The changing red and yellow ground, or blue and yellow, or blue and red ground of early days gradually gives way to a hard, uniform blue in Mycenæan times. The colors become muddied and impure. The late artist seeks for a wider range and greater vividness. But there is poverty of invention, the same motives are used in a lifeless way and the early spirited action is lost. Neutral gray, so pleasing in the earlier frescoes, disappears, and we have instead the introduction of violet, green, and other colors which were somewhat less conservative. Green was practically always a mixture of yellow and blue. The ornamental patterns especially show the degeneration in Mycenæan times of older Cretan motives.

The part which ornamental decoration played in the palaces of Crete and Mycenæ was very extensive, but the remains are not so numerous as we might hope. In the Middle Minoan period marble incrustation may have been employed in Crete as a dado decoration in the earlier palace. The reasons for such a conclusion are the imitations found in painting and ceramics. Stucco remains often show fields decorated in imitation of marble—yellow, with red and black wavy lines, or bluish white with the same colors.[43] Wave-like imitation of marble is comparatively rare but it is found beneath the Gryphon Fresco in the Throne Room. The "Toreador" Fresco is also framed by bands imitating stones and marble. Remains of stone and alabaster friezes with spirals, divided palmettes, and triglyphs have been discovered in Crete and on the mainland, Figure 181 (cf. Fig. 186), but none of marble. In Crete, the orthostates extant are everywhere of gypsum which may have been covered with stucco and painted.[44] The marbled decoration found probably represents an earlier baseboard of colored stone or marble.

The decorative patterns in Crete go back to Middle Minoan II. Bands of color were earlier employed in dado decoration and were often used as edges for the larger

[43] Sir Arthur Evans, *The Palace of Minos*, London, 1921, I, 356; G. Rodenwaldt, *Tiryns*, 1912, II, 23 ff. and Color Pl. III.

[44] G. Rodenwaldt, *Tiryns*, 1912, II, 28; Sir Arthur Evans, *The Palace of Minos*, London, 1921, I, 364, Fig. 264.

friezes, which always closed with a white band above and below. We have spoken of the spirals of Middle Minoan III, which were executed in blue and white against a darker blue or red ground, with touches of red and black (Figs. 137-138). Their perfection reveals a long period of skill behind them. The most common ornament in Cretan-Mycenæan painting was the tooth ornament which was used as a border for figure and ornamental painting, usually in two rows of color. Rosettes were also very frequently employed. The frieze from the older palace at Tiryns is typical of the class on stems (Fig. 182), a type that was also found in Egypt.[45] They seem to have been set on a marbled field of yellow, red, and white, bordered by a darker band dotted with red and white. The colors from the center were red, white, and blue, once repeated. Perhaps the most effective decoration preserved from Late Helladic II is a frieze of shields (Fig. 183) from the older palace at Tiryns. The design is a very complicated one. The main pattern is a series of spotted, oxhide, figure-eight shields—brown, black, and gray in color. They are placed against a decorated ground that of itself would be elaborate enough to form the ornamental border. Through the center runs a band of cream spirals with red centers and gray spurs, bordered by a gray tooth pattern and apparently set against a wavy marbled ground of yellow, gray, and red. The closing patterns above and below are running spirals of green, yellow, and white bordered again on either side by a gray tooth pattern. The centers of the spirals are white, the spurs blue. The striking feature in this marvelously designed frieze is the extensive use of green, which is rare in Cretan painting, and the prevalence of gray which practically disappears in the later palace style.

The most common ornamental band from the later palace is the up-and-down spiral, which began to have its vogue in the earlier palace (Fig. 184). The height of this band is about thirty-nine centimeters and the workmanship is very superior in parts, less good in others, leading Rodenwaldt to the conclusion that it was executed by several hands. The spirals here are black and blue outlined with white bands sown with dots. The rosettes have yellow and white fields surrounding a red center. From the corner of the spirals and from the points where they touch the lower margin arise conventionalized lotus flowers of white and blue with yellow in the middle. The central spears are blue, while the side leaves are yellow. The whole design is set against a ground of red. This particular pattern seems to have been common on the mainland and has not been found in Crete, except on pottery. It occurs in Egypt and a similar design is found on the stone ceiling of Orchomenos to which we shall return later (cf. Fig. 186).

We are now able to form some idea of the decoration of the palace walls in Crete and on the mainland. The lower part of the wall in early times probably had a marble

---

[45] G. Rodenwaldt, *Tiryns*, 1912, II, 33.

dado which was later imitated in marbled or painted stucco. Above this was a horizontal wooden beam which was doubtless often left in the original state and not covered with stucco. Proof of this is seen in the paintings of the frieze of women from Thebes and Tiryns, who seem to move on a beam of grained wood. Above this beam were the great figure friezes which were bordered with ornamental patterns, usually above and sometimes below. Higher than all this was another beam or a wooden cornice of some nature.

We are less fortunate in our knowledge of the character of the ceiling decoration but some few examples aid us here in our attempts at reconstruction.[46] Remains of a spiral pattern of plastic form with rosettes in the corners found at Knossos date in all probability from Late Minoan I or II (Fig. 185). The spirals are white, with polychrome rosettes of red and yellow color sown on the blue field. This pattern occurs sporadically in Egypt in the Twelfth Dynasty, frequently in the Eighteenth (*cf.* Fig. 76c). From Orchomenos comes the famous stone ceiling with spirals and lotus flowers, a design similar in character to the ornamental band described above[47] (Fig. 186). It belongs in Late Helladic II. The center field was bordered by rosettes. Remains from Knossos of flat decoration in large spirals probably also belong to a ceiling pattern.[48] Steps covered with stucco and painted with spirals have been discovered in the older palace at Tiryns.[49] We know that objects in the house, such as benches and couches, were ornamented in the same way.

Of the floor decoration we know more. We learn little about the subject from Knossos, much from Tiryns. That there were stuccoed floors at Knossos is evident from the floor underlying the magazine of the Medallion Pithoi.[50] In general, Knossos seems to have preferred in Middle Minoan II "Kalderim" paving, which means irregular slabs of thick limestone. Painted plaster has been found at times in the interstices of the slabs, so that these floors do not appear to have been covered with stucco. At the close of Middle Minoan II, finer polygonal slabs of limestone were employed. The interstices were filled with white or red plaster giving the effect of a mosaic. This practice led the Cretan workmen to call this type of pavement by the name "Mosaiko." In Middle Minoan III, gypsum slabbing was the rule. Below the gypsum slabbing, examples have been found of stuccoed floors, but they are unpainted. In many cases a double row of slabs runs around the walls at Knossos and, within this border, there was probably stucco decoration. The Throne Room at

---

[46] *B.S.A.*, VI (1899-1900), 44; Theodore Fyfe, *J.R.I.B.A.*, X (1902-1903), p. 118, Figs. 41, 42, Pl. I.

[47] Perrot and Chipiez, VI (1894), Fig. 220, p. 543. *Cf.* Fig. 221 (Reconstruction).

[48] Theodore Fyfe, *J.R.I.B.A.*, X (1902-1903), p. 121, Figs. 45-48.

[49] G. Rodenwaldt, *Tiryns*, 1912, II, 58 ff.; H. R. Hall, *Ægean Archæology*, London, 1915, Fig. 65.

[50] Sir Arthur Evans, *The Palace of Minos*, London, 1921, I, 209, 351.

Knossos has this border of well-cut gypsum slabs enclosing a more irregularly paved square of the same material. This stone floor and the benches had been covered originally with red and white plaster.[51] In the Cretan rooms paved with regular blocks may be sought the origin of the painted Mycenæan floors arranged in blocks of different colors.

At Mycenæ there have been discovered remains of painted floors which date from the time of the later palace at Tiryns.[52] They show that a single row of slabstones ran around the wall and within this in three sections were set colored squares of stucco separated by bands of dark red and sometimes with contours impressed with a string. The square fields were colored red, blue, or yellow and on each colored field alternating patterns were placed. On the yellow ground were circles or a wave pattern; on the red, zigzags or scales; on the blue, a wave pattern or imitation of stone. The simplest pattern preserved is the zigzag on a red ground. Here, dark red lines alternate with black lines dotted with white (Fig. 187). The lines are drawn free-hand and are executed with great regularity and exactness. The pattern was probably taken from textiles. The scale pattern was also set on a red ground and above the dark red line in the center is a black line with a white one below (Fig. 188). A similar pattern has been discovered on the garments of one of the women in the "Procession Fresco" from Knossos. The circle pattern has three colors—an outer black ring, followed by a dark red and an inner white, painted upon a yellow ground (Fig. 189). Rodenwaldt points out the similarity of many ornamental patterns in Egypt and Crete, namely, the zigzag, rosette, and net. More significant than these is the more complicated design used on the garment of the woman from Hagia Triada which occurs also in Egypt.[53] Both countries imitated textile patterns, but the idea of covering the ceilings with materials that were later imitated in painting can have arisen independently in the two places. On the other hand, the importation of Egyptian textiles into Crete may have caused some borrowing to be done. It is true, however, that the decorative art of Crete is almost entirely free from Egyptian influence. We can only say that whereas in Egypt the papyrus, lotus, and Nymphæa underwent energetic stylization and were rendered in strong colors drawn from nature, these practices were foreign to Crete until a late period.[54]

From the megaron of the later palace at Tiryns comes a floor pattern belonging to the Late Helladic Epoch (Fig. 190). In contrast to the remains from the palace at Mycenæ, it covers the entire floor up to the wall and there are no slabs of stone

---

[51] B.S.A., VI, 38, 54.

[52] G. Rodenwaldt, Mykenische Studien, I, Jahr., 34 (1919), pp. 87-106, Pls. 7-9.

[53] G. Rodenwaldt, Jahr., 34 (1919), pp. 103-104, Figs. 10, 11 (cf. Fig. 76 N). Cf. Sir Arthur Evans, The Palace of Minos, II, 2, pp. 732 ff.

[54] O. Kümmel, Ägyptische und mykenische Pflanzenornamentik, Freiburg, 1901.

to border the design. The pattern around the hearth is lost but the fragments from Mycenæ indicate that it abutted on the hearth, without any design fitted to the circular center. The field, as at Mycenæ, was divided into squares of color—red, yellow, and blue. In alternate red and yellow squares occurred the scale pattern; on the blue fields octopods or dolphins. An idea of this scale ornamentation may be gathered from the floor decoration of the smaller megaron at Tiryns (Fig. 191). On the red fields, the waves and blossoms of the scale pattern were black, the rings white; on the yellow field, the flowers were red. The wave-like pattern in the scale design may denote ground on which the flowers grew. The various squares were separated from one another by simple rosettes with red and blue border lines. The dolphins, which are descended from types found in the Knossian fresco, show strong conventionalization (Fig. 192), and the octopus has little of the beauty which it possessed in Late Minoan I (*cf.* the vase from Gournia, Fig. 165a). But the floor as a whole is extremely decorative and the animals have been conventionalized to that end. They are a greenish-gray color. Other floors with similar decoration were found at Tiryns.

As we survey the field of Mycenæan painting, we see in it little that commends itself as original. In general, the pictorial art shows the decadence and stagnation of Cretan inspiration and achievement. This art, however, just as the Cretan, had a very strong influence on the minor arts, and in ceramics we see the effect of the frieze composition which we have discussed—in vases such as the Warrior Vase from Mycenæ. This and similar works are probably Late Helladic and belong to an Argolid school. The Warrior Vase (Fig. 193) is a large krater decorated in the Mycenæan technique—a brownish varnish on a buff ground. The scene depicted is the departure of warriors for some combat. At the left a woman bids them a mournful farewell. We recognize the type of male figure as a descendant of the hunters on the Tiryns frescoes. At Tiryns, a vase fragment was found which also seems to hark back to the fresco of the hunt (Fig. 194). Two unhelmeted figures with shields and spears advance in front of a horse. Beneath the horse, a running dog is seen. The analogy is not compelling but it is possible to see the origin of such ceramic designs in the earlier frescoes. The vase belongs to the Late Helladic III, the Mycenæan age.

Crete refrained almost to the last from using the human figure as a motive in ceramic decoration, but when northern influence had reached the south and native artistic ability had been exhausted or driven out, we find sporadic examples of the human form conventionalized in geometric fashion. Among instances known are the late vase from Muliana, in Crete (Fig. 196). Cyprus took over some of the mainland motives, notably the women in chariots (Figs. 197-198). These are all Late Helladic, or later. They show the last gasp of Mycenæan art in the Ægean area. We recognize that the women going to the hunt have been adapted from a Tirynthian model. The

krater from Muliana is one of the latest pre-geometric vases and really belongs to
the transitional period between Cretan-Mycenæan painting and the mainland geometric. The style is debased Mycenæan. It dates after 1100 B.C. Iron weapons were
found with the vase. It is probably to be placed in the time of the Dorians. These are
all much later than the Fisherman Vase from Melos (Fig. 195), an almost isolated
example from the third city at Phylakopi.

The great epoch of Cretan power was over in Late Minoan II. The inroads of
foreigners, especially Achæans and Dorians, had put an end to her supremacy by
1200 B.C. Many of the Ægeans were then driven to the neighboring islands and to
the shores of Asia Minor. In conjunction with other peoples on the Asia Minor
shore, this civilization was later to burst forth in the brilliant epoch of Ionian art.
Whatever was left of Cretan love for nature, passion for movement and color, fondness for realism and truth to life, gave its heritage to the Greek world on Ionian
shores and we look in vain for such characteristics in Greece at a later time until
the Hellenistic age. The severity and rigidity of the Dorian successfully tempered
whatever survived on the mainland, and gave us that glorious "restraint" which we
admire so much, but which would not have appealed so strongly to the Cretan.
Perhaps the greatest contribution of Cretan-Mycenæan art to later times was the
feeling for landscape and the sea and a love of nature naturalistically rendered. The
treatment of spatial depth as found in their art may have had its influence on
later times. It is certainly true that the Cretan was well on the road toward space
representation. On the other hand, this kind of pseudo-perspective appears to occur
frequently before the true knowledge requisite for the solution of the problem has
been attained. Added to the things mentioned as essentially Cretan was a pronounced
taste for polychromy. We shall trace these characteristics later in Ionic art.

# V

# GREECE

## THE PRIMITIVES AND THE ARCHAIC SCHOOLS*

IT is no light matter to attempt to write the history of painting in Greece. We shall find ourselves handicapped at every turn, for time has dealt harshly with all that concerns the art in Hellas. In the first place, the monumental painting of ancient Greece is lost for us. The great masterpieces of Apelles, Zeuxis, and Polygnotos have perished down to the smallest fragment.[1] We may as well admit that we cannot reconstitute for ourselves the glory of the works of these famous painters. Their art was great because of the nameless quality which goes into every great work of art—a quality which emanates from the genius of the person who creates it. And though we may gain some idea of how vase-painters treated a subject which they "copied" from the wall-painters of the time, or we may see in the work of journeymen artisans at Pompeii examples of attempted reproductions of ancient masters, we shall know how to value these: they are the products of handicraft, conditioned by the demands of a particular technique or purpose. Although handicraft in ancient Greece, as in the case of the Orient today, was never entirely separated artistically from major works of art, the products of the artisan nevertheless belong on a somewhat lower plane. When they mirror greater paintings, they are but pale reflections of the originals. Most of us have seen artists copying works in galleries and we know what our own reactions usually are in regard to the fidelity of such reproductions: the spirit of the original is missing. No doubt the agony of Zeuxis in regarding the Pompeian "copy" of "Herakles Strangling the Serpents" would have been very great. We need but consider our own feeling in the case of Roman "copies" of Greek originals in sculpture to understand that

* The chapters on Greek painting were completed in 1921 before the appearance of E. Pfuhl's *Malerei und Zeichnung der Griechen*. Since the publication of my book has been unavoidably delayed, I have taken cognizance of Pfuhl's work as far as possible.

[1] A tiny fragment of blue in the Lesché at Delphi can hardly be thought to go back to Polygnotos and that is all we have. *Cf.* Frazer, *Pausanias*, V, p. 357.

a copy can never be an original. The truth is, we must regard the lost as lost and must recognize that we can never recover an original from secondary sources. But what we can call back is some idea of the drawing and at times the composition and color of certain ancient paintings. We can trace the growing power of the artist. We can see his struggle from silhouettes to outline work of significance, which expressed by means of contours the objects of the real world. We can follow his attempt to approach reality by modeling and his labors with rhythm, perspective, light, and shadow. Where we are in greater straits is in the matter of color and composition. We may turn to Etruscan tombs and find there an art following the development of Greek painting in its main outlines and we may consider color and composition there. But it is not really Greek. It can only whet our imagination, rarely satisfy it. Only in the case of a few Etruscan tombs, apparently painted by Greeks, do we escape a certain barbaric element. We may study white-ground vases and observe color effects there, which are often very beautiful, but we are dealing with ceramics and colors that were fired, and it is a far cry from them to the great "four-color" masters. Perhaps our best idea of an ancient Greek painting may be gained from the Alexander Mosaic at Pompeii where we may feel some suggestion of the composition of a great original combined with the four-color scheme of the older school of painting. But here also the effect of the brush-stroke is lost and we find a certain hardness inherent in the technique.

This is not to say that there is no painting left to us from ancient Greece or that we can form no adequate idea of it. There are remains, fragmentary enough often, on stelæ, or grave stones, on votive and funereal tablets of marble and clay; there are tomb- and wall-paintings from Southern Italy and from various Hellenistic sites, and there is a great body of paintings on clay, such as vases and plaques. There are paintings on wood and linen, such as the portraits found in Egypt. What we do mean to say is this: the remnants of Greek painting are relatively meager and few belong to her greatest epoch. The works of the leading masters are entirely lost and we must form any idea we may have of them from the testimony of ancient authors and from secondary sources which imitated them. Only in the case of Greek vases do we have contemporary evidence for the use of the brush and from vases in the main we must form our ideas of Greek drawing and composition. Vase-paintings offer us some of the most beautiful works of art from ancient Greece. But they are filled with the spirit of everyday life, its humor, triviality, and sensuous elements; they lack in part the grand, monumental quality of the major art. Despite the many remains which we possess, we are still unable to visualize as we should like an ancient Greek painting of the period of the Parthenon.

We find ourselves handicapped not only by the loss of material but also by the testimony of writers on painting. The ancient authors, who are our chief sources for

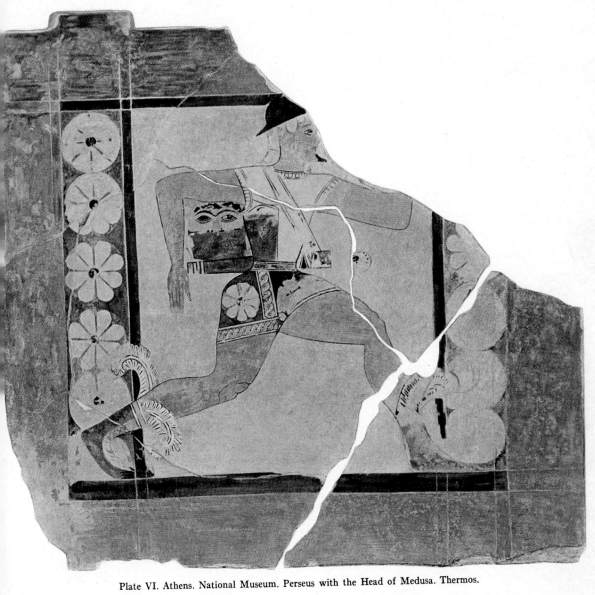

Plate VI. Athens. National Museum. Perseus with the Head of Medusa. Thermos.

Greek painting, do not give us as adequate a view of the art as we should like. In the first place, they are not so ancient as we should like—few of them going back beyond the Third Century. One of the earliest writers on the subject was the philosopher Demokritos. His works, "On Color" and "On Painting," περὶ χροῶν and περὶ ζωγραφίης, are mentioned and quoted by later authors, especially by Theophrastos, the favorite pupil and successor of Aristotle. Demokritos was born in 460 B.C. or a little later, so that his discussions of color probably apply to the painters of the Fifth Century. His work deals largely with the mixing of colors. According to his statements, there were four primitive colors from which the others were obtained by combination, viz.: red, yellow, black, and white. "Thus the tone of gold and bronze is obtained by mixing white and red. . . . If a touch of yellow[1a] is added the tone is very beautiful. . . . A purple tone is made from red, black, and white in this proportion: three parts of red for one of black and two of white. . . . One obtains an indigo color by mixing black and yellow, the black in the larger quantity. Green is composed of yellow and purple.[1a] . . . Black with a touch of blue is a combination of indigo and red.[1a] Yellow mixed with black gives brown"[1a] . . . (Theophrastos, De Sensu et Sensilibus, 13, 76). This is the kind of information which Theophrastos offers us in his book on "Sense Perception and Objects of Sense," quoting constantly from Demokritos. His information on the mixing of colors has led to the conclusion that the colors of the ancients were capable of some 819 changes! In any case, the palette of the artist working with only four colors was not a very limited one.

In the Pseudo-Aristotelian tract "On Color," περὶ χρωμάτων, the modifications to which color is susceptible are studied, together with theories of perception and observation of light. Various combinations of color are examined, their modification by light and shadow, by superposition and juxtaposition. Theories of color-contrast are advanced by Aristotle.[1b] The germ of our modern theory of the optical fusion of colors is found in a treatise by him.[1c] Aristotle and his followers knew that the painter, instead of mixing his colors on the palette, might allow this fusion to take place on the retina, through the juxtaposition of colors seen from a distance. In addition to the works mentioned, we have discussions of the subject by Plato but in no detailed way such as we should like. Plato's ideas about art seem to be closely bound up with morality. His theory of color shows an artist's pleasure in color.

One of our main writers on art, Pliny, often did not understand the authors from

[1a] The Greek word is χλωρόν. R. Schöne, Jahr., VIII (1893), n. 11, shows that χλωρόν is used in Ionic for yellow. The black referred to in the last two lines is κυανοῦν, a blue-black. The red is πυρῶδες, a flame-like red. Indigo here is woad.

[1b] Aristotle, Meteorolog., III, 375a.

[1c] Aristotle, De Sensu et Sensilibus, p. 439b, ll. 19 ff. De Sensu, p. 440a, ll. 7 ff., discusses superposition of color.

whom he drew. His sources were mainly Xenokrates of Sikyon, Douris of Samos, Antigonos of Karystos and Varro. Xenokrates' local patriotism led him to amplify the importance of painting in his native town and to trace the beginnings and significant developments of painting to Sikyon, neglecting somewhat the Ionic school of artists. Douris of Samos was responsible for much of the biographical and anecdotal material in the lives of the painters. At times we are fortunate in having long accounts of paintings such as the description by Pausanias of the works of Polygnotos at Delphi or Lucian's picture of "Calumny" by Apelles, but, in general, we could wish for earlier sources and clearer accounts—a glimpse into Euphranor's work, "On Symmetry," or "On Color"; or that of Melanthios "On Painting." Apelles also wrote several volumes on the theory and practice of painting. Lacking these, we must be grateful to Pliny for the attempt at a connected history of painting which he gives us.

Added to the difficulties which face us in our study of ancient painting as a result of the loss of originals and of works of contemporary criticism, is the fact that time has tended to relegate Greek painting to a subordinate position which it never occupied in antiquity. It is true that the genius of the Greeks was more essentially plastic than pictorial. That painting ranked as high among them as sculpture, if not higher, is, however, to be gathered from ancient authors. The accounts of works by Polygnotos, Zeuxis, and Apelles are far more exhaustive than is the case with the sculptures of Pheidias. Our idea of the relative importance of the two arts is, however, conditioned by the fact that our museums today are well stocked with examples of ancient sculpture, whereas painting has almost perished. We are likely to think of painting, therefore, as occupying a subordinate position in ancient Greece, which was not really the case. In fact, it is possible that it developed earlier than sculpture and played the leading rôle for a time, because the technique is not so laborious as that of the chisel. However, this cannot be proved. It is true that it developed more slowly than sculpture, especially after the Periclean Epoch, and although sculpture had attained its zenith by the end of the Fifth Century, painting was not really in control of its media until the age of Alexander. But that painting in early Greece occupied a leading position and even in the age of Pheidias greatly influenced sculpture is an undoubted fact. The arts must be reckoned as sister arts developing for some time along parallel lines and mutually influencing one another.

If we turn again to Greece in 1100 B.C.—to the point where we left the Mycenæan civilization with the invasion of the Dorians—we shall find a dark age ensuing. It was the period of the migrations, when the Cretans and Mycenæans were being driven from their island and mainland homes to the shores of Asia Minor and when the Dorians were making themselves masters of Greece. There is no mention of painting in the period. The pictures which Homer describes were wrought in metal or woven in garments, the finest of which were of Sidonian workmanship.[2] There were pictures on shields inlaid in metal, carrying on the Dædalid tradition of Crete, illustrated in the dagger blades of Mycenæ,—as the Chest of Kypselos on the mainland, a later descendant of the same technique, carried on the tradition of inlaying in wood. But if we wish to know what was being achieved with the brush, we must turn to the vases of the period. They show us that the rich plant and animal decoration of Cretan days was almost entirely lost, that art had begun to develop along new lines, with geometric patterns, and that the Greek had almost everything to learn when he started on his artistic career. He had as an inheritance the fine black glaze which the Cretan had handed down to him, together with a rich variety of decorative motives. Probably also in architectonic composition the earlier period had left its mark. But various contributions went into the formation of Greek geometric and its beginnings are by no means obvious. It is difficult to consider it a descendant of Pre-Mycenæan geometric, because of its glazed technique and different forms and decoration. On the other hand, it cannot be explained as a continuation of the Mycenæan style with its decadent schematization of living forms.[3] But it drew from both of these styles in shapes, technique, and motives. A latent artistic gift in the native peoples, surviving Mycenæan contributions, contact with new races, and an ability to transform to new ends artistic matter that was available, all contributed toward the making of Greek geometric. We should like to feel that the Dorians furnished the decisive factor in the art, although geometric vases occur in centers where the Dorians did not settle. Even there, however, the migrations were felt and had their influence. Further, geometric patterns were found all over the Mediterranean at the end of the Cretan period, of a simple type known as Proto-Geometric, dating from the Twelfth to the Tenth Century B.C. The artist made use of circles, zigzag lines, triangles, and the like. But the essence of the later style was northern, as a comparison with the pottery of the Balkan region and that of Central Europe

[2] Homer, *Iliad*, III, 125; VI, 289 ff. The ἐνώπια παμφανόωντα, "gleaming walls," were probably so described because they were plastered smooth and reflected the light. *Cf. Iliad*, VIII, 435 (Leaf). Leaf, *Iliad*, XXIII, 743, notes that the distinction between Sidonians as craftsmen and the Phœnicians as traders, is always observed in Homer. I owe the reference to Miss Milne.

[3] A. von Salis, *Die Kunst der Griechen*, pp. 17 ff., considers the Mycenæan Epoch a time of orientation and preparation; an age when discipline in art took the place of Cretan unrestraint—which seems to him to amount almost to anarchy. *Cf.* B. Schweitzer, *Untersuchungen zur Chronologie und Geschichte der geometrischen Stile in Griechenland*, I, Heidelberg. Diss. Karlsruhe, 1918; *Ath. Mitth.*, 43 (1918), pp. 1-188, II, for dating and development of styles in geometric art. E. Buschor, *Griechische Vasenmalerei²*, München, 1914, tr. by G. C. Richards, *Greek Vase-Painting*, New York, 1922. For a recent discussion of the geometric style, *cf.* Gisela Weyde, "Probleme des griech. geometrischen Stils," *Œster. Jahr.*, XXIII (1926), pp. 16 ff.

proves. Without the primitive style which the Dorians brought with them and without the impetus which their coming gave, the style could hardly have arisen. The soil from which the art developed was prepared for its coming and contributed its share along with the Orient, but to our thought the Dorians, with the rude style which they brought from the North, were essential. Many scholars believe that in Greek geometric art a native peasant style came to full fruition after the suppression of Mycenæan culture.[4] Even if we should admit this, which we are not prepared to do, we should be obliged to recognize the important part which the invading northerners played in its inception: without their appearance there would have been no Greek geometric as we know it. Out of the decadent and the primitive a new people caused a new style to grow.

The geometric artist took the simple material for decoration which he found at hand and created from it a rich system. It was a system which especially made use of straight lines and reduced the human figure to a kind of geometrical formula. The human torso was an inverted triangle and the chest was therefore seen from the front. In the head, which was treated as a silhouette in profile, a small space was reserved at times for the eye. The limbs as well as the head were rendered in profile. The figure was nude—the nudity of primitive art. In this, clothes were not an essential element and they hampered the clarity of the design.[5] It was not the real appearance of a man that was sought for and arrived at, but the idea of a man, based upon a "memory picture." The ornamentation was simple, consisting especially of the meander, triangle, checker, zigzag, rows of dots, swastika, cross, star, and circle. These were woven into a design that covered practically the entire vase in combination with friezes of human and animal figures (Fig. 199). Most of the human forms were parallel; bodies were elongated, the poses were stiff and movement awkward. The artist desired to leave no open spaces. He painted a bird and rosettes under the bodies of the horses depicted, or he filled in the space with zigzags. The finished product is reminiscent of textile work, but, though some of the patterns may have been derived from that source, it is quite an independent development.

Although the means employed to express the idea, "man"—a crude, black, opaque silhouette—seem extremely primitive and far removed from nature, it is necessary to remember that the artist was not seeking to copy nature. The formal element and the decorative end which he sought were the things which interested him most. We must grant that he had a genius for decoration. He cleverly adapts his main design to a frieze, the center of which may be heightened into a broad panel to give the

[4] F. Poulsen, *Die Dipylongräber und die Dipylonvasen*, Leipzig, 1905, p. 68; S. Wide, *Ath. Mitth.*, XXI (1896), p. 408; G. Richter, *A.J.A.*, XIX (1915), p. 391. New light on the evolution of the geometric style is promised from Crete, *J.H.S.*, 47 (1927), p. 245.

[5] E. Buschor, *op. cit.*, p. 32.

proper amount of space and the required emphasis to his composition. Here and there balanced metope-like sections fill in the corners with ornamental patterns. Certain centers such as Athens employed a system of decoration in three zones combined with the use of metopes, thus achieving a very striking decorative effect. This is attained mainly by the repetition of similar shapes which produce a certain rhythm and which form solid masses satisfactorily spaced over the background. These vases are the first artistic expression of the Greek painter and we recognize in them a strong feeling for design and an intense interest in things human. The art is essentially abstract, reducing its elements to the simplest schemes possible, and discarding all nonessentials. To make his meaning clear, the artist sometimes presents things which the eye could not have seen, in a kind of x-ray fashion, such as the dead man under the cover of his funeral couch.

The various examples of geometric art discussed above are known as "Dipylon" ware, or Athenian geometric. They were termed "Dipylon" from the double gateway at Athens where they were found. They served as funeral monuments and the paintings on them are usually, as here, connected with the honors paid to the dead. They depict mourning scenes, the dead laid out on the funeral bier, the chariot games in his honor, and similar subjects. Some few present fighting on shipboard and naval scenes. Occasionally mythological themes may be illustrated. This ware was essentially Athenian, but geometric pottery is found all over Greece and the Ægean, only it developed in different ways on different sites, growing out of the simpler and often clumsier Proto-Geometric ware, which followed closely upon the Mycenæan. This phenomenon emphasizes the isolation of the various small city-states which we know were quite independent of one another. The excellence and differences in the wares seem to depend upon the gift of the people who created them and upon their ability to take over new artistic elements. Outside contacts also played their rôle. Bœotian geometric, for example, showed a fondness for the πότνια θηρῶν type (Fig. 200). Here we see the mistress of the wild things represented—Queen of the earth with her lions, of the air as shown by the birds, and of the sea. The representation of the figure of the goddess in front view is quite distinctive and though angular lines are common, there is more of an attempt to make use of the curvilinear. The motive of the goddess between lions reveals connections with the East where this scheme was native. It is, in all probability, Hittite. Poulsen has gathered together the eastern motives occurring in geometric art and shows that "even in her darkest hour Greece was not without light from the Orient."[6] The greater use of curved lines and greater freedom in drawing appear to advantage in the Bœotian bowl of Figure 201, where the flying bird is less angularly rendered than in Dipylon vases (cf. Figs.

[6] F. Poulsen, *Der Orient und die frühgriechische Kunst*, Leipzig, 1912, p. 116, cf. pp. 108 ff.

250-251). The polychrome effect produced by the band of rosettes heightens the charm of this work. Although the examples cited may seem primitive because of the limited means which the artist employs and the simplicity of his expression, the important thing is that with this abstract linear style the artist has expressed not a little emotion and has aroused pleasure with his designs. The art gives promise of greater things to come.

While geometric wares were declining on various Greek sites, schools of painting were growing up in the Seventh and Sixth Centuries—under eastern impetus— e.g., at Corinth and the neighboring Sikyon, and in the East in Ionia. We can best judge of the achievement of these centers by an examination of their minor works of art, inasmuch as only these are left to us, together with literary traditions regarding the origin and development of their painting. Sikyon, an early center of painting in Greece, was probably the home of the so-called Proto-Corinthian class of wares, a group of miniature vases only a few inches high, decorated with three or four zones of ornament. Often the vases had plastic heads such as the lion of Oriental type on the Macmillan lekythos in the British Museum. Scenes of combat are commonly found and legends such as the Judgment of Paris or Herakles in combat with centaurs. These vases are masterpieces of their kind (Pl. VII*a-e*). Some examples date as early as the Eighth Century. They reveal the influence of metal prototypes. As Sikyon was a center to which Cretan artists migrated and which contained a flourishing metal industry, these facts, together with the alphabet, have led scholars to place the home of the ware in Sikyon. The earliest specimens were decorated in geometric fashion. Many were flat-bottomed jugs (Pl. VII*d*). Most of the vases were found in Argos and Ægina. They were distributed by Corinth and influenced the Corinthian style, which finally drove them from the market. Our examples show epic battle scenes (Pl. VII*a, e*), riders, hunting scenes, Bellerophon slaying the Chimæra (Pl. VII*b*), and Oriental animals. The colors are the cream of the ground, dark brown and reddish purple. Payne believes these vases were made in Corinth.

Since Corinth was a commercial center closely in contact with the East we should expect an artistic awakening there at an early date. We shall find that the city was credited with being the original home of painting in Greece. The character of this early painting may be seen, as far as we can judge of it, from vases and from painted terra cotta plaques and metopes. The earlier Corinthian vases reveal close contact with the East, especially in the tapestry-like patterns that cover the field. The ground, which is a creamy or greenish white, was strewn with black rosettes, the details of which were put in by means of incision. The figure patterns consisted of bands of animals following one another in procession, especially the curious hybrid types that were native in the East (*cf.* Figs. 202*a* and *c*). We find many panthers with faces in front view, lions,—often heraldically posed—sirens, sphinxes, antelopes,

*a*. London. British Museum.
Macmillan lekythos. Warriors. Hunt.

*c*. Boston. Museum. Hybrid lion;
warrior, panther, winged male figure.

*d*. Naples. Museum.
⸱-bottomed lekythos. Stag.

*b*. Boston. Museum.
Bellerophon slaying the Chimæra. Sphinxes.

*e*. Berlin. Lekythos.
Fighting warriors; chariot-race; hunt.

*f*. Paris. Cabinet des Médailles.
Chalkidian amphora. Herakles and Geryon.

Plate VII. Proto-Corinthian, Chalkidian, and Laconian Pottery.

*g*. Paris. Cabinet des Médailles.
Arkesilas cup. Weighing silphium.

boars, and horsemen. The details were incised with a sharp, pointed instrument, and, added to the creamy ground of the vase and the brown or black silhouettes of the figures was a rich use of reddish purple and white. But the main interest in this class of vases lies in the designs and in the treasure-house of patterns borrowed from the East. The work is essentially "Orientalizing."

Gradually, with time and with the development of artistic power, the Corinthian began to renounce these tapestry-like fields of decoration, to relegate the various animals to the shoulder of the vase or to a lower frieze and to reduce his strewn ornaments to a minimum. He became more interested in frieze decoration employing human figures. We, in turn, feel a conflict between the demands for decorating a vase and joy in a picture *per se*. Examples of the transitional type are seen in vases such as the Boston skyphos where the favorite Greek motive of two warriors heraldically grouped in combat is flanked by the old eastern pattern of the sirens (Fig. 202*b*). Here, we have a black-figured style in its beginnings. Incision is employed for details on the black silhouette. Red, however, is often used for the faces by preference.

By the Sixth Century, the Corinthian school was emancipated from purely decorative friezes of animals and strewn ornaments, and had developed an elaborate genre style in which human beings played the essential rôle. Usually, the subjects illustrated were mythological but the art was borrowed from everyday life. The vase-painter had learned more about drawing the human figure, so that we are not reminded at every turn of the primitive triangle which formed the basis of his work. This advance probably took place under the influence of the major art. An example of this development is evident in Figure 203, where the band of animals is placed on the surface of the lip and a line of galloping horsemen occurs below the principal frieze with rays above the foot. The main subject pictured is that of Herakles banqueting at the house of Eurytios. The composition has grown more ambitious than was the case in earlier examples, the drawing more skilful. Human figures recline at ease or move about with grace. The figure of Iole, the standing woman in the upper frieze at the right, has a great deal of archaic charm due to a certain freedom of pose and movement. Homely details, such as the cutting up of meat for the banquet and the dog tied under the couch, remind us of similar scenes in Etruscan painting. There may be some truth in the legend that Demaratos, the father of Tarquin, was driven from Corinth by the tyrant Kypselos and fled to Etruria, accompanied by Corinthian artists.[7] On the reverse of the same vase occurs the motive of heraldic pairs and groups of fighting warriors. Most dramatic is the design under

---

[7] Pliny, *N.H.*, 35, 16; *cf.* Cornelius Nepos, Fr. 35 (Halm); Cic., *De Rep.*, II, 19, 34; Tacitus, *Ann.*, XI, 14; Dionysios of Hal., *Ant. Rom.*, III, 46; Strabo, V, 219 f.; P. N. Ure, *The Origin of Tyranny*, Cambridge, 1922, pp. 239 ff.

one handle of the death of Ajax who has just committed suicide by falling on his sword (Fig. 204). Odysseus and Diomede stand awestruck at the deed. The artist has made of these figures a clever pyramidal group with the aid of the crossed spears, filling in the space at the bottom of the triangle with Ajax "on all fours." The design arouses a certain amount of amusement because of its naïveté. So also does the attempt to represent intense feeling by means of the stiffly posed figures who stand woodenly regarding the dead warrior. Emotion is suggested only in the attitudes and the raised hand of Diomede. But we cannot deny that the artist has conveyed his sincere impression of a very tragic event that deserves our sympathy. It is this great laboring with simple means which charms us so much in Greek archaic art—the efforts of an artist struggling more and more toward expression. From the technical point of view, the reserving of the white dog and the head of Iole against the unpainted ground of the vase is interesting; they are rendered in outline. There is a generous use of white and of purple for added details. The faces of the men are red, their bodies black.

These vases from Corinth show contact with the East and patterns derived from that source, together with a growing power to combine human forms into significant compositions. There is vastly greater freedom in drawing and truth to nature than we find in Dipylon ware. How very pictorial the designs often become may be seen from the Amphiaraos krater in Berlin which seems to have drawn its subject matter from the cedar chest of Kypselos, and to have imitated in color the technique of inlaying in gold and ivory.[8]

More evidence for the achievement of Greek painting in the Sixth Century than is obtainable from Corinthian vases alone, may be derived from a series of votive plaques in terra cotta which were excavated at Penteskouphia near Acrocorinth. They date in the Seventh and Sixth Centuries B.C. and though small in character and ceramic works by artisans, they are, however, drawn on flat surfaces, and thus are often better able to give us an idea of the major art than vases. In Figure 205 we see a number of these plaques ranging from four to six centimeters up to 0.20 meter to 0.30 meter. Many are perforated with small holes indicating that they were intended to be hung up in a sacred grove or *temenos*. Most of them have representations in black silhouette of Poseidon, whose favor was very dear to the Corinthian trader. Sometimes the god appears brandishing his trident or riding on a horse. Often he is seen in a chariot with Amphitrite. The striking thing to be observed in technique is that we find opaque black silhouettes without inner details, outline drawings with the brush and the regular Corinthian style found on vases,

---

[8] F.R., *Gr. Vas.*, Pl. 121; Paus., V, 17, 5—19, 10. *Cf.* H. Stuart Jones, *J.H.S.*, 14 (1894), 30 ff.; W. von Massow, *Die Kypseloslade, Ath. Mitth.*, 41 (1916), pp. 1-117. A. Furtwängler, *Meisterwerke der Griechischen Plastik*, Leipzig, 1893, pp. 723 ff.

consisting of incised details and added red (Fig. 206). Women's heads are almost always reserved in the creamy ground-color of the clay. The colors added for details are a rich, dark red and white. Many of the scenes are genre scenes depicting the trades pursued by the dedicators. Especially frequent are representations connected with the potter's trade, a thriving industry at Corinth. Sometimes we see plaques which picture a ship with vases hung up in it, an offering to the god to propitiate his favor in a commercial venture. Inscriptions found read: "Give us a happy voyage"; "We arrived from the Piræus." Representations of the potter's oven and wheel and of mines and vineyards occur. Summary indications of landscape are commonly found. The culmination of achievement in these plaques is seen in a work in Berlin, signed by the painter, Timonidas (Fig. 206, center). The plaque is painted on both sides. The subject presented on the obverse is a hunter with his dog. The pinax is practically entirely outline work, with the muscles finely indicated as in the stele of Aristion in Athens and with the use of a dilute wash in the rendering of the dog. In the broad, massive appearance of the figure, we have a new conception of the human body. There is little development in color shown. Dark red is used for the garment of the hunter while the arms and legs are outlined in yellow and reserved in the color of the clay. The dog looking up at his master is bright yellow with red spots on the shoulder and hind leg. The motive employed reminds us of the Alxenor relief.

These plaques for the most part show a renunciation of ornaments strewn over the field and a turning away from ornamental to pictorial composition. Far more than vases they reveal a joy in landscape and genre scenes. In spite of a slight suggestion that the artist is interested in spatial problems, the painting remains entirely flat. Nor is coloring developed to any extent: the opaque silhouette is employed very extensively. Sexes are usually distinguished by color, the heads of women being reserved in the ground-color of the clay while those of men are red or black. Red retouches are frequent for details, and violet also appears. These pinakes give us an intimate view of life in Corinth in the days of King Periander. The temple housecleaning which gave us these small vignettes was a very happy thing.

Even more important than these plaques for completing our notions of ancient Greek painting in the Sixth Century, and especially Corinthian painting, are some painted metopes from a temple of Apollo at Thermos in Ætolia. Art on this site was strongly influenced by Corinth and although the paintings extant are fictile works and, as such, used only colors that could be fired, we are perhaps nearer to monumental painting here than with any other primitive paintings in Greece. It is probable that the metope decoration of a temple possessed an artistic importance greater than that belonging to a Greek vase, though it will readily be seen that all fictile work is closely related and many assign the tablets and vases to the same artists. Certainly Timonidas made both, as we have a signed vase from his hand.

The plan and the date of the temple to which these painted metopes belonged have recently been determined. Beneath the remains of a temple of the Third Century are the foundations and ruins of a very early structure which Koch would date in the Seventh Century B.C.[9] To this temple he would assign the oldest metopes in question, which are the work of Corinthian masters. To the oldest period belong also the fragments of the lateral *simæ* with openings in the center of each slab, masked alternately by the heads of lions and of men. These were used as water-spouts. Between every two of these slabs were rectangular ones against which were set female heads of "Dædalid" type, with "pearl locks" and "layer wigs" (*Ant. Denk.*, II, Pl. 53 A, 1, 2). The later antefixes dating after 550 B.C. also ended in gaily painted heads modeled from clay. Such objects as these, Pliny tells us, were originally made at Corinth by Boutades, who invented modeling.[10] The later water-spouts were moulded heads of satyrs or of men, with beards and mustaches. Between every two of these slabs were female heads of Nesiote type wearing the *polos* or high crown (Fig. 207). The colors employed in the early antefixes were red, black, and white. The later examples show various shades of red, from crimson to orange.

The date of the metopes has been much debated. Probably Koch is correct in considering that the oldest belonged to a temple dating from the end of the Seventh Century B.C.[9] Other writers such as Hauser would date some of the paintings as late as 550 B.C.,[11] comparing the drapery on them with that on a vase by Exekias[12] (Fig. 235). Koch uses the satyr head on the same vase to prove that the later class of antefixes dates between 540 and 530 B.C., but points out that the larger metopes show an intimate relation with the *older* group of terra cotta heads in technique and in stylistic resemblances. First of all, the metopes are large, heavy plaques of coarse, reddish clay, not covered with the rather thick, second layer of better clay employed in the later class, but merely washed over with a clay wash and then covered with a paper-thin yellowish-white slip which has often peeled off. From the point of view of

[9] H. Koch, "Zu den Metopen von Thermos," *Ath. Mitth.*, 39 (1914), pp. 237-255, Pls. XIII-XV; *Röm. Mitth.*, 30 (1915), pp. 51-74.

[10] Pliny, *N.H.*, 35, 151-152.

[11] F. Hauser, *Griech. Vas.*, III, 68. Sixth Century, G. Sotiriades, *Ant. Denk.*, II, Pls. 49-53A, Text, p. 4; *Eph. Arch.* (1900), pp. 161-212; (1903), pp. 71-96. *Cf.* Rhomaios, *Arch. Delt.*, I (1915), pp. 225-279. Four stages were represented in this temple: "(1) a temple without a peristyle; (2) a temple with an elliptical peristyle; (3) a temple decorated with metopes and with a rectangular peristyle; (4) the temple of the classical period with stone columns and stone stylobate." *Cf.* E. Douglas Van Buren, *Greek Fictile Revetments in the Archaic Period*, London, 1926, pp. 64 ff. The quotation is from this work. H. G. G. Payne, *B.S.A.*, XXVII (1925-1926), pp. 124-132, argues for a date between 650 and 630 B.C. for the earlier metopes on the basis of the similarity of their style to Proto-Corinthian and early Corinthian vases.

[12] F. Hauser, *Griech. Vas.*, Pl. 131.

style, several things mark the painting of the larger metopes as archaic: the beard worn without a mustache, the proportions of the figures with their wasp-like waists, broad shoulders, and long legs; the shape of the skull and the treatment of hair about the forehead; the patterns on the garments; the lack of folds in drapery; the tendency to one-figure composition or to the use of fabulous animals in panels. The later class of smaller panels were apparently local imitations of Corinthian work.

The metopes were painted for the most part with mythological scenes (Fig. 208). Against the yellow wash of the ground, the designs were set off in color. The flesh of men was usually an orange red; white was used for women, black for hair, beards, and eyebrows. Purplish red was employed for garments and details. We have thus a modified three-color scheme—black, red, and white, combined with orange. Pure yellow is not yet used, but a kind of orange appears for the flesh of men.

The subjects depicted are varied in character: a Gorgon, the Chelidon myth, seated deities, the Perseus myth, a hunter bearing home his game, and Typhon (?). One metope represented Perseus wearing a cap, winged boots, and a short, close-fitting tunic embroidered with rosettes and a guilloche pattern (Pl. VI). Under his arm he carries the head of Medusa. He strides rapidly to the right, with such freedom that his right leg overlaps the rosette pattern of the border. The colors used are those found on all of the metopes from this temple: red, black, and white, with orange for the silhouette.

Probably the best example of painting from the temple is a metope depicting a hunter, returning home with game (Fig. 209). The figure is about twenty-three inches high. He wears a short, tight-fitting tunic, the upper part of which is half red, half creamy white reserved in the color of the ground, with decorative patterns in red, white, and black. The lower part is divided by ornamental bands into red and black divisions decorated with rosettes and finished with an archaic border. The colors which are used throughout are again red and black, against a creamy yellow ground, with orange for the silhouette. The figure is the thin-waisted Cretan type and recalls Dædalid sculptures such as the bronze relief of the hunters in the Louvre. The design is well composed, with a certain archaic nicety of balance. The composition, in fact, reminds one of the Sicilian metope of Herakles and the Kerkopes. One of the most interesting things about the painting is the monochrome silhouette in orange red—outlined with black—for the figure of the hunter. No minor details are indicated and there are no incised lines. The wild boar on one end of the pole is painted black; the stag at the other end, reserved in the ground-color. The weight of the game would seem to indicate that the hunter is Herakles.[12a] Probably these paintings are as typical as anything that we shall find for the early primitives of Greece

[12a] Cf. H. G. G. Payne, op. cit., p. 128. He argues that a local hero, not Herakles, is portrayed, because his hair is long. He considers the three divinities, goddesses, p. 126.

during the Sixth Century. It is very likely that most of the painting of this age was on clay. Already we have a genuine polychromy.

Prominent among other subjects depicted was a representation of three divinities, perhaps Apollo, Artemis, and Leto[12a] (Fig. 208). They are seated on a throne decorated with a frieze of gryphons and are much later in date, owing perhaps to a repainting. They may originally have dated from the earliest period. The metope is different in size from the others but this change may have occurred when it was re-used. The rosette decoration seems to indicate that it belonged to the same building as the other metopes, but was used again later. The background is a yellow-white and against this the three deities, garbed in richly embroidered garments of purplish red, white, and black, were painted. This metope, like the others, was bordered on either side by cream rosettes against a field of red. On another panel was a Gorgon head in red, black, and the yellowish white of the ground, with a huge tongue hanging out between two rows of enormous teeth. A design with two people talking and an inscription at the right, may be a representation of the myth of Itys. It is very archaic, the shape of the heads reminding one of certain bronzes of Dædalid type.

The Corinthian school of fictile art may therefore be said to exhibit several phases of decoration: the orientalizing, tapestry-like phase seen in vases, in which the patterns were purely decorative; a second phase, when designs became more pictorial and the figure compositions show a certain feeling for style. In this period sexes were distinguished, the flesh of women being usually painted white. The plaques of the third type exhibit opaque silhouettes and outline drawings and reveal a fondness for landscape elements and genre subjects. Details are often added in red. A more monumental type is represented by the Thermos metopes, in which orange red silhouettes outlined in black are found combined with a genuine polychromy. In color, the scale of the later "four-color" painters is not yet attained, pure yellow not being found. Compositions are simple but well handled and show a certain archaic precision that extends to minute details. The last two classes tell us most about the major art. Such was Corinthian painting in the days of the Kypselids. At this time, Corinthian wares penetrated to all markets—Italy, Sicily, and Ionia in particular. A study of Corinthian pottery is being prepared by Payne, *Necrocorinthia*.

Closely connected with Corinth, and, like her, one of the great trading centers of Greece was the city of Chalkis in Eubœa. Her pottery is not uninfluenced by the East. On the basis of the development in drapery and of inscriptions found, Rumpf has assigned the earliest vases to 550 B.C., the latest to 510 B.C.[12b] They belong to a relatively short period of time and show no prehistory nor any great development. As

[12b] Andreas Rumpf, *Chalkidische Vasen*, Berlin, 1927, esp. pp. 139; 134 ff.; *cf.* Pls. VI-IX for our example; *cf.* J. D. Beazley, in *Gnomon*, IV (1928), pp. 329-332. E. Buschor, F.R., III, p. 215, Pl. 152, dates the earliest vases *ca.* 570 B.C.

a typical example we may choose the amphora in the Cabinet des Médailles in Paris, which depicts Herakles in battle with Geryon (Pl. VII*f*). At the left the cattle of Geryon are nicely differentiated by the use of white and of purplish red. Athena holds the center of the scene with her close-fitting garment of purple and black, and her writhing, snaky ægis. She is giving her support to the hero Herakles who vigorously attacks his triple-headed, six-armed opponent. The bodies of Eurytios, the herdsman, and of his dog are trampled on by the combatants. Geryon's eastern affinities are evident in his "sickle" wings, and the garment and figure of Athena also have an Ionian look. The lotus buds—or perhaps they are even rosebuds— form an attractive border below the main design. The remaining decoration on the vase pictures a charioteer in a quadriga with the horses' heads neatly turned in profile because of the technical difficulties in drawing the front view and for the sake of pattern. The flying bird is reminiscent of Corinth. Other vases of this class which Rumpf has gathered together,—some 279 in number, including fragments—show varied subject matter. Many vases are decorated with eastern animals, often heraldically posed on either side of a palmette ornament with lotus buds. The cock is commonly found. There are many vases with ribald satyrs and mænads, others with riders, battle scenes and mythological representations. These vases carry on the Corinthian tradition where it breaks off, just as the Corinthian wares supplanted the Proto-Corinthian. The scene on our vase—the fight of Herakles with Geryon—was an old Corinthian theme, treated on the famous chest of the tyrant Kypselos.

Rumpf has added to the Chalkidian class the fabrics from the workshop of the Phineus Master, earlier held to come from one of the Cycladic Islands (*cf.* Fig. 215). They show a predilection for fat satyrs pursuing mænads. He has also pointed out the very strong Corinthian influence on Chalkidian vases and has shown that Ionian influence on this class has been overestimated, though perhaps not so much as he implies.

On other sites in Greece, such as Argos, the old traditions of the Mycenæan school lingered on in the Seventh and Sixth Centuries B.C. This school had renounced in favor of human figures the vegetable and animal forms held so suitable for vase-decoration by the Cretan. Traces of Mycenæan influence are evident in vases such as the Seventh Century krater of Aristonothos, from Cære (Fig. 210). The connection of this vase with the Warrior Vase from Mycenæ is easily recognizable from its shape and from the geometric schematization of its figures. The krater records epic material—a naval battle and the legend of Odysseus blinding Polyphemos. But the art is quite different in character from the Dipylon ware of the Eighth Century and shows no relation to centers like Corinth. Like the Warrior Vase, it made use of outlines for heads and in its schematization did not reduce its forms to a rigid rectilinear system.

While the Corinthian school of painting was emancipating itself from purely decorative friezes of tapestry-like patterns and becoming more truly pictorial, on the shores of Asia Minor and the neighboring islands another school was developing which is usually termed "Ionic." We should naturally expect that the people of this region, as the direct heirs of Cretan-Mycenæan civilization, would have a bent for painting and we should expect this painting to be of a certain character, knowing what we do of the creations of Ægean art. We should expect polychromy, fondness for action, a feeling for landscape, and certain motives surviving that were essentially native to the Mediterranean basin. Let us see what we find.

The Cretans and Mycenæans, crowded out of their footholds in the islands and on the mainland, in conjunction with native peoples on the shores of Asia Minor, created in the Seventh and Sixth Centuries B.C. a brilliant civilization which combined extensively Ægean and Oriental elements. Wherever this particular combination occurs, we shall call it "Ionic." Its characteristic marks are chiefly a creamy slip for the ground to be decorated; figures represented partly in outline, reserved spaces and Oriental motives. The centers of this culture were Miletos, Ephesos, Kolophon, Priene, Klazomenai, Phocæa, and neighboring sites (see Map, Plate XVI). In these cities a group of eminent philosophers grew up; here were created great works of poetry, of architecture and sculpture. We should naturally expect painting to play a rôle as well, and we find literary traditions showing that this was the case. We also discover minor works of art, which reflect after a fashion the heights achieved. Not only was the coast of Asia Minor an important center of this civilization, but the culture was widely spread wherever Ionian traders coasted or Ionic colonists founded new centers for the mother country. The common marks of this culture will therefore be observed in the islands, especially at Rhodes and Melos; in Cyrene in northern Africa and at Naukratis in Egypt; on the shores of the Black Sea and as far afield as Cære in southern Italy.[12c]

We are enabled to trace this civilization over the wide area which it covered by means of painted vases. To this Ionic class belong, *e.g.*, the Rhodian vases of Class A, which were probably exported from Miletos. Like the Corinthian class, with which they have no connection, they borrowed the animal friezes of the Orient and used them in tapestry-like patterns, but without incision (Fig. 211). They also frequently made use of heraldic groups. These devices, as well as the employment of the guilloche and lotus bud, prove close contact with the East. The colors used were crimson red, black, and the creamy white of the background. The heads of animals were usually left in outline, in contrast to those of Corinth, which were opaque sil-

[12c] On the range of this culture, see E. R. Price, *East Greek Pottery* (*Classification des céramiques antiques*, Union académique internationale, Paris, 1928). Miss Price distinguishes eleven classes of wares.

houettes. Not only do we find vases with purely ornamental patterns but also a class of plates with figure decoration. These exhibit a well developed style, showing a fondness for balanced designs. Representative of this class is the Euphorbos pinax in London (Fig. 212). It is interesting to compare the composition here with the Ajax group from the Corinthian vase discussed. On the Rhodian vase, stop-gap ornaments still abound and distinctly Ionic elements occur, such as the guilloche and the "Ionic eyes" for warding off evil. The colors are red, reddish-brown, yellowish-white, and black. Other plaques show an arrangement in metopes which frame heads of birds and animals and which are separated from one another by triglyphs. In general, bands of animals—goats, gryphons, sphinxes, and birds—form the subject matter of the paintings. A later class, B, influenced by Corinth, shows incision.

The achievement of the Seventh Century Ionic painter is well illustrated by a "Melian" vase picturing Apollo, Artemis, and two maidens (Fig. 213). Here we see a conventionalized goose frieze at the top, together with stop-gap ornaments which are sown over the entire field. The main frieze is a procession honoring the chief deities of Delos. The horses which draw the chariot of Apollo bear distinct traces of geometric conventionalization and are of the "Corinthian" type. We feel the primitive artist's intense desire to omit no detail which might make the scene clear. The heads of the quadriga are therefore given in outline—four heads and three manes. The bodies of the rear horses are outlined against the silhouette of the foremost horse. The early artist of geometric days begins with a seeming inability to observe anything as it appears in nature—everything is convention; his followers see everything and often fall into minute details while attempting to sift their material. The painter of the "Melian" vase is given to *minutiæ* but he does not let them overshadow his main theme—the glorification of the Delian cult. At the right, Artemis appears— a variant of the "Persian" type—with a stag in her hand. Her features show the large nose, eye, and chin of primitive art.[13] She advances to meet a chariot drawn by winged horses, in which Apollo and the Hyperborean maidens are approaching. The coloring is very vivid; the ground is a creamy white, the figure of Apollo a golden brown; garments, purplish red, black, and white. The women's heads are outlined in brown against the light-colored clay. We feel in the painting the pride of the trailing-robed Ionians in their island cult. It brought together Ionians from all over the world to celebrate the festival of the god.[14] No doubt there were larger paintings on

[13] W. Deonna, *L'Archéologie*, II, 1912, p. 173.
[14] E. Buschor, *op. cit.*, p. 55 (tr. by G. C. Richards, New York). The vase might perhaps more properly be called Delian-Melian, since numberless small vases of this style come from Delos-Rheneia. J. H. Hopkinson and J. Baker-Penoyre, *J.H.S.*, 22 (1902), pp. 46 ff. Excavations at Rheneia have revealed fragments of many vases which formed a part of the contents of graves brought over to Rheneia at the purification of Delos in 426-425 B.C. (*cf.*

clay panels in the Seventh Century not unlike the cult scene depicted here—expressing with simple means the dignity of a religion which attracted the island peoples to the Delian shrine. These "Melian" vases appear to have been made in the island of Delos.[14]

The Busiris vase from Cære also shows interesting Ionic elements (Fig. 214). It depicts Herakles' arrival at the court of the wicked King Busiris and his subjection of the Egyptians. The vase is very gay in color, the figures being placed directly against the yellowish ground of the clay. Herakles is painted a deep red, the six Egyptians are mulattoes and there is a plentiful use of black, white, red, and yellow in rhythmic arrangement over the surface of the vase. In addition to the striking polychromy of the vase, we are impressed by the humor of the scene in which Herakles makes away with six enemies "at one fell swoop"; by the skill of the painter in the delineation of types, such as the negro and the Egyptian; by the vivid action which fills the scenes—all "Ionic" qualities. Above the gaily colored palmettes are naturalistic myrtle branches (Fig. 257). The vase was probably made by a wandering Ionian, perhaps in Phocæa or Samos or northern Africa. In all probability it was not made in Cære.[15] Certain vases of this class are related in style to the sculptures of the column drum of the archaic temple of Artemis at Ephesos (*Ant. Denk.*, II, Pl. 28). They date therefore about 550 B.C. They derive their name from ancient Cære in Italy where they were found. Our example shows Herakles' revenge on the murderous Egyptian king who slew all foreigners visiting his shores. Incision is used in these vases even for outlines. The preference for color is quite pronounced. The bodies and the hair of the various figures are black, yellow, or red. White is put on over a wash. Various motives on the vase hark back to ancient Egyptian art; for example, Herakles slaying Busiris is a reminiscence of the ancient Pharaohs trampling on their enemies.[15a]

Another series of vases belonging to the Orientalizing group is a class earlier termed "Cyrenaic" but now generally known as "Laconian."[15b] At the shrine of Artemis Orthia in Sparta a temple "dump" revealed a chronological series of these vases dating from their origin in the Seventh Century through the development and

Thucyd., 3, 104). See F. Poulsen, C. Dugas, "Vases archaïques de Délos," *B.C.H.*, 35 (1911), pp. 350-422.

[15] Phocæa, F. Dümmler, *Röm. Mitth.*, III (1888), p. 179; Asia Minor coast, E. Pottier, *B.C.H.*, XVI (1892), pp. 260 ff.; Phocæa, *Cat.*, II, 534 ff.; Samos, F. Winter, *Jahr.*, XV (1900), p. 88; North Africa, G. Karo, *B.P.W.*, XX (1900), p. 368.

[15a] F. Matz, *Arch. Anz.*, 36 (1921), pp. 11 ff.; W. Wrede, *Arch. Anz.*, 38-39 (1923-1924), pp. 11 ff. Beazley was the first to call attention to these similarities, *J.H.S.*, 30 (1910), p. 52.

[15b] J. P. Droop, *The Dates of the Vases called 'Cyrenaic,'* *J.H.S.*, 30 (1910), pp. 1 ff. *Cf.* C. Dugas and R. Laurent, *Rev. arch.*, 9 (1907), p. 377; *Rev. arch.*, 10 (1907), pp. 36 ff.; C. Dugas, 20 (1912), pp. 88 ff.

decline of the ware in the Sixth and Fifth Centuries. In the earlier stages of this style, the vases, as is usual in the Ionic Class, were covered with a white slip but near the end this is given up. One of the most famous Cyrenaic vases is the Arkesilas kylix (Pl. VII*g*). In its subject matter it points to Egypt, as was the case with the Cæretan hydria described above. It represents King Arkesilas of Cyrene supervising the weighing and loading of silphium, one of the leading exports of Cyrene.[15c] As the king is probably Arkesilas II, the vase belongs in the first half of the Sixth Century.

The cup reveals the same keen observation, life, and humor which characterize the Cæretan class. Obviously the artist knew Cyrene and may have wandered to Egypt on one of the ships which was engaged in the transport of silphium. He has drawn an amusing picture—almost a caricature—of the King, seated on the boat on a folding stool with his hunting leopard under his chair, directing the slaves who scurry about with the loaded bales or who take "time off" to observe the ape and birds on the yard-arm. The flying curlew(?) and the lizard are mere decorative additions. The colors used are: yellow of the slip, black for silhouettes, black and purple for garments, brownish yellow on the bags, and white for the silphium. Bordering the design is an ornamental pattern of pomegranates. The subjects employed on other vases include scenes from daily life, dancers, warriors, Erotes with riders or revelers, and mythological themes. As Cyrene was founded by Spartan settlers from Thera, it is not surprising to find African themes on these wares. Another famous Laconian vase in the British Museum represents the nymph Cyrene with a branch of silphium in her hand.[15d] Winged genii fly round about her,—perhaps Boreads and Hesperids. Most Cyrenaic vases were probably made in Sparta, but some examples were doubtless produced in Cyrene itself.

Other important examples of Ionian wares have been found in the Egyptian cities of Naukratis and Daphnæ. Naukratis was a Milesian colony and much of its pottery shows relations with Rhodian-Milesian ware. The city was located on the western side of the Nile Delta and was founded in the Seventh Century. The vases date from the first half of the Sixth Century. The polychromy of Naukratite pottery is more vivid than that of the Rhodian-Milesian group—terra cotta red, black, white, golden yellow, brown, and purplish red appearing against the creamy ground. In the earlier period, the animal friezes of wild goats, deer, and geese, cultivated by the Rhodian artist, appear, painted on a white ground, often with the heads reserved in the slip and with polychrome details. In addition to the animals named, the lion and bull are commonly seen and friezes including the boar, dog, panther, hare, ram, duck, and cocks. On the inside of the vases dark paint is laid over the white slip. On this

---

[15c] Silphium is probably asafœtida. *Cf.* F. Studniczka, *Gnomon*, IV (1928), p. 236.
[15d] W. M. F. Petrie, *Naukratis*, London, 1886, I, Pls. VIII-IX.

ground, white and red ornaments or floral patterns occur. Human figures are rarely seen and these at first without incision. The vases are usually chalices with a conical foot, resembling Lydian bowls. In the latest stage of Class A, Rhodian elements disappear and incision comes in, perhaps under Klazomenian influence.

In Naukratite B, the "Chalice Komos" or "Revel" style is found and the animal decoration is seen on pyxides or round toilet boxes. These fabrics were often dedicated to various divinities, but aside from these dedications in Classes A and B, few inscriptions are found. Many other Orientalizing styles have been discovered in Naukratis, especially Rhodian-Milesian ware, and the Klazomenian-Daphnaic and Fikellura-Samian classes. The heterogeneous decoration of Naukratite pottery proper shows that the city was a kind of meeting ground of Ionians and various other peoples.

The Naukratite platter of Pl. VIIIa depicts a sphinx, with white flesh painted over the creamy ground. The profile is outlined in golden brown. Red, black, white, brown, and yellow form the color scheme. Bands of animals are seen in the second fragment, red, black, and white predominating against the yellow ground (Pl. VIIIb). Incised lines are combined with the contours.

At Daphnæ in Egypt, the site of an ancient Greek fortress, the archaic pottery has a dark ground for the most part. Imaginary monsters and animals are often pictured (Pl. VIIIc). In the later examples, polychrome designs are set off against the reddish yellow clay (Pl. VIIId). In the hydria represented here, a woman mounting a chariot is depicted and in the second vase, an ancient Godiva. The flesh of the woman is white in each case and the paint is laid directly on the reddish clay ground. The Lady Charioteer wears a brown chiton starred with white crosses and a purple mantle. Her horses are brown and white. The work is highly polychromatic. In the second example, we have an even gayer color scheme—dark brown for the flesh of the man, white for the woman and dog, and dark brown for the horse with purple additions (Pl. VIIIe). In these vases, the white portions are surrounded by a brown outline, at least in the case of the face. Inner markings are also rendered in brown by means of the brush or by incision on black. Incision is usually employed in engraving the outlines of men. The pottery of Daphnæ reveals a technique similar to that which is found on Klazomenian vases and it may in fact have originated in Klazomenai.[15e] We find the same curious combined technique of outline, silhouette, and incising on both sites. Folds begin to be rendered with incision rather than by means of the earlier colored surfaces.

The Klazomenian vases present practically a black-figured style. In our example (Pl. VIIIf), we see a band of sixteen women dancing around an altar. They have

[15e] R. Zahn, *Ath. Mitth.*, XXIII (1898), pp. 39, 49 ff.; H. L. Lorimer, *J.H.S.*, 25 (1905), p. 119.

b. London. British Museum. Lions and stag. Naukratis.

. London. British Museum. Sphinx. Naukratis.

d. London. British Museum. Woman mounting a chariot. Daphnæ.

London. British Museum. Hybrid monster. Daphnæ.

e. London. British Museum. Woman on horse. Man with dog. Daphnæ.

ondon. British Museum. Bird. Altenburg, Revelers. "Fikellura Ware."

f. Munich. Women dancing around an altar. Klazomenai.

Plate VIII. Ionic Pottery.

their "hands on one another's wrists," as Homer says, except for the two nearest the altar who hold wreaths. The upper part of their bodies is angular as is usual in this class and the garments cling closely, revealing the forms beneath. Elbow-sleeves are the rule. The outlines of the faces are incised as are the eyes, the brows, ears, neck-laces, girdles, and dress borders. The white of the flesh is put directly on the clay ground.

Common to the Klazomenian vases and to those from Daphnæ are the painting in white on the clay ground and the outlining of white with a brown line, especially in the case of faces; inner markings in brown paint or by means of incision on black, and the use of rows of white dots often placed between two incised lines. The forms of horses and the ornamented harness are also similar in the two classes.[15e]

Lastly, the Fikellura vases must be mentioned, found especially at Samos, Miletos, the Delta, and at Kameiros in Rhodes. They have been thought to be Samian,[15f] but may possibly belong to southwest Asia Minor. Characteristic of the class are the crescents at the bottom of the vase (Pl. VIII*g*), fabulous types, figures in vivid action, and the shape—a squat neck-amphora. A white slip is employed on the vases of this class and the black paint often tends to become brown or red. The technique is essentially that of Rhodian vases. The dancing revelers on our example have a thoroughly Ionian liveliness. Other vases represent running figures; hybrid beings such as the rabbit-headed man; animals, including the dog pursuing a hare; the goose, water-bird, and the like. Certain vases were covered with a net-like pattern.

Many other styles belonging to the Orientalizing classes do not fall under any of the categories mentioned. Thera, Crete, Bœotia, Cyprus, the Cyclades, and many eastern Greek sites possessed wares akin to those which we have discussed. We have chosen representative styles of the group, confining ourselves to the most important examples.

Instances of landscape occur on many Ionic vases and on Attic vases made under Ionic influence. The Phineus kylix is typical, with its waves over which the Harpies flee, its palm trees, and vines (Fig. 215). This vase, earlier assigned to one of the Cycladic Islands, shows the immediate stamp of Chalkis in Eubœa.[16] After Asia Minor fell into the hands of the Persians, Ionic art had a rebirth in Greece be-cause of the many artists who took refuge there. We can therefore trace the in-fluence of eastern landscape art on some of the vases found in Athens and on sites closely in contact with the East. Doubtless many of these vases were made by Ionic artists. Names of black-figured vase-painters such as Amasis and Nikosthenes occur to us as instances of this Ionic trend. Amasis probably came to Athens from Nau-

[15f] J. Boehlau, *Aus ionischen und italischen Nekropolen*, Leipzig, 1898, pp. 52 ff.

[16] A. Rumpf, "Zur Gruppe der Phineusschale," *Ath. Mitth.*, 46 (1921), pp. 169 ff.; *Chal-kidische Vasen*, Berlin, 1927, pp. 104 ff.

kratis; his name has an Egyptian sound. Nikosthenes may have taken from Ionia his metallic amphora and his experimentation with a white slip.[16a]

Other examples which show an Ionic fondness for landscape are to be seen in several black-figured vases of later date with representations of forests, vineyards, and olive groves. Of particular interest is a vase in Munich depicting the conclusion of one of the exploits of Herakles, where the hero is disemboweling the animal which he has slain (Fig. 216). Two spreading olive trees form the background for the episode. The branches are rendered in a soft, feathery fashion recalling the typical "Ionic branch" pattern so familiar in Dionysiac scenes.

Vineyard scenes are very common on vases of Ionian type. Ionia was in fact the home of "Dionysiac painting," with its train of satyrs and mænads bearing vine branches. Very often arbors occur where the grapes are being plucked and trampled down by fat satyrs. In Figure 217 we have a country scene derived more directly from life but showing the same fondness for patterns drawn from nature. The artist decidedly exaggerates the richness of the harvest with its huge bunches of grapes, but in his use of the pattern to cover the background he shows not a little ingenuity. This vase is an Attic work with Corinthian elements, but the artist has felt the influence of the East. It has a certain kinship with the unsigned amphora by Amasis in Würzburg, where corpulent satyrs are engaged in vintage scenes.[16b]

In Figure 218 is another example of an attempt at rendering a landscape. Here two large grapevines adorn the circle of the kylix and among the branches are birds' nests, insects, and bird life of all kinds. A figure of a man in the center who appears to be shaking the branches unites the two parts of the composition, but just what is the relation of the trees to the figure and to the background is not wholly clear. Suffice it to say that the artist's feeling for nature and his ability to render it satisfy our demands as far as the decoration of the vase is concerned. These landscapes, in contrast to those of Crete, are not realistically given but the scene is always a more or less typical one. Schematization, which the decorative end demanded, reduced the patterns to certain formulæ. These vases are Attic works of the Sixth Century which reflect Ionic influence in the use of landscape elements.

Vases such as the polychrome lekythos in Athens, with a representation of Odysseus and the sirens, also show the effect of this Ionic love for polychromy and landscape (Fig. 219). The vase in question has a creamy yellow ground and the sea is indicated by a brownish dilute wash. The diving dolphins settle any doubt as to the locality intended. Odysseus bound to the mast occupies the center of the compo-

---

[16a] Vs. this view, cf. S. B. Luce, "Nicosthenes: His Activity and Affiliations," *A.J.A.,* XXIX (1925), pp. 38 ff.; Albert Gallatin, "The Origin of the Form of the 'Nikosthenes Amphora,'" *A.J.A.,* XXX (1926), pp. 76 ff.

[16b] *J.H.S.,* XIX (1899), Pl. V.

sition and the sirens perched on rocks balance the design on either side. The conventional Ionic branch motive is added. The vase is polychromatic with an abundant use of white, purple, and black against the yellow ground. This theme was treated in much the same manner in vases of the red-figured style of the Fifth Century (*cf.* Tailpiece, Ch. VI).

From these monuments found at widely separated centers, we can gain an idea of the progress and continuation of Ionic painting from Ægean and Oriental traditions. Gradually, like the Corinthian class of vases, the Ionic group became emancipated from stop-gap ornaments which early covered the field, and in the Busiris vase we see a black-figured style in its beginnings.

But we can form a still clearer idea of Ionic painting from yet another class of art objects, fictile, to be sure, but of a more monumental stamp. The sarcophagi found at Klazomenai in Asia Minor also picture for us the development of Ionic painting in the Seventh and Sixth Centuries B.C. These terra cotta coffins, which the Ionians doubtless adopted under Egyptian influence, were of baked clay, usually wider at the top than at the bottom, but, when rectangular, closed by a gabled lid— few of which survive. The surface, as in most ceramic products of Ionia, was covered with a creamy white slip and the monument was then decorated on the broad face of the rim and at times on the interior of the coffin and the inside of the lid. Most frequently the ornamentation runs around the top face of the sarcophagus. The decoration thus formed a frame for the deceased lying in state. Two technical processes are observable, as in early Attic vase-painting: first, the black silhouette with an occasional addition of white or deep red, against a creamy ground; secondly, outlined figures reserved in the light ground of the slip with the background painted black. In both classes, details of the silhouettes were put in with a brush; white lines, or even red, were used on the black silhouettes; brown or red on the white.

Good examples of the earlier technique are found in Berlin, London, Paris, and New York. In the Berlin example a Persian winged Artemis (?) with lions is painted at the top between two charioteers. The design is beautifully balanced and the black silhouettes stand out in relief from the creamy ground (Fig. 220). There is often a certain delicacy in pattern amounting almost to affectation—evident in the head of the horse bent low, in the charming bell-shaped flowers on their thread-like stems, and in the element of conventionalization employed in the lions. It is noticeable that patterns such as the lion are borrowed from eastern tapestries and are therefore strongly conventionalized whereas animals like the boar are more naturalistically rendered. There is a certain restlessness in the composition due to the curling, winding lines. The Dorian loved the meander and triangle, swastika and zigzag; the Ionian is fond of the guilloche, spiral, and volute. There is an extensive use of fine, sinuous lines. The field is framed by an egg and dart moulding above, by rosettes below. Along the sides are running antithetic animals and heraldic boars, placed above ornamental patterns in which the guilloche plays the leading rôle. At the bottom occur other balanced groups, especially the one of a lion and a panther on either side of a dappled bull. The striking thing in the composition is the beautiful symmetry of the design. The spots on the bull and the heads of the lion and panther are reserved in the slip of the background, a technique that survived from Minoan days.

Even more instinct with life and action are two sarcophagi in the opposite technique. Figure 221 shows an advanced archaic composition with a theme similar to the one of Figure 220. The main design has merely been transferred to the opposite technique with the figures reserved in the light ground of the slip instead of being painted in black silhouette. A winged figure, identified by certain scholars as Athena, is flanked on either side by a warrior, each leading his horse. The element of pattern is handled with great skill. Every detail on the right finds its corresponding line on the left—the stepping, fiery horses, the dogs with raised forelegs, the flying birds, and the flowers. The pattern on the shield, the reins, and muscles of the horses are all indicated with delicately curving lines. The designs below introduce the centaur, the guilloche, goats, and a lion and a panther in heraldic design.[16c] Occasionally human heads replace antithetic and heraldic animals (Fig. 222). On this Berlin example, we find an heraldic group of a lion and a boar at the top reserved in the creamy slip of the ground with details in black and brown line, and a goat between panthers in silhouette and outline below. The sides, however, are ornamented with the heads of helmeted warriors facing one another, and with outlined heads of youths that remind one of the cycle of Euphronios in Attic vase-painting. We have in this example a combination of technical processes—the opaque silhouette in black, reserved technique in the warriors' heads, and a combination of outline and silhouette in the heads of the youths.

One of the finest sarcophagi is now in the British Museum.[17] The exterior of the cover (Fig. 223) is ornamented in the center with rows of fanciful creatures

---

[16c] R. Zahn, *Jahr.*, 23 (1908), p. 177, calls both animals, *lions*.

[17] Picard et Plassart, *B.C.H.* (1913), p. 378, Pls. X-XVI; *cf. B.C.H.* (1910), p. 469, Pls. XI-XII; *B.C.H.* (1921), p. 559; A. S. Murray, *Terracotta Sarcophagi in the British Museum*, London, 1898; Wace, *J.H.S.*, 41 (1921), p. 275. The number of sarcophagi now extant must be tremendously augmented since the systematic excavation of the cemetery has begun. "About forty graves with painted terracotta sarcophagi not later in date than the second half of the Sixth Century were excavated. The sarcophagi were often placed above one another, so that sometimes there are as many as six layers of them" (Wace). They were decorated with geometric and floral patterns and animal friezes. The covers were poros slabs. Numbers of Klazomenian vases were also found. M. G. Welter is preparing an account of the sarcophagi. *Cf. Jahr.*, 41 (1926), pp. 51 ff.

marching in procession—sphinxes and sirens. Above is represented a chariot-race—probably to illustrate the funeral games held in honor of the dead.[17a] Even in the Sixth Century such games as these were held in Ionia in memory of famous warriors and this formed one of the favorite themes of the Ionic painter. Over the chariots, winged beings fly, recognized by some as *Eidola* or *Nikai,* by others as a personification of the *Agon,* or contest for the prize. At the right, a vase stands on a tall column, the reward offered to the winner in the contest. In addition, the capture of the spy Dolon by Odysseus and Diomede formed part of the artist's subject matter. He is represented in the center of the group surprised by the two warriors. In the field below is a cavalry charge of historic import. Everywhere, we feel the rush and pandemonium of battle: horsemen attacking foot soldiers; fallen hoplites and comrades attempting to protect them. The scene represents the invasion of Cimmerian hordes who devastated Asia Minor in the Seventh Century. These episodes must long have remained in the memory of the people. The style is probably copied after an earlier painting of some battle. Some have thought that it goes back to the Defeat of the Magnesians by Boularchos. Figure 224 presents funeral games once more. Warriors are seen combating to the music of the flute; charioteers with bigæ occur and dancers with castanets which they are shaking to excite the horses.

From the sarcophagi painted at Klazomenai we may draw several conclusions: Ionic painting had a predilection for Oriental motives. The hybrid and eastern animals may even have been employed in secondary friezes in wall-painting. It concerned itself with three main themes in its figure painting: games in honor of the dead, battle scenes, and the chase. Only one example of the latter subject has been found. Probably epic material played a larger rôle in its subject matter than appears from monuments extant. It had a fondness for vivid action and for finely balanced compositions.

It is easy to see how the painter of sarcophagi worked. He traced a pattern on the clay while it was still moist. From this pattern, he obtained a double image by reversing it at the right, so that we have almost exact correspondence, as in many Egyptian scenes of fowling and fishing. After the drawing of the outlines, he filled in his silhouette with black or set about glazing the background with black. Details were later added with the brush. His lines were of unusual delicacy and fineness and by means of these light and sinuous strokes he was able to represent spirited action very successfully. But there is a touch of the affected here and there and we begin to feel the oncoming decadence which did not affect Athens until the period of strong Ionian influence, shortly before the time of the Persian wars.

In color, we are not able to judge of the mural art. Baked clay allowed the Ionic painter the use of a creamy ground, a discreet use of red and of white, and a black

---

[17a] L. Malten, "Leichenspiel und Totenkult," *Röm. Mitth.,* 38-39 (1923-1924), pp. 300 ff.

which might turn red or brown according to the way in which it was fired. We can hardly believe that the heirs of Crete and Mycenæ possessed so limited a color range when they worked with monumental compositions. After the middle of the Sixth Century, when the Persians had placed their yoke upon Ionia, we find few examples of these painted sarcophagi. The systematic excavation of the cemetery which is now taking place at Klazomenai, where these sarcophagi were buried, may soon tell us more of the art. It is interesting to compare the large class of Klazomenian vases with the coffins.[18] The vase-painter is fond of representing the human figure sheathed in a close-fitting garment. He has a predilection for long skulls with sloping foreheads and for almond-shaped eyes. Many similarities in technique and many patterns are common to the ceramics and the sarcophagi.

It is now time to consider what the remains of early painting in Greece and Ionia tell us of the monumental art and how these remains tally with the accounts of ancient writers in regard to the beginnings of the art. The origins of Greek painting are necessarily obscure. Aristotle named as its inventor, Eucheir, the kinsman of Dædalus, apparently from Crete.[19] This is only another way of saying that the Cretans, who were very "clever with their hands" passed on their art to Greece. Pliny laughs at the idea that the Egyptians claimed to have invented painting six thousand years before it arose in Greece,[20] but that both Egypt, through centers like Naukratis and Daphnæ, and Crete, through its Ionian revival and Mycenæ, played their part in the development of painting in Greece is very certain.

Pliny assigns the invention of painting to Corinth or Sikyon. He says that everyone agrees that painting arose from outlining shadows. The first person who had the idea of imitating the contour of the body directly with the aid of a line, was Philokles, an Egyptian, or Kleanthes of Corinth,[21] or some Sikyonian—perhaps a certain Kraton, mentioned by others. The name Philokles, whatever the worth of the legend, shows that he was no Egyptian. He was probably a Greek who lived at Naukratis and later perhaps went to Greece and taught his countrymen what he had learned there. Obviously many Greeks, especially Ionians, sojourned in Naukratis. Probably the painter of the Busiris vase from Cære had been there. But just what Philokles contributed to painting and what he would have learned in Egypt is another matter. Pliny seems to imply that the work was outline drawing. If he had studied painting in Egypt, the weight of evidence is all in favor of the view that

---

[18] *Ant. Denk.*, II, Pls. 54-57. See Bibliography on Klazomenian vases and pp. 128-129.
[19] Pliny, *N.H.*, VII, 205.                    [20] Pliny, *N.H.*, 35, 15.
[21] Pliny, *N.H.*, 35, 16. *Inventam liniarem (picturam) a Philocle Ægyptio vel Cleanthe Corinthio primi exercuere Aridices Corinthius et Telephanes Sicyonius, sine ullo etiamnum hi colore, iam tamen spargentes linias intus. Ideo et quos pingerent adscribere institutum. Primus invenit eas colore testæ, ut ferunt, tritæ, Ecphantus Corinthius.*

he would have worked with silhouettes filled in in flat colors and would have come back to Greece with no such rudimentary invention as outline drawing. But after Philokles or Kleanthes had made his invention, whatever it was, it is Aridikes of Corinth and Telephanes of Sikyon who "practiced" it, still using no color, but introducing lines within the composition. What they contributed, we also do not know. Many think the reference is to ornaments in the field. Probably it refers to the marking of certain lines in the figures, such as nostrils, inner markings, and minor details. The next stage in the development of painting is the filling in of the silhouette with solid color. These painters were monochrome painters.

The account by Pliny of the beginnings of painting up to this point is not wholly clear or convincing. Pliny himself does not seem to place great credence in it, saying that the origins are obscure and hardly fall within the scope of his work. In the first place, to judge from extant evidence, outline drawing in Greece does not precede silhouettes in solid color. The reverse seems to be the case, though very early they exist side by side. The account which Pliny gives appears to be a rationalizing record in which events proceed from the simple to the more complex. Outline drawing would thus precede monochrome silhouettes; monochromes, the polychrome work. The Dipylon ware shows us that the solid silhouette is probably the more primitive; after silhouettes, outline work appears, although, as said, both occur early together. With regard to monochromes, we can learn much about this stage, which was probably employed in Egypt at a time when Greeks of the Sixth Century were active in Naukratis, from vases, and from Seventh or Sixth Century Etruscan painting. Probably very few early paintings were black monochromes such as we find in pottery, though their use on Attic funerary plaques and on tablets by Skythes proves that they did exist. Painting with color was said to have been "invented" by Ekphantos of Corinth, who used powdered potsherds. That is to say, the red which we find on Corinthian plaques and which came to be the color used to designate the flesh of men was introduced at Corinth. Many silhouettes were undoubtedly in this color. Eumaros of Athens was the first to mark the difference between men and women in painting.[22] In other words, he probably made current the practice found in early painting of rendering the flesh of women in white in contrast to the reddish or brown color employed for men.

It is evident that such a succession and methodical list of inventions is purely imaginary and designed to explain the logical growth of the art. Obviously, certain known names of painters, the earliest remembered, were attached to certain "inventions." The truth is that among the earliest Greek paintings, monochromes played a leading part and sexes were early distinguished by color, red being espe-

[22] On the name, *cf.* A. Reinach, *Recueil Milliet, Textes grecs et latins relatifs à l'histoire de la peinture ancienne*, Paris, 1921, p. 76, n. 1. Pliny, *N.H.*, 35, 56.

cially employed for retouches and the silhouettes of men, although brown was also
used for the latter purpose. This practice was probably derived from Egypt.

The first real name in painting is that of Kimon who lived at Kleonai, a site near
Corinth.[23] His appearance marks a great step forward. He devised κατάγραφα
—whatever they may be—and varied the archaic stiffness of the face, causing the
figures to look back, up, or down. He marked the joints and emphasized the veins
and put in wrinkles and folds in the drapery. Without embarking upon the lengthy
literature of κατάγραφα, and arguing whether the term can mean profile drawings,
which obviously were in general use from the beginnings of painting, we shall accept
the view now more widely recognized, that the invention is the very significant one
of linear foreshortening.[24] We can best judge of the importance of his attainments
from certain vases connected with the names of Euthymides, Phintias, and others of
the Euphronian period. They show in vase-painting the tremendous step forward
made shortly after 510 B.C. under the influence of the major art. Not only were
figures so drawn that they might look backward and down, but poses grew much
bolder so that limbs and feet were foreshortened in front and rear view (Fig. 225).
Further, drapery began to take on the semblance of real folds. The greatest advance,
however, was in loosening up the rigid positions of the figures which were now
enabled to move with some appearance of natural ease. This invention of Kimon's
marks the point where the artist has learned to observe nature. It means the discarding of the black-figured silhouette and emphasis on outline work. It is doubtless
true that the transition from the black-figured silhouette to the red-figured technique
in vase-painting was largely due to the influence of Kimon. The breaking up of
frontality in sculpture at this time was also probably not unconnected with his
innovations. He must have worked with flat tones still, but with figures in a lighter
color set off against a darker ground. We have leapt forward in time from the early
Sixth Century, the age of Eumaros, to the beginning of the Fifth Century. Kimon
lived in the time of the Peisistratidai when the organization of the Panathenaic
games gave such an impetus to gymnastic exercises and furnished an opportunity
for studying the nude.

So much for Pliny's accounts of the origin and early development of painting. It
is evident from his discussion that Corinth and her neighbor Sikyon divided the

[23] Pliny, *N.H.*, 35, 56. *Hic catagrapha invenit, hoc est, obliquas imagines, et varie formare
voltus, respicientes suspicientesve vel despicientes. Articulis membra distinxit, venas protulit,
præterque in vestibus rugas et sinus invenit.*

[24] H. Brunn, *Ges. der gr. Künstler*, 1889, II, 8, considers that the correct rendering of the
eye in profile view is meant; F. Winter, *A.Z.* (1885), p. 201, the use of outline drawing instead of incision; A. E. J. Holwerda, *Jahr.*, V (1890), p. 258, thinks Kimon used the black-
figured silhouette.

honor of having the earliest painters and that there were vague traditions of the connection of the art with Egypt, Crete, and Ionia.

Pliny makes almost no mention of painting in Ionia in early times, but by piecing together scraps of information, we may gather some evidence on the point. He tells us that King Kandaules of Lydia paid for a painting by Boularchos—which represented the battle of the Magnesians—its weight in gold.[25] This need not have been very much money, unless the painting was on terra cotta, as some scholars believe. The legend may be invention. Important, if true, is the information that in the Seventh and Sixth Centuries painting was being practiced in these regions and the example cited is an historical battle scene. Reinach has attempted to show that the painting on the London sarcophagus with its representation of the struggle against the Cimmerians, harks back to the painting of Boularchos.[26] It need not necessarily go back to Boularchos' original, but it does seem to bear some relation to monumental painting.

In the Ephesian Artemisium, there was a picture by Kalliphon of Samos depicting the Homeric battle at the ships.[27] The painting was greatly honored in Pausanias' time because he cites it in his description of the Chest of Kypselos and the paintings of Polygnotos at Delphi. There was also a famous Sixth Century painting in the Heræum at Samos of which Herodotus tells us.[28] King Darius rewarded the architect, Mandrokles of Samos, for bridging the Bosphorus, and Mandrokles in turn dedicated a painting to the Samian Hera. It represented the army of Darius crossing the new bridge under the eyes of the King. In all probability, the painter was a Samian. We know further that the Heræum at Samos was a Museum in Strabo's time;[29] he tells us about the Samian picture-galleries. When we add to this the tradition that Saurias of Samos "invented" shadow painting by outlining his horse in the sun,[30] we seem to have a body of evidence which points to early painting in Ionic cities. The Ionians were not so fortunate as Sikyon in having their efforts recorded and preserved for posterity, and accordingly, much of the early tradition is buried with time. But we know that the wealthy sanctuaries in various Ionic cities abounded in works of art; and, beside the school of sculpture in Samos, there was undoubtedly a flourishing school of painting. There must also have been many other local Ionic schools in addition to the one at Samos. Herodotus refers to marble statues, bronzes, and paintings left behind when the Phocæans fled from the Persian yoke.[31]

The monuments which we have discussed, namely, vases and the sarcophagi from

[25] Pliny, N.H., 35, 55; VII, 126.

[26] A. S. Murray, Terracotta Sarcophagi, pp. 2-3; S. Reinach, Revue des études grecques, 1895, pp. 176 ff., thinks a victory of the Magnesians is meant, as a Greek painter would hardly have immortalized a Greek defeat.

[27] Paus., V, 19, 1.           [28] Hdt., IV, 88.           [29] Strabo, XIV, 637c (20).

[30] Athenag., Leg. pro Christ., p. 133, 3 (Geffcken).           [31] Hdt., I, 164.

Klazomenai together with the traditions enumerated, prove that there was an early school of painting in Ionia which may dispute priority with the Peloponnesian school. Ionic painting was the real heir of Cretan-Mycenæan art, and combined with these elements Oriental material. Its leading characteristics were polychromy, which contrasts with much of the early monochrome work of the mainland, love of symmetry and balance, fondness for lively action and for sinuous, winding lines. It was probably a gayer and more impulsive art even than extant monuments make it out for us. We recall the dancing bands of satyrs on vases and the running negroes on the Busiris hydria. It had, too, an interest in landscape which was fostered by contact with the East, especially Assyria. Such a painting as that of Boularchos implies a representation of a landscape with foreground, middle ground and background, however crudely this may have been depicted.

Athens appears to have had little share in the beginnings of Greek painting. It was Eumaros, a son of hers, who in his painting is said to have distinguished sexes by color, but no other mention is made of an Athenian as an "inventor" of painting, except of a certain Semon who is said to have invented drawing.[32] A survey of the early history of art in Athens proves, however, that painting was a decorative art there in early times, inseparably connected with architecture and sculpture. The primitive pediments on the Acropolis were radiant with color. One of the earliest of these, the "Hydra" pediment, depicted a combat of Herakles against the Lernæan hydra. It is a crude relief, in all probability cut with a knife, with the outer surface of the figures left flat. Nowhere is it much more than one inch in height. Its closest analogies are to be found in vase-painting, for its technique is really that of drawing. Color is extensively used—rose, dark blue, red, black, and green, with the color of the stone appearing here and there.[33] The background was usually blue; flesh, rose; hair, blue, red, or white; brows and eyelids, black; pupils, black, red, or blue.

Some idea of the way in which color was lavishly employed on these sculptures may be gathered from the "Typhon" group. The "Blue Beard" of the "Typhon" pediment from the old Hekatompedon, or temple of Athena, in Athens, was painted in colors that seem almost violent to us today.[34] A triple-headed monster is repre-

---

[32] H. Diels, *Laterculi Alexandrini, Abh. der Akad. der Wiss.*, Berlin, 1904, Col. VI, 14.

Σήμων Ἀθηναῖος. οὗτος          τύπον (?), ἵππου ἐν λευκῶι
εὗρε πρῶτος γραμμῆς          πίνακι ἀλείψας τὴν σκιάν.

[33] Guy Dickins, *Catalogue of the Acropolis Museum*, I, 1912, pp. 11 ff., 36, 57; Th. Wiegand, *Die archaische Poros-Architektur*, Cassel, 1904, Pl. VIII, 4.

[34] *Ant. Denk.*, I, 30. H. Lechat, "Note sur la polychromie des statues grecques," *Rev. des études anciennes*, X (1908), 161; M. Collignon, "La Polychromie dans la sculpture grecque," *Rev. des deux mondes*, 1895, I, 823; W. Lermann, *Altgriechische Plastik*, München, 1907; Th. Wiegand, *Die archaische Poros-Architektur*, Cassel, 1904; R. Heberdey, *Altattische Porosskulptur*, pp. 125, 127; G. Rodenwaldt, "Zur Polychromie der attischen

sented who was earlier known as "Typhon." Against the yellow ground of the poros stone, the colors employed seem especially vivid—blue for "Typhon's" hair, beard, and mustache; greenish blue for the iris, which may originally have been blue; yellow for the ball; red for lips and cheeks; black for pupils and eyebrows. The exposed parts of the body were a vivid rose red. The snake-like coils of his tail were decorated in parallel stripes of color—red, blue, and the yellow of the ground. The same colors were used for the wings. Brown and possibly some white appear. This elaborate use of polychromy over the surface may have been intended to cover up the crude material employed; it looks more like the satisfying of primitive taste by an orgy of color. The polychromy in this period was conventional and total. These early figures with their red bodies and blue hair and beards strike us as very grotesque, but they were doubtless artistic delights in the age of the Tyrants.

It will readily be seen from the above that red and blue were the dominant colors employed. It is interesting to see in early Greece the use of blue for hair and beards, a practice which occurs in Egypt from the time of the Old Kingdom, especially from the Fifth Dynasty. There, blue was frequently employed in places where we should today expect black. Koldewey calls attention to the fact that in the East the hair of men and animals always has a touch of blue. Where we think black, they thought blue.[35] It seems very probable that the influence in the East was from Egypt. The practice of using blue for black continued in the Orient down through Persian times, since we find a greenish blue used on the heads of the sphinxes from the Palace of Darius. Probably the green which appears on many of the Athenian poros sculptures was originally blue.

The use of marble, with the beauty and durability of its surface, brought a more limited employment of color over the surface of the material, although the range of tones was greatly extended. The problem of the amount of color on Greek sculpture has not yet been solved. It certainly varied with different periods. That it was always greater than modern taste would employ seems certain. The vividly colored architecture of Greek temples called for colored sculpture. Most handbooks, after discussing the total polychromy of the early poros pediments, seem to imply that marble sculptures had a very restricted amount in comparison and that this was confined to the hair, eyes, borders of garments, straps of sandals, and minor details unless the statues were small. This is misleading and a survey of the evidence reveals a greater use of color than is usually stated.

First of all, the problem is a dual one, relief sculpture varying in treatment from sculpture in the round. The reliefs of the time were undoubtedly rich in color, far

Grabstelen," *Arch. Anz.* (1922), pp. 170 ff.; Th. Homolle, *B.C.H.*, 14 (1890), pp. 497 ff.; Perrot and Chipiez, "La Polychromie artificielle," *Histoire de l'art*, VIII, 211 ff.

[35] R. Koldewey, "Das Ischtar-Tor in Babylon," *Wiss. Veröff. D.O.G.*, 32 (1918), p. 26.

gayer than statues in the round. It is hardly to be thought that if reliefs were set into a brightly colored architectural frame, they would have failed to add their note of color. We find traces of color on practically all extant friezes unless it be the Parthenon, where it undoubtedly occurred also, and we find it in masses. The backgrounds usually dark, were red or blue: blue is found for this purpose on the Siphnian Treasury, the Ægina pediments, on some Olympia metopes, the Theseum frieze, and Mausoleum frieze. Grave reliefs often had a red ground: the Locrian reliefs were set against blue. These reliefs, as well as the pediments and metopes which are so intimately connected with architecture, possessed large amounts of color on the drapery and accessories and also on certain parts of the figures. The garments and the armor of the "Sikyonian" and Siphnian Treasuries at Delphi were colored—some of the drapery in solid red. Athena's mantle on the Ægina pediment was red and so was Apollo's on the Olympia pediment. Helmets were often blue. The painting of the nude parts of figures is a more debatable point. Poulsen thinks entire figures were painted on the "Sikyonian" Treasury but the flesh was apparently not colored on the Siphnian Treasury. On the other hand, the Mausoleum frieze shows flesh tones in red, and on the Lycian sculptures the same is true. The colored masses were designed to emphasize the architectural elements. But there was no canonical scheme. Beside the prevalent blue of the background found in the Fifth Century, there was the white of the Alexander sarcophagus in the Fourth; beside the marble tone or *ganosis* of many reliefs was the red of the flesh tones on the Mausoleum. Rodenwaldt has pointed out that grave reliefs from the Fourth Century on often have a background in which the upper part was painted either red or another color; the lower part was yellow or an undetermined color. In such examples, the background was evidently thought of as a wall.[34] In the Sixth Century, the grounds seem frequently to have been uncolored. Against this neutral ground highly polychromatic figures were placed. The effect was the same as is found on black-figured vase-paintings, for the sculptured figures were predominantly red and black. After 520 B.C., as in red-figured vase-painting, light or red figures appear against a darker ground. This agrees with what we find on the "Sikyonian" and Siphnian Treasuries (*cf.* Poulsen, *Delphi*, p. 81).

When we turn to statues in the round the problem is more difficult of solution. *A priori* it seems unlikely that the Greek would have covered the flesh parts of marble statues with a wash. In that case he might have used poros or any poor stone. The beauty of the marble would be lost if this were his practice. The play of light and shadow on the surface would have been destroyed. It is evident that the Greek respected this marble surface in Fifth Century architecture and did not paint the walls of buildings in solid color. Let us examine the evidence for sculpture.

The Acropolis maidens of the early Sixth Century appear to have had about one-fifth of the entire surface painted. Red, blue, and green were especially used on the borders of the garments where the meander pattern is often found picked out in these colors.[35a] The hair was painted red as a rule but sometimes it was yellow. The lips were red, and the iris of the eye. Black was used for the eyebrows, pupils, and minor details. The polychromy was only partial. The remaining four-fifths of the statue was apparently rubbed with hot wax by a process known as *ganosis,* and seems not to have been painted in opaque color.

We are not able to determine the practice in the Fifth Century unless we infer it from what we find later—a dangerous proceeding. Of course, much coloring has been lost with time so that absolute proof is impossible. We have spoken of the solid painting of garments such as is found on the mantle of Apollo at Olympia and it was probably true that most sculptures in the round were decorated in this fashion with opaque washes of color for draperies. For the flesh we have no evidence except from later periods. The Mausoleum frieze is after all a frieze and the statues which we possess on which the flesh is colored are late—notably the head of Athena in Berlin and the head of a young girl in the British Museum. In the case of Athena, the flesh parts are left in the color of the marble, copying the chryselephantine original. The surface is polished. The lips were roughened and color was applied. Hair and brows were red, the iris, a dark brown, the helmet, yellow. The face of the young girl in the British Museum is rose-colored and is completely painted; the hair is blonde. But these examples are late, dating from Roman days, and it is possible that taste may have deteriorated with time. We should not be surprised to find the Roman covering his statues with paint. He was much influenced by the Oriental Etruscan who was accustomed to an orgiastic display of color on his works of art.

Turning to the Fourth Century, we have the Hermes of Praxiteles for evidence though in this statue much color has doubtless been lost. Here we know that the hair was red, the lips also; the latchets of the sandals were colored. For the nude parts we have no evidence of painting. The surface of the garment was roughened, while the flesh remained smooth. This indicates that the mantle was colored but the flesh was not.

From the Third Century we have some inscriptions from Delos—temple accounts relating to the expenses of decorating the statues—κόσμησις ἀγαλμάτων. These in connection with statements by Vitruvius and Pliny on the process of γάνωσις, or waxing of statues, tell us much that we know about the decoration of Greek sculpture. The Delian accounts record that the sponges used for washing the statue of Hera cost one drachma. Three drachmæ and three obols were charged for perfuming the statue—a curious expense to us. For the statue of Artemis similar charges were

[35a] The use of green is a debatable point, most writers accepting the view that the original blue has suffered a chemical change resulting in green.

made as well as for nitron, oil, linen, and wax. On some accounts charcoal is an expense—perhaps to heat the wax or possibly for the silversmith.

Just how was a statue decorated? It was apparently first washed with sponges in water mixed with nitron. Then oil and wax were rubbed into the pores, and the question is whether this was done over a colored coating or on the bare parts of the marble which were not colored. At certain times this may have been executed over the color. The possible proof is a statement by Vitruvius.[36] Here the wax was used to preserve the vermilion of walls, a color which was affected by sunlight. Vitruvius implies that waxing was also employed for this purpose in the case of marble statues. The Delian accounts seem to deal with the refurbishing of statues for the sake of their preservation. We shall quote the passage from Vitruvius in translation: "But anybody who is more particular and wants a polished finish of vermilion that will keep its proper color, should, after the wall is polished and is dry, apply with a brush Pontic wax melted over a fire and mixed with a little oil; then after this he should bring the wax to a sweat by warming it and the wall at close quarters with charcoal enclosed in an iron vessel and *finally,* he should smooth it all off by rubbing it down with a wax candle and clean linen cloths, *just as nude marble statues are treated.*" It is *possible* that Vitruvius' remark may apply only to the rubbing with wax and linen. The evidence seems, then, to indicate that the nude parts of marble statues were usually waxed and appeared a warm ivory color such as is seen today in the Venus of Cyrene or the Hermes.[36a] But late statues which are entirely painted and

[36] Vitr., *De Arch.,* VII, 9, 3. *At si qui subtilior fuerit et voluerit expolitionem miniaceam suum colorem retinere, cum paries expolitus et aridus fuerit, ceram ponticam igni liquefactam paulo oleo temperatam sæta inducat; deinde postea carbonibus in ferreo vase compositis eam ceram una cum pariete calfaciundo sudare cogat lietque, ut peræquetur; deinde tunc candela centunculisque puris subigat, uti signa marmorea nuda curantur (hæc autem* γάνωσις *græce dicitur); ita obstans ceræ ponticæ lorica non patitur nec lunæ splendorem nec solis radios lambendo eripere ex his politionibus colorem.* Pliny, *N.H.,* 33, 122, gives the same description with this variant: *sicut et marmora nitescunt.* For the Delian temple accounts, see Th. Homolle, *B.C.H.,* 14 (1890), pp. 497 ff., *cf.* H. Lechat, *B.C.H.,* 14 (1890), p. 552, No. II, *Polychromie;* Blümner, *Technologie,* III, 203; Treu, *Jahr.,* IV, 18; Perrot and Chipiez, *Histoire de l'art,* VIII, 211 ff.; Collignon, *La Polychromie dans la sculpture grecque,* Leroux, 1898. For illustrations of color, see *Ant. Denk.,* I, 3, Parthenos; I, 30, "Bluebeard"; 19, 39; *cf. Fouilles de Delphes,* IV, Pls. XXI-XXIV, Treasury of Siphnians; Hamdy Bey et Reinach, *Une Nécropole royale à Sidon,* Paris, 1892, Pls. 34-37. *Terracottas:* E. Pottier et S. Reinach, *La Nécropole de Myrina,* pp. 137, 362, Pl. 23; E. Pottier, *Les Statuettes de terre cuite dans l'antiquité,* p. 259; F. Winter, *Das Alexandermosaik aus Pompeii,* 1909, 2 plates; G. M. A. Richter, "Were the Nude Parts in Greek Marble Sculpture Painted?" *Metropolitan Museum Studies,* Vol. I, Part I, 1928; *The Sculpture and Sculptors of the Greeks,* New Haven, 1929.

[36a] G. Treu, *Jahr.,* IV (1889), p. 20 and note 2, and p. 22, points out that the wax lay *under* the colors on the head in the British Museum and on the one in Dresden.

passages such as the one of Vitruvius make a decision about the practice difficult. These Roman statues which, as in the case of the head from the British Museum, copy a type of a good Greek epoch, need not however, in their present state, necessarily reproduce the original coloring. It is possible that the flesh portions of statues were solidly painted after a certain period. We incline to think that in the Fifth and Fourth Centuries the nude parts were rubbed with wax and oil so that the marble took on an ivory tone. The cheeks were tinted, however, and in later times the flesh, as literary evidence indicates.[37] A realistic touch was thus given, although the coloring of Greek sculpture always remained conventional and decorative. Terra cotta figurines are sometimes adduced as evidence for color on sculpture but their size and material are so different from the monuments with which we are dealing that the evidence must be used with caution. They are brilliantly painted in solid colors—red and blue predominating. We have no evidence for the painting of flesh in color for marble sculpture in the round from the Fifth or Fourth Centuries, even on the statues that preserve extensive traces of color. On the other hand, reliefs show flesh tones. The Alexander Sarcophagus of the Fourth Century is a good example, with the flesh of the Greeks painted a light yellow and that of the barbarians, a dark yellow. The examples from the Fourth Century seem to be from the East, from Oriental sites. Our conclusion therefore is that the flesh of Greek statues in the round was not painted in solid colors unless in late Hellenistic or Roman times but that it was waxed with unbleached wax to give the warm ivory tone found in the Hermes and the Venus of Cyrene. Had the flesh portions of Greek statues been painted we should have found some trace of it along with the numerous traces of color on other parts of the marbles.

In architecture, the same fondness for polychromy prevailed in early times. There is no rule for the application of color, which seems to have varied with different materials and styles of buildings. Most of the early temples known to us, especially those of Sicily, were clothed with terra cotta in places which received much weathering. Such were the old Athenaion, or temple of Athena at Syracuse, the old temple C at Selinos, numerous temples in Magna Græcia and the Treasury of Gela in Olympia. The geison and the sima were customarily decorated in red and black combined with the reserved yellowish slip over the clay. Geisa were ornamented with geometric patterns similar to those found on Greek vases—lozenges, palmettes, meanders, the braid, triangle, rosette, and star.[38] This tendency toward polychromy was a part of the primitive Greek's childish love for color. It dates from the time when statues

[37] Lucian, *Imag.*, 7; Plato, *Rep.*, IV, 420, C-D; G. Treu, *Olympia*, III, Berlin, 1897, *Register, s.v. Bemalung.*

[38] W. Dörpfeld, R. Borrmann, *et al.*, 41 *Winckelmannsprogr.*, Berlin, 1881; R. Borrmann, *Handbuch der Architektur*, I, Band IV, *Keramik*, Stuttgart, 1897; *cf.* Baumeister, *Denk-*

of wood were brilliantly colored vermilion,[38a] when temples with wooden roofs were gay with the painted terra cotta decorations which adorned them. Cornices, metopes, and dedicatory plaques, such as the one of Medusa and Pegasus at Syracuse, show us this early temple decoration which was later to be suppressed with the introduction of marble, but which was nevertheless to influence the polychromy of later times.[39] These terra cottas date in the early Sixth Century B.C. and similar material has also been found at Gela and Camarina in Sicily. In fact the polychrome stage with terra cotta revetments, which preceded marble or stuccoed stone, is a very common one on South Italian, Sicilian, and Etruscan sites. Gutters, water-spouts, and antefixes were also painted in gay colors. We have already noted some of this decoration at Thermos, a northern Greek site.

This earlier polychromy in architecture was later transferred to marble where the colors were changed to suit differing needs to red, blue, and green. In the Doric order, the triglyphs were blue, the metopes red or blue when ornamented with sculpture, otherwise white. Horizontal members like the soffit of the cornice, the bed-mould of the metopes, and the tænia were red. Vertical members such as the triglyphs and regulæ were blue, though some earlier triglyphs of black are also found. Walls of poros were covered with stucco and then painted before marble came into use. This stucco might be mixed with any pigment desired. The backgrounds for pediments or sculptured friezes were red or blue. In the case of the Ionic order, color was used with more refinement, merely emphasizing the different features of the order. The architects of Doric buildings, however, were fonder of color and used it in crasser combinations.[40] Vivid reds, blues, and gilding were principally employed, blue mainly for the higher surfaces that were better lighted, red for backgrounds. Yellow and green were frequently used for minor details. Guttæ were sometimes red, sometimes white.

It was not until early in the Sixth Century that painting at Athens freed itself from its decorative connection with sculpture and architecture and began to exist more for its own sake. We have records of early paintings which were dedicated in a temple of Artemis Alpheionia not far from Olympia. Two of these were painted by Kleanthes of Corinth. Legend has it he or Philokles invented linear painting. He painted an Iliupersis, or Sack of Troy, and a Birth of Athena. Probably the primitive character of these early paintings gave rise to the report that Kleanthes

mäler, *s.v. Polychromie;* Mrs. E. Douglas Van Buren, *Archaic Fictile Revetments in Sicily and Magna Græcia,* London, 1923; F. C. Penrose, *The Principles of Athenian Architecture,* N. Y., 1888.

[38a] *Cf.* Frazer, *Pausanias,* II, 2, 6, commentary.

[39] P. Orsi, *Mon. Ant.,* 25 (1918), Pl. XVI, pp. 614 ff.; *cf.* A. Della Seta, *Italia antica,* Bergamo, 1922, pp. 117 ff. and Figs. 103-104.

[40] L. Fenger, *Dorische Polychromie,* Berlin, 1886, plates in color.

"invented" Greek painting. Aregon painted Artemis riding on a gryphon. The nature of these paintings we may assume from early works which we have examined and from representations of some of these themes on Athenian black-figured pottery. Doubtless, these paintings were, like those of Ekphantos, Eumaros, and the other primitives, not really paintings so much as drawings filled in with flat color. They must, in all likelihood, have been monochromes. The painters of this age were essentially draughtsmen, and no real mastery had been attained with the brush; they practiced mere outline and had not advanced to the point of grappling with complicated problems.

From 625 to 510 B.C. was the great age of tyrants in Greece, and under their power as so often in ages of domination by monarchs, art flourished.[41] We have seen that from the Seventh to the Sixth Century, under the Kypselids, Kypselos and his son Periander, the city of Corinth maintained a thriving commerce and sent her bronzes, pottery, and other industrial products all over the Greek world. In 585, their rule came to an end. In 565, Kleisthenes, the Tyrant of Sikyon, died. Undoubtedly, these rulers did much to foster art and to encourage the practice of painting in which Corinth and Sikyon played the leading rôle in early Greece. By 573, the great Pythian, Nemean, and Isthmian games were founded which helped to unify the Greeks and developed to some extent a national feeling. About this time Athens was brought to a high point by Solon who was later succeeded by tyrants— the Peisistratidai. Under these rulers, especially Peisistratos, 560 to 527 B.C., the arts were furthered, and inasmuch as Ionic cities were being harassed by the Persians, many Ionic artists found a haven in Athens at this time. Some were "invited" by Peisistratos to practice their calling in Athens. From 560 B.C. to 510 Athens was under the sway of these rulers and during this period we see her rise to eminence and attain an extensive commerce, sending her wares especially to Etruria. She was the more able to obtain a dominating position since Corinth's power had waned and the Ionian cities were losing their prestige.

We begin to see the Athenian stamp in painting about 560 B.C. but we must look to vases again to help us. In the François vase, a large krater found in Etruria and now in the *Museo Archeologico* in Florence, we find the national style developed. From the crude attempts of the Dipylon artist to this vase was a long stride, but it was not made in a single step; there are many transitional vases of the Seventh

[41] For an interesting presentation of conditions under the Greek Tyrants, see P. N. Ure, *The Greek Renaissance,* London, 1921, Chs. VI and VII; *The Origin of Tyranny,* Cambridge, 1922. Gyges of Lydia was the first tyrant, 687-652; Kypselos established himself at Corinth in 657 B.C., Periander his son ruling there from 625-585. Polykrates ruled in Samos from 540-522; Phalaris at Agrigentum, in 570. Not everyone will accept the theory presented that the tyrants owed their power to wealth acquired as a result of economic revolutions, but the material is handled in a very interesting manner.

Century showing geometric and Oriental influence. These are usually termed Proto-Attic. The old geometric forms still linger on but beside these a wealth of new subjects comes into vogue. Figure 226a, a jug from Athens, betrays the influence of geometric ware in its shape and in the crude band of dancing figures on the neck (Fig. 226b). But the main zone of decoration exhibits curvilinear patterns and heraldic lions of Oriental mien (Fig. 226b). Numerous motives on these vases are derived from the East, but borrowings from the Corinthian-Sikyonian school do not escape our notice.[42] As a typical example we shall take the Nessos amphora, where Herakles is shown slaying the centaur Nessos (Fig. 227a). Strewn ornaments are found over the field and the rosette and meander border the design. The artist works with the silhouette and already the red which Ekphantos brought in is used for the garment of Herakles. The vase employs violet-brown and black. On the other hand, the fleeing Gorgons are not painted white and "locality" is denoted by the dolphins (Fig. 227b). The stage reached by the Nessos amphora is roughly akin to that of the "Typhon" pediment in sculpture, though somewhat less crude. If it is true that the mustache comes in during the first quarter of the Sixth Century, the two monuments are not far removed in time, but the vase is of course earlier.[43] An advance in composition is to be noted in the case of the metope frame for the main design, but the use of violet-brown for the faces of Herakles and the Centaur shows that the work is laboring with primitive means. Very careful incision for outlines and details is found. This vase is followed by a series from Vourva near Marathon and by the so-called Tyrrhenian amphoræ, which form important groups in the Proto-Attic class but which may only be mentioned here in passing.

Turning to the Attic style of the Sixth Century, we see that the François vase corresponds in the important place which it holds in ceramics to that of the Kypselos chest in furniture. Each is a *chef d'œuvre* of its kind. The Attic vase, like the chest, is a great mine of mythological lore, arranged in zone-like compositions. Strewn ornaments have disappeared; the emphasis is on narrative (Fig. 228). Many of the myths which were to form a part of the repertoire of painting are already found here: the Achilles legend, with the funeral games for Patroklos and the slaying of Troilos; Theseus landing from Crete, and the marriage of Peleus and Thetis; the Calydonian boar hunt; the battle of the Centaurs and Lapiths; Hephaistos taken into Olympus, and the like. The colors used are black for silhouettes against the clay ground of the vase, white for the flesh of women and details, and purple. Some red was used for the flesh of men. Fairly successful attempts at balance, rhythm, group-

---

[42] E. Buschor, *op. cit.*, p. 66.

[43] Koch, *Ath. Mitth.*, 39 (1914), p. 244 and n. 2. The Nessos amphora is one of the earliest examples known of the occurrence of the mustache in vase-painting. On the François vase, 560 B.C., the smooth-shaven lip and the mustache both occur. The Moschophoros is without a mustache, Zeus of the pediment with the introduction of Herakles has it.

ing, rapid motion, and localization are all found. Traces of the primitive triangle are still seen in the depicting of the human torso, but a truer rendering of nature is apparent. The body is often twisted at the waist, bringing the trunk into front view. Often, too, the head faces in one direction while the feet go in the opposite. The "bent knee" formula is employed for swift movement. Isocephaly, or the placing of the heads of all figures, whether standing or seated, on the same level for the decorative effect, is the rule. But in general, the freedom of action and variety of pose seen here were not found in Dipylon ware and garments although sheathlike begin to give some idea of a figure beneath. The weak spot is the composition, which seems to have no beginning, middle, or end. There is no inevitable coherence of parts, so that certain groups in the central zone might well be interchanged without affecting the whole. The monotony is also rather pronounced. This vase was made by Ergotimos and painted by Klitias. Examples of the same potter's work appear to have been found at Naukratis in Egypt, and Gordion in Phrygia. This alone indicates the expansion of Attic commerce and the lack of provincialism among her artists.

In the period immediately following that of the François vase, there are numberless vases in the black-figured technique—some of them proudly signed by their makers, others by unknown masters. Most of the work is distinctly Attic. A part of these painters adopt Ionic motives, shapes, and technique; others were undoubtedly native Ionians themselves. The vases are usually painted in black silhouettes which stand out sharply from the reddish ground of the clay. Sometimes the color is applied directly to the clay; at other times, a red ocher was put on like a wash. When the design had been planned to suit the surface to be decorated, the figures were sketched in outline and filled in with a black varnish. After this, details such as eyes, hair, muscles, and folds of drapery were put in by means of incision with a sharp, pointed instrument. In this way, the black varnish was cut through to the surface of the clay and the lines are yellowish white. Sometimes they were even filled in with white, an Ionic device. The outlines of figures were not incised except in cases where they overlap. Details in white and purple were added last.[44] Purple was especially used for patterns on the drapery, white for the flesh of women, for shields, and ornamental patterns. The subjects chosen were commonly mythological, connected with the labors of Herakles, the Trojan war, the birth of Athena and Dionysiac legends, but some genre scenes occur.

Typically Ionic work is seen in the vases of the artist Nikosthenes.[44a] He was a very

[44] For the technical details of making a Greek vase, see especially Gisela M. A. Richter, *The Craft of Athenian Pottery*, Yale University Press, New Haven, 1923; Fowler and Wheeler, *Greek Archæology*, New York, 1909, p. 428. F. R., I, 13, 24.

[44a] Nikosthenes was probably the head of an *atelier* and employed more than one painter;

prolific potter who was fond of amphoræ of metallic form, with broad, flat handles (Fig. 229). The designs often show bands of satyrs and mænads dancing around the vase in pairs. The painting may be characterized by liveliness and spirit, as is the case here, where the decorative patterns are finely rendered—or it may be dull and careless. Red-figured and white-ground vases were made in his workshop. It is evident that he was an innovator, experimenting with various processes and forms.

The work of Amasis appears more individual.[45] In fact, some of his designs have an inimitable charm which Nikosthenes' painters lack. In the Bibliothèque Nationale is an amphora from his hand which reveals this difference (Fig. 230a). On one side Poseidon and Athena are represented; on the other Dionysos and two Mænads. In the case of the reverse, we see Dionysos garbed in a long robe and wearing a mantle about his shoulders. This dignified and elderly deity is represented as greeting two Mænads who hop toward him joyously with their arms about one another's necks (Fig. 231). The perspective has not turned out entirely as it should have, since the further Mænad is much larger in size than the one in front. The relation of the arms to the figures is also confused. But the artist shows spirit and imagination and he knows the value of a good decorative pattern. This is clearly evident from the design on the shoulder,—bands of warriors fighting in pairs (Fig. 230b). The vigor of the thrust lines of the spears, the beauty of balance, the arrested motion of the bowman in the center who is fleeing rapidly away with arms and legs outstretched, all contribute to the excellence of the pattern.[46]

One of the problems of the Attic painter from the days of Solon until the period of Kimon of Kleonai seems to have been to try to approach nature somewhat more nearly in rendering the human form. The vase-painting of this age is, however, essentially a decorative art and the first demand therefore is the decorative value of the pattern. For this, the masters of the Sixth Century had a fine sense. This superiority may be seen in such vases as the Dionysos kylix by Exekias (Fig. 232) and in the Cheiron vase in London (Fig. 270). Designs such as these mean that the painter has solved the problem of perfect spacing of his masses over the background and that he has an instinctive feeling for line. The artist works with fixed schemes. The beginnings of this are to be seen in Dipylon ware but in the vases of the early black-figured style the painter is strictly bound by these conventions. There are schemes for fighting, wrestling, running, dancing, locality, and the like. The su-

one of these is known as the Nikosthenes Painter. Epiktetos and Oltos also worked for him.

[45] G. Karo, *J.H.S.*, XIX (1899), p. 135; Pls. V-VI; F. Hauser, *Œst. Jahr.*, X (1907); Alice Walton, *A.J.A.*, XI (1907), pp. 150 ff.; Adamek, *Unsignierte Vasen des Amasis*, Prag, 1895; Loeschcke, *P.W.*, I, 1748, *s.v. Amasis;* J. C. Hoppin, *A Handbook of Greek B.-F. Vases*, Paris, 1924, pp. 27 ff.; Beazley, *Attic Black-Figure*, London, 1928, pp. 22 ff., App. II.
[46] *Cf. W.V.*, 1889, Pl. III.

periority of Greek art lies in the fact that the Greeks used their schemes as a limitation within which there might be infinite variety. This allowed each artist to represent beauty as he saw it and yet he worked with laws that were fixed enough to be laws.[47]

What the painter had learned about drawing the human figure and its value as a decorative pattern is seen by comparing two vases given as prizes in the Panathenaic games. The Burgon amphora of Figure 233 belongs in the early Sixth Century and the features show the exaggerations of primitive art. The figure of Athena is heavy, and we are not certain whether we have a front or back view, judging from the way in which the arm with the spear is attached. Her garment is almost entirely of purplish red, because of the early artist's love for polychromy. Contrast with this a vase executed near the close of the Sixth Century (Fig. 234). The artist here understands how to represent movement more gracefully. He has elongated his figure to meet the decorative demands of his vase. He has learned to draw folds in his garments and to gain the full decorative effect of the ægis. He has made use of his ornamental patterns by sowing them in color over the garment. The vase is less polychromatic than the Burgon amphora because purple has been largely given up. The prominent features of the face are no longer exaggerated and the design acquires a certain lightness of character which is well seen from a comparison of the shield devices.

The achievement of the black-figured painter was nothing short of extraordinary when we consider the medium with which he was working, a black silhouette, in which all details had to be put in by incision with a sharply pointed instrument. The work was that of an engraver rather than that of a painter. In Figure 235 we see a vase of Exekias dating after 550 B.C. All of the white lines mean incision and show the meticulous care needed to render hair, patterns of garments, and details. Exekias had a fondness for this kind of work and has produced beautiful examples such as this representation of heroes playing draughts.

But vase-painting worked with one technique, monumental painting doubtless with another. It is extremely questionable whether the black-figured silhouette was employed by wall-painters. That it was used, however, on other *fictile* works is evident from a series of Attic funerary plaques dating after the middle of the Sixth Century. It may be also that in monumental painting of the Sixth Century we are dealing almost exclusively with fictile work. Twelve of these plaques were found near the Dipylon Gate in Athens and must at one time have formed the terra cotta decoration of a tomb. They probably made a frieze-like decoration on four sides of rough masonry which supported a stele. Doubtless they helped to conceal the poverty of the construction. We do not know just how they were arranged but they

---

[47] P. Gardner, *Principles of Greek Art*, 1914, p. 239.

are divided into two groups in one of which the meander pattern at the top goes to the left, in the other, to the right. They measure about 0.37 meter in height by 0.43 meter in breadth and there are no suspension holes. The colors used are a lustrous black, yellowish-white, and a brown nearing purple. The artist began by painting all of the figures in black. Then the white and red additions were made, white for the flesh of women, brownish red for the folds of mantles and certain other details. Ornaments on garments and details of figures were incised. All of this was set off against the almost orange red of the clay.

The scenes on the plaques concern the death of a woman whose funeral rites are brought before us. In Figure 236 we have a group of eight women, five of whom are seated in sorrowful attitudes. One of the three standing holds a child in her arms. The central figure of the group, distinguished by her rich garment and a mantle over her head, is probably the mother of the dead woman, and the child, at the right, the orphan. The center of the monument must have been decorated with the main theme —the *Prothesis* scene. Here we see the dead woman wreathed with a crown, laid out on a rich funeral couch (Fig. 237). At the right, two women are bending over the bier. The Doric column in the fragment at the left denotes the interior of the house. Within, a man and woman are represented in attitudes of mourning, tearing their hair. In the upper fragment a second woman is shown in a similar attitude.

The scenes following present the *Ekphora* or funeral procession. In these fragments are several chariots and groups of men and women on foot. The mules which probably drew the funeral car are seen with a nude servant attending them (Fig. 238). The funerary procession was formed with the bier in front, with men and horsemen following.[47a] There are few remains of these figures but behind the mules we see four men on foot, one of whom is rather grotesquely represented with face in front view. There follow chariots in procession and mourning figures of men and women (*cf.* Fig. 236). Probably the procession of women formed one side, that of the men, the opposite side. In the front of the monument the dead woman was laid out in state. At the back were riders and four-horse chariots.

The composition of the plaques is unified, the drawing exact and sure. At times it possesses a certain archaic elegance. There is a distinct element of melancholy which runs through the whole frieze, aroused largely by poses and gestures. The art shows a decided superiority to the workmanship of the Corinthian plaques which were fashioned for ordinary traders, sailors, and peasants of Corinth. The Athenian plaques, on the other hand, were probably made by a good painter such as Eumaros to adorn the tomb of the wife of a rich Eupatrid of Athens.[48] The paintings give us

[47a] G. Hirschfeld, *Festschrift für J. Overbeck*, Leipzig, 1893, pp. 8 ff., doubts that the bier was in front.

[48] Perrot and Chipiez, *op. cit.*, IX, 254. Caskey suggests they may be metope-like slabs.

some idea of fictile art on a larger scale and it is very doubtful whether there was much mural work of a different character in the middle of the Sixth Century. Certain conventions are very closely adhered to—light silhouettes for women, dark for men; round, incised eyes for men, almond-shaped for women, white for one of the horses seen in perspective. The work has an archaic charm combined with strength and originality. These plaques belong in the age of Peisistratos when Solon's law limiting the luxury of grave monuments was no longer enforced.[48a] The Museum of Fine Arts in Boston has recently acquired two Attic plaques of this type but about half a century older. On one, the dead woman is represented laid out on a couch and mourned by two women. Above in the field, three geese fly to the right while below the couch is a siren—symbol of the soul of the dead. On the second plaque are three women with their arms raised to their heads in sign of mourning. Caskey points out that this plaque so closely resembles a Hydria of "Vourva" style that they may both be by the same hand.[48b] Rumpf assigns the Berlin plaques to Exekias (*Gnomon*, 1925, p. 334).

The museums of Athens and Copenhagen possess numerous fragments of other plaques of this character. Several have been published by Benndorf.[49] They show how much this kind of decoration was in fashion in the funerary architecture of the Sixth Century. A number of votive plaques have been found, from the end of the Sixth Century. A famous one of a goddess mounting her chariot with Hermes before her is signed by Skythes, who was also a painter of vases (Fig. 239).

Somewhat later than these monuments and showing the more advanced technique of light figures against a darker ground instead of the reverse, is a painted poros fragment from the Acropolis.[50] It represents a lioness in a rose red color against a dark greenish ground, which was originally blue. It probably formed a part of a pedimental composition and is one of our earliest examples of the new technique which came in near the end of the Sixth Century. The work is essentially linear in character.

One of the most important monuments in this technique is the painted marble stele of Lyseas, a rich Eupatrid of Athens who apparently owned stables of horses which competed in the Panathenaic races (Fig. 240). The ground of the stele seems to have been red, but it has lost most of its color. Against this we see Lyseas garbed in a white mantle with a purplish red chiton.[51] Almost the only trace of color is a

[48a] The "laws of Solon" may be Post-Solonian. Cic. *De Leg.*, II, 26, 64, seems to imply as much in regard to this particular law.

[48b] *Bull. of the Museum of Fine Arts*, Boston, 1927, p. 55.

[49] O. Benndorf, *Griechische und sicilische Vasenbilder*, Pls. I-IV.

[50] Th. Wiegand, *Die archaische Poros-Architektur der Akropolis zu Athen*, 1904, p. 230, Pl. VI, 3; *cf.* Milchhöfer, *Ath. Mitth.*, V (1880), p. 164, Pl. VI.

[51] G. Rodenwaldt, *Ant. Denk.*, III, Pls. 32-33; Loeschcke, *Ath. Mitth.*, IV (1879), p. 36, Pls. I, II.

reddish patch of this garment seen on the chest. As a priest of Dionysos, Lyseas holds in one hand a kantharos which was probably black, and in the other some green branches. His beard and hair were apparently reddish brown. The strings of his sandals and the border of his himation were certainly in colors. There is doubt about the flesh-color; it was in all probability left in the tone of the marble.[51a] The contours, which have practically disappeared, seem to have been in black; the lines are now white. The drapery, which begins to take on the appearance of real folds, calls to mind the inventions of Kimon. In other respects, however, the stele seems less advanced, especially in the immobility of the feet, flat on the ground. It is doubtless to be dated between 520-510 B.C. as it is similar to the Aristion stele in sculpture.[52] Both are ideal types of manhood having little value as portraits. In technique they are also closely akin. The recently published facsimile of the Lyseas stele executed by Gilliéron shows more clearly the nobility of the figure and the monumental character of the work.[51]

The horse and rider below Lyseas indicate the victory of a Eupatrid in a race, probably at the Panathenaic festival (Fig. 241b). The color of the rider was similar to that of Lyseas. The ground upon which the design was placed seems to have been blue, and not the white of the marble. In this stele of Lyseas we have polychromy and an advance beyond the earlier monochrome stage of painting. Girard would associate the monument with the period of Kimon of Kleonai and mark as one of his advances, the use of polychromy instead of monochrome work.[53] The colors were probably put on in *tempera* and whether or not a wax technique was used, we cannot definitely know. Langlotz connects the drapery of the stele with that of an amphora in the Louvre by Euthymides.[54]

[51a] Loeschcke held that the nude parts and the himation had no solid color but the natural color of the marble, "toned in the one case with brown, in the other, with white," *op. cit.*, p. 39. K. Müller assumes a light red for the flesh, the same color as the chiton, but thinned. *Cf.* note 52. E. Pfuhl, *Malerei und Zeichnung der Griechen,* München, 1923, I, 494, states that the fact that the flesh parts were more weathered than the chiton and ground indicates that the nude portions were unpainted.

[52] F. Winter, *Œst. Jahr.*, III (1900), p. 130, connects the Aristion stele with the Antaios krater of Euphronios. *Cf.* E. Langlotz, *Zur Zeitbestimmung der strengrotfigurigen Vasenmalerei und der gleichzeitigen Plastik*, Leipzig, 1920, p. 65. He establishes the stele in the Leagros period which he dates at 510 B.C. K. Müller, *Arch. Anz.*, 37 (1922), pp. 1 ff., argues from weathering that the ground of the Lyseas was blue; the flesh, light red; chiton, dark red; kantharos, black; color of face and hair, uncertain; lips, red; branches, green. The horse on the base of the stele, in his opinion, was left in the color of the marble. The boy's flesh was the same color as that of Lyseas. The ground was again blue.

[53] P. Girard, *La Peinture antique*, pp. 142 ff.

[54] E. Langlotz, *op. cit.*, p. 67, n. 4; *Louvre Album*, G 44, Pl. 92; J. C. Hoppin, *Euthymides and his Fellows*, Cambridge, 1917, Fig. 6, p. 61 and Pl. XVI.

Monuments such as the Lyseas stele are of great importance in the history of painting. They seem to indicate that painting was at least developing in a manner parallel to the development of sculpture at the end of the Sixth Century. There are also other specimens of this more advanced technique, for example, the head of a youth from Sunium—a rather free portrait in white outline on a red ground (Fig. 242). The color of the flesh is reddish, but we do not know that this was the case originally. The white lines, which may have been black in the beginning, indicate that it was not black. At present it is a red, lighter than the ground.[55] The monument belongs to the end of the Sixth Century, about 510 B.C. Pottier has pointed out its relation to drawings by Euphronios. Among other stelæ of the period is the one of Antiphanes in which a cock is sketched in black with feathers of red and blue against a ground of yellow.

Freer than these in style is a disc in marble of the physician Aineios. It dates from about 500 B.C. and may have been dedicated by some grateful patient. Only the shadow of a figure is left—a bearded man, seated on a high *klismos* (Fig. 243). Little color remains but the most important feature is the use of pure yellow on the garment over his knee. Black was employed for his hair, his beard, and also for the ground line. Blue is found on the letters and a few traces of red here and there indicate that the ground color was once more red. There is great freedom in the drawing and in the treatment of drapery. The head seems to be a portrait.[56] It is merely an outline drawing on which color was placed in *tempera* or in encaustic.

From the Athenian monuments which we have examined it seems very evident that until the end of the Sixth Century, a purely flat style was current among the painters of the time. The silhouette was employed and minor details were scratched or drawn in. The surfaces were covered with a few solid colors and the background commonly used for painting on marble was red. About the end of the Sixth Century, the first indication of linear and bodily perspective appears with Kimon of Kleonai. Such monuments as the youth on horseback against a dark ground, with anatomical details carefully indicated, may perhaps be considered to reflect his influence (Fig. 241a). It seems likely, as Girard supposes, that the change to light-figured silhouettes in vase-painting may have resulted from Kimon's efforts and we should therefore reckon the light silhouette against a dark ground and the marking of anatomical features as due in part to his innovations. Certainly painting on a large scale preceded vase-painting in the introduction of the light silhouette, as the fragment of a lioness referred to above indicates.

The Warrior Tablet from the Acropolis is another very interesting monument

[55] *B.C.H.*, VIII (1884), Pl. XIV, pp. 459-461.
[56] H. Dragendorff, *Jahr.*, XII (1897), Pl. I, pp. 1 ff. *Vs.* this view, *cf.* E. Pfuhl, *Die Anfänge der griechischen Bildniskunst*, München, 1927, pp. 2 ff., 19.

from the end of the Sixth Century. The figure of the youth is again a solid silhouette, this time in very dark brown against a light ground (Fig. 244). The fictile character of the work may have determined the color. The tablet represents a young warrior armed with a lance, and with a shield which bears a dancing, nude satyr as a device. The drapery about his loins is black with folds incised. His helmet and shield are mostly white, but the crest of the helmet, minor markings, and the satyr's tail are painted purplish red. White is used for the eyeball, and muscles are indicated by fine black lines on the brown; folds of drapery by incised lines on the black. The drawing calls to mind vase-masters of the late Sixth Century, such as Phintias. The fore-shortened shield is characteristic of work which in this period so strongly reflected the innovations of Kimon. The treatment of drapery is closely akin to what we find in Figure 303. The style is throughout strongly reminiscent of Phintias. It is certainly allied with vases of this circle and Hoppin may be correct in attributing it to Euthymides,[57] although he states that it shows resemblances in style to both masters.

The plaque is a brick 0.06 meter thick, 0.52 meter broad, and 0.39 meter high. It must have been about 0.70 meter high when whole. It is decorated around the edges with two painted bands, one of purplish red and one of black. Above in the field runs an inscription, *Glaukytes Kalos,* but the name Megakles had been erased to make way for this. We do not know the reason for the substitution. Buschor connects it with a Megakles banished in 486, and worthy of this praise twenty-five years earlier.[58]

Pausing for a moment to reconsider the achievement reached in the major art of Greek painting by the days of Kimon, we find in the earliest period, judging from the vases, from reliefs such as those from Prinias,[59] from traditional accounts, and from the earliest Etruscan paintings, that painting in Greece held to flat colored surfaces and was geometrically stylized. It undoubtedly avoided the extensive use of ornamental patterns found in vase-painting, nor did it, like vase-painting, have recourse to black figures unless in the earlier period. Probably few minor details were marked in the figures, and the coloring must have been very simple. In the severe archaic period, which is represented by the metopes from Thermos, polychromy took the place of the earlier monochromes. But until the end of the Sixth Century, the painting was flat like Egyptian painting and relief; the employment of the pure silhouette was universal.

The stele of Lyseas of the third stage marks a much freer epoch, in which the "innovations" of Kimon began to come into vogue. This monument shows a light silhouette against a dark ground, polychromy, and an ability to render drapery with

[57] J. C. Hoppin, *Euthymides and his Fellows,* 1917, pp. 89 ff.
[58] E. Buschor, *op. cit.,* p. 148.
[59] G. Karo, *Arch. Anz.* (1908), p. 123; L. Pernier, *Bollettino d'arte,* 1907.

folds. The greater achievement of foreshortening is not evident here but is seen in many vases of the early red-figured period. In the East at this time—in Ionia—landscape elements were also playing a rôle in painting, as the pictures dedicated by Mandrokles prove.

Down to the Fifth Century the colors seem to have remained largely black, white, and red. The red varied from brick dust to terra cotta and violet. Yellow was often reserved in the color of the ground; in the Thermos metopes the color seems to have been mixed with red, but the earliest use of a pure yellow occurs about 500 B.C. on the marble disc of the physician Aineios.[59a] More colors may have been employed in Ionia. Though the sarcophagi do not show others, the gaiety of early Etruscan painting would indicate as much. We can hardly think of Mandrokles' painting of Darius crossing the Bosphorus without a strip of blue sea. The fragile nature of green and blue when fired may have prevented their use on clay, but this cannot have been the reason for the failure to use them in Greece proper. The reason probably lay in the simple character and timidity of the art itself, which was after all much more a matter of pure drawing than of painting as we know it. It was not that the painter did not have these colors at hand; we have seen blue and green used extensively on the sculpture and architecture of the period; it was the simplicity of the early attempts in the field.

With Kimon undoubtedly some of the flatness customary in rendering the human figure was done away with. Work with the brush began to be significant. By gaining control of some of the real media of painting and by learning how to foreshorten, he gave to Polygnotos the opportunity for developing a grand style. Without Kimon and without the impetus which came into art after the Persian wars when temples and other buildings were extensively rebuilt, Greek painting might long have lacked the master spirit who placed upon it the stamp of nobility.

The work of Kimon was essentially dependent on draughtsmanship. Drawing was to the Greeks more important than color. Justness of outline was the thing sought for above all things by the great painters—the lines that revealed movement and form. Plutarch thought color of more significance in painting, believing it to be a source of greater illusion, but the more prevalent view is represented by Aristotle, who champions the superiority of drawing over color.[60] "Painting does not consist entirely in the mixture of colors, for one color sufficed for ancient painters. Only later, they used four, then more. Moreover, a drawing where shadow and light are indicated, even without the employment of color—is not that painting? In such

---

[59a] Yellow occurs earlier on the dog of the pinax by Timonidas, but was not used extensively as it appears to have been on the disc of Aineios. Cf. K. Müller, Arch. Anz., 1922, p. 3.

[60] Aristotle, Poetics, VI, 15; cf. Scholiast on Aratus, Phainomena, 828, quoting Plutarch; Plutarch, De Tranquill. An. 15.

drawings we see likeness, the restraint or boldness of the figures, although they are devoid of color."[61]

We have followed Greek drawing, especially on vases and fictile work in general, from the crude geometric stylization of the Dipylon age, through the period of monochrome silhouettes. Then, the artist was attempting to correct somewhat his earlier memory images by what he observed in nature although his work was often hampered by fixed schemes. By the middle of the Sixth Century these *schemata* for representing the human figure in rest and motion approached nature much more nearly. There was great archaic elegance in many vases of the period but as a whole the artists were bound by certain conventions which limited their development. Chief among these was the use of incision which the black silhouette demanded.

During the last quarter of the Sixth Century a change came about in vase-painting. Painters no longer always represented the human figure as a black silhouette, but, instead, they began to outline with the brush on the red ground of the clay the contours of their figures. Thus they allowed their forms to stand out in the ground color of the vase, filling the background with black. For the first time, the painter's brush was really emancipated. The artist had attained real freedom in drawing his contours and he had in addition the use of the brush for lines of drapery and for all details within the silhouette.

Much time has been spent in conjecturing the cause of this change. Some have asserted that it was the influence of Ionia where we have seen both black-figured and light-colored silhouettes, especially on sarcophagi.[62] Others have sought to explain its innovation on technical grounds arguing that the new style brought greater protection against porousness in the vase. The most likely explanation is that the vase-painters were following the major art of the period which had turned its attention to nature. In order to be able to draw more freely, the artists of the time changed from the black-figured silhouette to figures in light color.

We are not able to know the character of the drawing and painting of Kimon of Kleonai except as we can follow it on vases and on painted stelæ and tablets. Suffice it to say that about 525 B.C. we see a few ceramic innovators such as Nikosthenes, Andokides, Hischylos, and Epiktetos working in both techniques and often transferring to the red-figured style the black-figured designs. Where we begin to have real evidence of Kimon's extensive influence with vase-painters is in the work of painters like Euphronios, about 510 B.C. Here, in the Antaios krater in the Louvre, where Herakles is represented strangling the giant Antaios, we see the care in ana-

[61] Philostr., *Vita Apollon.*, II, Ch. 22.

[62] M. Heinemann, *Landschaftliche Elemente in der griechischen Kunst bis Polygnot,* Bonn, 1910, p. 82; E. Pottier, *B.C.H.*, 14 (1890), pp. 380 ff.; 16 (1892), pp. 243 ff.; G. Loeschcke, *Ath. Mitth.*, IV (1879), p. 41 (influence of marble-painting).

tomical detail and in expression of emotion which Kimon undoubtedly brought in (Fig. 245). The muscles of the stomach and the chest are rendered with great precision; the pectoral line is marked. There is a suggested attempt at foreshortening the giant's right foot. Moreover, expression is well rendered. The leering look in the giant's eyes and the mouth open in agony show the death grip in which Herakles holds his victim. The use of a dilute wash for hair and beard adds to the wildness of the monster, but chiefly the painting interests us because it gives evidence of greater skill in brushwork. The growing ability of the artist to render drapery is seen in the women's garments. Since the head of Herakles recalls to us the head of the warrior Aristion, we may therefore, with the evidence above, date the vase about 510 B.C. The pyramidal composition in the center and the carefully balanced masses in the background to right and left offer us an advanced composition which may have been influenced by sculpture or by painting.

The character of compositions in the days of Kimon we also cannot know with any degree of certainty. Vases such as the kylix by Euphronios in Munich with its elaborate grouping of figures (Fig. 246) indicate that the compositions of Kimon were nothing puerile and that we need not presuppose isolated figures strewn over the field, as some are inclined to do with Polygnotos. Here the overlapping figures, forceful and free action, stop-gap filling and balanced masses prove that the major art was rapidly advancing.

From the time of Kimon until after the middle of the Fifth Century, Greek vases drew a great deal of inspiration from the major art of painting in Athens. From them we learn much that we know about the drawing of the major artists and how it developed. We can trace the painstaking efforts of these artists in rendering the smallest details and in attempting to approach nature more closely; we can see their struggles toward self-expression.

Since drawing played so large a part in the equipment of the Greek painter and was such a significant element in his painting, we may pause for a time to consider drawing and design as it appears on Greek vases. The monumental painters were at no time behind the humbler artists in their technique and vases can indicate for us the progress of the major art. These small works of handicraft contemporary with the famous masters therefore possess for us a great importance in the history of Greek painting. This is the more true because the artisan in Greece was usually an artist and invented every time he used his brush. He repeated traditional types unendingly but never slavishly nor without contributing something new. Although he was dominated by an abstract conception of form, his designs are a combination of patterns drawn from nature and formal elements. It is largely the beauty of the drawing and design which appeals to us in Greek vases. If the lines found there were of such excellence, what might we expect of the master of line, Apelles! The archaic period which we have discussed together with the age of Kimon of Kleonai was the important era when the art of drawing developed so tremendously in Greece. Never after were painters so sincere and so true to the demands of their craft as in this period of striving to adjust nature to abstract ideas of form.

# VI

# GREECE: DRAWING AND DESIGN ON GREEK VASES[1]

THE arts of design—primarily painting, sculpture, and architecture—depend largely upon arrangement for their success—upon the scheme of lines, masses, spaces, and colors employed. We shall confine ourselves to the discussion of design as it appears on Greek vases. When we consider that, with the aid of these "thousand sketches on fragile clay, we can trace an evolution that lasted four or five centuries and created the art of drawing as practiced by all modern nations,"[2] it would seem worth while to study these drawings and to analyze the elements which contributed to the beauty of Greek design. The recent appearance of several books of importance dealing with the subject of Greek vase-painting makes more accessible for the student of Art and Archæology a wide range of valuable material for the study of these problems. The publications by Beazley[3] and Hoppin[4] catalogue and illustrate for us the most important works of

[1] Parts of this chapter were read at a session of the Archæological Institute of America in Baltimore, December, 1921. While some of the material treated was touched upon in Chapter V, it is discussed here from a new viewpoint.

[2] E. Pottier, *Douris and the Painters of Greek Vases*, tr. by B. Kahnweiler, London, 1908, p. 81.

[3] J. D. Beazley, *Attic Red-Figured Vases in American Museums*, Cambridge, 1918; *Attische Vasenmaler des rotfigurigen Stils*, Tübingen, 1925; *Greek Vases in Poland*, Oxford, 1928; *Attic Black-Figure*, London, 1928.

[4] J. C. Hoppin, *A Handbook of Attic Red-Figured Vases*, Cambridge, 1919; *A Handbook of Greek Black-Figured Vases*, Paris, 1924; M. A. B. Herford, *A Handbook of Greek Vase Painting*, London, 1919; K. Reichhold, *Skizzenbuch griechischer Meister*, München, 1919; E. Buschor, *Greek Vase-Painting*, tr. by G. C. Richards, New York, 1922; E. Langlotz, *Griechische Vasenbilder*, Heidelberg, 1922; P. Ducati, *Storia della ceramica greca*, Firenze, 1922; C. Dugas, *Greek Pottery*, tr. by W. A. Thorpe, London, 1926; G. Nicole, *La Peinture des vases grecs*, Paris, 1926; G. von Lücken, *Griechische Vasenbilder*, Berlin, 1921.

the vase-painters, giving us an appreciation of their achievement as well; they open up greater possibilities for the study of design and for æsthetic criticism.

With the heritage of more than three thousand years of artistic endeavor behind us, we are likely to forget that the Greek artist was obliged to solve for himself many problems which seem very simple to us today, such as the adaptation of shapes to spaces, rhythm, symmetry, foreshortening, perspective, light, and shadow. In the dim background of Greek prehistory, which was a prelude to, rather than an essential stage in the development of Greek art, many problems of composition had been successfully attacked and solved, but how much the Hellenic race really owed to the artistic gift of the Cretans in this respect is very uncertain. The amalgamation of the Minoans with peoples on the coast of Asia Minor after the breaking up of the Cretan civilization gave rise to the splendid outburst of Ionic art and probably handed on to Greece a touch of her genius for composition. It gave to her that fondness for the treatment of patterns drawn from nature and suggestions of landscape that we term "Ionic."

In striking contrast to the highly developed art of Crete, with its technical perfection and marvelous choice of fauna and flora for decorative purposes, is the art of early Greece. Much had been lost after the destruction of the Ægean civilization; some elements from Crete were later to influence Greece by way of the Argolid and the East, but, in its beginnings, Greek art was almost without conventions and artistic traditions, though some technical facility, some monuments and certain Ægean motives had been inherited from Mycenæan art.

In the geometric pottery of Greece, which reached its culmination in the Dipylon ware of Athens during the Eighth Century B.C., we see at once that the Greek painter displayed an instinctive feeling for design (Fig. 247; cf. Fig. 199). The way in which he has used his ornaments to decorate the various zones shows great skill in arrangement and combination. If, however, we separate out single details, such as a charioteer (Fig. 248), the work seems crude and almost grotesque. The primitive triangle for the torso of the man and the peculiar structure of the horses with their elongated legs strike the eye at once. The charm of the patterns is, however, undeniable. The repetition of the dark figures of the mourners in the upper zone of Figure 247, against the lighter ground of the clay, and the succession of charioteers below, arouse a certain feeling of pleasure. The artist has used the human figure as a schematic pattern and has succeeded well in his effect. No one would deny that the water-birds set between geometric checkerboard-patterns and the delicately drawn does of Figure 249 are æsthetically moving. These motives were used to adorn the necks of large amphoræ and they form delightful decorative elements. The wild duck of Figure 250 is somewhat more rigid in form but it is well suited to its function in the design (Fig. 251). The Dipylon vases are important not only

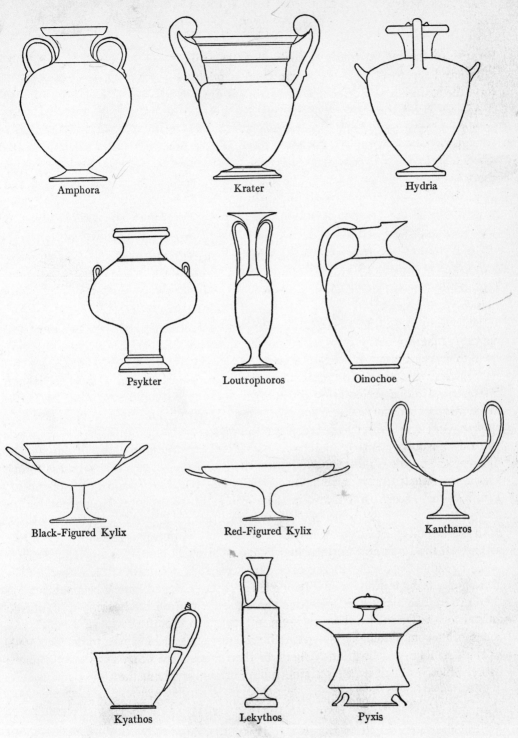

Amphora Krater Hydria

Psykter Loutrophoros Oinochoe

Black-Figured Kylix Red-Figured Kylix Kantharos

Kyathos Lekythos Pyxis

Shapes of Greek Vases.

because of the splendid feeling for design that they reveal, but also because they introduced representations of human beings and these representations continued to form the main interest of Greek vase-painters until the decline of Greek art.

After appreciating the good quality of the design, we may consider the means employed for expression and the reasons why the artist chose to represent men and animals in forms so far removed from nature. The Dipylon artist was quite independent of nature in his drawing and seems rather to have perverted it (Fig. 252). The truth is that he created his works of art with no regard for the real appearance of objects in nature. The image in his mind was a kind of typical picture with everything individual and accidental removed. The graphic expression of this was a scheme of lines in geometric form:[5] the torso of the human figure is a triangle, the legs are long and thin, the head rather bird-shaped; the corpse awkwardly lying on its side has the chest in front view, the head and legs in profile (Fig. 252). This last phenomenon, in which the various parts of the body are seen from different points of view, resulted from fidelity to a primitive mental picture, which usually retained objects in their broadest and most characteristic aspects. We must not consider that the artist was seeking to copy nature; he probably could not have done so had he chosen. He did not have his eye upon the object. The *schemata* which he evolved were his means of representing nature in rhythmic pattern. His main interest was in decoration and the figures became pure ornament. Gradually, as the artist began to observe, these purely mental images were altered and corrected, though Greek art for many centuries shows the struggle between the memory-picture and observation of nature in its twisted bodies, squinted eyes, and other discrepancies. It does not seem likely that the geometric artist produced these forms, as some have held, in his attempts to copy Cretan-Mycenæan, wasp-waisted figures.[5a] Primitive man, arriving at a certain stage of civilization, appears to conventionalize his figures in geometric forms, whether he lives in Peru, Elam, Egypt, or Greece.

In the Seventh Century B.C., when geometric decoration must have begun to pall somewhat, the Ionic and Corinthian schools, which were developed in Greece under Oriental influence, began to reveal a new style. They were doubtless inspired in great measure by tapestries and by objects in metal, clay, and ivory brought in from the East by Phœnician traders. From these they borrowed the hybrid and fantastic animals of the Orient. In their beginnings, they made use of a style of decoration in zones, often compressing or elongating their figures to suit the space to be decorated.

The Rhodian oinochoai, or pitchers, of the Ionic school (Fig. 253) exhibit many Eastern motives such as the striding sphinx or the gryphon, the goose, which may

---

[5] E. Loewy, *The Rendering of Nature in Early Greek Art*, tr. by J. Fothergill, London, 1907, pp. 10, 22.

[5a] É. Cahen, *Rev. des études grecques*, 38 (1925), pp. 1-15.

be domestic, the lotus, guilloche, and dotted circle. On other Ionic vases, the siren and lion occur and the panther with face in front view (Headpiece, Ch. V, Fig. 255). The whole field is usually strewn with ornaments like a fabric. As we have seen earlier, the East is the home of these bands of animals which follow one another and sometimes bite the one in front. The individual characteristics in drawing to be noted are the elongated forms of the wild goats which lend a certain elegance and delicacy to the zones of ornament and which emphasize the horizontal divisions of the decoration (Fig. 253). The majestic stride of the gryphon in Figures 253 and 254 is a repetition of the Oriental hieratic gait seen in the lions of the Procession street in Babylon. In contrast to this, truth to nature is observed in the heavy waddle of the goose and in the lightness of the browsing goats (cf. Fig. 211). Everywhere, there is freedom of pose, fine observation, and selection. The value of the gryphon as a conventionalized decorative animal is fully grasped (Fig. 254); the curve of the wings, the open beak, the tail with a swallow on it, show the more stylized motives, so employed as to gain their full value as pattern. One of the main interests of the artist has been elegance of form and the beauty of long, undulating lines. In order to accentuate these, he has not hesitated to lengthen the animals and to adapt them to the space to be decorated (Fig. 254). The effectiveness of the Rhodian goats as a pattern has recently caused them to be used in modern designs on circular bonbon boxes. The polychrome coloring of red, yellow, black, and white adds a note of harmony.

The Ionic vases from Cære, represented here by certain patterns (Figs. 256 and 257), show the fondness of the East for introducing plant motives and suggestions of landscape. Figure 257 from the Busiris vase, and Figure 255 as well, exhibit the polychromy of Ionia, derived directly from Crete, in their extensive use of black, white, red, and brownish yellow. But the striking thing about the Busiris vase is its naturalism, whether in the rendering of myrtle branches or in depicting the burly, thick-lipped negroes who form the Egyptian police guard. The hare running up the mound (Fig. 256) goes back to Assyrian art where animals are seen galloping over hills, often pursued in the hunt. The hare is truthfully drawn with long ears and a heavy coat, though its hind feet are those of a lion. The hill and trees, on the other hand, are strongly conventionalized. This design is a part of a vase-painting in which Europa, seated on the back of the bull, is landing after her long voyage from Crete. As she approaches, she terrifies the small hare, which races up the hillside. We have already noted the love for balance and symmetry in Ionic work and the fact that in many of these monuments, such as the sarcophagi, we have real pattern-designing with bilateral symmetry.

The school of Corinth, in contrast to that of Ionia, had a preference for heavier figures which are compressed or elongated according to a variable canon to suit the space to be filled (Fig. 258). Often the neck of some bird or that of a panther or sphinx is grotesquely lengthened to adorn the neck of a long, narrow alabastron, or perfume jug (Fig. 202c), and the legs of various animals are shortened or increased to suit the decorated space. The animals are used in a purely decorative fashion without regard for proportions. The lion employed as a conventionalized type is seen in Figure 259. The fine use of incision for details is especially noteworthy. These vases give the effect of tapestries even more than those of the Ionian class, especially because of the large number of "ground ornaments" such as the rosette (Fig. 258). The Oriental motives recur—for example, the panther with one head in front view and two bird-bodies (Fig. 260). This motive may be traced later in the capitals of Romanesque churches.[5b]

Corinthian figures are drawn differently from the Ionic, with heavier proportions and wings that are often broad and drooping in type and richly adorned with purple stripes. The sphinx of Figure 261 exhibits these features in drawing. The heraldic and antithetic animals of the East also occur, especially raging lions (Fig. 262). The animals represented were not studied from nature but the decorative element to be gained from the forms was the thing which interested the artist. He carefully balanced his masses over the field and made his designs conform to the various divisions of the vase. Horses are done in a rather dry, geometric way (Fig. 263), and though they are more recognizable than the grotesque, spike-maned representations of the Dipylon vases, they are not yet the type that would arouse a neigh from Bucephalus! They are, however, the forerunners of those on Attic vases of the black-figured style. This is the Corinthian formula for "spirited pair of horses." The second horse is recognizable by the two tails, the legs, and the outline of the second head. In the herd of oxen of Figure 264, the grouping of the cattle is skilfully managed with an occasional abbreviating of figures, although there are twenty-five legs! Euphronios was not much more clever in handling the same problem many decades later (Fig. 295).

After adapting and combining for some time geometric patterns, motives from the East and from various schools such as those of Corinth, Ionia, and Bœotia,[5c] Athens created a distinctive style of her own. Figure 265 shows some of the old formulæ of Dipylon ware living on, combined with elements from Corinth and other schools. The legs of the horses are long and thin, the bodies elongated and narrow. The heads and manes are conventionalized in the Oriental manner. In the drawing of the human figure some freedom is attempted but the artist does not feel the inconsistency of the body facing forward and the head backward.

[5b] Morin-Jean, *Le Dessin des animaux en Grèce*, Paris, 1911. The drawings of Figs. 248, 249, 250, 254, 256, 259, 260, 261, 262, 263, 264, 265, 269, executed by M. Morin-Jean, are reproduced here by his kind permission and that of the publisher, Henri Laurens, Paris.

[5c] *Vs.* this view, see E. Pfuhl, *Malerei und Zeichnung der Griechen*, München, 1923, I, 124.

By 560 B.C., the date of the François krater,[6] the old Dipylon ware had practically died out and Athens had developed a true archaic style, as we have seen from this vase. The animals in this period are frequently drawn with great delicacy and refinement; the proportions of figures become more slender and though the forms are often angular, there is greater grace. The cups of the "Kleinmeister" are beautiful examples of the decorative art from the middle of the century (Fig. 266). They have the charm of miniature work and the note of Attic restraint is already sounded. The "ground ornaments" which the Corinthian and Rhodian schools loved are not the things that satisfy the soul of the Attic painter. He is content to place a single animal in the center of the field and to wind a palmette on either side of the handles. This is an example from the hand of the painter Exekias, and is therefore to be dated about the middle of the Sixth Century. He proudly signs his work with his signature. At times a head of a man or a woman in outline (Fig. 267), two fighting cocks, or mythological scenes replace the animal figure. There is always simplicity of pattern, and the artist does not often care to crowd the zones with figures as his forerunners had done. Xenokles, Tleson, Hermogenes, Anakles, and Sakonides were some of the finest cup-makers of this epoch.[6a]

In the period of Exekias, there is greater nobility and greater truth to nature in the artists' conception of the human form (Fig. 268). But it is always evident that the pictures are typical ones—that at the basis of the artist's design are certain fixed schemes. Indications of muscular detail begin to emphasize the roundness of form. The artist becomes more interested in the rendering of hair and drapery, which are done with not a little precision and nicety. But even though drawing grows more significant, many of the rigid forms of an earlier age live on; the eye in front view is still seen in the profile face; there is no adequate memory-picture for the human hand; in many instances, the head still faces in one direction, the feet in another. The stiffness of these archaic forms was often intentional and was adopted for decorative purposes, but the practice of incising the details of figures greatly handicapped the freedom of the painter. The horses in Figure 269 reveal the primitive artist's love for representing even the things which he did not see in the way of horse's legs and hoofs. The angular drawing of the legs of the riders was intentional and was employed for a decorative end.

The vase-painting of Figure 270, which represents Peleus bringing the child Achilles to the centaur Cheiron, shows black-figured design at its best, although the

[6] Some date this vase as early as 575 B.C.; others near 550, as G. Dickins, *Cat. of the Acropolis Museum*, Cambridge, 1912, p. 10; *cf.* E. Langlotz, *Zur Zeitbestimmung der strengrotfigurigen Vasenmalerei und der gleichzeitigen Plastik*, Leipzig, 1920, p. 11.

[6a] For illustrations of these vases, see J. C. Hoppin, *A Handbook of Greek Black-Figured Vases*, Paris, 1924. *Cf.* A. H. Smith, F. N. Pryce, *Corpus Vasorum Antiquorum, Great Britain*, Fasc. 2, London, 1926, III, H, *e*, Pls. 12-16; Beazley, *Attic Black-Figure*, London, 1928.

ground this time is not the customary red but a creamy yellow. The field is divided in the center by a conventionalized tree and the masses of black are dextrously balanced on either side. The drawing reveals infinite care and charm. There are no superfluous lines. The branch over Cheiron's shoulder serves to fill in the upper field and to complete the rhythm. The dog helps to balance the masses of black on the right. The figures begin to move; the feet are no longer planted flatly on the ground. The jaunty way in which Achilles is held indicates immediacy of action.

The black-figured period was one of greater invention than is often recognized. This was the time when subject matter and various *schemata* were invented which the later red-figured style frequently adopted: Herakles and Theseus at their labors, Helios in his chariot, the Judgment of Paris, Dionysos with his bands, the Sack of Troy, the battles of the centaurs, the departing warrior, and the like. Balance, symmetry, rhythm, and perspective were attempted even in the time of the François vase. The Calydonian boar hunt from this krater (Fig. 271) reveals all of these elements in play. The rhythm arising from bodies in motion is seen in the runners on the Sixth Century Panathenaic amphora of Figure 272. The outstretched arms, one forward and the other back, and the raised left legs give a vivid impression of a two hundred yard dash. The artist's formulæ still remain very primitive; there is a reminiscence of the triangular torso produced by the narrow waists and broad chests; swift motion is represented by the "bent knee" scheme. This formula for rapid motion continued in the red-figured style where it was employed with greater skill (Fig. 273), the lines of one figure seeming to pass on to the next and to carry on the action. The artist often spares himself the trouble of drawing the human body by placing it behind a shield, though undoubtedly in this case he did so for the sake of the pattern.

The black-figured vase of Figure 274 is an interesting piece of work showing the advance in technique in the last quarter of the Sixth Century. There is still a suggestion of the East in the heraldic animals which form the lower border and the palmette has been conventionalized along the sides into a subtle pattern. But the striking elements in the design are the judicious spacing of light and dark and the rhythm produced by the various verticals; beginning with the columns, this is repeated in the female figures, in the water jars on their pedestals with the fountain heads above, and lastly in the metope and triglyph arrangement at the top. There is a clever effect of depth attained by placing a woman now before, now behind the columns of the spring-house. Variety is given to the scene by the use of the Ionic branch pattern. White is added for the flesh of women. The folds of the drapery begin to acquire thickness.

The black-figured vase-painter understood thoroughly the art of adapting his design to the shape of the vase to be decorated and to the particular portion of the vase, whether it was a frieze, a shoulder band, a metope-like panel, or a circle. On the shoulder panel of the amphora in Figure 275, the design is perfectly balanced on either side of a vertical line passing through the warrior standing behind the horse, which is also the central axis of the vase. Very often a panel extended from the base of the handles over the body of the vase, but the artist soon disposed of formal panels and gave himself freer rein, limiting his design with palmettes, as in the red-figured amphora of Figure 276. The design in the center of the kylix, or drinking cup, also evolved from a gorgon's head to patterns of single figures, such as the horseman of Figure 277, the forerunner of Euphronios' Thracian rider. But it is especially from works such as the interior of the cup of Exekias, representing Dionysos sailing over the sea with the vine, that we realize how skilful this adaptation could be (Fig. 232). The vine branch growing from the mast divides the pattern into two symmetrical parts. The graceful arbor above with its rich clusters of grapes is balanced by the leaping dolphins below, beautifully arranged in a group with very finely curving lines. The Panathenaic amphoræ also have skilfully ordered compositions disposed in finely balanced patterns, picturing the athletic contests (Fig. 278). A line drawn through the vertical axis of the vases often gives bilateral symmetry. But, whatever the shape to be decorated, the artist chose his pattern to suit it (Figs. 279-280). In the stamnos of Figure 279 painted by Oltos in the factory of Pamphaios, it was necessary to have a compressed, elongated pattern. The artist has therefore bent the figure of Herakles over the river god, Acheloös, in a death struggle. Instead of making Acheloös a bull-man, he has aided his design by making him half-snake, half-human. Even though the painter plays strange tricks with his figures and gives us practically dwarfs at times, as in the kylix of Skythes (Fig. 281), the beauty of the design covering the vase is in no way impaired, but rather enhanced. The spirited little figures are so satisfactorily spaced and combined with the palmette pattern that the whole composition leaves nothing to be desired. In this scene, Theseus is represented in the act of strangling the wily robber, Prokrustes. Wild landscape is denoted by a sharply pointed rock and a hare nibbling at a shrub. On the reverse, the hero attacks the sow of Krommyon. This vigorous drawing is the work of a Scythian slave, as his name indicates. The vase dates about 520 B.C. In Figure 282, the Xenotimos painter of the free style near the end of the Fifth Century has again produced figures of miniature proportions; but the masses of light and dark are arranged with such genius, because of the way in which the forms are silhouetted against the background, that the eye is entirely satisfied. The main scene is concerned with the birth of Helen. At the right is Leda; at the left, Klytaimnestra. In the center, beside the altar, Tyndareos is seen. The seated figure represents Peirithoos. In contrast to these delightfully Lilliputian figures are those of the design of Figure 280, which is again eminently suited to the space to be covered. It is a scene of three revelers, drawn by Hermonax in a measured style, with large forms and austere movements. The rhythm produced by the outstretched arms and the lines of the legs is quite pronounced.

One of the most difficult problems which the vase-painter had to face was the filling of the circle in the center of the kylix. This he met in various ways. In the earliest period, he cut off a segment of the circle and placed his figures upon it (cf. Fig. 287). Very often he represented a figure in swift motion, with the arms bowed outward and the legs bent in running, in the old "bent knee" attitude, as in the satyr in Figure 283. At times he twisted the form into a contorted position, as in Figure 284, a work of the Panaitios Painter. Here the head and one arm are bent forward, the other arm backward, while the right leg is a bit lengthened to fill the space. At other times he introduced an object into the field to balance the design, such as the fallen stick of the lyre-player of Skythes, in Figure 285. Here one notes not only the superiority of the design but also the marking of the breast muscles with strong lines and the rendering of the details of the abdomen in a dilute wash.

It is interesting to follow the evolution of the design from the single standing figure, rather stiffly posed, through the more agile moving forms. Floating figures also occur, such as Aphrodite on the goose (Fig. 286). This is found on a white-ground vase in the British Museum, assigned by Beazley to the Pistoxenos Painter. The elegance and precision of the drawing betoken a skilled hand. The introduction of a second figure into the design, producing a composition where two figures pivot on either side of a central axis, occurs very early (Fig. 287). The tripod above the mound in Figure 288, where the young Glaukos naïvely witnesses his own resurrection from death, marks the division in this white-ground kylix. The legend depicted here is the story of Glaukos, the son of King Minos. The child was accidentally killed. The King placed the seer Polyeidos in the tomb with the dead boy to bring him back to life. Luckily for Polyeidos, he killed with his spear a snake which he saw there. Immediately, a second snake brought an herb with which it revived its dead companion. Polyeidos profited by the lesson and brought Glaukos to life. Here, he is represented killing the serpent. This vase was painted by the Sotades Painter.

In general, the various artists are fond of emphasizing the central point of the vase. In Figure 289, the Brygos Painter has indicated it by breaking the circle above the head of Selene, with the moon. This design, because of the skilfully patterned drawing of the winged horses with their interlacing forelegs, is a graceful work of æsthetic significance and forms an effective composition for the interior of a cup. The origin of the motive is to be found in black-figured designs with Helios in his chariot.[eb]

We have mentioned only in passing the red-figured technique in Greek vase-

[eb] Cf. J.H.S., XIX (1899), Pl. IX.

painting. It probably arose because the artist felt the cramping limitations of the black-figured style and desired to use his talent in drawing to greater effect. He first sketched on the surface of the leather-hard clay, which had been covered with a red ocher wash, the outlines of his figures.[6c] This preliminary sketch, made with a blunt instrument, is visible on most vases today—a shining, colorless line, which was usually followed fairly closely in the final work, although it was sometimes altered. After the preliminary sketch had been completed, it was surrounded first by a narrow painted line, and then by a broader contour line, probably intended to keep the black glaze from running into the design. The details of the figures and the drapery the artist executed in relief lines, using the black glaze and applying it with an instrument which is still unknown. The glaze has recently been the subject of an extensive investigation by Professor Charles Binns of the New York School of Clay-working and Ceramics at Alfred, New York. The results of his work and the supposed constituents of the glaze are shortly to be published.[6d] The instrument used to apply the glaze may have been a feather brush made from a snipe's or swallow's feather, or a metal or reed pen, or a bristle from a pig or boar, or even a camel's-hair brush—but what it actually was can only be left to conjecture at the moment. The last stage in the making of the vase was the filling in of the background with the black glaze. This was done with a brush—at least in the case of larger surfaces— while the vase was turned on the wheel.

The significance of the freedom given to the vase-painter about 530 B.C., because of the introduction of the red-figured technique, can hardly be overemphasized, even though some of the earliest red-figured works are practically transliterations of black-figured designs. The Thracian rider of Euphronios (Fig. 290) and the amphora of Figure 276 are cases in point (cf. Figs. 277 and 270). In many of the early red-figured cups, the human figure is treated entirely as a pattern, as in Figure 291, and in this use, as earlier in the Dipylon and black-figured vases, the painter attained great success. Some of the best drawing of the archaic severe style is revealed in the work of Epiktetos, 520-475(?) B.C. His figures are almost miniature in character and show great refinement. There is a certain thinness and lightness of form and meagerness in the number of lines employed, which emphasize well the sober, restrained character of the work. The drapery is amazingly simple in its folds. Figure 292 gives a good example of the use of trim outlines and a neatly balanced composition. To quote the famous *dictum* of Beazley about Epiktetos: "You cannot draw better; you can only draw differently."[7] Figure 293 which presents a symposium or drinking scene from the hand of Epiktetos, exhibits similar

[6c] K. Reichhold, *Skizzenbuch griechischer Meister*, München, 1919, p. 4, thinks there was a second preliminary sketch in an oily solution which has entirely disappeared.

[6d] *A.J.A.*, XXXIII (1929), pp. 1-9.        [7] J. D. Beazley, *V.A.*, 1918, p. 18.

characteristics and contrasts strongly in its simplicity with much of the work of the Andokides Painter, where a love of rich and elaborate detail and a fondness for curved lines prevail. The vases of Epiktetos show Attic restraint. This one by the Andokides Painter seems much more "Ionian" in its ornateness and excess in decoration (Fig. 294). This man was doubtless a foreigner who had been trained in Naukratis or in some Ionian center and who came to Athens in the period of strong Ionian influence (Langlotz, *Zeitbest.*, p. 27).[7a] He was working there at the height of the tyranny which was suppressed in 510 B.C. Perhaps the clientèle which he served formed the élite of the aristocracy. They are much more elegant, with their long curls, their side whiskers and rich garments than the simple folk of Epiktetos. The cross section of Athenian life, which the Andokides Painter gives us, represents a rather mannered and precious group of individuals who doubtless constituted the upper stratum of society and who were a bit foppish with their rosebuds, elegant canes, and elaborate mantles. It was no unfortunate thing for Athens that their Oriental proclivities were brought to an end by the expulsion of the tyrants.

The masters of the ripe archaic period which follows were even more skilful in drawing than their predecessors. The Antaios krater of Euphronios is an excellent case in point (Fig. 245). Not only is there wonderful understanding of anatomy here, but a new handling of expression is found (Fig. 314). Interest in more elaborate compositions grows by leaps and bounds, as may readily be seen from the more complicated groups of Euphronios in Figures 246 and 295. A work of unusual charm from Euphronios' factory is the Theseus cup in the Louvre (Pl. IX), painted by the Panaitios Master, though more delicate in style than some of his other vases. This painter is especially fond of large-headed, thin-limbed figures with big noses and faces that are often vulgar in type. Here, we have a decided contrast— the light, boyish figure of Theseus borne on the hands of a Triton as he enters the halls of his mother, Amphitrite. Theseus had been insulted by King Minos while on his voyage to Crete with the youths and maidens who were to be sacrificed to the Minotaur. Minos had challenged Theseus to prove his divine descent from Poseidon by rescuing the ring which the king had thrown into the sea. Theseus has arrived before his mother, with the aid of Athena. He is shown receiving a wreath from her. The legend probably mirrors the passing of sea-power from Crete to Athens. The youthful figure of Theseus seen through transparent drapery, the majestic form of Athena with her elaborately pleated garments rendered in various parallel and zigzag folds and the attempt to draw Amphitrite's mantle over her head and shoulders in many rich pleats disclose an artist of invention. The Panaitios Painter

[7a] U. von Wilamowitz, *Aristoteles und Athen*, Berlin, 1893, II, 74, note 5, holds that Andokides was a client of the family to which the orator Andokides belonged. I owe the reference to Miss Milne. Beazley, *Attic Black-Figure*, p. 25, gives the black-figured designs to the Lysippides Painter.

Plate IX. Paris. Louvre. Theseus visits Amphitrite. Panaitios Master.

has been associated by many scholars with Euphronios and has, in fact, been thought to be the painter, Euphronios, in his later manner. He could much more justly be the Brygos Painter with whom he shares the long-limbed figures of men with large noses. They are often engaged in vivid action and possess a certain lifelike reality which contrasts sharply with the more abstract designs of earlier masters. Our vase is not executed in this broad, bold manner, but in a refined and more exquisite style.

There are few more beautiful cups than the Theseus kylix. Archaic patterns, such as the hair done in wavy strands and the stiffly outstretched hands, are turned to true coin by this artist. The use of perspective in the folds of the garments gives us borders rendered with some detail. The artist's sense of tactile value is not very pronounced. The charm of the drawing of the interior is increased not a little by the addition of the meander design and the perfect palmette pattern on the edge. The outer surface of this vase figures the exploits of Theseus (cf. Fig. 300).

In the kylix of Figure 296 from the factory of Pamphaios, and probably executed by the Nikosthenes Painter, we see to what lengths love of rhythm and balance could carry the artist. Two warriors and two youths with armor alternate with one another on either side of the vase, between two spirited Pegasi. In following the lines we observe the rhythm achieved by the painter and how the movement in one figure is taken up and passed on to the next. Even the small black spaces between the legs of the horses and men form charming patterns. The general effect of the whole design is that of fine, point lace. The patterns are admirably suited to the decorated surface. How this rhythm and balance could degenerate into dramatic and almost bombastic composition is seen in the later "Polygnotan" aryballos from Naples (Fig. 297), where the fighting Greeks and Amazons are posed in corresponding groups on either side of a central fallen Amazon, but where the strength and beauty of the design is in part lost because of the exaggeration of movement and pose and the emphasis on the third dimension. This vase was painted by Aison near the close of the Fifth Century (cf. Fig. 327).

In the third quarter of the Sixth Century, certain vase-painters began to interest themselves in the human body—its anatomical structure and muscular detail. About 520 B.C. they also began to show an active interest in linear foreshortening, representing the body in twisted and violent positions, the legs in front and back view. It is undoubtedly true, as has been said, that this was largely due to the influence of the wall-painter, Kimon of Kleonai, but also in part it was due to a certain desire to vary somewhat the monotonous types of an earlier age. It meant that the artist now turned directly to the study of the human form, instead of correcting his memory-picture of it by random observation. Greater interest is shown in the trunk of the human figure, which is presented in aspects not seen until now—obliquely and in back view.

The vase-painters who seem to have been most attracted by the new vogue were Euthymides, Euphronios, Phintias, and the Kleophrades Painter (510-470 B.C.). Euthymides and his school are fond of showing athletes in back view, but the results produced are sometimes rather inadequate. Figure 298 presents two typical figures in rear view and the difficulty which the artist has had with the hips, shoulder blades, and arms is very evident. The figure at the right, in fact, seems to lack a right arm and the left arm of the athlete on the left appears to fold back. The foot in front or back view also intrigued the painter, but he seems to have had no adequate idea of how to draw it. The heel often resembles a pad added to the bottom of the foot. This amphora has been attributed to Euthymides. Much more successful are the stalwart, fleshy figures on the back of the "Hektor" amphora in Munich (F. R. Pl. 14), signed by him as the painter. On this amphora he boasts that Euphronios never made a better vase, so that the two men must have been rivals. The efforts of the Kleophrades Painter, in Figure 299, were also fairly successful. The right hip of the youth in back view is incorrectly drawn, but the right foot is cleverly presented, so that several planes seem to be indicated. The painter has also attempted to foreshorten the foot in front view in the case of the two figures at the right. The style of the Kleophrades Painter has a certain massiveness about it. The figures are solidly built and are often heavy in type. The folds of the drapery are quite thick and voluminous.

The Panaitios Master in Euphronios' workshop was very canny in handling back views as the figure of Theseus in Figure 300 testifies. With the long, sweeping curve from the left hand to the foot, it forms one of the freest and most engaging figures from this period. The left leg is, in fact, lengthened to add to the effect. The artist has also drawn a face in front view in the case of Kerkyon at the left, and has not avoided the indication of locality by trees and rocks. The various planes, however, seem to be suggested rather than developed. The scene represents the labors of Theseus in wrestling and in capturing the Marathonian bull. The groups are satisfyingly balanced on either side of the tree in the center. On the interior is the design of Theseus visiting Amphitrite (Pl. IX).

With these painters, the new movement toward naturalism was one of vital importance and they rarely lost sight of it in their painting. But its effect was sporadic even earlier, and is observable in works of the Andokides Painter, such as the Berlin amphora of Figure 301. Here, the twisted figure at the right and the face in front view, together with the wrestler hidden behind his opponent, give evidence of the growing freedom. Epiktetos was not untouched by the new fashion, and Peithinos, a mannerist who painted in the factory of Chachrylion, seems to have felt its influence, if we may trust the evidence of Figure 302. The genuineness of this naïve fragment in Syracuse has been doubted by Perrot, but it seems a pity not to accept

it among the works from this factory, especially when we see that the youth is practically duplicated on a cup in the Louvre.[8]

We hear from Pliny that Kimon was able to make his figures look upward and
back and that he did away with the archaic rigidity of pose and movement. We see
these innovations reflected in works such as the kylix of Figure 303, attributed to
Euthymides. The freedom of pose in the fleeing warrior on this vase is very daring.
But in most cases foreshortening was more often suggested than achieved. Many
times it was avoided in various ways and the general effect of its presence produced.
An example of failure actually to indicate foreshortening, while achieving the general
effect of it, is seen in the Bald-headed Schoolmaster (?) of Figure 304, from the hand
of the Panaitios Master. Here, a more correct rendering of the back in foreshortened
view would have shown less of the left side, but the artist has not indicated the
rounding away of the surface from the spectator.[9] He has, however, turned his attention to nature, as the crooked nose, bald head, and thin legs of the Schoolmaster
prove.

That this tendency toward the use of foreshortening was a very widespread one,
is obvious from the numerous examples of it on vases. These attempts were as yet
hardly ever successful. An example of this is the dog of Figure 305 foreshortened in
back view, by the Kleophrades Painter, or the horse of Figure 306, with its head in
full front view, perhaps by Hypsis. The vase by Kleophrades represents a warrior
consulting the omens by inspecting the entrails of an animal. At the left is a Scythian
slave wearing a garment with long sleeves and legs. In front of him a small slave
holds a liver in his hands. Divination by regarding the aspect of the liver was not
uncommon in antiquity.

Foreshortening and the third dimension are better handled on a vase by the
Panaitios Master (Fig. 307). Here, the positions of the wrestlers are very complicated and the painter has marked his planes with some success. The knee of the
kneeling youth, with the ankle and the back of the foot indicated behind it, together
with the foot of the trainer in the rear, give a real feeling of perspective. But even
here the illusion is by no means complete. The artist tends rather to mark the
extreme planes. He arranges the planes behind one another like silhouettes. We have
the general effect of various "drops" in stage scenery. Perhaps the lack of knowledge
on the part of the artist and his inability to foreshorten were advantageous to his
designs, or his own infallible taste may have helped him to keep his designs flat. The
decorative end for which they were created on the curved surface of a vase after all
demanded that they be flat.

[8] E. Pottier, *Louvre Album*, II, 142, G 38. J. C. Hoppin, *op. cit.*, I, 166. J. D. Beazley,
*Att. Vas.*, p. 50, places the Louvre example in a class "related" to the works of Peithinos.

[9] Jules Berchmans, *L'Esprit décoratif dans la céramique grecque, Annales de la société
d'archéologie de Bruxelles*, 23 (1909), Figs. 26, 27.

The naturalistic movement which we have mentioned had its influence on the reliefs of the period no less than on vases. The newly discovered bases from Athens not only reveal a fondness for back views and for figures bent and twisted in exercise, but we see the same attack on the problem of the third dimension (Fig. 308). However unsuccessful these various attempts at foreshortening were—and there were very many unsuccessful ones—we must grant that the painters and sculptors of this period were doing their best toward the solution of a very important problem in art and that all of this striving was necessary for the final comprehension of linear foreshortening and perspective. For vase-painting, however, the significance of these innovations was not so great and flat designs remained the first demand for the artist.

It is not our purpose here to trace in detail the history of vase-painting in Greece; this would require much more space than may be devoted to the subject. We shall merely attempt to indicate in outline the characteristics of representative painters who were in part contemporaries of Euphronios, in part his successors, bringing the development from 500 B.C. down to the end of the Fifth Century. This means selection and passing over many anonymous painters whom Beazley has been drawing from oblivion. The history of red-figured vase-painting for a time centered around the "Big Four"—Euphronios, Douris, Hieron, and Brygos. The number of known painters has now increased so enormously that this group of artists and factory owners is somewhat overshadowed; nevertheless, the achievement of each of these men is of importance and is fairly representative of what was taking place on a large scale among great numbers of ceramists. But each artist had his individual stamp and that we must always miss by adopting the eclectic process.

One of the most interesting problems in drawing which we find in vase-painting from the end of the Sixth to the middle of the Fifth Century B.C., is the one which faced the artist in the rendering of the human eye. The early painter drew it from memory. He always presented it in front view—the most typical view—and placed it in the profile face. The pupil was a black ball which might touch both the upper and the lower lids. The corner of the eye near the nostril was always closed (Fig. 309, Nos. 1-6). This was not a very lifelike rendering and a few more enterprising painters, doubtless feeling this, occasionally used a circle with a dot (Nos. 7-11), Beazley suggests, to indicate a blue or light colored eye! Probably also the practice of placing the pupil more and more in the corner was an attempt to correct the memory-picture from observation. At any rate, we find a series such as is seen here, in Numbers 12-19, which gradually pushes the pupil more and more toward the corner, until we have many figures with squinted and crossed eyes. The circle of Euphronios and Euthymides frequently introduced the use of lashes, seen in Numbers 20-22. Finally, with observation of nature, the profile eye is opened on the side near the nostril, such examples as the triangle of Number 23 by the Brygos Painter helping to bridge the way for a correct rendering in later times (Nos. 24-29). The Panathenaic amphoræ, which retained the black-figured technique in the Fourth Century, give us a clear presentation of this chronological development in the drawing of the profile eye.[10]

In drapery, too, we may follow the same struggle toward perfection. First of all in black-figured vase-painting the garment was a sheath—the Doric peplos (Figs. 268, 271, 233)—until 540 B.C. Between 540 and 530 B.C. the chiton appeared beside the peplos, but in 530 with the advent of the red-figured style, the soft Ionic linen garment with sleeves became almost the exclusive fashion and we first find simple folds arranged on one side (Figs. 274, 234); then a double set of folds on either side of a central panel (Fig. 245); then two or three groups of folds, or an even distribution of folds over the surface of the chiton, and finally, the illusionistic effect of drapery (Fig. 332). It is possible to trace this progress as well on Panathenaic vases.[11]

There are innumerable ways in which we may follow the growing ability of the painters of this epoch. We may examine the rendering of hair, for example, which proceeds from formal locks in curls or strands to the use of dilute washes and finally to an impressionistic rendering of hair. We will study their achievement, however, by examining their compositions and drawing, observing how the artist proceeded from simple silhouettes repeated one after another in frieze-like fashion to more complicated groups and subtly balanced designs of overlapping figures; how he progressed from abstract linear designs to compositions filled with figures of pulsating vitality.

In a vase signed by the master Sosias as maker, we have a work connected by Hauser, Beazley, and others with Euphronios (Fig. 310). If it is from the hand of Euphronios, which seems doubtful, we must certainly believe that in his later period he became a mannerist.[12] The exterior represents Herakles' entry into Olympus; the interior, Achilles binding up the wound of Patroklos. Some have seen in the designs on this vase the reflection of an important painting, which may be possible, but which is by no means certain of proof. The excellence of the work may be due to the vase-painter alone. He shows himself a consummate artist, a keen observer, and a worker alive to the new movements of his age. For the first time, we find the eye correctly drawn in the profile face. The outline of the hair is no longer incised but is represented by a reserved red line. Elaborate foreshortening is also undertaken

[10] See especially *Mon.*, X, Pls. 47-48; G. von Brauchitsch, *Die panathenäischen Preisamphoren*, Leipzig, 1910, E. Norman Gardiner, *J.H.S.*, 32 (1912), pp. 179 ff.

[11] E. Langlotz, *op. cit.*, 1920, pp. 28 ff., 96, 107.

[12] F. R., Pl. 123. I note that Beazley now rejects it as a work by Euphronios, *Attische Vasenmaler*, p. 59. The motive of binding up a wound is found on a Chalkidian vase.

in the case of the right leg of Patroklos. Further, with simple means the artist has expressed well the suffering endured by the hero while his wound is being bound— not only in the pose but also by means of the open mouth with the teeth showing and by the wild look of the eye. The figure is certainly a picture of misery. This is increased by the lines in the face, the position of the head, and the hand held against his wound. The anxious concern of Achilles with his lips firmly set also adds to the note of distress. This design is one of the earliest examples of first aid on record, but the motive was invented earlier in the black-figured period[12] (cf. Fig. 315).

In the work of the Brygos Painter, from the first quarter of the Fifth Century, we see the influence of the major art in the complicated designs with overlapping figures and in the pronounced use of white, gold, and a diluted varnish which appears as a yellow or reddish brown (Fig. 311). In his Sack of Troy, shown here, we have the master at his best in rendering violent action. Traces of the old "bent knee" formula for motion still survive; but, beside this, many innovations now appear, such as the indication of hair on the body which, intentionally or not, aids in the modeling of the figure. There is further the use of a dilute wash on the disheveled hair of the fleeing woman, and polychromy. The armor is aglitter with gold bosses, and a yellow varnish is also found. The Brygos Painter influenced many of his contemporaries to design scenes filled with strenuous action. His drawing is sure and spirited and his figures are full of fire. There is a certain bigness about his style which belongs to an artist "thinking all round his mass." His name indicates that he was probably a Thracian. This scene represents the Trojans surprised in the night by the Greeks. Two Greeks are attacking fallen warriors, clad only in mantles. Andromache, anxious for the child Astyanax, belabors a Greek with a piece of furniture.[12a] The expressively drawn contours present us with figures full of vitality. They possess a firm stability—produced by a just equipoise between thrust and resistance. They reveal a comprehension of mass and of the softness of flesh.

The painter Douris, a contemporary of Brygos, appears in his earlier period to have been a follower of the Panaitios Master; later, he was influenced at times by the Brygos Painter. Many of his sketches are revel scenes or pleasant *symposia* where slender figures with small heads recline gracefully, or palæstra scenes where tall youths and men are silhouetted one after the other in frieze fashion against the background. He seems one of the least inspired of the great painters, his work maintaining a consistently high and usually conventional level. His style is essentially a linear, abstract style. In Figure 312, which depicts the contest between Ajax and Odysseus over the armor of Achilles, together with the intervention of Agamemnon, we see the influence of the Brygos Painter. There is neatness, precision, decided rhythm, and ease in action here. He is not the equal of the latter in expressing

[12a] Some writers term the club a pestle.

violent emotion, though his work is marked by a certain charm which is foreign to the passion and movement of the Brygos Master. Douris probably made this vase about 490 B.C.

Makron, the important painter in the factory of Hieron, combined some of the excellencies of the styles of Brygos and Douris, but there is less variety in his subject matter, which is mainly concerned with the representation of palæstra scenes and various amours. In his cup with Mænads in revel, we see the height of his attainment (Fig. 313). It is a purely decorative creation. The beauty of the work lies largely in the garments of the Mænads which follow the swift movements of the figures, but, in part, it is bound up with the blown hair, lithe gestures, and abandoned attitudes, and the way in which the Bacchantes fill the spaces. From the drapery of these figures to the François vase is a far cry.

Many of the works which we have been discussing were signed by the painters. Douris, for example, states that he painted the vase of Figure 312 and on the foot we see the signature of the potter, Python. Not all vases, however, have the name of the painter. Many are signed merely with the Greek word εποιεσεν, "made." We conclude, therefore, that in most cases this word represents the mark of the potter or of the factory and we have been obliged to search for the painters by means of stylistic criteria. The vases are datable in large measure by the names which occur on them of handsome young men belonging to the society of the time. For example, Douris on the vase of Figure 312 praises the beauty of Chairestratos; Χαιρεστρατος καλος. It is assumed that these *débutants* could hardly have retained their good looks more than twenty years, if so long as that. Vases which praise Leagros, Panaitios, and Athenodotos, begin about 510 B.C. We know of some fifty vases dedicated to Leagros. Lysis, Laches, and Glaukon, are first praised as "beautiful" from 490 to 475 B.C.[12b] The vases with *kalos* names were probably inscribed with the names of the handsome youths in question to please their various admirers.

We have said little about expression in Greek painting, largely because the faces of the severe period are singularly free from emotion. As a rule, only inferior beings such as brute centaurs, or giants, display in their features the tumult which arises within in times of stress. Euphronios has given us the best example of this expression of emotion in the head of the giant Antaios, which we have already had occasion to mention (Fig. 314). We have spoken of the open mouth with the teeth showing, the set pupil which betokens the death struggle and the limp forearm—all of which are portrayed in a masterful fashion. The diluted glaze used on the hair and beard also adds to the disheveled and barbaric effect. In the same way the painter of the Sosias vase expresses pain by means of the open mouth and drawn features, by lines in the

[12b] W. Klein, *Die griechischen Vasen mit Lieblingsinschriften,*[2] Leipzig, 1898; E. Langlotz, *op. cit.*, p. 117. Langlotz places these vases in the seventies.

face and a large, lugubrious eye (Fig. 315). A dilute wash is used extensively for marking muscles, wrinkles, and other details. A new and quite different fashion is adopted by the Kleophrades Painter. In his amphora in Munich which portrays a Bacchanalian rout, he has painted some raging Mænads, one of which concerns us here (Fig. 316). Her head is thrown backward in drunken frenzy; the whole figure, in fact, expresses passionate abandon. Nowhere has the fury of these onrushing attendants of Dionysos with their gleaming fawn-skins and vine branches, and their brandished *thyrsi* been so well portrayed. Others have painted such scenes with greater beauty, for example, Makron in the kylix of Figure 313; no one has portrayed them with greater feeling.

The direct observation of nature, which led to foreshortening, had its influence also in turning the Greek painter away from typical figures toward individualism in drawing, attempts at facial expression and the rendering of emotion. It had been customary before the days of Kimon to represent the aged Priam as an old man, bearded and partially bald, but he begins now on occasion to be realistic and homely (Fig. 317). The Greek painter in general preferred the ennobled human being of calm aspect. He chose an idealized type, not troubling about individual differences nor being interested in them. He did not wish to express passion in the faces of his figures because it interfered with the harmonious relation between the soul and body. Where individualism was essayed before the days of Kimon, it was usually attempted in connection with disgusting beings like Medusa or creatures like centaurs toward whom the Greek wished to express his loathing. After the age of Kimon, the painter occasionally became interested in giving the wrinkled warrior individual characteristics (Fig. 318); he now has a crooked nose, lined face, heavy curving eyebrows, in short, the traits that marked out the man more as he was in life (*cf.* Fig. 319). The old hag on the cup by the Pistoxenos Painter (Fig. 320), with her bent form, white hair, wrinkled face and few teeth, her glassy eye and long nose, shows well the new tendency. On this cup, the unruly young Herakles is seen going to his music lesson. His rolling eye and general attitude indicate that this expedition may end in disaster for the teacher. His old nurse acts as an attendant, shuffling along behind and bearing his lyre. Figures such as the unkempt Charon on the white-ground vase of Figure 321 are found, and pathos is often seen in faces, for example, in the mourning group of Figure 322. Even caricature arises; the kylix of Figure 323, where Æsop and the fox are shown, is an example of this tendency. In general, painting, working with a more facile medium than sculpture, attempted more experiments and was frequently attracted at this period by the realistic in art, though this was never carried as far as the realism of modern times. It merely implies the introduction of certain individual characteristics added to the type. The occasional use of a wash for shading, found on the bodies of centaurs on a pskyter in Rome (Fig.

*a.*

*b.*

*c.*

Plate X.

a. New York. Albert Gallatin Collection. Mænad. Hermonax.
b and c. New York. Metropolitan. White-ground lekythoi. Toilet scene : farewell.

324), gives evidence of a sporadic effort to model the form with shading. Beazley connects this vase with the Harrow Painter.[12c] Interesting innovations aside from the use of a dilute wash for shading on the shields, the hair, and the bodies of centaurs, are the falling figure in back view and the three-quarter faces. These experiments, like the levels used for perspective by Polygnotos, were by no means adopted by all the vase-painters. They merely indicate an age of invention in painting.

Vase-painting in the late archaic or transitional period, from 475 to 460 B.C., is represented by a number of artists of importance, among whom Hermonax and the Penthesileia Painter stand out as most significant. An excellent example of drawing by Hermonax may be seen on the Munich stamnos with a representation of the birth of Erichthonios (F. R., Pl. 137). The work is dignified and executed with care. The figures possess a certain austerity and loftiness of style and the artist shows his independence by breaking away from old formulæ (cf. Fig. 280). Our Pl. Xa gives a charming mænad from his hand, now in the collection of Mr. Albert Gallatin in New York. The beauty of the blown drapery as the figure rushes ahead, the sweeping action and ease of movement show that Hermonax has almost outgrown the trammels of archaism.

The Penthesileia Master who was a contemporary of Hermonax was a much more uneven painter, but he could rise at times to greater heights as he could also sink to much more abysmal depths of carelessness. His most famous piece is a cup in Munich (Pl. XI; cf. Fig. 373). Here, Achilles is shown falling in love with the Amazon queen, Penthesileia, at the moment when he drives his sword into her heart. The eye at last really sees and figures look into one another's faces. Although no deep romance may be read in this drawing, the interrelation established between the two figures by means of the eye is a new note. This vase follows the major art in its grand forms, rich coloring, and overlapping figures. The expression of *Ethos* also relates it to the classical painting of the transition, about 460 B.C. It has been said that "*Ethos* is the spiritual complement of the formal qualities of the classical style" with its measure, dignity, mood, and noble modesty (Pfuhl, *Masterpieces*, p. 57). All of these elements are seen in play in the Penthesileia cup, together with an extensive range of color. The mantle of the warrior at the left—perhaps Ajax—is red; that of Achilles, gray, with a brown and white border. The garment of the Amazon is a reddish color like the clay, but was originally different. Gold and white are found on the armor. There is a certain largeness of style which marks out the painter as a master of the grand manner, and this quality characterizes him at his best.

The second great mural painter to influence the vase-painter was Polygnotos, but it is very questionable how good this influence was. In Figure 325, a krater is repre-

[12c] *Att. Vas.*, p. 471. It is said to be "related" to the work of the Harrow Painter, but is not by his hand.

sented, done in the sublime Polygnotan manner with a suggestion of depth in the ground levels. It was apparently designed by the "Painter of the Berlin Hydria." The introduction of perspective on the Greek vase was a doubtful blessing and the innovation marks the beginning of a decline in the art. The indication of depth in a flat wall-painting was quite a different thing from its representation on the curved surface of a vase and the vase-painter was guilty, in the latter case, of violating the rules of his art. It was no longer a question of flat decoration as we see from Figure 326. Here, in a battle between Greeks and Amazons, we have the old problem of foreshortening attempted in an Amazon on horse, riding toward the spectator. The success of the effort is not miraculous—nor are the overlapping figures seen one behind the other so satisfying as the more reposeful silhouettes of earlier days which were arranged in frieze-like fashion. The style lacks clearness and the contours are not sharply defined. It was not possible for vase-painting to follow the major art of mural decoration in all of its technical progress. The vases that attempt to do so often become overcrowded and are not true to their decorative demands. Figure 327, a later aryballos by Aison, shows clearly this deterioration in composition (cf. Fig. 297). The simplicity and purity of design found in the earlier masters are abandoned. The restlessness of the composition leaves no place where the eye may find repose.

The age of Polygnotos also brought, in addition to the treatment of perspective, experiments in drawing the human figure in complicated poses and the head in three-quarter views. The krater of Figure 328 shows both of these innovations. The scene portrayed is the attack on Tityos and his mother Ge by the arrows of Apollo. The decorator, whom Beazley calls the Painter of the Ægisthus vase in Bologna, has tried a complicated pose in the sinking figure of Tityos. This has succeeded only in part, the trunk appearing in front view, with the legs practically in profile. Where his work interests us more is in the drawing of the face in three-quarter view (Fig. 329). What a difficult problem this was for the artist is seen by a glance at the line of the nose, the crooked mouth, and the left eye which is drawn too far to our left. Compare with this a vase by the Achilles Master (Fig. 330), where the feat is more successfully accomplished. Only the mouth is rendered a bit faultily here, the lower lip being too thick. If we hark back to the days of Amasis and contrast his Mænads with their arms about one another's necks (Fig. 231) with the motive here, we are able to discern the long road forward which painting has traversed.

The treatment of drapery was also attacked in new ways in the Polygnotan epoch. The old swallow-tailed folds of Euphronios no longer satisfied, nor the thin, transparent garments of Makron, often bellying out as if filled with wind. The artist now attempts on occasion to render folds by shading (cf. Fig. 350). This practice was carried into the later Fifth Century as may be seen in Figure 331. On the garment of the seated woman, Deianeira, we have the employment of "eye" folds which are

Plate XI. Munich. Achilles and Penthesileia. Penthesileia Master.

done in a yellowish wash. The origin of this technique is probably in painting and has been claimed for Polygnotos.[13] Its earliest occurrences in sculpture seem to be found on North Greek reliefs, on the Olympia pediments, and on the Boston Counterpart of the Ludovisi throne. In vase-painting it is especially to be noted on the Amazon krater in New York and the Orvieto krater in Paris, both of which were strongly influenced by the painters Mikon and Polygnotos. This was the beginning of a more illusionistic treatment of drapery which culminated during the fine style in impressionistic work such as we see in Figure 332. Here, short curved lines abound and shading, in the form of a dilute wash, is often used for folds. This vase, which belongs to the later classic style at the end of the Fifth Century, was painted, according to Beazley, by the Master of the Berlin Deinos. A group of Mænads are engaged in sacrifices and orgiastic rites before a tree trunk dressed up as Dionysos.

In direct contrast to the Polygnotan type of composition, with its interest in the third dimension, were the flat designs on vases with a white ground. The white-ground technique is the third important technique employed by the Greek vase-painter. In these vases, the ground was covered as a whole, or in part, with a slip of yellow, white, or brown and the designs were put on mainly in outline with a black, brown, golden yellow, or red color. Originally, the creamy slip may have been brought to Athens by Nikosthenes, as we have intimated earlier, from some Ionian center. The light-colored slip originated in prehistoric times. It was used with the outline technique on the Delian-Melian vase picturing Apollo in his chariot with the Hyperborean maidens (Fig. 213). Clay tablets covered with a white slip, such as the Warrior Tablet from the Acropolis (Fig. 244), and painting on marble may have influenced the style at the turn of the century (500 B.C.). Whatever the early contributions to the technique, the vases seem finally to have felt the dominance of the great wall-painters and to have turned from the early, sober, monochrome designs to the rich polychromy found near the end of the Fifth Century.

Vases with a white ground include mainly lekythoi, kylikes or cups, oinochoai or pitchers, kraters, aryballoi, the phiale or saucer, and pyxides.[13a] There are some forty fine cups,[14] the most famous of which are probably those by the Sotades Painter; the Hegesiboulos cup in Brussels; the Mænad of the Brygos Painter, which has a red-figured exterior, and some cups in the Louvre and Boston. They follow the same

---

[13] *Cf.* Chapter VII, n. 34.

[13a] See page 161, containing drawings of various vase shapes. *Cf.* L. D. Caskey, *The Geometry of Greek Vases*, Boston, 1922; The Metropolitan Museum of Art, *Shapes of Greek Vases*, New York, 1922.

[14] A. S. Murray and A. H. Smith, *White Athenian Vases in the British Museum*, Pls. XV-XIX; Furtwängler, Reichhold, *op. cit.*, I, 249 ff.; II, 24 ff.; H. Philippart, *Mon. Piot*, 29 (1927-1928), pp. 99-136; J. D. Beazley, *Greek Vases in Poland*, Oxford, 1928, pp. 27 ff.; F. R., III, pp. 91-94.

lines of development that one finds in the red-figured style, beginning with an archaic period and passing through a transitional stage to a fine style. The most beautiful cups were made by the Sotades Painter near the middle of the Fifth Century. They usually have delicate, thin walls. The outside of the cup is painted black or dark brown and the handles take the form of a chicken's merrythought or wishbone. The best painting from the factory of Sotades is characterized by great delicacy and refinement (Fig. 288). The potter, who was probably Sotades himself, is fond of modeling parts of his vases in relief. Many *rhyta* or drinking horns are known from his hand—one from Susa, one recently found at Meroë in Egypt and now in the Boston Museum and two from Capua. Mastoi, or breast-shaped vases, were also fashioned by him and a type of phiale, or saucer, known as the *mesomphalos,* with a boss in the middle. Sometimes this center was modeled in the form of a grasshopper. One of his most beautiful vases in relief is the Amazon of the Boston Museum (Pl. XII). Here a youthful, boyish figure, wearing a helmet and a close-fitting, long-sleeved garment, is seated on a spirited horse. The Amazon is executed in the white-ground technique and traces of color are still found. The ground below the horse is green, with a lion on one side and a boar on the other. The modeling of the horse is superbly done. The cup attached to the rider's back is decorated with red-figured designs. On the base is an inscription saying that Sotades made the vase. Another very interesting shape from his hand is the *astragal* in the British Museum, on which the Cave of the Winds is probably represented.[14a] The winds are shown as the tailpiece of Chapter VII. A sphinx rhyton in the British Museum, in which the sphinx is covered with white and the designs on the drinking-horn are red, is also typical of his combined relief and red-figured technique.

The earliest vase pictured here in the white-ground technique is an alabastron in London from the shop of Pasiades, dating about 510 B.C. (Pl. XIII*a*). The scene depicted is probably the lustration or purification of a house, which is being sprinkled with laurel branches dipped in lustral water. The ground is covered with a creamy slip. The chitons are rendered in yellow glaze, while the mantles are white. Black glaze is used to indicate outlines, folds, hair, and sandals. The heron is black with a yellow crest and breast feathers, and yellow lines border the design which is fairly archaic in character. The women are called Mænads by some scholars.

Among white-ground vases, the lekythoi hold the most important place. Aristophanes tells us that they were made for the dead (*Eccl.* 996), and designs on the vases themselves show lekythoi arranged on the steps of tombs, occasionally with some other shapes (Pl. XIII*d*). Furthermore, the subjects, which are largely connected with rites for the dead, indicate that they were made for use at the tomb. The

[14a] L. Curtius, *Der Astragal des Sotades, Sitzb. Heid. Akad. der Wiss. Phil.-hist. Kl.,* 1923, 4.

Plate XII. Boston. Museum. Amazon on horse. Sotades.

vases may be grouped into two main classes: A, the class with designs in glaze paint; B, the vases with lines in dull (matt) color. Under each of these two classes are many subdivisions. For example, in A, the vases differ greatly in the slip, presenting earlier a dirty yellow or brownish slip with designs in solid black. Either the flesh or garment—but not both—and the relief lines were in black glaze. Later, the glaze was thinned by diluting it to brown and an enamel white was added for the flesh of women. Finally, a very fine white slip was employed which became shiny when polished, and dull colors occurred occasionally. Sometimes the drawing was done with a golden yellow glaze. In Class B, which is the large class of outline lekythoi, the outlines were sometimes black; or, red was used for the figures and black for the ornamental designs, or figures and patterns might both be red. Polychromy became more important and the use of a slip, which, in contrast to the hard, creamy, lustrous one of earlier times, was chalky and flaked off easily. It was naturally much more perishable in character. In this stage, purple borders are found for garments or a solid red color, while other painters employed green for the drapery or blue, yellow, or purple.[14b]

The funereal lekythoi present four main subjects: the *prothesis* or laying out of the dead, and the mourning at the bier; the *depositio,* or placing of the body in the tomb; Charon preparing to ferry the soul to the other world; the rites at the tomb, or preparations for them.

In Plate XIII*b*, we have an example of the lekythoi with *prothesis* scenes. A dead youth lies on a funeral couch, mourned by two women and a young man. The painter has employed solid masses of color for the most part. The youth wears a red himation; behind the bier, is a mourning woman clad in a yellow chiton, with a red mantle drawn up over the head, while the figure at the foot of the couch also wears a red garment. The color scheme includes a dull black merging into purple, yellow, and dark red. This is the earlier palette, which occasionally employed an added white. Plate XIII*c* illustrates the *depositio,* or placing of the body in the tomb. This is probably modeled on the Homeric story of the carrying away of Sarpedon to Lycia for burial. In our vase, the hero is borne in the arms of Hypnos and Thanatos— Sleep and Death. The older, bearded man probably represents Death; the slender, youthful form, Sleep. Some have called these winged figures Boreas and Zephyros. Unusual beauty is found in the sweep of the lines of the wings, the bent figures, and the subtle symmetry of the design. The contours are drawn with elasticity and assurance. The figure of Sleep is filled in, in a quite unusual manner, with a red wash; the outlines are brown with dull black for the wings; red is used for sashes and drapery.

A very common scene on the lekythoi depicts the unkempt, individualized Charon

---

[14b] Arthur Fairbanks, *Athenian White Lekythoi,* N. Y., 1907, 1914 ("University of Michigan Studies," VI, VII).

calling with his barque to take the dead to the other world (*cf.* Fig. 321). Usually, Hermes leads the victim gently to the boat. Our example (Pl. XIII*f*) is drawn in thin red outlines. The same red, only thicker, is employed for the hair of Hermes and the dead woman, for the chlamys of Hermes, and for the pole of the boat. Gray is used for the souls which flit about Charon and for the folds of the red mantle. The garments of the woman and Charon are a gray-black with red folds, while the color of her chiton has been lost. Stylistically, this lekythos belongs with the earlier vases in dull colors. A few sharply contrasted colors are sufficient and much of the work is in outline, especially the boat and the forms of the male figures.

After the dead had been deposited in his tomb, it was customary for his relatives and friends to bring offerings (Pl. XIII*d*). This vase is especially interesting because it reveals how the lekythoi were used. In this case, they were arranged on the steps of the tomb, with wreaths hung over every second vase. Sometimes, filled with unguents, they were placed open near the bier. At times, they were thrown on the funeral pyre. At the left, beside the grave-stele, stands a young man wearing a blue petasos or traveling hat, and a brown mantle. His garment is bordered with white and the folds are black. He is probably the dead hero. Behind the stele rises a great mound. On the right, a young woman in a Dorian chiton—the sleeveless garment of wool—is bringing wreaths and fillets as offerings. The drawing, which is worthy of an artist of the Pheidian school, is done in a dark brown glaze without relief. Originally, the garment of the woman was probably red, as traces of that color still survive, while the fillet on the wall at the right is rose-colored. In contrast to vases *b* and *f* of Plate XIII, which belong to Class B, this vase is executed in an almost black glaze and belongs to Class A. Light brown and blue are sparingly used—a greenish blue for the wreaths. The work of the artist of this lekythos has been compared to that of the Achilles Painter—a master of the early free red-figured style.[14c]

How fine the simple, linear designs with the figures in two dimensions could be, is evident from the charming New York lekythoi of Plate X, *b* and *c*. Here, at the left, *b*, a toilet scene is represented. A woman is fastening the girdle of her *kolpos* while a second woman offers her an alabastron. The figure of the youth bidding good-bye on the vase, *c*, on the right side, reveals an extraordinary renunciation of detail on the part of the artist and great purity of draughtsmanship. The scene is drawn in lines of fine glaze; the mantles are red. Each of the figures was sketched before the garments were indicated.

To this same period of simple outlines and coloring belongs the *genre* scene on the

---

[14c] A. Fairbanks, *op. cit.*, I, 205; J. D. Beazley, *Greek Vases in Poland*, Oxford, 1928, p. 49, note 2, follows "Luce, *A.J.A.*, 1919, pp. 19-32, and Buschor after him in considering a number of lekythoi bearing the love-names, Dromippos, Lichas, and Diphilos to be early or fairly early works of the Achilles Painter."

*a*. London. British Museum. Purification of a house. Pasiades.

*b*. London. British Museum. *Prothesis* scene.

*d*. Athens. National Museum. Offerings at the tomb of a dead warrior.

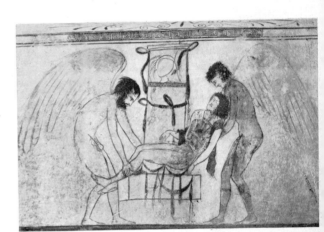

*c*. London. British Museum.
*Depositio*. Dead warrior borne by Sleep and Death.

*f*. Athens. National Museum. Hermes leading a woman to Charon's boat.

Plate XIII. White-ground vases.

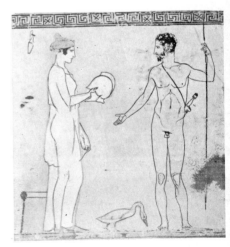

*e*. London. British Museum.
Warrior receiving a helmet from a woman.

vase of Plate XIII*e*. A young woman is handing over a helmet to a warrior. The outlines are strong and flowing. The contour drawing suggests the rounding of the forms admirably. Anatomical details are broadly treated. The goose relieves the baldness of the scene and adds to the beauty of the line-work. The figures are executed in brown, while red is used for the cap and helmet. Probably the artist wished to suggest that the warrior was leaving for his last battle.

In Figure 333 we have one of the finest white-ground lekythoi known in Attic vase-painting. Here we see the beauty of pure outline drawing at its best. The emphasis is on the flatness of the design and on purity of line. There is about the composition that nobility and quiet which characterized the finest works of Greek art. The painter has known how to draw his lines with assurance and strength and yet with an elasticity and grace that are very striking. All of the contours and inner details are drawn in a glaze that has been thinned to a golden yellow. In addition to this, there is the use of yellow on the chiton of the warrior and that of the woman and cinnabar on her mantle which has now turned violet. The ridge of the helmet and the bag on the wall are dark red. Some gray appears. The scene probably tells us again that the warrior did not return. The charm of the design lies in the restraint and in the simple beauty of the outlines. The chair contributes its part with the exquisite curve given to the back and legs. The vase belongs to the Pheidian class— a group executed shortly after the middle of the Fifth Century and marked by the qualities of austerity, nobility of form, and a certain grandeur of style achieved by the renunciation of all superfluous details.

In the example of Figure 334, we see a nude youth standing beside a grave-stele. His counterpart is to be found in figures on the Parthenon frieze, no more nobly executed than here. He also belongs in the Pheidian Age as does the young girl from the same vase who is bringing offerings to the tomb (Fig. 335). The drawing is done with great refinement and the figures possess an unusual charm. It is not certain that the maiden's garment was ever painted, but it would be very unusual for a young girl to be pictured nude on the lekythoi. We assume, therefore, that the garment has disappeared with time.

The white-ground lekythoi are dated mainly by their shapes, by the ornamental patterns, the hardness and general character of the slip, by inscriptions, such as occur in the Diphilos class of the transitional period, and by the rich polychromy which is found in the latest examples. The class with glazed lines is, in general, earlier than the class with matt colors. The white-ground vases date from about 500 B.C. to a period near the beginning of the Fourth Century. Most of them belong near the middle of the Fifth Century.[14d]

[14d] On chronology, see W. Riezler, *Weissgrundige attische Lekythen*, 1914, I, 59 ff.; E. Buschor, *Attische Lekythen der Parthenonzeit*, München, 1925, pp. 190-191, *et passim*.

In the early period of the white-ground technique, the vases shared the solid black silhouette with the black-figured style. Later, the red-figured technique was combined with the white-ground, as we see it on a vase from the factory of Brygos (F. R., Pl. 49). Here, the Mænad of the interior is painted on a white ground, whereas the scenes of the exterior are in the red-figured style. Probably, therefore, the white-ground vases were also made in the factories where red-figured ceramics were produced.[14e] In the earliest period, the same instrument was used in both styles to produce the relief lines, whether it was a pig's bristle, or a snipe's feather, or whatever. Later, the relief lines were abandoned. The vases should be appreciated rather for themselves and for the wonderful drawing found on them than for the knowledge they may possibly be able to give us of lost wall-paintings. In these vases, line is raised to the utmost importance, largely because the figures are in the same color as the background. This allows a pure play of line that is not found on vases of the red-figured style, where the background is blocked in with black.

The palette of the early group of vases was limited—red, yellow, purple, black, and white predominating. In the latest period, six different reds appeared: cinnabar, deep red, brownish red, light and dark purple, and a bluish red. The coloring at that time was no longer purely decorative. Blues and greens played a much larger part in the later class. The vases in matt colors really formed the polychromatic group. Probably the dilution of the original black glaze to brown and golden yellow led to the polychrome style.

A rough system of chronology would place the lekythoi with relief lines in glaze between 500 and 460 B.C. The *kalos* name, Glaukon, used by Euphronios, occurs in this period. On the vases which make use of an added white, the names of Diphilos and Dromippos are found. They belong in the transitional stage from about 465 to 450 B.C. Roughly contemporary with these are many of the vases which use a golden glaze. The class with dull paints range from about 450 to 400 B.C. Most of these must be dated from stylistic criteria, employed in a rather subjective manner. In the expression of feeling which they reveal and in the moving revelation of the way in which the Greeks faced death, the lekythoi remind us of the Attic grave-stelæ. The nobility of quiet grief is nowhere painted more sensitively. The artists of these vases seem to have outgrown figures constructed of purely ornamental lines and to have expressed the depths of human emotion in the presence of death. This emotion is rendered with austerity and true Greek moderation.

Similar excellence in outline drawing is apparent on monuments outside the ceramic field but closely analogous to vases in their general achievement, for example,

[14e] J. D. Beazley, *Greek Vases in Poland,* Oxford, 1928, p. 50, believes that the Achilles Painter "was one of the chief painters, perhaps the determining painter, of white lekythoi."

on the stele of Mnason from Thebes,[15] belonging after the middle of the Fifth Century, or the very beautiful colored drawings on ivory found near Kertch in Southern Russia and revealing a style dating from the late Fifth Century.[16] The grave-stele of Mnason, Figure 336, presents only a sketch done in fine, dotted lines. It was probably made for a painting in encaustic. The background has been picked out with the aid of a chisel and offers a rough, gray surface. The care in the preparation of the ground suggests that encaustic, or wax painting, was used. Over the sketch, a coat of color was originally placed. The lines of the drawing which we now see were not intended to be visible in the final work, but were merely to guide the painter and to hold the wax firmly. A mere drawing in crayon, or with the brush, could not have withstood the hot wax mixed with the colors, which was put on after the sketch had been made. It would have disappeared entirely. We shall have occasion to discuss the encaustic technique later. The workmanship is of unusual beauty and simplicity, and finds its closest analogy in Attic vase-painting about 430 B.C. The head is paralleled in some of the figures of the Parthenon frieze.

The colored drawings on ivory are some of our finest extant Greek drawings (Fig. 337). The fragments apparently formed part of the ivory veneer of a coffin. The drawing was incised with a sharp point and the surface covered lightly with color, traces of which remain. The lines show great freedom, delicacy, and sureness of touch. The two figures above belong to a scene of the Judgment of Paris and represent Aphrodite and Eros at the left with Hera at the right. Other pieces picture Paris and Athena. The spirit of the drawings is Meidian. They show the grace and grandeur of the gods of the late Fifth Century, but with this a tendency toward the delicate and playful, seen in the fluttering garments and rich decoration. Perhaps the finest fragments are those of the quadriga and charioteer, which probably formed part of a representation of the rape of the daughters of Leukippos. The pattern is admirably suited to the long, narrow bit of ivory which it adorns; the horses are spirited and rhythmically drawn; the charioteer is a splendid, lithe figure springing into action. Other pieces depict the preparations for the chariot race of Pelops and Oinomaos. These drawings give us a vague idea of our loss of originals of monumental scale from the late Fifth Century. They are usually dated in the middle of the Fourth Century but the style which they preserve is that of the age of Meidias.

Comparable in excellence to such works as these, are many of the patterns found on various red-figured vases of the early free style (460-420 B.C.). The drawing of Euphorbos with the young Œdipus in his arms (Fig. 338) is a fine bit of outline

[15] W. Vollgraff, *B.C.H.*, 26 (1902), Pl. 7; H. Bulle, *Der schöne Mensch*,[2] Pl. 309, G. Rodenwaldt, *Arch. Anz.*, 28 (1913), pp. 63 ff.

[16] E. H. Minns, *Scythians and Greeks*, 1913, Figs. 100, 101, 102; H. Bulle, *op. cit.*,[2] Pl. 311.

work by Beazley's Achilles Master. The artist has not consciously striven for grandeur or grace, but he has obtained both;[16a] the nobility and strength of the figure of
Euphorbos contrast charmingly with the delicate form of the child. The composition
is one of great simplicity. It is interesting to see that in this period drapery begins to
have the illusion of drapery, and hair, of hair.

From about 440 B.C., a large number of red-figured vases are extant with figures
silhouetted against the background in statuesque fashion—figures sublimely conceived and drawn with great breadth of style. Because of the qualities of restraint,
dignity, and austerity which these vases possess in a high degree, they must be placed
in the Pheidian class, discussed in connection with some of the white-ground
lekythoi. The models of this group, whether in sculpture or in the major art of
painting, must have revealed an unusual comprehension of the great and simple.
In contrast to the vases of the Polygnotan class, this class renounces all means and
motives at variance with the surface effect of vase-decoration and shows a fondness
for frieze-like compositions of figures in reposeful attitudes. Figure 339 contains two
examples of "Pheidian" design. The figures are noble types, quietly posed in each
case in a well-balanced composition which is carefully divided in the example below
by a crane introduced into the scene. The design in the upper panel is assigned by
Beazley to the "Painter of the Boston Phiale." The pelike from Lecce illustrated
below was painted by the "Chicago Painter." Both were masters of the free style.

In Figure 340, we have a finely arranged group of three figures and the artist has
preferred to express a mood. From left to right, Melousa, Terpsichore, and Mousaios
are represented. The majestic calm and serene beauty of the composition are attained
by emphasis on form and on simplicity and purity of line. There is a natural ease in
the poses of the figures and three-quarter views are, at last, correctly drawn. The
vase was executed by the Painter of the Petrograd Amazonomachy. He was a follower of the vase-painter Polygnotos, an academic artist of distinction, who had no
connection with the great wall-painter of that name. The same qualities are also
perceptible in scenes where vivid action is portrayed, as in the skyphos of Figure
341. These scenes are concerned with one satyr shading a woman with a parasol
and a second one swinging a young girl. Swinging apparently had a religious significance. The Pheidian character appears in the renunciation of all superfluous
elements and in the refusal to strive after grace or external effects. In Figure 342,
where Pelops is represented carrying off his bride, we see the same elements at play.
The composition depicts the horses and chariot of Pelops dashing along the shore
in measured rhythm. The mantle of Pelops flies out behind and his hair is blown in
the wind, the chariot wheels bend in swift movement; but, over all, there is that
Greek restraint which tempers the violent. This is perhaps the finest example known

[16a] J. D. Beazley, *V.A.*, p. 163.

in Fifth Century Greek vase-painting of the union of figures and landscape into an harmonious whole. This amphora was probably drawn by the Meidias Painter, who is famous for the exquisite beauty of his lines. They are most competently employed in depicting richly elaborated drapery and bold scenes of action. The Meidias Painter was a master of the on-coming florid style in the last quarter of the Fifth Century. Affectation enters into his work. This is seen in the poses of the figures, in the tilt of the heads and in the dramatic gestures of the hands. Technique becomes an end in itself. The lines grow increasingly softer. Artistic formulæ replace form.

After the days of Polygnotos, we often find deterioration in design arising from the overcrowding of the vase and from attempts at perspective. In Figure 343 we have a superior example of Polygnotan vase-painting. Although levels are attempted and figures are cut off by the background, the general treatment remains a surface treatment. We have a balanced composition with Selene, the moon, at one end on her horse. She is going down the sky, bayed at by a dog, while Helios, the sun, is coming up at the opposite end.[16b] In the center, the Dawn pursues Kephalos, a beautiful youth, and the little stars dive into the sea before the rising sun. This is Polygnotan "allusion." On the other hand, many Polygnotan vases were crowded with figures and the design passing up on the shoulder made an inferior composition, difficult to grasp. Even such a beautiful masterpiece as the Meidias vase is not so good from the point of view of design as many other vases less carefully executed (Fig. 344). In the scene depicted here, we have an illustration of the legend dealing with the rape of the daughters of Leukippos by Castor and Pollux. Their carefully balanced four-horse chariots decorate the shoulder of the vase. Below, in the precinct of Aphrodite, designated by an altar and a statue of the goddess, Castor is carrying off his bride. The vase-painter of this period, having gained the control of his brush, allowed his lines to run riot, or he modeled his figures with delicately curved lines as in Figure 345, so that the flesh seems soft. This is a vase by Aison picturing Theseus slaying the Minotaur with the aid of Athena.

From about 420 B.C., we see a gradual decline in vigor and strength of line, suppression of contour, recourse to nicety of detail and dramatic posture. The simplicity of the old days is gone. At this period, Aristophanes painted the Berlin Cup where Poseidon is seen slaying one of the giants, while Mother Earth rises from the ground to protest the slaughter (Fig. 346). There is a kinship in works like this to the later Pergamene sculptures. Aristophanes treats the battle of the gods and giants on the exterior of this vase, but more than two centuries before the marbles. In these vases, the work of the artist begins to be a bit finicky.

Even at the end of the Fourth Century, when Athens was no longer a great center of vase-painting as in the Fifth Century, and foreign markets had absorbed her

---

[16b] This is the dog of the hunter Kephalos and may be purely symbolic.

trade, the artist still understood the value of a good decorative pattern, as we see from the Panathenaic vase of 336 B.C. (Fig. 347). Here, Athena is represented between two columns, with her garment conventionalized into swallow-tailed patterns and the lower part of the body schematized into a swirl of drapery. The decorative value of the figure is undeniable but the design as a whole is not so fine because the figure of Athena extends upward on the neck of the vase and a certain affectation appears. It shows a return to a more rigid schematization, found in the beginning and in the decline of Greek art. The artist has traveled a long way from the triangular figures of the Dipylon and drawing and design have passed through many vicissitudes, from schematic forms to more naturalistic representations; from decorative figures to scenes filled with the artist's emotional expression. The Greek vase-painter was at his best when he remembered the canons of his art and adhered to flat composition and decorative demands. Periods of his activity stand out boldly when by sheer beauty of form and simplicity and purity of line he achieved his artistic end. It was only when he tried to follow the major art too far and when he understood too well the technicalities of his craft that the decline of vase-painting followed. Behind the beauty of his designs certain mathematical ratios appear to lie, the character of which has not as yet been finally determined.[17]

[17] Cf. J. Hambidge, *Dynamic Symmetry: The Greek Vase*, New Haven, 1920; L. D. Caskey, *Geometry of Greek Vases*, Boston, 1922; G. M. A. Richter, *A.J.A.*, 26 (1922), pp. 59 ff.; Rhys Carpenter, *A.J.A.*, 25 (1921), pp. 18 ff.

# TENTATIVE CHRONOLOGY OF SOME OF THE MOST IMPORTANT VASE-PAINTERS*

| | | |
|---|---|---|
| Middle Sixth Century B.F. Masters. | Klitias.<br>Earliest vases of Exekias, Amasis.<br>Little Masters (Kleinmeister). | Kalos names. |
| 550-530 | Later works of Exekias and Amasis. | Onetorides. |
| R.F. Masters.<br>530-520 | Amasis.<br>Early work of Andokides Painter.<br>Oltos.<br>Epiktetos.<br>Pheidippos.<br>Menon Painter. | |
| 520-510 | Nikosthenes Painter.<br>Ambrosios Painter.<br>Later work of Andokides Painter.<br>Hermaios Painter.<br>Cerberus Painter.<br>Oltos.<br>Epiktetos.<br>Skythes.<br>Euergides Painter.<br>Epeleios Painter.<br>Early work of { Phintias.<br>{ Euphronios. | Hipparchos.<br>Memnon. |
| 510-500 | Sosias Painter.<br>Peithinos.<br>Phintias.<br>Euphronios.<br>Euthymides.<br>Epiktetos.<br>Panaitios Master.<br>Kleophrades Painter.<br>Douris.<br>Late work of Skythes. | Leagros.<br><br>Chairestratos.<br>Athenodotos.<br><br>Panaitios. |
| 500-490 | Kleophrades Painter.<br>Panaitios Master.<br>Douris.<br>Brygos Painter.<br>Makron.<br>Berlin Painter.<br>Myson.<br>Eucharides Painter. | Chairestratos.<br>Panaitios.<br>Hippodamas. |

* Based on the work of J. D. Beazley and E. Langlotz.

# TENTATIVE CHRONOLOGY

### (Continued)

| | | |
|---|---|---|
| 490-480 | Kleophrades Painter.<br>Brygos Painter.<br>Onesimos.<br>Douris.<br>Makron. } Ripe period.<br>Berlin Painter.<br>Pan Painter.<br>Foundry Painter.<br>Tithonos Painter.<br>Eucharides Painter.<br>Seesaw Painter.<br>Triptolemos Painter.<br>Dutuit Painter.<br>Antiphon Painter.<br>Syriskos Painter.<br>Copenhagen Painter.<br>Flying Angel Painter. | Hippodamas.<br><br>Lysis.<br><br>Lykos.<br>Laches. |
| 480-470 | Berlin Painter.<br>Brygos Painter.<br>Douris.<br>Epiktetos(?). } Late work.<br>Makron.<br>Kleophrades Painter.<br>Foundry Painter.<br>Briseis Painter.<br>Tithonos Painter.<br>Pan Painter.<br>Triptolemos Painter.<br>Sabouroff Painter.<br>Seesaw Painter.<br>Syriskos Painter.<br>Copenhagen Painter.<br>Antiphon Painter.<br>Dutuit Painter.<br>Providence Painter.<br>Lewis Painter.<br>Pistoxenos Painter.<br>Penthesileia Master.<br>Sotades Painter.<br>Dionokles Painter. | Lykos<br>(485-75).<br>Laches<br>(485-75).<br>Glaukon. |
| 470-460 | Dionokles Painter.<br>Pistoxenos Painter.<br>Telephos Painter.<br>Penthesileia Master.<br>Hermonax.<br>Euaion Painter.<br>Lewis Painter.<br>Villa Giulia Painter.<br>Achilles Painter. | Glaukon<br>(475-65).<br>Diphilos.<br>Dromippos.<br>Alkimachos I.<br>Hygiainon. |

# TENTATIVE CHRONOLOGY

### (Continued)

| | | |
|---|---|---|
| 470-460<br>(Continued) | Niobid Painter.<br>Sotades Painter.<br>Sabouroff Painter.<br>Altamura Painter.<br>Douris (Latest work). | |
| 460-450 | Hermonax.<br>Penthesileia Master.<br>Euaion Painter.<br>Lewis Painter.<br>Villa Giulia Painter.<br>Achilles Painter.<br>Niobid Painter.<br>Sotades Painter.<br>Sabouroff Painter.<br>Altamura Painter. | Hygiainon. |
| 450-440 | Chicago Painter.<br>Villa Giulia Painter.<br>Achilles Painter.<br>Polygnotos.<br>Lykaon Painter.<br>Euaion Painter. | Alkimachos II.<br>Euaion. |
| 440-430 | Polygnotos.<br>Penelope Painter.<br>Lykaon Painter.<br>Painter of the Naples Centauromachy.<br>Achilles Painter.<br>Phiale Painter.<br>Kodros Painter. | |
| 430-420 | Penelope Painter.<br>Kodros Painter.<br>Washing Painter.<br>Kleophon Painter.<br>Painter of Berlin Deinos.<br>Phiale Painter.<br>Eretria Painter.<br>Shuvalov Painter. | |
| 420-410 | Aison.<br>Kleophon Painter.<br>Painter of Berlin Deinos.<br>Kadmos Painter. | |
| 410-400 | Aristophanes.<br>Meidias Painter.<br>New York Centauromachy. | |

# VII

# GREECE: POLYGNOTOS AND THE PAINTING OF THE FIFTH CENTURY

WHEN we left Athens in the days of Kimon of Kleonai, painting was beginning to struggle with the third dimension. It was becoming more conscious of nature and of the shortcomings in the older fashion of rendering it. The age was the period of the Peisistratidai—one of luxury in life and of experimentation and affectation in art.[1] Under the rule of the tyrants—Peisistratos and his sons—much Ionian luxury and Lydian decadence had been creeping into the muscles of the Athenians and nowhere is this clearer than in the art which was created immediately before and after the tyrants were driven from Athens in 510 B.C. We find a group of mannerists in vase-painting, of whom masters like Peithinos are representative. They show a rather playful handling of material, elaborate drapery, rich detail. There were also archaists who chose to go back to older modes of expression instead of inventing anew. Examples of their work may be seen in certain Panathenaic amphoræ. The Persian wars brought to a close the decadent court life, the eastern effeminacy, and the note of elaboration in art which had survived the annihilation of the tyrants. The Greeks develop a national consciousness as a result of the Persian invasion and there is a reaction against eastern standards reaching even to the gradual discarding of Ionian dress. In painting, the tendency is toward simplicity. We find the people, the mentors of art, throwing overboard the precious manner of an earlier age; reacting against the polychrome gaiety and intricate detail of much of archaic art. The Athenians were a different race—serious, self-conscious, proud. Something energetic comes into art to take the place

---

[1] A. von Salis, *Die Kunst der Griechen*, Leipzig, 1919, pp. 62 ff.

of the superfluous, coquettish, and trivial.[1] There is a certain largeness of style, a striving for spaciousness and grandeur. The art of the period breathes this fresh air of freedom.

Into this new heritage, Polygnotos, the Thasian, entered shortly after the Persian wars. He came from an Ionian island and his art is not uninfluenced by his training there, but his productions express the intellectual and artistic greatness of Athens after Salamis and Marathon. We must think of his genius therefore as essentially Athenian—an expression of the great awakening which swept over Greece at this time. We cannot forget, however, that he had lived on an island swept by sea breezes and that his wind-blown draperies revealing the form beneath probably have a Thasian element in them. It is possible also that his interest in landscape, slight and formal though it was, may have been native to the soil from which he came.

Polygnotos is the first Greek painter who can really be called a painter in the modern sense of the word. He lifted painting above the plane of colored drawing, and though much of his work remained archaic so that he seemed to the Romans one of the primitives,[2] his innovations must have been astounding, to judge from the praise of ancient authors. We are dependent for our knowledge of his work on literary tradition and on the numberless monuments in which his style was copied, paraphrased, or excerpted. These are mainly vases, but the sculptures of the Olympia pediments and the Parthenon bear marks of his influence and reliefs in far-away centers such as Etruria and Gjölbaschi in Lycia.

Let us see first of all what ancient writers say of Polygnotos, that we may form some idea of the character of his work. Aristotle gave him the palm in painting, looking to the end or purpose of art. It was the "moral uplift" in his paintings which interested the philosopher. He would have them viewed by the youth of Athens as an inspiration, because he painted men better than they were.[3] This ideal character of Polygnotan art is emphasized by many writers so that we may well expect heroic figures. Ælian also speaks of the greatness of his conceptions.[4] He created on a grand scale—works that lifted the spectator above the level of everyday commonplaces into a more ennobled atmosphere. Further he painted the soul behind the individual. He was a great master of *Ethos*, or inner greatness of character—in contrast to Zeuxis, who possessed none of this quality.[5] Under this, we may expect not only the permanent, essential qualities of human kind, but the depicting of mood and temperament.

[2] Quintilian, *Inst. Orat.*, XII, 10, 3.

[3] Aristotle, *Poetics*, 2. Πολύγνωτος μὲν γὰρ κρείττους, Παύσων δὲ χείρους, Διονύσιος δὲ ὁμοίους εἴκαζεν. Cf. *Pol.*, V, 1340ᵃ, 37.

[4] Ælian, *V.H.*, IV, 3. ὁ μὲν Πολύγνωτος ἔγραφε τὰ μεγάλα καὶ ἐν τοῖς τελείοις εἰργάζετο τὰ ἆθλα.

[5] Arist., *Poet.*, 6. ὁ μὲν γὰρ Πολύγνωτος ἀγαθὸς ἠθογράφος, ἡ δὲ Ζεύξιδος γραφὴ οὐδὲν ἔχει ἦθος.

Pliny, on the other hand, does not place Polygnotos among the real "luminaries" in painting, the first of whom was Apollodoros. Judging the art by its technical progress he gives the first place to Apelles. What Polygnotos did, in Pliny's estimation,[6] was to make a "first serious contribution to the development of painting by opening the mouth, showing the teeth, and varying the stiff archaic set of the features." These "innovations" were known before Polygnotos. We have seen pain rendered on the Sosias cup and on the krater of Euphronios by means of the open mouth and the teeth showing, and many early works of art reveal similar attempts. What Polygnotos accomplished was much more subtle than these archaic efforts toward the expression of emotion and pathos. We can gather an idea of his achievement from the description of his figure of Polyxena, "in whose eyelids lay the whole of the Trojan war."[7] We can imagine it from the description of Hektor in the "Underworld," where he is seated with his hands clasped around his knee, in the attitude of a man bowed down with sorrow.[8] We may also infer it from his treatment of subject matter in themes like the Iliupersis, or "Taking of Troy." Here, it was not the gruesomeness and brutality of battle which attracted him, but the lull after the storm—the sadness of the Trojan women; Helen still triumphant in her beauty in the midst of destruction; the plight of the exile, Antenor. He represented, then, the psychological effect of the disaster on the victims. We shall see also that he carried further the inventions of Kimon of Kleonai making use of the face in three-quarter and front views. In this way, some of the "archaic set of the features" was done away with.

Polygnotos made certain contributions to the treatment of drapery. Lucian says that the drapery of Kassandra in the "Taking of Troy" was worked out to the thinnest and finest, so that it was drawn together in soft masses, but for the most part appeared as if blown by the wind.[9] Other writers speak of the fineness of Polygnotan drapery and the word used, $\lambda\epsilon\pi\tau\acute{o}\tau\eta s$,[10] implies thinness and lightness of material in many small and delicate folds. Pliny adds that he was the "first to paint women with transparent garments and to give them headdresses of various colors."[11] The influence of this wind-blown drapery of Polygnotos on the sculptures

[6] Pliny, N.H., 35, 58. The translation quoted is from Jex-Blake, Sellers, The Elder Pliny's Chapters on the History of Art, London, 1896.

[7] Anth. Pal., XVI, 150 (Planud., IV). ἐν βλεφάροις δὲ παρθενικᾶς ὁ Φρυγῶν κεῖται ὅλος πόλεμος. The reference to Polygnotos rests on an emendation. Cf. A. Reinach, Recueil Milliet, I, 148, note 2.

[8] Paus., X, 31, 5. Cf. P. Girard, Mon. Grec., 23-25 (1895-1897), pp. 17 ff., Le Cratère d'Orvieto et les jeux de physionomie dans la céramique grecque.

[9] Lucian, Imag., 7. ὁ Πολύγνωτος δὲ ὀφρύων τὸ ἐπιπρεπὲς καὶ παρειῶν τὸ ἐνερευθὲς οἵαν τὴν Κασάνδραν ἐν τῇ Λέσχῃ ἐποίησε τοῖς Δελφοῖς, καὶ ἐσθῆτα δὲ οὗτος ποιησάτω ἐς τὸ λεπτότατον ἐξειργασμένην, ὡς συνεστάλθαι μὲν ὅσα χρὴ διηνεμῶσθαι δὲ τὰ πολλά.

[10] Ælian, V.H., IV, 3.                    [11] Pliny, N.H., 35, 58.

of the Parthenon has been pointed out by Schroeder.[12] The thin, transparent chiton over the nude form must have been rendered by fine parallel brush-strokes and must have awakened in the spectator a certain breathless surprise. We hear no more from ancient writers of the Polygnotan handling of drapery but we shall see from vases which reflect his influence that he probably also knew how to indicate folds in heavy material in a new way by shading. These are usually termed "eye folds."

In the matter of composition, the painting of Polygnotos was epoch-making. Of this we may form an estimate by comparing the description by Pausanias of his works at Delphi, with designs on vases of the transitional period from about 470 to 450 B.C. In this lengthy account of Pausanias—which goes about as far as words can toward describing the paintings for us—there is a continual mention of figures "above" or "below" or "in front of" others. To give an example from his "Taking of Troy": "On entering this building (the Lesché, or Club Room of the Cnidians), you perceive that all the painting on the right represents Ilium after its capture and the Greeks setting sail. Menelaus' crew is making ready to put to sea: the ship is painted with the sailors on board and children among them: in the middle of the ship is the pilot Phrontis with two punting-poles in his hands. . . . Below him is a certain Ithaimenes carrying raiment and Echoiax going down the gangway with a bronze urn. Polites, Strophios, and Alphios are taking down Menelaus' tent, which stands not far from the ship and Amphialos is taking to pieces another tent. Under the feet of Amphialos is seated a boy. . . . Briséis is represented standing, Diomeda is above her, and Iphis in front of both: all three seem to be scrutinizing Helen's form. Helen herself is seated and so is Eurybates near her. . . . Beside Helen stands her handmaid Panthalis, while Elektra, another handmaid, is putting on her mistress' sandals. . . . Above Helen, a man clad in a purple mantle is seated in an attitude of profound dejection. You might guess it to be Helenos, the son of Priam, even before reading the inscription. Near Helenos is Meges who is wounded in the arm. . . . Lykomedes, son of Kreon, is also depicted beside Meges with a wound on his wrist. . . . Euryalos . . . is also wounded on the head and wrist. These figures are higher up than Helen in the painting. Next to Helen is the mother of Theseus with her hair closely cropped and Demophon, one of the sons of Theseus. . . . The Trojan women are depicted as captives and lamenting. Andromache is painted and in front of her stands the boy grasping her breast; this child was killed by being hurled from the tower. . . . Andromache and Medesikaste wear hoods, but Polyxena has her hair braided after the manner of maidens. . . . Nestor is painted with a cap on his head and a spear in his hand and there is a horse in an attitude as if it were about to roll on the

[12] B. Schroeder, "Die polygnotische Malerei und die Parthenongiebel," *Jahr.*, 30 (1915), pp. 95 ff., esp. p. 117. G. Körte, *Jahr.*, 31 (1916), pp. 280 ff., denies the influence of the Ionic school, especially of Polygnotos, on Pheidias.

ground. As far as the horse, the scene is the sea-shore, and pebbles may be distinguished on it; but from that point it is no longer the sea."[13]

Or in the description of the "Underworld":[13] "The other portion of the painting, that on the left hand, represents Odysseus in hell, whither he has descended to consult the soul of Teiresias about his return home. The painting is as follows: there is water to indicate a river, obviously the Acheron; reeds are growing in the river and so dim are the outlines of the fish that you would take them for shadows rather than fish. There is a bark on the river and the ferryman at the oars. Polygnotos, it seems to me, followed the poem called the Minyad. . . . Accordingly, he has represented Charon as an aged man. . . . On the bank of Acheron, just below Charon's bark, is a man who had once ill-used, and is now being throttled by, his father. . . . Near the man who maltreated his father and is suffering for it in hell is a man punished for sacrilege. . . . Higher up than the figures I have enumerated is Eurynomos; the Delphian guides say that he is one of the demons in hell and that he eats the flesh of corpses, leaving only the bones. . . . I will describe his appearance and attitude in the painting: his color is between blue and black, like that of flies that settle on meat; he is showing his teeth and is seated on a vulture's skin."

These descriptions of Polygnotos' paintings at Delphi have caused endless attempts at reconstructions for more than 150 years. The results show wide differences and readily convince the student that no approach to probability is possible. The earlier efforts of Count de Caylus (1757) labored with pictorial illusion, spatial depth, and landscape charm—things but vaguely understood or not at all grasped in the days of Polygnotos. The restorations of F. and J. Riepenhausen, 1805, 1826, were executed in academic fashion, but were unconvincing, as was the work of Gebhardt, who made a noteworthy advance in symmetry of arrangement. Benndorf, while presenting a new basis for reconstruction, proceeded from an hypothesis impossible of proof, viz., that the relief scenes of the Heroön at Gjölbaschi in Lycia were dependent in motives and principle of arrangement on the paintings of Polygnotos. On this basis, he sought to restore the Iliupersis, or "Taking of Troy," in a double frieze of two rows one above the other, corresponding to the sculptures of the Lycian tomb.[14] The most artistic attempt, still unsuccessful, however, has been made by Robert (1892-1893). He employs motives taken from vases which copied Polygnotos, but he held that Polygnotan composition took little account of group-

---

[13] Paus., X, 25. Tr. by Frazer but with spellings changed and certain omissions; for the Underworld scene, cf. Paus., X, 28 ff. Quoted by permission of Macmillan & Co., London.

[14] For various reconstructions, see *Wiener Vorlegeblätter*, 1888, Pls. X-XII; G. Körte, *Jahr.*, 31 (1916), p. 284, takes up Benndorf's arrangement anew and approves it. Goethe began the system of three levels in his reconstruction, 1805. C. Robert, *Die Nekyia des Polygnot, Hall. Winckelmannsprogr.*, 16 (1892), p. 34.

ing, silhouetting its figures against the background and not placing any two figures on the same ground-line, in the fashion of "Polygnotan" vases. But he who reads may judge whether any true idea of the great painter's composition can ever be formed from the record of Pausanias.[14a]

The important thing to be gathered from these descriptions is the fact that the various individuals were arranged over the surface of the painting at different levels. Robert was the first to make clear this principle by collecting together a group of vases which show figures arranged on ground-lines at varying altitudes. Figure 348 presents his reconstruction of the "Taking of Troy" on this basis. The right half covers the description cited—the ship and tent of Menelaus, Helen seated, the Trojan women weeping, and the pebbly shore up to the horse at the left. The walls of Troy and the wooden horse appear in the background.

Let us turn from conjectural material to contemporary evidence. The "Niobid" or "Argonaut" krater, found at Orvieto and now in the Louvre, tells us more than many reconstructions can of this new principle of composition which can hardly have been invented in the potter's workshop but which belonged to the major art of wall-painting. In Figure 349, from this vase, we have a rocky landscape cut by ground-lines which indicate a region with hills and valleys. The scene is that of Apollo and Artemis pursuing the sons and daughters of Niobe. The Niobids lie slain on the ground or half hidden by hillocks, or they flee, pierced with arrows. The significant things are these: in order to distribute figures in numbers over an extensive surface, the painters of the period adopted a schematic arrangement for the area to be decorated. A high point of vision was chosen. Figures which would be behind others, appeared higher up; those lower down were nearer. The divisions of the ground were made clear by irregular lines. The landscape was not really landscape but a formal frame for the figure composition. The space was ideal space and there was the scantiest allusion to locality.

But does the reconstruction of Robert or the "Niobid" krater really tell us much about Polygnotan composition? The painter of the vase was working with a dark background against which, for the sake of clearness, it was necessary to silhouette his figures and where groups occur they are more or less open[15] (Fig. 350). This was necessary for clearness of form and outline. The demand for the apportioning of light and dark conditioned grouping. The employment of overlapping figures introduced light masses to too great an extent, as we see on the Amazon vase of Figure 326 and confusion resulted. Polygnotos had none of these difficulties to face. He was working with a neutral background of light color and could use various contrasting colors to make clear the details of his figures, so that undoubtedly they would not be

[14a] For Robert's reconstructions, see *Hall. Winckelmannsprogr.*, 16 (1892); 17 (1893); 18 (1895).

[15] R. Schöne, *Jahr.*, VIII (1893), p. 195. *Cf.* esp. p. 187 for Ælian passage.

isolated in the way in which Robert reconstructs them. There was, however, as in vase-painting, the same scrutiny of individual forms and attention to contours which should reveal form and motion. Furthermore, the ground lines which Polygnotos used would appear in darker color against the light ground of the wall.

The method of Polygnotan composition depends upon many laws, as Schreiber has pointed out,[16] but, to judge from the text of Pausanias and from vases, certain things are clear. First of all, Polygnotos chose for his paintings a high horizon-line. In the Iliupersis, the figures ranged from the walls of Troy at the top of the painting to the pebbly beach in the foreground, so that, with the tent and ship of Menelaus, at least three levels were indicated. But the figures higher up, which were thought of as being in the background, were not reduced in size and were virtually in the same plane as those in the foreground. There was no real perspective but the impression of its presence was attained; even to us who are accustomed to true perspective, "Polygnotan" vases suggest spatial composition. Scientific handling of the third dimension occurred later in Greek painting but the innovation of Polygnotos contained elements which contributed toward such a development. Painting in this period was at last freed from the trammels of frieze composition, without definitely attacking the problem of the third dimension.[17]

The compositions of Polygnotos are much more difficult to conceive. It is certainly true that the figures were placed at various heights freely, but they were composed in group arrangement. The text of Pausanias makes clear that in the Iliupersis the composition was a symmetrical one with three main points of interest: the center where Epeios was tearing down the walls of Troy; the figure of Helen at the right; and that of Kassandra at the left. Near Helen were four figures balanced by four above; on either side of Kassandra groups of two figures were added. Beyond these, there were other groups and isolated figures and the symmetry became less rigid. But the principle of arrangement seems to have been that of a balanced composition made up of complex groups, with the figures of greater importance in and near the center. Open spaces occurred between the groups, not accessories, as so often in vase-painting. There was a strict correspondence throughout, figures being grouped together by worth, honor, friendship, or a common fate. This symmetry of arrangement is evident at the very entrance where one saw on the right the ship of Menelaus ready to depart; on the left the bark of Charon and the Acheron. The scene on the right depicted earthly vanities and miseries; the one on the left, the rewards and punishments in the Other World. Throughout there was harmony of form and content and symmetry in grouping, at times subtly veiled and almost never rigid.

[16] Th. Schreiber, "Die Wandbilder des Polygnotos," *Abh. der Phil.-hist. Cl. der Kgl. Sächs. Ges. der Wiss.*, Leipzig, 17 (1897), pp. 1-178.
[17] H. Bulle, *Der schöne Mensch,*[2] pp. 605 ff.

The figures had necessarily to be adapted to the surface to be covered. This at Delphi was a rectangular Club Room built by the Cnidians.[18] The building was 18.70 meters long by 9.53 wide,—twice as long as it was broad,—and there was a door in the long wall on the south side. In the interior, eight pillars arranged in two parallel rows supported the roof, in which there may have been an opening for lighting purposes. Around the walls were benches for loungers. The paintings began on either side of the doorway on the south, continued along the short walls in all probability, and met at the middle of the north long wall, facing the doorway. In this way each picture was distributed in three different sections over three separate walls, forming a kind of trilogy.[19]

All of this evidence, however, does not give us back the Polygnotan paintings, which allow for innumerable combinations on the basis of Pausanias' text. Suffice it to say that in the Iliupersis the three main sections centered at the entrance around Helen and the Greeks preparing to depart; in the middle, about Epeios tearing down the walls of Troy; at the left, about Kassandra. Epeios was the grandson of Phokos and the Phocians were probably lords of Delphi at the time when the frescoes were painted, between 458 and 447 B.C. Polygnotos accordingly gave the central point of interest to this hero.[20]

The Polygnotan principle of composition, therefore, as far as we can make it out, was based on a formal system of levels; it dealt with concentric groups arranged in careful symmetry, the figures being bound together by various ties such as love, friendship, and common destiny. Dramatic contrast played an important rôle—the mourning Trojans and triumphant Greeks; the happy and damned in Hades, and the like. Probably also the triple form of composition is significant for Polygnotos, because it appears again not only in the "Underworld" scene at Delphi but in the "Battle of Marathon." Schöne's interpretation of the phrase in Ælian is probably correct.[15] Πολύγνωτος ἔγραφε τὰ μεγάλα καὶ ἐν τοῖς τελείοις εἰργάζετο τὰ ᾶθλα, would then mean that Polygnotos won the prize by his compositions which had a certain grandeur of style and completeness. According to Aristotle's definition,

[18] Th. Homolle, *B.C.H.*, 20 (1896), pp. 637-639; 21 (1897), Pl. XVII, p. 259. Frazer, *Pausanias*, V, 635-636 (Addenda); *Fouilles de Delphes*, II, Pls. V, IX; *Arch. Anz.*, XIII (1898), p. 45; *Jahr.*, 31 (1916), p. 287.

[19] G. Körte, *Jahr.*, 31 (1916), p. 288, thinks it more probable that only the south wall on either side of the doorway was covered with paintings.

[20] C. Robert, *Nekyia*, p. 76; Wilamowitz, *Phil. Untersuch.*, VII (1884), p. 223, *An.* 19; W. Klein, *Ges. der gr. Kunst*, I, 1904, p. 429; *cf.* A. Reinach, *Recueil Milliet, Textes grecs et latins relatifs à l'histoire de la peinture ancienne*, Paris, 1921, I, 90, for a discussion on the dating. The Cnidians could not have erected the monument until freed from Persian domination, in 468. The paintings were executed later, *ca.* 458.

τέλειον, means that which, like a tragedy, had a beginning, middle, and end. This definition may be applied to the triple arrangement of Polygnotan composition.[20a]

In the matter of colors, Polygnotos also made advances. He was one of the great "Four-Color" painters, but he undoubtedly had a far richer palette than the primitives of the Sixth Century. There, we found the use of red, black, and white, with a few instances of yellow. Polygnotos used these four, and by combining them, he was much nearer the polychromy of old marble-painting. Pliny says that the tetrachrome painters used white from Melos, red of Sinope, yellow ocher from Attica, and black —which we are told was sometimes made of wine lees.[21] Undoubtedly, yellow first came to have full importance under him.[22] We are not informed whether the colors were put on in flat tones or whether Polygnotos began the practice of mixing colors and of shading; we can only draw inferences. Apollodoros, who followed Polygnotos and who was a great shadow master, was probably the first person who really succeeded in the mixing of colors and in shading, but that Polygnotos was without colors like green, which could be had by mixing blue-black and yellow, seems unlikely when we recall figures like Eurynomos.

Further, red from Sinope would give several shades and so also would yellow ocher, when burned. Grape-black mixed with white would produce a bluish color. If certain blues were not used by Polygnotos, it was probably because the technique employed did not allow it. Indigo and *cœruleum*, Pliny tells us, could not be used *al fresco*.[22a]

It is obvious that the range of tones produced by the palette of Polygnotos was by no means a limited one. The combinations which Demokritos speaks of are very numerous. Many famous colorists have employed a very small number of colors; Rubens, for example, used seven. Velasquez was an eminent painter in gray. The important thing was not the number of colors, but the relation and harmony of tones. In color, there are two distinct elements: the hue, or colored appearance, and the value of the tone; *i.e.*, the degree of light or shadow that the tone produces. The value is the more important of the two. (Bertrand, *Études*, pp. 135 ff.) A modern example of a Four-Color painting may be seen, as Jex-Blake, Sellers have pointed out, in Titian's "Christ crowned with thorns" in Munich.

Further, when we find on vases the beginnings of shading, however modest, it seems improbable that the major art was less progressive. In Figure 350, there is a

[20a] Aristotle, *Poetics*, VII, 1450[b], 29; XXIII, 1459[a], 21; *Physica*, 3, 207[a], 13.

[21] Pliny, *N.H.*, 35, 50; 35, 42; Cic., *Brutus*, 18, 70; Vitruvius, *De Arch.*, VII, 10, 4; Quint., *Inst. Or.*, XII, 10, 3; É. Bertrand, *Études sur la peinture*, Paris, 1893, pp. 132-144.

[22] Pliny, *N.H.*, 33, 160. *Sile pingere instituere primi Polygnotus et Micon, Attico dumtaxat.*

[22a] Pliny, *N.H.*, 35, 49.

slight use of shading, especially in the "eye folds" of the garments of the Amazons; there is dirt on the foot of the fallen Greek in the center; there is shading on the interior of the shield. On the Villa Giulia psykter (Fig. 324), a small amount of shading occurs on the bodies of the centaurs, probably to suggest roundness, and the beards and hair are done in a dilute wash.[23] Polygnotos doubtless used in moderation both the mixing of colors and shading, but these practices were really in the beginning stages with him and it remained for Apollodoros to make the decisive break with archaic methods, to employ perspective in this connection and to surround his figures with light and shadow.[24] Just how the shading of Polygnotos may have appeared, is difficult to visualize. Perhaps the hatched shading on later lekythoi may give us an idea. But if we wish to know how a tetrachrome painting looked, we must turn to the Alexander Mosaic, which made use of the Polygnotan color scale[25] (Fig. 451). Here, we see at its culmination the Four-Color painting which had in Polygnotos its first representative vouched for in literature. The importance of the advance lay in the use of yellow ocher. With the addition of this color, the full development of the other colors by mixing became possible. As Winter has pointed out, a limited number of tones may be obtained from white, red, and black, but they give only dull and cold transitions. Yellow, however, placed beside these colors heightens their value; mixed with them, it produces all sorts of shades. Its adoption caused a development of mixed tones which was epoch-making for the development of painting.

The other important color employed by Polygnotos was a grape-black, made from wine lees.[26] It was the use of this black with the other three colors which gave the sober character to the painting of Polygnotos. It renounced gaiety. In contrast to this is the richer palette of marble-painting, which employed blue instead of black. These two methods of painting, one employing black, the other blue, developed from the Polygnotan period onward. The effect of the two methods is clearly seen by contrasting, as Winter has done, the polychromy of the Alexander Sarcophagus, which used blue, with the Alexander Mosaic employing black. Finally, the gayer tradition prevails.

What the ancients admired in the painting of Polygnotos was the sobriety of color. The emphasis was on extreme simplification of form which contributed to the nobility and grandeur of the figures. There was undoubtedly less attention given to

[23] F. R., *Gr. Vas.*, Pl. 15; E. Pfuhl, "Die griechische Malerei," *N.J.*, XXVII (1911), p. 177.

[24] E. Pfuhl, *op. cit.*, pp. 168, 180.

[25] F. Winter, *Das Alexandermosaik aus Pompeii*, Strassburg, 1909, pp. 2 ff., and colored plate.

[26] Vitruvius, *De Arch.*, VII, 10, 4; Plut., *De Defect. Orac.*, 47; Pliny, *N.H.*, 35, 42.

action than to pose and the figures possessed a sculptural dignity. Dionysios of Halikarnassos says:[27] "In ancient paintings, the scheme of coloring was simple and presented no variety in the tones; but the line was rendered with exquisite perfection, thus lending to these early works a singular grace. This purity of draughtsmanship was gradually lost; its place was taken by a learned technique, by the differentiation of light and shade, by the full resources of the rich coloring to which the works of the later artists owe their strength." It was thus largely by drawing and simple color that Polygnotos produced figures of such grandeur and of such power of expression. The colors were probably put on in the fresco technique on walls, or in tempera on panels, but the matter is a very complicated one, involving more than one possible method.[28] We shall return to this subject later.

The Persian wars supplied the artists of the seventies with new themes, although they still, for the most part, used the old ones, and left for them rich opportunities by destroying the works of their predecessors. Polygnotos' activity in Athens began shortly after the invasion and his career probably lasted until after the middle of the Fifth Century. He came from an artistic household where he was trained by his father, Aglaophon, a painter, and where his brother Aristophon followed this calling. He was probably invited by Kimon, who was in control of Athens, to help rehabilitate the city and he gave his services toward decorating the public buildings without pay. The Athenians rewarded him for this with the rights of citizenship. Possibly also he owed to his artistic talent the fact that he lived on intimate terms with the family of Kimon.

Records tell us of many public buildings in Athens which Polygnotos decorated, notably the Stoa Poikile, or Painted Porch; the Sanctuary of Theseus; the Anakeion, or Temple of the Dioscuri; and the Pinacotheca, or Picture Gallery. These paintings were probably earlier than the more famous ones at Delphi. In addition to these, he decorated the temple of Athena Areia at Platæa. Among the oldest frescoes in Athens were probably those in the Anakeion or Sanctuary of the Dioscuri.[29] Here were painted the marriage of the daughters of Leukippos by Polygnotos and a scene from the Argonautic expedition by Mikon, probably an older contemporary. We have no adequate means for restoring these paintings nor any sufficient data on which to form a very conclusive opinion of them. Archæological research has associated with the painting by Polygnotos a well-known vase in the British Museum by the

[27] Dionys. of Hal., *De Isæo Judic.*, 4 (tr. from Jex-Blake, Sellers, *op. cit.*, p. xxxi).

[28] A. Reinach, *Recueil Milliet*, I, 91; *cf.* C. Robert, "Marathonschlacht," *Hall. Winckelmannsprogr.*, 18 (1895), p. 104; *cf.* E. Berger, *Die Maltechnik des Altertums*, München, 1904.

[29] Paus., I, 18, 1. *Cf.* Körte, *Jahr.*, 31 (1916), pp. 266 ff.; Harpokration couples this painting with those in the sanctuary of Theseus as the basis of Polygnotos' admittance to Athenian citizenship.

Meidias Painter (Fig. 344). But the scene here is the rape of the Leukippides, which Pausanias does not mention, although it may be implied when he states that the "marriage" was depicted. Furthermore, the vase is to be dated in the last quarter of the Fifth Century and bears only slight traces of the influence of Polygnotos. This may be seen in the use of levels,—indicated by light, wavy lines,—and in certain types of poses such as are found in the frieze below and which are vouched for by Pausanias: the youth at the left with his foot high on a rock, or the figure of Asterope resting her arm on the shoulder of Chrysothemis. But there is no trace here of the *style* of Polygnotos, with simple, firm lines in drawing—as we conceive it from the testimony of ancient writers. The artist revels in a sea of beauty in which finely curved lines run riot. The necessity of using the greatest reserve in forming conclusions about Polygnotos from material so far removed in style and time cannot be too strongly emphasized.

On the other hand, there is a certain vase often associated with the Argonautic painting, which *can* give us ideas about composition and drawing in the period of Polygnotos and his circle (Fig. 351). This vase is usually called the Orvieto krater from the place of its discovery, but it is sometimes referred to as the "Niobid" or the "Argonaut" krater because it bears on the reverse the slaughter of the Niobids (Fig. 349), and on the obverse, a supposed reference to the Argonauts. The subject of the latter scene is not in the least certain. Robert connects it with the assembling of the Argonauts on their Colchian journey; Hauser considers it the gathering of Attic heroes before Marathon and associates it with the "Battle of Marathon" by Mikon. But two figures in the scene are certainly known: Herakles in the center, Athena at the left. There is little to connect it with the painting of the Argonauts, where great pains were lavished by the artist on the horses of Akastos. It is quite possible that the helmeted warrior with a serpent on his shield is Menelaus, who bore this device on his shield in Polygnotos' Iliupersis, in token of the prodigy at Aulis. More important than the subject matter is the composition, freely arranged at various levels and with the background half concealing a youth in armor at the left. This device was employed by Mikon in the painting of a figure named Boutes, of whom only the helmet and one eye were visible. This gave rise to the proverb, "Sooner painted than Boutes."[30]

If we examine the vase in detail, we gain some information in regard to "Polygnotan" types, poses, drawing, and style (Fig. 352). First of all, the figure of Athena is seen to be an idealized type with noble features and a sublimity that recalls the Lemnian Athena of Pheidias. She wears a soft linen chiton with fine parallel folds and a Doric peplos above, worn in the Attic fashion with a girdled overfold. Feihl has pointed out that the dress, treatment of hair, and ægis all belong to the transitional

[30] Zenobios, *Prov.*, IV, 28, θᾶττον ἢ Βούτης.

period and are typically "Polygnotan."[31] In the case of Herakles, we find again an ideal figure. The torso, with the chest marked off schematically into distinct fields, is curiously archaic. Some new poses appear, notably in the youth who places one foot high on a rock, and in the figure seated at the feet of Herakles, supposedly grasping his knee with both hands after the fashion of Hektor in the "Underworld" (Fig. 353). The device has not, however, been successfully carried out nor has the three-quarter view of the face with its thick lips and wry mouth succeeded. What is striking is the impression of freedom obtained in the various positions, especially in the reclining figure in the center. The treatment of the eye approaches correctness but the drawing is not wholly successful. The eye is an ellipse with the pupil a black dot on the upper eyelid. The whole composition has a certain majestic calm resulting from ideal types and quiet poses. Combined with this is a striving toward realism, seen in new positions, in lines in the face, as in the case of Herakles, and in individualized types like the bearded figure with the *petasos* (cf. Fig. 319). It is evident that the artist is entering upon new paths but much that is archaic survives and much that is attempted in a new way is only partially successful.

Close in time to the paintings of the Anakeion were those in the Sanctuary of Theseus at Athens.[32] This building was completed to receive the bones of Theseus in 475, so that the paintings may be dated between 475 and 465 B.C. Here were painted the Athenians fighting the Amazons, the Battle of the Centaurs and Lapiths, and Theseus' descent into the sea. Apropos of the Centaur battle, Pausanias says: "Theseus has already slain a centaur, but the others are fighting on equal terms. To those who may be unacquainted with the legend, the painting on the third wall is not clear, partly, no doubt, by reason of time, but partly also because Mikon has not painted the whole story." Pausanias makes no mention of Polygnotos in connection with these paintings but Suidas and Harpokration seem to assign them to him, although the passage in both writers rests on an uncertain reading, $\theta\eta\sigma\alpha\upsilon\rho\hat{\omega}$, changed by Reinesius to $\Theta\eta\sigma\acute{\epsilon}\omega\varsigma$ $\acute{\iota}\epsilon\rho\hat{\omega}$. Pausanias gives the painting "which is not wholly clear" on the third wall to Mikon. It represented Theseus descending to the halls of Poseidon to prove his divine birth by bringing up the ring which Minos had thrown into the sea (cf. Bacchylides, XVI).

If we turn again to Figure 350, we have interesting material for elucidating points of style and subject matter in the painting of the Polygnotan circle. On the neck of the New York krater is a representation of the Battle between the Centaurs and

---

[31] E. Feihl, *Die Ficoronische Cista und Polygnot*, Tübingen, 1913, pp. 12 ff.

[32] Paus., I, 17, 2; Harpokr., s.v. Πολύγνωτος. The Theseum was erected to receive the bones of Theseus brought from Skyros by Kimon in 475. Plut., *Cim.*, 8; *Thes.*, 36. It is not to be identified with the well-known temple of this name but lay east of the Agora and south of the Gymnasium of Ptolemy.

Lapiths—an event which occurred at the marriage of Peirithoos. In the center, Theseus is swinging his axe above his head for a blow at a boldly posed centaur. The figure of Theseus and that of the centaur carrying off a boy bring to mind motives from the west pediment at Olympia. In fact, the Centauromachy of the pediment and the one on the vase may have been inspired in each case by the fresco in the Theseum.[33] Characterization is cleverly handled in the bride's father at the right and a "lost profile" is avoided by partly covering with a mantle the face of the youth with a long spear. Motives and style are probably akin to the work in the Sanctuary of Theseus, whether the painting was by Polygnotos or Mikon.

On the other hand, the Amazonomachy of the same vase shows interesting innovations such as we know were introduced at this time in Athens by the major art of painting. Space seems more successfully conceived, with plants growing here and there in the background. In the group of Theseus and the fighting Amazons in the center, extensive use has been made of shading on the "eye folds" of the garments. This new practice, which we have had occasion to mention, is found on a number of North Greek reliefs, such as the Philis relief and the stele of a girl in the Palazzo Conservatori; it was probably derived from painting as it is confined largely to vase-painting and relief, and is doubtless to be classed as "Polygnotan."[34] Other striking features in the vase are the fallen Greek in the center, with shaded foot; the fallen Amazon, with the lower part of the figure cut off by a ground-line, and the sinking Amazon with face in three-quarter view, who plunges over the border of the design at the right.[35] This last device is typical of the entire painting which seems to be bursting its bounds in the painter's attempt to crowd on a vase the material of a mural composition.

The artist of the New York krater has not only been interested in combining on his vase subject matter from two of the paintings in the Theseum but he has also concerned himself with the technical problems of foreshortening and perspective, although the foreshortening is suggested rather than executed. How difficult some of these matters were for him is seen in the drawing of the legs of striding or lunging Amazons, especially the lunging one at the left. Possibly Polygnotos himself was not able to master these problems wholly, otherwise we should hardly have so many wry faces and misshapen legs on the vases of the period.

The third painting in the Theseum represented the legend of Theseus descending into the sea to prove his divinity. It was painted by Mikon. A late vase, the Bologna

---

[33] F. R., *Gr. Vas.*, II, 311 ff.; H. Oelschig, *De Centauromachiæ in arte græca figuris*, Halle, 1921 (Diss.); F. R., *Gr. Vas.*, II, 247, Fig. 88.

[34] L. D. Caskey, "The Ludovisi Relief and its Companion Piece in Boston," *A.J.A.*, XXII (1918), pp. 134 ff.; F. Hauser, F. R., II, 309; H. Brunn, *Kleine Schriften*, II, pp. 184 ff., 201 ff.

[35] This last point is cited by some writers as evidence for the non-Attic origin of the vase-painter.

krater, probably follows the design after a fashion, though it is undoubtedly far removed in style from Polygnotos and can tell us little of his art[36] (Fig. 354). The motives introduced by Polygnotos are decaying in the hands of this artist. They must quickly have become common property and have been modified to suit individual needs. It seems, however, not impossible that the vase-painter was imitating, after a fashion, the Mikonian masterpiece. The arguments adduced against this by Schreiber are rather rigid, especially when Pausanias says that the painting was not wholly clear in presenting the legend.[37] The fact that Helios appears beyond the rim of the ocean where the boat is beached seems only "poetic license." This may also be granted for the flowers growing in Poseidon's realms. The absence of the ring when the crown will suffice and when the Minos episode could not be wholly introduced, need not concern us too much. The framework of Polygnotan composition seems to be present; the style of the master is almost wholly lost, so that the vase is, after all, of little value to us except in so far as it reveals the survival of "Polygnotan" material in a later epoch, near the end of the Fifth Century. The design is probably a contamination of Polygnotan subject matter and some material from Dionysiac legend.[37a] The vase was painted by the Kadmos Painter.

The honor of decorating the Stoa Poikile, or Painted Colonnade in the Market-Place at Athens, has usually been assigned to Polygnotos, although Mikon also coöperated with him here.[38] Four paintings are mentioned by Pausanias. They included a battle between the Athenians and Lacedæmonians at Oinoë, for which no artist was named; the battle of Theseus against the Amazons, assigned by Aristophanes to Mikon;[39] the Iliupersis and the insult to Kassandra given by Plutarch to Polygnotos;[40] and the Battle of Marathon. We need not pause at length over these paintings of which we know practically nothing beyond the text, unless it be to discuss the Mikonian Amazonomachy. We possess today a large number of vases depicting battles between Greeks and Amazons and the task is to separate from the list of these "paraphrases" and "excerpts," material that is Mikonian and in the style of the Polygnotan circle. We can hardly hope to distinguish greatly between

[36] Against the use of this vase as a reflection of Mikon's art, see P. Jacobsthal, *Theseus auf dem Meeresgrunde*, 1911; G. Körte, *Jahr.*, 31 (1916), p. 286.

[37] Th. Schreiber, *op. cit.*, No. 30, pp. 128 ff.

[37a] The absence of the ring favors an early Fifth Century version of the legend. Sir R. C. Jebb, *Bacchylides, Introduction*, XVI, 227. I owe the reference to Miss Milne.

[38] Paus., I, 15; Pliny, *N.H.*, 35, 59. The Stoa was probably erected by Peisianax between 475 and 462. It was certainly finished in 456 because of the battle of Oinoë commemorated in it. A. Reinach, *op. cit.*, pp. 86, 136, dates the paintings between 469 and 462, as Kimon was banished in 461, or in 456, after he was recalled.

[39] Aristoph., *Lys.*, 678 and Scholiast; Arrian, *Anab.*, VII, 13, 5.

[40] Plut., *Cim.*, 4.

what is Polygnotan and what is Mikonian. Klein believes that much "Polygnotan" material really goes back to the older painter, Mikon, and this is probably true.[41] Where we can trace Mikon's style is in the bolder use of ground-lines, which cut off the figures by means of the background.

Aristophanes tells us that in the painting by Mikon the Amazons fought on horse. On a "Polygnotan" vase from Gela, certain Mikonian features appear (Fig. 355).[41a] These are, above all, the representation of rough ground by connected lines; a charging Amazon in Phrygian garb on horse and a lunging Greek warrior with his sword raised across his forehead. The style of the drawing and the restrained action are characteristic of the period and we may assume, because of the repetition of this one motive of the raised sword, that it belonged in the Mikonian repertoire of groups. But the various vase-painters made use of the mural material in different ways to suit their decorative needs and may have paraphrased or adapted this or that group for their own ends. One group presented a warrior with his foot high on a rock, on the point of attacking an Amazon on horse (Figs. 356 and 357). Klein considers that this probably formed the central part of the composition in Mikon's painting.[41] In a vase from Ruvo, now in Naples (Fig. 358), the vase-painter has shoved this group to the left and has attempted to place it in the background, whereas the center is occupied by a Greek hero hurling his spear at a sinking Amazon (*cf.* Fig. 359). In addition to these groups, there is sometimes found a composition of two combatants on foot, in which a Greek is staying the hand of an Amazon (Fig. 360). Possibly another group presented a Greek brandishing his sword above his head and combating an Amazon who had dismounted from her horse and who fought with an axe (Fig. 361). How these various groups were bound together into an harmonious whole, we cannot know. The vase-painters cannot take us far in this matter. They undoubtedly walked about the Stoa enjoying the paintings and deriving inspiration from them. Later, they painted certain groups and motives from memory. But each chose the material which attracted him artistically or technically. It was impossible for the vase-painter to give in his small compass an idea of a mural decoration containing more than one hundred figures, even if he had desired to do so. In most cases he was lured too far from the canons of his art in what he did present. Some masters, like the painter of the New York vase of Figure 326, were almost wholly absorbed with the matter of foreshortening and perspective. Others cared so little for this that we have almost a return to frieze-composition with the emphasis on nobly conceived forms. The New York vase of Figure 350 probably

[41] W. Klein, "Mikon und Panainos, Mikon und Paionios," *Jahr.*, 33 (1918), pp. 1-38.

[41a] This vase was painted by the vase-painter Polygnotos, but it also belongs to the class of vases that copied the wall-paintings of the mural painter. P. Orsi, *Mon. Ant.*, XVII (1907), Pl. 43.

comes nearest in approximating the style of the Polygnotan-Mikonian Battles with Amazons.

In Polygnotos' Iliupersis, the treatment of the theme was doubtless similar to what we found at Delphi in the picture dealing with the same subject—a representation of "Troy Taken" rather than "The Taking of Troy." In connection with the insult to Kassandra, ancient writers speak of the delicate color in her cheeks: the blood seemed to tinge her face with a soft hue.[42] The picture of Laodike by Polygnotos offered a portrait of Kimon's sister, Elpinike, with whom he had fallen in love. We shall see that so-called "portraiture" begins to play a rôle in this period and that attempts in this direction occur in the "Battle of Marathon," the fourth painting in the Stoa.

We do not know the author of the "Battle of Marathon." Pausanias and Pliny both name Panainos, the brother of Pheidias, but in his description of the painting, Pausanias cites no artist.[43] Several ancient writers mention Mikon as a co-worker, and many scholars assign the painting to both artists.[44] There is a statement in Ælian which gives to Mikon at least the execution of three figures and a dog, possibly of the whole painting, although he adds that some authors assign the work to Polygnotos.[45] The strongest evidence for Mikon's authorship is a passage in Lykourgos and one in the rhetorician Sopatros. These state that Mikon was punished by the Athenians because he painted the barbarians larger than the Greeks.[46] The conclusion to be drawn is that we cannot determine from the evidence who painted the picture, but probably it must be assigned to both Mikon and Panainos. Evidently Mikon had some connection with it because he was fined for painting the barbarians larger than the Greeks. Perhaps he was in charge of the whole and Panainos was working under him. Polygnotos probably had no part in this particular painting, but his name was associated with it because the entire decoration of the Stoa was often assigned to him in antiquity. The element of portraiture is new, but just how much of portraiture could enter in some twenty or thirty years after the event is uncertain. Furthermore, it seems unlikely that any very realistic attempt could be made in the case of the Persian generals.

The account of the painting does not suffice to give us any idea of it as a work of art. "The Bœotians of Platæa and all the men of Attica are closing with the barbarians. In this part of the picture, the combatants are evenly matched, but farther

[42] Lucian, *Imag.*, 7. This refers to the painting at Delphi.

[43] Paus., V, 11, 6; Pliny, *N.H.*, 35, 57; *cf.* Paus., I, 15, 3, where the painting is described, but no author named. W. Klein, *Arch.-epigr. Mitth. aus Œster.*, 12 (1888), p. 96.

[44] H. Brunn, *Ges. der gr. Künstler*, II, 14; F. Hauser, F. R., II, 249.

[45] Ælian, *N.A.*, VII, 38. *Cf.* Arrian, *Anab.*, VII, 13,5.

[46] Lykourgos, cited by Harpokration, *s.v.* Μίκων. *Cf.* Sopatros, διαίρεσ. ζητημάτ. Walz, 8, p. 126, μετὰ Μαραθῶνα Μίκων ὁ ζωγράφος τοὺς βαρβάρους γράψας μείζους τῶν Ἑλλήνων κρίνεται.

on the barbarians are fleeing and pushing each other into the marsh. At the extremity of the picture are the Phœnician ships and the Greeks slaughtering the barbarians who are rushing into the ships. Here, too, are depicted the hero, Marathon, after whom the plain was named; Theseus seeming to rise out of the earth; and Athena and Herakles. . . . Of the combatants, the most conspicuous in the painting are Kallimachos, who had been chosen to command the Athenians; Miltiades, one of the generals; and a hero named Echetlos."[46a]

According to Pliny the use of color had grown so greatly and the technique had been so perfected that real portraits were painted of the commanders on both sides— Miltiades, Kallimachos, and Kynaigeiros among the Athenians, Datis and Artaphernes among the barbarians.[47] We have already found names assigned to various figures in the Polygnotan paintings at Delphi; it was an archaic practice which Polygnotos did not discard. In the "Battle of Marathon," the name of Miltiades was not given because of his unpopularity, but his position and gestures clearly indicated who he was.[48] As to portraiture, Kallimachos and Kynaigeiros had fallen in the battle of Marathon almost a generation before the building was erected and Miltiades had long been dead. The Persian leaders were certainly not available for portraits. There can be no question of real portraiture but probably there was an attempt at characterization. Perhaps Pliny found in his source a notice to the effect that the "Battle of Marathon" contained pictures of this and that named person, and, judging from the importance of portraiture in his own time, drew the conclusion that the characterization of Panainos, which was something new and striking in the history of art, was the beginning of portraiture.[49]

It is difficult to visualize the "Battle of Marathon," as it is difficult for us to visualize any of the great mural paintings of the Fifth Century. Robert has again attempted a reconstruction based on vases. The plan of composition seems to be tripartite. At the right, the combat was just beginning; in the center, the Persians were fleeing and driving one another into the marsh, while at the left, shown here in restoration, the barbarians were pursued to their ships by the Greeks and many were killed (Fig. 362, left half). The painting gave an opportunity for depicting Persian costumes and armor, examples of which occur in numbers on the vases of the period.[50]

---

[46a] The translation is by Frazer.  [47] Pliny, *N.H.*, 35, 57.

[48] Æschines *vs. Ctesiphon*, 186; Cornelius Nepos, *Milt.*, 6, 3.

[49] J. Lange, *Darstellung des Menschen in der älteren gr. Kunst*, Strassburg, 1899, pp. 162 ff.; Jex-Blake, Sellers, *The Elder Pliny's Chapters on the History of Art*, p. 102, 5; for a reconstruction, see Robert, *Hall. Winckelmannsprogr.*, 18 (1895). E. Pfuhl, *Die Anfänge der griechischen Bildniskunst*, München, 1927, p. 3, note 5.

[50] B. Schroeder, *Jahr.*, 26 (1911), pp. 281 ff.; Savignoni, *Ath. Mitth.*, 23 (1898), pp. 404 ff. Schroeder follows Furtwängler in refusing Panainos a part in the Marathon Battle of the Stoa.

The paintings of the Pinacotheca in the Propylæa at Athens offered scenes from the Trojan cycle, and a certain parallelism is evident:[51]

| | |
|---|---|
| Odysseus carrying off the bow of Philoktetes | Diomede carrying off the Palladium |
| Slaying of Ægisthus by Orestes | Sacrifice of Polyxena |
| Achilles at Skyros | Odysseus in Phæacia with Nausikaa and the maidens |

None of these subjects are presented on vases of the Polygnotan period with a style which arrests our attention or which recalls characteristics of the master painter of this epoch as cited by ancient authors. Inferior works such as the Munich amphora treat the theme of Odysseus and Nausikaa. This vase-painting may reflect Polygnotan subject matter but, if so, it reflects nothing more (Fig. 363). Pausanias says that Polygnotos painted Odysseus at the river approaching the maidens who were washing clothes with Nausikaa. This is the scene represented here in abbreviated form, but the work of the painter is so poor that we can only surmise how remarkable such a composition might be in the hands of a great master. The material offered an excellent opportunity for the representation of abashment in Odysseus and confusion in the fleeing maidens; for *ethos* in the case of Nausikaa. Polygnotos certainly availed himself of this opportunity to the full; to the vase-painter, it meant little. A pyxis in Boston, dating in the last quarter of the Fifth Century, treats the theme again, little more convincingly, except for the type of Odysseus (Fig. 364). The figures common to the two vases—Odysseus hiding behind the branches which he has broken from a tree, and the maid standing on wet linen held between her feet—were probably not invented independently but may go back to Polygnotos as a common source.

We have not discussed the paintings by Polygnotos in the temple of Athena Areia at Platæa which must probably be dated early—shortly after the battle in 479 B.C.[52] Here, Polygnotos pictured Odysseus on his return to Ithaca, after he had slain the suitors.[53] We are able to recognize possible motives employed from a vase in Berlin and from certain reliefs on a tomb at Gjölbaschi in Lycia.[54] Both monuments are somewhat removed in time from the Polygnotan original and the composition has necessarily been adapted in each case to suit the needs of the artist, but both display motives which point to a common source. On the vase in Berlin (Fig. 365), we see

---

[51] Paus., I, 22, 6. *Cf.* F. Hauser, *Œst. Jahr.*, VIII (1905), p. 18, pyxis in Boston, Pl. I (color).

[52] Plut., *Aristeides*, 20; Frazer, *Paus.*, 9, 4, 1; *cf.* A. Reinach, *Recueil Milliet*, I, 150, n. 1.

[53] Paus., IX, 4, 2.

[54] Körte, *Jahr.*, 31 (1916), p. 257, denies that such a scene was represented by Polygnotos because Pausanias specifically states that he painted "Odysseus after he had slain the suitors," not in the act of doing so.

Odysseus drawing his bow against the suitors who are shown in confusion at the right, one with his back pierced by an arrow which he attempts to extract, a second helplessly stretching out his hands from the couch, and a third hiding behind a table. It is this group of suitors which is similarly represented on the frieze from Gjöl-baschi and which may have occurred in the Polygnotan painting (Fig. 366). Possibly even the "lost profile" of the suitor with an arrow in his back, found on the Berlin vase, may be Polygnotan, although for the most part Polygnotos avoided the "lost profile," using the shoulder and drapery to cover the face.[55] The maid-servants introduced at the left fill out the design in chorus fashion, wringing their hands or expressing in gesture the anxiety of the moment.[56]

Let us return once more to the paintings of Polygnotos at Delphi—probably his latest and most finished work. We have discussed the Iliupersis. Its companion-piece, the "Underworld Scene," like the painting of the "Taking of Troy," falls into three parts with the emphasis on the ends: at the left, the Acheron with the boat of Charon; at the right, Tantalos in water, grasping for the fruit which always receded. The *leitmotiv* of the picture is the attempt of Odysseus to consult the soul of Teiresias in regard to his return home. This occupied a prominent position in the timeless, spaceless whole, where the damned and blessed were pursuing their joys and sorrows: Orpheus was seated beneath a tree, holding his lyre; the two daughters of Pandareos were engaged at knucklebones; Chloris rested on the knees of Thyia; the blind Thamyris was shown dejected beside his lyre; the great sinners, Tityos, Sisyphos, and Tantalos, were represented suffering in the Underworld. New figures such as Oknos, or Sloth, played a prominent part. Sloth was shown weaving a rope which a she-ass ate as fast as it was woven. The group was symbolic of a fruitless task. Eurynomos, the devourer of corpses—an uncommon figure—also appeared. Robert's reconstruction (Fig. 367) may help to visualize the painting somewhat, but again it is futile to feel that any reconstruction is possible.

A design on a South Italian krater, which has been thought to represent Odysseus consulting the spirit of Teiresias and to have been suggested by the painting of Polygnotos, is interpreted by Wolters as the mad Ajax slaughtering sheep (Fig. 368).[56a] He considers that the supposed head of Teiresias at the feet of Ajax is not original, even if ancient. In any case, the vase is late, the style consequently freer, the proportions un-Attic, the forms soft. Furthermore, in the Polygnotan Nekyia, Odysseus was in the underworld, not on the earth. The hero sits on a pile of rocks, above a ram which he has slain. On either side, his companions—usually held to be

[55] E. Feihl, *op. cit.*, p. 40. He considers that Polygnotos may have introduced the lost profile.
[56] *Cf.* H. Bulle, *Der schöne Mensch,*[2] Pl. 306, text, p. 626.
[56a] Springer-Michaelis-Wolters, *Die Kunst des Altertums,*[12] 1923, p. 351.

Perimedes and Eurylochos—now transmuted into shepherds—are resting in easy poses, the one on his spear, the other with his sword above his head in "Polygnotan" fashion. In the Polygnotan painting, Odysseus crouched above the trench over which the ram had been slaughtered. Elpenor also appeared. Whatever the interpretation to be given the vase, it does not fulfil the Polygnotan demands, since Teiresias was represented approaching the trench.

There are no reproductions on vases of the Orpheus of Polygnotos, but a vase in Berlin on which the figure of Orpheus appears is as truly representative of the art of Polygnotos as any ancient vase, the Orvieto krater and the New York Amazonomachy alone excepted (Fig. 369). This vase depicts a mood and shows what was meant in part by Polygnotan *ethos*. We see the effect of the power of music on four Thracians. In the center, Orpheus is seated on a rocky height playing his lyre, with his head thrown back in inspiration and self-forgetfulness. At the extreme right, a Thracian, somewhat troubled by the music and not wholly sympathetic, wraps his mantle about him in aloof fashion. His comrade, more interested, fixes his gaze intently on the singer, as if trying to analyze the secret of Orpheus' power. At the left, the Thracian in front view has closed his eyes and dreamily follows the music. On his shoulder rests another Thracian who has abandoned himself entirely to the charm of the music and is wholly absorbed in it. Bulle sees in the vase four temperaments—the reserved, phlegmatic type; the choleric; the melancholic; and the sanguine.[57] The design on the vase has often been compared with the Giorgione concert. It has great psychological understanding and fine feeling. Not only does the vase give us an idea of Polygnotan *ethos*, but Polygnotan devices appear everywhere: in the poses of the youth with his foot on the rock and of the melancholy Thracian resting on the shoulder of his friend. In drawing, we have an interesting example of "Polygnotan" experiments and shortcomings in the case of the Thracian represented in front view. Here, the difficulties of drawing a face in front view are evidenced by the large nose and wry mouth. Where the artist failed most dismally was in drawing the shoulder in front view. The arm seems out of place and the result is very distressing. But the effect of the whole design is moving and the composition appears to have a Polygnotan quality.

Other works seem to echo the Nekyia. The painting with the blind Thamyris on a vase in Oxford (Fig. 370) may be borrowed from Polygnotos; the ground-lines and general style would appear to point to such a conclusion, though Körte insists that the Polygnotan Thamyris was bearded and had at his feet a broken lyre.[58] A composition on a marble panel by Alexandros, which depicts two girls playing knucklebones, may also be related to the Pandareos group of Polygnotos (Fig. 371). We

[57] H. Bulle, *op. cit.*, Pl. 305, text.
[58] G. Körte, *Jahr.*, 31 (1916), p. 279; *cf.* B. Schroeder, *Jahr.*, 30 (1915), p. 113.

shall have occasion to discuss this monochrome painting later. Many white-ground lekythoi with representations of Charon and his bark among the reeds of Acheron were probably also inspired by the Nekyia (*cf.* Fig. 321).

We have followed the career of Polygnotos, the first great name in Athenian painting as far as the texts of ancient authors and monuments of the Fifth Century, especially vases, allow us to go. The paintings from his hand marked the passing from colored drawing to pictorial composition, with modest attempts at mixing colors, at linear foreshortening and perspective, and a slight use of chiaroscuro. His painting was significant largely because of beautiful drawing, restrained coloring, and nobility of conception in subject matter. It broke away from the stereotyped representations of the day: in the Iliupersis, there was no hurling of Astyanax from the walls of Troy, but the child was seen at his mother's breast just before his doom. There was no Ajax overpowering Kassandra. New characters assumed importance, such as Epeios, who tears down the walls of Troy; Oknos, Eurynomos, Phokos, and others. Frequently, a mood was represented where feeling was restrained, and we are conscious of the tensity of emotion beneath the surface. But, with all of the innovations in subject matter, drawing, and composition—especially in the use of levels— the art of Polygnotos remained a limited art. Despite the fact that he introduced many significant innovations, painting was still in many respects archaic and was only beginning to gain control of its *media.* However, with Polygnotos and his circle, the art in Greece was finally separated from handicraft and became an independent and monumental creation. The walls of public buildings under Kimon were covered with historical and mythological scenes and historical composition assumed importance for the first time in the history of Greek painting after the days of Boularchos.

We have said little about the technique of Polygnotan painting. Following the ancient tradition current in Crete, Mycenæ, and Etruria, Greek painting in this period was probably most commonly *al fresco, i.e.,* painting on walls on a coating of wet plaster. This view has hardly been displaced although arguments have been advanced that the paintings were executed in the tempera technique on marble, or painted on wooden panels.[59] The theory that they were painted on wooden panels rests partly on the authority of the author, Synesius. According to him the paintings, which he says were on σανίδες—"boards"—were taken away by the proconsul from the Stoa. We know that Synesius is speaking from hearsay, and he may have drawn conclusions about Fifth Century painting from the panel-painting current in

---

[59] E. Berger, *Beiträge zur Entwickelungsgesch. der Maltechnik,* München, 1901-1912; *Die Maltechnik des Altertums,* München, 1904; *vs.* his view, *cf.* O. Donner, *Technische Mittheilungen für Malerei,* No. 1, Sept., 1903, Leipzig; H. Brunn, *Gesch. der gr. Künstler,* II, 42 ff. (wall); C. Robert, *Nekyia,* p. 37, painting on marble walls, as on grave stelæ; *Marathonschlacht,* p. 104; A. P. Laurie, *Greek and Roman Methods of Painting,* Cambridge, 1910, p. 49; *cf.* G. Körte, *Jahr.,* 31 (1916), p. 283, who argues for wooden panels.

his own time. The mere fact that the famous paintings of Polygnotos at Delphi and Athens survived so long was doubtless due to the fact that they were painted on walls and could not be carried away. Panel-painting first began to be of importance after Polygnotos. His fame rested on mural decoration and this was in all probability executed, for the most part, on wet plaster without a binding medium, although some use of tempera is possible.[60]

That certain paintings were executed by Polygnotos on wooden panels seems evident. Pliny states that a *tabula* by Polygnotos, the subject of which is uncertain, existed in the Portico of Pompey.[61] This, however, may have been a part of a larger composition. Just how walls could be arranged with wooden panels above the ortho-states is difficult to conceive. Körte's theory that they were placed in two frieze-like rows above one another, as Benndorf formerly suggested, on the analogy of the Gjölbaschi frieze, hardly wins conviction.[62] Under these circumstances, the paintings would have to be reduced in size and we can no longer think of them as conceived on a grand scale. On the other hand, largeness of style is distinctly implied by several writers. However, the paintings in the Pinacotheca seem to have been on panels. The condition of the walls, in Dinsmoor's opinion, points to some sort of panel arrange-ment.[62a] This fact and the so-called *tabula* of the "Warrior" in the Portico of Pompey are evidence for a certain amount of panel-painting. Mention is also made of works by Polygnotos in the encaustic or wax technique, but these probably played a very minor rôle.[63] We shall discuss this particular technique under masters like Pausias, who employed it extensively.

The paintings covered the upper part of the wall like a frieze. For their general appearance and frieze-like arrangement, Etruscan paintings can perhaps furnish the best guide. The background was a neutral tone and against this the figures appeared in color. The ground-levels and indications of water were naturally also in color.

The best evidence for the important rôle played by Polygnotan painting is the wide influence which it had on contemporary and later monuments, not only in Greece but over a wide "Ionic" territory. We need hardly speak again of the in-fluence of Polygnotan poses and drapery on sculpture. The garment worn by the Niké from the Parthenon is typical of the transparent, wind-blown drapery used in painting; on the other hand, the Boston "Counterpart," which has been proved to be closely connected with Polygnotos, shows "eye folds" in heavier drapery and this device would seem to have originated in painting of the Polygnotan era.[34] The Olym-

---

[60] Pliny, *N.H.*, 35, 123; Paus., I, 17, 3; IX, 4, 1. Synesius, *Ep.*, 136, ὁ γὰρ ἀνθύπατος τὰς σανίδας ἀφείλετο αἷς ἐγκατέθετο τὴν τέχνην ὁ ἐκ Θάσου Πολύγνωτος. *Cf. Ep.*, 54. Synesius, arch-bishop of Ptolemais, was in Athens at the turn of the century.

[61] Pliny, *N.H.*, 35, 59.               [62] G. Körte, *Jahr.*, 31 (1916), pp. 283 ff.

[62a] See Dinsmoor's note on the Pinacotheca in Ch. XI, p. 424, note 14[a].

[63] Pliny, *N.H.*, 35, 122; Lucian, *Imag.*, 23.

pia pediments, which bear the closest relation to Polygnotan painting, exhibit "Polygnotan" characteristics not only in the general treatment of subject matter but also
in the latent emotion felt before the impending disaster. Individualized figures are
found such as the seer and the maid-servants with their wrinkled brows. "Polygnotan" drapery appears and emotion is indicated by the open mouths and tense
expressions of the figures.

In the matter of poses, the "Ares" motive, where the youth clasps his knee with
his hands, seems to be Polygnotan and one figure resting on the knees of another.
Many mourning figures, such as occurred in the Underworld of Polygnotos, are probably to be traced on later sarcophagi. Further, crouching figures like the kneeling
maiden in the West pediment at Olympia and the knucklebone players of Alexandros
(Fig. 371) are probably also "Polygnotan" material.

One region which seems to have felt the influence of Polygnotos strongly was
Etruria. We might name several monuments which reveal his influence, but a few
typical examples will suffice—all not a little later than the time of Polygnotos
himself. One of the best examples is the Amazon Sarcophagus (Fig. 429). Here, the
group of a fighting Greek and an Amazon on horse is strongly reminiscent of Polygnotos and Mikon. The type is idealized as far as Etruscan taste would permit and the
motive of the sword above the forehead is employed again. Such a figure as that of
the Amazon would not be unworthy of Polygnotos. In the Etruscan Sarcophagus
from Torre San Severo, some themes employed by Polygnotos are depicted, but there
is no trace of Polygnotan style (Fig. 431): they include the sacrifice of Polyxena,
balanced by an un-Polygnotan subject—the sacrifice of Trojans at the tomb of
Patroklos; Odysseus sacrificing to call up the spirit of Teiresias, balanced by Odysseus threatening Circe. Probably the sculptor of this monument was acquainted
with the Greek prototypes of several of these paintings.

The artist of the Ficoroni Cista also achieved a "Polygnotan" composition, but
as Feihl shows, his style is that of the Fourth Century and his landscape is a real
landscape where figures and ground are fused together in an harmonious whole (Fig.
372). The landscapes of Polygnotos were probably not conceived as an organic
whole, to judge from vases of the period. This advance appears first in the Meidias
vase representing Pelops and Hippodameia (Fig. 342). On the cista, the ship of the
Argonauts with a figure going down the gangway is probably a direct borrowing from
Polygnotos' Iliupersis, but the style would appear to be much freer than that of
Polygnotos. Conception of space is more developed, also foreshortening, handling of
drapery, and treatment of the nude. In Polygnotos, there were probably no fat
figures—to judge from the best "Polygnotan" vases. On these vases, the construction
of the bony frame of the body is almost geometrical in its rigidity and the muscles
are those of an athlete. On the Ficoroni Cista, the forms are rounded, the flesh
"blooming."

Most of all, the Athenian vase-painters from about 470 to 450 B.C. were influenced by Polygnotos. Under the influence of the major art, vases began to take on a grandiose style. Some artists turned to polychromy in an attempt to follow the mural art—for example, the master of the Penthesileia kylix (Fig. 373). This cup depicts the dramatic moment when Achilles falls in love with the Amazon queen whom he has mortally wounded. The power of the artist to express emotion is seen by a glance at the eyes. The other striking innovation is the use of gray and brown in addition to the red, black, white, and gold of the vase. Other painters were more vitally interested in foreshortening and made a *tour de force* of their drawing. The New York Amazon vase of Figure 326 is typical of this. But the majority of painters were influenced in some way by this school, if only in the use of new motives—not merely the poses which we have enumerated earlier, such as the standing figure with his foot on a rock or one figure leaning on the shoulder of another, but sinking figures, usually shown in front view, and figures with a sword raised above the forehead. These motives and similar ones were endlessly repeated and new types were introduced. The wily Odysseus was probably created by Polygnotos. Further, the whole stock of accessories in vase-painting was enriched by him. We think first of all of the caps and the hats—the *piloi* and *petasoi* of the men, the snoods and kerchiefs of the women in gay colors. The splendor of the garments, among which often occurs a foldless, short chiton with a border of triangles, is striking in this age. The armor is especially decorative. There are rich helmets and corselets of old-fashioned type on which anatomical details are often indicated; there are shields with elaborate decoration, sometimes made of wicker-work and often crescent-shaped.

Most striking were the new movements introduced—lunging, striding, and falling backward. Figure 374, by an Athenian wit, caricatures some of these attempts. Here, foreshortened figures, such as the horse in back view, are grotesquely executed and the wicker shields and horsehair crests fairly daze the eye. One seems to hear a gymnastic director shouting: "Forward lunge—and back." The figures have lumpy noses and thick lips and were obviously intended to arouse a smile.

The influence of Polygnotos also made itself felt in the Orient, especially in the case of a tomb at Gjölbaschi in Lycia, the site of ancient Trysa (Fig. 366). This monument belongs to the end of the Fifth Century, but the artist drew from the artistic wealth of the age preceding. The inner walls were decorated with reliefs of Bellerophon, the Calydonian Boar Hunt, the Siege of Troy, the Slaying of the Suitors, and the Rape of the Daughters of Leukippos; the inner and outer walls were adorned with Battles of Amazons and Greeks and Battles of Centaurs and Lapiths. On the outer wall was also represented the Seven against Thebes. These scenes depict local battles under mythical garb as is often the case in Greek art. The reliefs of Lycia are like outline drawings standing out in strong relief, with a slight use of architectural background, where perspective plays a rôle. The monument discussed is half a century later than Polygnotos but it reveals the vitality of many of his innovations.

We have spoken of the contemporary painters of the Helladic school only in passing. Mikon, an older painter than Polygnotos, is believed by some scholars to have been just as important in the history of painting as the Thasian.[64] He was an Athenian despite all efforts to include him in the Ionic circle.[65] His father was Phanomachos and the name is rooted in Athens. It is difficult to dissociate his style from that of Polygnotos; perhaps the best that we can hope to do is to win a vague vision of the painting of the Polygnotan group. We are certain that Mikon made a practice of cutting off figures by the background, so that only half or partial figures often appeared. His treatment of spatial depth seems to have been more searching than that of Polygnotos. He was skilful in the painting of horses. Pausanias mentions the horses of Akastos in the picture of the Argonauts[66] and Ælian speaks of his representations of horses.[67] His paintings of Amazons are undoubtedly reflected on vases of the transitional period and probably many of the marvelously foreshortened figures and bizarre poses are Mikonian. His art would seem to have been more energetic and dynamic than that of Polygnotos, but this may be inherent in the subject matter. It is significant that the beauty of Polygnotan art lies partly in its static character; there is more standing, lying, and quiet posing than action. Mikon was a sculptor as well as a painter and was known for his figure of athletes. Klein would make him the creator of the Olympia pediments because of the closeness of these sculptures to paintings of the Polygnotan circle.[68] But this is only saying what has been felt by so many, that the pediments are pictorial in character and that the characteristics of the painting of the age are deeply impressed upon them. This led Hauser to assign them to Panainos, the third important painter of this epoch.[69] Thus by a confusion of names the pediment sculptures would have been attributed to Paionios whose work is far different in style. Schroeder thinks that Mikon inaugurated the damp-looking drapery, an example of which is seen in the Niké of Paionios. Paionios was a native of Thrace, and is considered by some a countryman of Mikon. Drapery somewhat like this was used by Polygnotos.[69a]

Whatever the claims of Panainos to the authorship of the Olympia pediments, and

[64] W. Klein, *Jahr.*, 33 (1918), pp. 1 ff.

[65] M. Fraenkel, *A.Z.* (1876), p. 227; B. Schroeder, *Jahr.*, 27 (1912), p. 343, from Thrace; M. Heinemann, *op. cit.*, p. 96, n. 1, Ionian; F. Studniczka, *Jahr.*, 26 (1911), p. 162, Athenian. *I.G.A.*, 498.

[66] Paus., I, 18, 1.                          [67] Ælian, *N.A.*, IV, 50.

[68] Klein, *Jahr.*, 33 (1918), p. 38. *Cf.* Paus., VI, 6, 1; *A.J.A.*, IV (1900), p. 346.

[69] F. R., *Gr. Vas.*, II, 324.                    [69a] B. Schroeder, *Jahr.*, 29 (1914), pp. 123 ff.

it would seem best to leave them nameless, he was closely associated with sculptors. He assisted his brother Pheidias at Olympia in painting the throne of Zeus and was commissioned to decorate the garment of the statue.[70] The paintings on the throne were on a set of screens—probably forming panels placed between the legs of the throne on two sides and the back, the side facing the door being painted blue. They depicted mythological scenes: Herakles and Atlas, and Herakles and the Nemean lion; the Hesperides; Theseus and Peirithoos; Salamis and Hellas; Prometheus and Herakles; the death of Penthesileia in the arms of Achilles; Ajax outraging Kassandra; and Hippodameia with her mother.

The question of the arrangement of these screens has busied archæologists, and the choice of a solution seems to lie between an arrangement in groups of three panels with two figures or the version of Gardner.[71] Murray considered that they formed a screen barrier surrounding the marble pavement in front of the throne and were placed between the pillars of the cella. But the objection to this is, as Gardner has indicated, that one could go under the throne, a possibility which Pausanias says the screens prevented. Further, Murray supposes the outside of the barriers blue, the inside covered with paintings by Panainos. But only the screen opposite the door is said to have been blue, the part of the throne which was covered, to a certain extent, by the legs of the statue. To judge from the description, the screens formed an integral part of the throne itself, and the nine themes were probably distributed in groups of three on the three sides. Gardner's view that such an arrangement would be unsymmetrical because we should have two pictures in which the figures stood in close dramatic relation—such as Herakles and Atlas, Theseus and Peirithoos, followed by a third consisting merely of two female figures—Greece and Salamis, Hippodameia and Sterope, may be correct. The matter, however, can in no way be settled. Gardner arranges them very artistically in three sections of four panels— and it may be in the manner of Panainos:

| * | * | | * | | * |
|---|---|---|---|---|---|
| Herakles and Atlas | Theseus and Peirithoos | Herakles and Nemean Lion | Ajax and Kassandra | Herakles and Prometheus | Achilles and Penthesileia |
| | | | | | |
| Hellas | Salamis | Hippodameia | Sterope | Hesperid | Hesperid |

[70] Paus., V, 11, 2, 5; Strabo, VIII, 354.
[71] A. S. Murray, *Hist. of Gk. Sculpture*, II, pp. 125 ff.; *Ath. Mitth.*, VII (1882), pp. 274-276; E. A. Gardner, "The Paintings by Panænus on the Throne of the Olympian Zeus,"

The actual nature of the paintings we cannot know. They doubtless presented many features characteristic of Polygnotan work and of the sculptures of the West pediment at Olympia. Blümner would place a female figure on either side of two metopes.

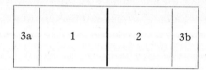

It seems wiser to follow the account of Pausanias and arrange the panels as he describes them from left to right, in sets of three. Since the coins show no pillars between each pair of legs, it may be advisable to follow Evelyn-White's arrangement, placing the pillars under the center of the seat and the panels below the crossbars.

Panainos is also said to have painted the shield of a gold and ivory Athena that Kolotes had made at Elis.[72] His most significant achievement was probably his work at Olympia and the painting of the "Battle of Marathon" in the Stoa, of which Mikon seems to have had charge. His originality perhaps lay in the direction of realism and in suggestions of portraiture, but we can form little idea of his style. He was a part of the famous group painting in this period in the new fashion.

Imperfect as our conception of the art of Polygnotos and his circle undoubtedly is, certain undeniable facts stand out: the painters of this period who followed the lead of Mikon and Polygnotos definitely broke away from archaic flat painting. There were fewer frieze-like compositions in which forms were silhouetted in a line against the background, but the main interest of the artist still lay in the beauty and dignity of individual figures. The subject matter of Polygnotos included many beautiful figures of women. We picture them in serene attitudes, revealing inner excitement by an intense or sad look in the eyes, or by simple gestures. There was no use of the nervous, excited type of head found later on South Italian vases and associated with the work of Aristeides. In contrast to archaic art which concealed feelings for the most part, this epoch showed a restrained expression of them and skilful representation of mood. Other advances lay in a greater technical facility. The painters of this epoch could draw better than the more archaic masters and attempted bolder problems of foreshortening and perspective. The result was that there were

J.H.S., 14 (1894), p. 233; cf. H. Blümner, "Die Gemälde des Panainos am Throne des Olymp. Zeus," Jahr., 15 (1900), p. 136; H. G. Evelyn-White, "The Throne of Zeus at Olympia," J.H.S., 28 (1908), p. 49; C. H. Tyler, "The Paintings of Panænus at Olympia," J.H.S., 30 (1910), p. 82; G. Pellegrini, Atti del Reale Instituto Veneto di scienze lettere ed arti, 74 (1915), pp. 1555-1574; A.J.A., 20 (1916), p. 488. Cf. Hitzig-Blümner, Pausanias, Comment. on V, 11, 6; A. Reinach, Recueil Milliet, I, 170, n. 1; E. N. Gardiner, Olympia, Oxford, 1925, p. 242.

[72] Pliny, N.H., 35, 54; Paus., VI, 26, 3.

more faces and bodies in three-quarter and front views—however unsuccessful the achievement may sometimes have been. In this age, the old *schemata* for representation were not discarded but were modified and corrected by observation and a number of new formulæ were added. Above all, the art remained on an ideal plane, although there are many evidences of its interest in more realistic representation. Its greatest power, according to Aristotle, lay in the fact that it could lift the souls of men above the commonplaces of life.

We are able to follow Polygnotan innovations and their far-reaching influence after the middle of the Fifth Century in stray monuments only. Polygnotos' departure for Delphi about the beginning of the Periclean régime may have been one of the reasons why Periclean buildings, so far as we know, had no paintings. We see in a group of vases often called Pheidian, a certain largeness of style and grandeur of conception which may be due to the influence of either sculpture or painting or both (Figs. 339-341). One of the main advances in the period from 450 to 430 lay in the softer rendering of flesh and rounding of the body. In contrast to the lean and sinewy "Polygnotan" figures found on the Orvieto krater, we have fleshier and more rounded forms, such as occur on the vase representing the Murder of the Suitors (Fig. 365) or the Theseus vase of Figure 345. The "lost profile" also occasionally appears beside the face in front and three-quarter views.

We seem to have a faithful copy of a late Fifth Century Greek original in a small monochrome painting on marble from Herculaneum (Fig. 371). This painting can tell us much about the developed use of the brush. Robert places the original of the work in the period between Polygnotos and Zeuxis. In the foreground, two kneeling maidens are pictured, Hileaira at the right, Aglaia at the left. Five knucklebones have been thrown by Hileaira and three have been caught on the back of her hand. The game is to pick up the rest without dropping any of those already caught. Her left hand seems to be filled with those which she has won, whereas Aglaia holds her last one pressed to the ground. In contrast to these two light-hearted figures in the foreground, is the more serious group in the rear composed of Leto, Niobe, and Phœbe. Here, a mood seems to be represented. A disagreement has taken place between Leto and Niobe who, as Sappho tells us, "were once friends full dear." In the center, Niobe, urged on by Phœbe, offers her hand to Leto, who seems none too eager to receive it. Robert assumes that they too have been playing knucklebones with disastrous results and that Niobe is attempting to appease her friend! It is not certain that the two parts belonged together in the original, although, as Bulle points out, there is an undoubted artistic value in the fine contrast between the carefree figures below and the anxious atmosphere above.[73] Robert considers them in-

[73] H. Bulle, *op. cit.*,[2] p. 638.

separable.[74] The folds of drapery in the case of the kneeling pair are similar to what we find on the Parthenon pediments and Bulle would therefore date the original of the painting in the thirties of the Fifth Century.[75]

The painting is interesting because of its technique. With some few others, it really represents for us the panel-painting of antiquity. The drawing, which is fairly fine, does not equal that of some of our better vases. The painting is a monochrome, or, more properly speaking, an oligochrome—the figures are executed on the marble ground in reddish brown paint and the hair and details are given in the same color. Only in rare instances does a second color appear—a bluish gray on the chiton of Leto, on the mantle of Niobe, on sandals, and a few other places. It is possible that other colors may have disappeared. There seems to be a slight attempt at rendering shadows. The nude parts of the figures are merely left in the ground color of the marble, outlined in reddish brown. The hair and folds of the garments show a darker tone which indicates the beginning of shading. The effect is almost that of charcoal work. The technique is probably that of tempera, in which the colors are bound to the background with some medium such as the white of an egg. Robert has shown that the paintings were not done in encaustic, but consisted of outline work in tempera, with a slight use of added color. The plaque was doubtless set into the wall as a decorative panel, and is a typical example of work by an ordinary master shortly after the middle of the Fifth Century. Its simplicity and largeness of style associate it with the grand manner of Polygnotos and the Parthenon pediments and the original probably dates shortly after the period of these monuments. It is, however, not at all improbable that this group of knucklebone players was copied from the one painted by Polygnotos in his "Nekyia."

In the Knucklebone players by Alexandros, an artist of the First Century, the tendencies of classical painting after the middle of the Fifth Century are clearly seen. The two maidens in the foreground form a closed group in which both figures are bent over in the same way, the heads low and inclined at the same angle. This severe symmetry is kept even down to the position and drawing of the pupil; in this respect it is almost pedantic.[76] As von Salis has pointed out, a painter of the Hellenistic age would have sought for contrast in the faces by the use of light and shadow and he would have set the scene obliquely in space. Here the design is placed severely

[74] C. Robert, "Die Knöchelspielerinnen des Alexandros," *Hall. Winckelmannsprogr.*, 21 (1897); P. Gusman, *La Revue de l'art ancien et moderne*, 1909, Pt. II, 117 ff.; L. Savignoni, *Bull. comun. di Roma*, 1897, Pl. VI. See also E. Pfuhl, *N.J.*, 1920, pp. 61 ff.

[75] B. Schroeder, *Jahr.*, 30 (1915), pp. 108 ff. On the basis of connections with vases, C. Robert dates the originals of these monochromes in the last quarter of the Fifth Century, although he shows in *Hall. Winckelmannsprogr.*, 23, that some may go down to the Middle Fourth.

[76] A. von Salis, *Die Kunst der Griechen*, Leipzig, 1919, p. 165.

in one plane with the heads in absolute profile. The painting is greatly enriched by an elaborate chiastic arrangement: Aglaia turns her back to us, whereas with Hileaira, the upper part of the body is seen from the front. The lines of the drapery have their own rhythm in each case and flow in opposite directions. This entire arrangement is without value for space illusion but was adopted solely to vary the two halves of the picture. The beauty of the work lies in the composition, the outlines, the drapery, and delicate shading.

The monochrome from Herculaneum presents us with the beginnings of shadow work. Robert considers it too advanced to be associated with the painting of Polygnotos and it is possible that it presupposes the appearance of masters like Apollodoros. But the use of shading is very slight. Pliny says that Apollodoros was the first painter worthy of real fame and the first to give reality to his pictures. As a result of his chiaroscuro, he was named the "shadow master," but his advance seems to have consisted in equipping the entire space in which his figures appeared with light and shadow, rather than in the shading of outlines. This latter practice may well have played its part in the paintings of Polygnotos to judge from vases, whereas the innovation of Apollodoros was largely concerned with perspective.[77]

But Apollodoros was not the first painter to investigate the matter of perspective. The attack on the third dimension really began in Greek painting with Agatharchos, the scene-painter from Samos. It was Apollodoros, however, who brought the art to a high degree of perfection, but Agatharchos had earlier created a revolution by his discoveries.[78] He employed perspective in order to gain the illusion of depth and wrote a treatise on the subject which caused the philosophers, Demokritos and Anaxagoras, to investigate the problem. Probably only the most elementary rules were treated by Agatharchos, but the basic principles of foreshortening and of lines converging toward a vanishing point must have been discovered. In his stage-settings, where temples and palaces were represented, he must have applied his perspective to architecture and it is in this field that his real innovation lay.[79] But there may also have been attempts at simple landscape representation, so that we may probably credit Agatharchos with the introduction of determinate backgrounds and suggestions of landscape. His main contribution undoubtedly lay in theater decoration and in perspective as applied to architecture. He probably decorated the front of the stage-building with architectural settings to which perspective was applied, and used certain landscape elements.

[77] E. Pfuhl, "Apollodoros, ὁ σκιαγράφος," *Jahr.*, 25 (1910), pp. 12 ff. *Cf.* R. Schöne, *Jahr.*, 27 (1912), pp. 19-23; E. Pfuhl, *Jahr.*, 27 (1912), pp. 227-231.

[78] Vitr., VII, *Præf.*, 11.

[79] P. Gardner, *J.H.S.*, 19 (1899), pp. 252 ff.; Pfuhl, *N.J.*, XXVII (1911), p. 180; R. C. Flickinger, *The Greek Theater and its Drama*, 3d ed., Chicago, 1926; James T. Allen, *The Greek Theatre of the Fifth Century before Christ*, Univ. of California Publ., VII, 1924.

We can date the activity of Agatharchos between 460 and 430 B.C. from two historical facts. First of all, he seems to have been responsible for the earliest painted scenery in Athens which doubtless came into existence in connection with the wooden stage-building of the theater of Dionysos about 460 B.C. Secondly, Alcibiades locked him up in his house and forced him to decorate it after he had refused on the ground of overwork.[80] This probably occurred about 429 B.C.

The innovations of Agatharchos were perfected by Apollodoros.[81] He first "opened the doors of art through which painters such as Zeuxis" and Apelles passed. He gave true glory to the brush and must be credited with gradations of color and with surrounding his figures with light and shade. He was a painter of space and may therefore be called the real originator of illusionism in painting. Apollodoros first observed the way in which light falls on an object so that the colors on the lighted side stand out brightly, whereas the unlighted part is so dark that little color shows. He was able to employ color, light, and perspective in a fashion which marks the beginning of painting in the modern sense of the term. Plato was opposed to this humbug of illusionistic painting because it created illusions which were really deceptive and made the large appear small, and the small large.[82]

Of Apollodoros' works we have only titles left us. In these, we observe an interest in experimentation, especially with light. They include Ajax struck by lightning, a priest in prayer, and the Herakleidai seeking protection in Athens.[82a] These paintings were not mural decorations in fresco, as most of the works of Polygnotos and Mikon had probably been, but they were panel-paintings and were placed on wooden boards covered with stucco. The technique was doubtless tempera, with a binding medium of gum or egg-white. Apollodoros not only gave to later times mixing and gradations of color, $\phi\theta o\rho\grave{\alpha}\nu$ $\kappa\alpha\grave{\iota}$ $\grave{\alpha}\pi\acute{o}\chi\rho\omega\sigma\iota\nu$ $\sigma\kappa\iota\hat{\alpha}\varsigma$, and progress in spatial perspective and the modeling of forms, but he emancipated painting from architecture and gave us easel-painting. After his time, mural painting practically disappears, its place being taken by paintings on wooden and marble panels.

Some idea of the changes which occurred in painting between the time of Polygnotos and Apollodoros may be formed from an examination of some white-ground lekythoi, in Berlin, in Paris and Madrid. The lekythos in Berlin depicts a mourning scene in which the newly found freedom of the painter is evident[83] (Fig. 375). The

[80] Plut., *Alc.*, 16; Andoc., *C. Alcib.*, 17. A. Reinach, *Recueil Milliet*, I, 178, n. 1, gives the dates 460-420.

[81] Pliny, *N.H.*, 35, 60; Plut., *De Glor. Ath.*, 2.

[82] Plato, *Rep.*, 602-603; 598 A. Plato does not refer to the work of Apollodoros but to the later exponents of the same tendency.

[82a] Some doubt exists whether the painting was by Apollodoros or Pamphilos. It is possible that each painted this subject.

[83] F. Winter, *Winckelmannsprogr.*, Berlin, 55 (1895); *cf.* M. Collignon, *Mon. Piot*, XII (1905), Pls. III-V, pp. 29 ff.

figures are no longer flat but in his use of shading and modeling, the artist lifts them from the background so that we feel their corporeal existence. This is observable in the case of the father who stands at the head of the couch. Furthermore, the use of a reddish brown ocher has allowed the artist to shade his draperies. The shadows and folds of the garments, the outlines, and hair are in a reddish brown.[83a] An important element is the use of shading by means of finely hatched lines.[84] This occurs on the breast and arms of the father. The innovations of Apollodoros were naturally far advanced beyond this and may more nearly approach the achievement credited by many to Zeuxis and seen on the Centaur monochrome from Herculaneum (Fig. 378). The technical method employed in this period is no longer a linear one; patches of color are introduced which were used to create the illusion of roundness and depth. The colors at this time were no longer placed over the surface in a regular line of march, as they were in earlier Greek works, where the change proceeded in a rigid fashion with a carefully alternating system of red, black, and white. They are much more subtly handled. In comparison with the advances made by Apollodoros, earlier painters would seem to have done little more than distribute tints within outlines.

The elaborate use of shading to model forms is clearly seen on later vases. The Talos vase from Ruvo is perhaps the best example that may be cited (Fig. 376). Although it borrows earlier motives such as the Polygnotan one of the beached ship of the Argonauts with a figure on the gangway, it is very advanced in technique and in the newness of its subject matter.[85] The scene represented is that of the bronze giant Talos expiring in the arms of the Dioscuri through the wiles of Medea. The vase is largely interesting to us for its technique and composition and for the beauty and nobility of its forms. The gleaming bronze of the giant's body is rendered in white, modeled by means of shading in a diluted brown varnish. The contours of the figure are thus strikingly rounded. Thinned varnish is also employed for shadows on the garments.

With Apollodoros, the era of the individual artist begins. The introduction of the wooden panel covered with stucco gave more opportunities for the artist to follow his particular bent. Apollodoros attempted to present the world around him in illusionistic fashion by perspective and by modeling forms with shadows. To us today, gradation of color and shading are so generally accepted as the accompaniment of true painting that we consider it one of the elementary concomitants of the

---

[83a] The undergarment of the central figure is a grayish green and there the shading is in a deeper green; the mantle of the man is a violet passing into red and the folds are rendered in dark red.

[84] M. Collignon, *Mon. Piot*, XII (1905), pp. 47 ff. *Cf.* A. de Ridder, *B.C.H.*, 23 (1899), pp. 325-332; E. Pottier, *Mon. Piot*, II (1895), p. 45.

[85] F. R., *Gr. Vas.*, Pls. 38-39.

art. It is somewhat difficult, therefore, for us to understand what a bold change was made at this time. The term "shadow master" as applied to Apollodoros may contain a touch of opprobrium because it involved illusionism and optical deception. Apollodoros was forced to defend himself against critics of the new school. The proverb cited by him in this connection—"it is easier to blame than to imitate"—shows that his path was not unbeset with troubles.[86]

The innovations of Apollodoros were carried further by Zeuxis, one of the greatest artists of the end of the Fifth and the early Fourth Centuries. Aristotle denied him *ethos* because he preferred the unusual and exotic in subject matter to the great, but his technical ability had advanced so far beyond that of Polygnotos that we seem to enter into a new world.[87] Quintilian says that he discovered the laws of light and shadow but this merely means that he carried to a high point the modeling of shadows and the inventions of Apollodoros.[88]

Zeuxis was probably a citizen of Herakleia in Magna Græcia and lived at the time of the Peloponnesian Wars, but he was trained also in Sicily, came early to Athens, worked at the court of Archelaos of Macedon, and spent his last days in Asia Minor at Ephesos.[88a] He was thus a cosmopolitan Greek but he is often classed in the Ionic school of painters. He was evidently gifted with an artistic temperament and the anecdotes which are associated with his name on this score are very numerous. He amassed great riches and paraded at Olympia with his name embroidered in gold upon his mantle. He often gave away his works on the ground that they were beyond price.[89] He was not above calling himself the best painter of his time and his contemporaries agreed with him.[90] He admired his own works so much that he is said to have died from laughing at one of his paintings of an old woman.[91]

The most that we know about Zeuxis is to be found in the accounts of ancient writers. He chose to paint new and strange subjects. Of these we have some thirteen titles: the infant Herakles strangling serpents, Tritons with wild eyes, Centaur families, Penelope, Marsyas bound, Helen at her toilet, and other mythological and genre paintings. One of his most famous masterpieces was his Helen, ordered by the people of Croton for the Temple there of Hera Lakinia. For this painting he chose five young women, as models, the most beautiful to be found in the city of Croton.[92]

---

[86] Plut., *De Glor. Athen.*, 2. Ἀπολλόδωρος ὁ ζωγράφος, ἀνθρώπων πρῶτος ἐξευρὼν φθορὰν καὶ ἀπόχρωσιν σκιᾶς, Ἀθηναῖος ἦν, οὗ τοῖς ἔργοις ἐπιγέγραπται· 'μωμήσεταί τις μᾶλλον ἢ μιμήσεται.'

[87] Aristotle, *Poetics*, VI, 11.          [88] Quint., *Inst. Or.*, XII, 10, 4.

[88a] The evidence for this is not very strong. E. Pfuhl, *Malerei und Zeichnung*, II, 682, opposes the view.

[89] Pliny, *N.H.*, 35, 62. Not much credence can be placed in these stories.

[90] Aristid., *Or.*, XLIX, περὶ τοῦ παραφθέγματος, 386 (II, p. 521, Dindorf).

[91] Festus, *s.v. Pictor*, p. 209, 10, M; 228 L.

[92] Cic., *De Invent.*, II, 1; Dionys. of Hal., *De priscis script. cens.*, I (V, 417 Reiske);

He did this in order that from all he might attain as nearly as possible his ideal of womanly beauty; for in one woman he felt that he could not find perfect beauty. Not only was his use of women as models a bold innovation but his nude Helen must also have been as unusual as the Praxitilean Aphrodite of Knidos. Hitherto, Helen had not been painted without a veil. His work was for this reason called "Helen the Courtesan"—in allusion to her nudity and to the fact that Zeuxis obtained a large sum of money by charging an admission fee to see her.[93] This painting was later taken to Rome and was set up in the portico of Philip, but a copy of it by Zeuxis apparently existed at Athens. Anticipating the admiration which the painting would arouse, Zeuxis placed under the picture an inscription from Homer which said that, "it was no great wonder if the Trojans and well-greaved Achæans endured long suffering for such a woman." This implied that his work had attained the Homeric ideal of Helen.[94]

The painting by Zeuxis which seems to have aroused the greatest interest in antiquity represented a family of centaurs. Lucian has given us a long description of this work which combined in a very subtle way human and animal instincts and qualities.[95] The original of the painting was lost in a storm off Cape Malea when Sulla was sending it to Italy, but a copy of it was preserved at Athens and this is the painting which Lucian describes. On a greensward, a centauress is seen; the upper part of her body was that of a beautiful woman; the rear, that of a horse. The equine part lay on the ground, the feet stretched out behind; the human part rested on one elbow, while one foreleg was advanced like that of a horse about to rise. Two small centaurs were seen with her, one held at her breast and nursed like a child; the other fed like an animal. The father centaur, on guard above, bent over smiling. Only a part of him was seen, including about half of his horse body. He was a wild, savage creature with tossing hair—an untamed inhabitant of the mountains. In his hands, he held aloft a lion cub to terrify the young centaurs. They regarded it without stopping their feeding. The alluring part of the painting, aside from the beauty of drawing, clever brush-work, happy play of color, management of shadows and proportions, which Lucian praised, was the mingling of animal and human elements— the striking contrast between the brute centaur and the beauty of the centauress who was half woman, half animal, with the transition almost imperceptible. The young centaurs were represented as wild and fierce but with an element of tenderness.

We cannot picture the painting to ourselves very clearly and no satisfactory aids exist to help us. The Berlin mosaic from the Villa of Hadrian which is often cited as

Pliny, op. cit., 35, 64. Pliny wrongly places the painting in the temple at Agrigentum, or else Zeuxis must have worked there also.

[93] Ælian, V.H., IV, 12.    [94] Valer. Max., III, 7; Ext. 3. Cf. Homer, Iliad, III, 156-157.
[95] Lucian, Zeuxis, 3-8.

a pendant to our painting is filled with Hellenistic atmosphere[96] (Fig. 377). The maker of the mosaic painted in stones the sequel to the Centaur Family of Zeuxis. The angered father of the stolen lion cub has revenged himself on the centaur family by wounding the mother centauress and the fierce centaur is bringing to a close the tragedy of the wild mountain landscape. The conception of the centauress is in the manner of Zeuxis and we may be certain that the many representations of centauresses in Pompeian and Roman art echo his innovations.[96a] The appearance of the tiger dates the original of the mosaic after 300 B.C.

Two paintings on marble from Herculaneum and some ceramic products found in Southern Italy, where Zeuxis spent his youth, have been thought to shed some light on his art, though the evidence is not very satisfactory. The painting on marble which shows Peirithoos attacking the centaur, Eurytion, and rescuing Hippodameia from his clutches, is believed by Robert to present many analogies to the painting of Zeuxis (Fig. 378). In the first place, we have a very individualistic conception in the case of the centaur, with the male torso separated from his horse body by a shaded fringe of hair. The body is modeled with hatched lines, which make the form stand out in plastic fashion. There are cast shadows in front of the rear feet of the centaur and the right foot of Peirithoos—the earliest examples known to us. The expression of emotion in the face is very subtly rendered by the arched brows and oblique eyes and by the open lips. Most important of all, the movement is not parallel with the front plane but proceeds into the background of the painting from left to right, so that the problem of the third dimension is attacked with some seriousness. The figure of Hippodameia is reduced in size because of its distance from the spectator. The painting, like the monochrome of Alexandros, is in red outline. A greenish color which passes into yellow is found on the garment of the maiden and a dark tone for shadows in the folds of the chlamys of Peirithoos. The painting, like its companions, was probably executed in tempera.[97]

A second marble tablet, in which Robert finds the influence of Zeuxis, represents the dedication of a charioteer victorious in the Panathenaic games or at those in honor of Amphiaraos (Fig. 379). Again the direction of the movement is not parallel to the front plane of the painting, but the quadriga dashes from right to left out of the background. The artist was thus concerned with the problem of depth in the same way as in the centauromachy of the panel just discussed. The scene depicted is the moment in the course when the charioteer guides his horses in such a way that

[96] E. Pfuhl, "Die griech. Malerei," *N.J.*, 27 (1911), p. 181.

[96a] H. Heydemann, *Hall. Winckelmannsprogr.*, VII (1882), pp. 12 ff.

[97] For these marble tablets, see C. Robert, *Hall. Winckelmannsprogr.*, XIX (1895), and XXII (1898); *cf.* W. Helbig, *Wandgemälde der vom Vesuv verschütteten Städte Campaniens*, Leipzig, 1868, 1241 (Theseus).

the Greek warrior accompanying him may leap down from the chariot-box and vie with his companions in a race. These men were called ἀποβάται. The contest thus became a combination of chariot- and foot-racing. The characteristics which in Robert's estimation ally the work with that of Zeuxis are as follows: the painting is an example of the *monochromata ex albo* which Pliny states were painted by Zeuxis.[98] Although additional colors, such as violet were used, the paintings are like drawings in red crayon, with hatched shading. The modeling of the body of the Greek and of the horses shows unusual skill. Further, the horses are Tarentine in type, the kind which Zeuxis must have seen in his youth. The head of the charioteer is rather large and the figure betrays the proportions which Xenokrates criticized in Zeuxis.[99] Whether or not one is able to accept all of Robert's arguments, it is obvious that the painting exhibits very interesting attempts in the matter of perspective and shading and that these developments were carried forward at this time by Zeuxis with great success. This monochrome is later than the painting of Apollodoros and shows a more advanced technique. It is difficult to feel in it much of Zeuxis' power in drawing or of his novelty in conception.

Two South Italian vases which Hauser would assign to the hand of the youthful Zeuxis are more dubious evidence for the master, and at best could only be his early productions. It is true that Zeuxis worked in clay, but we know nothing of the nature of these creations, or even whether they were paintings.[100] The vases in question were found near Herakleia, the early home of Zeuxis. The scene depicted on one of them is the episode of Odysseus and Diomede surprising the spy Dolon[101] (Fig. 380). It must be admitted that the drawing is extraordinarily clever and that the invention and droll humor involved are not unlike what we should expect from Zeuxis. Even the trees seem to be caricatured! But that Zeuxis is the author is much less certain. The sly figure of Odysseus at the left merits the Homeric epithet, and Dolon is the ugly spy of the Iliad. The handling of depth, shading, and the face in three-quarter view are all managed with unusual skill. The other vase supposedly from his hand is represented by Figure 368. Hauser also connects with Zeuxis the charmingly drawn head of a centauress on a vase fragment coming from Tarentum[102] (Fig. 381). It may well reflect the art of Zeuxis as female centaurs appear very rarely in pre-Hellenistic times. The vase shows great fineness of execution. The clay is covered with a reddish varnish and the relief lines appear on a gray ground. The finger nails are reserved and the technique is, in general, very advanced.

[98] Pliny, *N.H.*, 35, 64. Hauser, *Gr. Vas.*, II, 265. P. Milliet, *Études sur les premières périodes de la céramique grecque*, Paris, 1891, p. 163.

[99] Pliny, *N.H.*, 35, 64.      [100] Pliny, *N.H.*, 35, 66.

[101] F. R., *Gr. Vas.*, Pl. 110, 4; II, p. 264.

[102] F. R., *Gr. Vas.*, II, Fig. 94*b*, p. 265. *Cf.* J. D. Beazley, *Greek Vases in Poland*, Oxford, 1928, p. 72, note 4.

A famous work from the hand of Zeuxis represented the infant Herakles strangling the serpents. Several Pompeian wall-paintings are extant which treat this subject but they are far cries from the work of Zeuxis. Figure 382, from the House of the Vettii, illustrates one of these frescoes. It dates from the First Century A.D. and shows the impressionistic technique often found in Pompeian painting. The composition may follow the general lines of the panel by Zeuxis but the treatment of depth and light is very advanced and the painting bears a Hellenistic stamp. In the center is the young Herakles, with a writhing serpent held in either hand. At the right, Amphitryon is seated in an attitude of suspense and anxiety. Behind him, Alkmene flees away, terrified, and a startled servant at the left hastens toward the back of the room. The eagle of Zeus dominates the altar in the rear and contributes to the solution of depth. How much of Zeuxis we may recognize in such a painting, it is difficult to conceive. The figure of Amphitryon, and the fine expression of emotion in his face are the best things in the painting. It is doubtful whether Zeuxis had advanced so far in light effects as the master of this painting. Light from the left corner of the painting sends a flood of brightness across the forms of Herakles and Amphitryon, while sunlight from the rear bathes the figure of Alkmene. The vase by the Nausikaa Painter, formerly in the Castellani Collection and now in the Metropolitan Museum in New York, forms an interesting contrast to the later work of Zeuxis. It is in the older tradition of the second half of the Fifth Century.[102a]

The name of Zeuxis has also been connected with a late painting from Eleusis which belongs to the age of Hadrian (Fig. 383). Here, we are supposed to have an echo of the Throned Zeus of Zeuxis. The god is seated in majestic fashion with a Niké in his right hand, while his left arm rests against a scepter.[103] It is possible that the Throned Zeus may have formed part of a painting which included Alkmene and Herakles strangling the serpents. In any case, the painting from Eleusis does not seem to add anything to our knowledge of Zeuxis.[104] The modeling of the figure is mainly achieved by means of red brush strokes on the more yellowish red color used for the flesh.

Although we have discussed at length the painting of Zeuxis, it is obvious that we do not know as much as we should like to know about his work and that we have no real idea of any one of his great paintings. We may perhaps be able to gain from Lucian's description some slight notion of the composition and nature of the "Centaur family," but even this is not very satisfactory. Granting the handicap, we may say that Zeuxis stood for certain things in art and of these we may have some conception. The first thing is realism. We need only to read the anecdote about the boy

[102a] Cf. A.J.A., 30 (1926), p. 40, Fig. 9.
[103] P. Girard, La Peinture antique, Fig. 117; Eph. Arch., 1888, Pl. V.
[104] Cf. A. Reinach, Recueil Milliet, I, 198, n. 3.

whom he painted carrying some grapes to gather an idea of his style. The grapes were so real that the birds came and pecked at them. This displeased Zeuxis because he felt that had he painted the boy better, the birds would have been afraid of him. The artists of this period were thus engaged in an attempt to present the world of reality in such a way that the illusion would be complete. This is evident from a second anecdote which recounts the rivalry between Zeuxis and Parrhasios.[105] In a competition, Zeuxis painted some grapes which the birds attempted to eat. Parrhasios, in turn, displayed a curtain so cleverly painted that Zeuxis was deceived and ordered him to draw it back that he might view his work. On being told his error he gave Parrhasios the prize, saying that he himself had deceived only birds but that Parrhasios had deceived him, an artist.

The illusionism of this age was made possible by the advanced technique employed in shading and by the greater understanding of perspective as revealed in Zeuxis and Parrhasios. The brush had now "come into its own." For the first time in history objects were probably presented according to the way in which the eye sees things. The relations of masses were adjusted and objects further away were made smaller in size. Never before had the optically correct interested man. Probably also high lights and color effects were developed at this time.

In the matter of color, Zeuxis used only the four which Polygnotos had employed, but coloring must have been much more naturalistic and gradations of tone and softening of outlines gave entirely new effects. The emphasis of Zeuxis' art was on τέχνη. He cared nothing at all for sublimity in subject matter, or for ethical greatness. He was interested in making his figures stand out in relief by the aid of modeling; he desired to place them in a natural background, to express subtle emotion. His principles of composition were truly pictorial.

Parrhasios, an Ephesian and a contemporary of Zeuxis, was a master of contour. Pliny tells us that he interested himself in the problem of symmetry in painting, that he "added vivacity to the features, daintiness to the hair, and charm to the mouth." His chief glory seems to have lain in the contours of his figures, and in his ability to draw them in relief in such a way "that they appeared to fold back and to express what was behind."[106] In other words, the outlines suggested what the eye could not see. Parrhasios must have done away with the dryness of line and vigor of contour of earlier Greek painting by shading and suppressing the outlines, modeling shadows, and causing the figure to melt into the light and shadow which surrounded it. He knew how to round his contours in light and was so good at drawing them that he was called the "legislator," his figures of gods and heroes being used as models.[107] His perfect mixing of color, of which Diodoros speaks, was also an aid in achieving this end.[108]

[105] Pliny, *N.H.*, 35, 65.
[107] Quint., *Inst. Or.*, XII, 10, 5.

[106] Pliny, *N.H.*, 35, 67-68.
[108] Diod. Sic., *Exc. ex* XXVI, 1.

The personality of Parrhasios was no less eccentric than that of Zeuxis. He called himself "habrodiaitos," "the friend of pleasure." He lived luxuriously, wore a purple robe, a golden crown, and sandals with golden latchets. He often carried a staff with golden spirals. He boasted endlessly of his art, claimed to be descended from Apollo, and insisted that he had often seen in a dream the Herakles of Lindos whom he painted. Worsted by Timanthes at Samos, where he exhibited his "Ajax in the contest for the armor of Achilles," he remarked that he was sorry in the name of his hero who had been worsted a second time by an unworthy rival.[109] He was accustomed to sign his paintings with inscriptions complimentary to himself, such as: "Parrhasios, a friend of pleasure but one who respects virtue, painted this picture— son of brilliant Ephesus, a legitimate son of Euenor, the first of the Greeks in my art."

About twenty-four works from his hand are known and most of these show a humanizing of legend which was perhaps due to the influence of Euripides. They represented Philoktetes wounded; Odysseus feigning madness; the punishment of Prometheus; Theseus; a priest with a young acolyte; two hoplites; a Thracian nurse; Æneas and the Dioscuri, and other themes. His "Philoktetes" seems to have aroused much comment because of the sadness in the eyes of his hero.[110] He painted "Prometheus" so well that an anecdote arose that for his model he had tortured to death an old prisoner sold by Philip from some Olynthian captives. This would have caused Parrhasios to live fifty-two years after the death of Socrates, which spoils the story.[111] Among his most famous paintings were his "Theseus" fed on roses[112] and his "Demos," or picture of the Athenian people.[113] In the latter painting, the most striking thing was the skilful blending of opposed moods and conflicting emotions. At one and the same time the people were seen to be "fickle, passionate, unjust, changeable but exorable, compassionate and pitiful, boastful, proud and humble, bold and cowardly"—in a word, everything at once. This seems to be a "rather large order" and we can scarcely believe that it existed in one painting. Parrhasios evidently understood how to express the finest shades of feeling, when many conflicting emotions could be read in one face.

Timanthes, the last painter of the "Ionian" group, probably came from Kythnos, though Sikyon is also mentioned as his home, doubtless because he worked there for the most part.[114] Like Parrhasios and Zeuxis, he showed much technical skill in his

[109] Pliny, *N.H.*, 35, 71. Ælian, *V.H.*, IX, 11; Athen., XII, 543C; XV, 687B.
[110] Anth. Pal., XVI, 111; A. Reinach, *Recueil Milliet*, I, 229, n. 3.
[111] Seneca, *Controv.*, X, v (34).
[112] Pliny, *N.H.*, 35, 129; Plut., *De Glor. Ath.*, 2; F. R., *op. cit.*, III, 54. In the "Theseus fed on roses," the flesh was soft and "blooming," *cf.* Fig. 345.
[113] Pliny, *N.H.*, 35, 69. (Tr. by Jex-Blake, Sellers.)
[114] Quint., *Inst. Or.*, II, 13, 13; Eustathios, *ad Il.*, p. 1343, 60; Pliny, *N.H.*, 35, 73; Cic., *Orat.*, XXII, 74. E. Loewy, *Œst. Jahr.*, XXIV (1929), pp. 1-41.

painting and a great deal of imagination. It was said of his efforts that one always recognized more in his paintings than was painted.[115] His greatest power lay in his ability to depict emotional states. Nowhere was this more evident than in "The Sacrifice of Iphigeneia."[116] In this work, Iphigeneia stood before the altar at the moment when she was about to be sacrificed. Nearby was the priest Kalchas, deeply moved; Odysseus was shown still more affected by the tragedy, and Menelaus overcome with grief. So great was the sorrow of Agamemnon that the artist, unable to paint his emotion, veiled his face from sight. This painting in the hands of Hellenistic artists took on even more pathos and more of the dramatic. It is to some such painter that we owe the well-known Pompeian version of the subject (Fig. 384). In this instance, varying degrees of emotion are attempted, and Agamemnon is veiled in inexpressible sorrow. Iphigeneia, however, no longer stands before the altar, but is carried in the arms of Odysseus and Diomede, while Kalchas is seen at the right with uplifted knife. Agamemnon appears beside an archaic statue of Artemis at the left. Above, the goddess assumes bodily form, while a nymph brings on a stag as a substitute for the human sacrifice. The forms are conceived in one plane like a relief and there is practically no attempt at spatial composition. The painting is far removed from the Greek work of Timanthes but perhaps in the expression of deep emotion in the figures of Agamemnon and Kalchas, it may betray some slight reminiscences of his most famous masterpiece. The work is uneven and *gauche* at times. An altar relief in Florence, with the false inscription, Kleomenes, presents a much closer similarity to the original in its central group and in the veiled form of Agamemnon.[117]

Timanthes also painted subjects of less heroic stamp. One work from his hand depicted the Cyclops asleep and some satyrs beside him measuring his thumb with a thyrsos. As Reinach has pointed out, this painting is probably the forerunner of a series of Hellenistic works, such as the Pigmies surrounding Herakles asleep or the children about the Nile. This theme may have been inspired by the "Cyclops" of Euripides.

We have followed the course of painting in the Fifth Century from the first crude beginnings under men like Kimon of Kleonai down to the finished works of Zeuxis and his contemporaries. At the time of the Persian wars, painting was still in swaddling clothes, making use for the most part of only three colors, black, red, and

---

[115] Pliny, *N.H.*, 35, 74.

[116] Pliny, *N.H.*, 35, 73; Cic., *Orat.*, XXII, 74; Quint., *Inst. Or.*, II, 13, 13; Valer. Max., VIII, 11, *Ext.* 6.

[117] See W. Amelung, *Röm. Mitth.*, 20 (1905), p. 306, for the altar relief of Kleomenes. *Cf.* J. Lange, *Die mensch. Gestalt*, Strassburg, 1903, 74, *Anm.*, 1, who condemns the Pompeian painting strongly. Better opinions of it are expressed by G. Loeschcke, *Die Enthauptung der Medusa*, p. 13; *cf.* P. Herrmann, *Denkmäler der Malerei*, Pl. 15.

white, and using them as flat tones. Kimon became the *Bahnbrecher* for Polygnotos by attacking linear foreshortening, which, however, even then, must often have been suggested and indicated rather than solved in any satisfactory way. Long after Kimon's time, Greek painters avoided foreshortening in many clever ways, as the Egyptians had done earlier, painting in one plane. Polygnotos followed Kimon and made many startling innovations, especially in the indication of depth by means of levels, in the use of yellow in addition to red, black, and white, and in the expression of mood and character. He was a true artist and much of his renown lay in the ethical greatness of his conceptions and in the nobility and grandeur of his forms. But he was without a scientific knowledge of chiaroscuro and perspective which came in with Apollodoros and Zeuxis and which gave to painting the mastery of basic elements. Optical illusion began to play its part and modeling of forms, together with an appreciation of the true value of light and shadow.

Probably by the end of the Fifth Century the painters were mostly Four-Color painters, as various traditions seem to indicate. Though Zeuxis and Parrhasios were greater masters from the technical point of view than Polygnotos had been, the content of their works was inferior. They chose the dramatic situation, the pathetic and the exotic subject matter rather than the lofty and sublime themes which had characterized the artists of the sixties. Their work tended toward genre painting and realistic treatment of material. The trivial and obscene also found their place in art. By the close of the Fifth Century, painters had in some measure begun to understand perspective and chiaroscuro. They had not, however, shown any interest in atmospheric effects, landscape *per se,* or rich coloring. Painting was emancipated from drawing under Parrhasios and Zeuxis, and no longer sought for the vigor and definiteness of outline which had been the end and aim of the artists of the early Fifth Century. Instead, we have the "living line" of Parrhasios—perhaps something like the *morbidezza* of modern artists. Most of this great advance in painting came in fifty years. By the age of Alexander, the art was to reach its zenith.

# VIII

# ETRURIA AND SOUTHERN ITALY

T HE history of Etruscan painting remains to be written.[1] Perhaps, as Cultrera suggests, many more tombs must be excavated before we can acquire an adequate amount of datable material upon which to pass accurate judgment.[2] In any case, the researches of Milani, Martha, Dennis, von Stryk, Weege, Ducati, and Poulsen form the beginnings of what must finally result in a monumental work of great importance. For Etruscan painting is interesting not only in itself but also for its wider bearing on the customs and history of the people and for its relation to Greek painting. Where Greek mural painting fails us, Etruscan tomb-decoration can often furnish a reflected picture of its achievement, more satisfactory at times than contemporary Greek vases, because executed on the flat with a wider range of colors such as the mural painters must have used. In the meantime, discoveries in Etruria, notably the Apollo from Veii, are gradually enlarging our views of the artistic capabilities of this almost mythical race.

It would be inadequate to discuss Etruscan painting without mentioning something of what we know about the people who created it. We shall pass lightly over the Etruscan problem which has vexed so many minds, accepting the view of Herodotos and Horace and other ancient writers, that they came to Italy from Lydia, and that they are in essence Asiatic.[3] How they came we shall not attempt to say, but probably as early as the Eighth Century B.C., they were occupying various parts of Italy; and in the Seventh and Sixth Centuries, they were ruling Rome and had important cities at Tarquinia (the modern Corneto), at Clusium (Chiusi), Cære (Cervetri), Volsinii (Orvieto), Perousia (Perugia), Veii, Vulci, and other sites (Fig. 385). That they

[1] This chapter was completed in Italy in the summer of 1921, before the appearance of Poulsen's book, *Etruscan Tomb Paintings, their Subjects and Significance* (Oxford, 1922). I have allowed my own account to stand, merely inserting references to his work.

[2] G. Cultrera, *Not. d. Sc.* (1920), p. 266.

[3] Hdt., I, 94; Hor., *Sat.*, I, 6, 1; *Odes*, III, 29, 1; *vs.* this, Dionys. of Hal., *Ant. Rom.*, I, 30. Recent research among Italian scholars seems to favor an autochthonous origin for the Etruscans. *Cf.* L. Pareti, *Le Origini etrusche*, Firenze, 1926. For an eastern origin, see D. Randall-MacIver, *The Etruscans*, Oxford, 1927.

were a rich, luxury-loving people, ancient writers are fond of telling us, and the tomb-paintings confirm their statements.[4] The Romans strove to discredit them whenever possible and to veil their subjugation to them, but Polybios[5] warns us against accepting a biased judgment of the Etruscans based on the period of their decline.

In the time of her power, Etruria possessed great wealth, due largely to the minerals and grain in her territory. She surrounded herself with costly works of art —bronzes and vases from Ionia and Corinth; tapestries, ivory, and silver from the East; Greek vases from Attica; and terra cottas and imitative works of her own fashioning. She had at least an outward love for art. She built elaborate archways, walls and bridges, temples and tombs—some of which are extant today. The tombs give us an idea of what the decoration of Etruscan palaces may have been, but better still, they tell us of Etruscan life and beliefs about the world beyond and something about methods of painting.

The Etruscan, like the Egyptian, believed that the soul led a life beyond comparable to the one on earth, especially in its desire for pleasure and entertainment. Accordingly, the dead were housed in underground hypogæa, oftentimes hewn out of the rock (Fig. 386), and, in the case of the wealthy, adorned with paintings. The interiors usually imitated the houses of the living. In the earlier period, the paintings show scenes of hunting, banqueting, dances, and games—events in which the dead had delighted while alive. At a later period, when Etruscan imperialism was on the decline, these gay and lively scenes changed to gloomy pictures of the trials through which the soul must pass to attain its ultimate perfection and freedom from the body.[6]

Among the hundreds of thousands of tombs that were once known in the necropoles of Etruria, there exist today only about seventy painted ones, most of which are in Southern Etruria. Many that were uncovered earlier have been destroyed by vandalism and time, so that the number of vivid Etruscan paintings is fast growing smaller, and, unless new tombs are discovered, we shall probably become more and more dependent on publications for our impressions of these works of art. It is to be regretted, however, that at present reproductions are not being made in color and that the colors on many walls are rapidly disappearing because of dampness. A few museums are fortunate in having colored facsimiles. Of these, the reproductions in

---

[4] Athen., IV, 153 d: Timæus, *Frag.* 18, Müller, *Frag. Hist. Græc.*, I, 196; Athen., XII, 517 d.

[5] Polybios, II, 17, 1; F. Weege, *Etruskische Malerei*, Halle, 1921.

[6] F. Weege, *op. cit.*, pp. 23 ff., believes that this change was due to Orphic-Pythagorean teaching brought into Southern Italy by the Greeks. *Vs.* his view, see C. C. Van Essen, *Did Orphic Influence on Etruscan Tomb Paintings Exist?* Amsterdam, 1927.

the Ny Carlsberg Glyptothek at Copenhagen are the finest, though far from accurate.

Some of the oldest Etruscan paintings which we possess are the Seventh Century ones from the Tomba Campana in Veii, about twelve miles from Rome.[7] The tomb was hewn in the living rock. At the entrance were vaulted doors leading on the right and left into side chambers but the two main rooms are placed one behind the other and are approached by an arched door flanked by reclining sphinxes. Earlier writers speak of lions but older pictures of the one remaining decapitated animal show that they were sphinxes with female heads. When the front chamber was first opened, skeletons were seen lying on huge mounds of stone, on either side of the rectangular room. The bodies had been buried in state with candelabra, bucchero vases, and other objects at the head and feet. On the back wall, on either side of a central doorway which leads into the rear chamber, are the paintings which belong to this tomb. When the spectator's eyes become accustomed to the light, the striking phenomenon is the profuse use of red, yellow, and gray against a gray-blue ground. The ground was originally covered with white paint, but because it was put on in a thin layer over the greenish brown tufa, it appears as a bluish gray. The gray of the figures was originally a black which was thinly applied over the white ground. The appearance of the colors is therefore deceptive, as red, yellow, and black alone were used against a white ground.[7a]

The subjects presented are difficult to interpret. At the right, we see a diminutive rider on a very tall horse, holding a cat-like animal on a leash behind him (Fig. 387). The horse is guided by a male figure of the archaic "Apollo" type, with bulging muscles and long hair, and is preceded by another male figure with a hammer over his shoulder. The scene is probably one of hunting, as Harmon has suggested.[8] Tamed panthers and leopards were especially used for this purpose in antiquity and it seems more likely that this interpretation is the correct one rather than the view that we have here a ride of the dead to the underworld under the guidance of Charon, or a scene of Hephaistos taken into Olympus.[9] Above the painting is a rich border of red and yellow lotuses painted against a white background; along the side, triangle

[7] L. Canina, *L'antica città di Veii*, Roma, 1847, Pls. 28-32; G. Micali, *Mon. Ined.*, Plate LVIII; G. Dennis, *Cities and Cemeteries of Etruria*, 1848, 2d ed., 1878, 3d ed., London, 1883, I, 33 ff.; J. Martha, *L'Art étrusque*, Paris, 1889, pp. 421 ff.; F. von Stryk, *Studien über die etruskischen Kammergräber*, Dorpat, 1910; T. L. Seeman, *Die Kunst der Etrusker*, Dresden, 1890, Pls. VI, VIII, IX; A. Rumpf, *Die Wandmalereien in Veii*, Leipzig, 1915 (Diss.).

[7a] A. Rumpf, *Die Wandmalereien in Veii*, Leipzig, 1915, pp. 7-8.

[8] A. M. Harmon, *A.J.A.*, 16 (1912), pp. 1-10; *cf.* F. Weege, *Jahr.*, 31 (1916), p. 165; *vs.* this view, *cf.* Poulsen, *op. cit.*, p. 7, who argues that it is not a hunting leopard because it has a short tail.

[9] E. Petersen, *Röm. Mitth.*, XVII (1902), pp. 151 ff.

patterns in red, yellow, and black (Fig. 389). Below this group of figures occurs a second panel with a long-legged, winged sphinx (Fig. 388). A deer (?) trots behind, while a panther rests its forefeet against the tail and haunch of the sphinx. The significance of the scene is not clear; the painter seems to be copying Oriental patterns. On the left side of the door, balancing the hunting scene, is a nude boy on a tall horse with a lioness or pard in the rear (Fig. 389). The panel below contains a lion and two other animals, possibly dogs.

The various compositions have tendrils and palmettes strewn about the field in an incomprehensible manner, probably, as various writers suggest, because the artist was copying Oriental motives and did not understand what he was drawing. The work is crude and naïve, the composition unwieldy and unsuited to the space. In their crudity, the paintings remind us of the sculptured frieze of horsemen from Prinias in Crete. The background was originally white. The nude bodies of the men are done in red,—as is the case throughout the history of Etruscan painting,—the hair in black or white.[9a] The various ornaments are half red, half yellow. The animals are the most bizarre part of the composition, being painted in various zones of color— red, yellow, and black. Over these zones are strewn dots of contrasting color, red on yellow, and *vice versa,* recalling the primitive technique seen in the work of the cave man at Marsoulas. What has particularly delighted the artist is this use of contrasting color. It is found not only on other portions of the body but also on the legs of the animals which are rendered one in red, the other in yellow, as we have seen them on the warrior stele from Mycenæ. The ornaments are also divided into red and yellow parts. The painting as a whole has the effect of tapestry and probably answered this purpose on the wall of the tomb. The models for the design are to be sought in the Orientalizing wares which were being imported into Etruria at the time, especially "Melian" vases, and objects such as tapestries brought in by Phœnician trade from the Orient. Rumpf suggests the influence of tapestries from Crete and the Cyclades in the Seventh Century, citing as analogous the style of the frieze of horsemen from Prinias. The frescoes are interesting as our earliest examples of Etruscan painting.[10] The second room shows six shields in a line, with stripes of red, yellow, and black.

The designs are executed in the fresco technique. In other words, the painter first prepared the wall for his work by putting upon it a coat of white lime plaster. Just how he prepared the wall depended in great measure on the stone of the tombs on the various sites. For example, at Chiusi, the paintings were placed directly against the rock without any intervening coat of plaster, and on some sites, such as Volterra,

[9a] The gray was probably originally black—the most destructible color in the tombs.

[10] L. Pernier, *Annuario,* I (1914), Fig. 19. For other tomb-paintings, badly preserved, however, see A. Rumpf, *op. cit.,* pp. 61 ff. (Cosa, Cære, Chiusi, etc.); F. Weege, *Etruskische Malerei: Veii, Chiusi, Orvieto,* in press, De Gruyter, Berlin.

the character of the stone was so crumbly that paintings could not be employed at all. At Veii, Corneto, and most of the centers important for painting, this layer of white plaster is found. It is usually very thin, from one-quarter to one centimeter in thickness—much thinner than in the case of wall-decorations at Pompeii, because the tombs were damper. When he had laid on his plaster, the artist drew his figures in the wet stucco with a pointed instrument and then later put in the outlines in red or yellow paint. The outlines thus formed were later filled in solidly in flat tones, the colors being placed directly on the wet plaster, to which they were bound by the action of the lime, no binding medium being used. Etruscan painting proceeds from the outline and in the earlier examples is merely a matter of pure flat painting with the figures in dark silhouettes against a lighter ground. Later, the reversed technique of spaces reserved in a light ground also occurs, as in Greek vase-painting, and we find both technical processes employed in the Stackelberg Tomb. Occasionally, for added details, the distemper process was used; that is, a binding medium was employed to put on other colors after the fresco had dried. This practice has probably given rise to the theory held by some writers that the paintings were done in *tempera* and not in the *al fresco* technique. In the older class of frescoes, the preliminary sketch in red which preceded the painting of the silhouette, is often visible. These red contour lines were outlined with black.[10a]

The tombs at Corneto range in time from the Sixth to the Second Centuries B.C., and furnish a splendid opportunity for a chronological survey of Etruscan wall-decoration. Here one of the earliest schools of Etruscan painting with fixed traditions was developed. Today, the traveler to Corneto-Tarquinia winds up a hill from the station through misty plains and olive groves to the modern town and from there sees a rocky ridge on which the ancient city stood. Few stones from the site remain in place but the old road which led from the height down to the harbor is still traceable and over this the chariots of the Tarquins must have passed many times. The hills opposite the Acropolis are literally honeycombed with tombs and here and there from the plain rises a tumulus of earth to bear witness to the vast city of the dead which stretched over this region. The sightseer descending into the tombs is struck first of all by the richness and gaiety of color which still prevail after all these centuries and by the vividness of the life painted on the walls. It is as if one were visiting an ancient city, not the burial places of the dead. The tombs are rather small, averaging about three yards in width by five or six in length. Most of them contain but one chamber, which imitates rather closely the room of an Etruscan house, with a broad beam down the center of the ceiling and a sloping roof—sometimes with heavy crossbeams indicated. The central beam is frequently painted in red, and the remainder of the ceiling may be in variegated checkerboard designs of

[10a] A. Rumpf, *op. cit.*, p. 8.

red, blue, and yellow. Or a small ornament of four dots placed together, sometimes painted red, sometimes black, forms a design which resembles the type of pattern found on old-fashioned wall paper. In some tombs, the patterns are very simple; in others, the ceiling is covered with luxuriant vines. At times the central beam is adorned with concentric circles in red, blue, yellow, and black.

One of the earliest tombs found here is the Tomba dei Tori, or Tomb of the Bulls. It belongs to the first half of the Sixth Century, and is interesting because it gives, in all probability, one of the earliest representations of a Greek mythological subject. The tomb itself is simpler in type than the Campana, without side chambers, but with two parallel rooms behind the main chamber. On the rear wall of the first room, between two doors, Achilles is represented surprising the young Troilos as he comes to a fountain to water the horse of Priam (Fig. 390). Achilles wears a Corinthian helmet, greaves, and a red loin cloth.[11] The form is not badly rendered, with less geometric schematization than was seen in the Campana tomb, and motion is fairly well expressed. The proportions of the horse and the length of the legs of Troilos give evidence, however, of the exaggerations of primitive art. The body of the horse, in contrast to the horses at Veii, is rendered in a uniform yellowish color, but the mane, tail, and hoofs are a grayish blue. The color again proves the artist's delight: the checkerboard pattern on the fountain is in blocks of red, blue, and white; reddish brown is employed for the flesh of Achilles and Troilos, and the whole painting is framed above by parallel bands of red, yellow and gray, white and black. These colors seem almost as fresh as when they were laid on. The branch, or tree pattern, below, with fillets intertwined, gives variety in color and design. The development of this motive in Etruscan art into a connecting background is interesting to follow. The pediment at the top is rather effectively decorated, although the figures are somewhat large for the triangles. The interesting part is the lengthening of the Chimæra and the horse of Bellerophon to fill out the space. Fine contrasting colors are used— blue on the wings and ruff of the Chimæra against a yellowish color for the body; red for the tongue; red for the horse of Bellerophon, blue for the jacket of the rider and yellowish white for his cap and breeches. Zones of color are found on the Chimæra, but not on the horse. The whole design presents the appearance of a tapestry even more than was the case in the Tomba Campana. Many other paintings in the Tomb of the Bulls are obscene in character[12] and show how unrestrained the lives of the Etruscans must have been if they ventured to decorate the houses of the dead in this fashion. The suggestion of Ducati that these were stock subjects, shared with Ionia, does not lead one to alter this opinion.[13] The paintings were put directly

[11] *Ant. Denk.*, II, Pls. 41-43; O. Montelius, *La Civ. prim. en Italie*, Pl. 303, 2; F. Weege, *Etr. Malerei*, Pl. 96, cf. E. Petersen, *Röm. Mitth.*, 17 (1902), pp. 149 ff.
[12] *Ant. Denk.*, II, 42a. Cf. *Not. Sc.*, 1892, pp. 261-263.
[13] P. Ducati, *Atene e Roma*, XXVII (1914), p. 137.

on the wall and the pigments flake off easily. They are not in the fresco technique.[14]
The bulls, which give the name to the tomb, are found in the triangles over one
of the doorways and in the zone between the main design described and the pediment. In the latter instance, the human-headed bull especially reveals Oriental
influence.

Contemporary with these paintings from the Tomba dei Tori, which have about
them an Ionic atmosphere and which were probably painted by an Ionian, are some
terra cotta plaques in the Louvre, found in a tomb at Cervetri, the ancient Cære.[15]
Ionic influence in this city is known to us from the class of vases found there which
are called Cæretan hydriæ (Figs. 214, 256-257). They are marked by a searching
realism and a love for nature. To judge from their size and decoration, one series of
these panels belonged to a single monument (Fig. 391). They represent a procession
of men and women approaching an altar from the left, while from the right a warrior
with a bow rushes on, followed by a winged demon bearing a woman in his arms. We
shall have occasion later to discuss these winged deities who play such a prominent
part in Etruscan works of art and who are the forerunners of our Christian angels
and devils. Suffice it to say that the scene represented is probably funereal; relatives
come to mourn for the dead woman, to perform some ceremony, and probably also to
engage in games in her honor. The group of "sorrowing old men" may also belong
with this series. The "Prince," seated before a statue of a divinity, is unconnected.
The colors are very somber—red, brown, black, and creamy white prevailing. The
execution is, in general, very fine. The slabs were first covered with a white slip and
on this the designs were sketched and then painted in in red and black. The flesh of
the women was reserved in the color of the slip. The forms are stiff and have a
heavy Ionic stamp. The structure of the wall with a cornice above and the representation of a horizontal crossbeam on which the figures move, together with the colored
panel-like orthostates below, recall the structure of Mycenæan walls as seen in the
paintings from Tiryns and Thebes.

With these plaques belong some slabs in the British Museum.[16] The designs present two seated sphinxes of Corinthian type which may have adorned both sides of
the entrance to a tomb. Approaching these sphinxes was probably a funeral procession (?) of men and women in curious costumes. The group published by Murray
is one of the most typical and represents two men greeting one another, one bearing

[14] G. Körte, *Ant. Denk.*, II, Pls. 41-43; text, p. 4.

[15] *Mon.*, VI, Pl. 30; J. Martha, *L'Art étrusque*, Pl. IV (colors); H. B. Walters, *History of Ancient Pottery*, II, 1905, p. 319; E. Pottier, *Cat. des vases antiques de terre cuite*, II, p. 412; P. Ducati, G. Giglioli, *Arte Etrusca*, Roma, 1927, *Pittura*, Figs. 12, 13, 14. See A. N. Modona, *Pitture etrusche archaiche, le lastre fittile policrome ceretane*, Firenze, 1928.

[16] A. S. Murray, *J.H.S.*, X (1889), Pl. VII, p. 243; Brizio, *Bullettino dell' Instituto Arch.*, 1874, p. 128.

a branch, the other a standard with a bull on the end.[17] On the right stands a woman with a spear and a wreath. The design is executed entirely in red, black, and white against a cream-colored ground. Above is an elaborate guilloche, or braid pattern.

At Corneto, some Sixth Century tombs have been found which are marked by an Ionian fondness for realism, by a predilection for heavy, soft forms and by liveliness in action. Some display an Oriental bent for animal life and for Ionic patterns such as a lion and a panther rending a gazelle. One of the best-known tombs of this group is the Tomba degli Auguri or Tomb of the Augurs (Fig. 392), so named from the bird of omen flying in the field and from the supposed figures of augurs. On the rear wall, on either side of a painted door, a figure wearing a white garment, pointed shoes, and a dark mantle lined with red stands in an attitude of mourning. The main interest in subject matter, however, centers in the funeral games depicted on the long walls (Fig. 393). On the right, two thickly built, nude wrestlers are represented, engaged in a hand-to-hand bout. The bowls which were used as prizes stand in the background. At the left are seen a bearded official in charge of the games, a slave with a stool over his shoulders, and a second figure—possibly a slave—asleep.[18] At the right, cruel sport of some kind is taking place, in which "Phersu," a masked figure wearing a pointed cap, plays a prominent part. A dog on a leash guided by Phersu has attacked a man with his head in a sack. The design shows only too well Tuscan love of realism and brutality. The figure at the left with the "hockey-stick," formerly thought to be an augur, is probably an umpire. The artist borrowed from Ionia the heavy figures of the wrestlers, as a glance at the Cæretan hydriæ will show. The scene has little to recommend it artistically but is of greater import for Etruscan games and for the Etruscan word "Phersu," from which the Latins probably derived the word *persona,* meaning "mask." The colors, which are well preserved, are mainly reddish brown, black, creamy white, and greenish blue. On the opposite wall, the figure of "Phersu" recurs, but much of the design is lost.[19]

Of greater charm are the frescoes in the Tomba della Caccia e della Pesca (Figs. 394-396)—The Tomb of Hunting and Fishing. They form some of the most interesting compositions in Etruscan art and show in what direction the Etruscan artist might have developed if he had not followed Greek lines so closely and if he had depended somewhat more on his own inspiration. The Tomb of Hunting and Fishing reveals a love of realism and of nature which seems to have been characteristic of the Etruscan people. No close models exist in the Greek for such scenes as the hunt in

[17] A. S. Murray, *op. cit.,* Pl. VII, color; H. B. Walters, *Art of the Greeks,*[2] 1922, Pl. LXIII.

[18] Poulsen suggests that the man at the left is a spectator who is about to be seated on the stool borne by the slave. The "sleeping slave," he terms a mourning figure.

[19] Poulsen considers Phersu worsted in his attack on his muffled opponent and fleeing.

the pediment of Figure 394, the nearest analogy being the hunter of the Thermos metope (Fig. 209). The scene is taken from life and the artist has observed with great care the dogs on the scent, and the hunters with their game. The lively, dancing figures on the side walls, separated by the branch pattern, are also individually Etruscan. These scenes form the decoration of the first room. Etruscan, too, is the family meal in the pediment of the rear chamber (Fig. 395), with the reclining pair attended by nude slaves and a flute-player. Even though a Greek symposium is the model for the design, there is nothing that suggests Greek art in the final product. No one of the scenes mentioned is remarkably successful from the point of view of composition, or in the drawing of the human form. The figures are crowded into the space and there has often been a desire to cover all of the available surface with patterns. The color is one of the most interesting features, rich blues alternating with violet, red, brown, yellow, black, and white. Where the artist has been more successful is in his seascapes. Here, the human element has been treated as secondary to the delight in nature. The gray-green sea with rocks banded with zones of red and blue; the flying birds,—some red, some blue, others in black outline,—caught in momentary attitudes of settling on the waves or flying up suddenly from the rocks,—are the things that have interested the artist. The impressionism in the rendering of the birds reminds one of Japanese work. Figures 395 and 396 show how successful the artist was in catching the life in such scenes and in holding it fast. The figures of the men in the gaily colored boats are treated very sketchily. They are engaged in fishing, slinging, harpooning, and apparently in robbing the nests of sea-birds. At any rate, the bold composition on the left wall in the upper panel of Figure 396, which adds not a little to the vivid action of the paintings, seems to indicate some such venture. There is real joy on the part of the artist in the sea and in the flying birds. The inspiration for such scenes may have come from Ionia, for we are familiar with the Ionian love of the sea, but there are no models which suggest a close analogy.[20] The only thing which mars the design is the senseless use of wreaths, placed by the Etruscan against the background as if a wall were represented and not the open sea and sky. The colors in this tomb are remarkably brilliant. They are still conventionally used; one horse is red and has a yellow tail, a second is blue with a red tail and mane. The scale of the figures is entirely non-Greek. They are presented as purely subsidiary to the main interest, which is the sea.

In the same period,—in the first half of the Sixth Century,—belongs the Tomba delle Leonesse, with hunting leopards, which have wrongly been termed lionesses,

[20] Cf. M. Heinemann, op. cit., pp. 48 ff. She accepts the view of Loeschcke that we have a Todessprung depicted here; the leap from the Leukadian rock is a crystallization of this same ritual; sometimes a boat stood by to rescue the victim and bear him to the other world. But why the slinging and harpooning?

in the pediment. On the rear wall are scenes of dancing; [21] on the side walls, separated by painted columns, reclining figures. Figure 397 shows a youth of this type, remotely resembling in his physiognomy the Cretan Cup-bearer. He is represented toying with an egg. Below these figures is a very beautiful decorative design of leaping dolphins and of birds flying above the waves (Fig. 398). The dolphins are in green or blue with red stripes. At the top of the design runs a lotus-palmette pattern in red, blue, and green.

The Tomba dei Vasi Dipinti, or Tomb of the Painted Vases, is to be dated in the second half of the Sixth Century (Fig. 399). Another family repast is pictured, similar to the one in the pediment of the Tomb of Hunting and Fishing and with the familiar unbridled dancers on the side walls, separated by the branch motive. Attic Greek connections begin to make themselves felt, not only in objects such as the black-figured amphoræ and cups which are represented on the right wall, and which furnish an indication of date, but even more in the rendering of the form, which becomes thinner and more athletic in type. The artist is also more concerned with the twisting and turning of the human figure in motion. The Tomba del Vecchio, or Tomb of the Old Man, offers yet another banquet scene similar to the ones which we have been discussing (Fig. 400). The individualism in the head of the old man is striking and recalls a fine piece of characterization on a painted Etruscan sarcophagus of the Sixth Century in the British Museum (Fig. 401). The homely details which the Etruscan, and which the Roman after him, loved to incorporate in his art, are seen in this painting in the guinea-hens under the couch, and in the realistic portraiture. The woman on the couch may be a courtesan. This tomb is unfortunately fast being ruined from moisture and very little of the design can now be made out. To this tomb should be added as roughly contemporary, the Tomba del Barone, or Tomb of the Baron, named after Baron Kestner one of the Germans who first worked in these tombs. The designs represent youths leading horses and conversing with a woman in a gray chiton and brown mantle; or they depict youths on horse on either side of a central group consisting of a man and a youthful male flute-player addressing a woman (Fig. 402). The technique of this tomb is peculiar. The artist seems to have experimented with distemper on the plaster stucco. A shadowy outline of color, formed by the absorption of the pigment in the plaster surrounds each figure (Fig. 403). Apparently, the dampness of the tomb prevented a successful outcome for his experiment (cf. p. 257). There is a generous use of bright green and brown on many of the garments and caps. The decoration on these walls is very effective, the silhouettes standing out isolated against the lighter ground. [22] One of

[21] *Ant. Denk.*, II, Pl. 42.

[22] F. Poulsen, *op. cit.*, p. 21, following G. Körte, considers that a Greek artist was responsible for this tomb, hence the quiet atmosphere. Greek letters have been found where the

the most interesting features is the blue hair and beard of the man mentioned above. The coloring recalls the early poros figures like the Bluebeard from the Acropolis. The heads are Ionic in type. Another important tomb of the period is the Tomba delle Iscrizioni or Tomb of the Inscriptions. Palæstra pursuits and very lively revels are depicted.[22a] The slenderer proportions of the figures, the freedom in drawing and in the representation of movement show that the artists are becoming more proficient. The animals are still conventionally drawn but there is more naturalism in the athletic scenes.

How dominant Greek influence became at the beginning of the Fifth Century is seen in tombs such as the Stackelberg Tomb, the Tomba del Triclinio, dei Leopardi, and the later Tomba della Pulcella. The Stackelberg Tomb, or Tomba delle Bighe,— Tomb of the Chariots,—has been well published by Weege.[23] It belongs to the turn of the century and gives a picture of funeral games with seated spectators watching them (Figs. 404a-405). The sports include dancing and athletic pursuits, such as boxing, wrestling, jumping, discus-throwing, and chariot-races. The influence of vase-painters like Euthymides is seen in the foreshortening of figures in back view— for example, in the grooms harnessing horses to the chariots (Fig. 404b). Ionic elements are to be found in the frieze above the main panel and in various details (Fig. 405). Dark silhouettes are used against a light ground in the narrow frieze above, and forms in light colors against a deep red ground below. The artist may have been a Greek from an Ionian colony in Southern Italy, as Weege suggests, but the scene depicted is thoroughly Etruscan.[24] The colors employed are red, blue, black, yellow and white, with some gray and green. The outlines in the smaller frieze are incised.

One of the best preserved tombs of the Fifth Century is the Tomba dei Leopardi —so called from the hunting leopards in the pediment[25] (Fig. 406). The interior is in very good condition; the checkerboard pattern on the ceiling is resplendent with vivid hues of red, yellow, blue, black, and green. The main scene opposite the door depicts a banquet of Greek type, but with women reclining with men on the same

artist reckoned up his day's wages. The scene depicted presents preparations for a *pompa*, or procession, and a dancing festival. There is a certain similarity between the work found in this tomb and some of the figures on Cæretan hydriæ, e.g., Louvre, E, 699, E. Pottier, *Louvre Album, E-G*, Pl. 53. The extent of East Greek influence on Etruria is as yet undetermined. Further excavations in Ionic territory are much needed.

[22a] Poulsen, *op. cit.*, Figs. 7-8. (*Cf.* Headpiece, Ch. VIII.)

[23] F. Weege, *Jahr.*, 31 (1916), pp. 105-168.

[24] The main interest in the subject matter, as Poulsen notes, is the representation of an Etruscan audience seated on typically Italic stands at the games. This is the only Etruscan example and it is Etruscan, not Greek. See F. Weege, *Jahr.*, 31 (1916), pp. 151 ff.

[25] F. Weege, *Jahr.*, 31 (1916), pp. 153 ff., esp. p. 161; Pls. IX-XVI; Figs. 25-31; O. Montelius, *op. cit.*, Pl. 304, 2.

couch.[26] The execution of this wall is dull and monotonous when compared with the one on the right (Plate XIV). Here, the design is replete with rhythmic motion, graceful attitudes, and lively colors. There is beauty in the play of line; there is delicacy of pattern. The Etruscan, like the Cretan and Ionian, was able to draw scenes of lively action better than those of repose and the dances are always superior to the banquet scenes. The rush of action in the figure of the flute-player is one of the best examples of drawing in the tomb. The colors are also very fine, the mantle of the musician being white with a border of blue and a narrow red stripe. Rich reds with stripes of green and white are also found on other mantles. The artist has frequently made use of a taut string against the wet plaster—for example, to mark the lines of the mattresses and colored bands in the banquet scene.

The height of achievement in Etruscan painting is reached in the Tomba del Triclinio, or Tomb of the Triclinium, in Corneto.[26a] The familiar banquet scene, with men and women in elaborate costumes reclining on luxurious couches, recurs here (Fig. 407). (*Cf.* Duell, *op. cit.*, Pl. I, color.) In the pediment above and on the ceiling, the vine pattern is employed in much the same way as in Eighteenth Dynasty tombs in Egypt. The reclining youths in the corners find their prototypes in vases of the period of Euthymides and Euphronios. Beside the doorway, riders in rich mantles, seated sideways on their horses, are seen in heraldic composition; above, in the angles, are tame-faced hunting leopards (Fig. 408). (*Cf.* Duell, *op. cit.*, Pl. IV, color.) The scenes described are badly preserved, except for the ceiling (Duell, *op. cit.*, Pl. V, color), and the finest effects are gained from the revels which line the side walls. Here the dancers and flute- and lyre-players, separated by trees and foliage, are rendered with a charm and grace that are unsurpassed in later work (Fig. 409). (Duell, *op. cit.*, Pls. II-III, color.) The beauty and precision in the drawing are striking. Combined with this, there is an unusual charm in the various trees, in the positions of the women dancers, and the quaint costumes. But the ease in motion, the grace in the bending of the heads and arms and the beauty of the nude forms, show what a far cry it is to the Tomba Campana at Veii. The colors begin to be used more in accordance with nature. Sometimes they are gorgeously rich. The dancing youth in the upper half wears a light blue mantle with a yellow border and the women have dotted yellow chitons and red mantles with yellow borders. The great achievement of the artist lies in the freedom attained in drawing the human figure. The flute-player who wears a yellow-bordered, filmy mantle of blue caught up over his

[26] F. Poulsen, *op. cit.*, pp. 32 ff., argues that the reclining women in Etruscan painting are not *hetæræ*, the view held by Weege and others, but respectable married women.

[26a] Prentice Duell, *The Tomba del Triclinio at Tarquinia, Mem. of the Amer. Acad. in Rome*, VI (1927), pp. 9 ff., Pls. I-V (color). Accurate reproductions of the paintings illustrated in Figs. 407-409 may be found in Duell's article. The reproductions used by me are from old and unsatisfactory copies.

Plate XIV. Corneto. Tomb of the Hunting Leopards. Musicians and revelers.

arms illustrates well this progress (Fig. 410). The lightness of movement contrasts strikingly with what is found in the Tomba degli Auguri. Scenes of abandon are remarkably rendered and probably hark back to Greek vase-painting, to figures like the Mænad on the Munich vase of Kleophrades (Fig. 316). A good example of this is seen in the woman dancer of Figure 411. The Etruscan artist is copying Attic art in the Tomba del Triclinio, and he has created a composition full of freshness and infused with the joy of living. This *joie de vivre* is the dominant note in the decoration of the earlier group of Etruscan tombs. The painter may well have been a Greek for the language which he speaks is Greek.

By the middle of the Fifth Century, these scenes of joy and delight in banquets, dances, and games, seem to have been more and more interrupted by gloomier elements relating to death. This was due, according to Weege, to Orphic influence coming into Etruria from Southern Italy; according to Poulsen, to the decline of Etruscan power. The Tomba della Pulcella, or Tomb of the Young Girl, shows a combination of this lighter aspect of life with the more somber side (Fig. 412). The banquet scene is still retained, but the branch pattern has become a background of foliage against which the reclining banqueters are placed. Figures such as the young girl before the couch are rendered with great fineness; she it is who gives to the tomb its name. But in the niche, below the central pediment, winged deities like the Sleep and Death of white Athenian lekythoi, are seen caring for the dead. On either side of the alcove is a male figure, one playing a lyre, the other a flute. The atmosphere of the paintings is Greek and many patterns reflect those found on Attic white-ground lekythoi. The heads of the figures resemble in type the youths and maidens on Greek vases of the severe style. But for the heaviness of the garments worn and the elaborate drapery of the couches, the work might pass as Greek. Etruscan painting is now held in thrall by Attic art, having already served its apprenticeship to Oriental and Ionic art. The predominating color is a brownish red, with contrasting green, yellow, and black. The contours have been incised before they were painted. Many of the remaining paintings in this tomb have been defaced.

The period from the end of the Sixth Century until the middle of the Fifth is the time when Etruria gives evidence of closest contact with Greece. During this time, many thousands of the Attic Greek vases found in Etruscan necropoles and originally believed to be of Etruscan workmanship were imported into Etruria. These were largely the objects which inspired the Etruscan painter who was always more ready to copy than invent, though when he was forced to devise for himself, he was fairly equal to the task. The motives which he took over were not always worked into such well-balanced, finished compositions as we find in Greece, and though there is often rhythm arising from the rather monotonous repetition of single elements, there is not that symmetry and subtle harmony of composition which must have characterized the best Greek mural decoration of the period. On the other hand, many of the best tombs were probably the work of Greeks, especially those at Corneto.

Turning for a moment from the tombs at Corneto which are so valuable to us for a study of the development of Etruscan painting, we may consider a group of tombs of the Fifth Century from Chiusi—the ancient Clusium. They present features similar to those which we have been discussing but differ from the tombs at Corneto in being decorated only on the upper part of the walls; the lower portion was left in the natural color of the stone. One of the earliest is the Tomba della Scimmia, or Tomb of the Monkey. Palæstra scenes are represented and performances of dwarfs, giants, and jugglers. In general, the paintings are inferior to those at Corneto and this tomb illustrates some of the differences (Fig. 413). The figures of the four men at the left, who are probably officials in charge of the games, show a certain stiffness and angularity. The horses of the oncoming chariots are wooden in type and monotonous in pose. The colors are thin and transparent—almost like water colors—and were placed directly on the rock with no intervening layer of plaster. The scenes of wrestlers and armed riders and the dwarf and giant are done with more spirit. The monkey at the right, which gives the name to the tomb, may or may not represent Ionic influence. Other scenes depict women jugglers and various entertainers.

The Tomba del Colle Casuccini shows well the invasion of Attic influence at Clusium. Figure 414 gives a representation of a symposium which is a fairly good duplicate of what is found on red-figured vases of the severe style, though the draperies of the couches are Etruscan and the garments of the youths are heavy and lacking in beauty. The palæstra scenes are rendered with animation (Fig. 415). The chariot-race has a unique charm due to the repetition of the dapper figure of the charioteer in a biga. The drawing of the figures is adequately executed but the artist shows little originality. For the most part, we find in these tombs Etruscan ideas and customs clothed in Greek forms. Figure 416, from the tomb of the monkey, shows again the local interest in performances of dwarfs and giants.

After the period of the paintings from Chiusi which we have been discussing, there is a gap in our chronological survey, the next frescoes which we have to consider falling in the early Fourth Century. The scanty importation of Greek objects of art during this period may be partly responsible for this situation; more likely it is due to the blow dealt the Etruscans by their expulsion from seats of power. The fact remains that Etruscan art leaps from a severe stage represented by tombs of the later Fifth Century such as the Tomba della Pulcella and those at Clusium, into the free style of the Fourth Century. Examples of the later group are the Tomba Golini at Orvieto and the Tomba dell' Orco at Corneto. They were influenced by the innovations of the Greek painters, Apollodoros and Zeuxis, and must consequently be placed late.

The Tomba dell' Orco, or Tomb of Hades, is one of the most famous Etruscan tombs and is interesting because it shows the infusion of Greek mythological details into Etruscan beliefs and the influence of the great shadow painters of Greece, such as Apollodoros, in the rendering of light and shade. The form of the tomb is difficult to reconstruct and it may have been made up of several tombs. It extends over a wide range of territory. The paintings, scattered about on various walls, show certain similarities in style. Some were destroyed by the French in an attempt to remove them. The funeral banquet, which is one of the main episodes represented, takes place in the gloomy underworld in the presence of Hades and Persephone (Fig. 417, top). At the right, Hades is seated on his throne, with Persephone standing beside him. A dark blue, cloud-like mist surrounds their heads. Hades is represented wearing a wolf's head as a helmet (Fig. 420), whereas Persephone is a dread power like Medusa, with snaky locks. Before the pair stands the triple-headed Geryon, who doubtless carried out behests in connection with the souls of the dead. On another wall the Cyclops appears, done in gruesome Etruscan fashion with rolls of fat on his ponderous body and with one enormous eye in the center of his forehead. Odysseus is represented piercing the eye of the giant with a heavy pole (Fig. 417, bottom). The Cyclops doubtless ate the flesh of condemned souls in the underworld, like Eurynomos as described by Pausanias in the paintings of Polygnotos.[26b] On the long wall before the rulers, a procession of epic heroes advances (Fig. 418)— Agamemnon,[26c] the seer Teirisias, Ajax, and others now lost. On the branches of asphodel various souls are seen flitting about, or, as Weege believes, attempting to wrest themselves free.

Other paintings show Theseus and Peirithoos bound fast in the underworld (Fig. 417, center) and tormented by demons for attempting to carry off Persephone. In the hideous figures of the Cyclops, of Tuchulcha, and Charon, we observe some of the horrors with which the Etruscan peopled the underworld. Tuchulcha has a donkey's head, the beak of a parrot, and the wings of a bird of prey (Tailpiece, Ch. VIII). The soul was believed to be tormented by such demons as these until it could win its liberation from the body. In the lower panel of Figure 418, the winged deity is probably hastening to the banquet of the blessed. Near the Etruscan buffet, a nude slave of Polykleitan type ministers at the feast. The winged demons and deities pictured are probably the forerunners of the devils and angels of mediæval and modern times. Figure 419 reproduces a death demon, this time with a blue nimbus (?) about his reddish hair. He is the ruler of the souls of the dead and carries a hammer as a symbol of his power. In the circus at Rome, even in Christian times, two men impersonating Mercury and the Etruscan Charon appeared to bear away the bodies of the dead slain in the gladiatorial combats.[27]

[26b] F. Weege, *Etr. Mal.*, p. 28.
[26c] According to some authorities, this figure is Memnon, not Agamemnon.
[27] Tertullian, *Ad nat.*, I, 10; *Apol.*, 15; F. Weege, *Etr. Mal.*, p. 115, n. 92.

The influence of Greek wall-painters is very evident in the mythical content and in the technical details of this tomb. Etruscan beliefs have been thoroughly modified by Greek thought. Further, the figures of Hades and the banqueters surrounded by blue-black mist follow the innovations of light and shadow in vogue after Apollodoros. The head of Hades (Fig. 420) is remarkable for its breadth and nobility of style and reflects the grandeur of Fifth Century Greek painting. It seems to have influenced one of Michelangelo's sketches.[28] The head of one of the banqueters—a young, golden-haired woman named Velia, the wife of Arnth Velchas—shows also the simplicity and serene beauty which we associate with the greatest Greek masters of the Fifth Century (Fig. 421). Perhaps no painting in all of the underground tombs possesses the charm of this small portrait head with its cameo-like features and soft colors. It is an exquisite piece of workmanship with the refinement that belongs to the best Greek art. These frescoes probably date in the Fourth Century; but with all of their beauty in execution and adherence to Greek forms, we do not know that they were executed by Greeks. The painter may well have been an Etruscan trained in Greek methods. The Cyclops and the Medusa-like Persephone seem to indicate this. In these works we see the complete surrender of Etruscan painting to Greek forms; the subject matter remains partly Etruscan.

The theme of the wandering and torment of the soul must have become very common in art from the Fourth Century on, because of the many allusions to pictures of the underworld and the many representations found on Orphic vases of Southern Italy.[29] The Tomba del Cardinale in Corneto, which probably belongs to the Third Century, treats this theme and gives an idea of the difficulties which the soul encountered while wandering through its 10,000 years to win ultimate freedom and purification.[30] It is one of the best examples of tombs of the decadence, interesting because it presents the torture of the soul in the underworld and because it shows how, after the Fifth Century, the Etruscan peopled this region with sinister spirits and demons (Fig. 422). The paintings have suffered greatly from exposure and are in a very bad condition. A woman in a cart drawn by two demons, one black, the other light, is being taken to the underworld. Behind the gateway to the lower world, a crowd of victims tormented and driven by demons is seen. One woman is dragged along by two dark, winged demons with hammers. Out of the soil which produced such works as these, the frescoes in the Campo Santo at Pisa were later to arise and the Inferno of Dante.[30a]

The tombs of the Fourth Century are sharply separated from those of the earlier

[28] F. Weege, *Etr. Mal.*, Fig. 67.                    [29] F. Weege, *op. cit.*, pp. 31 ff., Figs. 27-34.
[30] F. Weege, *op. cit.*, pp. 36-37; Inghirami, *Mon. Etr.*, IV, Pl. 27; C. C. van Essen, *op. cit.*, argues that no scenes of torture are represented in the Tomba del Cardinale; *cf. La Tomba del Cardinale, Studi Etruschi*, II, Firenze, 1928.
[30a] Weege, *op. cit.*, pp. 49 ff.

period in subject matter and in execution. The poses and movements of the figures are easy and free, foreshortening is understood, and the forms are sometimes modeled with light and shadow. The themes presented are often essentially Greek and some of the designs may have been influenced by Orphic-Pythagorean teaching about the wandering and purification of the soul.

Closely akin to the Tomba dell' Orco, is the Tomba Golini at Orvieto, dating from the Fourth Century.[31] The rulers of the underworld are depicted as usual and the funeral feast is represented as taking place in their presence (Fig. 423). Two brothers recline on a couch at the right and their names are indicated by inscriptions. The scene is lighted by candelabra of a curious type—the candles being held in the beaks of birds. Flute-players enliven the banquet and a light-footed, nude attendant ministers at the feast. One of the important scenes pictures the interior of the kitchen and the preparation for a banquet (cf. Fig. 424). The larder is filled with beef, birds, and venison hung from the wall and the slaves are busy preparing the food to the music of the flute. Details are given with a precision found only in Egyptian tomb-reliefs and one feels that the scenes serve the same magical purpose. The names of the servants are added to ensure the pleasure of their service in the world to come. The occupants of the tomb whose portraits are presented here are doubtless enjoying the eternal banquet in the realm of Hades.

Near the end of the Fourth Century or in the early Third, the Tomba degli Scudi, or Tomb of the Shields, may, in all probability, be placed[32] (Fig. 425). The three-quarter and front views of the figure become a simpler matter for the artist and the forms are modeled with chiaroscuro. The brush strokes are heavier and more hastily executed. The artist has acquired the mastery of his craft and with it comes, as so often in the history of art, the decadence. It is possible to feel a certain provincial character in the painting and a departure from more purely Greek methods of expression toward local Etruscan forms. The old commonplace—the symposium—is reproduced with slight variations.

At the end of the Fourth Century, the famous paintings from the François Tomb, discovered at Vulci in 1857 and now preserved in the Torlonia Palace in Rome, are also to be placed. These paintings are inaccessible to scholars. Inadequate copies of them may be seen in the Museo Gregoriano of the Vatican. On the left wall were scenes from the Trojan and Theban cycles of myths. They treated subjects popular with Greek mural painters, such as the insult of Ajax to Kassandra, which formed the theme of one of Polygnotos' masterpieces; Eteokles and Polyneikes; and Achilles

[31] Martha, L'Art étr., Figs. 266, 279, 281, 292 (after Conestabile, Pitture murali).

[32] Poulsen, op. cit., p. 34, dates the tomb at the end of the Fifth Century on the basis of the similarity of one of the female figures wearing a diadem to the Hera Borghese. It is certainly later than the Tomba dell' Orco and the Tomba Golini.

slaying Trojan captives as an offering to Patroklos. Balancing these Greek themes, we see on certain walls local Etruscan history. The legend pictured is the story of Mastarna freeing his friend, Cæles Vibenna (Fig. 426). In other words, these Etruscan paintings apparently represent some very early events in the history of the struggle between Rome and Etruria.[33] Cæles is doubtless the Etruscan hero from Vulci who settled the Cælian Hill, and Cnæve Tarchu, who is being put to death by a second warrior, is one of the Tarquins. He is not, however, Lucius Tarquinius, after whose death Mastarna became King. According to our painting, Aulus Vibenna and Mastarna overpower a Tarquin and then free Cæles Vibenna, who was probably a prisoner in the camp of Tarquin. Mastarna has been identified as Servius Tullius. In execution, we find the same freedom which characterized the Tomba degli Scudi. Three-quarter views occur and figures are foreshortened with skill. The forms and motives are all Greek but the conception of the painting is Etruscan, as are the tense expressions and cruel faces.[33a]

After the Fourth Century, Etruscan painting gradually declined, as the Tomba del Tifone shows. This is one of the largest tombs in the necropolis at Corneto, distinguished by a great central pillar which was needed to support the roof, and by three stone benches rising one above the other like steps and extending the length of each wall. The latter were used for the sarcophagi. On the huge, square pillar, were painted representations of the winged giant Typhon (?), whose legs end in serpent tails. He is supposedly holding up the roof, like an Atlas figure (Fig. 427). Poulsen dates this tomb in the first half of the Fourth Century, but the figures seem to bear the marks of Hellenistic art. The so-called Typhon, with the snaky legs, calls to mind figures found in the Pergamene frieze. The tomb is probably to be dated in the Third or Second Century. In the same tomb, a procession of figures also occurs— probably funereal in character—which seems to be the prototype for the Roman triumphal procession. Men with musical instruments and elaborate robes are represented in solemn procession, guiding a youth to the underworld. An ornamental border of dolphins sporting above the waves is one of the most interesting parts of the decoration; it runs around the various walls of the tomb, above the figure paintings (Fig. 428). The colors are mainly reddish brown and black.[33b]

[33] G. Körte, *Ein Wandgemälde von Vulci als Document zur römischen Königsgeschichte, Jahr.*, XII (1897), p. 57. *Cf.* W. Helbig, *Führer*, I³, pp. 322 ff.

[33a] For some fine, new reproductions of paintings from this tomb, see F. Messerschmidt, *Volcenter Malereien, Die Antike*, IV (1928), pp. 103-107, Pls. 12-20. The portrait of Vel Saties, Pls. 12, 13, is a splendid characterization. Even finer than this are the heads of the dying Etruscan warriors, Pls. 18-19. In contrast to these are the idealized Trojans, Pls. 16-17, and the Goddess Vanth, Pl. 15. *Cf.* Ducati and Giglioli, *Arte Etrusca*, 1927, Figs. 38-41, *Pittura*.

[33b] Ducati and Giglioli date the tomb in the Second Century and compare the fantastic figures with serpent limbs to the giants of the Pergamene altar (183-174 B.C.).

A second tomb of this period has lately been uncovered at Corneto. The designs are more purely decorative and the tomb has been named the Tomb of the Festoons, from the shields hung on the walls with festoons between.[34] On either side of the doorway, Charon was painted with his hammer, but only the figure at the right is preserved today. The interesting part of the tomb lies in the inscriptions, partly in Etruscan, partly in Latin, showing that the sepulcher belonged to a period when Etruscan power was declining as Rome advanced.

The number of tomb-paintings in Etruria dating after the middle of the Fifth Century is very limited. This is largely due to the fact that her power was being gradually diminished and, with it, her wealth. After the expulsion of the Tarquin kings in 509 B.C., the Etruscans must still have retained much of their original strength. Lars Porsenna, at any rate, was able to exact from the Romans a "voluntary tribute" for a definite period.[35] In 474, Hiero of Syracuse destroyed the Etruscan fleet; in 438, Etruria lost her power in Campania through the fall of Capua before the Samnites. Soon afterward, the Gauls drove the Etruscans from the Po Valley. But the greatest blow fell in 396 with the loss of Veii, the rival of Rome.

Etruria never developed a strong, centralized state and Italy was never united under Etruscan dominion because of this lack of political unity. In the twelve Etruscan cities, native princes subjugated and ruled the Italian population, occasionally sallying forth for adventure and invasion. But these centers were never united together into a strong, central power, perhaps because of local jealousies, perhaps because the indolent, luxurious life of the Etruscans did not incite them to action except when the necessity was imminent. They were finally subdued by Rome at the end of the Third Century and their disappearance from the scene of history is almost as mysterious as their appearance. They were doubtless absorbed by the native population. Schulze has shown that many Roman patricians were descendants of the ruling Etruscans and that intermarriage with the Etruscans lasted until the end of the Republic.[36]

In the account of the paintings which we have given, almost no mention has been made of the sarcophagi which have been found in great numbers on all Etruscan sites. They are usually of terra cotta with sculptured figures on the lids (*cf.* Fig. 401). They are vividly painted in color—brownish red, yellow, blue, black, white, green, and lavender prevailing. The examples in the British Museum, in Florence,

---

[34] G. Cultrera, *Not. d. Sc.* (1920), pp. 248 ff.

[35] Dionys. Hal., *Ant. Rom.,* V, 26, 35; Plut., *Quæst. Rom.,* XVIII; Pliny, *N.H.,* 34, 139.

[36] W. Schulze, *Zur Gesch. lateinischer Eigennamen, Abh. d. Kgl. Ges. der Wiss. zu Göttingen, Phil.-hist. Kl. N.F.,* V, 5 (1904), pp. 62 ff. *Cf.* Herbig, *Indogerman. Forschungen,* XXVI (1909), pp. 367-380; *B.P.W.,* XXXVI (1916), 1440-1448; 1472-1480, on the Italic elements in the inscriptions of Clusium and in words like *Roma* from the early Latin word, *rumin,* "breast."

and in the Villa Giulia at Rome are characteristic, but by far the finest painted sarcophagus which has been discovered is the one in the Museum of Florence (Fig. 429). It is made of alabaster and the decoration is executed in tempera, with the aid of a binding medium. It dates from about 300 B.C. On the sides and ends, battles between Greeks and Amazons are painted.[37] The style approximates Greek work very closely; in fact, were it not for a certain rough-and-ready vigor in the faces of some of the Greek warriors and certain slips on the part of the Etruscan who has represented some of the Amazons nude or wearing strange costumes, we might be tempted to believe that a Greek painter had executed the work. It is valuable, therefore, because it presents us with an example of painting in the Greek style at the end of the Fourth Century. The colors are freshly preserved—pale lilac, blue, yellow, red, white, and black prevailing.

In Figure 429, from one of the long sides of the sarcophagus, a Greek warrior is seen charging an Amazon mounted on a horse. The motive is "Polygnotan." The ground for the design is a pale violet and against it these two central figures stand out in vivid color. The flesh tones of the Greek warrior are a brownish red and he wears a deep red tunic. His shield, which is skilfully foreshortened, is blue on the interior, with a yellow edge. He wears a silver-white corselet with gold decoration. At the right, an Amazon mounted on a gray horse has her sword uplifted across her forehead in "Polygnotan" fashion. She is clothed in a violet tunic and red trousers. Her hair is a rich chestnut and her eyes show well the artist's ability to depict emotion. The group is doubtless dependent on Greek monumental painting of the Polygnotan period. It is more effective than the three combatants of Figure 430, which adorn one end of the monument. Here, the old motive of the fallen warrior attacked from either side by an Amazon is depicted. The colors are extremely well preserved, especially the deep red garment of the Amazon at the right and the red tunic and blue shield of the Greek. The composition as a whole lacks a certain dash and sharpness and we miss in the painting the idealism which belonged to similar scenes by Greek masters.

A second sarcophagus of importance has recently been found near Orvieto. On it are represented, in relief, myths from the Trojan cycle. They can probably be traced back to Attic paintings of the Fifth Century (Fig. 431). The sculptures include the sacrifice of Trojan prisoners at the tomb of Patroklos by Achilles; the sacrifice of Polyxena at the tomb of Achilles by Neoptolemos, Odysseus threatening Circe, and Odysseus sacrificing to call up the spirit of Teiresias.[38] Some of these themes had

---

[37] A. della Seta, *Italia Antica*, 1922, p. 228, Fig. 251; S. Colvin, *J.H.S.*, IV (1883), pp. 354 ff., Pls. 36-38 (color). Ducati and Giglioli, *op. cit.*, p. 66, give the technique as encaustic. Some writers call the material of the sarcophagus marble.

[38] E. Galli, *Mon. Ant.*, XXIV (1916), pp. 5-116, Pls. I-IV (color); *Art and Archæology*, VI (1917), pp. 229-234; *A.J.A.*, XXII (1918), p. 214.

attracted Polygnotos. The conception is brutally Etruscan (Fig. 431), so also the strident polychromy, consisting largely of red, yellow, and blue. There is no beauty in the monument, which probably echoes Polygnotan paintings and which may be dated near the end of the Fourth Century or in the early Third.

There must have been a vast amount of painted terra cotta decoration in Etruria from the Sixth to the Third Century, as Pliny intimates and as excavations are proving. The recently discovered Apollo at Veii is a fine example of Etruscan work in painted clay from the Sixth Century. The flesh is reddish brown, the garment yellow, with added details in purplish black. Many antefixes from Etruscan temples, now in the Villa Giulia, give a slight idea of the extensive use of painted terra cotta among these peoples.[38a]

We have not spoken of the colors used by the Etruscan. They were mainly earth colors—several yellows, light red, and purplish red; blue made from copper ore, and a carbon black. The yellow ochers were sometimes roasted to obtain red. Purplish red seems to be a variety of hæmatite.[39] Green, which was sparingly used, was probably a mixture of yellow and blue. The figure designs were usually arranged in friezes, the remainder of the wall being marked off according to its architectural structure. Very often, a wave pattern decorated the bottom of the wall, while an ivy or myrtle pattern corresponded to the cornice above. In the pediment, animal patterns frequently occurred, especially in the earlier epoch. These were later replaced by human figures. Bands of color were used above and below the main frieze, usually red, black, and yellow. The clay plaques from Cære show the divisions of the wall very clearly; they have orthostates in color below the frieze.

The technique of the paintings seems to have been *al fresco*. Weege, in his recent publication, champions this view, set forth earlier by Donner and Martha. Some use of distemper appears to be vouched for in the Tomba del Barone and it may be that in the majority of tombs details were added in this technique. Duell thinks that the spreading of colors in the Tomba del Barone is due to the coarse *intonaco* used and its thin application over the rock. He believes that the colors were mixed with lime water and applied *al fresco secco*. Because the plaster was poor and the stone porous, they were absorbed. The evidence seems to indicate that the paintings were sometimes applied to the bare walls of the tombs; often they were placed on a thin layer of plaster. Here the technique was *al fresco*. Pfuhl in his recent work seems to favor the distemper process but this is not the generally accepted view. The latest investigation of the Tomba del Triclinio by Duell confirms earlier research and indicates that the colors were incorporated with the layer of lime plaster.

[38a] G. Q. Giglioli, *Ant. Denk.*, III (1926), Pls. 45-55, Pls. 52-55 (color). See A. della Seta, *Museo di Villa Giulia, Roma,* 1918, I, for fictile decoration.

[39] For an authoritative account of the pigments used in the Tomba del Triclinio at Corneto, see especially Prentice Duell, *Mem. of the Amer. Acad. in Rome,* VI (1927), pp. 61 ff.

The technical details of the painting were much the same for the various tombs.[40] After the lime plaster of the wall had been prepared and cartoons of the design were at hand, the horizontal lines marking off the divisions of the wall were incised with a stilus. Guiding lines—both horizontal and vertical—were also incised for the main frieze. These were to regulate the arrangement of the figures over the surface. After this was done, the complete decoration was incised in the plaster of the wall. A coat of yellow paint was then used to cover the wall. The incised lines, visible beneath this coat, were covered over with a light red pigment put on with a brush. The wall was thus decorated with the complete design in outline form, executed in red lines. After this, the various colors were put on *en bloc* within the outlines in solid silhouette—garments, nude parts, furniture, etc. The last detail was the drawing in in black line of the major part of the decoration. The original incisions and the red outlines were thus for the most part covered by the final processes, although the black outlines did not always follow the preliminary drawing in red. These red outlines, so clearly visible today in the Tomba del Triclinio beneath the supposedly transparent garments, were, in Duell's opinion, probably not seen originally. The yellow and blue of the garment have deteriorated; the more permanent red outlines have remained. The appearance of transparency, which we have today, did not exist originally. No traces of the human figure are seen beneath red garments which are better preserved, because of the permanency of the color.

We have followed the course of Etruscan painting from its beginnings in the Seventh and Sixth Centuries, to its decline in the Third and Second Centuries. It shows great dependence on foreign models throughout, following first the lead of Oriental art and copying models found in tapestries, ivory, and metal from the Mediterranean. Phœnicia and Crete influenced the early period. Later, when Ionian wares began to make their way into Etruria, Ionic art won the upper hand. During both of these periods, it is possible not only that Etruscan artists practiced their craft in Etruria but that rich Etruscans may have brought in foreign artists to decorate their tombs. We know from Pliny that there was a migration of foreign artists to Etruria from Corinth,[41] and Ionia probably also contributed its quota. During the period when Ionic art was strongly influential, there developed a native bent toward realism. This seemed for a time likely to produce original Etruscan creations—for example,

---

[40] I have taken my account of the colors and the technical details from the work of Prentice Duell, *op. cit.*, pp. 47 ff. This method is certain only for the Tomba del Triclinio at Corneto, but as the incised outlines are found in the Tomba della Pulcella and elsewhere and a similar technique is observable in South Italian Tombs, we may conclude that the tombs had certain common characteristics in this respect and probably did not vary greatly. We have seen that the artist of the Tomba del Barone was an experimenter but he was apparently an exception.

[41] Pliny, *N.H.*, 35, 152.

in the Tomb of Hunting and Fishing—but this tendency very soon disappeared and Attic art won the ascendency.

The work of the Etruscans is thus seen to be a borrowed art and this accounts for some of its most glaring defects—misunderstanding of what was being copied, monotony, and lack of spontaneity. The decorators who painted the Etruscan tombs were not always born artists with an irrepressible desire to express their emotions and ideas; they were painters schooled in and dependent on the art of other peoples, adapting it to their own ends. As a result, the paintings are more often interesting for the light which they shed on Etruscan customs and beliefs than they are for their artistic merit. At times their close adherence to Greek models may conjure up the glory of the lost art of painting in Greek lands in the Fifth and Fourth Centuries. At times, there is a real joy in the dance, in scenes of hunting and fishing, or in the drawing of some charming head or figure. But, in general, the impression left behind by most Etruscan paintings is that of sluggish loungers at luxurious banquets; of fat and flabby wrestlers and boxers at games. There is a certain delight in the ugly and brutal, and even in the sinister. Often we are aware of exquisite beauty of line in the drawings and the compositions usually give pleasure, but there is nothing subtle about the work of the Etruscan and too often he betrays a wretched lack of taste. What he loved most was an orgy of color. He employed his pigments decoratively, for the most part, against a yellow ground. With the means at his command, however, and with a borrowed art as a basis, he is to be commended for what he accomplished. Perhaps his greatest achievement was the reflection of Etruscan life which he produced. If Etruscan life was brutal and cruel, it is not surprising that this side should be prominent in their paintings. We cannot forget the citizens of Cære, who, although distinguished for their sense of justice and their courage, stoned their Phocæan captives to death;[42] or Mezentius, their king, who tied the dead and living captives together to rot side by side. If the Etruscans were given to luxurious feasting and much drinking, that too should occasion no surprise when presented in their tombs. The practice of women reclining at banquets on the same couches with men which caused the Greeks to criticize the Etruscans for their immorality,[43] probably also has a sufficient basis of truth; but, in general, women of good birth and breeding seem—from the paintings at least—to sit upright at the symposia. Doubtless the life of the Etruscans had about it much sensuousness and luxury which were decidedly antagonistic to the severe standards of the early Romans and which, therefore, frequently called forth bitter criticism. But Rome in the end took much from her and probably also some of her corruption.

The problem of dating the tombs has always been difficult because they were early

[42] Hdt., I, 167; Poulsen, *op. cit.*, p. 52.
[43] Athen., XII, 517; IV, 153; Dionys. Hal., IX, 16.

despoiled of their contents. The dating rests in general on stylistic grounds—comparison with Orientalizing wares, Cæretan hydriæ, Ionic vases, black-figured vases, and the vases of both the early and the late severe styles, such as those of Euphronios and his followers. Some paintings are to be dated after the introduction of chiaroscuro in Greece. The great age is the archaic period and the real bloom was over by 450 B.C. In all, there were about one hundred years of splendor in Etruscan art.

## SOUTH ITALIAN PAINTING

DURING the Fifth and Fourth Centuries when Etruscan power was waning, the Oscans of Southern Italy began to assume prominence. They occupied towns of importance in Campania at Cumæ, Nola, and Capua; in Lucania, at Pæstum, the ancient Poseidonia; in Samnium, and also in Apulia, at Ruvo (Fig. 432). We do not know much about these people. They fought against Rome in the Samnite wars and were worthy enemies. They passed on to Rome certain institutions, such as gladiatorial combats and Atellan farces, but our ideas of their civilization are somewhat vague. Their tomb-paintings are of especial interest to us because they bring the people before us as they were in life—departing for and returning from battle; engaged in banquets, dancing, and busied with various pleasures. Sometimes a woman is pictured at her toilet, or we see the dead laid out on a funeral bier.

The Oscans were doubtless led by Etruscan example to use painted hypogæa for their dead. There are almost no tombs of this character in Greece, but they were common in Italy on Etruscan sites. Although many Etruscan tombs are visible and accessible today, the Oscan examples have been destroyed and of the fifty excavated we have frescoes from about twenty-six in various museums of Southern Italy. Most of this number are in Capua. Some of the lost paintings have also been preserved in drawings.

The frescoes in question belong for the most part to the Fourth Century, but there are a few examples from the Fifth. The one which can be most certainly dated is a lost fresco from Capua,—No. 15—which represented two men at draughts, with a seated boy at the right and a nude youth standing at the left.[44] In this tomb was found an amphora with a representation of Achilles and Penthesileia, dating between 450 and 440 B.C. (Fig. 361). This places the fresco somewhat after the reputed founding of Capua by the Etruscans—after 473 B.C. The matter of dating the various frescoes is dependent upon objects discovered within the tombs and upon stylistic criteria. With regard to the question of style, Helbig has pointed out that, although in the beginning Campanian painting shows Greek spirit, combined with Italian national art, later, the national spirit triumphs and emancipates itself from the Greek.[45]

[44] F. Weege, "Oskische Grabmalerei," *Jahr.*, 24 (1909), p. 108, Fig. 4.
[45] W. Helbig, *Annali dell'Instituto*, 37 (1865), pp. 282, 288.

On stylistic grounds, a few frescoes may perhaps be assigned to the Fifth Century. Among these, is one from Nola representing a woman seated on a throne (Fig. 433). The figure is severely drawn in dark brown outlines. She wears a white garment, a red cap decorated with a border of meanders and rosettes, and a white veil. Her hair and the folds of her costume are brown. In one hand, she holds a red pomegranate; in the other, a bluish bunch of branches, possibly myrtle. The simplicity of style and the severity of the profile would appear to place the fresco in the Fifth Century. Her dignity is such that she has on occasion merited the name of Kore.[46]

A group of women dancing and led by a choregos also seems early and may belong to the Fifth Century (Fig. 434). It came from a tufa grave at Ruvo, the long sides of which were decorated with eighteen women led by a citharœde, the short sides by nine women under the conduct of a choregos. The colors are very vivid. Against a yellow ground, the gaily hued garments of the figures stand out sharply. Sometimes they wear long chitons of blue, and crimson headcoverings with yellow borders. The garments vary in color, but red, dark blue, yellow, black, and white alternate to form rich contrasts. The arms of the women are interwoven in the rhythmic movement of the dance. The youths are garbed in white garments with red borders and wear red girdles and shoes. Above the painting is a black stripe and a red. The regular profiles and severe style again suggest the Fifth Century and Greek influence.

Weege inclines also to date in the Fifth Century some paintings from Pæstum which have been lost and which now exist only in inadequate drawings. To judge from the drawings, which when compared exhibit many divergencies, the paintings represented a procession. This consisted first of all of a man, perhaps a charioteer, followed by two women in a chariot. Behind these was a nude youth on horse, bearing a severely wounded comrade on his back. A man with two lances walked beside the horse and at least three other persons followed. The most significant group in the composition is the one depicting the return of the nude horseman with his wounded companion (Fig. 435). We can gain little idea of the original from these drawings. Abeken remarks that they show less Greek spirit than Italian character but we are unable to form an adequate judgment from our evidence. The beauty of the central group is apparent in all of the copies. The limp form of the wounded warrior is rendered with great feeling.

Other paintings from Pæstum may belong to the early Lucanian period of this city (Fig. 436). Here a procession of warriors is seen, some of whom seem to be welcomed home. At the left, a woman in a yellow chiton and red mantle holds out a

[46] L. Farnell, *Cults of the Greek States,* III (1907), Pl. XI; *cf. A.Z.,* VIII (1850), p. 146, Pl. XIV. See Weege, *op. cit.,* p. 130. He is uncertain whether the fresco belongs in the Fifth or the Fourth Century.

bucchero cup to a warrior richly equipped with a red garment, a golden girdle, cuirass, greaves, and a feathered helmet. He carries a lance with trophies hung at the end—a fringed red, blue, and white mantle and a golden girdle. He is followed by a companion with similar armor who wears a gray costume with a red border and rests his right hand on a shield with a blue ground. A second warrior on horse, garbed in a red costume with a blue border, and a man in a white mantle complete the scene. Below the red ground line is a rich wave pattern in blue against the yellow wall.

On the right side of the tomb, two other groups occur—a bearded man on horse with a second horse beside him, and a youthful rider welcomed home by a woman (Fig. 437). The figures are drawn with spirit. The chestnut-colored horses are particularly well executed. The red costume of the youth with its blue border and the white garments of the other figures with red patterns add liveliness to the color scheme. Above are decorative borders of meanders and rosettes in red, blue, and white. The costumes and armor are Oscan but the paintings are Greek in spirit. The motive of offering a cup to a returning hero is typically Greek.

A large number of important Oscan paintings of national stamp are to be dated in the Fourth Century. They often depict warriors or genre scenes. In Figure 438, we have a proud Oscan knight, sitting erect on his horse—a trim figure elaborately costumed and decked out in rich armor. He wears a white garment and a golden girdle decorated with red bands and white bosses. A mantle with yellow, red, and gray stripes hangs down his back. His head is adorned by a red-crested, golden helmet with cheek pieces. His horse is decorated with splendid trappings—yellow feathers, a gold nose piece, and two red bands with golden ornaments. The pride, the quiet dignity, and high spirit of the Oscan race are all embodied in this fresco. The colors are the usual vivid reds, yellow, blue, brown, black, white, and gray.

Other frescoes from this period include the fragment in Figure 439a, which belongs to a painting with figures of almost life size. It pictures a woman with a box in her left hand and a flower in the right. She is dressed in a brownish red garment with a broad stripe down the center and wears a black and red cap from which hangs a veil. Red occurs on the cheeks. Similar in character is a second painting in Dresden (Fig. 439b). Here, the woman holds a dove in one hand and a rose in the other. Before her stands a maid-servant with a bucchero cup. We probably have portraits of the dead in the more important figures of these frescoes. They possess little if any artistic merit.

Another genre scene representing a seated woman with a mirror in her hand and a servant girl with a basket standing before her may belong in the same period (Fig. 440). The fresco comes from Cumæ and shows how the paintings were arranged on the wall surface. The lower part of the wall was covered with red, forming a kind of socle. Above this, separated by a wave pattern, came the main part of the figure painting. The background was a creamy yellow. Still higher, was a fourth section in the ground color of the wall. The predominant colors are red, yellow, black, and white. The figures extended over the socle and the intermediate part of the wall instead of being confined to the central frieze.

Shortly after 300 B.C., the fresco which depicts two warriors in combat may be dated (Fig. 441). The painting is wholly Oscan in subject matter and spirit, and is far different in character from our earliest examples dating from the Fifth Century. In this case we see two grim fighters dressed in short red and blue striped chitons with red neck and arm bands. They carry round, yellow shields with red designs in the center and wear gold greaves and helmets with cheek pieces. Both are severely wounded in the legs and the pain suffered is indicated by their tightly drawn lips. This is doubtless a representation of a gladiatorial combat. We know that these were common in Campania and that they came to Etruria from this source. The scene is taken from life and is filled with stern realism.

We have said little of the technique of South Italian paintings. The tombs were hewn in the rock or constructed of great square blocks of tufa, peperino, or travertine, with roof beams set against one another and resting on the side walls. They were erected for Oscans of distinction.[46a]

The interior was carefully prepared for the paintings, which were executed in fresco. A layer of white or yellow plaster, sometimes forty millimeters thick, was first placed over the entire surface except the ceiling, which was left undecorated. This practice contrasts strongly with the elaborately adorned ceilings of rich Etruscan tombs. About one-third of the wall below was often reserved in red, forming a sort of baseboard. Above this, very often came a red stripe which marked off the second third of the wall. This was usually adorned with figure decoration in frieze arrangement. Still higher was a black and a red line, marking the top section of the wall. Sometimes, the lower section was separated from the main frieze by a wave pattern between two lines; the upper section by a meander and rosette device. From these upper lines or from the meander and rosette patterns which usurped their place, fillets, drinking-cups, garlands, and other objects were sometimes suspended, as if from nails. The place of honor in the paintings was opposite the entrance and here the portrait of the dead usually occurred.

The figures were outlined with a brush in yellow on the surface prepared for the fresco. The outlines were then filled in. In the case of men a red color was employed for the flesh; in that of women, the wall ground was used to render flesh tones and red was added for the cheeks, lips, and eyelids. The contours were next drawn in in black lines which often disregarded the yellow sketch, so that both may be seen on occasion. The colors used were red, black, which is often gone; yellow, especially

[46a] For technical details, see Weege, *op. cit.*, pp. 126 ff.

for objects of gold; gray, often for silver; blue, sometimes for metal; red, for neck-
laces, garlands, and garments. True green is not employed but blue takes its place.

The majority of paintings which show the beard are to be dated before or about
the middle of the Fourth Century, inasmuch as the beard was out of fashion in the
age of Alexander. Furthermore, pure profiles are usually to be dated earlier than
three-quarter attempts. The paintings are of greater interest for what they tell us
of the Oscan people than for any significant contribution to art. Nor are we able to
disentangle very successfully Etruscan and Greek influences, though it is obvious
that both peoples had some effect on these monuments.

# IX

# GREECE: THE PAINTING OF THE FOURTH CENTURY

THE technical skill attained by Greek painters in the Fourth Century was so superior to what had been achieved by the masters of the Fifth, that we are accustomed to place the height of the art in the days of Apelles. This is justified by what we know but we must not forget that the way to this supremacy had been prepared by Apollodoros and his successors and that the art of the Fourth Century rested upon Fifth Century foundations.

As far as remains or copies of Fourth Century painting are concerned, our position is no better than it was in the preceding era. Furthermore, we no longer have so valuable a guide in Greek vases, inasmuch as the ways of the two arts may be said to have parted by the close of the Fifth Century. The Greek vase-painter was unable to follow the course of the major art in its developed use of light and shadow, perspective and color effects. In addition to this, the blow dealt Athens by the Peloponnesian War seems to have crippled her ceramic industry and power of production. To be sure, we have a number of Athenian, Kertch, South Italian, Bœotian, and white-ground vases, which show us the use of pictorial innovations, but, in general, vase-painting in this period is far less important as a reflection of monumental painting and as an index to artistic power in drawing and composition than we find it a century earlier. Other works help us little more: Etruscan mirrors, wooden sarcophagi, and grave-stelæ offer but a pale reflection of the original greatness of Fourth Century painting. Our best aid is to be found in Pompeian wall-painting, mosaics, and a few marble panels.

Perhaps we shall gain a clearer idea of the artistic achievement of this age if we begin with some of the available literary evidence and follow it with a discussion of the actual remains which elucidate this material. The important difference between the painting of the Fifth and Fourth Centuries lay in the rise of significant schools.

There were great centers of pictorial art in the Sixth and Fifth Centuries, such as the ones at Sikyon, or Athens, but we do not hear of courses of instruction under prominent teachers and systems and rules of guidance laid down for the neophyte and for the talented artist. In the Fourth Century there was certainly one great school at Sikyon which attracted painters like Apelles, and there were apparently others at Thebes and at Athens.

The most important teacher in the Academy at Sikyon was Pamphilos. His master was Eupompos, but we know little of the older instructor beyond certain statements of Pliny. He tells us that Eupompos was a contemporary of Parrhasios and Timanthes and a rival of Zeuxis, and that he painted a victor in an athletic contest holding a palm.[1] The type created by him is probably traceable in a group of monuments which depict a youth of Polykleitan type holding a palm in his left hand and raising a crown to his head with his right. A reflection of this painting may perhaps be seen in an old fresco in the Palazzo Rospigliosi at Rome (Fig. 442). Eupompos worked at Sikyon when the sculptor Polykleitos was at the end of his career and when the latter's pupils were beginning to migrate to Sikyon. Perhaps his "Victor" formed a canon for the athletic type in painting as Polykleitos' Doryphoros had done in sculpture. In any case, Eupompos represents in painting the same tendency found in sculpture in the work of Polykleitos. His achievements were so significant, according to Pliny, that from his time the Sikyonian school of painting existed beside the Asiatic school of Zeuxis[1a] and Parrhasios and the Helladic of Polygnotos and Mikon. In other words, after Eupompos, there was an Ionian, an Attic, and a Sikyonian school of painting. He claimed to follow no teacher but only nature.

The Macedonian Pamphilos, a student of Eupompos, is largely known to posterity because of his great pupils, Apelles, Melanthios, and Pausias. Some of his fame, however, rested on the fact that he caused drawing and painting to be introduced into the schools of Greece as a subject to be taught to free-born boys.[2] The training gained under Pamphilos included the study of arithmetic, geometry, optics, color effects—in fact, everything in the art of painting which could be taught. The emphasis in the school was on *ars*, not *ingenium*. Academic accuracy and perfection were sought after, theories were brought into a system, and an attempt was made to teach the basic laws which govern the art. The master strove for *dispositio* and for *mensura*, rating the study of symmetry and proportion very high. We see that the

---

[1] Pliny, *N.H.*, 35, 64; 75. For the type see Milchhöfer, *Arch. Studien H. Brunn dargebracht*, 1893, p. 62; *cf.* A. Furtwängler, *Masterpieces*, p. 256; W. W. Hyde, *Olympic Victor Monuments*, Washington, 1921, p. 160.

[1a] E. Pfuhl, *Malerei und Zeichnung der Griechen*, 1923, II, 687, finds no reasons for associating Zeuxis with the Asiatic school.

[2] Pliny, *N.H.*, 35, 77.

Sikyonian school excelled in the development of the technical and formal side of painting. Pamphilos was one of the greatest painters of his time because of his adherence to rules.[3] He reduced the technique of painting to a science and artists of ability, like Apelles, considered this training of such value that they were willing to give twelve years of their lives to it. We know practically nothing of the original work created by Pamphilos himself, as we have little more than titles. These include the Herakleidai as suppliants seeking protection in Athens, the victorious Battle of the Athenians at Phlious in 366 B.C., and Odysseus on a raft. A family group from his hand may have been the prototype of farewell scenes on grave-stones, such as the stelæ from Pagasæ.[4]

It was Pausias, one of the pupils of Pamphilos, who developed to a high degree of perfection the encaustic technique which he had learned from his old teacher.[5] We are not absolutely certain how this process was employed but we know that the painting was done with heated wax on wooden or marble panels. We find statements about the use of this method in the days of Polygnotos but it remained for Pausias to make it famous. He employed it especially in the coffers of ceilings. Here, he painted small figures—pictures of boys and, in all probability, the little Erotes which were the forerunners of the *Amoretti* found in Alexandrian and Pompeian painting. His ceilings must have required a knowledge of optics. Reminiscences of this kind of work may perhaps be seen today in the painted and stucco decoration of certain late tombs on the Via Latina in Rome.

There are several theories as to how wax was applied on surfaces to be decorated when the encaustic technique was used. The important element was heat and the process was not so much one of "burning in" the design, as of employing warmth. The method varied with the material on which the painting was executed and with the climate of the country. According to Pliny, three processes seem to have been employed: painting with wax by means of a metal *cauterium,* or spoon-like instrument; painting with the aid of a *cestrum,* or sharp pointed tool, which was probably a burin and incised the design on ivory or marble; and painting with a brush. Wax painting probably originated in Egypt, as it seems best suited to a warm climate and, if heat was not present, it had to be produced. In Egypt there was no difficulty in keeping wax mixed with powdered colors in a softened condition. The danger would rather be in the opposite direction. The wax might be applied in a fluid state with a

[3] Quint., *Inst. Or.,* XII, 10, 6.  [4] A. Reinach, *Recueil Milliet,* 1921, I, 256, n. 2.
[5] Pliny, *N.H.,* 35, 123. For the technical processes employed, see Pliny, *ib.,* 35, 149; *Encausto pingendi duo fuere antiquitus genera, cera et in ebore cestro, id est, vericulo, donec classes pingi cœpere. Hoc tertium accessit resolutis igni ceris penicillo utendi, quæ pictura navibus nec sole nec sale ventisque corrumpitur.* The best explanation of these three processes is given by Laurie, *Greek and Roman Methods of Painting,* Cambridge, 1910, pp. 37 ff. *Cf.* esp. pp. 57 ff., p. 51, n. 1; p. 60. *Cf.* Pliny, 35, 147, and table of contents, Bk. XXXV.

brush or might be worked with a heated *cauterium* when it was being applied. This instrument was probably often used for retouching after the colored wax laid on with the brush had grown cold.

As one proceeded farther north, the difficulty of keeping the wax soft would increase. At St. Médard, a bronze box of several compartments was found with silver lids perforated with square holes. It was doubtless filled with charcoal for melting the colors and for heating the *cauteria,* examples of which were found here. It may also have served to keep the panel warm.

How the *cestrum* was employed is not clear. Probably it served merely as a burin to engrave the design. After the incision, the painting may have been executed in a wax tempera—and the colors fused by means of heat. The various methods seem then to be: (1) painting on wood or marble with a *cauterium,* keeping the panel and metal instrument heated. With this hot metal tool the colored sticks or cakes of wax could be moulded on the panel into the desired picture. This technique produced a mosaic-like surface of color in relief. (2) Painting on ivory or marble with the help of a *cestrum,* or sharp pointed implement, which incised the design that was later to be filled in with color and fused with heated tools. (3) Painting on each of these materials or on canvas with a brush dipped in fluid wax. This latter process with the brush was employed for larger surfaces such as the painting of ships and certainly for backgrounds, as in the case of the Fayûm portraits. We shall return to these methods later in our discussion of Græco-Roman painting. The general effect produced by wax painting, especially when the *cauterium* was used, must have approximated modern results in oil. The coloring was more brilliant and possessed greater richness and depth because of the uneven surfaces and the juxtaposition of various colors. Blue played a rôle here, and green and red in various shades. The process, however, was a laborious one and for this reason was usually confined to small pictures. Which one of these processes was employed by Pausias is not known. Doubtless he made use of the brush and *cauterium* on tablets of wood or marble. Earlier examples of painting on marble, however, reveal the presence of the *cestrum.*

Pausias was not only proficient in the encaustic technique, but he seems as well to have painted large pictures and to have been skilful in the use of perspective and in modeling his figures. Pliny tells us that he painted a "Sacrifice" of some oxen in which "wishing to display an ox's length of body, he painted a front and not a side view of the animal and yet contrived to show its size." Instead of putting the high lights in white and the less salient parts in dark color, he painted the animal entirely in black and "gave substance to the shadow out of the shadow itself, showing great art in giving all his figures full relief upon the flat surface and in indicating their form when foreshortened."[6] This was simply a feat in modeling without the use of

[6] Pliny, *N.H.,* 35, 126. The translation is quoted from Jex-Blake, Sellers. *Cf.* 21, 4; Paus., II, 27, 3.

extraneous colors. This painting was displayed at Rome in the Portico of Pompey and may have influenced later works of art. A mosaic recently found by Shear at Corinth, in which the modeling is done in the local colors, seems to reflect his art.[7] The foreshortening of the ox in back view may also have been derived from Pausias. The subject matter is known to us from Græco-Roman reliefs, such as those of the Ara Pacis and the Boscoreale cups. Pausias also painted a famous picture of Methe or "Drunkenness," in the Tholos at Epidauros. She was shown drinking from a crystal cup and her face was seen through the bottom of the glass. All of these paintings give evidence of remarkable technical progress. Much of Pausias' strength must have lain in chiaroscuro and rich coloring. It is probable also that he was the first painter of genre scenes. His "Wreath-Maker," for which his beloved Glykera was the model, may be reflected, as Reinach suggests, in the "Psyches" of Pompeii or remotely in the "Flora" from Stabiæ (Plate I). The extensive use of garlands found in Græco-Roman reliefs and on painted and sculptured monuments from Alexandria may have had its origin in the painting of this artist.[8] He excelled in small pictures and oftentimes chose to paint flowers and children. He was famous for his obscene pictures and paintings of hetæræ. The precious and mannered art of the Hellenistic age is believed by some scholars to have originated with him. He must have been a facile painter. A panel, depicting a child, executed in one day, won the title, "Hemeresios," "Day's Work."

Of Melanthios we know little. He wrote on painting, as Pamphilos had done before him, was superior to Apelles in composition, painted with the aid of Apelles the Sikyonian tyrant Aristratos beside a chariot of Victory, and appears to have succeeded Pamphilos as the head of the Sikyonian school.[9] His writings dealt especially with symmetry.

The most famous student in the Sikyonian school, and indeed the most famous painter of the Fourth Century was the Ionian Apelles. He was probably born at Kolophon about 370 B.C., and studied at nearby Ephesos, where he was given citizenship. For this reason, he was sometimes called an Ephesian.[10] He was at the height of his power between 332 and 329 B.C., "contributing more to painting than all the other painters put together."

Of this inimitable master no work is preserved nor have we a copy of any known

[7] T. L. Shear, A.J.A., 29 (1925), pp. 391 ff., Fig. 9.

[8] E. Breccia, Alexandrea ad Ægyptum, guide de la ville ancienne et moderne et du musée gréco-romain, Bergamo, 1914, p. 251; Fig. 103, p. 249; Fig. 105, p. 252. Musée égyptien, III, 1915; cf. Mus. Borb., IV, Pl. 47; Niccolini, Domus Vettiorum.

[9] Quint., Inst. Or., XII, 10, 6; Pliny, N.H., 35, 80; Vitr., VII, Præf., 14 (Melampus or Melanthius); Diog. Laert., IV, III, 18; Plut., Arat., 12-13.

[10] Suidas, s.v. 'Απελλῆς (Kolophon); Strabo, XIV, 642 (Ephesos); Pliny, N.H., 35, 79 ff. (Kos).

painting from his hand.[11] His fame, which is vouched for in antiquity, continued throughout the Renaissance. He was especially known as the painter of "Calumny" and of "Aphrodite Rising from the Sea." He was also the portrait painter of Philip and Alexander. It is difficult to disentangle from the stories and proverbs of antiquity a clear idea of the man and his work. He seems to have combined the freshness, grace, and charm of Ionia with a practical Dorian training in the school of Pamphilos at Sikyon. His artistic temperament thereby gained a singularly happy balance and the great appeal which his works aroused may have been due in large measure to this fortunate combination.

Apelles was a much-traveled, cosmopolitan artist. We find him living his early life in Ionia, studying at Sikyon, painting at Kos his famous Aphrodite, visiting Protogenes in Rhodes, spending much of his time at the court of Philip of Macedon, and incurring the hatred of the painter Antiphilos and the enmity of Ptolemy at the latter's court in Alexandria.

The most famous painting by Apelles was an Aphrodite executed for the Temple of Asklepios at Kos. He was apparently inspired by a living model here, either Phryne or Pankaspe. The painting represented the goddess emerging from the waves and pressing the sea-foam from her dripping hair. It aroused tremendous admiration in antiquity and was finally brought by Augustus to Rome and placed in the Temple of the Divine Julius in the Forum. Tradition says that Apelles was making a second Aphrodite at Kos at the time of his death. Antiquity praised the flesh tones of the nude Aphrodite and the beauty of the figure, the lower part of which no one could restore when it was damaged. It commended the dripping foam and the purple waves.[12] The fame of this painting may perhaps have influenced Botticelli's "Birth of Venus" in the Uffizi at Florence. It inspired several works of sculpture in antiquity which preserve the type, notably a torso in the Louvre.[13]

The portraits by Apelles also ranked high among the ancients. One of these depicted Alexander in a triumphal chariot and War with his hands bound behind his back. An equestrian portrait of Alexander won renown as well, because the animal was so realistically rendered that other horses neighed at it.[14] Of Antigonos he made a famous profile likeness concealing the King's blindness,[15] while his family group of Archelaos with his wife and daughter is one of the earliest known to us.[16]

[11] Most scholars do not accept the theory of Six that the type of Herakles found in the painting in Naples which represents Herakles finding Telephos may go back to a work executed by Apelles at Pergamon. Cf. Jahr., 20 (1905), pp. 169 ff.

[12] Pliny, N.H., 35, 91; Anthol. Pal. XVI, 178-182; Cic., De Nat. Deor., I, 27, 75.

[13] The Venus Anadyomene in the Vatican may go back to this type. Cf. Ch. Picard, La sculpture antique, 1926, II, Fig. 78.

[14] Ælian, V.H., II, 3; Pliny, N.H., 35, 95.

[15] Pliny, N.H., 35, 90; Quint., Inst. Or., II, 13, 12.          [16] Pliny, N.H., 35, 96.

Among mythological paintings, after his Aphrodite, Artemis leading a band of maidens who were sacrificing was well known. His Herakles was also famous. Although seen in back view, it "seemed not only to suggest but actually to give the face."[17] Apelles had a predilection for "unpaintable" subjects, such as a Thunderstorm, with *Astrapé,* "Lightning"; *Bronté,* "Thunder"; and *Keraunobolia,* "Thunderbolt." These may have formed part of a painting embodying the legend of Semele. So renowned was his "Calumny" because of Lucian's description of it that more than twenty paraphrases are known since antiquity.[18] Apelles painted it to express his rage at Antiphilos, a rival painter who had slandered him to King Ptolemy. He was falsely accused of having aided Theodotos of Tyre in a conspiracy against the Egyptian ruler. The account by Lucian runs as follows: "On the right sits a man with very large ears, almost like those of Midas, extending his hand to Slander while she is still at some distance from him. Near him, on one side, stand two women— Ignorance, I think, and Suspicion. On the other side, Slander is coming up, a woman beautiful beyond measure, but full of passion and excitement, evincing as she does fury and wrath by carrying in her left hand a blazing torch and with the other dragging by the hair a young man who stretches out his hands to heaven and calls the gods to witness his innocence. She is conducted by a pale ugly man who has a piercing eye and looks as if he had wasted away in long illness; he may be supposed to be Envy. Besides, there are two women in attendance on Slander, egging her on, tiring her, and tricking her out. According to the interpretation of them given me by the guide to the picture, one was Treachery, the other, Deceit. They were followed by a woman dressed in deep mourning, with black clothes all in tatters—Repentance, I think her name was. At all events, she was turning back with tears in her eyes and casting a stealthy glance, full of shame, at Truth, who was approaching."

This description inspired Botticelli's painting of "Calumny" in the Uffizi at Florence (Fig. 443) and led Dürer to attempt a similar theme.[18a]

Our actual knowledge of Apelles and the character of his painting is thus seen to be rather meager. Only the titles and descriptions of some thirty works are left us. Our imagination is aroused by the form of Aphrodite shimmering through the seafoam and by the majesty of Alexander who had bound even War in fetters. Apelles

[17] Pliny, *N.H.,* 35, 94. *Cf.* Six, *Jahr.,* 20 (1905), pp. 169 ff.

[18] Lucian, *Calumny,* 2-5. The translation quoted is by A. M. Harmon, *Lucian,* 1913, I, 365, Loeb Series; *cf. Burlington Magazine,* XXIX (1916), pp. 183 ff. (Breu). R. Förster, *Die Verleumdung des Apelles in der Renaissance, Jahr. der Kgl. Preuss. Kunstsamml.,* VIII (1887), pp. 29 ff.; 89 ff.; XV (1894), pp. 27 ff.; H. P. Horne, *Sandro Botticelli,* London, 1908, p. 258. Lucian has obviously confused Theodotos of Tyre with someone else. The conspiracy of Theodotos dated in 219 B.C.

[18a] One of the painted reliefs on the throne in Botticelli's picture reproduced the Centaur Family of Zeuxis.

must have achieved great refinement in the matter of light and shade and must have displayed in his work a real feeling for values. He painted Alexander as Zeus, with a thunderbolt which appeared to project from his hand and which gave to the face and breast of the conqueror a somber hue. Plutarch says that he did not paint the flesh of Alexander its natural color, but darker and browner. Probably he was an adept in tone painting and may have achieved something similar to Rembrandt's picture of his brother with the golden helmet.[19] The painting of Alexander as Zeus is reflected in a gem of the Hellenistic period in Petrograd.[20]

If we try to discover the secret of this master's greatness, we must admit that it probably lay first of all in his own genius which gave rise to the particular grace that he claimed characterized his work. In addition to this, he must have been "a master of perfect design and marvelous modeling." He probably employed chiaroscuro much in the manner of Rembrandt. His groups and processions seem to have included few individuals but he was probably very clever in arranging them in perspective. Pliny says he was a "Four-Color" painter using for black a burned ivory.[21] There is little doubt, however, that he did not always limit himself to such a narrow palette. His works were executed on panels in the tempera technique. Furthermore, he employed a dark, transparent glaze over his paintings, the secret of which was his own. This lent depth and sobriety to the colors, softening their brilliance and protecting the works themselves.[22]

It is almost impossible to picture to ourselves a work of Apelles or to gain any real idea of his composition, coloring, or chiaroscuro. All that we can do after reading descriptions of his paintings is to examine a few Pompeian wall-paintings, the great Alexander Mosaic, and vases here and there, trying to form some estimate of his achievement. This can never be very satisfactory but we shall turn to these after a consideration of a few other painters of this group and of the contemporary Theban-Attic school. The pupils of Apelles may indeed have painted the panels of the funeral chariot of Alexander.[23] Alexander was represented seated in a chariot, surrounded by Macedonian and Persian troops with a bodyguard preceding.[23a] One panel depicted the elephants which came behind the escort; the third was decorated with cavalry; the fourth with ships of war. Ktesilochos, the best-known pupil of Apelles, liked to paint travesties of myths. One of his works represented Zeus at the birth of Dionysos,

---

[19] Pliny, N.H., 35, 92; Six, Jahr., op. cit., p. 169.

[20] Jahr., IV (1889), p. 69; III, Pl. XI, 26.

[21] Pliny, N.H., 35, 42. Cf. 35, 50; 92.          [22] Pliny, N.H., 35, 97.

[23] K. F. Müller, Der Leichenwagen Alexanders, Leipzig, 1905; Diod., 18, 26-27. J. Six, Deutsche Literaturzeitung, 26 (1905), pp. 1266 ff., Rec. Müller; E. Petersen, N.J., 15 (1905), pp. 698 ff.; H. Bulle, Jahr., 21 (1906), pp. 52 ff.; W. Helbig, Untersuchungen, p. 45.

[23a] U. von Wilamowitz, Jahr., 20 (1905), p. 105, takes these to be reliefs. Cf. A. Reinach, op. cit., p. 361, n. 5.

wearing a woman's hat and groaning painfully. Nikophanes was noted for pictures of courtesans and was considered among the most eminent artists of his time. He followed Polygnotos in painting Oknos or Sloth.[24]

The most prominent rival of Apelles was Protogenes, who came from Kaunos, a subject city of Rhodes, in Caria.[25] Apelles granted this master equality with himself in execution but criticized his elaboration and his labored efforts. Protogenes was apparently poor and painted ships for a long time at Rhodes. Later, he executed in the Propylæa at Athens his "Paralos" regarded by some as a personification of the Attic shore, and "Ammonias." These may be the patron heroes of the holy state triremes. He apparently signed this work with some tiny ships, pointing to his humble beginnings. His leading work was called "Ialysos," after the hero who founded the city of that name in Rhodes. On this painting he worked for seven years. Ialysos was represented as a hunter with a dog running beside him. When Protogenes was unsuccessful in painting foam on the dog's mouth, finally, in a rage, he threw a sponge at the panel and successfully accomplished his aim. The work would therefore seem to have been executed in tempera with a binding medium of egg or glue, but the story cannot be taken too seriously since it is told of other painters. He painted this picture in four coats for the sake of protection. Among other works from his hand was a satyr resting against a column—a motive which recalls the Faun of Praxiteles. In addition, he painted the mother of Aristotle, King Alexander, an athlete, and several mythological subjects.

The remaining masters of this period are often little more than names. Another prominent figure was Aëtion, who painted the Marriage of Roxana, the Bactrian princess, to Alexander.[26] Lucian's description of this work inspired the painting by Sodoma in the Farnesina and probably a drawing of Raphael's in Windsor Castle. A marriage chamber was shown with the nuptial couch. Roxana was seated with lowered eyes, Alexander standing before her offering her a garland. All about, Loves were smiling, one drawing aside the veil of Roxana, another seizing Alexander and leading him toward the bride. On the other side, Loves played with the armor of the king. Nearby stood Hephaistion with the marriage torch, leaning against Hymenaios, a beautiful youth. It is doubtful whether this painting is at all reflected in the Aldobrandini Wedding of the First Century B.C., as some have thought, inasmuch as Aëtion's composition embodies a Hellenistic and playful spirit. It is interesting, however, to see the influence of this painting on later works of art. The Erotes head

[24] Pliny, *N.H.*, 35, 140; 137.

[25] Pliny, *N.H.*, 35, 101. C. Torr, *Class. Rev.*, 1890, p. 232: Protogenes painted votive tablets of ships offered by sailors for deliverance from shipwreck. Cic., *De Nat. Deor.*, III, 37; Juvenal, XII, 27.

[26] Lucian, *Herodotus or Aëtion*, 4-6.

a long list of figures toying with the arms of world conquerors (Pfuhl, *Malerei und Zeichnung der Griechen,* Abb. 664, 668).

A jealous rival of Apelles, who seems to have been a very progressive painter, was Antiphilos of Alexandria. Lucian recounts, as we have seen above, the story of Antiphilos' slander of Apelles to King Ptolemy.[27] It arose from envy and ended, according to the narrative, when Ptolemy gave Antiphilos to Apelles as a slave. The incident was supposed to have caused Apelles to paint his famous "Calumny." Whatever the basis of the story—and it seems to be a false tale—the fact is clear that Antiphilos was the court painter for Ptolemy at this time and resented the intrusion of Apelles.

The accounts which we have of Antiphilos and his work show that he was very much interested in lighting effects, in genre painting which went over into caricature and probably in a new method of illusionistic painting. Antiphilos, in fact, was doubtless a much more vital figure for the progress of the art of painting than the more conservative Apelles. Let us examine the notices about the man and some of the eleven works cited from his hand.

Pliny tells us that Antiphilos was especially commended for a painting of a boy blowing a fire and for the reflection cast by the fire on the room and on the boy's face.[28] Another work portrayed a satyr with a panther-skin shielding his eyes from beams of light.[28a] Effects gained by light greatly interested the artists of this period. In Aëtion's marriage of Roxana with Alexander, use was apparently made of this in the torch borne by Hephaistion no less than in his painting of an old woman carrying lamps.[29]

Another branch of painting which interested Antiphilos was genre painting. One of his compositions represented wool-weaving, with a group of women busily engaged in their tasks. In other words, this artist was the Teniers of the ancients. Among his comic paintings was one of a man called Gryllos in a ridiculous costume. Pliny states that after this time, all such caricatures were called Grylloi. Reflections of work of this nature may be seen in a painting from Herculaneum which caricatures Æneas in flight with his father Anchises and son Ascanius. All three figures are depicted with dog heads or those of baboons[30] (Fig. 444). This fondness for

[27] Lucian, *Calumny,* 2-5; *cf.* Pliny, *N.H.,* 35, 138; 114.

[28] Pliny, *N.H.,* 35, 138.

[28a] Some writers think this gesture refers to a dance called σκώπευμα, Athen., XIV, 629. *Cf.* Photius, *Lex. s.v.*

[29] Pliny, *N.H.,* 35, 78; F. Wickhoff, *Wiener Genesis,* tr. by Mrs. S. Arthur Strong, *Roman Art,* London, 1900, p. 153.

[30] Pliny, *N.H.,* 35, 114; A. Reinach, *Rec. Milliet,* I, 386, n. 1, discusses the Egyptian source of caricature among the Greeks, citing the legend of Herakles and Busiris or Herakles and Antaios, the pygmies and cranes, negro and dwarf types, etc.

the grotesque probably led the Romans of Cæsar's day to decorate their villas with pictures by Antiphilos.[31]

But even more than his experimentation with light, with genre subjects, and with caricature, another side of Antiphilos interests us. It is a certain *facilitas,* or speed in painting, which Quintilian praises in him and which may possibly be connected with Petronius' account of *compendiariæ,* "short cuts" in painting.[32] Petronius states that these abbreviated methods, invented by the Egyptians, led to the decline of Roman painting. The remark doubtless alludes to the introduction of the impressionistic technique which evidently had its origin in Alexandria as Weisbach and others have pointed out.[33] Although we have very few extant examples of Hellenistic art embodying this technique, it seems evident that it originated there and spread later to Italy. This is likely because of the Hellenistic origin of most of the Pompeian styles of decorative painting and the improbability that figure painting alone would have had no influence. Furthermore, Roman mosaics which reveal the presence of this method —such as the one of Dioskourides—are obvious copies of Hellenistic originals and the Fayûm portraits are excellent examples of the impressionistic technique surviving in Egypt at a later period. The Dionysos mosaic from Delos also shows this manner.[34]

It seems possible, therefore, that the "short-cut" method in painting, which the Romans criticized so strongly and to which they attributed the decline of the art, may have originated in Alexandria with Antiphilos. He was evidently interested in light effects. This element in painting almost always interests the impressionistic artist who inclines to paint the world of nature in momentary aspects conditioned by light, air, color, and movement. Furthermore, a tendency toward caricature often involves a similar gift. The caricaturist seizes the most significant features of his subject for travesty and sketches them hastily. The artist in this field has, as a rule, the impressionistic gift of seeing. *"Facilitas"* in Antiphilos probably points, then, in the direction of impressionism. This technique indicates and suggests, by a sketchy method in which fixed outlines are broken up, the essential features of the matter for representation. It is no detailed, polished, and laborious manner. Color is an art of patches and flecks juxtaposed, with the task of fusion left for the eye of the spectator. Probably Antiphilos painted in this facile and easy style which did not supply

---

[31] Varro, *Rerum Rust.,* III, 2.

[32] Petronius, *Satyr.,* 2, 9, *pictura quoque non alium exitum fecit, postquam Ægyptiorum audacia tam magnæ artis compendiariam invenit.*

[33] Werner Weisbach, *Impressionismus,* Berlin, 1910; Quintilian, *Inst. Or.,* XII, 10, 6: *facilitate Antiphilus, concipiendis visionibus, quas* φαντασίας *vocant, Theon . . . est præstantissimus. Cf.* Jex-Blake, Sellers, *The Elder Pliny's Chapters on the History of Art,* p. 145, n. 18; p. 143, n. 16; p. 238.

[34] *Mon. Piot,* XIV (1908), Pl. 15 (color).

every detail but left something to the eye and imagination of the onlooker. The method found no more favor than the inventions of Apollodoros had done at an earlier period, but it had far-reaching consequences for the future of painting. That impressionistic painting was possible in this age is evident from passages in literature such as the Pseudo-Aristotle, *De Coloribus*, 3, 8, probably by Straton (*flor.*, 287-270 B.C.). (*Cf.* K. von Prantl, *Aristoteles über die Farben*, München, 1849; T. Loveday, E. S. Forster, *The Works of Aristotle*, VI, *De Coloribus*, Oxford, 1913.)

We may gain a slight notion of the possible achievement of this period in the impressionistic technique from a number of works which copy Hellenistic originals. One of these is a mosaic by Dioskourides of Samos which probably follows a painting of the Fourth Century B.C.[35] (Fig. 445). Street musicians are seen, represented in animated action, depicted in a manner quite characteristic of the age. The brush strokes of the original, with the color differentiated in the finest values, are traceable in the mosaics. At the left, a woman flute-player appears with a diminutive man, while a comedian plays a tambourine at the right, and the figure in the center uses cymbals. Similar figures are found among certain terra cottas from Myrina. The mosaic is realistically executed. The artist has been interested in light effects and in shadows. The colors employed are yellow, violet, gray, red, blue, brown, green, and also white. The cement bed in which the stones were set was also colored, as is often the case in mosaics which copy Hellenistic works. The mosaic probably belongs in the Second or First Century B.C.

Impressionism in color is reflected in a Pompeian piece from the house of the Vettii (Fig. 446). Here two cocks are represented ready for a fight—one standing on a small table on which rest an urn and some fillets. At the right is a third cock with a branch of victory in his mouth—symbol of the fallen foe who lies under the table. In the rear at the right is a herm. The work is a Pompeian piece going back to a Hellenistic original but the tendency seen here to paint in patches of color may very well have had its origin in the days of Antiphilos.

For Antiphilos, therefore, we are inclined to hold the brief that he was an original painter working in the impressionistic manner, contributing far more to the future of painting than his great enemy Apelles. Additional works from his hand are: The deliverance of Hesione by Herakles, which is probably reflected in a Pompeian wall-

[35] M. Bieber and G. Rodenwaldt, *Jahr.*, 26 (1911), pp. 1 ff.; Herrmann, *Denkmäler der Malerei*, Pl. 106, text, p. 135, argues against drawing conclusions from these mosaics for the technique of Hellenistic painting. H. Bulle, "Untersuchungen an griechischen Theatern," *Abh. der Bayer. Akad. der Wiss., Philos.-phil. hist. Kl.*, XXXIII (1928), pp. 282-283. Bulle argues that Dioskourides was the painter of the original of the mosaic and that he lived in the Second Century B.C. This is proved by the voluminous quality of the drapery. The scene presents a *thyroma*, a type of stage popular in the East in the Second Century B.C.

painting (Helbig 1129);[35a] Dionysos; a youthful Alexander; Hippolytos terrified by a bull sent up from the sea; Kadmos and Europa, and a group composed of Athena, Philip, and Alexander.

Yet another painter of this period who deserves mention is Theon of Samos.[36] He is said to have painted Orestes slaying his mother and the madness which followed— a composition which is probably reflected on certain sarcophagi. He also painted Thamyris playing his lyre and a hoplite full of fury and ready to make a vigorous attack. The latter was so vividly drawn that one seemed to see the combat beginning. The artist heightened this effect by dramatically sounding a trumpet before exposing the painting to view! Theon's work was obviously realistic and sensational. Numerous other artists might be mentioned from the period, notably Peiraïkos, a painter of odds and ends. He probably belongs at the end of the Fourth Century and his work very obviously connects with the Hellenistic Age. He was a painter of small genre pictures, such as barbers' shops, cobblers' stalls, asses, food, and trivial subjects. He won for himself the title "Rhyparographos," a painter of low life.[36a] Athenion should also be mentioned, who would have been incomparable, had he not died young. Among his famous paintings was Odysseus detecting Achilles in woman's costume, which is discussed later.

So much for the Sikyonian school, its great pupil, Apelles, and his Alexandrian rivals, friendly and hostile. Let us turn now to another group of painters of this age —the so-called Theban-Attic school. Probably this was not a school so much as a group of artists who had certain characteristics in common. The center of their activity was first Thebes, later, Corinth and Athens. Their greatest representatives were the two Aristeides, whom it is difficult to disentangle—the founder of the movement and his grandson.

Aristeides the Elder, the father of Nikomachos, was famous for the portrayal of emotional states. His work in painting corresponds to that of Skopas in sculpture. One of his best-known pictures was a representation of a siege of a city, in which a dying mother was seen with her child creeping toward her breast. On her face was written terror lest the child should drink blood.[37] Alexander removed this work to Pella. Aristeides was fond of the pathetic in painting and some of his work borders on the decadent. Pliny says he was the first artist to paint the soul and human emotions, by which he is merely saying that Aristeides emphasized in his painting emotional states in his subjects. From his hand were a sick man, a suppliant with a

[35a] For other treatments of the same subject, see Helbig, Nos. 1131, 1132.
[36] Pliny, N.H., 35, 144; Ælian, V.H., II, 44; Quint., Inst. Or., XII, 10, 6; Plutarch, Mor., 18A.
[36a] Rhyparographos was a pun on rhopographos which meant a painter of odds and ends. Pliny, N.H., 35, 112.
[37] Pliny, op. cit., 35, 98.

very "speaking" expression on his face, and a girl dying with love for her brother. Probably all of these works are by Aristeides I rather than the grandson, since Pliny would hardly say that an artist at the end of the Fourth Century was the "first to paint emotional states of the soul." His colors were said to have been hard.

The younger Aristeides seems to have painted Leontion, the mistress of Epicurus, and a Battle Scene with the Persians which contained one hundred individuals. The latter was executed for Mnason, tyrant of Elateia. The works of the two Aristeides cannot be disentangled with certainty but at least these two appear to belong to the grandson because of the chronology involved.

Some idea of the way in which emotion was expressed on the faces of figures during the Fourth Century may be gained from vases found in Kertch and in Southern Italy.[38] Here the lined and troubled visages give an agitated and restless atmosphere to the compositions. A good instance may be seen in a South Italian vase in Naples which represents Achilles slaying Trojan captives at the tomb of Patroklos (Fig. 447). The sorrowful expressions and nervous, excited heads probably represent something similar to what Aristeides and his pupils attempted. The vase is no less interesting for its developed use of light and shadow on the pyre and on the armor. Certain amphoræ from Ruvo with their pathetic expressions, their small, round heads with short curly locks and deep eyes wide apart, their swelling muscles and fluttering garments correspond to reliefs from the Mausoleum and enable us more easily to picture the major art of painting in this period. The lines of these vases are short and broken up in contrast to the long sweeping strokes of an earlier age. The heads are frequently in three-quarter view and there is much use of foreshortening. The eyebrows are raised, the foreheads lined, the lips set.

Euphranor of Corinth, the pupil of Aristeides, was both a sculptor and painter and seems to have been a very versatile artist. He painted the twelve gods, perhaps reflected today in recently discovered Pompeian wall-paintings.[39] He also pictured Theseus "fed on beef" in contrast to Parrhasios' hero who had "fed on roses"[40] and Odysseus feigning madness. His paintings had a sculptural quality as Pliny says that "he first gave heroes their full dignity and mastered the theory of symmetry." Criticism of his style states that he made the body too slim, the head and limbs too large. He wrote on symmetry and color and seems to have taken up anew the study of nature. Historical and allegorical subjects interested him. He painted the cavalry engagement which preceded the battle of Mantineia and a panel of Democracy and the People. His creations were probably marked by a combination of the technical

[38] On South Italian vases, cf. G. Patroni, *La ceramica antica nell'Italia meridionale*, Napoli, 1897. Cf. Furtwängler, Reichhold, *op. cit.*, Pls. 88, 89, 90.

[39] Pliny, *N.H.*, 34, 50, 77; 35, 111, 128-130; Paus., I, 3, 3; *Not. d. Sc.*, 1911, p. 420.

[40] Pliny, *N.H.*, 35, 129.

excellence of Sikyonian painting and the dramatic quality which belonged to painters like Aristeides of the Theban school.

Another prominent artist of this period, whose works are reflected in several Pompeian wall-paintings, was Nikias of Athens.[41] He studied under a pupil of Euphranor's and was also closely associated with the sculptor Praxiteles. He was accustomed to paint the statues of Praxiteles and was preferred by this sculptor for the task above all other artists. He apparently devoted himself to his art with such enthusiasm that he often forgot both bath and breakfast. One of his most famous pieces was a Nekyia, or underworld scene. Probably the crowded ghosts appeared here in a mass. He was fond of painting legendary heroes, battle scenes, and women. Among the latter are mentioned Danaë, Kalypso, Io, and Andromeda. The painting of Io watched by Argos in the house of Livia on the Palatine is generally accepted as a copy of Nikias' painting (Fig. 448). It is executed in the grand manner and pictures Io seated on a rock guarded by Argos. In the background Hermes appears.[42] The same grandeur and plastic style are evident in copies of Nikias' Andromeda (Fig. 449). Here, against a rocky background, Perseus aids Andromeda to descend. At the left the expiring monster is seen. The treatment of spatial depth, of light and coloring is similar in the two paintings—yellow, violet, and blue predominating with some use of red and brown. These paintings show the artist's painstaking care with light and shade and the relieving of figures against the background, which Pliny mentions. Nikias appears also to have painted a marble tomb, doubtless in the encaustic technique. Some have seen in the grave-stelæ recently found at Pagasæ, in Thessaly, possible reminiscences of this work. The example by Nikias which Pausanias saw at Triteia in Achæa represented a young and beautiful woman seated on an ivory throne with a maidservant holding a parasol beside her.[43] Before her was a youth in a white chiton and a purple chlamys; beside him a servant with darts and dogs on a leash. In other words, the decoration of the tomb followed a type with which we are familiar in sculptured monuments of the Fourth Century. The general effect made by these encaustic paintings may be gleaned from an examination of a Fourth Century grave-stele of Tokkes of Aphyte, found in Attica[44] (Fig. 450). It represents an aged man. The tombstone seems to have been painted solidly in body color on the marble ground, without any engraving or reserving of surfaces free of

---

[41] Pliny, op. cit., 35, 27; 130-133; Ælian, V.H., III, 31.

[42] Perrot, Rev. arch., XXI (1870), Pl. XV; cf. Herrmann, Denkmäler der Malerei, Pl. 53; Helbig, Nos. 131-139. H. Bulle, op. cit., pp. 309-311, argues that the Palatine copy of Io guarded by Argos is the best copy extant. The pillar and tree he considers additions of the copyist. The backgrounds of the Io and Argos and of the Perseus and Andromeda were influenced by stage-settings in his opinion.

[43] Paus., VII, 22, 6.     [44] Milchhöfer, Ath. Mitth., V (1880), pp. 185 ff., Pl. VI.

pigment. It is now a question of marble *painting* in contrast to the drawing on marble of an earlier period.

Many paintings by Nikias were taken to Rome and were given places of prominence in public buildings there. His "Nemea" was brought from Asia by Silanus and placed in the Curia. Pliny tells us that she was shown seated on a lion and holding a palm branch in her hand.[45] An old man above whose head was a picture of a two-horse chariot formed a part of the composition. He probably represented the judges of the games; the picture above was symbolic of the contest in which the victory was won. The painting was executed in the encaustic technique. In the Temple of Concord was a Dionysos by Nikias, while his Hyakinthos was dedicated by Tiberius in the Temple of Augustus. The Alexander in the Portico of Pompey was from his hand. Possibly the originals of certain paintings from the Tor Marancio which depict a number of women renowned in antiquity for their passionate, unhappy love affairs may go back to Nikias. Such is the suggestion of Reinach, who enumerates the following: Kanaké, in love with her brother; Myrrha, with her father; Pasiphaë, with the bull; Scylla, with Minos; and Phædra, with Hippolytos.[46] There is, however, no real proof for this view. (*Cf.* Fig. 626.)

The fame of Nikias rested in part on the dexterity of his technique, but even more on his mastery of chiaroscuro and on the grace and refinement of his works. His "Nemea," as has been said, was done in the encaustic method as were probably also the tombstones from his hand. Doubtless the *circumlitio* which he carried out on the statues of Praxiteles was executed in this process. In this work, details—such as hair, drapery, latchets of sandals, eyes, and lips—were done in color, with the aid of wax. The art of Nikias, and indeed the work of other Greek painters of the Fourth Century, was especially influenced by the drawing of the Sikyonian school. This influence has been traced in engraved mirrors and in cistæ of this period.[47] The style of drawing in this period may be reflected in a mirror owned by Mr. E. P. Warren of Lewes, England.[48]

Contemporary with Nikias was a painter from Eretria, Philoxenos by name, who, like the younger Aristeides, was a pupil of Nikomachos. This Philoxenos painted for King Cassander a battle scene between Alexander and Darius which, Pliny adds, was a picture second to none. It was in all probability this painting that served as a model for the famous mosaic found in the House of the Faun at Pompeii. At any

---

[45] Pliny, *N.H.*, 35, 27.　　[46] Reinach, *Rec. Milliet*, I, 292, n. 3; *Ausonia*, 1906, Pl. II.

[47] Furtwängler, Reichhold, *Griechische Vasenmalerei*, II, Fig. 18. Some mirrors were made at Corinth. *Cf.* Dumont et Chaplain, *Les Céramiques de la Grèce propre*, 1890, II, Pl. 31, pp. 243 f.

[48] *Cf.* Six, *Jahr.*, 20 (1905), p. 165, who assigns to the influence of Pausias certain drawings on a mirror owned by Mr. Warren.

rate, the claims of Philoxenos seem to outweigh those of the Alexandrian lady, Helena, or even of Aristeides. As the mosaic in question has the greatest claim to be considered a copy of a Fourth Century painting and is one of our best monuments for studying the art of this period, we shall consider it in detail (Fig. 451). The battle between Darius and Alexander can only be the one which occurred at Issos. Since it was made for King Cassander, the work dates after 318; or, if one is insistent on the King's title, between 305 and 297 B.C.

If we turn to the mosaic at Pompeii, certain things are evident at a glance. The wonderful composition, which scarcely belongs to Pompeii and which may go back to the Third Century, had as its prototype a four-color painting. Nikomachos, the teacher of Philoxenos, was a four-color master, which increases the probability that Philoxenos was responsible for the great original. Winter has pointed out the importance of the color scale—black, white, red, and yellow—for the sober effect of the mosaic. The absence of blue precludes the richness which one finds on the Alexander Sarcophagus.[49] The moment is represented when Alexander, charging from the left, has just driven his lance through a Persian nobleman whose horse has fallen. King Darius is deeply agitated over the disaster and stretches out his hand as if to aid the victim. A second Persian has dismounted from his horse in an effort to help his distressed countryman. In the dangerous onset, the charioteer of Darius turns the King's chariot swiftly to the right. The impression of the violence and tenseness of battle is increased by the irresistible dash from the left; by the swerving of the King's horses to the right; by the overlapping masses of human beings and horses, and by the fallen armor. Although few figures are employed in the composition—some thirty in all—they are massed with great ingenuity. It is no longer a case of placing figures actually behind one another above each other in space in order to represent the third dimension. The artist emphasizes depth by means of the foreshortened horses in the foreground, by giving the figures behind an abridged form—sometimes only the heads or helmets appear—and by the skilful use of the tree and the spears in the background. We have a definite impression of various planes and of figures behind one another in space. The fallen armor in the foreground was undoubtedly intended to accentuate this effect. Again, the movement is not all in one direction, as in earlier works, so that the lines of movement and the intermingling of figures heighten the impression of seething masses of combatants. The mosaic is a gripping representation of a vital moment, done with the simplest means. Our emotions are engaged over the final outcome: our sympathy is aroused by the misfortune of the King; we are anxious that Alexander's boldness may succeed. He has evidently lost his helmet in the charge and Persians press around him. He becomes a more heroic figure because of the nobility of the foes pitted against

[49] F. Winter, *Das Alexandermosaik aus Pompeii*, Strassburg, 1909 (color plate).

him. The composition is a balanced one with the figure of Darius uniting the two parts. The painter has not, like Polygnotos, chosen a high horizon line, but stands a little higher than his figures and close to them. Emotion is vividly expressed in the gestures and in the faces of the figures. The head of Alexander is fiery and spirited (Fig. 452). The faces of the Persian King and his followers are filled with disquietude, pain, and terror (Fig. 453); the foreheads are lined and the deep-set eyes, with their intense expressions, remind us of the work of Skopas; the sad face of Alexander's doomed victim is rendered with great skill. The technical ability of the maker of the mosaic may be gathered from the head of a Persian in Figure 454.

The artist shows little interest in nature; his concern is with men. Landscape is treated in the baldest fashion imaginable, with only a few elements from nature introduced, such as the gnarled tree, a rock here and there, or rough ground. In his employment of light and shade, slight use is made of cast shadows. Modeling is usually done with light tones as the foreshortened horse shows, but also with local colors such as Pausias used. High lights appear here and there. The real glory of the painting, however, for those who have seen this work in the Museum at Naples, lies in its emotional appeal. Added to this is the charm of the cool, restrained coloring and the skilfulness of composition. Fourth Century artists have at last learned to set events in space, to render vivid action with spirit, to compose with power, to convey emotion. The mosaic is 5.12 meters by 2.71 meters and the figures are of monumental size.

The painting by Philoxenos had its effect on many later works of art. Even in the Fourth Century it appears to have influenced the famous Alexander Sarcophagus, where its echo in the Alexander group seems unmistakable. Similar reminiscences may possibly be found on South Italian vases,[50] and on Etruscan urns of a later epoch. It is merely a coincidence that Velasquez' Surrender of Breda makes use of similar artistic means, such as the grouping of figures and the introduction of lances to indicate depth.

Although we must reckon with a work done in a laborious technique—where small cubes of stone and glass, two to three millimeters large, put together with minute care, do not allow the gentle transitions in color that were possible in painting—the mosaic is nevertheless a wonderful reproduction of a great work of art. The copyist has misunderstood many things; the mosaic has been repaired and has lost much of its original beauty. With all this, we have a most dramatic battle scene where heroic figures are set in a landscape with a cool gray sky above. Bulle has pointed out that we also possess a fine study of the feelings of four individuals—the fiery, irresistible Alexander; the loyal general who dies a courageous death for his King; a faithful

[50] Furtwängler, Reichhold, *Gr. Vas.*, II, 150 ff. Ducati denies influence here. *Cf.* note 65°. Rizzo, *Boll. d'Arte*, V (1925-1926), pp. 529 ff. *Vs.* this, A. Ruesch, *Il bassorilievo con motivo della battaglia di Alessandro*, 1927.

friend who tries to bring help; and a noble King deeply affected by the sacrifice of his aide.

We have spoken of the severe coloring. All of the tones lie within a certain color scale—from white to yellow and red, through gray, brown, and brownish violet to black. No trace of blue is found, which accounts for the impression of restrained color. All of the intermediate tones from reddish and yellowish gray to deep brown and brownish violet are made of yellow, red, and black with more or less addition of white. The evidence from this mosaic seems to point to the fact that the four-color palette was in use in Greece during the age of Alexander. The colors employed were Melian white, Attic ocher, red from Sinope, and a black known as atramentum. The black of Polygnotos was sometimes made from wine lees, that of Apelles from burnt ivory. Blacks from carbon, pitch, burnt bones, and lampblack were not unknown.[51]

Pliny's account of Philoxenos adds certain interesting details which concern us in our discussion of the technique of his painting. He says that Philoxenos, rivaling the rapidity of his teacher, Nikomachos, invented some shortened methods of painting.[52] We do not know in what these short cuts consisted but we have argued, in the case of Antiphilos, that they were probably the beginnings of the impressionistic manner. Winter may be correct when he suggests that the "short cuts" of Philoxenos consisted in drawing not the whole figure but in giving the impression of figures massed behind one another by cutting off those in the rear with the figures in the foreground.[53] The method begun by Mikon in his figure of Boutes has reached a certain degree of perfection in the Alexander Mosaic. The figures in the foreground are complete; those behind are merely indicated by their heads, helmets, etc. The picture is thus composed into the depth of the background.

Philoxenos seems in other ways to have been an apt pupil of Nikomachos. He painted three Sileni engaged in a wanton debauch—a work which probably reflected Nikomachos' "Bacchantes surprised by Satyrs." We have said little of Nikomachos but it is evident that he was a Theban painter of note who not only trained Philoxenos in painting but also his brother, Ariston, and his son, Aristeides II. From him Philoxenos took his speed in execution as "no one was swifter in the art than Nikomachos."[54] Among his works are enumerated: "The Rape of Persephone" which is possibly reflected in a painting from the Tomb of the Nasonii belonging to the

[51] Pliny, *N.H.*, 35, 41; Vitr., *De Arch.*, VII, 10.

[52] Pliny, *N.H.*, 35, 110: *Hic celeritatem præceptoris secutus breviores etiamnum quasdam picturæ compendiarias invenit.*

[53] Winter, *op. cit.*, pp. 8 ff.

[54] Pliny, *N.H.*, 35, 108-110. J. Gildemeister, F. Bücheler, *Rh. Mus.*, 27 (1872), pp. 536 ff. The story that Nikomachos had painted at his portrait of Antipater for forty years instead of the forty days actually spent on it is borrowed from a Syriac version of a lost treatise falsely ascribed to Plutarch.

Second Century A.D. (Fig. 596); Cybele on a lion, recalling the Nemea of Nikias; Scylla; and a Victory bearing aloft to heaven a victorious quadriga. The latter is supposedly copied on the Blacas gem in the British Museum[55] (Fig. 455). The conception is a new one. Nikomachos combined strength and charm with a facile hand. He painted a portrait for Antipater in forty days. Antipater found the price high, whereupon Nikomachos answered that he had painted at it for forty years. Whether or not we understand by *compendiariæ*, technical innovations or the beginnings of the impressionistic manner, Nikomachos appears to have been blamed for being the father of the invention.

A number of lesser painters were probably also connected with the Attic school. Of these we shall mention only a few whose influence on later works of art was significant. Among these were Kydias of Kythnos whose picture of the Argonauts was bought by Quintus Hortensius the orator for more than 140,000 sesterces. This painting may have inspired the Ficoroni Cista (Fig. 372) discussed above as an Italo-Etruscan work of art with possible Polygnotan connections. Kydias is mentioned by Theophrastos as the discoverer of *miltos*—a red coloring derived from a burnt ocher.

Athenion of Maroneia in Thrace was preferred by some to Nikias. His coloring was harder but produced a more pleasing effect because of his technical skill. The painting by him which interests us most is Achilles discovered by Odysseus among the daughters of King Lykomedes at Skyros (Fig. 456). A number of Pompeian wall-paintings copy this theme but no one can definitely be traced back to Athenion. The difficulties are these: Polygnotos also treated this subject, and we are dealing with certain types which cannot be distinguished. Secondly, one cannot argue that a painting such as Figure 456 may not go back to Athenion because the coloring is so different from the sober tones which Athenion must have used. The artist of the Pompeian picture may have been a colorist who paid little attention to the scale of the original which he copied. Certainly this is the most spirited composition of all and is the one which we should prefer to connect with Athenion's name, but there is no assurance that the attribution is correct. It is quite possible that the work in the house of Holconius at Pompeii may reflect his painting better (Fig. 457). The simpler composition, the lack of depth, and the more womanish type of Achilles may argue for an earlier original, but the reasoning is very weak. The figure of Deidameia at the feet of Achilles is typically Pompeian. The contrast between the dark form of Odysseus at the right and the lighter figure of Achilles adds strikingly to the womanish character of the youthful hero.

The painters of the Theban-Attic school were not interested in severe academic

[55] Cf. *Jahr.*, III (1888), Pl. XI, 10; IV (1889), 60 ff.; Springer-Michaelis, *Kunstgeschichte*,[10] Fig. 584; [12]Fig. 596.

exactness, in contrast to the painters of Sikyon. They cared little about the scientific training and technical skill of the Sikyonian masters. Their aim was ease and versatility, grace of movement, charm of manner, the expression of human emotions. These were the qualities which brought fame to their work. The subject matter which an Aristeides chose would doubtless have seemed decadent even to Pausias. The method of execution would entail a much softer treatment of flesh and greater attention to refinement of color. Their paintings were more skilfully conceived in space, their knowledge of shading and perspective was more advanced, although they had probably spent less time studying these subjects.

We have spoken only of known masters, whose fame in the Fourth Century is attested by Pliny and other writers. There are a large number of nameless painters whose works have come down to us in later copies. These tell us not a little about the achievement of the Fourth Century artists. After the Alexander Mosaic, the work which is probably of most importance in this epoch is the Niobe painting from Pompeii. It was painted on marble and is about forty centimeters high (Fig. 458). Its significance for the representation of space at this epoch cannot be too greatly emphasized.[55a]

The scene represented is the slaying of the daughters of Niobe. The tragedy is enacted with only four figures. The architectural setting of the palace gives a calm background for the disturbed events in the foreground. It further aids in producing the impression of depth in the work. The composition is cut diagonally by the scepter of Zeus which acts like a "flash of lightning" across the painting. On the left, Niobe guards her youngest daughter and turns her eyes toward heaven for aid. At the right, the old nurse bends over another child who is dying in her arms. The entire composition is built into the third dimension. The center is slightly shifted to the left but the figure of Niobe dominates the scene. The painting was probably done with more colors than we have today; possibly only the under painting remains. The colors found at present are yellow and violet, strongly contrasted, with red and green playing a secondary rôle. The drawing is of the finest and compares favorably with work on vases of the Fourth Century. The original must be dated somewhere after the middle of the Fourth Century, and appears to have been Attic work. Foreshortening and shading are excellently handled.

A number of Pompeian paintings which have come down to us suggest by outstanding qualities that they were copied after famous Greek originals of the Fourth and Third Centuries. It is dangerous to argue that these works present a perfect

[55a] H. Bulle, *Untersuch. an griech. Theatern*, pp. 327-329, Pl. 25, considers that the architecture of this painting comes from the *paraskenion* of a stage of the Segesta type. The artist has misunderstood the architecture which he was copying. He dates the original picture in the first half of the Third Century. Bulle also considers the palace front in Fig. 456 the *regia* of the *thyromata* stage, p. 327.

picture of the painting of this period. The question of copying is always a hazardous one and we do not know whether or not the Pompeian artist, like the Greek vase-painter, chose only motives or parts of paintings which interested him and rethought his material. Probably he did in many cases. In general, however, the paintings of Pompeii are very like one another. They are conceived and carried out in much the same way, so that they seem to belong to the same school. This school was the one which flourished at the court of Alexander and his successors, the Diadochi. The mere fact that we have the subject of Io guarded by Argos repeated six times at Pompeii and once at Rome—as Boissier has pointed out[56]—suggests that the artists prepared a certain number of paintings on which they practiced and which they reproduced whenever copies were wanted. Their power of execution was always inferior to the conception involved, which tends to show that the work was not carried out by the person who had conceived it. In other words, the Pompeian and Roman artists reproduced and adapted well-known Greek paintings of the Hellenistic age. These paintings therefore give us an insight into the works of Greek masters of the Fourth and Third Centuries—untrustworthy as some of this evidence must be.[57] We can recognize in them, however, certain things which they have derived from their Greek models: love of space of trifling depth, figures done in relief fashion, symmetrical grouping, no landscape *per se*, no eye for atmospheric effects comparable to what we find today, or for the beauty of light.

A typical Pompeian work derived from a Greek original is to be seen in the painting at Naples which represents Achilles about to surrender Briseis (Fig. 459). It is painted in the epic manner and presents us with an example of Greek *megalography*. The scene is dominated by the figure of Achilles who is shifted from the center slightly to the left. Our attention is riveted on him because of his angry expression and gesture and because of the warm brown flesh tones and crimson mantle which mark him out. To the right the figures turn obliquely into the background. Patroklos, who is depicted in rear view, leads Briseis slowly forward, and Achilles, with a sweeping gesture, sets her free. She is shown in tears. Her yellow chiton contrasts strongly with the crimson garment of Patroklos. Depth in the painting is emphasized by the bodyguard massed in the background against the dark violet tent, by the diagonals of the tent and throne, and by the shields which are judiciously placed behind the principal actors in the drama, and which, like aureoles, surround their heads. The composition is a masterful one. Contrasting moods at play give an atmosphere of anxiety to the scene: the righteous indignation of Achilles is

[56] G. Boissier, *Rome and Pompeii*, N. Y., 1905, pp. 370 ff., after W. Helbig, *Wandgemälde*, Nos. 131 ff.

[57] T. Ely, *J.H.S.*, XVI (1896), pp. 143 ff. *Pompeian Paintings and Their Relation to Hellenic Masterpieces.*

opposed to the quiet calm of Patroklos and the weeping sadness of Briseis. Behind Achilles, the wrinkled, grieved face of old Phœnix appears, while at the left are the embarrassed heralds of Agamemnon. The coloring is cleverly used. In the background is the dark violet of the tent; in the foreground, the crimson mantles of Achilles and Patroklos; while the middle ground is dominated by the delicate yellow and blue on the garments of Briseis and the heralds, together with the bright yellow and silver of the helmets and armor. The painting is probably a fairly close copy of a good Greek model. The calm expressed and the deep emotion are characteristic of the Fourth Century; the Hellenistic Age would hardly have treated the material so simply.[58]

Another Pompeian painting which is probably derived from an original of the Fourth Century is found on a wall in the House of the Vettii. It depicts the fate of the young Theban King, Pentheus, torn to pieces by the Mænads (Fig. 460). The composition is carefully centralized—all eyes and hands being drawn toward the figure of the King in the center. Movement is not developed parallel to the front plane of the painting but goes diagonally into the depth of the picture. There is little attempt to deepen the space; it is filled rhythmically with figures much as in vase-painting, and remains the same everywhere, the upper figures being cut off by the background. The light is from the front and slightly to the left, and strikes with the same strength all elements of scenery and landscape. This uniform effect of light from one point is basically different from that found in paintings of a later period,[59] and dates the original work as early. The prevailing colors are the yellowish brown of the ground against which the rich blue of Agave's garment at the left and the violet chiton of the Mænad at the right are strongly contrasted. Yellow, violet, and blue are also found on the garments of the figures in the background. Warm flesh tones occur throughout the painting. Much use is made of chiaroscuro to emphasize the cloud of passion which sweeps across the scene and which seems even to send the garments fluttering before it.

A work from Herculaneum, which betrays the influence of the Fourth Century in its principal figure, is the painting depicting Theseus after the slaying of the Minotaur (Fig. 461). The heroic form of the victor furnishes the main interest in the painting, all the more because the Minotaur in the foreground is almost effaced. The figure of Theseus is a combination of Praxitelean grace, of Lysippan tenseness, and

[58] *Cf.* H. Bulle, *Der schöne Mensch,*[2] Pl. 314 and text.
[59] A. von Salis, *Die Kunst der Griechen,* Leipzig, 1919, 171. H. Bulle, *Untersuch. an griech. Theatern,* p. 309, argues that the date of the Pentheus and Dirce paintings is the end of the Fifth Century. Pfuhl places the Pentheus at the end of the Fifth (p. 621) and the Dirce in the second half of the Fourth Century or a little later (p. 788). Bulle considers the levels in the Pentheus painting to be an amplification of Polygnotan treatment of depth.

Scopaic fire, as Pfuhl has pointed out.[60] He looks far away, failing to see the children who crowd around him to express their gratitude at the death of the monster. On the right, is the entrance to the Labyrinth; at the left, Artemis, the guardian of the hero, is seated on a cliff. The artist, who was almost certainly an Athenian, has concentrated his attention for the most part on form and on the expression of emotion.

The interest in light seen in the painting of the Punishment of Dirce (Fig. 462) at once relates the work to the Pentheus fresco discussed above. Other links are the passionate emotion expressed and the fire of action. Both are in the House of the Vettii at Pompeii and were probably by the same master. The moment depicted is the instant just before the bull is set free by Amphion and Zethos to trample Dirce underfoot and thus avenge the sons for her treatment of their mother. The painting possesses certain similarities to the Hellenistic sculptural group by Apollonios and Tauriskos but also many differences. It was clearly derived from an original which is also reflected on certain Etruscan urns. The light, as in the Pentheus painting, falls evenly from one point.

We might enumerate many other paintings from Pompeii which copy originals of the period under discussion, such as the Punishment of Ixion, Thetis and Hephaistos, and Odysseus and Penelope,[61] but we have examined enough copies to gain some idea of the aim and achievement of Fourth Century painters. There seems to have been a return to the more noble subject matter of the days of Polygnotos in many cases. In coloring, yellow, violet, and bright blue were commonly employed with the complementary use of red and green beside white. Probably the earlier masters used four colors alone and their various combinations; but, in general, a wider scale was handled by most painters. The problem of the third dimension was seriously attacked and figures were set into their surroundings. Depth, however, was never very pronounced and in the matter of landscape no real beginnings were made. Landscape elements appear very rarely, as we saw in the Alexander Mosaic. Composition becomes more elaborate, often without rigid symmetry. The centralized type occurs beside the more subtle examples where the vital point of interest is pushed to one side, as in the Niobe painting or in the Surrender of Briseis by Achilles. Lighting effects absorb the attention of artists to a great extent, but the light falls from one point and is evenly distributed over objects and landscape, as in the Pentheus fresco. The expression of human emotion interests most artists. Foreshortening, chiaroscuro, and perspective are handled with increasing skill and the practice of placing figures above one another to indicate depth is superseded by the clever device of cutting off figures in the background by those in front and representing only parts, such as

---

[60] E. Pfuhl, *Malerei u. Zeichnung*, II, 790.
[61] Herrmann, *Denkmäler der Malerei*, Pls. 39, 139, 54.

heads, helmets, and the like. In general, painting in the Fourth Century emphasizes painting rather than drawing; it becomes much more a matter of color, light and shadow, and the arrangement of masses. It has passed from the decorative stage into the emotional.

We have left aside in our discussion many lesser painters and many whose names have been associated with important works; for example, the Alexandrian woman Helena, who painted a battle of Alexander and Darius, considered by some scholars to be the original of the Alexander Mosaic. In general, we have presented only those artists whose works may mean something more than a name today and whose paintings appear to have significantly influenced later times. There are also a number of objects dating from 400-300 B.C., from which we may increase our knowledge of Greek drawing, composition, and use of color during the period under discussion. These include engraved mirrors, Fourth Century vases, reliefs, and grave-stelæ.

After 400 B.C. we find some charming works like the mirror in the British Museum (Fig. 463). On the cover of this, Pan and Aphrodite are playing at knucklebones. The incised outlines are drawn with great beauty and seem to suggest roundness of form. In addition to this, hatched lines occur quite frequently on the drapery of Aphrodite and on the figure of Pan. The couch, on which the contestants are seated, is very cleverly drawn in perspective. The atmosphere of the work is distinctly one which announces the Hellenistic age, but the forms hark back to Greek works of the Fifth Century. That the figure is Aphrodite and not Peitho, seems probable from the presence of Eros and the goose.

A school of engravers of bronze mirrors probably existed at Corinth in the Fourth Century; at any rate, some fine examples have been found in this region—a circumstance which leads us to this supposition. In Figure 464, on a cover found near Corinth, we have the heroic figure of Corinth enthroned, crowned by Leukas, the daughter colony of Corinth. The figures are nobly conceived. The head of Corinth resembles the Zeus type in sculpture in the Fourth Century and, in general, marks of the Fourth Century are seen in the drawing of the throne, in the flowers inserted in the open spaces, which recall designs on vases of Southern Italy, and in the subject matter. Personification of cities was common in ancient art. We have records of various peoples crowning cities—for example, of the people of Syracuse crowning Rhodes.[62] The cover is an accomplished piece of work, the drawing that of a finished master. Since it was found near Corinth, we are inclined to connect it with the Sikyonian school of artists who were so significant at this time and who gave so much attention to the subject of drawing. How very refined and delicate such engraving on mirrors could be, a mirror-cover in New York, in the Metropolitan

[62] Polybios, V, 88. *Cf*. Dumont et Chaplain, *Les Céramiques de la Grèce propre*, 1890, II, pp. 176 ff.

Museum, bears witness (Fig. 465). Here, two women are represented in a toilet scene, one arranging her hair, the other holding up a mirror. The motive of the one at the right recalls the Aphrodite of Apelles. The grace in the lines of the drapery and the beauty of the hair and features readily show to what heights Greek artisans of this period could rise. This mirror also appears to be connected with the Sikyonian school which we have been discussing.

Certain grave-stelæ which have come down to us from Thebes are remarkable for the preliminary sketch made by the artist before the monument was painted. We have already spoken of the stele of Mnason, a work of the Fifth Century. Somewhat later in time and style is the stele of Rhynchon, executed by a master of the Fourth Century (Fig. 466). The technique of the painting is interesting, being a combination of the distemper and encaustic processes.[63] The outlines and details of the figure were first incised. Within this outline was a polished surface on which the encaustic technique was used, the incisions preventing the color from spreading into the background. The surface between the outlines and the frame of the picture was picked out with a pointed instrument, forming a roughened area to which the painting in distemper adhered. None of the sketch which we now see was visible when the monument was completed; it was merely intended as a preliminary guide and as a technical aid before the color was applied. The drawing is free and bold, dating after the first quarter of the Fourth Century, as the short curved lines used for anatomical details and the elaboration of the pattern on the interior of the shield tend to prove. The design of Bellerophon slaying the Chimæra is one of the most charming bits of drawing on the stele, although the youth enjoying a lesson on the lyre is done with minute care. In antiquity, the entire stone was covered with color, so that the beauty of the preliminary sketch which we enjoy today was wholly lost, since it was covered over by the wax. Probably the background was a solid red, while the figure and drapery were put in in various gay colors.

In the field of relief, a monument from Eleusis recently published by Rodenwaldt adds to our knowledge of the use of color on Attic relief[64] (Fig. 467). It is a small fragment of a votive relief 20 centimeters high and 27.5 centimeters wide, belonging in all probability about 400 B.C. Against a background of rich blue, two figures, a youth and a veiled woman, are seen turned toward the right. The outlines of the faces and hands are in red line, as are details of the eye, such as the lids, brows, and circle of the iris. The torch at the right apparently belongs to a Kore standing in front view and holding a torch in either hand. The relief, which has an Attic quality, as Rodenwaldt points out, is most important because of its color. The blue ground is preserved around the boy's head; brown is seen on the hair and yellow on

[63] W. Vollgraff, B.C.H., 26 (1902), pp. 554-570, Pl. VIII.
[64] G. Rodenwaldt, Jahr., 36 (1921), pp. 1 ff., Pl. I (color).

Demeter's (?) veil, in addition to the red mentioned. The surprising thing about the relief is the use of red for the contour lines of the face, neck, hands, and outlines of the fingers. This practice was known to us earlier in the case of Roman reliefs such as the ones from Neumagen in the Trier Museum.[65] Behind these Roman reliefs lay a Greek tradition, as the Eleusinian monument proves. From the Fifth Century, blue was the prevalent color of the ground, but beside it in the Fourth Century, we find the white ground of the Alexander Sarcophagus. Side by side with the marble tones or ganosis for the flesh is the painting with solid colors, seen on the frieze of the Mausoleum. The outline in red on the Eleusis relief adds a further method, sharply relieving the silhouettes of the heads against the blue ground. If the relief were larger or higher, the same need for the colored outline would not be felt and it is not found in these cases. However, there are probably other examples of the red contour line which have not been distinguished. Rodenwaldt shows that the archaic grave-stele of the Sixth Century in the Metropolitan Museum made use of this practice. Around the head of the Maiden in Berlin, which was originally a part of this monument, was a broad, red contour line and the fingers also were outlined in the same color. The brush-strokes may be seen with the aid of a magnifying glass against the red of the ground. Since the contour lines were in a different shade of red from the ground, they no longer served the purpose of lifting the figures from the background, as is the case in the relief from Eleusis; rather, the figures were toned into the background by this means.

We have said that the vases of the Fourth Century are of much less value for the study of the major art of painting than those of the Fifth Century. Not only is this true, but they are less artistic and have not the same appeal as the Fifth Century examples which date from the period when Athenian power was at its height. Although vases continued to be made in Attica, it was no longer a great center of ceramic industry as in earlier days.

We can readily follow the development and the decline, which occurred in this period, in Panathenaic vases. These begin in the Sixth Century and continuing in the black-figured technique throughout the Fourth Century allow us to trace the artist's mastery of drawing and design. We see him struggling at first with rude memory pictures and, later, correcting these from nature; we follow him as he learns to draw the eye correctly in profile view and to put folds in drapery, at first very stiffly but finally in impressionistic fashion. Gaining control of his brush, he interests himself almost wholly in pattern. His designs in the Fourth Century wander up on the neck of the amphora and do not, as earlier, emphasize the structure of the vase. The shapes of the vessels also show deterioration.

[65] A. Grenier, *La Polychromie des sculptures de Neumagen, Rev. arch.,* III (1904), pp. 245 ff.

If we examine a series of Greek vases of the red-figured style from the end of the Fifth Century, we shall find that they followed two varying traditions—one, the pretty, delicate, refined, and subtle style which Meidias inaugurated; the other, the grand style of the Parthenon, to which vigor in movement and action were added. The amphora from Melos in the Louvre exemplifies this second trend (Fig. 468). It represents a battle of gods and giants. In the center, Zeus is fighting Porphyrion. Dionysos and Poseidon are at the upper right hand; Hermes in the foreground. Herakles and Athena appear at the left of the center and Apollo and Artemis are scaling the heights, fighting as they go. The chariot of Zeus is driven by Victory. Certain figures, like the one of Porphyrion in back view, are apparently copied from greater works of art and are repeated elsewhere. In addition to the extensive use of short curved lines, one finds the employment of a dilute wash for details of shading, and a copious use of white. The author of this Gigantomachy, who probably also painted the Talos vase, preferred his figures in three-quarter, front, or back view. He was skilled in foreshortening, as the right leg of Herakles and of several sinking giants in the foreground shows. The monumental character of the composition makes us feel that the work is derived from an important original. The overlapping figures are more suitable for a wall-painting than for the limited surface of a vase.

For the most part, we must look to centers outside Athens for our knowledge of Fourth Century vases—to Kertch in the Crimea, to Southern Italy, to Cyrene in Northern Africa, and to Bœotia. In these classes of vases, we frequently find the degeneration of Attic themes and modes of expression. In some examples, Dionysiac and Eleusinian subject matter is treated. The striking thing about most of the vases is the extensive use of color—violet, rose, red, green, and yellow, beside the favored white and gold of the Kertch group.

Attic vase-painting may be said to have breathed its last with the Kertch class. This group of vases is well exemplified by the pelike of Figure 469, which presents Zeus consulting Themis. The protagonists are deciding how the burden of the earth may be lessened by the Trojan War. At the right Selene and Hesperos are withdrawing while the two women at the left are probably Aphrodite and Peitho. Athena, Hermes, and Niké balance the design in the center. Themis is seated on the omphalos. One notes at once that the outline which was so important in Fifth Century painting plays little part here. The figures are sometimes silhouetted against one another. White is used for the flesh of women, for the ivory throne and silver helmet. Lilac is found on the garments of Athena and Themis; blue on the wings of the Niké; red on the crest of the helmet; yellow on the omphalos. Foreshortening and perspective are employed with skill in the central figure of Zeus and on his throne. The drawing may perhaps be connected with the Sikyonian school and reminds us of the figure of Corinth on the mirror in Figure 464. The troubled face of Zeus is rendered with the pathos of an Aristeides. However, following Attic taste, the use of perspective and of emotion is not carried to such a length as we should find it in easel-painting. The Athenian artist—and these vases were in all probability made by Athenians—understood too well the decorative demands imposed upon him by his craft. He avoided breaking the surface of his vase by buildings drawn in perspective and remained truer to the canons of his art than did South Italian masters. While he no longer composed in frieze-like fashion and while the freedom found in the use of new motives and in the treatment of drapery is very striking, he still employed figures of heroic proportions posed in passive attitudes. These were arranged one above another, or beside each other—for the most part in one plane. The decoration tended to be flat decoration with certain figures standing out in white, sometimes with the addition of gold or various colors such as blue, green, or rose. Many vases of this Kertch class have genre scenes on them—such as the preparation of a bride for marriage or a toilet scene.

Athenian colonies were sent out to Italy as early as the days of Pericles. The vase-factories found in this region are direct offshoots of the Attic ones. From Lucania they spread to Campania, Apulia, and Southern Etruria. The rise of these factories effectually suppressed Attic imports. Probably most of the artists working in them were Athenians who had migrated there after the Peloponnesian disaster. Only occasionally were they supreme masters and very few of them sign their works, as Attic masters in Greece were accustomed to do in pride and for commercial ends.

In general, structural considerations did not play an important part in the decoration of South Italian vases. We find a pronounced use of architecture drawn in perspective in the center of the vase, breaking up the old, flat decoration of an earlier age. The silhouette style, which had now exhausted its possibilities, is discarded. A decided interest on the part of the artist lies in the expression of emotion in the faces of the actors. Many of these features take away from the purely decorative quality of the designs.

Among South Italian vases, the Apulian class holds a prominent place. The most important center of manufacture was probably Tarentum but the ware has been commonly found in Ruvo, Canosa, and Bari. These vases are usually very large kraters made of yellowish clay.[65a] They are decorated with designs executed in black or a brownish dilute wash, with a copious use of white and sometimes of red and yellow. The neck frequently bears a female head, Helios in a quadriga, or some other device, combined with volutes, tendrils, or palmettes. The ivy and laurel wreath are common patterns on the mouth or rim of the lip. A large number of the class have designs in two or three levels, oftentimes with an architectural pattern in the center —a tent, temple, or *ædicula* of some kind. A good example of the Apulian type with

[65a] The clay of the vases from Ruvo was red.

two levels is a vase from Naples on which the story of Orestes and Iphigeneia is sketched (Fig. 470). The center is occupied by a bloodstained altar with a laurel tree growing behind it. Orestes is seated in a somewhat dejected attitude, while Pylades stands at the left. The hero is doubtless pondering his fate, doomed as he is to become a victim to Artemis. His sister, Iphigeneia, and a priestess approach. The temple with its open doors appears in the background partly cut off by hilly ground. Two divinities are seated above on the left of the temple—a white dotted line indicating the difference in level from the foreground. They are Apollo, the guardian of Orestes, and Artemis, the inhabitant of the temple. The palmettes under the handles are elaborately developed while above the main design runs an "Ionic" frieze of lions pursuing a deer. At the top the favorite vine pattern, a wave pattern, and an egg and dart complete the decoration. This vase probably belongs to an earlier period than the "Darius" vase (Fig. 471). The composition is simple. The artist pays some attention to perspective in the drawing of the altar and the temple, and represents emotion by attitudes rather than by expression. The influence of tragedy and the stage is common on South Italian wares.[65b] The date of the vase is about 370 B.C.

The "Darius" vase belongs to the developed Apulian class and dates after the middle of the Fourth Century.[65c] It is one of the largest and the most beautiful of the group and is decorated on the neck with a battle of Amazons and some Bacchic rites. On the back occurs the scene of Bellerophon slaying the Chimæra (F. R., II, 143, Fig. 46), whereas the front scenes recall the great historical struggle of Greece against Asia. In the center, King Darius is seated on his throne with his advisers around him. A Persian, standing on a round platform, addresses him. Below, the King's treasurer receives tribute, while above the gods occupy the scene. In the center is Zeus, with Hellas beside him and Athena near. At the left, are Apollo and Artemis. Seated beside a herm, at the right, is the figure of Asia. Apate or "Treachery," a woman with snaky locks and firebrands in her hands, beckons her on against Hellas. Beside Zeus stands Victory. The painting is symbolic of the protection afforded Greece by the gods against Persian encroachment.

The arrangement in three levels is typical of the developed Apulian class; so also are the following: the soft flesh of the figures of the men, the flying garments which are unmotivated and which in their patterns often show the influence of the theater; the frequent attempts at perspective and the elaborate foreshortening. Faces filled

[65b] L. Séchan, *Études sur la tragédie grecque dans ses rapports avec la céramique*, Paris, 1926.

[65c] For an earlier dating, see P. Ducati, *Storia della ceramica greca*, 1922, II, 456. Ducati considers that Philoxenos did not influence these vases. Furtwängler dated the Darius vase at the end of the century because of the form of the Alpha. F. R., II, 154. He thinks the vase may have been inspired by a revival of the "Persians" of Phrynichos. *Cf.* O. Jahn, *A.Z.*, 1860, pp. 41 ff.

with emotion such as those of the Persian addressing Darius, or Apate, or the suppliants begging release from taxes, are characteristic also. These vases exhibit a certain richness and floridity, to which the color adds not a little.

Apulian vases do not come from the earliest center of vase-industry in Southern Italy; the Periclean colony in Lucania was probably the oldest. The Lucanian group is distinguished by a very strict adherence to Attic standards and reveals few local peculiarities of taste. Oftentimes it is difficult to separate Lucanian fabrics from work made in Athens. A fine example of this Attic quality is seen in the vase which represents the expiation of Orestes after he has slain his mother (Fig. 472). He is seated on the altar at Delphi, before the omphalos, with the Furies guarding him. Behind him, stand Apollo and Artemis. The shade of Klytaimnestra rises in the background to incite the Furies. The purification is symbolized by a pig held by the god above the head of Orestes. The forms have an Attic grace about them. The heads are idealized types, and differ from Athenian work in being somewhat large. The style is a conservative one with a rare use of accessory colors; the drawing is rather severe. There is much less white than on Apulian and Campanian vases and the general appearance of the vases is much less gaudy than is the case in other South Italian wares. Ground-lines are rare; dots occur on this vase beneath the feet of the Furies. The influence of Æschylean drama seems obvious. The krater dates about 430 B.C. In style, the various figures recall those of the Parthenon pediment, as Hauser has pointed out:[66] the figure of Orestes, that of Theseus; the sleeping Furies, the so-called Fates. The vase is probably a copy of a great original painting.

An interesting series of signed vases is probably to be included in the Lucanian group. Two painters, Assteas and Python, have painted a number which show close connections with the theater. Because of the mixture of Ionic and Doric in the inscriptions and because of the fact that several vases by Assteas have been found at Pæstum, Hauser localizes their activity in the ancient Poseidonia.[67] As there seems to be a close connection between the work of the two men, he assumes their workshops were in the same place and that they belong to the same period. The cross stroke of the *a* in the name, Assteas, dates the work of the painters in the last decades of the Fourth Century.

Python painted a krater now in the British Museum which is of interest for our study of these two artists (Fig. 473). The subject portrayed is not wholly clear. Alkmene, seated on an altar, is obviously appealing to Zeus, apparently against her husband Amphitryon. The cause of her husband's rage we do not know. It has been suggested that he was not pleased with the reception given him by his wife on his

[66] F. Hauser, Furtwängler, Reichhold, *op. cit.*, II, 330 ff.; *cf.* V. Macchioro, *I ceramisti di Armento in Lucania, Jahr.*, 27 (1912), pp. 265-316, Fig. 3.

[67] F. Hauser, F. R., *Gr. Vas.*, III, Pl. 130, p. 60.

return from the wars and determined to take vengeance on her.[68] She fled to an altar, where Amphitryon and Antenor followed her. On our vase, they are proceeding to light the fire which will turn the altar into a funeral pyre. Alkmene calls for the aid of Zeus, who sends a thunderstorm and a deluge to put out the flames. The Hyades provoke a tempest from above and surround Alkmene with a kind of rainbow. The added figure at the right is the Dawn. Of interest in the painting is the type of composition, arranged in two divisions, one above the other, with full figures below and half figures above. These half figures are secondary and in some instances act somewhat as spectators. This arrangement, which becomes a stereotyped one in the vases of this period, was probably drawn from Fourth Century painting.[69] We see a reflection of it in the Iphigeneia painting from Pompeii which is supposed to echo a work by Timanthes (Fig. 384). We must conclude that the vase-painters composed much as did the great easel-painters of the Fourth Century. The vase-painting seems more primitive than the easel-paintings because all the local colors are missing and the figures are silhouetted against a black ground. On the other hand, this method of composition may have been derived from the stage-setting of the theater of this period. A vase by Assteas which depicts *Hercules Furens* shows a stage-setting of this type.[70] Here, the mad Herakles is about to hurl his children into the fire. In the background are three windows where Mania, "Madness," Iolaos, and Alkmene appear. The stage with three windows seems, then, to have existed in Southern Italy in the late Fourth Century. Many of the vase-paintings of Assteas and Python reveal strong influence from the stage in subject matter, setting, and costumes. An example by Assteas illustrates a scene from one of the Phlyakes or farces of Southern Italy.[71] Here, two youths are trying to wrest money from an old man who plants himself firmly on his money-chest and appears on the point of being torn in two by his opponents (Fig. 474). The vase is interesting for the light it throws on the ancient stage. In tragedy, the influence of Euripides prevailed. His plays were revived in Magna Græcia from the Fourth Century on.

The third class of South Italian vases, the Campanian group, is much less important for our purposes. The vases are mostly small, of buff clay, and decorated with masses of white, carmine red, and yellow. Plates with representations of fish were common. Many comic scenes occur and subjects drawn from everyday life. Sepulchral themes are also found. Local elements appear in the armor and dress; e.g., on

[68] A. S. Murray, *J.H.S.*, XI (1890), pp. 225 ff., quoting Engelmann.

[69] F. Hauser, *op. cit.*, III, 61. *Cf.* with this type of composition the Pompeian painting of Pentheus torn to pieces by the Mænads (Fig. 460).

[70] F. Hauser, F. R., *Griech. Vas.*, III, 62.

[71] R. Zahn, F. R., *Griech. Vas.*, III, 178-207; M. Bieber, *Die Denkmäler zum Theaterwesen im Altertum*, Berlin, 1920, Pl. 84.

the vase in Figure 475. Here we have an Apulian warrior garbed in the dress of his native land. The chiton is very short; the breastplate, made of three metal discs arranged in a triangle, is typical of the country as is also the crested helmet. The wave pattern below is commonly found on this class of vases. The similarity of vase-paintings of this type with some of the South Italian tomb-paintings of the same period is perfectly obvious.

At the end of the Fifth Century, ware with figures moulded in relief became common in Attica. A number of Kertch vases in this technique are known. One very interesting example signed by its maker, Xenophantos, an Athenian, depicted a hunt of a Persian prince and suggests motives on the Alexander Sarcophagus. More important for our purposes and roughly contemporary, but not from the hand of Xeno-phantos, is a vase in relief representing the contest between Athena and Poseidon for the land of Attica (Fig. 476). Poseidon has produced a salt spring with his trident but is worsted by Athena, who, through the creation of the olive, wins the privilege of giving her name to the land. As this subject was treated in the west pediment of the Parthenon, our vase has figured in the reconstruction of these sculptures, although there is no sign of a retreat on Poseidon's part such as one sees in Carrey's drawing. At the left of the design, Dionysos supports Athena, while the Niké flying toward her and the snake hostile to Poseidon, announce her victory. At the right, the judge, Cecrops, is seated. Behind him, Amphitrite flees as a result of the adverse decision. The temple is the Erechtheum. The figure above at the left may be Eris, "Strife," or an Athenian arbitress. The central group of Athena and Poseidon was gilded in details such as the trident.

Xenophantos was apparently an Athenian who had taken up his residence at Kertch, the ancient Panticapæum in the Crimea. There he produced some of the splendid, richly colored vases, which the luxury of the age demanded. In fact, the surprising thing about the vases from the Crimea and Southern Italy is the evidence of opulence which they reveal and the presence of a certain striving for general effects of splendor. Whether these vases were manufactured in Athens and exported, as some have argued, or were made on the local sites by Greek artists, or even in some cases by Italians trained by Greek artists, they disclose characteristics of the best period of Greek art, combined with sure signs of decadence. One of the most elaborate of these vases in relief presents the Eleusinian circle of deities.[72]

We have not spoken of certain Bœotian fabrics connected with the worship of the god Kabeiros, a Thracian deity with a distinct likeness to Dionysos. These vases apparently began in the Fifth Century and continued in the Fourth Century until the destruction of Thebes by Alexander in 335 B.C. The scenes present travesties of

[72] *Mon. Ant.*, XXII (1914), Pls. C-CII. *Cf.* F. Courby, *Les vases grecs à reliefs*, Paris, 1922.

mythological subjects, such as the Circe legend, and representations of events associated with the worship of the god Kabeiros. As in the case of the Panathenaic
amphoræ, the black-figured technique was used throughout, though the glaze is
usually diluted to a brown. It was applied directly to the buff-colored clay. The
striking thing is the clever work in caricature. The vases seem to have certain
features in common with the class of South Italian fabrics which are decorated with
scenes from the Phlyakes, or even more with the later vases from Hadra in Egypt. The
most famous example of the type is probably the Circe cup in the British Museum
(Fig. 477). Circe is seen standing with a potion-cup in her hand before the somewhat
bedraggled Odysseus. Behind the hero is the loom of the enchantress and one of
Odysseus' companions metamorphosed into a boar. The negroid characteristics in
the profiles and the exaggerated details are a far cry from ordinary Greek work and
bring before our eyes some of the strangest phenomena known in the art of Greece.
The grotesque character of the representations may be an outgrowth of the celebra-
tions in honor of the god Kabeiros, who, like his counterpart Dionysos, favored
dramatic events. The vases were dedicated to Kabeiros. In one example, we see one
carried in a procession by a woman. The cult was popular in Samothrace and Lem-
nos. Many vases have only floral designs such as the ivy or the vine. The shape is
usually a deep bowl with ring handles.

Rather sophisticated in character and provincial in style is a second Bœotian vase
which depicts Herakles drawing water from a fountain (Fig. 478). The design is
executed largely in outline in a black-brown pigment on yellow clay. The vase
belongs to a limited group apparently made at Tanagra. Another example of this
class in the British Museum represents a woman playing kottabos. Still another has
a charming seated figure of a chthonian goddess possibly Demeter or Persephone.[73]

With this brief survey of vases, our discussion of Fourth Century painting ends.
It was a period of great importance for the major art but, on the whole, one of
decadence for ceramics. The facility attained in drawing which gave rise to such
ease in ceramic decoration, oftentimes led to careless and faulty execution. Not
infrequently the use of white for buildings, of gold for various objects, together with
purple and red for garments, produced a gaudy and florid effect. The easel-painters on the other hand, with their ability to give relief to their pictures and with
their interest in light and in the third dimension, carried their art forward into the
realms of true painting. Their coloring was more naturalistic; the background and
accessories became more significant. They modeled their figures out of the local

---

[73] Cf. S. Wide, *Ath. Mitth.*, 26 (1901), pp. 143 ff. and Pl. VIII. He associates them with
Mykalessos because of the presence of Herakles and Demeter who were worshiped in this
center. Tentatively, he proposes a dating for the vases in the second half of the Fifth
Century, while recognizing the freedom in execution which characterizes them.

coloring; they foreshortened with skill and used perspective cleverly, setting their scenes before backgrounds of moderate depth. The illusionistic painting of Apollodoros had obtained control of all means for rendering space, light, or shadow, without exhausting them or trying to do so. The human figure, however, remained the artists' paramount interest and other attractions such as space and setting were always secondary. The painting probably still appeared sculpturesque and, though dramatic subjects came to the fore, a certain traditional nobility of form remained inherent in the figures.

While Athens was developing her painting in the Fourth Century and wandering artists were carrying her traditions over the Greek world, there arose in Greek towns, as far afield as Southern Russia, works of painting which essentially followed Greek traditions but which were often marked with a strong barbaric and provincial stamp. Some of these works should probably be mentioned as a kind of appendix to Fourth Century painting. They bear witness to the strength of Greek influence in remote places. The tombs of Scythian, Thracian, and Macedonian kings and princes give evidence of this vitality.

From the first half of the Fourth Century we have the grave-stele of Apphe, discovered on a road leading from Kertch (Fig. 479). It is, as Minns remarks, a unique work on Scythian soil.[74] The drawing is beautifully done. The outlines were lightly incised on the stone and the space within was originally filled in with color which has since disappeared. The scene represents a woman clad in a brown mantle with a red border, looking down at a child which she holds in her arms. He wears a red cap and a white shirt. In front of her, in our drawing, a herm is shown but other writers have interpreted this as a woman holding a pine cone and a box. Above, against a brown ground, was painted a red inscription which records that the stele is that of Apphe, the wife of Athenaios. White bay leaves crowned the top. The beauty of the work lies in the utter simplicity of the design.

The late Fourth Century is represented by paintings from the Taman Peninsula. Here, in the vault of a chamber tomb covered with a mound now known as the Great Blisnitza, painted cornices were found and in the central coffer of the step-vaulted ceiling, a head of Persephone[75] (Fig. 480). The goddess is silhouetted against a dark blue ground. With this are contrasted the warm flesh tones, her reddish veil with

---

[74] E. H. Minns, *Scythians and Greeks*, Cambridge, 1913, p. 306, Fig. 219. *C.R.*, 1882-1888, pp. 19-20 and Pl. (color).

[75] For an account of these paintings in Southern Russia, see M. Rostovtzeff, *Ancient Decorative Wall-Painting*, *J.H.S.*, 39 (1919), pp. 147 ff., where some of the results presented in his Russian work, *Ancient Decorative Painting in the South of Russia*, Petrograd, 1914, are made available for English readers. In *J.H.S.*, *l. c.*, Fig. 1, Professor Rostovtzeff gives a sketch of the interior of the Blisnitza tumulus. *C.R.*, 1865, text, frontispiece (color).

darker red stripes, and her gaily colored red and yellow flowers with their green leaves. Her hair and eyes are dark brown and she wears beads of gold.

Professor Rostovtzeff further points out that, in the Fourth and Third Centuries on several South Russian sites, we find examples of a "structural" system of wall-decoration in the painted vaults there. One from Kertch, belonging to the Fourth Century, shows "a very primitive decorative scheme" (Fig. 481). The wall, although of stone, is treated as if it were made of brick and is separated into four distinct parts corresponding to the "structural" system of a wall of unbaked bricks. In these walls of unbaked brick, large stones were used for the base. To join the bricks to the base, a course of wood or twigs was necessary and a similar course was required at the top to fit on the roof. This "structural" plan is followed in our example. At the top or cornice, the artist has resorted to the very simple pattern of fillets, wreaths, and oil-vases hung on pegs. The remainder of the wall corresponds to the central portion, intermediate part, and base of the wall. The base was red, the middle part, yellow, and the intermediate part corresponded to a wooden course. Professor Rostovtzeff has shown that this "structural" system of wall-decoration, dating back to Egypt and remaining almost unchanged in later times, led to important decorative principles in the ancient world. The central, undecorated part became the background for Greek, Etruscan, and Italian figure-painting.

Few painted tombs dating from this epoch have been found in Greece proper. Ross mentions one on the island of Ægina[76] and Vollmöller has published a chamber grave in Eretria.[77] Others are known in Tanagra,[78] Thessaly,[79] and Macedonia.[80] The painted vaults of Macedonia are closest in style to the early tombs of Southern Russia. They belong to the tumulus type and were designed for kings and princes in this region.[81] The finest example shows a rider on horse attacking a barbarian enemy and dates well after the age of Alexander (Fig. 482). The design is painted on dry stucco on a white ground. The excellence of the painting lies in the expression of movement. The artist also had a feeling for color; yellow and blue are used on the rider, with some red; red, green, and yellow on the cringing barbarian. We have

[76] Ross, *Archäologische Aufsätze*, I, Pl. II. This grave may belong to the Fifth Century.

[77] K. G. Vollmöller, *Über zwei euböische Kammergräber, Ath. Mitth.*, 26 (1901), pp. 333 ff.

[78] E. Fabricius, *Ein bemaltes Grab aus Tanagra, Ath. Mitth.*, X (1885), pp. 158 ff. Part of a horse probably belonging to the dead,—weapons, etc. On other walls garlands are mentioned in a frieze. Fabricius dates this tomb in the Third Century.

[79] *Eph. Arch.*, 1908, 16; *cf.* 1909, pp. 27 ff. (Arvanitopoullos). He dates the tomb in the Third Century.

[80] Kinch, *Beretning om en Archäologiska Reise i Makedonien*, København, 1893. *Cf.* Danske Vid. Selsk. Skr., 7 Raekke, IV, 3, 1920, pp. 283 ff., Pl. I.

[81] Heuzey et Daumet, *Mission archéol. de Macédoine*, Paris, 1876, pp. 226 ff., 243 ff., Pls. 15, 16, 17. *Cf.* pp. 231, 247, and Pl. 18.

spoken of some of the tombs of Southern Italy where Greek and Etruscan cultures met and influenced the traditional type of painting and tomb. One of the best examples in Greece is the tomb at Eretria.[82] It is a chamber tomb with a dromos, adorned above with stucco imitating marble and with a blue socle below. The chamber proper shows traces of more than one period of decoration. The outer layer today has a white ground on which designs were painted in tempera in dull, chalky colors which were easily washed off with water. Near the top of the wall was a row of iron pegs which formed a point of departure for the artist. These pegs carried painted wreaths, bands, flowers, and the like. Under the present painting, a dark blue ground is evident everywhere. Real objects were apparently hung on iron pegs on the wall at this time. Later, in the painting visible today, the wall ground was made white and the objects hanging from iron pegs were painted in color. They apparently hang from pegs which touch the outer edge of incised concentric circles. Some wreaths were formed from these circles in two rows. Over the door between the iron nails hang three fillets. This decoration of objects hung from pegs is found in Fourth Century tombs in Southern Russia (cf. Fig. 481).

[82] Cf. n. 77.

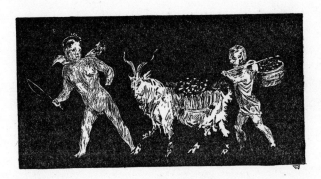

# X

# HELLENISTIC, GRAECO-ROMAN, POMPEIAN, AND ROMAN PAINTING

BY 300 B.C., Greek painting had become master of space, color, and light. It had shown no interest in landscape for itself, but man had remained the dominant concern of the artist. In one hundred and fifty years, painting had passed through many stages on its way toward developing perfection in technique—from the tinted profiles of the early Fifth Century, through the modeling of forms with light and shadow, to a more properly pictorial manner in which scenes were occasionally set against a background of nature. From the Third Century onward, the attention of the painter was directed toward giving an illusion of the real world in his creations and toward the expression of emotion. The one great development left for the Hellenistic age was landscape. This appealed to the Hellenistic artist because it formed a part of the realism toward which he was striving. In fact, we shall find that two main tendencies mark the art of this epoch: an interest in the realistic and in the picturesque.

With the Hellenistic age, the independent city-states were submerged in a more universal culture.[1] The center of painting under the Diadochi, the successors of Alexander, was no longer to be found in Greece; the scepter of power had passed to Rhodes, Antioch, Pergamon, and Alexandria. The Orient became Greek—at least superficially—and art changed just as life and taste and letters had changed. But there was no great break with the work of the past, nor did painting alter by leaps and bounds. The idealism of the Fifth and Fourth Centuries was shot with realism and the representation of genre scenes, which began in the Fourth Century, became

[1] W. W. Tarn, *Hellenistic Civilisation*, London, 1927, gives an excellent survey of Hellenistic civilization; *cf.* J. B. Bury and others, *The Hellenistic Age*, Cambridge, 1923.

very common; the Grylloi of Antiphilos were carried on in the caricatures of this period. The Hellenistic baroque element had its germs in sensational painters like Theon; in the pathos of sculptors like Skopas and in the excess of Fourth Century masters. Fondness for realism gave rise to paintings of still-life, and probably also to the pronounced interest in rhopography, or "odd bits" drawn from daily existence. Life—pulsating, unadulterated life—was what the Hellenistic artist cared about.

Whether or not there were any great schools of painting in the Hellenistic age, we cannot be certain. Hellenistic painting is imperfectly known to us and must in great measure be judged from secondary sources, such as Pompeian wall-painting and mosaics. More important than the schools and more rewarding as a study are the various *types* of paintings developed in this period. Megalography,[2] or figure painting on a grand scale, is still found, especially in centers like Pergamon. Mythological subjects were employed. Very often an idyllic element was combined with figure painting, as, for example, in the picture of Polyphemos and Galatea (Fig. 543), or in the Tired Silenus receiving a drink (Fig. 498). Frequently, a playful element or a fondness for the pretty and exotic, the coquettish and the trivial, mark the paintings of the period. In this development, Aëtion in his "Marriage of Alexander and Roxana," had had a part and also the older Timanthes in his "Satyrs measuring the thumb of a sleeping Cyclops." Myths were frequently parodied and the scandals of the Olympians, of demigods and mortals, occupied a place in the limelight. The pornographic pictures begun by Parrhasios and Pausias culminated in this epoch and were seized upon later by the Pompeian artist. The stage also had its influence on art. Daily life, which, in the Hellenistic age, became a leading theme for the artist, often appeared in painting in its more ignoble aspects. Ugly and brutally realistic scenes were depicted, drawn directly from existence and similar in tone to the material presented on the stage by the comic poets. The age falls into two main divisions—an early, creative phase, followed by a later one of creative exhaustion and decline. Art collecting became an important pastime. Picture galleries were established. There had been collections of paintings earlier: in the Fifth Century there were votive paintings in the Heræum at Samos and in the Pinacotheca of the Propylæa at Athens. In the Hellenistic age, the Sikyonian painters had a hall at Sikyon given over to their masterpieces. There were public and royal galleries and possibly private ones, especially at Pergamon, and rulers such as the Attalids and Ptolemies vied with one another in collecting. In contrast to the increasing poverty in great work by creative masters, decorative wall-painting developed much more rapidly. The walls of houses and palaces must have been gorgeous with color. The

---

[2] This term may even be applied to landscape. Vitruvius, VII, 5, 2. G. Rodenwaldt, "Megalographia," *Röm. Mitth.*, XXIX (1914), pp. 194-199.

wealthiest homes were encased on the interior with slabs of gaily colored marbles and were hung with brilliant tapestries. Probably marble reliefs also formed a part of the mural decoration, as the series of Hellenistic landscape reliefs would seem to indicate. In addition, mosaics on the floors enriched the interiors. We know that in the tent of Ptolemy II (*ca.* 275 B.C.), paintings were placed between the columns, and hanging tapestries alternated with them.[3] The interiors of less elaborate homes were covered with colored stuccoes and were doubtless also adorned with wall-decorations in the form of tapestries.

We will consider first the possible schools of painting and the known artists of note who may have been connected with them, turning later to the different classes of Hellenistic painting, in order to form some idea of the achievement of this age. During the Hellenistic epoch, there were prominent painters working at Sikyon, as there had been in the Fourth Century, and, in fact, from the earliest times when painting first arose in Greece.[3a] Whether these Sikyonian masters carried on the academic traditions of the school of the Fourth Century, or whether there was an actual school in the Hellenistic period, we do not know. Two prominent names point to Sikyon—Timanthes II and Nealkes. Timanthes made famous the victory of the Sikyonian noble, Aratos, over the Ætolians.[4] Aratos restored the democracy in the Third Century and, out of hatred for the tyrants, destroyed all pictures of them. Not even the entreaties of Nealkes could prevail upon him to spare a work of Melanthios and Apelles, but he insisted on blotting out the figure of the tyrant Aristratos. The nature of Timanthes' work, we do not know. Plutarch says that he "represented the battle in a painting full of life." This combat occurred at Pellene about 241 B.C. A. Reinach suggests that Timanthes II may have been the grandson of the first Timanthes—the late Fifth Century artist.[5]

Nealkes is a more vivid figure than Timanthes II. That he was a friend of Aratos is evident from the story cited above.[6] He was apparently best known as a painter of genre scenes. Fronto, in speaking of him, asks if anyone would expect *magnifica* from Nealkes, implying that his forte lay in the opposite direction.[7] We learn that

[3] Athen., V, 196[e]-197[c]; F. Studniczka, *Abh. der Kgl. Sächs. Ges. der Wiss.*, Phil.-hist. Kl., 30 (1915): *Das Symposion Ptolemaios II; cf.* F. Caspari, *Das Nilschiff Ptolemaios IV, Jahr.*, 31 (1916), pp. 1 ff.

[3a] Charles H. Skalet, *Ancient Sicyon, with a Prosopographia Sicyonia*, Baltimore, 1928, pp. 127 ff. ("The Johns Hopkins University Studies in Archæology," No. 3, edited by David M. Robinson).

[4] Plut., *Arat.*, 32, 3.

[5] A. Reinach, *Rec. Milliet*, I, 394, n. 2. This chronology seems highly improbable. It is more likely that he was the great-great-grandson of Timanthes I.

[6] *Vs.* this view, *cf.* Jex-Blake, Sellers, *The Elder Pliny's Chapters on the History of Art*, p. 166; *cf.* A. Reinach, *Rec. Milliet*, I, 395, n. 6.

[7] Fronto, *Ad Verum*, I (Naber), p. 113.

he painted a foaming horse and since he had not been successful in representing the foam and the hot breath from the nostrils, he resorted to the expedient which seems to have been a stereotyped one for enraged Greek artists—that is, he threw a sponge at the painting and obtained his effect.[8] The genius of Nealkes was revealed, Pliny intimates, in a painting of a naval battle between the Egyptians and Persians.[9] Here, "wishing to show that it was fought on the Nile (the waters of which are like those of the sea), he indicated by a symbol that which art alone could not express, painting an ass drinking on the river's brim and a crocodile lying in wait for it."[10] As Reinach, following Münzer, has shown, the battle referred to is one of those which finally resulted in the subjugation of Egypt by Artaxerxes Ochos.[11] In derision, his name, Ochos, was changed by the Egyptians and the Greek mercenaries who fought with them, to *Onos*, "donkey," so that the ass has more significance than at first appears. The symbolism of the Egyptian crocodile watching the Persian donkey refers to historical events dating about 350, but might still be applicable in the time of Aratos. Either we must suppose an earlier Nealkes as grandfather of the friend of Aratos, or we must believe with Reinach that the event was painted one hundred years later to flatter the Egyptians with whom the Sikyonians had close relations at this time. The adjusting of the evidence, in any case, is difficult but the latter explanation seems more likely. This work of Nealkes appears to be reflected in a Pompeian wall-painting of humorous design which represents a man attempting to pull a stubborn, thirsty donkey from the clutches of a crocodile (Fig. 483). The scene is placed in an Egyptianized landscape, with a baboon in the foreground. Probably the genre element in the work is not unlike the attempt of Nealkes. Nealkes had several pupils: first, his daughter; secondly, Erigonos, who ground his colors and who later rose to be a famous artist as the teacher of Pasias; and last of all, Xenon of Sikyon.[11a]

Whether or not there was an Alexandrian school of painters seems difficult to decide. Antiphilos, who lived there before the founding of the city, is not known to have had any pupils. Only one name points certainly to Alexandria—that of Polemon, which is mentioned by Pliny in passing.[12] Far more interesting to us is Demetrios, the *topographos*, or landscape-painter. His Egyptian origin cannot be proved, but he appears to have been a painter of note received at the court of Ptolemy VI, Philometor, whom he later befriended when Ptolemy was exiled by his brother.[13]

---

[8] Pliny, *N.H.*, 35, 104; Plutarch, *De Fort.*, 4.

[9] Pliny, *N.H.*, 35, 142; *cf.* E. Pfuhl, *Gött. Gel. Anz.*, 172 (1910), p. 821.

[10] The translation is quoted from Jex-Blake, Sellers.

[11] Münzer, *Hermes*, 1895, p. 532, n. 2; A. Reinach, *op. cit.*, p. 395, n. 6; Münzer supposes there were two painters with the name Nealkes.

[11a] The name rests on an emendation.

[12] Pliny, *N.H.*, 35, 146. Athen. IV, 184[b], seems to imply an Alexandrian school.

[13] Val. Max., 5, 1, 1; Diod. Sic., *Exc.* XXXI, 18. A. Reinach does not identify this Demetrios with the one whose father was Seleukos. *Cf. Rec. Milliet*, I, 405, n. 2.

Most scholars now incline to believe that the term *topographos* can hardly be applied
to mere map-making and that in Demetrios we have the first attested Greek landscape-painter of note.[14] Ptolemy was driven out of Egypt in 164 B.C., so that Demetrios was apparently a painter of the Second Century who probably influenced later
Pompeian wall-painting in the field of landscape. Serapion, a painter of the late
Hellenistic period, who worked in Rome, was probably also of Egyptian origin,
to judge from his name. He painted a giant picture in Rome which covered the whole
of the balconies by the old shops.[15] He was a good painter of *scænæ,* or stage
fronts, but could not paint human figures. In other words, he was probably a scene-
painter, painting the settings on the fronts of stage-buildings. His work may have
lain in the field of landscape. The learned grammarian, Dionysios of Thrace, painted
his teacher, Aristarchos, with tragedy ἐν τῷ στήθει,[16] "on his breast," wishing to say
that in all that concerned tragedy he spoke from memory and expressed what he
knew by heart. What this painting must have been seems difficult to conjecture.
Some have supposed a mask to represent Tragedy, on the breast of Aristarchos. It is
almost impossible to think of a female figure reposing on the chest of Aristarchos!
The novelty of the conception has caused the work to be cited, but it is just this
novelty which escapes us. It can hardly be something set into the breast of the figure.
The painting belongs somewhere near the middle of the Second Century, since
Aristarchos died about 140 B.C. Euanthes is the last important artist connected with
Alexandria who can be more than a name to us. Achilles Tatius gives several long
descriptions of paintings by him.[17] The accounts are in bad taste and do little more
than embroider for us the subject matter. In the Temple of Zeus at Pelusium his
Freeing of Andromeda by Perseus and of Prometheus by Herakles were exhibited.
Perseus was represented attacking the monster. Euanthes, unlike Nikias, who chose
to represent a later moment when Perseus was freeing Andromeda, preferred the
dramatic aspect of the engagement. The description of Andromeda is a piece of fine
writing in which her eyes are described "as violets which had just begun to fade";
her fingers "hung like bunches of fruit from a vine." The paintings may even be
fictions of Achilles Tatius, but as he came from Alexandria, they may have existed,
though they were not certainly painted in his time.

It is unfortunate that accounts of the Alexandrian school are so fragmentary. We
should like more information on impressionism, landscape, the famous "short cuts"

---

[14] W. Helbig, *Untersuchungen über die campanische Wandmalerei,* Leipzig, 1873, pp. 138,
169, 289, 322; K. Woermann, *Die Landschaft in der Kunst der alten Völker,* p. 219; *Die
Landschaftsmalerei bei Griechen und Römern,* in *Von Apelles zu Böcklin,* Eszlingen, 1912,
pp. 24-25; *cf.* E. Pfuhl, *Gött. Gelehrt. Anz.,* 172 (1910), p. 820.

[15] Pliny, *N.H.,* 35, 113.

[16] Eustath., *Ad Il.,* p. 974, 9, has the phrase—φέροντα ἐπὶ στήθους τὴν τραγῳδίαν.

[17] Achilles Tatius, *Leukippe and Kleitophon,* III, 6.

which ruined Roman painting and which were invented here, and numerous other matters.

In Asia Minor, there were great centers of painting in the Hellenistic age. There was doubtless a Pergamene school of painting just as there was one of sculpture. In a city as rich as Pergamon in the days of the Attalids, painting must have flourished. The King, Attalos II, paid enormous sums for original works and also sent his own painters to Greece to copy celebrated paintings for his gallery.[18] An inscription from Delphi speaks of three painters who copied there—Kalas, Gaudotos, and a third lost name, ending in -ides. We have a record of one famous Pergamene painting which represented a Victory over the Galatians and which appears to have had its counterpart in the sculpture of the time. In other words, painting and sculpture were developing along similar lines in Pergamon in the Third and Second Centuries before Christ.

The best copy of a work of the Pergamene school which we possess today is the famous fresco of Herakles discovering his son Telephos in Arcadia (Fig. 484). This is painted in a massive style and calls to mind the execution of the giants on the altar at Pergamon. The figures are of heroic mould. At the left, Arcadia—a colossal and powerful personification of the locality—is enthroned. She is as mighty as the rocks among which she sits. Her yellow garment falls in heavy folds and a rich wreath of flowers surrounds her head. The repose of the goddess is emphasized by the upright staff in her left hand. The figure contrasts in color and in power with the winged divinity at the right, who points out Telephos to Herakles. She may be Dike-Themis or Parthenos, and was perhaps the guardian of the child. Her mantle is red. The figure of Herakles is strongly individualized. The brushwork on the head is done in broad strokes with patches of white here and there—a manner which is opposed to the sculpturesque treatment found in the head of Arcadia. Two distinct methods of painting are evident here: first, the old Attic style of the Fifth and Fourth Centuries, dependent on line, and exemplified in the head of Arcadia (Fig. 486); secondly, the new impressionistic method in which the painting was done in patches of color. The latter technique may be seen on the head of Herakles (Fig. 485), and on the young satyr behind Arcadia. This youthful figure, with his shepherd's crook and pipe, and his engaging smile, has been called an ancient Franz Hals.

New and old elements exist side by side in this painting. In addition to the technical details noted, the old Greek method of representing landscape by personification and allusion is present here. The wildness of the locality is indicated by the lion; the place itself, by Arcadia and the satyr. The beginnings of still-life are seen in the basket of fruits resting beside Arcadia. The animal scenes of later times may

[18] M. Fränkel, *Gemälde-Sammlungen und Gemälde-Forschung in Pergamon, Jahr.*, VI (1891), pp. 49 ff.

have originated in figures such as occur here in the foreground. The skill of the artist is revealed in the arrangement of the diagonals; in the pairs of heads posed similarly and inclined in the same direction, but alternately dark and light; and in the clever way in which he emphasizes the Telephos group by setting it against the rock of the foreground. The spirit of the work and the details call to mind the Telephos frieze from Pergamon, and we may assume that both works copy a great original. Telephos nurtured by a hind and guarded by an eagle occurs on Pergamene coins. The grandiose manner in which our painting is executed is on a par with the conception. It is far finer in this respect than the reliefs. The picture is symbolic of the glory of the Attalid house, which claimed descent from Telephos. It is a mature composition of Pergamene origin.

A copy of an earlier work may perhaps be found in a small Pompeian fresco in which a Hellenistic general is shown decking out a trophy in the presence of Victory (Fig. 487). The head is individualized and probably represents Attalos I standing beside a token of victory. The armor includes a Gallic horned helmet, and a cuirass on which muscles are indicated recalling the trophy reliefs from the hall of Athena at Pergamon. The painting shows the restraint of early Hellenistic work. In coloring we find three leading tones: the purple mantle and green chiton of Attalos contrasted with the grayish blue-green mantle of the Niké. The weapons are shining gold.

In addition to the megalography of the Telephos painting, Pergamon developed painters of still-life and of animal scenes. An example of still-life is found in the mosaic by Sosos from Pergamon.[19] He made the one known as the "Unswept Floor" for the dining-room of a house in Pergamon. In this work, scraps of food which had fallen from the table were shown strewn about in confusion. The original of Sosos was apparently copied by Herakleitos in a mosaic found in Rome in 1833 on the Aventine and now in the Lateran Museum[20] (Fig. 488). The central mosaic has been lost, but about the middle portion ran four narrow mosaics with designs of flora and fauna found along the Nile—ducks, Nile-plants, crocodiles, fish, the ibis, etc. Adjoining this band on three sides, was a white field covered with remains of food—a chicken's foot, sea-animals, part of a wishbone, bits of fruit and vegetables—and a mouse about to nibble at a morsel. The mosaic is made of pieces of glass and colored stones, and the designs are naturalistically rendered with cast shadows. The colors are fresh green, red, brown, yellow, white, and black. The fourth side of the mosaic was decorated with six scenic masks. Between these, vases and other objects alternated. The decoration with masks is typically Alexandrian. The mosaic is signed by

[19] Pliny, N.H., 36, 184.
[20] B. Nogara, I mosaici antichi, Milano, 1910, pp. 3-5, Pls. V-VII; W. Helbig, Führer,[3] II, 49.

Herakleitos, who was probably an artist living in the time of the Roman Empire. It apparently formed a part of the decoration of a dining-room. The taste of the owner —and of Sosos, in fact—is a matter which need not be discussed. He must have been the Trimalchio of his day. There is a similar but fragmentary mosaic in North Africa.[20a]

The destroyed mosaic in the center of the room may well have been a copy of Sosos' "Drinking Doves" which has come down to us in three copies. Figure 489 represents a Roman transcript from Hadrian's Villa, but a second mosaic, found at Pompeii, is probably a free Hellenistic rendering of the original. Pliny describes the work of Sosos so accurately that we are able to recognize the prototype of the later copies.[21] In our reproduction, four doves are perched on the edge of a metal basin filled with water and one of them is drinking. The waters are shaded but there is no reflection of the dove which Pliny praised in the original. The mosaic is a fine study in light and shadow. With this chiaroscuro, the doves are modeled; it gives the metallic quality to the bowl and renders the shadows of the water. The mosaic has often been copied and is still being paraphrased in Italy today. In one Hellenistic example, parrots have been substituted for the doves, except in one instance, and other details such as fruits and a marsh-lynx have been added.[22] The coloring is lively—brown, red, blue, green, and yellow being used. Another example of still-life is seen in a mosaic representing a basket of gaily colored flowers (Fig. 490), a type which may have developed from the wreaths and flowers begun by Pausias. Still finer is the painting of Figure 491, where peaches and a glass vessel containing water present us with a type of painting known as *Xenion*. In these Xenia, the various kinds of foods offered to guests visiting a rich household were represented. The ancient practice of receiving traveling guests who desired at all costs to avoid the bad inns of the time, probably led to a kind of lodging system under which the guest received the raw food from his host and prepared it himself. The still-life paintings of Pompeii often represent such rations. Fruit, eggs, fowls, vegetables, fish, and other foods are common in these pictures. Our Figure 491 offers some impressionistically rendered peaches which have a very modern look. In fact, it seems hard to realize that the painting in question is about 2000 years old. The artist is in full command of shading, perspective, and the use of color.[22a] The color of the shelves on which the

[20a] E. Petersen, *Arch. Anz.*, 18 (1903), p. 13. I owe the information to Professor Rostovtzeff of Yale University. V. Spinazzola, *Le arti decorative in Pompeii*, p. 183, for the doves.

[21] Pliny, *N.H.*, 36, 184; *cf.* Helbig, *Führer*,³ I, 438-439. *Cf.* P. Herrmann, *Denkmäler der Malerei*, p. 12, n. 1. The mosaic from Pompeii has a shadow of the drinking dove.

[22] O. Keller, *Die antike Tierwelt*, II (1913), Fig. 19, p. 46 (color).

[22a] H. G. Beyen, *Über Stillleben aus Pompeii und Herculaneum*, Haag, 1928, pp. 34 ff., Pl. VII; *Jahr.*, XLII (1927), pp. 41 ff., Pls. I-II.

fruit is placed ranges from violet above to brownish red below. The glass is a greenish white with reflections from the water in a grayish green. The peaches are unripe, the leaves a Veronese green.

There were undoubtedly many other artists working at Pergamon whose names are lost to us. The famous Pompeian painting of Herakles and Omphale (Fig. 497), which has been called an antique Rubens, may well be a copy of a Pergamene work, but we have treated in this section only artists and copies of originals definitely connected with Pergamon, as far as our evidence points.

We cannot prove that there was a school of painting at Rhodes. We infer it because there was a famous school of sculpture in the island and because certain names of painters are identical with those of Rhodian sculptors. We should like to know whether the sculptor Tauriskos, who came from Tralles, and who made the famous group of Dirce trampled by the bull, was also responsible for the painting which deals with the same subject (Fig. 462). The sculptured group and the Pompeian painting obviously follow a common original which may fall anywhere between the middle of the Fourth Century and the end of the Third, and which was apparently a painting.

One of the most famous artists of the Hellenistic age was Timomachos of Byzantium.[23] He lived, according to Pliny, in the time of Julius Cæsar. The Dictator is said to have paid eighty talents, or about $80,000 for his Ajax and his unfinished Medea. He is known to have painted in addition: Orestes and Iphigeneia *in Tauris;* a portrait of a gymnastic trainer; a picture of a distinguished family, and two men in cloaks, about to speak, one sitting, the other standing. Several of these paintings have come down to us in Pompeian copies, the most famous of which is the Medea.

Two Medea types—a seated and a standing one—occur in Campanian painting. The one which we prefer to link with Timomachos comes from Herculaneum and is in a fragmentary condition, only the figure of Medea being preserved (Fig. 492). She stands in deep meditation, pressing her sword closely to her. Her eyes betray pain and anger. The painting is a masterful study of a soul torn by conflicting emotions. The tragic pathos of the figure is heightened by the drawn lips, open mouth, and tense brows. This Medea formed part of a group which was apparently similar to the copy seen in Figure 493. Here, the Pompeian artist has probably added to his original in perspective and in lighting effects, but the composition doubtless echoes the original of Timomachos. The figure of Medea is less fine than the one from Herculaneum but the outward calm and inward desperation indicate the same emotional turmoil. Medea, in this case, stands out illumined in bright sunlight coming from the front and bathing the bodies of the children. Her anxious attitude is contrasted with the carefree play of the children seated at the altar on which they

[23] Pliny, *N.H.*, 35, 136.

are soon to be sacrificed. In the door stands the old pedagogue, who is perhaps a Pompeian addition to the painting of Timomachos. Even in the altered copy, we feel the greatness of the original and observe the simple means employed to express the intense emotion of this gigantic battle of the soul. Violet and yellow, with some blue, mark the garments of Medea; the old pedagogue wears a grayish-green mantle while those of the children are deep red and blue.

Some of the spirit of a fine original still lurks in a painting found at Pompeii, which depicts Orestes and Iphigeneia among the Taurians (Fig. 494). The work may go back to Timomachos but this can in no way be proved. In the center, the priestess, Iphigeneia, with an idol of Artemis on her arm, prepares to descend the steps of a temple, the upper part of which is destroyed in our copy. The barbarian King, Thoas, is seated at the right with his spear-bearer beside him, while at the left stand the captives, Orestes and Pylades, their hands bound behind their backs. They are guarded by a spear-bearer with a yellow tiara drawn over his head. The two friends are finely contrasted (Fig. 495)—the spirited, fiery head of the defiant Pylades forming a splendid foil for the dejected and resigned Orestes. The crimson mantle of Orestes is also opposed to the yellow one of Pylades, while Iphigeneia wears a white garment and stands before a pale violet curtain. The crown on the head of one victim and the flaming altar indicate the bloody sacrifice which is to occur after the purification. The brooding calm of Orestes and the intense excitement and anger of his companion are moods such as Timomachos liked to portray, as we have seen in his Medea. The breathless moment before a tragedy, the pathos of a situation and contrasting moods especially interested him. The painting is to be connected with Euripides' tragedy, "Iphigeneia among the Taurians," although it varies from the tragedy in many respects, e.g., in the meeting between Thoas and his captives. Iphigeneia is on the point of purifying her victims. Judged from an artistic point of view, the painting ranks high. Orestes and Pylades are superb Greek figures, probably created for an original which depicted the meeting between the youths and Iphigeneia. Two other paintings which portray this legend present no suggestion of connections with an important original.[24] A third example from the house of Cæcilius Jucundus (Herrmann, Pl. 118), is superior to these. Yet another example has been found in the recent excavations at Pompeii in the Street of Abundance.[24a]

We have no monument which gives us a satisfactory idea of the Mad Ajax of

[24] Herrmann, *op. cit.*, Pls. 117, 119. H. Bulle, *Untersuch. an griech. Theatern*, pp. 314-315, considers the background a stage background as also in the case of Fig. 493, *cf.* p. 279, note 1.

[24a] I owe the information to Professor Rostovtzeff of Yale University. See also H. Philippart, "Iconographie de l'Iphigénie en Tauride d'Euripide," *Rev. belge de phil. et d'histoire*, IV (1925), pp. 5 ff.

Timomachos. We recognize the type from several works among the minor arts, e.g., a terra cotta lamp. The hero is seated beneath a tree resting his head on his hand in an attitude of brooding dejection. He has his sword in his hand and is pondering suicide. Before him is a slain animal.

A number of Eastern painters, whom it is difficult to localize, painted interesting works of art. Ktesikles is known, according to Pliny, from an affront which he offered to Queen Stratoniké, who received him without honor. "He painted her lying in the arms of a fisherman, her reputed lover, and had the picture exhibited in the port of Ephesos after he himself had sped away with all sails set. The queen, however, did not allow the picture to be removed, as both portraits were excellent likenesses."[25] Artemon seems also to have painted a portrait of this queen and a composition which represented Danaë and pirates marveling at her.[26] There are some Pompeian paintings which treat the latter theme, but the charm of the original is certainly lacking.[27] Artemon's Herakles and Deianeira, which is reproduced in several Campanian paintings, is more possible for us to conceive.[28] One of the best copies, which may go back to Artemon, is seen in Figure 496. The moment is represented when Nessos begs Herakles for permission to carry Deianeira across the Evenus river, which it was necessary for them to ford on their journey. Deianeira stands in a chariot drawn by two horses and is on the point of taking the small Hyllos in her arms. She is dressed in a violet chiton and wears a white veil drawn up over her head. Herakles appears to regard the centaur with distrust. The stream is vaguely seen in the foreground. In the background are trees and a wall. The outcome of the event was an attempt on the part of the centaur to outrage Deianeira. As a result of this, he was shot through the heart by Herakles. The color scale reveals a predominating yellow, with brownish red for flesh tones, much use of green and some violet. The cool effect of the color scheme in the painting is very pleasing.

Other paintings by Artemon are little more than names to us—the Apotheosis of Herakles, and Laomedon, Herakles, and Poseidon. There were many other painters working at this time in the Greek East, about whom we know so little that it is not worth while to discuss their works in detail. On the other hand, the compositions of certain nameless masters have a greater importance for us today and tell us more of the accomplishment of the artists of the time. One of these men painted the panel of "Herakles and Omphale," a picture preserved for us today in a copy from the House of Marcus Lucretius, at Pompeii. As the beauty of the work lies largely in the masterful use of color, we shall not reproduce it here in its entirety. Herakles is

---

[25] Pliny, *N.H.*, 35, 140. The translation is quoted from Jex-Blake, Sellers.
[26] Pliny, *N.H.*, 35, 139.      [27] *Cf.* Helbig, *Wandgemälde*, No. 119.
[28] *Cf.* Helbig, 1146 (Alinari 12026)—treated with mastery and apparently after a good original; Herrmann, *Denkmäler, Farbendruck*, V, and Pl. 147.

represented in the toils of Omphale. The muscular giant is leading an effeminate life, serving the Queen of Lydia, to atone for his murder of Iphitos. He is shown tormented by his captors. At the right, Omphale, wearing his lion skin and carrying his club, casts a cold glance of scorn at him. A Love pipes in his ears and he is made sport of by all the Dionysiac rabble. The painting is the creation of a colorist like Rubens, the achievement of a man accustomed to working with masses. The upper part of the picture is a stream of greenish blue; the lower half makes much use of crimson and rich yellow. Against these grounds the warm flesh tones stand out. Figure 497 gives a detail of the painting. The garment of Omphale is yellow with a blue border, while Herakles wears a red mantle lined with blue. In our reproduction, the head of the distressed Herakles, who is supported by Priapos, is seen above, while below is Omphale, with the fine head of a Lydian servant behind her. As has been said, the work may be copied after an original of the Pergamene school. The forms are heroic in scale and fill the entire space except for a small stretch of blue above the heads. Of the eleven people represented, only three full figures are seen, but the impression of a crowd is well given. In spite of the pitiful position to which Herakles has been reduced, he still dominates the scene.

The pictures which we have been discussing are mainly examples of Greek megalography, dating from the Third and Second Centuries B.C. In addition to these, there exists an extensive group of figure paintings which possess a certain idyllic charm and which give us a very characteristic side of Hellenistic art. One of the best of these is the Tired Silenus of Figure 498—a painting on marble from Herculaneum. It may even copy a Fourth Century composition but the spirit is that of Hellenistic painting. At the right, Silenus, weary from his ride, is seated on a rock, drinking from a rhyton offered him by the daughters of King Pandion, Procne and Philomela.[29] One sister stands beside the tired donkey at the left and covers him with her mantle. Only the front of the animal and the rear indicated in perspective are seen. Two trees round out the composition. The coloring has suffered greatly; some greens and browns are faintly visible today with violet, red and yellow.

The playful and coquettish element, known to have existed in certain Hellenistic paintings, is found in many Pompeian copies. This more trifling treatment of subject matter began in the days of Aëtion, as we saw in his Marriage of Alexander and Roxana. In the composition which represents Ares and Aphrodite (Fig. 499), two Erotes are busily playing with the armor of Ares, but the coquettish attitude of the goddess, Aphrodite, would not have been possible in the earlier work. To the beauty of the rich coloring, where purple, blue, and gold predominate, is added the grace of the figures, the contrasts of light and shadow and the diagonal cleverly cutting the field.

[29] C. Robert, "Der müde Silen," *Hall. Winckelmannsprogr.*, 23 (1899).

We could enumerate other pictures which show this playful element even more clearly—for example, the wrestling match between Pan and Eros before Dionysos and Ariadne (Fig. 500), or the Lovers with the nest of Loves.[30] We shall not elaborate our thesis but shall turn rather to a consideration of certain additional types of compositions characteristic of the Hellenistic age. Among these were character painting, scenes from everyday life, and animal paintings. These became the forerunners of modern canvases of this kind.

Pliny mentions a painter Kalates, who executed small scenes from comedy. His clever observation of life and joy in the popular, the homely, and ugly, are doubtless reflected in two mosaics by Dioskourides of Samos.[31] One of these, we have had occasion to mention when we were discussing the beginnings of the impressionistic technique (Fig. 445). There we noted the striving for realism in the handling of a street scene where strolling musicians were performing. The mosaic probably goes back to a prototype of the Fourth or Third Century B.C. but in its present form was doubtless made about 100 B.C. It apparently copied the spirit, the strength, and the impressionistic use of color of the original. The composition is a simple one. Light and shadow are handled with great dexterity. A second work by Dioskourides represented a young woman consulting a pharmaceutria, or a magician dealing in love magic.[32] The scene recalls the second Theocritean idyll and the mimes of Herodas. Two women are seated at a table advising with an old witch in regard to a love affair. One acts as an agent for her friend. At the right is a small maid-servant.

Of a piece with works of this nature were the genre scenes depicting brothels, processions, the circus and the amphitheater, scenes in fullers' shops, such as Simos painted, or the barber shops, cobblers' stalls, and eatables of Peiraïkos. These men were the Dutch masters—the Jan Steens and Van Ostades of ancient times—working with everyday life in all its phases. "Odd bits" such as these have come down to us in degenerate form in Pompeian copies.

One of the most charming paintings extant from antiquity gives us a scene taken from everyday existence (Plate I, color). In the "Flora" found at Stabiæ, near Pompeii, we have an ancient piece full of freshness and life. A young woman is shown gathering flowers and filling a basket which she carries on her arm. The blossom which she plucks at the moment seems almost an afterthought as she turns in passing and breaks it lightly from the stem. Her soft, filmy garments of yellow and bluish white seem to be gently blown by the wind. They have slipped from her right shoulder leaving it bare and adding greatly to the beauty of the figure which is seen in back view. The graceful turn of the body and the softness of the cheek have been

[30] Herrmann, *Denkmäler*, Pl. 17.

[31] M. Bieber and G. Rodenwaldt, *Jahr.*, 26 (1911), pp. 1 ff. See Ch. IX, note 35.

[32] Herrmann, *Denkmäler*, Pl. 107. Herzog, *Herondas*. I owe the reference to Professor Rostovtzeff.

well caught by the painter. The drawing is delicate and refined. Here and there the painter employs patches of color impressionistically. The hand breaking off the flower, the hair, and the plants are done with unusual ingenuity with daubs of color put on in impressionistic fashion. Nowhere is there any sharp outline. The painting is beautifully luminous. As has been said, "It is woven of morning vapor and clear sunlight." The figure is set against a gray-green ground. Its modernity seems striking to us today.

In the Hellenistic age, although the human figure remains the dominant interest of the Greek artist, other elements come to the fore to share in this preoccupation. Among these is a fondness for landscape and for scenes with animals. In earlier Hellenistic art, there was a predilection for paintings with animals. An example of this type of picture may be seen in an excellent mosaic from Pompeii, which belongs to the period of the First Style of decoration (200-80 B.C.). A lion is shown rending a panther in a rocky landscape (Fig. 501). Despite the faulty foreshortening and proportions of the lion, the mosaic is executed with real power and is filled with the violence of wild life. The artist has presented a vivid scene of brute force, rage, and suffering. In the space at his disposal he has cleverly arranged two wild beasts in mortal conflict beside a stream. Unlike the usual Greek artist, the maker of the mosaic had seen lions and panthers and he was able to depict their vital struggles and indomitable rages with genuine mastery. The cat-like body of the panther and his spotted hide with its furry texture have all been well observed. The lion stands triumphant over his groveling foe, digging his huge claws into the bloodstained body of his enemy. He appears to be still trembling from the blow which has laid low his victim; his muscles are tensely drawn and we can fairly hear the roar of fury emitted from his huge body. The representation of animals for their own sake probably came from Alexandria. We read of various kinds of beasts being led in the processions and festivals of Ptolemy Philadelphos.[33] Ptolemy had a zoölogical garden containing panthers, lynxes, leopards, some oxen from Africa and India, wild asses from Syria, a giraffe, a rhinoceros, and a white bear—to say nothing of rare birds. Many Pompeian works of art have representations of animals which were at home along the Nile and in the deserts of Africa. These bear no relation to the fauna of Southern Italy. Such a painting is Figure 502, from Pompeii, in which the antelope, elephant, and other animals of Northern Africa are presented. Unless the Italians were picturing their zoos, these works of art have no connection with the animal life of the country. This fact becomes more evident when one looks at Pompeian mosaics. A very large number reflect the fauna and flora of the Nile valley (Fig. 503). In this example, we see a rhinoceros, an ichneumon, water-birds, a uræus, and other Egyp-

[33] Athen., V, 197c. Cf. esp. pp. 200 ff.; G. Loisel, *Histoire des ménageries*, I, 1912; George Jennings, *Noah's Cargo*, London, 1928.

tian animals. The ibis and hippopotamus are favorites on the mosaics. Probably the animal hunts which came to play such an important part in Pompeian painting were also copied from those of the Ptolemies and eastern potentates. Walls covered with giant hunting scenes have been found in the new excavations in the Street of Abundance at Pompeii. These pieces may have been influenced by the Roman *venationes*, but an interest in animals of strange types doubtless arose among the Romans as a result of their contact with Northern Africa and Egypt. The paintings may thus illustrate the animal lore of the Hellenistic period. This theory would explain some of the strange beasts painted on the walls of a tomb at Marissa in Palestine (Figs. 556-559).

Another mosaic from Pompeii pictures a cat attacking a fowl, while below is a representation of live ducks and sea-food (Fig. 504). This animal piece shows the same clever observation of nature that we found in the lion mosaic but is drawn from domestic sources rather than from wild life. It is in a class with the doves of Sosos. The lower section combines still-life with animals and may belong to the Xenion type of painting referred to earlier (p. 310). Figure 505, on the other hand, might be a cross-section from the aquarium at Naples. It betrays as keen an interest in the life of the sea as the makers of the mosaics had in the fauna of Northern Africa. Tracing out the various kinds of fishes represented here would delight the soul of an ichthyologist. The average student is satisfied to observe that they are extraordinarily fishy and active and terrifyingly realistic at times. A second mosaic from Palestrina presents similar subject matter. It is a seapiece containing a shore with a shrine of Poseidon and green water with fishes and crayfish swimming about.[33a]

Sometimes these animal pieces form part of a landscape and are more important as landscape than for the representation of the fauna. Such is the case in Figure 506, where we see a lion rending a bull in a rocky region. The clever foreshortening of the bull, the high lights on the body and the modeling of the figures bespeak a practiced artist. But it is rather the action, the mastery of the third dimension and the handling of light in the mosaic, which interest us. These may all represent certain advances on the part of the maker over his Hellenistic original. They indicate, however, that the Hellenistic workers were setting their events in natural surroundings and were started on the way toward compositions of unlimited space. In the background of the mosaic a startled cow is seen beside a stream. The composition is set obliquely in space.

Idyllic landscapes, which combined animal and figure representations, frequently occur. One of these depicts a goddess seated under a tree, while near her sheep and goats graze in rolling country with a stream in the foreground (Fig. 507). The

[33a] R. Delbrück, *Hellenistische Bauten in Latium,* Strassburg, 1907, I, 59. I owe the information to Professor Rostovtzeff.

impressionistic method is extensively employed here, even for details such as the fleeces of the sheep. This peaceful scene is a decided contrast to one of the finest landscapes which we possess from antiquity (Fig. 377). The space here is not unlimited, but the artist has mastered the third dimension. We have spoken of this mosaic as a pendant to the centauress of Zeuxis and have noted there the Hellenistic character of the work. This is observable in the fine use of chiaroscuro; in the perspective; in the contrast between animal and human traits; in the dramatic fury of the enraged centaur revenging himself on his enemies; in the feeling for nature, and in the opposed moods. The scene represents a centauress killed or wounded by a tiger. The centaur now wreaks his revenge on the marauder. It is an idyll of wild life set with consummate ability in a rocky landscape. The colors used are yellow, brown, red, lilac, white, and green.

Landscape came to Italy from Hellenistic Greece. It grew out of a revulsion in Alexandria and other eastern sites against life in cities. Added to this was the impetus gained from contact with the wonderland of the Orient, where parks and gardens flourished. A return to nature seemed to offer some solace for the jaded, artificial existence in cities like Alexandria. Accordingly, we find recourse to nature not only in the poetry of Theokritos, but in the "Hellenistic" reliefs and in Alexandrian landscapes. That landscapes and seascapes came from Egypt seems probable from the content of many landscape-paintings. We have spoken earlier of the Nile scenes and of the Egyptian flora and fauna found in painting and mosaic. Even more conclusive proof for the Egyptian origin of certain landscapes are the scenes where dwarfs and pigmies are engaged in battles with crocodiles and hippopotami (Fig. 508). Here, the subject matter points directly to Egypt, as do the architecture and the impressionistic technique. The spirit of rollicking sport, the droll humor and the element of caricature are all quite typical of Alexandrian taste. Thoroughly Egyptian is the Præneste mosaic from the Temple of Fortuna, dating somewhere between 80 B.C. and 200 A.D. (Fig. 509). Here an Egyptian landscape is represented in flood. The foreground is filled with temple and ritual scenes, bits of army life, banquets, hunting, and scenes on the land. At the top of the mosaic, following the old Egyptian convention, is a desert inhabited by wild animals. Here, hunts are in progress. This mosaic may have grown out of an interest in animal lore but it looks more as if the artist were copying some great original from the Nile Valley. The Egyptian character of the architecture, the Nile boats and the faithful observation of the Nile animals suggest this (Fig. 510), although it is true that the artist sometimes falls short in depicting the wild life of the desert. It may have been such scenes as this that Demetrios, the *topographos*, painted. The mosaic pictures life in Egypt in the late Ptolemaic and Roman periods.[33b]

[33b] For various theories as to the date of the Præneste mosaic, see R. Delbrück, *Hellenist-*

Portraiture was another branch of art which held a prominent place in Hellenistic times. We have records of so-called portraits as far back as the days of Polygnotos, when Panainos, the brother of Pheidias, is supposed to have painted some of the Persian and Greek generals engaged in the battle of Marathon. This report doubtless meant nothing more than that certain individualized features were added to a type. The first real portraiture probably began with Apelles in the age of Alexander. At this time, individualism came into its own. The numerous portraits of Philip and Alexander undoubtedly laid the foundation for the genre, although we do not seem to hear of painters who devoted themselves exclusively to portrait-painting. About 100 B.C. Iaia of Cyzicus painted portraits, especially of women. They were done in encaustic on ivory, and were probably the earliest miniatures known. Koinos made portraits that were fitted into family-trees. Masters of this kind must have illustrated Varro's *Imagines,* a book with seven hundred portraits of famous Greeks and Romans, published by Atticus.[34] The character of these works of art may be gathered from a series of portraits on glass, dating from the Third Century A.D.[35] The likenesses on these discs were worked out in gold leaf. They are very interesting realistic family groups and portraits of individuals.

Our ideas of Hellenistic portraiture are formed, for the most part, from a series of Græco-Roman paintings on wooden panels.[35a] Most of these were discovered more than twenty-five years ago in northern Egypt near Cairo, in a region known as the Fayûm. At centers such as el-Rubaiyat, Hawara, and Antinoë, over four hundred portraits have been found painted on panels of sycamore, linden, or, in some cases, cedar wood. They had belonged mainly to Greeks, Romans, and Jews in Egypt in the First and Second Centuries A.D. They occupied a section colonized by the Ptolemies. Because of their contact with the Egyptians there, the inhabitants adopted the Egyptian practice of mummification for their dead, but instead of using

ische Bauten in Latium, Strassburg, 1907, I, 83 ff.; cf. pp. 50, 59 ff., O. Marucchi, Bull. Com., 23 (1895), pp. 26 ff., Pls. I-II; 32 (1904), pp. 258 ff.; Atti Accademia Pontif., X (1910); Dante Vaglieri, Bull. Com., 37 (1909), pp. 212 ff.; Ralph Van Deman Magoffin, "A Study of the Topography and Municipal History of Præneste," Johns Hopkins University Studies in Historical and Political Science, XXVI (1908), pp. 49 ff. Some authorities place the mosaic in the time of Sulla, others in the time of Hadrian or later. R. Pagenstecher, B.P.W., 40 (1920), pp. 551 ff., notes the discovery of a mosaic with Nile scenes and pigmies at Thmuis in Egypt. This proves in his opinion the Egyptian origin of the Præneste type of mosaic. No date can be assigned to the Egyptian example.

[34] Pliny, N.H., 35, 147, 139.

[35] C. Albizzati, Röm. Mitth., 29 (1914), pp. 240 ff., Pl. XV, Vetri dorati del terzo secolo dopo Cristo. Cf. bibliography on glass.

[35a] F. Studniczka, "Imagines Illustrium," Jahr., 38-39 (1923-24), pp. 57 ff., gives a study of early Hellenistic painted portraits of Theokritos and the family of Demetrios Poliorketes as seen in later copies, such as the Boscoreale frescoes in New York and Naples. See p. 332.

an anthropoid coffin, they often placed a painted portrait of the deceased over the head of the mummy, fastening the picture carefully in the bindings of the mummy-wrappings or inserting it in the cartonnage of the mummy-case (Fig. 511). The use of the anthropoid coffin with the head end in the form of a modeled mask goes back to an early period in Egypt. The Græco-Roman population adopted the mask made of canvas, cartonnage, plaster, or wood and used it beside the painted portrait. In some places, one style was preferred to the other but the two types are contemporary. In the Fayûm, painted portraits were preferred; in the South, the mask. Some sites have both. Masks are commonly found from the First to the Third Century A.D., but later ones exist.

The painted portraits are of inestimable value today, because they give us some splendid examples of ancient portraiture and because they tell us, along with painted stelæ from Pagasæ, the most that we know about the encaustic technique. They also give us an idea of the skilful use of impressionism by the painters of the period. Although they were not executed by great artists and although they vary greatly, they furnish some notion of the general level of work of a cross-section of the painters. Lastly, they are of great interest ethnologically, in that they furnish us with excellent material for the study of the types settled in Egypt in this period.

The portrait-paintings were made for the most part during the lifetime of the individual and were designed to be hung in the houses of the living. Many of them have holes made for this purpose and some still have cords for attachment. One was found beside the body, not fastened in a mummy-case, but set in a frame with a cord attached. At the death of the person painted, the portrait was taken down and cut to fit above the head of the mummy. Pieces of the panel that were chipped away have been found in the wrappings. That the likenesses were executed as a rule during the lifetime of the individual is shown by the fact that there are almost no portraits of old people and that a fifty-year-old portrait is sometimes found with an eighty-year-old mummy.

The panels were carefully executed by several methods, depending in part on the background and on whether wood or linen was to be used. First of all, the encaustic technique was employed, which demanded primarily the use of colors mixed with wax in a kind of paste. These were laid on with a brush or cauterium. The metal cauterium was heated for the purpose of fusing the colors over the surface. Very often tempera painting was combined with the encaustic method; i.e., the background, garments, and minor details might be brushed in in tempera, leaving the head and neck to be done in the encaustic process. Other examples are wholly in the duller tempera method. In the case of the latter, a ground of chalk or gypsum had to be prepared over the panel to prevent any dampness from going through. This ground heightened the luminosity of the colors. It is practically always found when linen is used. The greater number of portraits are done in encaustic. The coloring of the hair and flesh was laid on with a metal tool, while the garments and the background were put on in encaustic also, but with a brush flowing with color. This use of the brush often gives a silky, shimmering glitter to the colors and heightens their power.[35b]

The portraits are mostly life-size or somewhat smaller. They usually show the head, shoulders, and breast, but sometimes only the head and neck. The full-length ones are late, and, in general, it follows that the more of the figure shown, the later the portrait. The sitter is usually seen in front or three-quarter view against a gray-blue or yellow ground. The light on the face is often from the right but on occasion it comes from overhead. The colors are mostly laid on for their effect from a distance and usually are handled impressionistically. Near at hand, one sees that the sticky wax colors have been put on with a spatula and fused into one another in a kind of mosaic effect (Fig. 512). The color of the face is often brown with rose on the cheeks and forehead. On the lips, various shades of red are found. Frequently, there is a streak of white down the bridge of the nose. The relief of the pigment as it stands out from the surface adds to the effect of light and shadow and gives depth to the coloring. The encaustic technique represents the nearest approach made by the ancients to effects gained in modern times by oil painting.

The fact that one mummy-panel in Cairo has on the back of it certain observations to be followed in the painting—notes, as it were, on the sitter—indicates that the panels were not painted in front of the individual, at least in all cases. They are so very lifelike in quality, however, that it seems almost inevitable that some of them were made from life. In general, Hellenistic portraiture probably depicted types with certain individual characteristics added. In Figures 513 and 514, we have the Greek type of youth individualized in the two cases, while Figure 515 might be the sister of the pair. She is black-haired, with brown eyes and with a warm reddish yellow for flesh tones. She wears a purplish red garment, white beads, and golden earrings with drops. Far more individualized and interesting from the technical side is the portrait of a man dating, to judge from the beard and hair, between 161 and 169 A.D.—the age of Lucius Verus (Fig. 516). The impressionistic handling of color here is unusually successful. Figure 517, now in the National Gallery in London, is the portrait of a woman of twenty-five with a rather thin face and sallow complexion. The eyes and hair are brown; the lips, red. A very little rose is used on the cheeks and a reddish violet garment contrasts well with the bluish-gray ground. Her necklace and earrings have a dark green coloring, with some white and gold. She is dated by Petrie about 130 A.D.

A charming portrait of a child is seen in Figure 518. She is dressed in a yellow

[35b] See Ch. XI, pp. 425-426.

garment with red stripes and looks on the world with dark brown eyes of wonder. Most of the portraits show rather large, luminous eyes. This may have been the result of the "make-up" common in Egypt, which was used to exaggerate the size of the eyes, or, it may have been in part an artistic convention, because large eyes were apparently always considered beautiful in that region. Not only do many portraits have this feature, but a large number also have long, oval faces, narrowing toward the chin; broad brows, and prominent noses. These similarities indicate a type behind the vital rendering of the individual. The modernity of Figure 519 is very striking and the panel shows once more the elaborate use of the spatula and the impressionistic handling of color.

Among the finest examples of portraiture which we have today are those seen in Figures 520-523. The head of a man, now in the Ny Carlsberg in Copenhagen, presents a very ruddy-faced, unsensitive Roman with a thick neck—a type seen frequently in Italy today (Fig. 520). The portrait is painted on linen and makes use of red lines on the forehead for wrinkles and shading. Patches of white occur on the nose and lips and the shading on the lower part of the cheeks and chin sometimes passes into a yellowish green. Yellow also appears and brownish red. Although the upper part of the head is lost, we feel the individual before us very vividly.

Also on linen is the portrait of Aline (Fig. 521). This woman died at thirty-five, as the inscription from the tomb tells us. The figure is a rather matronly one. The features are heavy and full. The face is modeled by means of red, hatched lines— the same technique found in Fifth Century vase-painting (cf. Fig. 375). The ground of the portrait is a gray-brown, which is dark on the side of the light and brighter on the shadow side. The flesh tones are yellow to red, the chiton gray, with violet shadows. The portrait probably dates about 171 A.D. The method used is tempera. The eyebrows are of a greenish cast and are rendered by short, upright brush-strokes. The hair is dark brown and falls in ringlets about the face. She wears a golden necklace and earrings. This mummy was one of five found at Hawara, the ancient Arsinoë, in a chamber built of sun-dried bricks. The group included the father and mother and three children. The father and one child had gilded masks; the other three mummy-portraits, painted on linen.

In Figure 522, we have the head of a plainer, older woman with the face of an invalid. The hair is done in very simple fashion, pulled back closely, recalling the mode in the days of Faustina, about 140 A.D. In fact, most of the portraits are dated from the treatment of the hair, from jewelry, and from certain inscriptions. In the case of men, the presence or absence of a beard forms a criterion for dating. The flesh in this example is a yellowish color, the hair brown, the garment white. The woman wears no adornment of any kind. The heavily shaded eyes, with furrows beneath, and the lines around the mouth indicate physical suffering.

Plate XV. Cambridge. Girton College, Library. Hermione, Teacher of the Classics.

The head shares certain traits with one of the most interesting portraits of antiq-uity—namely, the likeness of Hermione (Plate XV, color). The plainness of the hair, the thin face, and sad eyes where no smile appears, are common to the two. Hermione was a teacher in Egypt in the Second Century A.D., and was probably one of the earliest women who taught the classics, although she doubtless shared this profession with Sappho, Pamphila, and perhaps Corinna. However that may be, her head is the first portrait which we possess of a woman teacher. The face of Her-mione is a joyless one. We do not know whether to sympathize with the young who came under her eye, or to regret, rather, that the profession was so uninspiring. In any case, the Hermione type seems to be self-perpetuating in the academic world. The portrait is on linen and makes much use of yellow for the flesh, tinged with a rose coloring, which is deepened around the mouth and about the eyes. The hair is brown. The reddish lids give to the eyes a heavy, tired look. The inscription reads, *Hermione grammatike,* i.e., Hermione, "Reader in the Classics."

The portrait of a youth in New York with a gilded wreath about his head is a masterpiece of impressionistic workmanship (Fig. 523). About the mouth is a streak of white; patches of white occur on the forehead, around the eyes, and down the bridge of the nose. A generous use of it is also made about the dark brown iris of the eye. The pigment stands out in relief over the painting. The ground is gray, the lips and ears rose, the flesh tones brownish yellow. The eyelashes are brownish black. This also appears on the brows.

Full-length portraits are found in the late period. A fine example of this type is to be seen in the Metropolitan Museum. They continue into the Byzantine Age.

The painter began by sizing or preparing his panels. In the case of the distemper technique, he covered the ground with a preparation of chalk or gypsum. Next, he outlined the head of his figure with a black line and indicated the mouth and eyes. Then he often brushed in the ground and drapery, proceeding afterward to the face and hair. Where distemper alone was used, he worked with a brush entirely. If wax was employed, he probably put in his background and garments first, with a brush dipped in melted wax, but he might of course employ tempera for this. Following these preliminaries, he laid a wax paste over the face and neck, putting it on with the aid of a heated metal instrument and keeping the panel warm while at work. This technique was a slow one and is probably the reason why tempera was often com-bined with the use of wax for the face.

The surprising things about the portraits are their freshness and convincing truth. The essential traits are expressed simply and directly and accessories such as gar-ments and adornments are subordinated in the interest of form, line, and color. Except for the large staring eyes, they seem very modern to us today. This is because of their realistic character and the impressionistic method employed. If portraits of this nature were made in the first three centuries of our era, we may well believe that the earlier Hellenistic age produced some splendid examples of the art. A comparison between some of the portraits from the Fayûm and Roman examples will show—as the paintings themselves do—that Greek portraiture dealt primarily with types. Proceeding from the type, the artist, who was really an artisan, individualized his material and presented a very speaking likeness of his subject. In most cases, the portraits are probably from life and are not drawn from memory.

The use of the encaustic technique apparently arose from an attempt on the part of the painter to bring in greater warmth of color and strength of light than could be obtained with the tempera process. These examples of portraiture prove that the painters gained the same richness of effect which modern artists have obtained with oil. Skill in painting impressionistically reached a high level with this technique. In fact some of the best examples of ancient impressionism which we possess are to be found in this series of paintings.


## DECORATIVE WALL-PAINTING

DECORATIVE wall-painting played a minor part in the adornment of houses in the Hellenic world. We have the story of Alcibiades who made the artist, Agatharchos, a prisoner, until he painted the walls of his house,[36] and we have an account of the decoration by Zeuxis of the palace of King Archelaos of Macedon.[37] In the Fourth Century, there was probably a moderate amount of ornamentation on the upper part of the walls of buildings, if we are to judge from the decoration of Hellenistic tombs. But we may gain an even clearer idea of the decoration of houses in the Third and Second Centuries from buildings and houses at Pergamon, Priene, Delos, Thera, Olbia, Kertch,—the ancient Panticapæum,—and Pompeii.

The mural system of decoration in Hellenistic Greece and Italy was based on the old Hellenic structural system of the wall, with its quadruple distribution into baseboard, intermediate joining course, central portion, and cornice. We have explained how this arrangement grew out of the materials employed in the wall (p. 300). This structural division into horizontal sections, Rostovtzeff traces as far back as Egypt.[38] It is found in paintings like the Cretan fresco (Fig. 134) and the Mycenæan wall-decoration from Tiryns (Fig. 179). From Crete, it probably passed to Ionia; thence to Etruria and Greece. Buildings such as the Propylæa in Athens and the Stoa of the Athena Sanctuary at Pergamon reveal this same arrangement.[39] It is found before

---

[36] Andocides, *Contra Alc.*, 17; Plut., *Alc.*, 16.          [37] Ælian, *V.H.*, 14, 17.

[38] M. Rostovtzeff, "Ancient Decorative Wall-Painting," *J.H.S.*, 39 (1919), pp. 144-163.

[39] W. Dörpfeld, "Gesimse unter Wandmalereien," *Ath. Mitth.*, 36 (1911), pp. 87 ff. *Cf.* p. 52.

the "First Pompeian" style in certain structures in Egypt, Southern Russia, and Italy —but the decoration followed different lines in different regions, three main types being observable—the Alexandrian structural style, the Oriental, as seen in Asia Minor and Southern Russia, and the Italian.[39a]

In the tomb of Sidi Gaber, near Alexandria, we have a continuation of this old Greek structural style[40] and a forerunner of the later Pompeian styles. In this building (Fig. 524), there are two rooms preserved today. In the first, there is a blue socle, followed by a row of alabaster rectangles above. These are united with the upper part of the wall by a black band. Above the black band are fields of solid color—red with blue above—while at the top is a cornice. In the second room, which contained the funeral couch, the colors change. The bottom is red. Above this is gray, while at the top is a broad blue-gray surface, adorned with typically Hellenistic garlands. The characteristic element in this Greek structural style is the *horizontal zone-decoration*. This arrangement is slightly altered in the second room of Sidi Gaber, where we find Doric pilasters supporting a narrow red field above and resting on one below. This decoration lightens the upper part of the wall and foreshadows the development of the second style.

A further stage in the history of decorative wall-painting may be seen in Delos.[41] In Figure 525, we discover once again the Hellenic emphasis on the horizontal divisions of the wall. This type of wall did not readily admit of pictures because of the heavy use of rectangles in different colors, but we occasionally find a frieze employed, as in this case. Here, Erotes are seen busily engaged in sport or occupied about an altar with offerings. This kind of decoration probably influenced the small friezes of the fourth style in the House of the Vettii at Pompeii. In the Delian example, one sees a red socle at the bottom of the wall, with black orthostates above, separated by a white field. There follows the frieze of Erotes, while above this, the wall is marked off into white rectangles of equal size, outlined with red. These blocks of stucco are in relief. This is a mark of the First style, which was essentially an *architectonic plastic style* in stucco. The various blocks and details, such as pilasters and cornices, were of stucco moulded in relief.

The upper part of the wall in Delos was sometimes treated more freely, with innovations such as Doric pilasters supporting a coffered ceiling seen in perspective (Fig. 526). As Delos was completely destroyed in the eighties of the First Century we might expect to find here forerunners of the Second Pompeian style and our example shows that a beginning was made in this direction. The lower part of the wall still

---

[39a] Rostovtzeff proposes to call the First Pompeian style, the Hellenistic structural style.

[40] R. Pagenstecher, *Nekropolis*, 1919, p. 170. This description is borrowed from Pagenstecher's work.

[41] M. Bulard, "Peintures murales et mosaïques de Délos," *Mon. Piot*, XIV (1908).

adheres to the old structural type. In the upper half are red and yellow blocks of stucco and narrow strips imitating marble or else decorated with a meander pattern and bounded by a moulding. The new element consists in decorating the part of the wall above the cornice and in giving *with the brush* an illusion of a building seen in perspective. The third dimension and the relieving of the heavy stucco work are well handled in the coffered ceiling and its supporting members. This wall-decoration at Delos is the richest representative of the Oriental branch of the structural style which we possess, though some good examples occur at Panticapæum[42] (Fig. 481). Similar types come from Priene,[43] from Magnesia on the Meander[44] and from Thera.[45]

The vertical divisions found on some of the Delian walls are not isolated examples. Such decoration is seen in Greek architecture of the Hellenistic age. Dörpfeld has pointed this out in the case of Pergamon and other sites.[46] The upper part of the walls sometimes had windows or niches. What is new in the Italian group is the opening up of the wall to give a view into space and the extensive introduction into the upper part of the wall of niches, and the like; "the rich development both in real architecture and in painted imitations." In Italy, the vertical divisions predominate and are emphasized—doors and window-frames, columns, pilasters, and the like. This creative departure from the Hellenistic structural decoration finally culminated in the architectural style, a product peculiar to Italy.[46a]

A typical example of the First style at Pompeii is seen in Figure 527, from the house of Sallust. Doors and pilasters in relief emphasize the verticals, while the stucco of the wall is painted in gay colors from the yellow socle to the top. Black, yellow, and violet, red, and green occur on the stuccoed blocks. Marbling effects also play a rôle. In the upper part of another wall from the same house we find decoration somewhat similar to the Delian example of Figure 526, except that Ionic half columns replace Doric pilasters.[47] From such examples, and from the Delian frieze, a development to the Second style was not far to seek and we find it coming in about 80 B.C. Probably, paintings such as the Odyssey landscapes (Fig. 529) indicate the next stage of progress after the Delian frieze.

The Second Pompeian style and its origin have been a matter of much discussion.

[42] Rostovtzeff, *op. cit.*, and Pl. VI, 1 and 2.

[43] T. Wiegand and H. Schrader, *Priene*, Berlin, 1904, pp. 308 ff.

[44] C. Humann, J. Kohte, C. Watzinger, *Magnesia am Mæander*, p. 138, Figs. 149, 150.

[45] Hiller von Gärtringen, *Thera*, III, 145, 148, and Pl. IV; 162, 164; Pls. I-II, Fig. 154.

[46] W. Dörpfeld, *loc. cit.*

[46a] Rostovtzeff uses the term *architectural* for the Second, Third, and Fourth Pompeian styles. *Architectural* is equivalent in this discussion to the Second style.

[47] A. Mau, *Geschichte der decorativen Wandmalerei in Pompeii*, Berlin, 1882, Pl. I, b, c, d, g, k.

What led the Italians to break up the wall with vistas into the open? Some have thought it was the influence of the theater, where painted stage-settings and backgrounds for the actors gave an impetus to scenes in perspective. However, the tendency to open the upper part of the wall and so lighten the somewhat heavy mural effect, we have seen earlier in the First style at Delos, where attempts at perspective and space representation are already present. The numerous vertical divisions of the First style and the upper part of the wall broken by niches, windows, and the like, no less than the frieze found at Delos, prepare for the Second style. We may say, then, that the germs of the Second style already existed in the First, but that the Second had a peculiarly individual development in Italy and one that emphasized particularly the architectural side.

Some authorities have wished to emphasize the influence of stage-decoration on the Second Pompeian style, citing as an illustration certain wall-decorations from the house of Fannius Sinistor at Boscoreale (Fig. 528), now in the Metropolitan Museum in New York. Vitruvius, the great architect of the Augustan age, in discussing the stage-decoration of the ancients, says: "Tragic scenes are pictured with columns, pediments, statues, and other objects suited to kings; comic scenes exhibit private dwellings with balconies and views representing rows of windows; satyric scenes are decorated with trees, caverns, mountains, and other rustic subjects delineated in landscape style."[48] From this account, it is evident that architectural structures played a part in the adornment of the Hellenistic theater.

The walls of the cubiculum of Fannius Sinistor illustrate the early stages of the architectural style with views of moderate depth. They may possibly follow the manner of Hellenistic stage-decoration and may illustrate the *scœnarum frontes*. Examples of the tragic background may be seen where the round tholos occurs; of the comic, in the view at the right, with its balconies and windows. The satyric setting is illustrated at the left, where a rocky cave and fountain are found in the foreground with a vine-covered pergola above. However we are to interpret this evidence, the paintings exhibit the use of perspective applied to architecture and an interest in landscape illusionism. Between the pilasters one looks into landscapes of limited depth in which architecture plays a part. It is quite possible that the Hellenistic theater did influence the Second Pompeian style as Herrmann has claimed.[49] From the theater the artist brought into the house a type of decoration which was not wholly suitable for its purpose.

An excellent example of the Second style with landscape vistas is found in a series

[48] Vitr., *De Arch.*, V, 6, 9.
[49] P. Herrmann, *B.P.W.*, 39 (1919), pp. 1227 ff. *Rec.*, R. Pagenstecher, *Alexandrinische Studien*, 1917. A. M. Friend, "The Portraits of the Evangelists in Greek and Latin Manuscripts," *Art Studies*, 1929.

of paintings from a house on the Esquiline, the walls of which were adorned with scenes from the Odyssey (Fig. 529). We know from Vitruvius that this subject was a favored one.[50] The frieze consists of episodes from the wanderings of Odysseus. They are united by pilasters painted red. Between these one looks as if through an open window into an extended landscape with far-distant views. The method is a continuous one. The source of this continuous narrative style, which joins together a series of episodes by means of a connected background is the Hellenistic East. The best and earliest example known today is the small Telephos frieze from Pergamon.[51] Architectural and landscape elements play a prominent rôle here.

In the Odyssey paintings, which are our best ancient landscapes, we have a frieze some fourteen meters long and two meters high, consisting originally of eight panels joined together by painted red pilasters. The first five are preserved and give us the adventures of Odysseus in the land of the cannibalistic Læstrygones, on the island of Circe and in her palace. The sixth is destroyed. There follows the seventh depict- ing the Entrance to the Underworld and a part of the eighth dealing with Sinners in Hades. The loss of half a panel was due to an opening broken in the wall. The arrangement of the wall-decoration here could have developed from the First style as it is seen in Delos. The pilasters in the Odyssey landscapes are painted red, with yellow capitals, and the wall between is treated as open space.

We have found that the real prototype of the continuous narrative method goes back to the Hellenistic East. The Odyssey landscapes are Hellenistic in their origin. We shall return to them in our discussion of landscape where they will be taken up as an outgrowth of Hellenistic landscape-painting. Their Hellenistic affinities are observable in the Greek inscriptions, in the personification of the Spring, the Beach, and the like, and in the continuous narrative style. On the other hand, the develop- ment toward *unlimited* space is a Roman contribution, although the Hellenistic age undoubtedly deepened the space-composition of earlier days. Pfuhl has suggested that in the Odyssey landscapes we see the older Hellenistic taste; in the Boscoreale paintings, Italian floridity. But there is much that is Roman in the Odyssey land- scapes, such as the subordination of figures to the landscape and much that is Greek in the Boscoreale frescoes such as the scale of the figures and the stage-like back- grounds. The scenes in our illustration depict Odysseus in the land of the Læstrygo- nes and the destruction of his ships.

A more definitely architectural style may be found on the walls of the house of Livia on the Palatine. In the fresco representing Io watched by Argos, which was probably copied after Nikias (p. 279), the *painted architectural elements* framing prospect views, present the essential characteristics of the Second style (Fig. 530).

---

[50] Vitr., *op. cit.*, VII, 5, 2.

[51] *Altertümer von Pergamon*, III, 2 (1910), Pls. XXXI-XXXII. *Cf.* Lawrence, *Later Greek Sculpture*, New York, 1927, Pl. 41[a].

Much use is made of perspective and the figures are reduced in size and fitted into landscape surroundings. The central panel is usually surrounded by an architectural frame. The emphasis on the distant view and on the architectural framework is distinctly Italian and in this direction lay the originality of the Roman. This development was prepared for by the peculiar form of the Italian First style. In addition to the horizontal divisions, vertical elements appear everywhere. From the socle to the cornice the walls are divided by columns, pilasters, doors, windows, niches, and half columns. Real architecture is apparently copied.

Another important Italian contribution was polychromy. The rich red grounds on either side of the central panel are contrasted with fresh green at either end and light browns. Black is used as a ground for the small panels in the socle, or it outlines various architectural members. Yellow and grayish white are commonly found. The delightful panel at the right (cf. Fig. 543), where Polyphemos is seen pursuing Galatea against a Campanian background of soft brown mountains, is especially beautiful because of the bluish green of the sea and the sepia coloring.[51a]

In addition to this architectural decoration with prospect views, the old megalography of earlier Greek times lived on in the friezes of the Second style. Excellent examples of this are observable in the painting of the Aldobrandini Wedding and in frescoes on the walls of the Villa Item near Pompeii.

The Aldobrandini Wedding is a fresco on stucco, about eight feet long (Fig. 531). It was found in a house on the Esquiline and remained in the Villa of Cardinal Aldobrandini until 1811. In 1838, it was taken to the Library of the Vatican. Whether it is a copy of an earlier Greek work or a late creation of a Neo-Attic master with eclectic tendencies remains uncertain.[52] The wall in the rear seems to argue for the latter; some of the forms point to an earlier date. The background is a grayish violet wall which seems to suggest more than one room—a central one, or thalamos, in which the marriage couch is placed; one at the left, and perhaps a vestibule at the right. Above the wall, greenish blue appears. In the middle of the painting, on a couch spread with a dark green coverlet, the modest bride sits, wearing yellow slippers and a white garment drawn up over the back of her head. Beside her is Aphrodite, or Peitho, with a violet mantle wrapped around the lower part of her figure. She appears to be pleading with the bride. Hymenaios, a lovely youth, crowned with a green and

---

[51a] According to Baumgarten-Poland-Wagner, *Die hellenistisch-römische Kultur*, Pl. VII, text, the panel at the right comes from a neighboring room. *Vs.* this view, G. Perrot, *Rev. Arch.*, 22 (1870-1871), p. 47, who places the fresco on the back wall of the room which has Io and Argos on the right wall.

[52] E. Pfuhl, *Gött. Gelehrt. Anz.*, 1910, p. 824, argues that the painting is a creation of a Neo-Attic classicist who may have derived much inspiration and even whole figures from creations of the Hellenistic Age. *Cf.*, also, W. Helbig, *Führer*,[3] I, 267. *Vs.* these views, *cf.* H. Bulle, *op. cit.*, Pl. 316, pp. 654 ff. Pfuhl, *Malerei und Zeichnung der Griechen*, II, 875.

yellow garland and garbed in a dark red garment reclines against the foot of the couch. At the left, Charis, or Peitho, leans on a pillar and pours perfume for the bride. A group of three figures is found at either end. At the left, the mother, a matronly figure in white, with a yellow chiton, tests the warmth of the bridal foot bath which two servants are preparing. Music is beginning at the right. A woman strikes the lyre. A figure in yellow shakes some perfume or incense into a metal basin with a high foot. Perhaps her companion who wears a pointed crown is the one who sings the marriage hymn. The participants in a marriage procession are represented here, after they have arrived at the marriage chamber. It is the moment when Hymenaios will summon the bridegroom during the singing of the epithalamium. Some have interpreted the woman pleading with the bride as the *pronuba*. In this case, the youth at the foot of the couch would be considered the bridegroom or his attendant. This does not seem probable.

The picture belongs to a great tradition and may be a copy, although most scholars incline to see in it a creation of a Neo-Attic classicist who drew from earlier material. The coloring is especially striking—golden brown and yellow, green and gray, violet and red brown predominating. The stronger colors emphasize the center. The figure of Hymenaios is done impressionistically. Broad red brush strokes have been put on the brown of his flesh in parallel fashion to indicate the modeling and flesh tones.[53] The painting was executed in a rather hasty, sketchy way. The same manner is used on the lips, forehead, cheeks, and nose. This painting and the Odyssey landscapes are well published, partly in color, partly in photographic process, in the monumental work of Nogara.[53]

The Greek serenity and calm of this painting contrast strongly with the agitated atmosphere and vigorous action of the paintings on the walls of the Villa Item near Pompeii. Here, in the Triclinium, the artist has depicted certain rites in honor of Dionysos, performed in the presence of the god and Ariadne (Fig. 532). Almost opposite the entrance occurs the figure of Dionysos reclining in the arms of Ariadne. At the left is an old Silenus accompanied by two satyrs. One is holding a mask, the other is gazing intently into a bowl, divining events by looking into a vessel filled with liquid. Here images of future happenings, or of the god of the oracle might be seen.

The paintings begin at the left of the entrance (Fig. 533). At the end are two women and a young boy scanning a scroll. He is doubtless a youthful servant of the god, considered by some to be Dionysos himself. He is reading a ritual for the seated woman who is thought to be initiating her companion at the left into the mysteries. In the panel which follows, a priestess is seated at a table. She is, in all probability,

[53] B. Nogara, *Le Nozze Aldobrandine* (*Collezioni dei Palazzi Apostolici*), II (1907), Pls. I-VIII; Color Plate VII.

unveiling an offering to the god—perhaps the gift of the woman initiate at the left. A young priestess assists her, while from the left a maiden much like the "Maid of Antium" approaches with a plate of offerings. This group is followed by one of three satyrs—an old satyr enthusiastically playing the lyre and two seated figures, one playing the pipes, the second—a young girl satyr—offering her breast to a kid (Fig. 534). Toward these satyrs, a woman flees in terror, drawing her mantle over her head. She has probably witnessed the unveiling of the phallos which is represented as taking place in the panel immediately following the divination by the satyrs and the group of Dionysos and his consort. A woman is kneeling beside a *liknon*, unveiling the *sacra* of Dionysos. At sight of the phallos, a young girl has fled and buried her head in the lap of an older woman (Fig. 535). A winged figure, who may be Diké, Justice, or Teleté, the personification of the mysteries,—like an avenging angel driving Adam and Eve out of Paradise,—raises aloft a lash to inflict a ritualistic flagellation. At the right of these figures, a nude woman, seen in back view, strikes a pair of cymbals and begins a dance. She is probably a happy initiate. Perhaps the noise was intended to drown the cries of the initiate or to increase bacchic frenzy. The wall at this point is broken by a window, on the other side of which a woman is shown at her toilet. She is assisted by a servant and by an Eros holding a mirror. This may represent the attiring of an initiate for the mysteries. At the left of the entrance a second seated woman is represented.

These paintings are not only of extreme interest because of their mystical subject matter—the presentation of a ritualistic flagellation, the uncovering of the sacred *liknon*, or basket, and divination by gazing into a bowl—but also because of their style. Against a background of the so-called First style, with a colored socle and red panels above, life-size figures are painted as if they were standing on a stage, or podium, seen in perspective. The figures are modeled out of light, as it were, and stand out in strong relief before the wall which is emphasized as a wall by the use of panels and pilasters. Figure 536 shows the use of the impressionistic technique in modeling the sprightly figure of a dancing satyr. The method employed is similar to the one which we found in the case of Hymenaios in the "Aldobrandini Wedding." The face of this satyr also reveals the vigorous realism frequently seen in the heads of the figures.

The work is conceived as a true mural painting, not as a series of panels set into an architectural frame, as so often happens.[54] This affects the coloring, as Miss Cooke has shown, and results largely in flat tints that are best suited to the decorative style. Furthermore, the composition forms a continuous narrative in which the principal actors and chief groups are made to stand out by the device of placing pilasters

[54] Miss P. B. Mudie Cooke, "The Paintings of the Villa Item at Pompeii," *J.R.S.*, III (1913), pp. 157 ff., gives an excellent account of the paintings.

behind them. On the whole, a great advance in pictorial power is evident in this work. The painting is executed in tempera and makes especial use of cinnabar in the wall fields, violet brown for the pilasters, and yellow, green, and lilac. In contrast to the frieze-like character of the Aldobrandini Wedding, which is governed rather by plastic laws, we have here a fine example of Greek megalography dominated by pictorial laws. In all likelihood, it follows a Hellenistic original, perhaps one from a sanctuary of Dionysos at Smyrna. Miss Cooke argues this on the basis of inscriptional evidence which proves the prominence there of the cult of Dionysos Breseus.

The frescoes from Boscoreale give us copies of Hellenistic wall-paintings which reveal artistic power and mastery of light and shadow. They probably date after the age of Sulla. We have seen that some of the walls were painted with a strong feeling for architectural decoration and for views of limited depth (Fig. 528). In addition to these scenes, there were colonnades rendered in perspective, set before panels brilliantly painted in red, green, yellow, purple, and white. In the Tablinum were fine festoons of fruits and leaves hung from bulls' heads, while a mask, a bell, or a basket is suspended from the center of each garland. The figure decoration in its types shows a certain similarity to the designs occurring on the frescoes from the Villa Item. On the back wall of the Triclinium, or dining-room, against a sacral landscape, Aphrodite and Eros appeared; on the right, the Graces; at the left, Dionysos and Ariadne. On the right or east wall, now in the Metropolitan Museum in New York, two figures were seated in the center—a man partially nude, and a woman; at the left, a woman playing the lyre was seen, with a young girl behind her chair (Fig. 537); while at the right, was a standing woman with a shield. The heads are strongly individualized and writers have been inclined to recognize in the paintings the owner of the Villa; his daughter playing the lyre, and, in the case of the aged man, perhaps his old father (Fig. 538). More recently, Studniczka has wished to see in these figures, members of a Macedonian ruling family. The nude male figure is identified by him as Demetrios Poliorketes, accompanied by his sister.[55] The paintings from the west wall of the Villa are preserved in the Museum at Naples. A stern-looking man with a spear is seated, gazing at a matronly woman. Studniczka sees in these figures Antigonos II, Gonatas, the son of Demetrios Poliorketes, and his mother Phila, a distinguished woman of character and ability. The elderly man, who looks like a philosopher, may, in his opinion, be one of the young king's teachers, possibly Menedemos. Other paintings belonging to the Villa depict a courtesan playing the lyre (Fig. 537), and Ptolemais, the daughter of Demetrios' sister and his last wife. She is seen bearing a shield in her hand. The paintings are probably historical but it

[55] F. Studniczka, "Imagines Illustrium," *Jahr.*, 38-39 (1923-1924), pp. 64-110; Pls. II-III. The woman is really the sister-in-law of Demetrios. *Cf.* Rostovtzeff, *Mystic Italy*, New York, 1927, p. 86.

is not at all certain that the persons concerned can be identified by name. It is possible also that the heads are to be considered early examples of Hellenistic portraiture. The background for the designs is a brilliant vermilion red and against this the life-size figures stand out effectively. The garments of the women are lilac and white.

These splendid, full-blooded figures, whose expressive faces and vigorously modeled forms seem to be the forerunners of creations by Italian masters like Mantegna and Benozzo,[56] form a contrast to the so-called Farnesina paintings, from a house by the Tiber (Fig. 539). Here, we find no such vivid representations of pulsating life as existed in the Boscoreale paintings, where the realistic element may be a purely Italian contribution. In the Farnesina frescoes there is a cold classicism which begins to border on affectation. Against a ground of white, Aphrodite is seated in rather stately fashion on a high throne. Before her on a footstool stands Eros; while behind her, leaning over the back of the throne and arranging the veil about her *polos,* is a youthful figure who may be called Peitho. In type she is rather like the maid-servant frequently seen on grave-stelæ. The Hegeso monument or the one in the Cleveland Museum occur as parallels. There are many reminiscences of early Greek art. At times the style borders on the archaistic but the master has chosen from the entire inheritance of the past and there are echoes of archaic art as well as of that of the Fifth and Fourth Centuries. The elegance of the drawing recalls at times the sketches on white-ground lekythoi. The outlines are in red, and a red wash is used for the hair. Aphrodite wears a white robe with blue stars. Peitho is dressed in greenish blue. The wings of Eros are blue and violet.

The house from which these paintings came has a number of interesting features. Among these are the vaulted ceilings, now in the National Museum in Rome, which are decorated with stucco reliefs, picturing landscapes, victories, mysteries, and bacchic scenes. There are also some unusual paintings on a black ground which hark back to Alexandrian models and which represent judgment scenes (Fig. 540, top). In these, victims are being dragged before a judge, perhaps Bocchoris of the Egyptians. The figures are rendered impressionistically. Many Egyptian elements appear on these paintings such as the sphinx and the costume-types. Between the candelabra below the "Judgment" frieze hang garlands of leaves impressionistically painted. This wall may be seen in restoration in Figure 540. Below the garlands are the famous landscapes on a black ground. These are executed in a reddish yellow with a sketchy, almost Japanese impressionism and audacity of brushwork. Another fresco from the same bedroom as the Aphrodite panel depicts the nurture of Bacchus by Leukothea. The figures are set against a background of architecture which prob-

---

[56] *Cf.* especially the fine figure of the old man leaning on a staff (Fig. 538). F. Barnabei, *La Villa pompeiana di P. Fannio Sinistore,* Roma, 1901, Pl. VII; *cf.* Pls. VI and VIII.

ably represents the *peribolos* of a sanctuary. The name Seleukos scratched on the wall points to a Syrian Greek as the author of these paintings.

The mention of the Farnesina landscapes brings us to a general discussion of landscape in ancient Greece—a rather complicated subject. It will perhaps be profitable to consider in detail Greek ideas about nature before taking up the Hellenistic examples which concern us here.

First of all, the Greek conception of nature was in complete contrast to what we find in modern times. Instead of a river, the Greek saw a river-god; instead of the fiery ball of the sun, a youthful charioteer in a quadriga. In other words, he personified all aspects of nature. This practice isolated the various natural phenomena rather than unified them into an harmonious conception of nature as a whole. It seems, in fact, to have prevented the Greek for a long period of time from looking at nature with a single eye, merely because his mind was diverted by a multitude of entities which made up her realm. Just how complicated his conception was, we realize when we consider the rendering of certain aspects of nature on vases, for example, on the Blacas krater about 420 B.C. (Fig. 343). Here, we see the sun rising in his chariot at one end of the composition, with the little stars diving into the ocean before him. Further on, the Dawn pursues Kephalos, a beautiful youth, while at the left the Moon, bayed at by a hound, descends on her horse. This is a cross-section from the Greek conception of nature and we can imagine how complex further additions could make it.

In the second place, even if we had the lost Greek landscape-paintings, we should not expect to find in Greece certain things which are common in our landscapes today; for example, subtle atmospheric effects, blurred outlines, or the luscious greens and grays that dominate landscapes washed by rainstorms. The landscape of Greece was sharply outlined in brilliant sunlight and hard outlines would be the first thing the Greek painted, not scenes softly modeled in chiaroscuro, or veiled in mist. Furthermore, in a country which rarely saw rain, one could not expect the colors and shades that belong to northern regions, nor can we expect an unusual interest in trees and streams in a country where few existed. In addition to all this, we must remember that for a long time the mountains and the sea were enemies rather than friends of man. It was not until these things were tamed to the uses of mankind that they could be thought of as objects beautiful for contemplation. Furthermore, the charms of nature would probably not be fully appreciated until the growth of cities had brought so much unrest that men were glad to flee to the country for peace and quiet. At such a time, her joys would begin to be sung and painted. This period did not arrive until the Hellenistic age.

We see, therefore, that Greek belief did not favor the concrete representation of objects in nature and that love for nature was probably a late development. There was, however, a landscape art in Greece, even in the Sixth Century, as the reference to a painting of Darius crossing the Bosphorus[57] proves and as many vases bear witness. Most of these vases belong to the Ionic class which we have discussed (pp. 129 ff.), and come from centers where Oriental and Cretan-Mycenæan influences met. In such regions we might expect a renascence of landscape art and we have seen this influence at work in the vases of Figures 215, 218, 256, 257. In general, however, even the Ionian artist was somewhat restrained in his use of elements drawn from nature and usually considered especially their value as pattern, conventionalizing them to that end.

It is an undeniable fact that the artist of the Fifth Century was not interested in nature. His concern was with men. Until the middle of the century he was attracted by the representation of the third dimension only in a superficial way. The interest of Polygnotos in landscape was of the slightest. Most objects in nature were represented symbolically: a tree was a symbol for a forest, a pebbly shore or dolphins for the sea.[58] Throughout the Fifth Century, we find similar symbols: a column stood for a house or temple; a door, for an inner room. The fondness of the artist for his environment was not comparable to his interest in human beings and nature received almost no attention.

Interest in the third dimension grew with Agatharchos, the scene-painter of the Fifth Century. We do not know how advanced his stage-scenery was, but the work was sufficiently concerned with the handling of spatial depth to lead to an investigation of the subject of perspective. This was really the beginning of the development of landscape-painting. We can imagine that Agatharchos' stage-scenery for the tragedies of Æschylus involved a temple or palace painted in perspective with landscape elements sparingly used. It was a case of perspective applied to architecture rather than to landscape. This stage-scenery and, more particularly, the settings or "panels" which formed a background for the actors may have developed in Hellenistic times into a kind of architectural style foreshadowing the Second style at Pompeii, although connecting links are lost if this is true. We gather from various Greek writers that this stage-painting was architectural in character. About 430 B.C. Apollodoros began a real attack on the problem of the third dimension by his use of chiaroscuro. He advanced beyond modeling the outlines of figures and surrounded them in space with light and shadow. That the Fifth Century did not make any tremendous progress is, however, to be inferred from vases. The Fifth Century vase which most successfully combines landscape elements and human figures into an harmonious whole shows a certain meagerness in its treatment of nature (Fig. 342).

[57] Hdt., IV, 88.
[58] Janet M. Macdonald, *The Uses of Symbolism in Greek Art*, Chicago, 1922.

It is, of course, only a vase, dating from the last quarter of the century, but the restraint and simplicity of means which characterize it are doubtless typical of the Greek handling of landscape near the close of the Fifth Century.

Several important innovations became prominent in the landscape of the Fourth Century. One of these was an insistence on the deepening of the third dimension; the other, the matter of impressionism in art. We can measure the first advance in compositions like the Alexander mosaic (Fig. 451). Interest in spatial depth extended also to interiors. In general, it is probable that the depth indicated at this time was always limited; that the environment was never more than a background. The figures were never really inserted into the depth of the pictures. The Pompeian copy of Nikias' "Perseus freeing Andromeda" doubtless reflects the achievement of this period in the matter of the third dimension and landscape backgrounds (Fig. 449). The Ficoroni Cista (Fig. 372) might also be cited to illustrate this progress.

Even more significant for the eventual development of landscape-painting was the use of the illusionistic method. Interest in space composition doubtless led to observation of light effects. In any case, we have argued that certain developments took place in Alexandria in the Fourth Century which point to an introduction of impressionism in painting.

One of the first writers to criticize "humbug" in painting was Plato. He believed that painting must be an exact imitation of proportions and colors. The failure to paint in the old, plastic fashion, with insistence on outline and drawing, as artists, with very few exceptions, painted from the days of Polygnotos to the time of Apelles, is apparently what Plato is criticizing. He seems to refer to the work of men like Agatharchos and Apollodoros—men who were painting in perspective and who were using chiaroscuro. The contours of their figures were not sharply defined, but the outlines were blurred and rounded off.

Plato was not the only critic to find fault with the new manner in painting.[59] Roman writers blamed the decay of their own painting on the Egyptian invention of "short cuts."[60] We have contended with Weisbach that this refers to the practice in Alexandria of the illusionistic method, a much more rapid manner than the linear style. The rendering of forms by color contrast is a more speedy method than that by contours. We have also followed Weisbach in naming Antiphilos as the master who appears to have developed the new fashion. This invention was of profound importance for the future of landscape-painting. It meant a sketchy, undetailed

---

[59] Plato, *Critias*, 107; *Sophist*, 235-236[b].

[60] Petron., *Satyr.*, 2, 9. Pfuhl, *op. cit.*, §975, suggests that *ars compendiaria* may mean a sketchy rendering of landscape. We find this, *e.g.*, in the impressionistic landscapes on the black walls of the Farnesina. *Cf. Jahr.*, 25 (1910), pp. 26 ff.; F. Wickhoff, *Roman Art*, London, 1905, p. 124 (tr. by Mrs. S. Arthur Strong); H. Stuart Jones, *Quart. Rev.*, 210 (1909), p. 442; A. Reinach, *Recueil Milliet*, p. 254, note 2.

rendering of objects, the choice of a distant point of view, the rendering of forms by color contrast and figures set *into* their surroundings. It meant, in general, the substitution of the optic point of view for the tactile-optic. We have no Alexandrian example of this new method and there is, of course, a certain danger in arguing from some late mosaics and from Pompeian and Roman painting about Alexandrian achievement in space composition and illusionism. Probably the figures always retained an imposing character in Alexandrian work and the use of illusionism was doubtless confined more or less to landscape. The most that we can say now is that the beginnings of the illusionistic manner appear to go back to Fourth Century Alexandria and later works tend to show that its nature was similar to what we have described.

We have a series of reliefs dating from the Third Century and after, which disclose the pictorial trend of Hellenistic art and the introduction of landscape into the sculpture of the period. These reliefs fall into three classes: mythological, pastoral, and genre. The pastoral group has sometimes been assigned by scholars to Alexandria. Dickins would give the mythological ones to Rhodes, the intimate and domestic scenes to Pergamon.[61] Wherever these landscape reliefs were produced—and this is still a much-debated problem—their style is, for the most part, Alexandrian.

We have mentioned earlier a series of reliefs which are of great importance in the history of landscape, namely, the group from Pergamon which relates the adventures of Telephos. They date from the Second Century and tell a continuous story, one isolated episode after another making up the life of the hero. Change of scene is indicated by a change of background—a significant, pictorial background instead of the blank wall against which earlier reliefs had been placed. There are trees with finely detailed foliage, a plane tree and an oak; there are rocks which define the region where Telephos was exposed. In addition, there are architectural elements. The reliefs are conceived in perspective but the figures are the dominant interest of the sculptor and they are never subordinated to the background which acts more or less like a theater "drop." On the basis of the Telephos reliefs, some writers assign the origin of the class to Asia Minor.[61a]

Other interesting examples of Hellenistic relief with landscapes are the pastoral ones. A fondness for the representation of landscape may have come into Alexandria after the expedition of Alexander to the East. The impression made on the Greeks at this period by the parks, gardens, and strange surroundings of the Orient, may have helped to produce the new vogue. But other influences were also at work. Alexandria was the wealthiest and most splendid Greek city of this age, with a very artificial

[61] Guy Dickins, *Hellenistic Sculpture*, Oxford, 1920, pp. 16, 29 ff.

[61a] *Cf.* Paul Arndt, *Denkmäler griechischer und römischer Sculptur*, Brunn-Bruckmann, München, 1912, Pls. 621-630, text (J. Sieveking).

urban life. From this complexity of existence the populace doubtless sought relief in dreams of simple country pleasures. This is mirrored in the poems of Theokritos which had great popularity because they presented a refuge from the jaded life of the city. The "Alexandrian" reliefs are the exact counterparts of the idylls. They bring before us a similar love of nature. They were small panels set into the walls of houses and often depict rustic scenes. The farmer who is driving his cow past a ruined building, gives us a good idea of the landscape relief which had an Alexandrian origin. These reliefs are the work of a painter in stone who made a very restrained use of background, nowhere subordinating his figures to the setting or including them in it. Sometimes an architectural setting was used, as in the relief of Dionysos visiting a mortal. The figures, however, remain the paramount interest of the sculptor, as is always the case whenever they occur. The constant placing of the figures before the background and the absence of a wax-like technique which indicates a model are some of the touchstones which determine the Greek origin of these reliefs.

That there were landscape-painters in Alexandria, we have seen in our discussion of Demetrios and others (p. 306). We have also argued that many of the Egyptianizing landscapes, such as the pigmy ones, or those with Nile flora and fauna, and, in all probability, the hunting scenes had their prototypes in Hellenistic originals. We have traced back to Alexandrian sources architectural landscapes with views of moderate depth, such as the relief of Dionysos visiting a mortal. In discussing the decadence of fresco painting in the Augustan age, the architect Vitruvius outlines the history of decorative wall-painting. "The ancients," he says, after some primitive beginnings, "began to represent the forms of buildings and of columns, and projecting and overhanging pediments; in their open rooms such as exedræ," "they depicted the façades of scenes in the tragic, comic, or satyric style; their walks . . . they decorated with a variety of landscapes. In these paintings there are harbors, promontories, seashores, rivers, fountains, straits, fanes, groves, mountains, flocks, shepherds; in some places there are also pictures designed in the grand style, with figures of the gods or . . . the battles at Troy, or the wanderings of Odysseus with landscape backgrounds."[62]

We have spoken of the Odyssey landscapes earlier (p. 328), and have given reasons for believing that Hellenistic prototypes lay behind them (Fig. 529). In these paintings, three things strike the observer at the outset: the impressionistic method used, the subordination of figures to the landscape, and the feeling for unlimited space which we have not found before. The figures are actually placed *in* their surroundings and appear to move and belong there. The entire painting with landscape and figures is conceived as an entity. The forms are not treated plastically as in earlier Greek art, nor do they occupy the major part of the composition. They have no sharp

[62] Vitr., *De Arch.*, VII, 5, 1-4. (Trans. by M. H. Morgan.)

outlines but are seen from a distance and the illusion of form is given by contrasting color hues. Spatial composition greatly interests the artist. He gives proof of this in his wide vistas out to sea and in the continuation of the paintings horizontally.

One of the most attractive paintings of the group is the representation of the Underworld (Fig. 541). At the left, is the ship of Odysseus; in the center, the entrance to the Underworld. Through the mouth of a great, rocky cavern the bright light of the outer world falls upon the shadow realm of ghosts. The artist is a master of light effects and the shadows and lights are handled illusionistically with great skill. Here and there reeds and grass are growing. These are rendered with fine swift brush-strokes and merely suggest plant life. The figures are vigorous little patches of light or shadow, with a sharp articulation of joints. The colors used are the bright red of the framing pilasters with their yellow capitals, the bluish green of the sea, the brownish yellow rocks and blue-green grass, the bright green pools and the reddish flesh-tones of the figures, with some added yellow and brown. Only one example of the series makes use of architecture, the one in which the palace of Circe is represented. Our interest, however, and that of the artist who painted the scenes, lies more in the vistas out to sea. An example of this is seen in Figure 529. In the central panel, where the ships of Odysseus are destroyed by the Læstrygones, the painter indulges his taste for distant prospects. The point of view taken is entirely an optical one. The figures move inward emphasizing the unlimited space in which they are placed. At the mouth of the bay are some gray-green cliffs, tinged with violet. On the bluish green sea, dark brown ships are seen. The flesh of the men is a reddish brown. The landscape is executed broadly and the figures are impressionistically handled with patches of color. A cleft between two rocks is a favorite motive.

The impressionistic manner which we have wished to derive from Alexandria, following Weisbach, attained a great development at the hands of artists in Italy during the late Republican and Augustan ages. The limited space composition of Alexandria took on a much more unlimited aspect and the figures, far from retaining their former classic dignity and proportions, became brisk little actors on a more extensive stage. There was real inclusion of figures in their surroundings; movement and action became more realistic and natural.

The artist's mastery of the brush and his ability to render form by a few strokes is seen in Figure 542, where Odysseus visits the land of the Læstrygones. In the section at the right, the movement of the figures in action is particularly well rendered. They are mere manikins. The colors melt into the background—bright yellow, brownish red, and green playing the leading rôles. The scene here depicts the combat of the companions of Odysseus against the cannibals. At the left, the Greeks meet the King's daughter and ask their way. The reclining woman is a personification of the spring, as the inscription *Krene* tells us; while, at the left, above the head of the sailor, is the word *Aktai,* "beach." The scene is a rather idyllic one with flocks pasturing in the middle distance and foreground. Valleys between rocky cliffs occur here.

Other paintings with mythological subjects have been found in the house of Livia on the Palatine. The story of Galatea fleeing from the giant Polyphemos is depicted here in the new technique (Fig. 543). The figures and surroundings form a unity. There is a certain lack of definition in the background which may, as some have thought, be drawn from the region around Naples. The landscape is again an idyllic one in which the mythological figures play a secondary part. The rather playful touch obtained by placing Eros on the shoulder of Polyphemos, and by making the small figure drive the huge giant, is Alexandrian. The contrasts of light and shadow are skilfully handled. The view is again a distant one but more limited than in the case of the Odyssey landscapes. A single conical mount forms the background.

Another class of paintings which Vitruvius mentions are vistas of a type found in the yellow frieze from the House of Livia on the Palatine (Fig. 544). Here, the point of view of the artist is a high and distant one, and the landscape, distributed into eight sections by painted columns, is rendered in impressionistic fashion. The scenes are more or less what one might see when traveling by. The landscape belongs to the "sacred-idyllic" class with temples, tholoi, altars, herms, statues of gods, and the like. The buildings are shown in fairly correct perspective, those in the foreground being larger. The painter has sought for the typical in landscape and in motion. These monochromes furnish some of the most interesting panoramas from ancient times. The work is done in swift brush strokes with brown shadows and white lights against a yellow ground. Above, in the foreground at the right, is a shepherd with his goats. His dog appears to be pursuing a traveler.[62a] To the left of the center, fishermen seem to be hauling in their nets. Below, one sees a man leading a camel, a second man crossing a bridge, and scenes of worship.

Closely akin to this frieze in technique are the sketchy scenes in yellow on the black wall from the Farnesina house in Rome, which we have mentioned above (Fig. 540). In contrast to the small narrow frieze just discussed which was placed near the top of the wall, the middle of the wall in this case is occupied with paintings, separated from one another by degenerate candelabra. It is a landscape with sacred-idyllic subject matter. Arches surmounted by statues, round pavilions, temples, men, trees, and animals are scattered about in a free fashion. These paintings in impressionistic vein are among the most charming from antiquity and show a Chinese dexterity of brushwork. Rostovtzeff has proved from a study of the buildings that these designs, as well as those from the house of Livia, are Hellenistic in origin.

Vitruvius mentions further, among his landscape subjects, harbors. This type of painting is doubtless reflected in Figure 545. The scene is carried out in impression-

[62a] This does not appear in our illustration which presents a section of the wall.

istic fashion with especial attention to the third dimension. The work is very sketchy but gives a vivid representation of piers washed by the sea, and suggests well the types of buildings seen around a harbor. In the foreground are fishermen.

In Figure 546 we have an inundated landscape. The chiaroscuro does not clearly mark where the land leaves off and the sky begins. In the foreground is a sacred island on which is a tree hung with fillets. Here altars are seen and shepherds sacrificing. The coloring and certain details are akin to what we find in the Farnesina paintings on the white wall, but the painting is considerably later.

During the Second style, there arose a landscape painter of some distinction named Studius, Ludius, or Tadius, who is called by Pliny the inventor of garden and villa landscapes.[63] He was a painter of the Augustan age and a series of landscapes of this period has been connected with his name. He is said to have decorated walls with representations of villas, harbors, landscape gardens, sacred groves, fishponds, streams, and shores. Some of the paintings which we have been discussing, such as the yellow frieze of Figure 544, may thus go back to this artist. He also brought in the fashion of painting seaside towns on the walls of open galleries. A number of scholars have connected garden scenes from the Villa of Livia at Prima Porta with the name of Ludius, whether rightly or wrongly seems undeterminable (Fig. 547). They are very charming formal enclosures with soft, feathery, green trees, sometimes burdened with yellow fruits; gaily colored flowers and birds are seen along the path which is bordered on either side by a low railing. The paintings are rendered with some feeling for depth; the effect, however, is rather that of a theater drop. It is this lack of interest in the third dimension and the very great precision in detail which suggests to me that they may not be the type Ludius used, especially since he must have availed himself of a distant viewpoint in his seaside towns and harbors. His style seems to me rather that of the yellow frieze of the House of Livia where some of his subject matter is also found.

Examples of a novel type of landscape are common enough especially in the Third and Fourth Pompeian styles. Some of those of the Third style have gardens in the background which recall the ones from Prima Porta but are visible behind an architectural façade which is not Italian. Rostovtzeff sees in these a reminiscence of the hunting or pleasure parks of the Hellenistic Kings of Egypt or Syria.[64] In the house of M. Lucretius Fronto at Pompeii, a group of villa landscapes of the Third style were found which are of distinct interest for the light which they shed on the Roman country house. In a gently rising landscape with three mountains in the background a country place is set among trees (Fig. 548). It consists of a series of

[63] Pliny, N.H., 35, 116.
[64] M. Rostovtzeff, "Die hellenistisch-römische Architekturlandschaft," Röm. Mitth., 26 (1911), p. 48.

colonnades, small detached houses, and a walled-in waterway in front adorned with statues, and furnished with a grassy path. The landscape is done in illusionistic fashion with hazy softening outlines for the mountains and rapid brush-strokes for the trees. The architecture has been shown by Rostovtzeff to be typically Italian.[65] Figure 549, which belongs to the Fourth style, shows a combination of the Roman villa type at the right, with a sacred, slightly Egyptianizing landscape at the left. Space composition has interested the artist who has indicated the two shores and emphasized the distant view by placing warships on the waters.

We have seen from our survey that the Alexandrians and the Romans created landscape in the modern sense. There was never any subtle achievement in aerial perspective or atmospheric effects. There were no twilights or early morning mists.[65a] Most of the landscapes lack something intimate and have about them a typical element. The art always remained a decorative one. Real landscape did not begin for Greece until the Hellenistic age which developed in all probability the illusionistic method of handling landscape as well as the sacred-idyllic architectural examples, certain villa landscapes, and possibly also the wild animal ones. Space representation was not important with the earlier painters and it was not until stage-scenery developed this feeling for the third dimension that the use of chiaroscuro and perspective made landscape-painting technically possible. The change from the formal plastic style to the coloristic probably occurred at Alexandria although both styles were employed throughout the later history of ancient painting. We shall return to this subject in our treatment of Roman illusionism and its history in later times.

We shall pass now from the subject of landscape which became so important in the Second Pompeian style in Italy and shall consider a number of Hellenistic monuments which add to our knowledge of painting from the Third to the First Centuries B.C. Here belong the Delian frescoes published by Bulard[66] which form a peculiar class, dealing largely with religion. On altars and on walls near altars, scenes connected with the worship of the Genius and the Lares were painted on very poor stucco. In our example (Fig. 550), two male figures are seen, each with one leg advanced and both arms outstretched moving lightly and rapidly toward one another. Behind each is a palm branch and an amphora. Above is a figure much larger in size wearing a short tunic. Bulard thinks this representation an illustration of events which took place during the *ludi compitalicii*. The nude men may be wrestlers at the

[65] M. Rostovtzeff, "Pompeianische Landschaften und römische Villen," *Jahr.*, XIX (1904), pp. 103 ff., Pls. V-VII.

[65a] See Pfuhl, *op. cit.*, p. 885, where a sunset is mentioned. Moonlight scenes were not unknown, as the painting of the Trojan Horse proves. F. Wickhoff, *op. cit.*, p. 149. The Odyssey landscapes give us the best idea of the atmospheric effects gained by ancient painters.

[66] M. Bulard, "Peintures murales et mosaïques de Délos," *Mon. Piot*, XIV (1908).

games, in which we know that slaves took part, at the time of the *compitalia*. The palms and amphoræ also point in this direction. The figure above is probably a representation of Mercury. The scenes show the influence of Italian merchants upon the religion of Delos. The frescoes belong in the Second and First Centuries B.C. None are later than the year 64 B.C.[66a]

More interesting even than the subject matter is the execution of the paintings. They are done with extreme facility, so much so that one feels the carelessness of a practiced technique. The artist is very hasty and daubs on his colors "as if with an ox's tail." We have a passage from the poet Nævius in which he criticizes the artist Theodotos, who painted altars before the houses for the *compitalia* in the Third Century B.C.[67] He berates him because, shut off by a barricade, he painted as roughly as if he were painting with an ox's tail the *Lares Ludentes*. Our paintings may quite well follow the manner of Theodotos, although most of them belong to the First Century B.C. They are summarily sketched in a speedy fashion. The type in our example may correspond to athletic paintings dedicated in the Third Century B.C. to the Lares Ludentes. They are executed against a neutral ground. The male figure at the left is in red silhouette, the one at the right is a dark gray. Behind each is a green palm inclined outward and an amphora outlined in brown. Above these men, who resemble hastily executed wrestlers on Greek vases, is a male figure in a green tunic and red boots holding in his hand the end of his red pallium or cloak and a caduceus. These silhouetted forms move with easy spring in sprightly action. In spite of the negligent execution of the frescoes, the sketches reveal a mature knowledge of form and a pleasure in visual effect. The artist seizes the momentary action with ease. Whether he is drawing outlines, or shading sketches, or using washes for silhouettes, he shows a mastery of the brush. Where drawing exists, the strokes are broad and thick.

The second Delian fresco which we publish sets forth another religious scene (Fig. 550). In the center Juppiter Liber is seen; on either side, Ceres and Libera; at the right a man is placing a wreath on his head. At the left is the centaur, Sagittarius, sign of the Zodiac under which the master of the house was born. In the center, a crown dedicated to "Zeus Eleutherios" is hung. The same hasty and spirited work appears here as in the preceding example. The lightness of action found in the wres-

[66a] M. Bulard, "La Religion domestique dans la colonie italienne de Délos d'après les peintures murales et les autels historiés," *Bibl. des Écoles Françaises d'Athènes et de Rome*, Fasc. CXXXI, Paris, 1926.

[67] Nævius, *Tunicularia*, Ribbeck, *Com. Roman. Fragm.*,[3] p. 27.

. . . *Theodotum*
*Compeiles <pingens> qui aras Compitalibus*
*Sedens in cella circumtectus tegetibus*
*Lares ludentis peni pinxit bubulo.*

tlers has been caught in the centaur. The figures are executed in the same impressionistic manner. The ground line of the painting is red, the frame red and green. The face and arms of the better-preserved female figure are yellow tinted with brown, details being given in dark brown. Contours and folds of the tunic are black, of the *kolpos,* red; the short cuffs(?) are green. The wreath of Libera(?) is green; the horn of plenty, yellow. The face, arms, and legs of the first male figure are a yellowish brown; of the one at the right, brown. The centaur is red, with contours and details in a darker red. These mural paintings are the work of artisans with practiced hands but they are not highly artistic productions.[67a]

More important artistically, though still the work of artisans, are the painted grave-stelæ from Alexandria and Thessaly. The Alexandrian ones have suffered greatly and very few are so preserved that they can give us any real pleasure.[68] Most of the stelæ belong to the Third Century B.C. and doubtless grew out of the painted Alexandrian reliefs. This was probably not the case with the scenes depicting funeral banquets which, though poor, may be dependent on Attic art. Of the ninety-five stelæ enumerated by Pagenstecher, twenty belonged certainly to the graves of soldiers, probably more; twenty-five have representations of women and children, and some are unrecognizable. The soldiers were Macedonians, Thracians, Galatians, and various peoples from the Peloponnese, Crete, Africa, Asia Minor, and the islands. They did not often use the Attic schemes of shaking hands or of the dead man standing by a seated relative. They represented the dead alone or with his squire or a small son. The squire carried the armor of his master or gave him a drink. The types represented are seated and standing figures; parting scenes in which individuals are shaking hands, soldiers on horse or standing,—usually in front view—children at play, and banquets of the dead.

A representative example of these stelæ may be seen in the one from New York of a Galatian cavalryman (Fig. 551). Reinach has pointed out the influence exercised by Galatian mercenaries in Egypt on the works of art found there.[69] With their fondness for realism and their curiosity about everything new, these artists stamped

[67a] M. Bulard, "Description des revêtements peints à sujets religieux," *Exploration archéologique de Délos,* IX, Paris, 1926.

The interpretation here is taken from M. Bulard, *La Religion domestique dans la colonie italienne de Délos,* Paris, 1926. It is quite possible, however, that the figures are Greek.

[68] R. Pagenstecher, *Nekropolis,* 1919, Chap. II, p. 32, especially Figs. 19, 22, 28, 53 (Helixo). *Cf.* p. 65 for a list of places where stelæ were found and the race to which the individual belonged.

[69] A. Reinach, "Les Galates dans l'art alexandrin," *Mon. Piot,* XVIII (1910), pp. 37 ff. *Cf.* A. C. Merriam, *A.J.A.,* III (1887), pp. 261 ff. and Pl. XVII (color). R. Pagenstecher, *Nekropolis,* Leipzig, 1919, does not list Fig. 551 as a Galatian stele. He enumerates eleven stelæ. *Cf. Expedition Ernst von Sieglin,* Band II, Teil I A, Pls. III-IV.

their art with certain realistic traits, as the sculptures prove. The stelæ, however, remain essentially Greek works. The majority appear to have been found at Hadra and are now scattered about in the museums of Europe and America, fourteen of them being known. The example pictured here is set within an architectural frame bearing a pediment and an architrave which originally carried an inscription. Of this one can now read only the letters *elot*. The ground of the stele is rose. Against this a chestnut-colored horse is rearing and attempting to break away from a young man who wears a conical cap and a yellowish white tunic held in by a belt. Behind him is a smaller figure, probably a groom, who appears to be watching the proceedings. The horse is done with spirit, his head thrown upward, his ears back, and his eyes full of fire. This realism is a mark of Galatian taste in art, but in other ways the stele does not seem typically Galatian. In general, these artists of the Third and Second Centuries—the period to which the painted gravestones belong—did not trouble to represent characteristically Celtic details except for Galatian armor.[69a] Reinach explains this on the ground that they were soon assimilated to the Greek population, as their names show. They were in the service of the Ptolemies at Hadra and soon took on Greek ways and manners. The stelæ are the works of Greek artisans and remain primarily Greek in spirit and in accessories.

The technique of the stelæ can be touched upon only in a general way. In most cases the preliminary drawing takes care by means of dark lines, not only of outlines and inner details, but also of folds of drapery, details of hair, latchets of sandals, etc. Apparently, these lines were supposed to remain visible. The Alexandrian group belongs in the field, then, of encaustic painting in its preliminary drawing, but whether the details were in encaustic is more dubious.[70] In most cases, the stone is covered with a stucco layer and this makes possible another technique such as tempera. The background was usually painted in a solid color—red, yellow, or blue. The architectural parts were in strong colors. Frequently a pale rose is found here. Violet was used extensively. For the flesh of men, reddish brown is found, following the old Egyptian convention; for that of women, a lighter color passing into rose. For the eyes, white was employed; for the lips, red; for hair, black, yellow, or red. The garments were often violet or purple. Shoes were red or black. The ground line was always yellow. The colors follow closely those of Alexandrian reliefs.

In these stelæ we have original examples of early Hellenistic painting. Pagenstecher has shown that the drawing and the conventions used in representing the human form were the same that were employed in Pompeian painting. They are seen

[69a] Pagenstecher, *op. cit.*, dates the stelæ from the founding of Alexandria through the Third Century only.

[70] Pagenstecher, *op. cit.*, p. 70. I have followed Pagenstecher's account of the technical details. The outlines, in my opinion, were probably invisible, as at Pagasæ.

in such examples as the soldier from Shatby (Fig. 552). We find here no classic proportions. The legs and arms are long and thin, the joints small. The outlines are hard and angular, the execution very hasty. These same hard outlines appear in Hellenistic black-figured vases and in the paintings on the altars at Delos. A close second to the soldier from Shatby is seen in the hunter from the Casa degli Epigrammi at Pompeii. The right foot is firmly planted, the left bent outward. The proportions of the arms and legs, their length and thinness all agree. Here, according to Pagenstecher, are the roots of the individuality of the art earlier designated as Roman. All this is Hellenistic material and is present in Alexandria in the Third Century. The development of space on the monuments is well illustrated by the Helixo stele in the Alexandria Museum (Pagenstecher, *op. cit.*, Fig. 53). The figures are relegated to the background and a wide space is left in front. Three planes are designated—the foremost one which consists of the ground covered with a mosaic, and the roof; the central one with the figures; the back one with the wall. The stripe in the foreground adds to the depth. The stele is earlier in time than the Hediste one from Thessaly of which we shall speak later (Fig. 553). The Alexandrian examples at Hadra fall between 280 and 150 B.C. The Hadra vases, which may be dated by the inscriptions between 284 and 249, also aid in establishing the chronology (Fig. 562).

Other stelæ have been found at Sidon. Many of these represent mercenaries belonging to the Seleucid garrison there in the Second Century B.C. They are cruder in style and less Greek but resemble the Galatian stelæ in the types employed.[71] They date in the Second Century and in later times. They are very modest works of art, with a figure of a man or a woman in front view, or a reclining figure, often occupying the background. Decorations of branches and garlands occur, especially at the top of the panel. Still other stelæ come from Cyprus, and Western Sicily.[72]

The most important stelæ from the period under discussion are those which came to light some years ago at Volo, the ancient Pagasæ in Thessaly. The space between the older town wall of the Fifth Century and the outer wall of the First Century B.C. was found to contain some fifteen hundred stelæ. About four hundred were discovered built into the walls there and dating from the Third and Second Centuries B.C. They were painted on marble in the encaustic technique with the aid of a spat-

[71] Ch. Clermont-Ganneau, "Stèles peintes de Sidon," *Gaz. archéol.*, III (1877), pp. 102-115, Pls. 15, 16; H. Lammens, *Rev. arch.* (1898), II, p. 109; *Perdrizet, ibid.* (1899), p. 42; III (1904), p. 234. Th. Macridy-Bey, *Rev. biblique*, I (1904), pp. 401 ff.; 547 ff., Pls. I-III, XII.

[72] Renan, *Mission de Phénicie*, Paris, 1864; Pl. XLIII; L. Jalabert, *Rev. Arch.* (1904), pp. 1 ff.; Murray-Smith-Walters, *Excavations in Cyprus*, London, 1900, p. 93. G. Mendel, *Catalogue des sculptures grecques, romaines, et byzantines, Musées Impér. Ottomans*, Constantinople, 1912, I, 258 ff.; *Memorie dei Lincei*, XV (1917), pp. 574 ff.

ula. Although many of them have lost their color, just as was the case with the Alexandrian stelæ, more than twenty examples are still so well preserved that we are able to judge of this feature as well. On two hundred others, traces of color are found.

M. Arvanitopoullos, their discoverer, overestimated the paintings for a time, holding that they gave us a very good idea of the work of painters in the encaustic technique, such as Nikias. They seem to copy Greek easel-paintings and are among our best examples of handicraft from the Hellenistic age. They give us no inkling, however, of the painting of masters like Nikias. They bear much the same relation to the major art of painting that sculptured grave stelæ bear to the art of sculpture.

The Pagasæ stelæ show many close affiliations with funerary reliefs but also many differences. They were apparently fashioned by a local school of artists. The style is not a distinctively individual one, but goes back to Attic models for much of its quality. The scenes, however, are not preponderantly farewell scenes, such as one finds on Attic grave reliefs. Figures shaking hands occur, but usually one finds a seated man or woman with one or more standing figures. Beside these, there are funerary banquets and some thoroughly individual representations, such as a youth with armor, or a small squire bearing armor.

One of the most famous examples of the class is the Hediste stele (Fig. 553). Here, an interior is skilfully pictured. In the foreroom, a dead woman is lying on a couch. At the foot of the bed, her husband is seated. The upper part of the stele is well preserved and the distressed head of the husband shows the artist's ability to portray pathos. Behind the dead woman, at the right, is an old nurse with the child in her arms. The inscription below tells us that it died shortly after its mother. Through an open door in the rear, a young girl is seen. Our interest in the painting lies largely in the ability of the artist to depict emotional states and in his mastery of the third dimension. This is the only painting in which the figures are not arranged beside one another in relief fashion. They are also considerably smaller in scale in relation to the surface to be decorated than other figures which we have met, and a great deal of space is left above the heads. The colors are violet for the wall and pillars above; yellow and red on the pillow and mattress; red for the coverlet over the child; red for the dress of the nurse, and red for her headband. The colors are perfectly fused, so that one sees no trace of the technical processes. The inscription tells the sad end of the mother who died in childbirth and of the child who followed her shortly afterward.[73] The stele belongs to the *naiskos* type.

To this same class, we must add the grave monument of Stratonikos (Fig. 554). The architectural features of this stele are similar to those of the Hediste one, but no free standing akroteria are preserved in this example. The architecture acts as a frame for a farewell scene. Stratonikos is seated at the right on a blue and pink

---

[73] For the Greek inscription, see *Arch. Anz.*, 25 (1910), 157.

cushion, which covers a stool with yellow legs. He wears a yellowish chiton of fine material and an himation over the left shoulder. The folds are outlined in dark gray. The hair and shoes are reddish, the flesh a deep yellow. He clasps the hand of a dark-skinned youth who stands before him and who is dressed in a red chiton and a white chlamys. The figure of Stratonikos is much more graceful and easy, so that some writers have thought of two artists. The inscription tells us that he was the son of Straton. "His soul which has now left his body we knew well. Here rest his remains—a sad grief to his mother and sister."

Yet another stele bears on its surface a picture of a young mother drawing her child toward her (Fig. 555). In its expression of tenderness, the scene is akin to some of the representations found on Greek lekythoi or on Attic grave-stelæ. The conception is new. The graceful, youthful figure of the woman with her head slightly inclined toward the child is one of the most arresting known to us on these monuments. It shows the combination of idealism and realism which is so very appealing in many of these works.

Rodenwaldt has pointed out that the stelæ from Pagasæ are not so important for the history of ancient painting as they are for color and technique.[74] The execution is of varying degrees of excellence, from the rather careless work seen on the stele of Peneïs and Herodotus, where the colors, put on in mosaic-like fashion, are not really fused, and where the pastes are sometimes not pressed together at the edges, to the Hediste stele where the execution is so fine that we cannot trace the technical processes. The surface of the stone where the painting appeared was not worked differently from the rest, nor was there any preparation of the surface for grounding the colors. Many of the stelæ have a preliminary sketch in grayish black, not only for the contours but for details of garments and the like. This sketch is at times so minutely careful that it seems impossible to believe it was covered up. It does not appear on well-preserved examples and in some instances we can trace color over the black lines. The preliminary drawing was executed with a brush but no brush was used in connection with the wax over-painting. The drawings were well preserved because they were burned in. The colors employed were violet or red on the ground and red-brown, yellow, pink, blue, rose, gray, and green. Already the Hellenistic colors begin to assert themselves—the pinks, violets, and pale greens which remind us of water colors. The colors were body colors. No stylistic development is observable in these works.

The stelæ date mostly in the Third Century, although some belong in the Second. This is proved not only from stylistic criteria but from a soldier's inscription which shows that he fought in the battle at Thebes won by Philip in 217 B.C. The walls of Pagasæ were destroyed in the wars with Rome in 197 B.C. and the years following.

[74] G. Rodenwaldt, "Zu den Grabstelen von Pagasæ," *Ath. Mitth.*, 35 (1910), pp. 118 ff.

They were reconstructed about 50 B.C. at which time the stelæ were built into the towers and walls. Their final publication by the discoverer, Arvanitopoullos, is awaited with much eagerness.[75]

Rodenwaldt has shown that the stelæ give pleasure by their variety and by a new approach to the treatment of the subject. They are not, like the poorer class of sculptured grave-stelæ, so monotonous in the repetition of types. They were made to order and the painter catered more to the wishes of the purchaser. They go beyond the sculptured grave-reliefs in introducing landscape surroundings and interiors. In this respect they show a certain affinity with Greek votive reliefs. Only one example is a known copy of an easel painting.

In addition to the stelæ discussed above, there are two gravestones from Chios which, in their engravings, recall work on metal. They are of dark blue marble. The surface has been polished, the designs engraved, the background roughened. Whether or not the forms were painted in, we do not know. The ground was probably in color. The more famous of the two is the stele of Metrodoros (Kekulé, *Griech. Skulptur*, 1907, p. 301; *Beschreibung der antiken Skulpturen*, Berlin, 1891, pp. 289-291, Figs. *a, b, c*). It is a square pillar. Each of the four sides contained a central panel, bordered above and below by engraved designs. On the front of the monument the inscription was cut at the top of the central field. This field although now badly defaced, must, in all probability, as Vollgraff suggests, have been used as a ground for encaustic painting in color.[76] Above this blank panel, which originally contained some design, are three engraved friezes: at the top, there are ivy or vine leaves; below this, sirens are engaged in playing various musical instruments; still below this, a battle of Centaurs and Lapiths was represented. At the bottom of the main field were pairs of horses driven by a Niké. Similar designs bounded the central fields of the other three sides. On the right side, in the center, an athlete is depicted shooting arrows, with his slave behind him (Kekulé, *Griech. Skulptur*, 1907, p. 301). In the background is a plane tree; at the left, a pillar surmounted by an urn. The back of the stele contained a second representation of an urn on a pillar. In addition, palæstra implements were shown—strigils, an oil-flask, and the like,—hung from a nail. The fourth side is practically destroyed. A second Chian example represents a woman playing a lyre with a small maid-servant beside her. (*Ath. Mitth.*, XIII (1888), p. 197.)

Certain examples of Hellenistic painting in Palestine reveal Greek traditions with an admixture of Oriental elements. Two tombs from Marissa from the end of the Third Century, or the beginning of the Second, have been published by Peters and

---

[75] A. S. Arvanitopoullos, *Eph. Arch.*, 1908, pp. 1 ff., Pls. I-IV.

[76] W. Vollgraff, *B.C.H.*, 26 (1902), pp. 559 ff. A. W. Lawrence, *Later Greek Sculpture*, New York, 1927, Pl. 42.

Thiersch and are of extreme interest because of the fusion of Greek and eastern elements found in them.[77] The form of these rock-cut tombs is definitely Hellenistic. They consist of underground halls with vaulted roofs, containing long rows of *loculi,* or burial places. They are entered by means of a dromos and steps. The type spread from Alexandria to Carthage, Cyrene, Egypt, Syria, and Phœnicia. The decoration is by a Greek or by someone schooled in Greek traditions. In Tomb No. I, at the end of the long hall, was a rectangular recess with a gabled roof. This niche contained the funeral couch so characteristic of the Greeks. The doorway was gaily decorated in color (Fig. 556). Facing the spectator was an entrance framed by a *naiskos* painted in red. On either side of this doorway was a Panathenaic vase of Hellenistic shape—one, black, with a red band and top, the other, with a pink band and top. The round yellow table at the left with lions' feet for supports is also Hellenistic. Typically Ptolemaic are the eagles with their outspread wings and scraggy necks which make them look as if they had been given a bath. Their outlines were drawn in black but they were painted a brilliant red. They are similar in type to those found on Ptolemaic coins and were probably associated with the Phœnix in the minds of the people. The festoons are also Hellenistic. They continue on the walls on either side, and, below them, run the famous animal friezes which we shall discuss. Thiersch points out that the fire is probably a Persian contribution and that the candelabrum of Tomb II is Phœnician. The tomb is interesting not only for its decoration but also for its historical connections. We have in this case "a Phœnician settlement on Jewish-Idumæan soil under Egyptian-Syrian rule, with a culture which, with the exception of some Persian influences, is chiefly Greek."[78] It shows anew the dependence of Phœnician art on Greek.

If we follow the paintings on the side wall, we shall find a hunting scene, the motives of which are borrowed from the Greek. They recall the Sidonian sarcophagi, *e.g.,* the Alexander hunt (Fig. 557). The same Persian costume is even found—the dark red breeches and short tunic girded at the waist; the chlamys with its long sleeves and the characteristic cap of Phrygian type. The decorated saddle-cloth is also paralleled in the Sidonian sarcophagi. In color, red and yellow prevail. The heavy festoons are dotted red and brownish black against a neutral ground. The garments and the horse trappings are red and yellow. The outlines and tree are brown. The animals are both imaginary and real. Most of the actual ones have their home in Africa. Among those represented, we find the rhinoceros, the hippopotamus, crocodile, giraffe, elephant, oryx, wild boar, lion, leopard, bull, gryphon, a wild ass, a lynx, and a porcupine. What led the people of Palestine to place these designs on the

[77] J. P. Peters and H. Thiersch, *Painted Tombs in the Necropolis of Marissa,* London, 1905 (Palestine Explor. Fund).

[78] *Cf.* Thiersch, *op. cit.,* p. 92.

wall of a tomb? Some have thought that the man buried there was a collector or purveyor of animals—a kind of Hagenbeck, as Merrill remarks, collecting animals for his royal master in Egypt or Syria. Probably it was merely an interest in the strange fauna of the Nile which led to the practice. We have seen this interest at play at Palestrina, in Italy, and at Pompeii. The great zoölogical gardens of the Ptolemies and their famous processions in which strange animals were led probably gave rise to an interest in zoölogy.[78a] Scientific study of these animals was doubtless common in Alexandria. These facts may have caused the painters to introduce into the tomb of a man who liked to follow the chase all sorts of unusual eastern animals. This is not the only instance of decoration of this nature in Syria. An animal frieze has also been found in the ruins of the "Palace" of Hyrkanos at Arâk el-Emir dating about 175 B.C.[79] There is also a glass vase of the Hellenistic period with a hunting scene on it not unlike the one from Marissa.[79a]

Figure 558 is taken from the south wall and shows clearly the hasty but vigorous workmanship of the artist of Tomb I. At the left is a conventionalized tree. An oryx with nicely drawn horns approaches, followed by a gryphon with red wings and much use of red for details. A wild boar faces in the opposite direction. Even more exotic are some figures from a section of the north wall (Fig. 559). A human-headed lion and an extraordinary long-eared lynx gave the artist's imagination full play. Both are executed almost entirely in broad strokes of red with gray outlines. The tree is grayish brown.

In execution the paintings follow the methods found on Greek vases. The designs were incised lightly. Then the contours were marked out in gray with freedom, after which color was applied. The range of color is limited—red, yellow, gray, white, and black prevailing. In Tomb II, where musicians are seen, green is lavishly used. The work is, on the whole, heavy and careless but shows a facile hand and not a little vigor. Thiersch points out that the paintings have their closest analogies in Hellenistic stelæ from Sidon.[80] Further examples of tomb-paintings of this age may be found in Italy where the Etruscan-Oscan tradition continued, in Apulian tombs, in one from Corinth, and in stray examples here and there in the East or in Mace-

[78a] Athen., XIV, 654[b]. Cf. Ælian, V.H., IV, 19; W. W. Tarn, *Hellenistic Civilisation*, London, 1927, p. 251; George Jennings, *Noah's Cargo: Some Curious Chapters in Animal History* (*Egypt, Babylon, Assyria, Africa, etc.*), London, 1928 (Black & Co.).

[79] Duc de Luynes, *Voyage à la mer morte*, 1864, III, Pls. 30-32; Howard C. Butler, *Syria; Architecture, Section A*, Leyden, 1919, Pl. I, pp. 1-25. Butler inclined to date the structure, which he did not consider a palace, in the time of Ptolemy II (285-247).

[79a] I owe the reference to Professor Rostovtzeff of Yale University. Cf. Helbig, *Führer*,[3] II, 212, 1486-1489.

[80] Thiersch, *op. cit.*, p. 86, note. Cf. p. 346.

donia. The art in these places is national in subject matter only; the forms are barbarized Greek forms.

Before leaving the subject of Hellenistic wall-painting we should mention two styles which had their origin in the Hellenistic age but which flower from the First to the Third Centuries A.D. These were the carpet or floral style in painting and the incrustation method. These styles arose, as Rostovtzeff has pointed out, "to supplant the structural style in the East and to fight the architectural style in the West." (*J.H.S.*, 39 (1919), p. 161.)

Rostovtzeff traces the naturalistic flower style back to Egypt, referring to such monuments as the Tell el-Amarna pavement (Figs. 62-66). Both the carpet and the true flower styles occur on Hellenistic ceramics, mosaics, and glass vases. The idea is to reproduce on walls, floors, ceilings, or on various objects, the effect of a richly woven carpet or material covered with flowers. Examples of the carpet style have been found in Cyrene and in the mosaics of Northern Africa. It occurs, according to Rostovtzeff, on the recently discovered ceiling of a house on the Palatine, dating in the period of the Second style, and in many Pompeian houses of the Fourth style. The walls were covered from dado to cornice with a rich carpet of red or yellow. Published examples of these styles as they occur in the Hellenistic age are not common, and we shall trace the style as it developed later, in our survey of monuments of the Empire.

In the naturalistic style, the flowers are not arranged symmetrically and may be conventionalized. They are strewn about among plants, birds, animals, and garlands. The style probably originated in early Egypt and was revived by the Ptolemies. It invaded mural decoration in the First Century B.C. Examples of this fashion may be found in the painted tombs at Kertch beginning in the Augustan age. It came to its height in the First and Second Centuries A.D. Some house-shrines in Pompeii are decorated in this manner and mosaics in Africa in later times bear witness to its persistence there. It was widely spread over the ancient world in the Christian Era. It grew out of the naturalistic trend in Hellenistic and Roman art.

On the other hand, the incrustation style, or "painting with slabs of colored marbles," came to Italy from the Hellenistic East. The palace of King Mausolos in Caria is the first example of this style cited by Pliny and Vitruvius. The practice probably came originally from Mesopotamia. The artist set into walls, floors, and ceilings, slabs of marble, metal, or glass, fitting them together in a sort of mosaic pattern with geometric designs. The manner must be studied today in poor copies in tomb and house decoration at Pompeii and elsewhere. It has no connection with the First Pompeian style. It is often found in the Fourth style at the base of the wall, as, for example, in the house of the Vettii. It became common in the First and Second Centuries A.D. In the late Roman Empire, as Rostovtzeff points out, "the flower and incrustation decorative style was *the* style." South Russian examples dating from the First and Second Centuries A.D. will be examined later in our survey (Figs. 601-603).

To the monuments discussed we may add the field of ceramics. The main centers of production were Italy, Egypt, and Southern Russia. By the Third Century, the Red-Figured style had mainly run its course and other styles came to the fore, notably the Black-Figured, white-ground, relief, and polychrome styles. We shall find the artist frequently using light colors against a black or dark ground as in Gnathia ware, or employing black or polychrome designs against a white field, as in the vases from Canosa. The white-ground class is composed for the most part of sepulchral vases decorated with polychrome designs. They show an attempt to adapt the major art of painting to the ceramic field. Two types are found: (a) vases with a firmly adhering white slip on which monochrome decorations in a brownish yellow or red violet were placed; (b) vases with a very flaky white slip decorated with gayer polychrome coloring. To the second group belongs the vase pictured in Figure 560. It is a kantharos with high, graceful handles. A creamy, friable slip covers the exterior. On the outer edge of the lip runs an egg and dart pattern in black and red. The body of the vase bears figure decoration, together with branches in bluish green and white under the handles. On the obverse, which is shown here, a nude youth with an himation around his shoulders is carrying a lighted torch in his right hand and a red tambourine in his left. On the back, occurs a draped female figure holding a mirror. These types are inherited from earlier South Italian ceramics. Many other vases in this class, especially some from Carthage, show charming floral decorations with vine patterns and ivy branches. These are often oinochoai painted in red against a white ground.[81] The clay of this class is like that of vases from Canosa, and they were probably made in ancient Canusium. Figure decoration is found less frequently. Flowers, masks, musical instruments, birds, small animals, and dolphins become common. These appear to be a degenerate form of Attic vases with a white ground.

The vases from Canosa preserve a less pure Attic tradition. They commonly present a white ground on which designs are painted in rose, green, red, blue, and other colors, but sometimes the ground for the decoration is rose-colored, or even blue. The vases are frequently adorned with figures in relief or statuettes. The decoration may be placed on the handles, body, or neck; in fact, the most pronounced characteristic of this class is the combination of the coroplast's work, together with the polychromy of the painter's art. They belong mainly to the Third and Second Centuries, though earlier works are known. An example of this class may be seen in Figure 561, a pitcher with a very thin neck and elegant handle. The ground of the vase is a rose

[81] E. Pottier, *Mon. Piot*, XX (1913), pp. 163 ff., Pls. XI-XII, color.

color. The figure decoration on the neck is in relief and is executed in a creamy white and rose. It consists of a Cupid and female heads. On the body of the vase is a quadriga guided by a woman who is preceded by Eros. She is dressed in a red garment which is deeper than the ground. The horses are white with blue collars and with details in a diluted brown. At the extreme right, one sees a hippocamp with four wings. The colors are red, rose, yellowish white, yellow, black, and blue. They were put on over a white coating. Many askoi of bulging shape are found in this class. They are adorned with vivid decorations in rose, blue, and yellow, and with rather homely, modeled statuettes. (*Röm. Mitth.*, 29 (1914), Pls. IX-X, color.) They are more genuinely typical of the class than the pitcher just described. Often the shape of the vase is that of a human head. The two main trends of ceramics in the Third and Second Centuries—in the direction of relief and polychromy—are seen in these examples. The Museum at Syracuse has some fine Hellenistic vases from Centuripe with moulded figures on the rim, and, in one case, a Pompeian red ground. Lavender, green, and white figure in the decoration. One large krater has a representation of Bacchus.[82]

Another important class of Hellenistic vases with a light ground for the decoration consists of the sepulchral hydriai from Hadra in Egypt. Hadra was the eastern necropolis of Alexandria and the hydriai were used to contain the ashes of Greeks who died in Alexandria. Pagenstecher and others who have studied this class point out that there are two types: (a) those which use the natural clay as a background against which the decoration is silhouetted in a brownish black, and (b) those which employ a yellow or a white slip of paint.[83] The first class is the more important for us. In it occur the funerary inscriptions which date the monuments in the time of the ruler, Ptolemy Philadelphos, *i.e.*, from 284 to 249. Pagenstecher shows the similarities in technique and ornament between this class from Hadra, the Bœotian Kabeiric pottery, and some Apulian works. These vases "are the chief representatives of a class found with various forms of expression throughout the Mediterranean." The class was not made by Theban artists who wandered to Alexandria after the destruction of Thebes; the forms are different, the hydria prevailing at Hadra and occurring nowhere in Kabeiric pottery. The ornamentation is also different. Common to both classes is the use of the ivy branch and the decoration in brown

[82] For Hellenistic Sicilian vases, *cf.* P. Orsi, *Not. d. Sc.*, 1912, p. 420; B. Pace, *Ausonia*, VIII (1913), pp. 27 ff. On vases from Canosa, *cf.* Ch. Picard, *B.C.H.*, 35 (1911), pp. 206-207; E. Pottier, *Mon. Piot*, XX (1913), pp. 163 ff.; M. Jatta, *Röm. Mitth.*, 29 (1914), pp. 90 ff. See bibliography, *Hellenistic Vases*. G. Libertini, *Centuripe*, Catania, 1926.

[83] R. Pagenstecher, "Dated Sepulchral Vases from Alexandria," *A.J.A.*, XIII (1909), pp. 387 ff.; *cf.* C. Dugas, E. Pottier, *s.v. Vasa*, in Daremberg and Saglio, *Dict. des ant.*, p. 654; Reinach, *Mon. Piot*, XVIII (1910), pp. 65 ff. H. Pomtow, *B.P.W.*, 30 (1910), pp. 1090 ff.; R. Pagenstecher, *Röm. Mitth.*, 27 (1912), p. 120.

directly on buff clay. The Hadra vases were not produced immediately after the city of Alexandria was founded. Not a sherd has come from Abusir which belonged to that period.

A group of Hadra vases in New York shows the peculiarities of this class (Fig. 562). The decoration occurs mainly on the shoulder and belly of the vases. At the left, in the upper row, one sees the use of the ivy band; in the second vase, the laurel wreath; in the third, a hunting scene of some spirit. The fourth has reminiscences of Apulia in the palmette and floral decoration. In the lower row, ivy occurs on the shoulder, while heraldic gryphons neatly designed are seen in the metope. Vases with ivy branches, wave patterns, and late palmettes follow. Outlines are often incised, as in the Kabeiric class. A very large number of these vases have traits in common with other branches of Hellenistic art, but not so many as the white-ground class, which show certain affinities with the stucco decorations from Delos.

In connection with the vases from Hadra may be mentioned two interesting examples with polychrome painting on a white ground, published by Six (Fig. 563). The one below is taken from a vase owned by Six and contains a representation of a Panathenaic amphora awarded at the games.[84] This amphora is combined with a conventionalized palm branch, ribbons, and a torch into a still-life painting. The figures of the athletes on the vase are sketchily done in silhouette, and though of more degenerate form recall the Delian paintings (Fig. 550). The colors are a red-rose ground for the athletes, black for the silhouettes, blue for ribbons and palms, brownish red for the torch, and grayish brown for the vase. Above the design on the hydria owned by Six (Fig. 563) is depicted a painted medallion from a vase found at Hadra and now in New York. In the center, a Medusa head is represented. The color is handled impressionistically. The medallion is brown with a rose stripe on the outer edge; within this is a blue field which sets off the head of Medusa with her auburn hair. The modeling and the flesh tones reveal the work of a practiced artist (cf. Röm. Mitth., 27 (1912), Pl. IV). The colors were applied in tempera. Six inclines to see in the silhouettes of the athletes an illustration of the much-discussed compendiariæ or "short cuts" in ancient painting mentioned by Petronius.

Gnathia vases comprise one of the Hellenistic groups of ceramics with a black ground. They were manufactured in Southern Italy. The name is obviously a misnomer as the vases were probably not made at Egnatia. They have been found at Oria; at Bari, and Ruvo in the Apulian country; in Campania, in Sicily, at Melos, and on other scattered sites. They were apparently imported into Faliscan and Etruscan territory as well as to Sicily and Cyprus. This pottery is often distinguished by a series of plastic vertical ribs up and down the body of the vase. Its chief characteristic is a black glaze covering the whole field. The influence of metal wares is obvious

[84] J. Six, *Ant. Denk.*, III, Pl. 34, text, pp. 33-34.

in the shapes, handles, and glaze. Against this rather metallic-looking ground, designs of Erotes, satyrs, animals, birds, garlands, and flowers are painted in opaque colors —white, yellow, and red (*cf.* Fig. 564). The patterns usually consist of a frieze or metope of figure decoration on the shoulder or body of the vase, or a twining vine or ivy branch around the center. These *rinceaux* are often very graceful in design. The vases were at the height of their beauty at the beginning of the Third Century.

While this pottery was being produced in Magna Græcia, Tarentum was the real capital of the region and the intermediary between Hellenic civilization and Italy.[85] She probably exported many small vases with white decoration on a black ground. She was mistress of the sea and carried her trade up the Adriatic to Ancona and Adria and inland among the Samnites. Because of her prominence, she has usually been considered the source of Gnathia ware, but it is unfortunate for the hypothesis that practically no Gnathia pottery has been found at Tarentum. Examples have come from Metapontum which was closely in touch with Tarentum, so that the home of this class may be Tarentum. One must admit, however, that absolute proof for this theory cannot be produced. The pottery has obvious connections with the Apulian class and represents one of the last efforts of the Greeks in ceramic painting. Tarentum was taken in 272 by the Romans and the independence of Magna Græcia virtually came to an end at this time. Artistic Greek or Italiote painted pottery is not made after 200 B.C. A good representative of Gnathia ware from Magna Græcia is seen in Figure 564. The general appearance of the vase suggests the influence of metal work. Around the belly is a running floral pattern, with a swan in the center; on the neck are Erotes guiding a chariot drawn by gryphons. The spirit of the designs and the motives are typical of Hellenistic art.

An additional group of Hellenistic vases that should not be passed over in silence are the so-called *pocula*. They have been found for the most part in Etruria and Rome and are held by some scholars to be Campanian, by others to be Etrusco-Latian. About fifteen examples are known.

These vases consist of small phialai, or plates, covered with a black varnish and bearing designs in color, usually yellow, brown, orange, and white. The patterns include a female head, Erotes playing—sometimes standing on a dog and driving it— and ornamental designs, such as ivy. Some merely have dedications to Ceres, Bellona, Juno, Saturn, Vesta, Vulcan, or Æquitia. All inscriptions are in Latin, which was very commonly in use in Campania in the Third Century, the period to which these vases belong. One of the most interesting examples is now in the Villa Giulia in Rome. It represents an elephant of war carrying two soldiers in a tower on her back

---

[85] Charles Picard, "La Fin de la céramique peinte en Grande-Grèce," *B.C.H.*, 35 (1911), pp. 177 ff. On Gnathia ware, *cf.* P. Ducati, *Storia della ceramica greca*, 1922, II, 479 ff.; G. Leroux, *Lagynos*, Paris, 1913. On Apulian geometric of the Daunian, Peucetian, and Messapian classes, *cf.* M. Mayer, *Apulién*, Leipzig, 1914; F. von Duhn, Ebert, *Reallex.*, I, 202 ff.

and followed by a baby elephant. As elephants were first used in Italy in the war with Pyrrhus, this vase adds another argument for a Third Century dating (280-270 B.C.).[85a]

After painted vases had run their course in Southern Italy, relief wares came into prominence. We have already spoken of the pottery from Canosa. As relief wares interest the student of ancient painting less, although their designs embody Hellenistic patterns, we shall note in passing only the painted examples—omitting a discussion of Megarian bowls, Calenian ware, and Arretine pottery. This relief technique is found all over the Hellenistic world—in Southern Russia and at Kertch, no less than in the regions mentioned. The examples from Kertch begin in the Fifth Century. Some of them are quite effective, such as the sphinx, or the head of Aphrodite.[86] They are richly polychromatic, with a use of white for the body, blue for the eyes, gilt for hair, a rose color for the face, and red for other details. The classic example of such relief work is a Fourth Century vase in Petrograd with designs in relief drawn from the Eleusinian circle. This vase was found at Cumæ. Here, the glaze covering the hydria is black. The figures are gilded and painted. The Acropolis vases in relief copy metal prototypes. Yellow is the dominant color on the dark glaze.[87] Fine examples have also been found in Southern Russia and at Kertch, notably the vase with hunting scenes made by Xenophantos. (Rayet and Collignon, op. cit., p. 263.)

While this pottery with plastic reliefs was taking the place of painted wares in most parts of the Greek world, a desire for painted ceramics continued among the Pontic Greeks. Accordingly, we find a class of distemper vases with exceedingly heavy walls and poor potter's work but with some very interesting painting (Fig. 565). Sometimes the clay was left in its natural dirty yellow color; in our example, it is colored black. On this ground a combat is represented between a Greek and an Amazon. The Greek has reddish brown flesh with high lights and wears a red chiton, a helmet crested with red and a blue scarf. His shield is a grayish white. The flesh of the Amazon is a yellowish white. Her shield is bluish and bears a red-haired gorgon

[85a] G. Q. Giglioli, *Corpus Vasorum Ant., Italia, Fasc. III, Villa Giulia, Fasc. III*, IV, b, q, Pls. III, V (color). P. Ducati, *Storia della ceramica greca*, II, 481 ff.; H. B. Walters, *op. cit.*, I, 489 ff.; Rayet and Collignon, *op. cit.*, pp. 332 ff.

[86] E. H. Minns, *Scythians and Greeks*, Cambridge, 1913, Figs. 250-251, pp. 344-346; Rayet and Collignon, *La Céramique grecque*, Paris, 1888, pp. 271-272, Figs. 103-104. *Cf.* G. Treu, *Griechische Thongefässe in Statuetten- und Büstenform*, Berlin, 1875, 35 *Winckelmannsprogr.; C.R.*, 1870, Pl. I.

[87] Vase in Petrograd, *Mon. Ant.*, XXII (1913), pp. 696 ff., Pls. C-CII. P. Ducati, *Saggio di studio sulla ceramica attica del sec. IV. a.c., Memorie delle Reg. Accad. dei Lincei*, 1916, p. 89; F. Courby, *Les vases grecs à reliefs*, Paris, 1922. C. Watzinger, *Ath. Mitth.*, 26 (1901), pp. 50-102.

in the center. A blue cap, yellow chiton, and red scarf add further color to the whole effect. The wave pattern and the egg and dart above are done in red, as is the meander below. The artist has used a kind of tempera process, but has not known well how to fasten his colors which readily flake off. Probably these vases were made in Kertch. They show some skill in drawing and painting but potter's work of a miserable quality.[88]

Other painted monuments belonging to the Third Century reveal in their Hellenistic motives certain features of design which are common to the vases discussed. At Anapa in Southern Russia a wooden sarcophagus has been brought to light which discloses old Hellenistic patterns such as *rinceaux* and Nereids riding sea monsters[89] (Fig. 566). The main body of the sarcophagus is in the natural color of the wood but the architrave, the center panels in each side, and the vertical panels in the corner posts are red with carved decorations in gilded wood. In the panels of the corner posts are charming arabesques of acanthus leaves; on the architrave are fighting barbarians. The main design is made up of Nereids who ride sea horses and who bear the armor of Achilles. This panel is framed by cymatia and a bead ornament, while below the architrave occurs the egg and dart with the bead and reel. A coin of Lysimachos found with the sarcophagus dates the monument in the Third Century. Minns points out that this agrees with the style of the Nereids which are ultimately derived from Skopas. Another painted sarcophagus from Abusir (Watzinger, No. 4) contains, at the gabled end, the head of a woman painted on a blue ground in the midst of floral ornaments.[90] The tendrils are white, the blossoms red. A conventionalized olive branch fills the panel below. The long sides were adorned with inlaid bands decorated with the laurel pattern, and with a guilloche in white, red, and blue.

Similar motives occur on Hellenistic glass vases. These have been studied by Rostovtzeff but his work is not accessible to most scholars.[91] He proves that their patterns are Alexandrian in origin. On a bowl from Olbia occur a brownish red gazelle, with black back and white belly and some red partridges with blue breasts and yellow heads. Laurel branches, flowers recalling the lotus, geese, ducks, and peacocks are found on other examples. In Figure 567 we have a glass cinerary urn of

---

[88] E. H. Minns, *op. cit.*, pp. 347-348; Stephani, *C.R.* (1874), Pl. II, 5-8; (1878-1879), Pl. I, 5 (color), our example.

[89] E. H. Minns, *op. cit.*, pp. 324 ff.; *C.R.* (1882-1888), Pl. VI, 5, color.

[90] C. Watzinger, *Griechische Holzsarkophage aus der Zeit Alexanders des Grossen*, Leipzig, 1905, Pls. I-II, 1 (color).

[91] M. Rostovtzeff, "Painted Glass Vases of the Late Hellenistic Times and the History of Decorative Painting," *Bull. de la Com. Imp. Arch.* (1914) (Russian); *Rec.*, Morin-Jean, *Rev. arch.*, V (1917), pp. 310 ff. *Cf.* E. Michon, "Verres peints antiques," *Bull. de la Soc. des Antiq. de France*, 1913. W. C. Hayes, "An Engraved Glass Bowl in the Museo Cristiano of the Vatican Library," *A.J.A.*, XXXII (1928), pp. 23 ff. See bibliography on glass. V. Spinazzola, *Le arti decorative in Pompeii*, pp. 220-221.

blue and white color, decorated with bas-reliefs in which genii and a vine branch interwoven in graceful patterns betray very clearly their source of origin. The grapes are being picked and trodden to the music of flutes. In addition to the floral designs there are various animals. This example was found in a tomb at Pompeii. The shape was first formed in an opaque, white, glassy substance, after which, a transparent blue glass vase was blown inside the first. The figures were then carved on the white outer layer in a style akin to what is usually found on sardonyx cameos. The decorative style of Alexandrian glass-makers in the Hellenistic age was taken up by artists of the Roman Imperial epoch, especially in the making of pavements and ceilings. From the First to the Third Centuries A.D., a homogeneous style arose, traceable especially in mosaics, in Southern Russia, Syria, Egypt, Asia Minor, Palmyra, Great Britain, and Africa. The repertoire usually includes animals—such as a gazelle resting,—baskets of fruits and flowers, pomegranates, and partridges. These are not arranged symmetrically. Egyptian flora and fauna commonly appear.

With this survey of Hellenistic work our discussion of Greek painting proper comes to an end, although we shall make use of some of the later South Russian material and of copies of Hellenistic paintings in our summary of Græco-Roman work. We have seen that the Hellenistic epoch made great strides forward on the technical side. As a result of this advance in skill, stage scenery and landscape with backgrounds of limited depth came to occupy a prominent place. Both of these were made possible by the advanced proficiency in handling perspective and chiaroscuro. We have suggested that illusionism was employed in the case of landscape backgrounds, and that the use of illusionism began in the Hellenistic age. Mosaics such as the one from Delos in which Dionysos is represented, indicate a thorough knowledge of the impressionistic method.[92] Encaustic painting was also handled with skill and use was made of the impressionistic manner. Portraits of the Hellenistic age may have been executed in this method.

Various new types of compositions were invented by Hellenistic masters and old ones were elaborated. Mythological scenes in megalographic form were still favored but the artist turned rather toward the material of everyday life for his inspiration. Consequently, we find street scenes, scenes from daily affairs; still-life, and animal pieces where strange beasts were depicted with a scientific, Alexandrian inquisitiveness. Caricatures, like the Grylloi, occurred; pornographic scenes from brothels and low places; portraiture; and a rich system of decorative wall-painting which had developed out of the old Greek structural system. The artists were painters in our sense of the term. How far they advanced as colorists, we cannot know. The mosaics suggest a very rich palette. We cannot tell in the case of Pompeian wall-paintings how much is Hellenistic and how much Italian. In their ornamental patterns, exten-

[92] Bulard, *Mon. Piot*, XIV (1908), Pl. 15 (color).

sive use was made of floral designs, both formal and free. Beautiful *rinceaux* were developed which were sometimes woven into all-over patterns like carpets. We see here the germs of the decoration of the Ara Pacis and of later Roman work.

The Hellenistic age was one of creative force but also one of on-coming decadence. The strength of the Fifth Century had been forgotten, and the graceful thing, the refined and elaborated pattern, the sinuous in line, the filmy effect in blown drapery—such as one sees in the Flora—came to take its place. These achievements were more comprehensible to the ordinary man in the street and were often more restful to contemplate. They appealed directly to the emotions and called for little intellectual effort. They had more relation to everyday existence and contained less elevation and nobility. Art became more cosmopolitan—a thing to be appreciated by the masses and a mirror of the life of the times.

## ROMAN PAINTING

Roman painting during the period from the Third Century B.C. to the First Century A.D. is something more than Hellenistic painting in Italy. Rome was the last great center of Hellenistic art, as Pergamon, Alexandria, and Antioch had been centers of artistic endeavor before her. But she displays originality in certain fields and transforms her inheritance into a new creation in others, so that her efforts should not be dismissed as "nothing more than Hellenistic painting." Her art continued Hellenistic Greek traditions. It was formed of foreign elements, but it was nationalized by the assimilation of these elements to a completely Roman conception. In other words, we must distinguish between a Græco-Roman art which is merely Greek art in the Roman period, and Roman art which was an evolution from Greek, Italic, and Etruscan traditions but at the same time a creative thing.

Among the earliest Roman paintings known were those in the temples of Ardea. Pliny tells us that they were more ancient than the city of Rome and that they were in good condition in his day.[93] He does not give their subject matter but informs us that the painter was a Greek, Lykon by name. After decorating the Temple of Juno, he was given citizenship and took the name of Marcus Plautius. On his picture, hexameter verses were written stating his achievement and adding that the painter was "born in wide Asia." The hexameters prove that he could not have lived earlier than the time of Ennius, *i.e.*, between 239 and 169 B.C.[93] This same artist painted at Lanuvium two nude figures, Atalanta and Helen, side by side. Cære is said to have had much older pictures than these. There are some terra cotta paintings of the Sixth

[93] Pliny, *N.H.*, 35, 17; 115. *Cf.* Servius on *Æn.*, I, 44. C. Cichorius, "Zu römischen Malern," *Rh. Mus.*, 76 (1927), pp. 325 ff. The name *Lyco* was read by M. Hertz, *Breslauer Progr.*, 1867, for *loco*. Cichorius thinks that Lykon was the painter and poet Plautius, whose comedies passed under the name of Plautus. Varro, *ap.* Gellius, III, 3, 3.

Century extant from this site which show Ionic Greek influence, and which belong to the days of Etruscan rule [94] (Fig. 391).

At the end of the Fourth Century, a patrician, Fabius Pictor, painted the Temple of Salus.[95] This was executed in 304 B.C. and as it was vowed in the second Samnite war it may have been connected with these events in subject matter, though this is not essential. Dionysios of Halikarnassos speaks only of the drawing and the brilliance and harmony of the colors. The first definitely historical paintings mentioned by Pliny are those dedicated by Messala in 264 B.C. Fabius was followed by another Roman, the tragic writer, Pacuvius, who painted the Temple of Hercules in the Forum Boarium.[96] The subject matter we again do not know, but if Pacuvius' pictorial power with his brush equaled that of his pen, it was no insignificant achievement. Following these Romans, the art seems to have been practiced little by men of good birth and only stray names occur until the Augustan age, when painting again assumes a dignified position.

More important than these primitive works, which give us little information about painting in the Third Century beyond the fact that it was being done by Greeks or followed a Greek tradition, are the historical paintings which date from the Third Century or earlier. These were concerned largely with military exploits and triumphs and often have the peculiar feature of including the geography of the victor's campaigns. They formed an unusual combination of topography and military detail. In them were depicted scenes of cities taken by assault; personified provinces which had been conquered; operations in campaigns and the disastrous effects of the battles on the vanquished.

Typical of this class was the painting celebrating a victory by Manius Valerius Maximus Messala, in 264 B.C., over the Carthaginians and Hiero at Messina. It was probably executed on wood. Once the subject was treated, other examples followed: Scipio Africanus commemorated his exploits at Zama in 202 B.C. in this way, and Lucius Scipio celebrated his Asiatic victory over Antiochus in 188 with a painting of similar nature.[97] From the picture of the Prætor, L. Hostilius Mancinus, however,

[94] A. S. Murray, *J.H.S.*, X (1889), Pl. VII, 243-252; Mon. VI-VII, Pl. 30. A. N. Modona, *Pitture etrusche arcaiche, le lastre fittili policrome ceretane*, Firenze, 1928.

[95] Pliny, *N.H.*, 35, 19. Dionys. Hal., *Exc. ex libro*, XVI, III, 6. A. G. Roos, *Mnemos.*, 38 (1910), p. 283, n. 5. A. Reinach, "Fabius Pictor, les Fresques du temple de Salus et les origines de la peinture à Rome," *Studi Romani*, II, 233 ff. Eugénie Strong, *Art in Ancient Rome*, New York, 1928, I, 55-57. The name *Fabius* on the painting may have caused the story to be invented. Valer. Max., VIII, 14, 6. Fabius' paintings probably covered the long walls of the cella.

[96] Pliny, *N.H.*, 35, 19; *Cf*. L. Urlichs, *Die Malerei in Rom vor Cæsar's Dictatur*, Würzburg, 1876.

[97] Pliny, *N.H.*, 35, 22; Appian, *De Bello Punico*, VIII, 66. Raoul-Rochette, *Peintures antiques inedites*, 1836.

we may form a better idea of the class. He exhibited in the Forum "paintings of the site of Carthage and the various attempts to storm it," while he himself stood by the picture and told the story to the spectators.[98] This painting apparently aroused national enthusiasm and patriotic emulation and was doubtless a cause for the further development of the genre. It may have resembled in certain respects the paintings of the founding of Rome now in the Terme; i.e., a series of incidents were probably represented in frieze arrangement and the figures in some cases were set against a background of architecture. The walls of the city and the general character of the site were represented, together with certain aspects of the attack and defense. In 174 B.C. at the triumph of Sempronius Gracchus over Sardinia, a painting representing the victory was executed in which there was a plan of the island combined with the various combats.[99] This work seems to have exhibited, then, a combination of topography and history. The representation was probably a map-like plan on which battles were painted in the localities in which they occurred.

It is easy to see how these paintings arose, as Courbaud has shown.[100] Paintings on wood were carried in the triumphal processions and were set up in the Curia or dedicated in temples or exhibited in the *atria* of private houses. They began with portraits of the triumphant general, clad in a purple-bordered toga, on foot or in a chariot. Personifications of conquered cities—a taste derived from Greece—had their part in these processions. Beginning with Marcellus, who had a personification of the city of Syracuse in his painting, we find many examples of this practice.[101] Most notable of all was the procession of Scipio Asiaticus behind whose chariot followed one hundred thirty-four portraits of cities which he had taken.[102] This was elaborated by Cornelius Balbus who had not only captive cities personified but the streams and mountains of the conquered country as well.[103] This presented to the eye of the spectator "a complete geography of conquered Africa."

These geographical and historical paintings, together with the personifications of captured cities derived from Greece, were woven into more unified compositions at the end of the Republic, and events before and after the victory were added to form a continuous narrative. For example, in a painting of the triumph of Pompey, the defeat and death of King Mithridates, together with the death of several of his

---

[98] Pliny, *N.H.*, 35, 23.    [99] *Livy*, 41, 28.

[100] E. Courbaud, *Le Bas-Relief romain*, Paris, 1899, pp. 197 ff., Juvenal, *Sat.*, VIII, ll. 2-10. I have drawn on Courbaud's account of early Roman painting and on Urlichs' in this discussion. The earliest triumphal painting was that of the Consul, L. Papirius Cursor, hero of the Samnite war in 272 B.C.

[101] Livy, 26, 21; *cf.* Courbaud, *op. cit.*, p. 199, n. 4, on *simulacrum*. P. Gardner, "Countries and Cities in Ancient Art," *J.H.S.*, 1888, pp. 47-81.

[102] Livy, 37, 59.    [103] Pliny, *N.H.*, 5, 36. Raoul-Rochette, *op. cit.*, p. 316.

daughters and the destruction of the house, formed a part of the representation.[104] At Cæsar's triumph, a number of pictures traced the disasters of the civil war and the moving scenes of the deaths of the vanquished leaders. Appian tells us that the painting of Lucius Scipio hurling himself into the sea and the suicide of Cato brought groans from the spectators.[105]

Such was Roman painting in the early Republic. It was essentially a representation of scenes taken from life with all of the local detail which the Roman liked in his art and which he may have inherited in part from the Etruscan. Etruscan artists were responsible for some of the earliest paintings in Rome. The father of Tarquin brought with him artists from Corinth when he came to Etruria. Etruscan artists decorated the Temple of Juppiter Capitolinus and we may well believe that they played a very important part in Rome in the Sixth Century. They themselves represented triumphal scenes in some of their paintings, although the examples which we possess are late. However, as triumphs and processions played an important part in their lives, we can imagine that some of the paraphernalia of processions also came to Rome from Etruria. Appian traces the Roman festive processions at triumphs and funerals back to Etruscan prototypes.[106]

Most of the artists of these paintings were, however, Greeks. We have the name of Metrodorus who painted the scene of Lucius Æmilius Paullus triumphing over King Perseus in 168. After the campaign of M. Fulvius Nobilior in Ætolia, in 186 B.C., many artists accompanied the general to Rome to take part in the triumphal games.[107] These were probably the men who executed the triumphal paintings. In their works, they introduced personification, which was common in the art of Greece and they adapted their ideas to Roman demands. The first historical battle paintings date from 264 B.C., the period of the wars with Carthage, when Greek influence was becoming very powerful. We see, then, that it was not possible for the Romans to escape this Greek tradition. The workmen were Greek. They brought Greek methods of composition, Greek technique and style. They were forced to cater to Roman taste and the result is a curious combination of national literal-mindedness, as seen in the geographic-historic representations, with Greek conceptions such as the personification of cities and the more emotional scenes of disaster in which the artists of Fourth Century Greece had shown some interest. It is barely possible that the Alexandrian *topographos*, Demetrios, whom we have mentioned above (p. 307), may have been guilty of some such landscape representation as the Latin text suggests for the setting of triumphal scenes, but we prefer to think not. These historical-topographical pictures may have been the forerunners of works such as the reliefs on the columns of Trajan and Marcus Aurelius.

[104] Appian, *De Bello Mithridatico*, 117.  [105] Appian, *Bellum Civile*, II, 101.
[106] Appian, *De Bello Punico*, VIII, 66.
[107] Livy, 39, 22. These are interpreted as actors, musicians, and dancers by Weissenborn.

We have several Roman frescoes which can give us a certain idea of this Græco-Roman painting in the early Republic. One of these was found in a tomb on the Esquiline Hill in Rome (Fig. 568). It presents a military scene arranged in several zones above one another. Of these, three are preserved in part, and a section of the fourth. The artist has used a creamy yellow background against which he has placed his figures on rigidly marked horizontal ground lines. In the upper panel, M. Fannius, apparently an Oscan or an Umbrian, as seen from his dress, addresses a Roman soldier, Quintus Fabius(?). Behind Fannius is a wall with crenelated towers—dark brown in color—and a trumpeter. In the second frieze, Fannius and Fabius again address one another, while at the right soldiers in white tunics are shown, rising behind one another in three tiers. The artist transforms his depth into height. Below, is a combat where warriors armed with oval shields and wearing feathers on their helmets are engaged in fighting. The costume indicates that we are dealing with Samnites. The painting is to be dated about 200 B.C., to judge from the inscriptions and the beardless heads. The coloring is largely a reddish brown against the creamy yellow ground, combined with green, blue, yellow, black, and white. Greek tradition is followed in the arrangement by friezes, in the neutral background, and in the foreshortening. The paintings call to mind tomb-paintings from Pæstum, Figs. 436-437.[107a] They are now located in the Museo Mussolini.

A second historical fresco of importance is the one in the National Museum in Rome, depicting scenes connected with the founding of Lavinium, Alba Longa, and Rome (Fig. 569). It formed a frieze running above the upper row of niches in a columbarium on the Esquiline. A series of events is represented some of which are mythological, others more properly historical. In the upper panel at the right, which comes from the west wall of the tomb, men are seen with materials ready to build a city, while at the left Latins and Trojans are shown in combat with the Rutuli. The Latins are armed with oval shields, breastplates, and swords, while the Rutuli are nude and carry oblong shields. The name of the woman standing near the tower and wearing a violet garment and green mantle must remain uncertain. It is probably the local divinity. The scene appears to represent the founding of Lavinium.

If we follow the paintings in the order in which they occurred in the tomb, we see

---

[107a] W. Helbig, *Führer,*[3] I, 553. *Cf.* Eugénie Strong, *Art in Ancient Rome*, N. Y., 1928, I, 55 ff. The frequent references to pictures in Roman writers of the Second Century indicate that painting played an important part in the life of the people. Plautus has many allusions to paintings and Nævius in his *Tunicularia* criticizes the careless work of Theodotos which was hastily executed "with an ox's tail" (Fig. 550). Charles Knapp, "References to Painting in Plautus and Terence," *Class. Phil.*, XII (1917), pp. 143 ff. *Cf.* Hor. *Sat.*, II, 7, 96 ff., where the slave's enthusiasm over pictures of famous gladiators executed in red chalk and charcoal is described, "their legs spread out stiffly and as true to nature as if they were really striking, fighting or parrying blows." These probably resembled the Delian frescoes.

on the south wall a Victory advancing toward an armed warrior. At his feet lies a fallen enemy, while on the left the fight continues. The Niké is clad in a red chiton and wears a yellow mantle with a blue border. Perhaps the victor is Æneas and the fallen warrior Turnus, but there are obvious difficulties in the way of this interpretation. These are, first of all, the insignificant figure of Turnus, and second, the fact that Æneas is probably shown combating Turnus where the fight continues by the Numicus River. If we turn to what appears to be the painting of this incident in the lower panel, we see at the right the giant figure of Æneas wearing a crested helmet and charging an enemy. Who the foe is cannot be proved, but the weight of evidence seems to be in favor of Turnus. It is probably not Mezentius, because the two figures shaking hands in a peace compact are Mezentius, who is named in an inscription, and Ascanius. Behind the two warriors, the river god Numicus (*sic*) is seated with a rush in his hand. An inscription leaves no doubt as to his identity. The painter appears to have adhered to the version in which Æneas perished at the Numicus River. At the left, follows a scene of the building of Alba Longa. The goddess of the city, designated by an inscription, is seated before the walls wearing a turreted crown (Fig. 570). The remaining subject matter on the south wall is difficult of interpretation but probably refers to the differences between Lavinia and Ascanius after the death of Æneas. The figures represent Lavinia, a goddess of the region, Ascanius, and the goddess of Alba Longa. Lavinia is seated, sad in demeanor, with the goddess of Lavinium, perhaps Anna Perennis, before her. The nymph is apparently trying to reconcile Ascanius with his stepmother, but seemingly without success. The figure of Alba Longa at the right refers to the new foundation of the city.

The scenes on the east wall which are not illustrated here depicted the story of Rhea Silvia. They are badly defaced. The decision that Rhea Silvia must become a Vestal is given by King Amulius of Alba in the presence of her father Numitor and the wife of the king. The scene following this presented Rhea Silvia surprised by Mars. Victory, landspeople, a river god, and a goddess of the region appeared in the painting as subsidiary figures.

On the north wall, which is badly damaged, the story of Romulus and Remus was painted; the river god was shown, rudder in hand; the life of the twins with their foster father was depicted and at the end was the founding of Rome. The nurture of the twins by the wolf did not appear. The ground of the paintings is light yellow. The colors used were: red for the flesh of men, greenish blue for the stream, yellow and red for the garments of women with occasional use of green. The frescoes probably belong to the end of the Republic. The various scenes appear not to have been influenced by the Æneid of Vergil.

The language of these paintings is Greek. The crowned goddess who sits beside the walls of Alba Longa resembles the Hellenistic type of Tyche. Many other figures, such as the nymph, Anna Perennis, are classical in mould. But the subject matter is Roman history and the vigorous realism of the building scenes is Roman. The paintings have suffered from a late occupation of the columbarium in the Third Century A.D. when some of the walls were made ready for new frescoes. There is a good facsimile of the paintings in color in the Palazzo Conservatori. In some ways a study of these is more satisfactory than an examination of the original work which has suffered greatly. The colors are sober and dark—reds, greens, and yellows predominating with some employment of purplish red. The paintings have been hastily executed but reveal a mastery of form and an ability to group figures well in a composition of moderate depth.

We have a record from the end of the Republic of painted scenery used at the games of Claudius Pulcher. This was so realistic in character that crows came to settle on the painted tiles. Foreign pictures appeared in Rome in great numbers after Mummius' sack of Corinth in 146 B.C. and we are told that huge prices were bid for these spoils. Attalos offered $100,000 for the Dionysos of Aristeides, whereupon Mummius grew suspicious and withdrew it from the sale. We know that Augustus dedicated many famous paintings in the Temple of Cæsar and in his Forum and that Agrippa also showed an interest in obtaining costly works of art. These acquisitions must have influenced the taste of the age.[107b]

We have already spoken of decorative wall-painting in Italy. We have shown that it came from Hellenistic Greece and that it was based on the structure of the wall upon which the designs were painted. From the very beginning, the Italian style revealed a preference for vertical wall divisions rather than for the horizontal zone system of Greece. They developed the vertical divisions into an architectural framework. Prospect views were made an important element in this framework and these gave the Roman a chance to further his bent for tridimensional compositions. The Odyssey landscapes represent, in this respect, a distinct advance over their Hellenistic forerunners. This elaborate architectural style with distant views was the characteristic style of the late Republic and of the Augustan age, although landscapes of moderate depth also appear (Fig. 547).

In our discussion of the Augustan age, we should not omit to mention Vitruvius' condemnation of the decadence of fresco painting in his time.[108] After recounting how "the ancients required realistic pictures of real things" in their much-used apartments, their *atria* and peristyles, he goes on to explain that the Romans no longer have truthful representations of real objects but "monstrosities." He traces the rise of interior decoration from its beginnings when marble slabs were used to the second stage where buildings were represented and where various scenes were copied from the tragic, comic, and satyric styles of stage-painting. He enumerates the subject matter of these paintings which we have quoted in our discussion (p. 327). He adds:

[107b] Pliny, *N.H.*, 35, 23 ff.          [108] Vitr., *De Arch.*, VII, 5.

"Subjects which were copied from actual realities are scorned in these days of bad taste. We now have paintings of monstrosities rather than truthful representations of definite things. For instance, reeds are put in the place of columns, fluted appendages with curly leaves and volutes instead of pediments, candelabra supporting representations of shrines and on top of their pediments numerous slender stalks and volutes growing up from the roots and having human figures senselessly seated upon them. . . . Such things do not exist and cannot exist and never have existed. . . . How is it possible that a reed should really support a roof, or a candelabrum a pediment with its ornaments, etc.? . . . The fact is that pictures which are unlike reality ought not to be approved."[108a] Vitruvius then proceeds to criticize the work of Apatourios of Alabanda which followed this style. Apatourios painted the *scæna* of the little theater at Tralles with a kind of architectural decoration which may quite possibly go back in its origins to the work of Agatharchos in the Fifth Century. We are unable to trace the development of stage decoration after Agatharchos. That it continued into the Hellenistic age we know from stray references. That it influenced the decoration of houses in the Second style seems likely. But Apatourios was probably not an innovator in this decoration which Vitruvius mentions. His date is late—the Augustan age[108b]—and he is probably making use of a new and foreign style which came from Italy. Vitruvius shows that his work tended toward the fantastic. He represented in his scenes "columns and statues, centaurs supporting architraves, rotundas with round roofs on them, pediments with overhanging returns, cornices ornamented with lion heads, and then on top of all, an episcænium in which were painted rotundas, porticoes, and half pediments, and all the different kinds of decoration employed on a roof." Criticism is made here of placing houses, columns, and pediments on top of a roof. Apaturios did not answer the objections of his critics but humbly altered the decoration to conform more to reality.[108c]

It is very possible that scenes in perspective came to Italy from the Hellenistic

[108a] Trans. by M. H. Morgan with some alterations.

[108b] H. Brunn, *Gesch. der griech. Künstler*, II, 192, argues that Apatourios is a generation earlier than Vitruvius.

[108c] A. M. Friend, *Art Studies*, 1929, thinks that roofs of houses were represented in perspective behind other houses, as in the Boscoreale frescoes, but that Likymnios did not understand this innovation of Apatourios and thought one was on top of the other. Professor Friend was good enough to send me the advance proofs of his very excellent article. I wish to acknowledge my appreciation of his kindness. His thesis is that the one-storey type of architecture seen in the Boscoreale frescoes goes back to Agatharchos and the stage scenery of the Fifth Century, whereas the two-storey type represents the enrichment of Apatourios and followed the scenery of the Hellenistic theater. *Cf.* H. Bulle, *Untersuchungen an griechischen Theatern*, 1928, pp. 273-277; 327, for the Boscoreale frescoes and their relation to stage scenery. On stage-painting, see G. Ferrari, *La Scenographia*, 1902.

theater and that private houses were decorated with a style that originally served another end. Possibly Agatharchos, in painting the home of Alcibiades in the Fifth Century, made use of a decoration similar to that which he had employed in his theatrical backgrounds. Although we have not found houses decorated in this fashion in the east there is no reason to think they may not have existed. This second or "architectural" style in Italy lasted from 80 to 10 B.C., when a new ornate style arose.

Further examples of painting of the Augustan age may be seen in a series of pictures from the Columbarium of the Villa Pamfili.[109] One hundred and twenty-six paintings are preserved, wholly or in part. They depict in some cases mythological scenes, a number of which are copied from well-known works of sculpture, such as the Farnese bull or the Prometheus from Pergamon; other themes treated are the Death of the Niobids; Endymion; and Herakles in battle with the Centaurs. The subject matter also includes still-life pieces with fruits, animal scenes, jugglers, people in the street, and landscapes. Parodies of various events with pigmies as actors occur and the old theme of the Battle between the Pigmies and Cranes is renewed. The tomb includes a scene which probably represents the Judgment of Solomon. The paintings are often extremely sketchy in character and embody an impressionistic handling of figures and landscape. Rostovtzeff has shown that the single representations formed a running frieze with the episodes mostly separated by red lines.[110] For the first time we meet here a new type of landscape which appears often in Rome and Pompeii, the pure Egyptian landscape with and without pigmy figures. The figures are the most important things in the landscape, which is sacred-idyllic in type. The buildings include the schola with a tree, sacred gateways, statues of gods, herms, altars, temples, the porticus, tholoi, etc. These friezes with landscapes appear at the same time as the prospect views. The landscapes in the Villa Pamfili are such as a traveler might see in passing by. The development of panoramas begins in this period. The yellow frieze from the House of Livia on the Palatine is typical.

The source of the Third Pompeian style is contested. Rostovtzeff derives both the Third and Fourth styles independently out of the Second Pompeian class. As the Third has many Egyptianizing ornaments it is possible that its origin is Alexandria.[111] In many ways it is a mirror of Augustan culture. The architectural elements were relegated to a minor position and, where they are used, they take on a much more ornate character. The main idea of the artist was to represent walls on which easel-paintings of some distinction appeared to be hung. The various paintings might

---

[109] E. Samter, "Le Pitture parietali del Colombario di Villa Pamfili," *Röm. Mitth.*, VIII (1893), pp. 105-144; Huelsen, *ibid.*, pp. 145-165. *Arch. Anz.*, XIII (1898), pp. 47 ff.

[110] M. Rostovtzeff, *Röm. Mitth.*, XXVI (1911), pp. 26 ff., Figs. 6-8.

[111] A. Ippel, *Der dritte pompeianische Stil*, Berlin, 1910.

contain mythological scenes, landscapes, or even Erotes with floral patterns. Figure 571 presents a detail from a wall of the Triclinium of Epidius Sabinus. Against a black wall at the left, green garlands and a flying Eros are seen; while at the right, the color passes from yellow to green, red, and gray. Below is a charming garden scene with delicately colored flowers and green bushes. The colors are purple, green, bluish lavender, reddish brown, black, white, and yellow. The work is very detailed and shows exquisite craftsmanship. This style, which usually made use of mythological scenes in the central panels of a tripartite wall, flourished from about 10 B.C. to 50 A.D. Certain of the larger panels greatly interest us; e.g., the Punishment of Eros (Fig. 572). In this example, Greek figures of idealized type are combined with a background of rocks and trees impressionistically executed. But the artist merely places his figures before the background and concentrates his attention on form. Drawing interests him even more than color. There are no changing, melting tones but hard colors are employed which add a certain strength and severity to the work. The scene represents Aphrodite waiting to inflict punishment on the whimpering Eros, who is being led toward her. On her lap rest his bow and quiver which have been taken away from him. A second Love peeping over her shoulder appears to take pleasure in the prospect. The background acts as a drop in the theater. Herrmann points out that such a figure as that of the woman at the left might well occur in a painting by Mantegna. The forms are plastically handled. The colors used are green for the trees, violet and white for chitons, a light blue for the mantle at the left, and yellow for the one of Aphrodite. Sometimes an architectural background is combined with figure decoration, as in the painting of Jason before Pelias (Herrmann, Pl. 75). Here the figure of Jason in the foreground is too small, much smaller than that of Pelias who stands on the steps in the background. This attempt in the Third style to combine impressionistic landscapes with figures of some size and dignity is often something of a misfit. It looks as if the artist were copying Hellenistic Greek originals in which the figures had not yet become an integral part of their surroundings. The painter of the original was merely learning how to adapt a background which was not neutral to his figure decoration. The setting remains more or less like a curtain "drop."[111a]

Even more beautiful for the grace of the figures and the modeling of the forms out of light are certain floating centaurs with bacchantes and other secondary figures from the so-called Villa of Cicero (Fig. 573). In the upper panel, a bacchante has sprung on the back of a young centaur whose hands are bound behind him. She

[111a] H. Bulle, op. cit., pp. 311-315, considers the backgrounds of the Punishment of Eros and of Jason before Pelias as copied from stage scenery. The painting with Aphrodite and Eros goes back to an original of the Fourth or early Third Century and copies a stage of the Segesta type. See G. Rodenwaldt, Die Kunst der Antike, 1927, Pl. 27 (color).

plants her foot firmly against his back and draws her thyrsos for a mighty blow. One feels the quivering play of the muscles and the violence of the assault.

In the lower panel, depicted here, a small boy reclines on the arm of a centaur and receives a lesson on the lyre. The gently floating movement of this group contrasts strongly with the bold action of the upper panel. The figures in both cases are handled impressionistically. The sharply falling light arouses the illusion that figures flooded by bright sunlight are floating through the air. These works are essentially Greek creations on Italian soil.

During the Third style, a peculiarly Roman type of landscape arose—the so-called villa landscape (Fig. 548). We have mentioned examples of this type from the house of M. Lucretius Fronto at Pompeii. In the middle of the side fields on two long walls of the Tablinium, villa landscapes are found. This type of landscape apparently had its prototype in Egypt or in Syria where a palace was often shown with a background of architecture or a park with trees.[112] The architecture there, however, is basically different from what we find in the Roman villas. In our example, we see a complex of buildings where waterways enclosed by stone run along the shore. There are gardens with trees and green footpaths. In the background cypresses, plane trees, and pines grow at the foot of the mountains. The villa is the kind which Statius describes—a country house which consisted of several independent buildings. Here, the portico plays a prominent part, and also long colonnades running by a water front adorned with herms and statues. The landscapes include temples, nymphæa, gardens, and parks. They are rendered in illusionistic fashion with soft outlines for the mountains and splotchy brush-strokes for the trees. We have noted that the architecture has been shown by Rostovtzeff to be typically Italian.[113] The paintings are of interest for the light which they shed on the Roman country house. In general, however, the Third Pompeian style seems to be more Greek in character than Roman. The villa landscape is one of the exceptions, although it probably took its point of departure from Hellenistic Greece.

The Fourth style took up the Second Pompeian style and developed it in a fantastic fashion. The architecture becomes soap-bubble architecture: the columns are open, plaited spirals; the delicate slender stems support roofs and second storeys. Typical of this style is a wall partly painted and partly in stucco from the Stabian baths at Pompeii (Fig. 574). Here the architectural supports are extremely tenuous at times and the wall is broken up into a mass of projecting and receding members.[113a]

[112] M. Rostovtzeff, *Röm. Mitth.*, 26 (1911), pp. 47 ff., Figs. 26, 27, 28; pp. 72 ff.; *cf.* A. Gnirs, "Forschungen über antiken Villenbau in Südistrien," *Œst. Jahr.*, XVIII (1915), pp. 101 ff. (Beiblatt) and Fig. 52.

[113] "Pompeianische Landschaften und römische Villen," *Jahr.*, 19 (1904), pp. 103-126, Pls. V-VII.

[113a] G. von Cube, *Die römische "Scenae Frons" in den pompeianischen Wandbildern,* 4

One gets prospect views in some instances, and a strong bent for developing the third dimension is evident. The steps into buildings and the open doors emphasize this predilection. Color is used to add to this effect. The dates for the Fourth or intricate style are usually given as 50-79 A.D. It came in at least as early as the reign of Claudius and lasted until the destruction of Pompeii. Most of our Pompeian wall-paintings, of which there are more than 3,500, date from this period. One may study the style well in the House of the Vettii at Pompeii where the walls are covered with paintings copying earlier Hellenistic masters. The colors have a brilliancy which approaches their original state when they were laid on almost two thousand years ago.

Some rooms in the House of the Vettii are decorated with a socle imitating marble—an example of the true incrustation style or the inlaying of marbles in marble. Above this dado one frequently finds a triple vertical division of the wall space with a megalographic composition in the center, such as the punishment of Ixion, while architectural details and views into the open are seen on either side of this. A second storey decorated with statues and architecture rises above these. At times the wall is adorned with painting from the socle to the ceiling. At the bottom, which is often black for the sake of protection, delicate garlands are twined from one division to another and single figures mark the tripartite arrangement. Above this, run the friezes of Erotes so familiar from reproductions. These long friezes are only a few inches high and the small figures are represented at all sort of tasks—goldsmithing, making and selling oil, fulling, making wine, etc. The daily pursuits of the Pompeians are idealized in these busy little actors. Typical examples of this decoration are seen in Figure 575. Here, at the left, two sturdy *putti* are caught in a tense moment at the anvil, while in the center a third Eros weighs out some gold for a dignified, seated customer. Other Erotes are seen plying hammers or bellows. The industrious activity of these Lilliputian figures adds to their charm. The artist has caught them in momentary poses when they are busy with very significant affairs! In the example at the right is the beginning of a chariot race which ends in a spill for one contestant and a proud victory for his opponent. The charm of these small figures is further seen in the pictures of those who drive crabs and dolphins (Fig. 576). The paintings are wholly in the impressionistic method. They are executed with extreme haste in splashes and daubs of paint, but the general effect obtained is most beguiling. The spirited passage over the sea is depicted in a masterful way and the usual sturdy application to the vigorous task in hand is evident. The ground for these designs is generally black, but sometimes red.

*Stils*, Berlin, 1906. Von Cube cites the paintings from the Stabian Baths in support of his theory that certain walls of the Fourth style derive their decoration from the *scænarum frontes*. *Cf.* Fig. 574.

Above the Erotes, floating figures frequently occur against a brilliant ground of Pompeian red. Vitruvius finds fault with this lavish use of red in his day but one sees the need for brilliant color in the dimly lighted Pompeian rooms, where darkness so readily devours the color. The floating figures are modeled out of light and stand out vividly from this ground as if surrounded by light and air. They are impression-istically handled and need to be seen at a distance. Above the floating figures are architectural details with statues, views, and figures—the whole giving the effect of a second storey.

We have had occasion earlier to refer to the frescoes which cover the walls in the period of the Fourth style. They are like so many easel-paintings copying, in many cases, works of well-known masters. They are essentially Hellenistic and it is from them, in great measure, that our ideas of Hellenistic painting are formed. Most of them are mythological in character and many are examples of Greek megalog-raphy.[114]

But there were various fields of painting beyond the examples mentioned which were successfully handled by artists of the Fourth style. We shall consider a number of these. One was landscape. Rostovtzeff has discussed in detail the architectural landscapes of the Fourth style in his work which we have cited so often. Egyptianiz-ing landscapes with pigmies occur and villa landscapes, usually of the seacoast variety. The most usual type of the latter class has a triple portio. There are a number of landscapes with tombs and sacred buildings which show Egyptian influ-ence and others which lack this. In general, the architecture of the Hellenistic land-scapes points to Asia Minor and Syria. Here belong the *schola* with a tree, a round sanctuary, pavilions, sacred gateways, etc. Egypt appears to have taken over the sacred landscape, to have reworked it, and to have given it to Italy.

Illusionism seems more and more to enter into the execution of the Italian land-scapes during the period of the Fourth style. A typical example of this developed method, carried to a height inconceivable in Hellenistic Greece, is seen in a painting from Herculaneum depicting the worship of Isis (Fig. 577). Here, we have an Egyptian temple flanked by sphinxes and palm trees, with an ibis at the right. On the steps indicated by a few bold dashes of white, are rows of women impression-istically rendered. They form a vague, undefined, indistinct mass, their heads modeled within two bands of dark shadow. The white garments of the priests con-trast strongly with their dark skins. The composition depends upon the arrangement

[114] G. Rodenwaldt, "Megalographia," *Röm. Mitth.*, 29 (1914), pp. 194-199. The term does not necessarily involve largeness of scale, since Vitruvius cites the Odyssey landscapes as examples of megalography, but it is concerned with a certain elevation in subject matter and distinction in style. On the other hand, these Odyssey landscapes may have been quite different in type from our present examples.

of colored masses and patches. The development and perfection of this method of painting took place on Italian soil. The painting probably represents the bringing on of the Holy water, at the opening of the temple, as described by Apuleius, *Metamorph.*, XI, 20.

The culmination of the illusionistic method in the Fourth style is seen in the well-known fresco of the Trojans bringing the Wooden Horse into Troy by Night (Fig. 578). Shrouded figures are huddled together in a very impressionistically executed landscape. In the foreground, one sees architecture, statues, and a tree; in the rear, a mountainous height reaching up to the top of the painting. The artist of the fresco has been true to nature in his observation of a moonlit landscape. The surfaces lighted by the moon broaden out brightly, while the deep shadows become blacker. The reflections on the faces of the men are indicated by red splotches on the cheeks. The art is one of light and shadows strongly contrasted, as is evident in the group pulling in the horse. The use of broad brush-strokes for shadows is clearly seen. There is no care or precision in rendering the figures, which are executed solely in color contrasts, not in line. The excitement and intensity of the moment have interested the artist who has renounced all detail for the general effect. Everything is seen in momentary action. The colors are largely yellow and dark brown.

The illusionistic manner remained the favorite Italian fashion beside the older plastic tendency. Its use is seen in local subjects, such as the fight between the people of Pompeii and their neighbors at Nocera (Fig. 579). In this scene, the use of perspective in connection with the amphitheater is wholly incorrect but the general effect is very good. The figures are impressionistically handled and are shown in vigorous action. In the foreground are some sketchy trees and men. The subordination of figures to the landscape and architecture is one of the most striking features. They are greatly reduced in size and resemble puppets rather than men.

Certain seascapes reveal the perfection of this illusionistic method. Figure 580 with representations of galleys on the sea is typical of this class. When the Roman used this illusionistic style successfully, it gives a very modern impression. We may take as an example the fresco of Paris on Mount Ida (Fig. 581). The space here is not limited in its general effect and the figures are an integral part of the landscape. This illusionistic manner was carried into later times as we shall see from paintings in the Tomb of the Pancratii belonging to the Second Century and from descriptions by Philostratos of paintings in the Third Century. It was used later in the catacombs and has been handed down to us in illuminated manuscripts.

During the period of the Fourth style we find a number of portraits. It is interesting to compare these with the examples discussed from the Fayûm (Figs. 511-523). Certain conventions and stereotyped poses were adopted by the painters which remind us of practices among photographers in more modern times. Women were often represented holding up to the lips a stilus—the ancient lead pencil—while in the other hand a folding writing-tablet was held. One well-known example of this style in Naples has been called the poetess of Herculaneum. She is probably no more a poetess than the less romantic wife depicted with her husband (Fig. 582). They have long been known as Paquius Proculus and his wife. Paquius has now been rescued from his social oblivion as a baker and been given a more dignified background, while it has been shown that the portraits do not belong to Paquius Proculus and his wife but to the Terentii.[115] We have a faithful representation of two citizens of Pompeii. The pair are posed against a neutral ground, originally yellowish green in color. They are as lifelike in appearance as the artist could make them. The wife has reddish brown hair and is dressed in a crimson garment. The husband, on the other hand, wears a white mantle with yellow or gray used for folds. He has a scroll in his hand indicating that he was probably a lawyer. His hair and beard are dark brown. The heads are very sober and the individuals not too intelligent in appearance. The work is clear-cut and truthful. More use is made of trivial details than in the Fayûm portraits. No characteristic feature is omitted by the Roman artist. The fresco technique has been used and color is handled impressionistically. In the portrait of the husband, who is probably Terentius Neo, as Della Corte thinks, there is a streak of yellowish white down the bridge of the nose; the eyelashes are daubs of brown; the flesh is yellowish in color with whitish yellow and rose for modeling. The flesh of the wife is rose-colored; the lips red. Delle Corte believes that the pair were people of distinction. While their portraits do not reveal any very scintillating qualities, there is a certain simplicity, honesty, straightforwardness, and conservatism about them that may be commended. They were steady, honorable members of the citizenry who formed the backbone of the late Republic and early Empire. They were probably dull and without a sense of humor, but their characters were above reproach and they were worthy members of the community. They probably represent fairly well the golden mediocrity of Pompeii in its last days.

The distinguishing characteristic of the Fourth style is its trend toward illusionism. Beside the large copies of famous masters which occupied the center of each wall there were many small landscapes in panels below or at the sides and in these the new method may often be seen. The large pictures do not appear in a frame as in the Third style but the frame encloses an extensive panel of uniform color, in the middle of which the painting was placed. The effects of the new illusionistic style may be seen most clearly in some of the floating figures. Here, as Wickhoff points out,[116] we have the impression that figures "are hovering in an atmosphere less

[115] M. Della Corte, "Publius Paquius Proculus," *J.R.S.*, XVI (1926), pp. 145-154; "Publio Paquio Proculo," *Memoria presentata all'Accademia Pontaniana*, Napoli, 1928.

[116] F. Wickhoff, *Roman Art* (tr. by Mrs. S. Arthur Strong), New York, 1900, p. 145.

brightly lit up than the wall upon which they are painted and in front of which they appear to float." This effect is accentuated by the slanting rays of light falling on the figures from an assumed central opening in the ceiling. "This heightens the illusion that figures are hovering in a dark part of the room, so that by slightly stippling the background round their outlines, especially the extremities, the atmosphere between them and the wall is made visible." He points out further that "the relief is not produced by toned shading but by colored spots and strips, like a glittering rain." In the case of a seascape from the Macellum at Pompeii, Wickhoff sees an effect produced by a few definite tones comparable only to the backgrounds of the portraits of Goya. "Over the deep blue of the southern sea galleys are gliding, represented by means of two or three broken shades of the complementary colors of the water (cf. Fig. 580). When looked at from the right distance the two chief colors blend in the contours, the ships, etc., to a gray, which as it forms on our retina far surpasses in brilliancy the gray produced by the mixture of pigments. In the body of the ship, on the other hand, the yellow is intensified by the mass of surrounding blue, so that above the graduated tones of the yellow seems to lie another yellow which is the subjective complementary color of the great bulk of the picture. This last yellow removes everything material in the coloring and produces an effect of mobility otherwise unattainable. By means of this retinal impression a vivacity is imparted to the picture which rivals the palpitating surface of the illuminated sea."

In the development of illusionism, then, lay one very definite advance made by the Roman painter over the Greek. In the development of the third dimension toward unlimited space lay another. In general, many of the Pompeian artists followed Greek masters in their choice of subject matter. We have seen that this was the case in the megalography of the period. In the same way, we find the familiar Hellenistic examples of still-life, genre scenes, and the like. Only the very development of this illusionism of which we have spoken gave a vividness to the Pompeian examples which we can readily feel in comparing the copy of the "Unswept Floor" of Sosos of Pergamon with real Pompeian examples (cf. Fig. 491). In the Pompeian examples, the transparency of glass, the fuzziness of a peach, or the silveriness of fish "is brought out by means of a few unconnected strokes and points dashed off by the brush in a scheme of middle tones which tend now to greenish, now again to brownish." Textures are rendered with extraordinary proficiency.

The curious thing about the Pompeian paintings is that there is no real development in composition or in technical method. The color scheme differs and the technical handling, but the paintings remain on much the same level. No new types were created as none were created in sculpture in this period. The artists were eclectic and chose from all the wealth of the past.

Roman innovations in subject matter appear frequently in the case of religious scenes. A familiar instance may be found in the numerous representations of the Lares (Fig. 583). In the center of a painting from the House of the Vettii, the Genius of the master of the house is represented with portrait-like fidelity, while on either side are the youthful Lares, with tunics girt up, dancing on tiptoe. Each carries a situla and holds aloft in one hand a rhyton. Below, a snake approaches an altar on which offerings have been placed. The colors used are red, yellow, green, blue, and white. The work here is executed with more care than is often the case with these scenes. For example, in a similar representation from Pompeii (Helbig, No. 56), the figures are extremely sketchy in character. In the latter example, a wreathed altar is depicted in the center. Beside it, the Genius of the master of the house is represented, holding in his hand a horn of plenty. At the left, balancing this figure, is a flute-player. Behind him, a small servant brings on a pig for sacrifice; while at the right, behind the figure of the Genius, is a second slave with offerings. The Lares complete the scene at either end, appearing larger in the foreground.

Other examples of Græco-Roman wall-painting may be seen in some frescoes recently excavated in the Street of Abundance at Pompeii.[117] Here, several sacred processions are represented. In one instance, the statue of Venus seated on a throne is borne by priests while above, on a yellow ground, appear colossal heads of various gods—the Sun, Jupiter, Mercury, and Luna. One of the most interesting frescoes is that of Venus Pompeiana, the tutelary divinity of Pompeii, who is depicted in a chariot drawn by four elephants (Fig. 584). On either side of her are subsidiary figures—the goddess, Fortune, standing on a globe and holding a horn of plenty, while, at the right, is a second divinity who may be Abundantia or a Genius.[118] The type of Venus drawn by elephants in a chariot which resembles the prow of a ship is probably derived from Egypt. She rests her left hand on a ship's rudder and wears a long blue chiton and mantle. Her turreted crown is set with eight large emeralds. Below the main painting are some smaller figures evidently engaged in the fuller's trade.

This fresco occupied the front of shop No. 7. On the opposite pilaster was a painting of Mercury coming out of his temple (Fig. 585). The sanctuary was represented as a small yellowish-brown *ædicula*, with a high podium and deep vestibule. The god is quite a dapper figure with his garments blown backward by the wind. He wears a petasos and carries a caduceus and a large wallet—the symbol of his activities as a god of gain. His tunic is white with a red border and he wears a violet mantle. The gods appear to have actually walked among men, when the Pompeian could conceive them in this vivid fashion! Below the painting of Mercury is a shop girl standing behind a counter and showing felt slippers to a customer seated on a bench at the right.

[117] G. Spano, *Not. d. Sc.* (1912), pp. 106 ff., Figs. 3-7; Della Corte, *ibid.*, pp. 137 ff., 176 ff.

[118] *A.J.A.*, 27 (1923), p. 303.

We have said nothing about the technique of Pompeian wall-painting which is a much-mooted question and which should be settled and can be settled only by some very careful chemical analyses. Since the work of Donner in Helbig's volume on the Pompeian wall-paintings, scholars have held until fairly recently that the pictures were executed in the fresco technique with some additions in tempera.[119] Many of the best authorities still support this view.[120] Recently, however, two Germans, Berger and Raehlmann, have attempted to disprove this belief.[121] Raehlmann made microscopic and chemical investigations and claims that the walls were painted in various techniques: in some cases, they were executed *al fresco;* in others, the upper layer of the stuccoed wall was colored as a mass and, in the latter instances, the paintings might be applied to this stucco in tempera or in fresco. Where white, yellow, or some reds were used as a wall-ground, the technique was *al fresco;* where blue, green, and brown were employed, the process was not fresco, because the physical properties of these color materials were apparently unsuited to this technique and demanded painting on a dry ground. Berger argued for a solidly colored upper wall surface with a wax coat. Raehlmann, on the other hand, disagreed with Berger in the belief that there was a wax coat above. Raehlmann holds that no wax was found in the analyses.[121a] The presence of organic matter in the paintings proves to his satisfaction that many of these works were executed in tempera. Very recently, Laurie has taken up the matter anew apropos of chemical analyses and experiments with the wax technique. He came to the conclusion that Donner was correct and that Berger was wrong.[120] Laurie believes that the paintings were mainly in fresco and were sometimes polished with wax.[121b] The organic matter found does not, in his opinion, argue for a binding medium such as egg or glue, as it may have been present originally in the material by accident or may form part of one of the pigments, as, for example, a pigment prepared from murex or madder. The most reliable view appears to be a combination of the various opinions. It is, in substance, that the majority of the wall-paintings at Pompeii were executed in fresco but that in cases where the materials were not suitable for this technique, tempera was used. We shall return to this subject in the chapter on the technical methods and colors employed in ancient painting (Ch. XI).

[119] O. Donner, "Die erhaltenen antiken Wandmalereien in technischer Beziehung," in W. Helbig, *Wandgemälde Campaniens*, Leipzig, 1868, I-CXXVII. A. Eibner, *Entwicklung und Werkstoffe der Wandmalerei*, München, 1926.

[120] A. P. Laurie, *Greek and Roman Methods of Painting*, Cambridge, 1910; F. Gerlich, "Die Technik der römisch-pompeianischen Wandmalerei," *N.J.*, 21 (1908), pp. 127-147 (modified fresco technique). Eibner, *op. cit.*

[121] E. Berger, *Die Maltechnik des Altertums*, München, 1904; E. Raehlmann, *Über die Maltechnik der Alten*, Berlin, 1910.

[121a] Some wax has been found, but it is modern.

[121b] Wax was used on vermilion walls and possibly on marble in Laurie's opinion.

Painting in Rome in the Julio-Claudian Era followed the classical Greek tradition for the most part. It was Neo-Attic in its general tendencies and reflects eclectic features. The baroque element, however, is already heralded and with the age of Nero we find it in full sway.

From the reign of Tiberius we have a monument known as the Columbarium of Pomponius Hylas.[122] It reveals a decorative style which is most suitable for the small structures to which it was applied but which is less fitting for a giant building like the Golden House of Nero, where it was later adapted. In Figure 586, a detail of the ceiling of the columbarium shows a combination of delicate floral motives together with birds and animals. Other examples have Cupids or putti playing about amid plant spirals and blossoms. Victories, or Horæ(?), also appear at times among the tendrils. This rather finicking style was thoroughly in keeping with the limited surface of a columbarium where the fine details were not lost but when this "columbarium style" is carried over into larger constructions such minutiæ escape the eye. In our painting, the designs are exquisitely wrought with just enough conventionalization of pattern to satisfy.

On entering the columbarium, we find certain *ædiculæ* executed in stucco relief and in color. These are rather heavy and baroque in style. In one pediment, Cheiron is represented instructing Achilles in playing the lyre; on the frieze, Oknos is plaiting a rope which a she-ass is devouring. Both of these themes are good Greek material coming down from an earlier period. The vault of the apse is decorated with the arabesques already mentioned. The colors found in the columbarium are: a flesh color for the figures; green, lavishly used, for garments, for the wings of Erotes, and for leaves; red for blossoms, and occasionally for stems and architectural details. Bright blue, yellow, dark red, and white are employed in the architectural details. The style of decoration found in this columbarium was carried into later tombs and into the catacombs.

From the First Century A.D. we have an interesting painting of the myth of Orpheus and Eurydice (Fig. 587). At the left is a door opening out from the realms of Pluto into the world above. Before it stands a very mild Cerberus and the seated janitor does not appear very threatening. The moment of the myth is represented when Orpheus, just on the verge of reaching the outer world, turns back to look at Eurydice and loses her. Terror is seen in the face of Eurydice and in her attitude which contrasts interestingly with the nonchalance of the janitor and the dawning realization of the deed in the face of Orpheus. In the background, the dim figures of Pluto and Persephone are barely recognizable. At the extreme right, Oknos, or "Sloth," is seated plaiting a rope which a she-ass eats as fast as he makes it. The

[122] Thomas Ashby, "The Columbarium of Pomponius Hylas," *B.S.R.*, V (1910), pp. 463 ff., and Pls. XXXVII-XLVII. (Drawings by F. G. Newton.)

performance is symbolic of a fruitless task. Oknos was a creation of Polygnotos in the Fifth Century. This fresco keeps the old Greek frieze-like composition of the Fifth Century but it appears to copy a late eclectic work which preserved much of the early tradition. The inscriptions naming the figures and the type of tomb construction date the painting in the First Century A.D. The color of the background is blue; the garment of Eurydice, brown; of Orpheus, gray and yellow; of the janitor, green.

Unfortunately, the remains which we have from the reign of Nero are fairly meager but frescoes from the famous "Golden House" give us an insight into the artistic achievement of this age.[123] Weege has made a very thorough study of the Golden House and has traced its history from the beginning. After the burning of Rome in 64 A.D., Nero was able to carry out his desire of uniting his Palatine home with the gardens of Mæcenas on the Mons Oppius and his others on the Esquiline. The size of this entire enclosure was colossal. Martial, in his second epigram, gives us some idea of its location and of the topography of the site while Tacitus and Suetonius tell us about its luxury.[124] It occupied a region one mile square in the center of Rome and included parks, colonnades, "pools like the sea," and buildings "like a city." It was equipped with baths, fountains, statues, gardens, aqueducts, and every kind of pleasure spot. The dining-room had a revolving ceiling of ivory, from which roses were scattered over the guests. The destruction of this palace was begun by the Flavians as a political policy and the Colosseum and Baths of Titus were built over some of the structure and grounds. It was partly burned under Trajan, which doubtless hastened his plan to build his baths. In later ages, it was visited by many famous artists who made sketches from the walls and covered the place with graffiti. Among these visitors were Giovanni da Udine, Raphael, Pinturicchio, and Michelangelo. They copied the arabesques and drawings which were called "grotesques" because they were found in underground ruins or *grotte*.

Pliny gives us some information about the paintings of the Golden House.[125] He says that "Fabullus"—the artist responsible for the paintings in the Domus Aurea— "painted for a few hours only in the day and treated his art seriously, always wearing the toga, even when mounted on the scaffolding. The Golden House was the prison of his art." Evidently, like Agatharchos, he was "persuaded" to carry out his task with force. Of this extraordinary house with its paintings only a small part has been

[123] F. Weege, "Das Goldene Haus des Nero," *Jahr.*, 28 (1913), pp. 127 ff.; *Ant. Denk.*, III, Pls. 13; 14-18 (color); *cf.* R. Lanciani, *The Ruins and Excavations of Ancient Rome*, N. Y., 1897, pp. 358-362, and bibliography; H. Jordan, C. Huelsen, *Topographie der Stadt Rom*, Berlin (1907), I, 3, pp. 273 ff.

[124] Tacitus, *Annals*, XV, 42; Suetonius, *Nero*, 31; Pliny, *N.H.*, 33, 54.

[125] Pliny, *N.H.*, 35, 120; 34, 84. The passage is taken from Jex-Blake, Sellers. The MSS. give *Famulus*, which seems to be corrupt for *Fabullus*.

recovered and this section probably belonged to a reception building. The principal part of the palace is doubtless to be sought to the north behind the Palazzo Brancaccio. Weege publishes certain paintings which have not been reproduced before.[125a] They come from rooms Nos. 60, 70, and 80. No. 60 is the so-called Volta Dorata. The room is spanned by a barrel vault, the decoration of which is still very beautiful, in spite of the destruction that has taken place. In Figure 588, we have a copy of a lost part of the ceiling made from a careful drawing by Francesco d'Olanda. When reproduced in color the effect is almost entirely one of contrasting reds and blues. The ground of the central panel and of the interior of the circle is a bright blue, framed by a red square. This same scheme is carried out in the smaller circles which have blue grounds and are set on a darker blue square framed by red. The backgrounds of all the figure panels are blue and many of the details are in red or a flesh color. Red, blue, white, yellow, and flesh tones make up the color scheme. The system is one of round and square fields framed by the egg and dart, by astragals, leaves, consoles, etc. The stucco work is very fine. The paintings themselves have been so badly defaced, for the most part, as to be scarcely recognizable, though Weege publishes Hippolytos' departure for the hunt; a satyr and nymph; the surprise of Ares and Aphrodite by Helios and Hephaistos, and a few other mythological themes. Reproductions of other paintings are found in ancient drawings. Only four of the pictures are still visible from the original twenty-one of the Volta Dorata. The stuccoes have mostly been scratched away for the gold.

In our reproduction (Fig. 588), which presents some of the lost paintings and stuccoes preserved for us by Francesco d'Olanda, we have in the center one of the erotic adventures of Zeus. He is carried through the air on the back of an eagle, bearing in his arms a nude woman or Ganymede. Above the pair is an Eros; at the left, Athena armed, and Hermes. In the round pictures, one sees a nymph on a dolphin; a nymph on a sea horse, another on a goat, and one on a bull. In the square corner fields, a maiden is pictured, in two instances, with a vase(?); once with a trumpet and once with a wreath. In the square fields by the round pictures were paintings of Venus with a Love; satyrs with women, etc. The other fields were adorned with stucco figures. Among these are represented: Pans and a nymph; a horseman with captives and a warrior; a shepherd under a tree with his flock; Cybele drawn by panthers or peacocks; a warrior in a chariot charging to the left, with a nude man in front and a small figure behind; a satyr on a mule with a crowd following; six nude figures shooting with bows at a herm. Michelangelo apparently copied the latter.[126]

The walls of this room are covered largely with débris but from descriptions it is

[125a] The paintings from room 60 were published earlier.
[126] F. Weege, op. cit., Fig. 24, p. 178.

evident that they bore a frieze, above which were four compositions with figures of almost life size. Scenes from mysteries appeared here and other subjects less easy to explain. More interesting because of their better preservation are the ceiling decorations of the long corridor which have been published in color.[127] This passageway was in the form of a barrel vault with sixteen windows through which light fell. The effect recalls that of the cryptoporticus on the Palatine Hill. A surface of more than sixty meters is preserved, with vault decoration. This inspired in Renaissance artists an enthusiasm that has lasted to our own time. Figure 589 gives a reconstruction of the broad middle zone of the ceiling which is decorated with several square red fields arranged in parallel diagonal rows and adorned with white birds. In between the rows of diagonals are birds, winged sphinxes, and gryphons, panthers and centaurs. These motives are all strongly conventionalized. The birds resemble flowers in the grotesque handling which they have received. The wings of the sphinx are curled into delicate patterns. The ground is neutral with a rich use of red and yellow, especially on the figures of the centaurs and panthers; a grayish yellow is employed for the sphinx; red, blue, yellow, and olive green for the ornamental patterns. The ceiling decoration gives the effect of tapestry.

In the east half of the corridor, ornamental patterns are found which are reproduced in Figure 590. On both sides are beautifully stylized plant motives. Several squares are seen inside of one another, framed at times by patterns such as sphinxes with lyres, vine leaves, or, as here, by gryphons heraldically posed on either side of a kantharos. These stripes of arabesques had a tremendous influence on Renaissance artists and were much copied. At times one finds flowers, eagles, lions, dolphins, the acanthus; the foreparts of animals and guilloche patterns. The painting is executed impressionistically. Weege publishes two paintings from room 80, one of which has for its subject matter the parting of Hektor and Andromache,[128] the other the legend of Paris and Helen. Hektor and his wife are represented standing before the dark city wall. He wears a golden helmet, short blue chiton, a golden breastplate, greaves, etc. Andromache is dressed in a long blue chiton with a yellow mantle. She holds her small son in her arms. Behind her is the nurse in a white mantle and purple chiton, followed by a maid-servant in blue. The flesh of the hero is red. The painting is framed by a blue and a red line. Numerous copies of this painting by artists of later times prove conclusively how very untrustworthy most of these attempts were. Andromache becomes an old woman and the child reaching toward Hektor disappears entirely and leaves only her outstretched arms.

The delicate decorative work of the Claudio-Neronian age had its successors in later times. A corridor of a house in the Via de' Cerchi belonging to the Second—or

[127] *Ant. Denk.*, III, Pls. 14-18 (color).
[128] F. Weege, *Jahr.*, 28 (1913), Fig. 63 and Pl. 21 (color).

perhaps even the Third—Century A.D. is painted in this style.[129] It was adorned with floral and ornamental patterns. Highly conventionalized red gryphons heraldically posed on either side of a floral design with twining tendrils, form charming friezes. Behind the gryphons, vases in red and black are seen. Red dolphins, which are almost like curling plant stems, add to the decorative effect. The upright floral designs made of honeysuckle, spirals, and blossoms recall Neronian designs, even in the color scheme. Ashby suggests that this style was influenced by the Columbarium style, which was imitated in the Neronian age.[130]

After the destruction of Pompeii in 79 A.D., relatively few wall-decorations are found until the days of Hadrian and the Antonines. Numerous mosaics from Hadrian's Villa show something of the achievement of artists in the handling of the third dimension and in setting their figures freely in open space surrounded by light and air. Figure 591 gives an idea of the growing power of these masters in making their backgrounds circumambient air. Here two sacrificial scenes are represented. Against a yellowish white ground, which suggests the light of evening, several figures are silhouetted, with an altar in the center of each field. The figures are placed in the background in both instances by means of a wide stretch of ground in front. In the mosaic above, rich red mantles are worn by the two figures at either side, while the chitons are brown or blue. Blue is used for the altar, red for the flame. The central figure is dressed in brown. In the lower field, a goat is being brought on for sacrifice while at the right a woman comes forward with a wreath. The trees add life and distance in each case. The lower panel has the freshness of a Giorgione. One loses much when the color is not reproduced. There are the same rich blues, reds, and yellows as before and some green, gray brown, and violet.

Typical paintings of the Second Century are preserved in a series of works from the Villa Negroni, a number of which were copied in modern times.[131] They can be accurately dated by a brick stamp, which proves that the house was built after 134 A.D. They are of great interest to us in showing that the decline in decorative wall-painting was by no means sudden but that painting was maintained at a high level for a long time. Figure 592 recalls at once the Second style. Fantastic architecture rarely occurs. As Mau points out, the picture occupies the middle of the wall but the architecture fastens the attention of the spectator. The wall is divided into three horizontal sections[131a]—a socle, which sometimes appears under the central panel

---

[129] Mrs. Strong, *B.S.R.*, VIII (1916), Pls. V-VII (color), pp. 91 ff. The corridor may belong to the pedagogium, dated by Miss Van Deman in the time of Domitian or later.

[130] T. Ashby, *B.S.R.*, VII (1914), p. 123.

[131] Camillo Buti, *Pitture antiche della Villa Negroni*, Roma, 1778; *cf. Notizie istoriche della Villa Massimo*, Roma, 1836, pp. 213 ff. H. Krieger, "Dekorative Wandgemälde aus dem II. Jahr. nach Christus," *Röm. Mitth.*, XXXIV (1919), pp. 24-52, Pls. I-III.

[131a] One series, 3, has only two horizontal sections.

only; a middle section in which figure decoration on a large scale is heavily framed in red and is set into a pavilion-like structure, and an architectural section above the cornice which often presents a view into the open. On either side of the great central field are large panels in solid color. Characteristic are the dark blue ones which are almost black and which are surrounded by a dark green frame. The panels of the first three Pompeian styles are occasionally undecorated. On our panels no figure decoration is found. In the side fields of our uppermost illustration there are small panels outlined in red on a white ground. They bear a horse's head at the top and some interlacing floral patterns below. The pavilion-like structure has an upper storey with columns of pure Ionic type. In the second illustration below, we see marble-incrusted pilasters supporting the arch above. The central barrel vault is upheld by delicate candelabra which end in Tritons. On either side above the cornice are pointed tower-like structures such as were affected by the Second style. In the central panel, Venus is represented with Loves playing about her. One is apparently turning a somersault in his enthusiasm. The side fields are grayish white framed in red and there is no socle below them.

Krieger points out that the architectural element is strongly emphasized in these paintings and that there is a definite reaction against the playful architecture of the Fourth style. The artist consciously archaizes and then goes further than his model. There is little of the Third style in the paintings. Painting the socle black and the architectural parts white is characteristic of the third manner. In coloring, the artist of the Second Century breaks with one school of Pompeian painters of the Second to Fourth styles. Instead of painting the socle, principal surfaces, and prospect in a consistent ground color, he treats the large enclosed fields as units and separates them clearly from the vistas. He makes use of red for narrow and broad frames and for large wall surfaces. He uses dark and light blue beside one another, often for garments. In addition to these colors, there occur flesh tones, brown, yellow, black, white, and occasionally green. The contrasts are not so strong as in the Fourth style and in general the color recalls that of the Third manner. On the other hand, the use of fantastic architecture, even though slight, brings to mind the Fourth style; this is true also of the landscapes; of the preference for large figures which are wholly or partly nude. Sea animals, dolphins, tritons, and fantastic sea monsters and swans are common. Furthermore, figures set on a light or dark field without further background recall the Fourth style.

In contrast to the painters of the Second style who sometimes executed walls with no socle but with only a narrow stripe below, the master of the paintings from the Villa Negroni combined on the same wall panels with and without a socle. As in the Second style, the side fields are no longer flat ornamental surfaces but are characterized corporeally by means of frames. The artist of the frescoes appears to have heeded Vitruvius' dictum about fantastic architecture and tries to bring some reason into the gay, fantastic architectural painting. In doing so, he harks back to the Second style and borrows a little from the Third.

Certain paintings on the walls of Hadrian's Villa, some of which are preserved in drawings at Eton College, should be compared with the Negroni frescoes in forming an estimate of the painting of the Second Century A.D. (Fig. 593). Here, we find a low socle sometimes encased in marble and a rich architectural structure above. In our central ædicula is a woman wearing a red mantle. She is probably Venus. On the left stands Mercury with his caduceus; at the right, Diana, clad in a green garment and carrying a torch. The second storey is strongly emphasized. Pilasters carry an entablature which supports a pediment. The central part of this structure has been cut away, in order to emphasize the throned figure of Zeus. This device is seen in architectural façades at Petra. Above, garlands are suspended. Krieger thinks that the presence of the smooth Tuscan shaft is evidence of the Italian origin of Pompeian decoration from the Second style on. This column is found in the Negroni paintings and in the Tomb of Nasonii. It is a case of conscious archaizing.

Close in type to the paintings from the walls of Hadrian's Villa are certain examples from the Tomb of the Nasonii.[132] Six originals from this monument are at present in the British Museum, fresh in color and apparently, for the most part, ancient. The tomb passed as destroyed for a long time but is still preserved, along with a great part of its stucco covering and a considerable amount of painting, as Rodenwaldt has shown. Most of what is gone has been cut out, but some of the stucco has fallen. The paintings were published by Bellori six years after their discovery in 1674. For publication, some colored copies and engravings were made by Bartoli. Colored reproductions were also in the possession of Cardinal Massimi. Some of these sketches and paintings may be found today in the Royal Library at Windsor Castle.

The character of the decoration is readily seen from a sketch of part of the ceiling (Fig. 594). The center is occupied by a figure of Pegasus set in a circle. From this center radiate four rectangular fields of decoration. The upper pavilion-like section in each of these is decorated with a landscape, while below are two floating figures facing an elaborate candelabrum. Between these rectangular sections are lunettes, one of which is occupied by a shepherd and a maiden (Fig. 595). These extremely graceful figures form an idyllic scene in a thoroughly harmonious composition. The types go back to Fourth Century originals, as Rodenwaldt points out, but they may

---

[132] G. Bellori, *Picturæ antiquæ cryptarum Romanarum et sepulcri Nasonum*, Rome, 1750; early ed., 1680; *Le Pitture antiche del Sepolcro de'Nasonii*, 1706;[2] A. Michaelis-E. Petersen, "Das Grabmal der Nasonier," *Jahr.*, 25 (1910), pp. 101 ff., and 5 pls.; G. Rodenwaldt, "Gemälde aus dem Grabe der Nasonier," *Röm. Mitth.*, 32 (1917), pp. 1-20.

have been made from later copies. The figures are plastically handled but there is an attractive play of line combined with this plastic clarity. There has been some reworking of the painting, especially on the head of the shepherd and the green garment of the maiden. The mantle of the shepherd is violet; the dress of the maiden, green outside and violet inside. The tree trunk is green and the ground is the same color but lighter.

From this tomb a mythological scene which goes back to an early prototype is also preserved (Fig. 596). Our painting was probably copied from an eclectic one which retained certain features of the Fifth Century model. The chariot shows that it was not borrowed directly from a Fifth Century work. Further, it was probably not modeled after the painting by Nikomachos—at least closely—because his panel was doubtless richer and more varied in the grouping of the horses. The scene represents Pluto carrying off Persephone in his chariot. The horses are fairly well rendered but a certain monotony is felt. Even if we allow for the restoration on the arm and head of Persephone, the action is extremely weak. The figure of Pluto is entirely preserved, except for a fleck on the upper arm. His body is reddish brown; his mantle, violet, with greenish shadows. The flesh of Persephone is lighter in color and she wears a yellow garment. The ground varies from gray green to brown. The background is a neutral white, the horses darker and lighter brown. At the right, Hermes is to be imagined, to judge from the drawing of Bartoli in Windsor.[133] The painting is about seventy-one centimeters high and ninety-eight centimeters wide. There are some restorations on the horses' legs, on Persephone's body, and on the left chariot wheel. The paintings have been carefully studied by Rodenwaldt and this summary is largely drawn from his excellent account. According to Eisler, the Rape of Persephone has a mystical significance.[134]

Among the ornamental figures preserved from the ceiling is an Eros (Fig. 597). The design is so typical of what we find in paintings of the Third and later Centuries that we venture to include it. Cupid stands on a decorative scroll design and holds a small vase aloft in his right hand. The flesh is a reddish brown, the wings brownish with some green. There is a large amount of restoration on the face, wings, crown, and garment. In addition to this and a second decorative figure of Eros, there are winged Victories, Bacchic groups, and ornamental plants, and flowers which recall similar ornaments in mosaics from Hadrian's Villa. These floral designs are executed with less fineness than the figure paintings which were probably made by the best

[133] A. Michaelis, *Jahr.*, 25 (1910), *Beilage* 4, No. 12.

[134] For an interpretation of the supposed symbolism in the tombs on the Via Latina, the Tomb of the Nasonii, the Columbarium of the Villa Pamfili, etc., *cf.* R. Eisler, *Orphisch-Dionysische Mysteriengedanken in der christlichen Antike*, Leipzig, 1925, pp. 123 ff., 159 ff., 173 ff.

masters of the time and which represent fairly well the style of the Second Century A.D. In opposition to the somewhat restless and thoroughly individual art of the Fourth style, we have here, as Rodenwaldt has shown, no impressionistic technique, no cast shadows, no play of light. The whole conception of painting is completely changed. There is much that connects these frescoes with the Third style but they have been copied from copies and the style is ruder; the colors, brighter. The walls are divided into two parts only. The architectural painting shows that the tomb has nothing to do with the Third style. It is to be dated in the age of the Antonines. Isolated monuments in Rome, such as mosaics and the tomb on the Via Latina, prove that this structure is akin to these in style.

The so-called tomb of the Valerii on the Via Latina is dated by a brick stamp of 159 A.D. in the period of the Antonines. The barrel vault of the sepulchral chamber bears some of the most beautiful stuccoes which we have from antiquity. It is covered by an "all-over pattern of circular medallions," twenty-five in number, which are in relief. These circles contain, in six cases, Bacchic figures—a satyr and a mænad; in six others, Nereids borne by marine monsters; in the twelve remaining, Nereids riding sea animals or Triton figures. Our Figure 598 presents graceful Nereids riding on sea monsters, or borne by Tritons. The square panels contain little Cupids or rosettes. The ground around the squares is adorned with conventionalized patterns. In the lunettes, arabesques fill the spaces except for a central oblong panel. The foreparts of animals form the ends of spirals and human figures are woven among the tendrils. The central medallion contains a veiled woman riding on a gryphon. These stuccoes give a splendid idea of the decorative ability of the Roman artist in the Second Century A.D. We shall see that the motives employed have a long history in art.

In the second tomb on the Via Latina—the monument of the Pancratii—stucco reliefs illustrating epic scenes are combined with decorative designs and small painted landscapes.[134] In Figure 599 we see the growing tendency toward the rococo. The reaction against the mannerism of the Fourth style, which set in under Hadrian and which produced the effects of simplicity and strength found in the wall-decorations of the Villa Negroni and the Tomb of the Nasonii, has begun to fail. The artist is interested once again in the illusionism which characterized the Fourth style. His landscapes and his friezes with various birds, flowers, and baskets of fruits show this (*Mem. Amer. Academy, Rome*, IV (1924), Pls. XXX-XXXII, XXV). There is not the calm atmosphere found in the works just named. A certain interest in vivid action and a fondness for decorating every available space herald a return of the restlessness of the Fourth style. However, the decorations show the persistent excellence of Græco-Roman painting in the era of the Antonines.

A house in the Via de' Cerchi offers interesting survivals of the Second style of

decoration from the time of Marcus Aurelius or Septimius Severus.[185] These paintings belong to a private house which was built against the southern slope of the
Palatine, while the front is near the northeast end of the Circus Maximus. It has
been wrongly called the Domus Gelotiana. The paintings of one room depict a
podium with a central opening flanked by groups of two columns resting on high
pedestals. Before this architectural façade, servants are engaged in welcoming and
serving guests (Fig. 600). One holds a garland, another a table napkin, both of
which were offered to guests when they entered the dining-room. A third has in his
hand a short staff with a knob on the end of it. He is doubtless the master of ceremonies—the head-waiter, as it were. On the floor, near the center of the room lies
a fly-brush, made of the tail and hoof of an ox. At the right, a fourth servant enters
with fruits in a dish or basket. Before him stands a box which may have contained
the silver.

The floor is painted dark green, the podium and architectural details are a light
or a reddish yellow; the columns, dark red. The servants wear white, purple-
banded, short tunics. The men are smooth-faced. The architectural background is
reminiscent of the Second style and the life-size figures in front recall the Villa Item.
Here, the architecture gives rather the impression of a loggia which serves as a
background, whereas the Second style concerns itself with prospect views which
were apparently intended, in many cases, to imitate easel-paintings placed on the
wall. The art cannot be said to be of the highest. As Mrs. Strong points out, it has
been called "crude, vulgar, and commonplace." The latter is perhaps the most just
epithet. The date of the painting is arrived at by means of the bricks. Miss Van
Deman assigns the room in which the frescoes occur to the time of Septimius Severus.

Closely related to monuments which we have been discussing, for example, the
paintings from the Tomb of the Nasonii, are some frescoes from Ostia.[186] They extend
in time from the Second to the Fourth Centuries A.D. Fornari concludes from his
study of the paintings that the walls of Ostia come under none of the four styles distinguished by Mau, but that they show a mixture of elements. They strongly recall
the paintings of the Fourth style and sometimes those of the Second with some
echoes from the Third. This agrees entirely with what we have found in paintings of
the Second Century A.D., such as those of the Villa Negroni and the Tomb of the
Nasonii. In the paintings from Ostia, there is a careful division of the wall into three
parts horizontally and vertically. On the whole, however, a decided falling off in

[185] Mrs. Strong, *B.S.R.*, VIII (1916), pp. 91-103, Pls. III-VII (color); VIII-IX; Ch.
Huelsen, *Röm. Mitth.*, VIII (1893), pp. 289 ff.; D. Marchetti, *Not. d. Sc.*, 1892, pp. 44 ff.

[186] F. Fornari, "La Pittura decorativa di Ostia," *Studi Romani*, I (1913), pp. 305-338,
Pls. 29-35; G. Calza, *Mon. Ant.*, 26 (1920), pp. 375 ff. (esp. pp. 402 ff.), Pls. II-III; *Ostia:
A Historical Guide to the Monuments*, pp. 51 ff.

artistic ability is seen in these paintings. There is less technical skill and they are executed more hastily. One of the greatest interests which they offer us is the possibility of tracing various repaintings above one another and of following the way in which these were executed. This can be done in some cases at Pompeii. We are able to see in these instances that the stucco worker began at the top of the wall and came down.

We have said that the flower decoration and the incrustation method came to supplant the architectural styles in the Second and Third Centuries A.D. Evidence of the carpet style of decoration is to be found in Cyrene and in the mosaics of Northern Africa.[137] Its influence may be traced in Hellenistic ceramics and in glass vases. Rostovtzeff cites a newly discovered ceiling on the Palatine decorated in this manner at the time of the Second style; he knows of ten unpublished examples of this type of decoration in Pompeii dating from the period of the Fourth style. The artist abandoned the architectural features and covered the wall from dado to cornice with a rich carpet of red or yellow.[138] The style probably originated in Egypt and made its way farther east, as we have said (p. 352), arising in the beginning from the practices of nomadic tribes who hung their tents with carpets. The flower style in Southern Russia, as it is found in a vault discovered in Kertch in 1895, is reproduced in Figure 601. Here the floral decoration is strewn over the surface of a lunette above the door. The branches and flowers, with birds here and there, are not symmetrically disposed over the space to be decorated, but the general effect is pleasing. Below are figures of Kalypso and Hermes, symbols of parting. In general, the triple structural division of the wall is kept in this style but any one of the three parts may be used for floral decoration. The patterns may be conventionalized or natural. The ceiling of this same vault from Kertch is pictured in Figure 602. In the center is the head of Demeter surrounded by a wreath to which is attached a hanging fillet. Over the surface of the ceiling, plants and birds and flowers are strewn at random.

The incrustation style, on the other hand, as Rostovtzeff tries to show, was probably born in ancient Mesopotamia, where it was the custom to face walls built of unbaked brick with alabaster, glazed tiles, and stones of various colors. Our first record of this incrustation style, or "painting with marbles," connects it with the palace of Mausolos in Caria in the Fourth Century B.C.,[139] but it was older. In this

---

[137] Pacho, *Voyage en Cyrénaïque*. Rostovtzeff divides the flower style into the carpet style and the naturalistic flower style. There are no examples of the carpet style in South Russia, where all of the designs are naturalistic. R. M. Smith, E. A. Porcher, *A History of the Recent Discoveries at Cyrene in 1860-61*, p. 31, Pl. XXI.

[138] M. Rostovtzeff, *J.H.S.*, 39 (1919), pp. 161 ff.

[139] Pliny, *N.H.*, 36, 47; Vitr., *De Arch.*, II, 8, 10.

style, the same triple wall division found throughout the structural style was kept, and a whole or a part of the wall was decorated with slabs of varicolored marbles. This decoration did not emphasize the wall divisions. The idea was merely to inlay marble slabs of one color in those of another and to achieve a polychromatic effect. The designs are usually geometric in character, but occasionally figure patterns were employed. Roman floors of the days of Nero—an example of which is to be seen today on the Palatine Hill—doubtless reflect this technique in their geometric patterns. Such designs in marbles of various kinds are common in the later Empire in the great baths. In Kertch, the incrustation style was frequently combined with the floral style and with figure scenes (Fig. 603). Barbaric as the mural decoration of the tomb wall is, we nevertheless have in this instance an interesting combination of the two styles as they were used in the Orient. The decoration of the lower part of the painted wall imitates slabs of gaily colored marble inlaid in geometric patterns with marble blocks of another variety. The various fields are separated by painted pilasters. In the upper part of the wall, flowers, "in the form of an ornament shaped like a light and a dark pink heart with pairs of green leaves (apparently a conventionalized rose)" are sown. With this as a background, horsemen wearing pointed caps and bearing long spears are riding to meet one another in battle, while in the background at the left are foot soldiers with shields. The ceiling of this tomb reveals the same combination of incrustation and floral decoration. Minns comments on the "centipede-like" garlands of yellow,[140] which are also seen in Figure 602, and which were probably derived from textiles. In the other portions which are not reproduced here are flowers and garlands interspersed with birds and animals such as the peacock, boar, dog, lion, deer, and leopard, while above the funeral couches are geometric patterns inlaid in squares and circles of different colors to represent marble. The decoration belongs to Rostovtzeff's second class. The first class deals with walls represented as masonry, the second one with those representing marble lining and the third with the group imitating embroidery. Rostovtzeff holds that the third style came between the other two and that it overlaps both. In any case, we have in this catacomb, which is usually known as Stasov's, a union of marble inlays combined with embroidery-like patterns. The latter appear to have originated in textiles.

When we examine in detail the very amusing colored plates of this tomb, we find a barbarian love of color combined with a childishness in drawing which reminds us of the Bayeux tapestry[141] (Fig. 603). The marbling effects are set on squares of gray, rose, or yellow. Against this the patterns are put in contrasting colors. On the

[140] E. H. Minns, *Scythians and Greeks*, Cambridge, 1913, pp. 316 ff.; V. V. Stasov, *Compte-Rendu*, 1872, Pl. III, Text; M. Rostovtzeff, *J.H.S.*, 39 (1919), p. 152, Pl. VIII; *Iranians and Greeks in South Russia*, Oxford, 1922, pp. 160 ff., Pls. XXVIII-XXIX.

[141] V. V. Stasov, *Compte-Rendu*, 1872, Pls. V-XVI (color).

yellow squares, we have a gray lozenge, green rays, a yellow circle and red dots. On the gray squares, the lozenges are rose, the rays white on a green ground, and the center again yellow with red dots. We are most intrigued, however, by the figure design at the top. Here the field is strewn with heart-shaped blossoms of dark and lighter rose, and with wing-like green leaves. Against this background, warriors, who remind us of soldiers in the battle of Hastings, are riding to attack one another in battle. Some wear pointed caps and coats of mail. Their mantles, always red in the case of the dead hero, fly out behind. The second group wears coats of gray or brown, and trousers. Which are barbarians and which Bosphorians is difficult to know. Probably, as Minns suggests, the Bosphorian came to wear very much the same sort of costume as the barbarian. The mailed warriors are doubtless Bosphorians; the dark-haired, fierce warriors, Taurians; the shaggy-haired figures, Scythians. In our painting a Panticapæan chief with his men is defending his land against encroachment, in all probability. The horses may be gray or yellow. Although Stasov overemphasizes the "Oriental" elements in the tomb, some of the designs certainly suggest the East and especially Persia.[142] Minns states that there is nothing which cannot be paralleled from Hellenic sources except the barbarian portraits and costumes and this is probably true. On the other hand, the conventionalized trees and the drawing of animals such as the deer, the lions, and the panthers, suggest the Orient. Here and there, winged Genii and Erotes of strange kind are also found.

The earlier Kertch style where the wall imitates masonry may be seen in the tomb of Anthesterios of the First Century A.D. (Fig. 604). Above the socle are four courses of stones separated by black lines and outlined in brown. Those of the top row in some cases bear figures. In the upper frieze, above the cornice, Anthesterios, wearing a blue and white shirt and brown trousers, is seated on a black horse. He receives a cup from a small boy dressed in brown and red. The seated woman probably connotes a funeral feast; the hero, the departing warrior. At the left is a brown tent with people inside; behind is a tree, with a quiver hung on it, and on the side wall is a green and a brown horse. A figure resembling Anthesterios is repeated at the right, riding a brown horse and leading a black one. Rostovtzeff sees in Anthesterios "a landed proprietor who spends most of his time in town; in summer during the harvest season, he goes out to the steppes, armed and accompanied by armed servants, taking his family with him. He supervises the fields and defends his laborers and harvesters against the attacks of his neighbors—Taurians and Scythians." In our painting, Anthesterios, the dead man, armed and followed by a retainer, is riding toward his residence, where his family is assembled beside the tent.[143] The work is

[142] V. V. Stasov, *Compte-Rendu*, 1872, Pls. V, VII, VIII, XI.

[143] M. Rostovtzeff, *Iranians and Greeks in South Russia*, Oxford, 1922, pp. 160 ff. *C.R.*, 1878-1879, Pl. I, i-iv; Minns, *op. cit.*, p. 312.

extremely crude and barbaric. To judge from a coin found in a tomb it dates in the second half of the First Century A.D. The Stasov catacomb is later than this. In one of the Kertch examples opened in 1891, the familiar motive of two peacocks drinking from a standing cup is seen opposite the door.

The closest parallel to these vaults from Kertch is to be found in a tomb from Palmyra of 259 A.D.[144] (Fig. 605). It is much larger in type and the size has allowed the artist freer rein. In this monument, we find heralded many characteristics of Byzantine style. Minns points out that conditions in Palmyra were much the same as in Bosphorus, as far as mixtures of races were concerned. Figure 605 shows a room with a lunette on which was represented the myth of Achilles discovered among the daughters of King Lykomedes. Below, on pillars between the grave shafts, are medallions which bear portraits of the dead—a bearded man with a parchment roll and a woman with a veil over her head, strongly recalling in type the figure of Bithnanaia in the recently discovered fort at Dura-Salihiyeh in the desert of Syria (Fig. 606). The medallions are held aloft by winged female figures dressed in white. They stand on blue globes under which is a large, green acanthus leaf. Below them are violet squares with red borders. Within these are yellow lozenges which bear green circles. This decoration imitates marble incrustation. At the bottom of the wall are panels with distinctly "Ionic" patterns—a lion, a panther, or a hunting animal attacking a gazelle, a deer, or an antelope. In other cases, we see a peacock or five flamingoes(?). One pillar contains a vine pattern woven over it in interesting design. The tomb combines several styles: mythological painting; portraits supported by Victories; floral style and decoration in the incrustation method.

The tomb type and certain pictorial features found here were developed by Byzantine masters. The arms of the structure are in the form of a cross and contain niches for sarcophagi. The central room is vaulted; the others have barrel vaults. This type of building is the forerunner of monuments like the Mausoleum of Galla Placidia at Ravenna. Strzygowski holds that the sources of Palmyrene and early Christian art in the Orient are the same and that similarities to Christian art are seen here in painting and in sculpture. Apart from local influences, especially Persian, the broad foundation of both is Hellenistic art. The tomb at Palmyra is really an example of late Hellenistic art, although it is a Jewish monument. It shows paganism at its decline and illustrates how the Jews, despite rigorous prohibitions,

---

[144] B. V. Pharmakowsky, "Painting in Palmyra" (*Bull. of the Russian Arch. Inst. in Constantinople*), 1903, VIII, Pt. 3; J. Strzygowski, *Orient oder Rom.*, Leipzig, 1901, pp. 11 ff.; F. Cumont, *Rev. de l'histoire des rel.*, 62 (1910), pp. 142 ff. F. Cumont, *Fouilles de Doura-Europos*, p. 166, dates the frescoes at the beginning of the Third Century. *Cf.* Chabot, *Choix d'inscr. de Palmyre*, 1922, pp. 96 ff. For bibliography on Syrian painting, see Cumont, *op. cit.*, pp. 165-168.

were, like the Christians of the age, caught by the existing fashion of decorating hypogæa with pagan motives and even of employing pagan artists to decorate them.

The principal decoration of the catacomb lies in the winged figures who support the portrait medallions. They are Hellenistic material descending from early Greece. The motive is not found in the catacombs of Rome. It is native in Christian art in the Orient and we can see these Victories become Christian angels in that region. Strzygowski traces, in monuments under Byzantine influence, the motive of the Niké standing on a globe and bearing aloft a portrait.[145] One of the best examples is found in the Capella S. Zeno in S. Prassede, in Rome. Here, the angels hold up a medallion adorned with the head of Christ. They have also acquired the *nimbus*.

Closest in style to the paintings which we have discussed from Palmyra are some newly discovered frescoes in a fort at Dura-Salihiyeh.[146] The site lies in Syria on the right bank of the Euphrates between Bagdad and Aleppo. During the World War it was in the center of the struggle. Professor Breasted was able to examine these paintings and to copy some of them through the courtesy of the British army who furnished him with a military escort. Immediately afterward the region had to be evacuated and some of the most important paintings have since been destroyed by fanatic natives. The work done at this time under grave danger was, therefore, of the greatest value to students of painting.

The frescoes at Dura-Salihiyeh are in the northwestern corner of a fort which occupied a strategic position as the extreme outpost of Rome's Oriental frontier. It guarded the passage of the Euphrates. In this fort there were three important rooms containing paintings. In room I designs decorated all of the various walls. On the north wall was represented a military scene of a Roman tribune, Julius Terentius, sacrificing with his soldiers to the Emperors in the presence of the Roman *vexillum*, or standard.[146a] To the left of this group one sees the Palmyrene gods—Baal, Yarhibol, and Aglibol. Below the images of these gods the Fortune of Palmyra and the Fortune of Dura were worshiped as goddesses. The identity of these divinities

[145] J. Strzygowski, *Orient oder Rom.*, 1901, pp. 26 ff., Figs. 8, 9 (S. Vitale). *Cf.* Stuhlfauth, *Die Engel in der altchristlichen Kunst,* who derives the angel from Rome.

[146] J. H. Breasted, "Peintures d'époque romaine dans le désert de Syrie," *Syria*, III (1922), pp. 177 ff.; *Oriental Forerunners of Byzantine Painting*, Vol. I, (Publ. of the Orient. Inst., Univ. of Chicago), 1924. Clermont-Ganneau, F. Cumont, *Les Fresques d'époque romaine relevées par M. Breasted à Sâlihîye sur l'Euphrate, Les Travaux archéologiques en Syrie de 1920 à 1922*, Paris, 1923, pp. 48 ff.; F. Cumont, "Les Fouilles de Sâlihîyeh sur l'Euphrate," *Syria*, IV (1923), pp. 38 ff.; *Fouilles de Doura-Europos*, Paris, 1926. E. Diez, *Belvedere*, 1924-1925, finds evidence of Far Eastern influence in the paintings. F. Sarre, E. Herzfeld, *Archäologische Reise im Euphrat- und Tigris-Gebiet*, Berlin, II, 1920, pp. 386 ff.; III, Pls. LXXXI-LXXXIII.

[146a] F. Cumont, *Fouilles de Doura-Europos,* now rejects this idea.

is made clear by inscriptions. They fill the left field of the painting. Below the gods are personifications of the river god, the Euphrates; of Dura, in the form of a child rising from the waters; of the spring, which symbolizes the waters of Palmyra, in the form of a woman; and a representation of a lion, symbol of the city.[146b] At the right of the fresco a group of twenty-four soldiers was depicted, clad in short tan tunics with a purple stripe at the bottom. They face the spectator. The tribune occupies the center of the composition a little to the right. Beside him is a vivid crimson standard with a golden yellow fringe and wreath. The design is uninspired and is concerned with Roman subject matter. It is more interesting as an historical document, depicting the official worship of a Roman military garrison. Julius Terentius, a Roman military tribune, presents himself at the head of a Palmyrene cohort of archers worshiping the Emperor and the local Syrian divinities.[146a] Cumont dates the fresco in the age of the Severi when the worship of Syrian deities was encouraged. The garrison was composed of legionaries and Palmyrenes. The former worshiped the deified emperor according to Roman rite; the others according to Syrian ritual.[147] Its relation to the paintings of room II, the sanctuary proper, is difficult to explain. The paintings are hastily executed and make use of black, reddish brown, gray, yellow, and sometimes rose.

The walls of room II were covered with white plaster. Against this ground, a religious scene was painted in a process which Cumont states was not distemper or fresco but which resembles fresco more. He argues that the porosity of the plaster alone held the colors fast. The most important paintings were found on wall C-D (Figs. 606-607). Here the figures executed on a large scale were placed on two levels, one above the other. Against a rose-pink architectural background with three doors of greenish yellow color is the figure of a woman named Bithnanaia. She is engaged with three priests and several members of her family in religious rites. She wears a white garment and a brilliant magenta veil over her head. Her jewels indicate that she is a personage of importance. She recalls the veiled portrait head mentioned in connection with the Palmyrene catacomb. At the right are four men attired in white with lavender borders and holding green branches. At the left (Fig. 607), three ministrants are busy with sacred ceremonies. The most striking figure in the group is a dark-skinned, bearded priest (Fig. 608), who strongly suggests the modern Oriental type of religious ascetic. The priests wear pointed white caps as Lucian says they did in Syria[148]—probably a survival from Hittite days—and white, flowing garments with long sleeves. The leader of the group is placing a branch in a

[146b] F. Cumont, op. cit., now thinks this a symbol of Atargatis.

[147] Cf. F. Cumont, "Le Sacrifice du tribun romain Terentius et les Palmyréniens à Doura," Mon. Piot, 26 (1923), pp. 1-46, Pl. I. See note 146[a].

[148] Lucian, De Dea Syria, 42.

tall blue vase filled with water. In his left hand are knives, a saucer, and a pitcher, all of which are gray-blue in color, except that the knives have rose-colored handles. The impassive face of this figure is painted in dark brown tones with only a grayish cast for the beard and white for the eyeballs. The contours are outlined in black. The figure at the left of the priests is Conon. He is the head of the family depicted here, whose names are given, for the most part, on the lower part of the figures. The striking thing about the composition is the frontality of the figures.

The nature of the architectural façade is difficult to figure out. It seems to represent the front of a temple with a projecting entablature supported by square columns. The color is a rose-pink. Just such an architectural background for the figures is found in the Eighth Century A.D. at Kusejr Amra. The two figures at the left stand on the rose-colored step of this building. From the central door, Bithnanaia has just emerged. The threshold on which the third figure and Bithnanaia are placed is in black and white. The last four figures seem to bear no relation to the architecture but appear to float in the air. On the south wall of room I, Cumont found a second ritual scene. The figures are shown again in frontal view. Most important was the discovery of the artist's name—Ilasamsos, "The Sun is God." The name is purely Semitic and shows that we have an Oriental practicing the art.

There is little use of modeling in the figures, the tones being mostly flat.[148a] The forms are elongated and this fact, together with their arrangement in a long line, calls to mind the Ravenna mosaics of Justinian and Theodora. The light on the faces is well handled. In the case of the architecture, it falls from the right. One figure in white has rose stripes on his garment. There has been thought to be an attempt to render the effect of light falling on it. The colors used are magenta, red, brown, purple, orange, maroon, various shades of green, yellow, blue, gray, black, and white. Some figures are painted with black outlines, others lack this entirely. Chiaroscuro seems to have been little employed in the case of the figures outlined in black.

The paintings raise several problems: (1) the history of Syria in this period and the reasons for a Roman camp here; (2) the character of the religious rites depicted with Oriental elements; (3) the relation of paintings such as these Syrian ones and those from Palmyra to Byzantine works of art. Mesopotamia did not become a Roman province until 114 A.D., after which a fort may have been needed to guard Roman transports, but it was not until the expedition of L. Verus against the Parthians in 162 to 165, or even those of Septimius Severus in 195 and 198, that a large part of Mesopotamia became definitely Roman. The ritualistic scene, where the family of Conon assist at a religious event, is unique of its kind. The bare feet of the high priest recall customs mentioned in the Bible and found in Oriental religions

---

[148a] Authorities argue that two painters were at work on this fresco because there is almost no modeling on Conon and the chief priest but a great deal on the other figures.

today; the branch ceremony brings to mind Jewish practices. The sacrifice on the flaming altar, together with the rite of the branch and vase, remind us of the adoration of the elements, fire and water, as practiced by the Chaldæans.[149]

What have the two scenes, Roman and Oriental, to do with one another? In one case, Conon, a distinguished head of a family, makes a sacrifice in the presence of all his descendants. His daughter and granddaughter as well as his sons and grandsons assist him. In the second example, we have a purely military scene. The paintings do not belong to the same date. The purely Oriental ritual scenes are earlier and date from the period of the autonomy of Palmyra well before the time of Zenobia. They are placed by Cumont in the second half of the First Century A.D. between 65 and 75.

Of very great interest is their importance for the history of ancient painting. Cumont points out that we know little of Græco-Syrian painting,[150] and that we gain our best ideas of it from this monument and from the catacomb published by Strzygowski. The physical types resemble those found in Palmyrene sculpture; the garments and headdresses are the same, so also the jewelry. According to Breasted, the arrangement of the figures *de face* in the same line, with feet resting as if they were floating through the air, recalls the Ravenna mosaics.

After this account of the paintings from Dura-Salihiyeh was written, Cumont studied the site in detail and published his results in a monumental work.[150] He has established that the city was a Hellenistic foundation which was colonized by Nikanor and named after the birthplace of his master, Seleukos Nikator, Dura-Europos. It became an important center on the route from Antioch eastward to Seleucia on the Tigris. The walls are practically those of the Macedonian enceinte. The word *Dour* in Assyrian means *fort* and Cumont is inclined to believe that there was an Assyrian stronghold on the site before the establishment of the Macedonian colony, Europos. He emphasizes strongly the importance of the paintings in the history of ancient art. They are our best examples of Græco-Syrian painting and reveal, in their style, Hellenistic traditions carried on in the east with Oriental admixtures.[151] They are the forerunners of Byzantine painting in the East and form a very vital link between Assyrian-Persian traditions and Byzantine art. Certain characteristics heretofore regarded as distinctive of Byzantine art are found to be centuries older. In Dura we have the finest surviving Oriental forerunners of Byzantine painting out of which

[149] F. Cumont, *Syria,* III (1922), pp. 206 ff. Cumont has discovered from inscriptions that the fort on the site before 165 was garrisoned by Palmyrene soldiers under the sovereignty of Parthians. The Roman garrison dates from 165 A.D.

[150] F. Cumont, *Fouilles de Doura-Europos,* Paris, 1926.

[151] *Cf.* Djemal Pasha, *Alte Denkmäler aus Syrien, Palästina und West-Arabien,* Berlin, 1918. *Cf.* Alois Musil, *Kusejr-Amra,* Akad. Wien, 1907; Pères Jaussen et Savignac, *Mission archéologique en Arabie,* III, 1922, pp. 78 ff., Pls. XXXVI ff.

arose the Pre-Renaissance painting of Europe. They therefore give us the lost ancestry of Byzantine art.[152]

The paintings of Dura illustrate the Oriental style and methods which later penetrated Christian art. Such paintings in the pagan temples of Syria later furnished the models for the wall-paintings of the Christian churches of that region. When the overthrow of Zenobia allowed Christianity to spread, as Breasted has shown, the temples appropriated by the Christians were decorated with paintings like those at Dura. The successors of Ilasamsos painted the Virgin, Savior, and Apostles in the same style, technique, and composition as those of Dura. The influence of this Græco-Syrian painting is seen in later times in the funerary chapels of the monastery of Bawît in Upper Egypt, which date from the Sixth Century A.D.[152] and on other Egyptian sites such as el-Khargeh. It is found in the earlier Cappadocian paintings which show the continuity of Syro-Hellenistic painting in remote districts.[152]

The Oriental and the Roman paintings were executed by native artists of the Palmyrene School. The Oriental group has a more monumental character. The forms are imposing and plastic in type. They exhibit little or none of the illusionism which developed to such a degree in Italy. The Greeks in the Neo-Attic style kept to the older Attic tendency and this is what we find in the Hellenistic East and later in Byzantine painting. The illusionistic method, on the other hand, became the favorite Italian manner of painting and was especially prominent in the Fourth style of painting. After the Fourth style had run its course there was a reaction visible in paintings like the Negroni frescoes and the Tomb of the Nasonii which renounced impressionistic methods and displayed a bent for classical figures of plastic type rather isolated and set off in architectural surroundings. By the Second Century A.D., we see the impressionism of earlier days beginning to return in monuments such as the Tomb of the Pancratii with its illusionistic landscapes, and from this time on the two styles existed side by side in various works of art. In the Third Century, Philostratos in his Imagines describes the kind of painting current in his time and we recognize again the presence of the illusionistic style. The value of his work for the history of painting is probably not very great. Many of his descriptions appear to be purely imaginary.[153] This illusionistic method was handed down in manuscripts of

[152] Cf. Gabriel Millet, "La Scène pastorale de Doura et l'Annonce aux Bergers," Syria, VII (1926), pp. 142 ff.; O. M. Dalton, East Christian Art, 1925, p. 247, n. 3. On the Bawît frescoes, see J. Clédat, Le Monastère de Baouît, Mém. de l'Institut d'archéol. du Caire, XII (1904), p. 79; Pls. LI-LII; J. Clédat in Cabrol, Dict. d'arch. chrét. s.v. Baouît; G. Maspero, Rapport sur les fouilles entreprises à Baouît, Acad. des Inscr. et Belles-Lettres, 1913, 287 ff. On the Cappadocian paintings, see G. de Jerphanion, Une nouvelle province de l'art byzantin: Les Églises rupestres de Cappadoce, Paris, 1925-1928.

[153] We have not considered Philostratos a very reliable guide and have been inclined perhaps to minimize his work. Cf. for a different view, F. Wickhoff, Roman Art, tr. by Mrs. Strong, London, 1900, pp. 158, 163-164.

the Fourth Century and was used for the most part in the catacombs. In contrast to this, centers like Ravenna, which in the later period drew their inspiration from the Christian East, show a fondness for painting based essentially on line.

If we return once more to the floral style, we find a tomb in Cyrene which in its flat, carpet-like decoration offers a close parallel to some of the types that we have been discussing.[154] These floral patterns are present in Italy in late tombs. Examples of the style may be seen in some designs in the Corsini MS. which Lanciani attributed to Gaetano Piccini.[155] They copy old paintings and mosaics. Figure 609 shows designs taken from the walls of sepulchral chambers unearthed in 1710 in the Vigna Moroni on the Appian Way, opposite the tomb of the Scipios. In each case, floral patterns are strewn at random over the walls and in the sepulchral niches. In No. 1, a woman is reclining on a couch; in No. 2, two women are seen playing on musical instruments. Other examples have peacocks or small objects. Hanging garlands are also found. The ceiling of one room is decorated with the head of a woman and six radiating diagonals which represent columns. The same strewn flowers, birds, and garlands also appear here.

Mosaics of Northern Africa, especially those of Uthina and Timgad, reflect the popularity of the floral and carpet styles. In the so-called Villa of the Laberii at Uthina,[156] we find a vintage scene which shows the floral style in its most charming aspect (Fig. 610). The design forms an all-over pattern. Around the edge of the mosaic is a heavy band of fruits and flowers with four masks—satyrs, Pan, and fauns. In the center, Dionysos is giving the vine to Ikarios, King of Attica, who is seated at the right. The beauty of the mosaic lies in the vines which grow in pairs from vases in the four corners and which interlace in pleasing but not rigid symmetry over the background. Small putti are busy among the branches gathering grapes or letting them down in loaded baskets into the vases by a long rope. Birds of gay-colored plumage are seen among the foliage and along the border—peacocks, swans, flamingoes, and various other kinds. The delicate intertwining vines and the busy Erotes lead us back to Hellenistic art. The villa belongs at the end of the First Century A.D., or to the beginning of the Second. Dionysos wears a blue mantle thrown over his left shoulder and gathered about his waist; the bearded slave before him has a short yellow tunic; Ikarios is clothed in green, with an orange mantle. This picture resembles a tapestry in the fineness of its execution. The birds which flit

[154] R. M. Smith and E. A. Porcher, *A History of the Recent Discoveries at Cyrene in 1860-1861*, p. 31, Pl. XXI.

[155] R. Engelmann, *Antike Bilder aus römischen Handschriften*, Leiden, 1909, Pl. X; R. Lanciani, "Picturæ antiquæ cryptarum Romanarum," *Bull. Comun.*, 1895, p. 165; Thomas Ashby, "Drawings of Ancient Paintings in English Collections," *B.S.R.*, VII (1914), pp. 1 ff.

[156] P. Gauckler, "Le Domaine des Laberii à Uthina," *Mon. Piot*, III (1896), pp. 177 ff., Pls. XX-XXIII.

about are bright colored with iridescent plumage. The Erotes have the same gay-colored wings and their pudgy little figures are done in rose color. Another mosaic from the same villa gives a landscape with scenes from African rural life (Fig. 611). A farm is depicted with various pursuits which take place on the land, such as hunting, watering the horses, guarding sheep, and the like. As Gauckler observes, the perspective is childish and the work uneven.

Mosaics from Timgad are especially interesting for what they tell us of the carpet style of decoration. The idea of the artist in this type of decoration was to give the wall, ceiling, or floor the appearance of a richly woven carpet or material. An idea of these materials may be gained, according to Rostovtzeff, from examining linen and woolen clothes which have been discovered in the graves at Antinoë and various towns of Egypt.[157] The decoration is floral in character and the blossoms may be natural or stylized. Many examples of the carpet style have been found at Cyrene,[158] but we shall deal only with those coming from the North African site of Timgad. A good example of the style is seen in a mosaic from the house of Sertius, a man who belonged to one of the wealthiest families in the town (Fig. 612). This mosaic came from the floor of the Tablinum or reception room, but it is now on the wall of the Museum at Timgad. It is formed of rosettes and conventionalized flowers and leaves surrounded by a luxuriant border of fruits and foliage. The general effect is that of a rich carpet. Even more elaborate in its "all-over" pattern is a second mosaic from a house in the southeast quarter of the city (Fig. 613). The decoration is composed of acanthus leaves and stems arranged in elaborate spirals and bearing in the center in two cases a vase with fruit and flowers. Six birds of brilliant plumage rest on the curved stems and flowers. A panel in the center has a design of Venus rising from the waves, and two Tritons. The beauty of the ornamental pattern is, however, far greater than that of the figure decoration. The colors are largely blue, green, and red, in the floral designs, with some yellow, gray, white, black, and sepia. The *rinceaux* are unusually elegant and luxuriant. The design is not rigidly symmetrical. Other fine examples so conventionalized that they have lost much of their floral character are illustrated by Ballu.[159] An example of the strongly stylized carpet style is

[157] On Hellenistic clothes and tapestries, *cf.* O. Wulff and W. F. Volbach, *Die hellenistischen und koptischen Stoffe aus ägyptischen Gräbern*, Berlin, 1926; W. F. Volbach, "Die Stoffe aus Antinoë in den Berliner Museen," *Arch. Anz.*, 41 (1926), pp. 238 ff.; G. Borovka, "Die Funde der Expedition Koslov in der Mongolei," *Arch. Anz.*, 41 (1926), 341 ff.; W. Sherwood Fox, "Hellenistic Tapestries in America," *Art and Arch.*, V (1917), pp. 161 ff. *Victoria and Albert Museum. Catalogue of Textiles from Burying Grounds in Egypt, Vol. I, Græco-Roman Period*, 1920. W. F. Volbach, Ernst Kuehnel, *Late antique Coptic and Islamic Textiles of Egypt*, London, 1926; J. Strzygowski, *Orient oder Rom*, Leipzig, 1901, pp. 90 ff.

[158] Pacho, *Voyage en Cyrénaïque*. O. von Falke, *Kunstgesch. der Seidenweberei in Europa*, Berlin, 1913; Ph. Lauer, *Mon. Piot*, XV (1906), pp. 107 ff.

[159] A. Ballu, *Les ruines de Timgad*, Paris, 1911, p. 86; *Guide illustré de Timgad*, pp. 136-138. *Inventaire des mosaïques de la Gaule et de l'Afrique*.

seen in a mosaic from the Baths of a Society known as the Filadelfi (Fig. 614). Here the floral patterns are woven into designs in which urn-shaped objects with tendrils and heart-shaped forms play a leading rôle. Rosettes and stylized leaves suggest the origin of the pattern which makes a very attractive design. In the center, the myth represented is probably that of Apollo and Daphne. Above the picture runs the inscription: "Long life to the Filadelfi!" The colors are especially sepia, flesh color, black, red, and brown against a white ground.

If we follow the floral style after Hellenistic times, we find traces of it in monuments such as the Catacomb of Domitilla in Rome.[160] The ground for this catacomb was apparently given as a cemetery for the Christian Church by Flavia Domitilla, a grandniece(?) of the Emperor Vespasian, but it was originally a sepulcher of the Flavian family. At one of the ancient entrances to this catacomb frescoes are found dating from the end of the First Century A.D. Vines are represented growing from acanthus-like centers. Among their branches, birds flutter. In the panels and in the circles, small putti, or Loves, are seen, executed in Pompeian fashion. Despite the heated controversy over the origins of Christian art, its beginnings in Rome seem to have been but an application of old, pagan forms and conceptions to a new purpose. We accordingly find the walls strewn with familiar patterns taken over from pagan art. In our Figure 615 walls are represented which are decorated with red garlands and roses strewn about at random, while in the panels framed with yellow, the myth of Cupid and Psyche is depicted. Psyche, a childish figure with butterfly wings dressed in a green garment, is gathering flowers while Love places them in a basket. These figures are symbolic of Divine Love and the Soul. Each wall and arcuated niche is bordered by a bright blue line which contrasts with the creamy yellow ground and the red flowers. Green is used for the garments and a reddish flesh color is common. This painting may be dated at the beginning of the Third Century A.D. Older examples of frescoes in the vault of the long corridor disclose vines heavy with grapes, among which genii and birds were originally painted. Most of these figures were destroyed by barbarians. These ancient decorations were symbolic for the Christian. The vine is one of the most common symbols: *Ego sum vitis, vos palmites.* Additional decorations of geometric designs in red, blue, and brown, containing putti and dolphins as central motives, continued the ornament of the ceiling. Impressionistic landscapes are found among the tomb-decorations.[161] Probably most of the art is symbolic: the fisherman, for example, alludes perhaps to baptism or to Christ's saying: *faciam vos fieri piscatores hominum.* Some scholars, however, reject a symbolic interpretation for the designs.

[160] O. Marucchi, *Roma sotterranea cristiana*, Roma, 1909, I, 77 ff., Pls. X-XVII; *Le Catacombe romane*, 1905; J. Wilpert, *Le Pitture delle catacombe romane*, Roma, 1903; *Die Malereien der Katakomben Roms*, Freiburg, 1903.

[161] Marucchi, *op. cit.*, Pl. XX.

More elaborate floral decorations are to be found in the Fourth Century mosaics of Santa Costanza in Rome.[162] This was probably erected by Constantine as a tomb for his daughters. Here both strewn floral decorations are found and those which approach more nearly the carpet type. In Figure 616, we see the first type in which birds, branches, fruits, flowers, vases, and various other objects are disposed without plan over the ring vault of the Mausoleum. Our example forms a section of the mosaic decoration. In the center is a blue bowl on which doves are perched—a motive recalling the work of Sosos of Pergamon. The mosaic seems in its heterogeneous use of objects to have followed a Hellenistic original in style as well as in subject matter. All kinds of things are found here—drinking-horns, pitchers, pomegranates, a palm, a shell, pine cones, a melon, lemons, figs, doves, peacocks, pheasants, etc. The branches with birds on them occur also in the catacombs. The colors of our mosaic are sober. Against a grayish white ground, blue predominates with green, brown, black, white, orange, red, yellow, gray, and gold. The artist has not aimed at brightness.

In Figure 617 the old vintage scene is repeated but individualized. In the center is a head, probably that of a boy, as there is a trace of a *bulla* left.[163] From the four corners, vine branches spread from an acanthus and wind themselves over almost the entire surface of the panel. Among the richly loaded stems, where birds are perched or flying, wingless putti are engaged in plucking grapes. In two corners, heavily laden carts drawn by oxen are proceeding to the wine-presses where putti are trampling down the grapes. The design seems to be purely decorative, but it has a symbolic meaning. Similar scenes are found in the catacombs and some occur in the Januarius crypt of the Second Century. The design forms an "all-over" pattern similar to the one found at Uthina in Northern Africa and goes back in its beginnings to Hellenistic art. The colors are again predominantly blue against a white ground with the same added colors as in Figure 616.[163a] We might follow the floral style in Dalmatia, Phœnicia, and the Balkans or trace it back to the palace of the Attalids at Pergamon. Enough has been said to show its origin and course of development. In the Fourth Century A.D. we find Hellenistic subject matter and a purely Hellenistic style still flourishing.

Still another portion of the mosaic decoration in the ring vault of Santa Costanza shows its dependence on earlier Greek tradition (Fig. 618). This consists of a series

[162] J. Wilpert, *Die römischen Mosaïken und Malereien der kirchl. Bauten vom IV-XIII Jahr.*, Freiburg, 1917², III, Pl. VII and text, p. 289.

[163] *Cf.* J. Wilpert, *op. cit.*, I, pp. 290-291. The vine is traced by scholars to Syria.

[163a] Gold is not used in this example. The Januarius crypt is in the Catacomb of Prætextatus. See Wilpert, *Pitture*, Pl. 34.

of medallions joined to one another by a braid pattern and decorated with winged putti, Psyches, various kinds of birds, sheep, and a cross-shaped ornament. The figures are mostly blue and brown against a grayish white ground. The braid pattern adds a touch of red, green, and yellowish white. Around the animals is a geometric design in green. This type of ceiling decoration is seen earlier in a fresco from the Stabian baths at Pompeii (Fig. 619). The field in this case is separated into squares where Erotes, floating female figures, birds, and geometric patterns adorn the field.

At the turn of the century, about 200 A.D., belong some newly discovered frescoes, found in Rome near the Porta Maggiore. They have been the subject of much debate. The problem involved is whether the material represented is pagan or Christian. It is possible that the artist who made them may have desired to create this impression in the mind of the spectator viewing them. The interest for us lies partly in the interpretation of the subject matter but also in part in the way in which fresh themes were dressed up in old garments. The paintings in question were discovered in Rome a few years ago in the Viale Manzoni. The tomb is an underground structure, built on several levels, with a rather complicated plan.[164] It was found by workmen who were digging foundations for a garage. They came upon a vault elaborately decorated with paintings. The room was 4.43 meters by 4.93 meters and was connected by stairways with several smaller chambers built of brick and with others hewn in the rock. A floor mosaic bearing an inscription proved that the monument was the tomb of Aurelius Felicissimus and that it was built for his fellow freedmen and for his "fratres." Around the walls were numerous arched niches which originally contained sarcophagi.

In the large vaulted room which we have mentioned, the walls were decorated with eleven standing male figures from 1.04 to 1.13 meter tall, dressed in white tunics with red borders. Over the tunics, white cloaks were worn. Some of the figures have scrolls in their hands, some extend an arm as if addressing an audience. They are barefooted. Were they supposed to represent the twelve Apostles? Paribeni believes them to be our earliest and best examples of Christian art and would accept these figures therefore as apostles. On the other hand, twelve smaller figures were painted in lunettes, but this time, men *and* women are found. Bendinelli, who first published the paintings, seems to feel that the monument was built for members of a Christian

[164] G. Bendinelli, "Ipogeo con pitture scoperto presso il Viale Manzoni," *Not. d. Sc.* (1920), pp. 123-141; Pls. I-IV, Milano, 1920; "Il Monumento sepolcrale degli Aureli al Viale Manzoni in Roma," *Mon. Ant.*, XXVIII (1923), pp. 290 ff., Pls. I-XVII (III, VIII, IX, XI, XIII, in color); R. Paribeni, *Antichissime pitture cristiane a Roma*, Boll. d'arte, 1921; O. Marucchi, *Nuovo Bull. di archeol. crist.*, XXVI (1920), pp. 53 ff.; XXVII (1921), pp. 44 ff., 83 ff.; XXVIII (1922), pp. 1 ff.; 128 ff. M. Rostovtzeff, *Mém. pres. par divers savants à l'Acad. des Inscript. et Belles-Lettres*, XIII (1923), pp. 10 ff., Pl. VI; *Mystic Italy*, N. Y., 1927, pp. 148 ff.

but "heretic" community, arguing this from the representations of the "Twelve Apostles" and the "Good Shepherd."[164a] Whether we interpret the scenes as pagan or Christian, there are obvious difficulties. Lanciani holds that "in the whole set of frescoes we detect the purpose of representing scenes from the gospel in a disguised form, without running the risk of detection by pagan visitors."[165] This interpretation appears wholly plausible. On the other hand, the view recently presented by Styger may be more nearly correct.[166] He argues that much so-called symbolism has been read into Christian monuments and does not really exist. It is quite possible that the Christians in taking over pagan art used its subject matter without very much understanding of the contents. According to Styger the themes echo the usual decoration of Christian interiors of the time. They are narrative subjects with no more symbolic significance than Pompeian decorations. They were the familiar and favorite themes of the early Christians, chosen for their narrative interest.

In the Viale Manzoni frescoes, the figure of the Good Shepherd carrying a ram on his shoulders is represented four times. A pagan would recognize this as an ancient motive. A male figure seated on an elevation has a scroll in his hands. Below him, sheep are pasturing. This is probably Christ on the mount. It partakes, however, of the Orpheus motive.

The large figures of the eleven apostles are of excellent workmanship. Figure 620 illustrates the heads of two of these. They are thoroughly individualized and give the impression of being splendid portraits. They have been interpreted as the apostles Peter and Paul. If this is true, and it seems probable, they are the earliest extant portraits of these apostles although earlier ones must have existed. They are the finest figures in the group of eleven. The faces are painted reddish brown with flecks of white here and there. The hair and beard are also handled impressionistically; the color, in this case, is a grayish yellow. The mantles are white with brownish yellow for shadows and with red borders. The head at the left is a masterful study. The figures stand out in relief from the background which is white.

Quite in contrast to these is a picture of Christ on the mount (Fig. 621). He is seated on a wooded hillside with a scroll in his hand. Below, in a gentle landscape with brown bushes and green trees, sheep are pasturing. The garment worn by Christ is a bluish white. His hair is reddish brown. The composition recalls the scenes with Orpheus as a central figure. The representation of Christ possesses none of the majestic quality which distinguishes the forms of the apostles.

[164a] In the *Mon. Ant.*, Bendinelli leaves the matter open as to whether they were apostles or Old Testament Prophets, but seems to favor the latter idea. He finds little evidence for considering the owners of the tomb members of heretical sects.

[165] R. Lanciani, *Illustrated London News*, Jan. 14, 1922, p. 54.

[166] P. Styger, *Die altchristliche Grabeskunst*, München, 1927. *Cf.* C. R. Morey, *A.J.A.*, XXXII (1928), pp. 138-139.

If the scenes and figures which we have described may possibly be Christian, others offer greater difficulty and appear at times to suggest no explanation in Christian terms. The landscapes are especially problematic. In Figure 622 we have a Hellenistic type of landscape in the upper half of the lunette, above the figures of the apostles. At the top, rustic buildings seen in perspective are placed in the background. Before these, cattle are pasturing and resting, while the donkey at the left has been taken to be an allusion to Christ's entry into Jerusalem. The grounds for this seem fairly slight. Below, a scene occurs which was earlier considered to represent Odysseus and Penelope together with the suitors. It may hold some allusion to the myth of Circe. According to Wilpert,[167] it is the clothing of the naked; the woman is probably Aurelia Prima, the unmarried sister of the owner of the tomb. She is weaving wool for the clothing of the poor. The leading colors are reddish brown for the animals and some of the buildings; white for the ground and for the tunic at the right; flesh color for the figures, and green.

Another Hellenistic landscape has groups of people within a huge colonnaded enclosure while at the right is a fenced-in garden, and, in the middle ground, a road.[168] Another example depicts a city at the right, at whose gate a group of citizens stand welcoming a galloping horseman.[169] He is followed by a crowd of men. These paintings seem to be entirely concerned with local events but they may have had some hidden symbolism. Wilpert decides that they are gnostic but eclectic. He dates them in the time of Septimius Severus and his successors. He interprets the triumphal entry of the horseman into the city as the arrival of the gnostic Epiphanes, a youth seventeen years old and the author of a work, περὶ δικαιοσύνης, which he holds in his hand. The Christian elements in the tomb are difficult to explain away and the more likely interpretation of the frescoes seems to be the one which considers most of them pagan works of art adapted to Christian ends. We must also bear in mind that the artist had no other language to use than the one which had been handed down to him by Hellenistic-Roman art. We may therefore expect the Hellenistic type of landscape when he desires a setting for his scenes and the Orpheus type of representation readily lends itself to the "Good Shepherd" theme. A cross painted green was discovered by Wilpert on the wall of the tomb. This symbol points to a Christian owner.

Another monument recently found six miles from Rome on the Via Triumphalis contains interesting frescoes also dating from the Third Century A.D.[170] It is a sub-

[167] J. Wilpert, *Mem. Acc. Pont.*, I, 1924, Pt. II, pp. 1-43.
[168] Bendinelli, *Mon. Ant.*, XXVIII (1923), Pl. XI (color).
[169] Bendinelli, *op. cit.*, Pl. X.
[170] Patroni, *Rendiconti Lincei*, XXXII (1923), p. 252; G. Bendinelli, *Not. d. Sc.* (1922), pp. 429 ff., Pls. I-II.

terranean tomb which belonged to Octavius Felix (Fig. 623). At the left, Hermes, the guide of souls to the underworld, is signaling to a small chariot drawn by doves in which Eros is represented carrying off the soul of a child. It has been suggested that this is Octavia Paulina who was buried in the tomb. In the center of the scene is a column surmounted by a statue of Hecate. Around it a meadow is depicted in which children are gathering enormous blossoms. In the right foreground, Athena appears in armor. Whether these are the Elysian fields or the upper world is uncertain. It looks as if Hermes were clearing a way for the entry of the soul into the Elysian realms. In another fresco children are playing near a shrine which is indicated by a column with a vase on top of it and a near-by tree. Patroni has suggested that the scene in this tomb represents the game known as the Judgment of Paris. It was played by children in the Elysian fields, each girl becoming Psyche when she had found an Eros.[170] The paintings are executed in tempera.

This painting with its representations of children recalls some frescoes found at Ostia, belonging possibly to the First Century A.D.[170a] They portray in one instance a crowd of children, apparently boys and girls, preparing for a religious procession. In the second example, they are shown engaged in a sacrifice before a statue of Diana. In Figure 624 a group of five are seen at the right, clad in cloaks of green, yellow, violet, and grayish white. They bear baskets of flowers and grapes hanging from T-shaped staffs which are adorned with sculptured heads. A leader appears to be giving directions to the group. At the left, a second company is standing before a statue of Diana with torches uplifted toward her. The scene recalls Horace's hymn of the maidens and boys who sing to Diana and Apollo. There is not a little childish charm about these serious-faced children engaged in their solemn task with quiet earnestness. The background is red; the street, grayish. The second painting from Ostia in which some children with crowns are drawing a cart on which a ship is placed has been variously referred to the Festival of the May and to the *Navigium Isidis*. It doubtless refers to some Roman celebration occurring in spring.

In the Third or Fourth Century a painting from Porta San Sebastiano must be placed which represents Amorini(?) engaged in a chariot-race (Fig. 625). It may have belonged to the tomb of a child. In a lunette, a chariot-race conducted by putti drawn in bigæ is found. At the top, on the right, the driver lashes a pair of reddish brown mules. Before him is a chariot drawn by two antelopes(?), while in the foreground a third contestant driving two yellow tigers looks back to see if his opponents are approaching. The fourth chariot is nonchalantly driven along, drawn by two yellow panthers. In the center is a *spina* composed of reddish brown bushes. The motive of chariots guided by Loves is an old Hellenistic conception. There may be

---

[170a] *Cf.* M. Rostovtzeff, *A History of the Ancient World, II, Rome,* Oxford, 1927, Pl. LVII, p. 267. *Cf. Mystic Italy,* p. 170, note 19, for bibliography.

an allusion to the pleasures allotted to shades of children in the other world. The scene is full of vivacity and movement.

A series of paintings from Tor Marancio preserves reminiscences of the dignity belonging to Fifth Century monumental figures combined with a certain sentimentality.[171] They offer studies of some of the famous women of antiquity who came to grief through passionate and unlawful love affairs. Among those coming down to us are Pasiphaë, Phædra, Kanake, Myrrha, and Scylla. Medea or Byblis was once thought to have been portrayed. The paintings were found in 1817 in an ancient villa, near the Porta San Sebastiano. According to the inscriptions inscribed upon them they must be dated in the Third Century. The finest examples are Pasiphaë (Fig. 626) and Scylla. Pasiphaë is represented in passionate contemplation, standing beside the cow which Dædalus fashioned for her. The artist is especially interested in the study of mood and expression. This predilection is excellently handled in the figure of Scylla. She is pictured beside the city wall of Megara with the lock of her father Nisos in her hand. She is considering the betrayal of the city into the power of her lover, Minos. The desperation of her passion is clearly seen in her face. The colors used on Pasiphaë have suffered greatly but the grayish blue chiton can still be distinguished. The outlines are a reddish tint. The paintings reveal a certain Hellenistic sentimentality and foreshadow the decline of the art. In addition to these heroines, a number of dancing figures found on the same site are published by Nogara (*op. cit.*, Pls. 38-42).

In a house discovered in 1887 on the Cælian Hill, under the Church of SS. Giovanni e Paolo, there were found some pagan and Christian frescoes dating between the Second and the Fourth Centuries A.D.[172] On the shore of the sea a goddess is seen, resting on a rock. She is probably Thetis, though some have called her Venus. Beside her is one of her sisters, a Nereid, while the bronzed youth on the right may be interpreted as Dionysos. On the water, which is inhabited by frisking dolphins, boats are guided by putti. The color is still well preserved. The dimensions of this fresco are the greatest of any paintings left to us from ancient Rome. On the ceiling of the large room was a vintage scene. Among the vines, which grow from acanthus leaves in the four corners of the room, putti are busy. Examples of marble incrustation cover the

[171] B. Nogara, *Le Nozze Aldobrandine*, Milano, 1907; *Ausonia*, I (1906), pp. 51 ff.

[172] Padre Germano di S. Stanislao, "The House of the Martyrs John and Paul," *A.J.A.*, VII (1891), pp. 31 ff.; *La Casa celimontana*, Roma, 1894; G. Gatti, *Bull. Comun.* (1902), pp. 163 ff. Eugénie Strong, *Art in Ancient Rome*, 1928, II, p. 129, Fig. 443. *Cf.* O. Wulff, *Altchrist. und byz. Kunst*, I, 59, Fig. 47; p. 87, Fig. 68. J. Wilpert, *Die römisch. Mosaïken und Malereien*, Freiburg, 1917, II, 631 ff.; IV, Pls. 126-129; 131, 215, 1 (color); P. Marconi, *La Pittura dei Romani*, Roma, 1929, pp. 106-107, Figs. 144-145. Wilpert states that all of the rooms are done in fresco. This is correct and the view of Padre Germano that they are encaustic paintings is to be rejected.

walls up to the painted decoration. Figure 627 depicts a frieze from this house which recalls the type of ornamentation first found in Rome in the Augustan age in the Columbarium of Pomponius Hylas.[172a] Several genii wearing green or red mantles appear between large ducks, peacocks, and other birds, before a creamy white ground hung with gaily colored garlands. The painting is fresco, not encaustic. The work has been executed impressionistically. The figures of the genii are a reddish brown; the ground on which they stand is green. In the Tablinum, the walls are painted to imitate marble panels of the isodomic style. On the vaulted ceiling are marine monsters, flowers, masks, and several Christian subjects: In contrast to the paintings of the genii which date in the Second Century, these later frescoes belong to the Fourth or Fifth Century. One of the most interesting of the mural decorations is found in the so-called Oratory of Pammachius. The beheading of three martyrs is pictured here—the earliest extant representation of a martyrdom (O. Wulff, *Altchristliche und byz. Kunst,* I, 1914, Fig. 68). The victims are blindfolded and have their hands bound behind their backs. Pompeian technique and subject matter are combined in this house with Christian themes.[172b]

Recent excavations in the columbaria and tombs under San Sebastiano have revealed paintings and stucco reliefs belonging to the First and Second Centuries A.D.[173] These tombs which were adapted for inhumation burials before the end of the Second Century have remarkably beautiful decorations in the form of stucco reliefs. In one of them is a peacock in a shell-like niche, while in another the ceiling is covered with a vine branch laden with grapes and with delicately woven tendrils (Fig. 628). The paintings commonly depict floral patterns with birds; birds in heraldic composition on either side of a vase with fruits, and hastily executed figure patterns of insignificant value. A neighboring building of the middle of the Second Century A.D. was decorated with paintings which figure a seaport.

Numerous remains in the provinces, especially in the field of mosaic, should be mentioned from this period, particularly those of Britain, Gaul, and Belgium. In addition to the mosaics which we have discussed from Northern Africa, there are paintings at Sousse, el-Djem, Gigthis, and additional sites. Rostovtzeff has compiled a bibliography of this provincial material, much of which is found in publications difficult of access to scholars.[174] New tombs of the Second and Third Centuries A.D.

---

[172a] The Columbarium of Livia on the Appian Way is perhaps earlier.

[172b] Wilpert dates the fresco of the Genii in the Fourth Century; of Thetis, in the Second; of the Christian subjects, in the Fourth. *Cf. op. cit.,* Pl. 131 (color).

[173] Paolo Styger, *Il Monumento apostolico della Via Appia secondo gli ultimi scavi della Basilica di San Sebastiano,* Roma, 1917; O. Marucchi, *Bull. Com.,* 43 (1916), pp. 249-278; *Nuov. bull. arch. crist.,* 27, 1-14, 6 Pls.; A. Profumo, *Studi romani,* II (1916), pp. 415 ff.; G. Mancini, *Not. d. Sc.* (1923), pp. 53 ff., Pls. X-XVIII.

[174] M. Rostovtzeff, *J.H.S.,* 39 (1919), pp. 157-159.

are constantly coming to light. Shear publishes one from Sardis, decorated with the familiar garlands, peacocks, baskets of fruits, flowers, vines, and birds.[175] At Gargaresh in Tripoli, an excellent tomb of the Fourth Century has been discovered.[176] The more important of the two niches has a portrait-medallion in the center, supported by female figures garbed in green and rose "Dalmatian" tunics. Above this design were winged figures holding a crown; below, quadrigæ engaged in a race. At either side of the main designs were candle-bearers in long tunics. The paintings are entirely pagan but may be symbolic. Allusions to the cult of Mithras occur. The portrait of the dead woman, Ælia Arisuth, a Semite or Phœnician, is excellent, possessing a certain elegance and dignity. It is not greatly inferior to some examples from the Fayûm.

It is impossible to enumerate the many paintings dating from the Christian era which have come to light in recent years, especially in Rome and other parts of Italy, in Egypt, and in Northern Africa and Sicily. Some interesting paintings found at Corinth in the chambers of the spring of Peirene will shortly appear in the Corinth Publication. They belong to two periods. The earlier ones present garlands on a yellow ocher ground and belong to the Roman refounding of the city in 46 B.C. Some walls are decorated with conventionalized flowers which grow erect, rising almost to the top of the wall. The second and more interesting group belongs to a period of redecoration in the Second Century A.D. At this time, the earlier paintings were covered over with black paint. A coat of dark blue was then laid over this backing, which formed a ground for marine designs with red borders. Here were pictured lobsters, an eel, a cuttlefish, oyster shells and various sea animals. A wainscoting of dark green extended to the floor below these designs. The paintings were executed in tempera and waxed. They have been copied by Mr. Prentice Duell who was good enough to give me advance information in regard to them.

The Alexandrian Catacombs should also be mentioned.[176a] In style, they are similar to the Roman examples, but they show a much fresher illusionism and a greater ability to combine figures with surroundings. The frescoes outside Alexandria are poor and decadent and reveal attempts to copy Syrian style. Examples may be seen at el-Bagawat, dating from the Fifth Century.

A very fine group of paintings has recently been found in an apse-shaped room on

[175] T. L. Shear, "A Roman Chamber-Tomb at Sardis," A.J.A., 31 (1927), pp. 19-25, Pls. III-VI (Pl. IV, color).

[176] P. Romanelli, "Tomba romana con affreschi del IV secolo dopo Cristo nella regione di Gargáresh (Tripoli)," Notiziario Archeologico, III (1922), pp. 21-32.

[176a] O. M. Dalton, B.A.&A., pp. 282 ff. (bibliogr.); Bull. di arch. crist., 1865; O. Wulff, op. cit., I, 93 ff.; Bock, Matér., p. s. à l'archéol. de l'Égypte chrét., 1901; J. P. Richter, Expedition Sieglin, Ausgrabungen in Alexandria, 1908, pp. 30 ff.; G. Pinza, N. Bull. di arch. crist., 1901, pp. 6 ff. (Cagliari). A. M. Lythgoe, Bull. Metrop. Mus., New York, 1908, pp. 203 ff.

the Via Salaria in Rome, in the necropolis there. It was probably used for some religious purpose, apparently by Christians.[177] The structure dates in the age of Constantine. One room contains a deep basin with an apse-like end and a vault. The basin was a spring-house, in all probability, as there is a mouth opening into it below the niche. The wall of the apse imitates Numidian marble below and is painted above. At the top, a kantharos is represented with birds painted on either side. The field is adorned with birds and flowers. At the left of the niche, a spirited figure of Diana is seen striding through a wooded landscape with a stag and a deer leaping to right and left of her. She resembles Diana of Versailles in her pose and in her short garment. She wears a crown of laurel, and is depicted bow in hand, drawing an arrow from her quiver. To the right of the niche a nymph, apparently her companion, is playing with a deer. The paintings probably belong to the Fourth Century. The painter was an accomplished master of light and shadow. Diana wears a short red chiton, and a flying rose mantle. The chiton of the nymph is also red. The flood of light which surrounds Diana and lights up the woods is an unusually fine achievement in ancient art.

Some excellent mosaics have also been discovered in a Roman villa at Zliten in Tripoli near the border of Tunis.[178] The author inclines to date them in the First Century A.D. The most significant example which decorated a room opening from a long corridor consists of a central section of colored marbles inlaid in eight squares with geometric patterns, alternating with eight circles where fish, eels, and various sea animals are executed in mosaic. The richly polychromatic pavement gives some conception of the wealth and splendor of North African villas. The border around this section is, however, more important for the art and life of the times. Gladiatorial combats are represented in mosaic—red, yellow, green, gray, lavender, and rose predominating in the color scheme. The scenes are depicted with great truth to life. On the north and south sides of the room gladiators are seen fighting in their native costumes and armor; on the east and west sides were *venationes*, or beast hunts, and scenes of torture. One example of particular cruelty depicts the *damnatio ad bestias*. Prisoners fastened upright in small wagons are being wheeled into the arena where they are attacked by lions and panthers. The orchestra is present: two musicians play horns; one has a tuba and a woman is performing at a water-organ. The bier on which the dead were carried out is not forgotten. The mosaic is particularly inter-

[177] R. Paribeni, *Not. d. Sc.* (1923), pp. 380 ff., Pls. I-III; *cf.* K. Lehmann-Hartleben, *Arch. Anz.*, 41 (1926), pp. 98 ff.; J. Wilpert, *Atti Pont. Acc. Rom. d. Arch. Rend.*, II (1923-1924), pp. 57-82.

[178] S. Aurigemma, "Mosaico con scene d'anfiteatro in una villa romana a Zliten in Tripolitania," *Dedalo*, IV (1923-1924), pp. 333-361 (color plate); pp. 397-414; V (1924), pp. 197-217 (color plate); *I Mosaici di Zliten*, 1926; "In a Roman Villa at Zliten," *Art and Archæology*, 23 (1927), pp. 161-169.

esting because of the types of gladiators represented: Samnites with their typical costumes; Thracian fencers; Murmillones with bell-shaped helmets. Yellow-skinned Garamantes are tortured. One scene depicts an ostrich hunt. The appeal for mercy by the victim to the editor of the games is a common motive in the mosaic.

A second mosaic decorated in the carpet style with floral volutes growing from acanthus leaves, and with birds and animals on the branches and blossoms, calls to mind the Ara Pacis. Aurigemma dates this in the Augustan age, but the sea monsters around the destroyed central disc suggest a later period.

The practice of illuminating books with pictures was an old Egyptian custom. We have seen some examples from the Book of the Dead belonging to the Eighteenth and later dynasties (Figs. 78-79). These richly colored illustrations for books were taken over by Hellenistic Greece and gradually spread over the Greek world. Vellum was invented by Eumenes II, King of Pergamon from 197 to 159 B.C., but the first reference to an illuminated vellum manuscript comes from Martial in the First Century A.D. A Vergil written on vellum and inscribed as a gift by Martial bore a portrait of Vergil.[179] This book is lost, but one of the few examples of manuscript illustration from classical times is a Vergil which contains a portrait of the poet.[180] This is a work belonging somewhere between the Fourth and Sixth Centuries A.D. The portrait occurs three times and presents a serious-minded, almost melancholy figure of the writer, seated with a *capsa* at the right and a bookstand at the left (Fig. 629).

But three illuminated manuscripts of classical age are extant, the two Vatican Vergils and the Iliad in Milan. It is doubtful, as Mr. Herbert points out, whether there was ever any very great fondness for illuminated books among the Romans.[181] This art implies a miniature technique which was alien to the temperament of the Roman, who cared usually for things on a large and imposing scale. Among the extant manuscripts, the First Vatican Vergil, by its dexterous technique, gives evidence of being a representative of a well-developed school of illumination.[182] It now contains fifty miniatures, some full page, others smaller. Black, red, and white bands frame the pictures, which were apparently painted by three different hands. One of the most skilful artists was the illustrator of the Georgics (Fig. 630). He was

---

[179] Martial, Epigram XIV, 186.          [180] Cod. Vat. Lat. 3867 (Codex Romanus).

[181] J. A. Herbert, *Illuminated Manuscripts*, London, 1912², pp. 1-35. I have drawn my account of manuscripts largely from his chapter on Classical Manuscripts. On book illumination in antiquity, see H. Gerstinger, *Die griechische Buchmalerei*, Wien, 1926; Th. Birt, *Die Buchrolle in der Kunst*, Leipzig, 1907, pp. 269 ff.; O. Wulff, *Altchrist. und byz. Kunst*, Berlin, 1914, I, 280 ff. (Bibliography, p. 306).

[182] Pierre de Nolhac, "Le Virgile du Vatican," *Notices et extraits*, XXXV, Pt. II (1897), pp. 683-791; *Fragmenta et Picturæ Vergiliana Codicis Vaticani*, 3225, Rome, 1899 (*Codices e Vaticanis selecti phototypice expressi*, Vol. I); Venturi, *Storia*, I, 311 ff.; Nolhac, "Les Peintures des MSS. de Virgile," *Mél. d'arch. et d'hist.* (1884), p. 305 (on colors).

able to design a landscape with great freedom, to represent space and perspective plausibly, making use of aërial as well as of linear perspective. He did not outline his figures, which melt into the background. He handles trees and flowers impressionistically and lays his pigments on in thick layers. The colors are rich and deep. Flesh tones are red, following Pompeian wall-painting. Trees are dark green. The manuscript is dated on paleographic grounds in the Fourth Century. The painting is done in tempera. White of egg was probably used as a medium. The background is carefully colored to give effects of light and distance. The colors which are graded into one another are: blue, green, rose (horizon) gray, yellow and green (foreground).

The Second Vatican Vergil, sometimes called the Codex Romanus, is distinctly inferior in execution to the First. The manuscript is much more nearly complete but contains only nineteen miniatures, bordered by gold and red. The sad portrait of Vergil illustrated above is from this manuscript. The artist was not a very gifted individual. His drawings of the Eclogues are so childish that they seem almost like parodies of the scenes and were considered such by Wickhoff (Fig. 631). He makes use once more of outlines which, in this case, are very heavy in character. He does not know well how to render space and appears on the point of reverting to the old pseudo-perspective found in the beginning and in the decline of painting. We see here the decadence and breaking up of the impressionistic manner and the beginning of a return to linear technique. Two shepherds are shown, one engaged in piping, another resting on his crook beside his flock. The idyllic atmosphere is well caught. The execution of the animals and flowers is extremely naïve, but very decorative. It reminds one of a tapestry.

In addition to the Vergil manuscripts, there is also extant an illuminated Iliad in the Ambrosian Library at Milan.[183] This had originally two hundred and forty miniatures of which fifty-eight survive. A certain largeness of style suggests that these small paintings may have been copied from Græco-Roman mural paintings of the Augustan age, which are now lost. The work is uneven and has childish conventions, such as a walled space containing six soldiers to represent Troy. On the other hand, individual figures are often good, e.g., Thetis, Apollo, Night, etc. The gods wear colored nimbi—Zeus, a purple one; Aphrodite, green; others, blue. The paintings are much stained and worn. Colors employed include: white, blue, green, yellow, purple, and much red. The compositions are framed in red and blue. The manuscript dates in the Fourth or Fifth Century.

Furthermore, we have a series of illustrated manuscripts of the Comedies of Terence dating from the Ninth and later centuries.[184] The best one is the Ninth

[183] *Homeri Iliadis pictæ fragmenta Ambrosiana phototypice edita*, Milan, 1905.

[184] E. Bethe, *Terentius. Codex Ambrosianus H 75 inf. phototypice editus*, Leyden, 1903 (De Vries, *Codices Græci et Latini*, Vol. VIII); J. Van Wageningen, *Album Terentianum*,

Century Vatican example, No. 3868. At the beginning is a portrait of Terence with two actors in comic masks. There follows an *œdicula,* or architectural frame, with masks of the characters arranged in shelf-like fashion. One also finds illustrated scenes from the comedies themselves in which the actors are violently and angrily gesticulating (Fig. 632). The poses and methods of rendering drapery are ancient and have been taken over into later art. This Ninth Century example copies, seemingly with a good deal of fidelity, a classical tradition. The figures, in their proportions, movement, and costumes, remind one of figures in the Vienna Genesis. The painting is executed in thick tempera. To judge from the style, the archetype was probably a manuscript dating from the Fourth Century. That it is not later seems likely because of the strong illusionistic tradition evident in the omission of contours on the lighted side of the figures.

Morey has recently studied the Vatican Terence and the other Terence manuscripts with the idea of making a Terentian Corpus of the miniatures and presenting a discussion of their styles.[185] In his examination of the Vatican manuscript, he discovered the signature of the miniaturist, Adelricus. In Fol. 3, in the *œdicula* containing the masks of the Andria, on the raking cornice of the pediment, the following words were found at the left: *Miserere mei Ds se . . .* (probably to be restored as *secundum magnam misericordiam tuam*). At the right was the signature, *Adelricus me fecit.* As the list of monks at Corvey contains the names of Aldricus and of a certain Hrodgarius who signs the Vatican manuscript, as the scribe, at the end of the Phormio, together with the name of the Abbot Warinus (826-856) and his predecessor, the date and provenance of the manuscript are established with certainty.

Morey believes that the Vatican Terence (C) was copied from a manuscript illustrated by a Greek painter of the Asia Minor School.[185] This Asiatic school produced the miniatures of the Vienna Genesis, of the Gospel of Rossano, and of the fragment of Matthew from Sinope. He dates the original between the Vienna Genesis (Fourth

Groningæ, 1907; O. Engelhardt, *Die Illustrationen der Terenzhandschriften,* Jena (Diss.) (1905); J. C. Watson, "The Relation of the Scene-Headings to the Miniatures in Manuscripts of Terence," *Harvard Studies,* XIV (1903), pp. 55-172. K. E. Weston, "The Illustrated Terence Manuscripts," *Harvard Studies,* XIV (1903), pp. 37-54; L. Webber Jones, "The Archetypes of the Terence Miniatures," *Art Bulletin,* X (1927), pp. 103-120. A photographic corpus of Terentian Miniatures is in preparation by C. R. Morey and L. Webber Jones. The text will discuss the complex problems of miniature style. Martin Schanz, Carl Hosius, *Gesch. der röm. Literatur,*[4] 1927, I, 123; E. Bethe, *Jahr.,* XVIII (1903), pp. 93 ff. "It is not impossible that the medallion portrait of the poet, Terence, in a Carolingian MS. in the Bibliothèque Nationale is directly descended from some contemporary *imago clipeata,*" Eugénie Strong, *Art in Ancient Rome,* I, 65. H. Omont, *Comédies repr. des 151 dess. du Ms. lat. de la Bibl. Nat.,* Paris, 1907.

[185] C. R. Morey, "The Signature of the Miniaturist of the Vatican Terence," *B.P.W.,* 46 (1926), pp. 879-880. *Cf. Rendiconti Pontific. Accad. Romana di Archeologia,* 1925-1926, for the date of the archetype of C. *Class. Weekly,* 20 (1926-1927), p. 154.

or Fifth Century) and the Gospels of Rossano and Sinope (Sixth Century). The archetype of the Vatican Terence, therefore, was illustrated in the Fifth Century.[185a]

The Vatican Terence is the most complete of the manuscripts of Terence. It contains all of the six comedies in their entirety and is illustrated throughout with colored miniatures. These miniatures are found at the opening of each scene. The coloring is as follows: brown and yellow for the architectural frames; tunics of slaves, bluish to grayish white, with orange or brown scarfs often thrown over the shoulder; the tunics of the young men, brownish red or blue; for other male characters, yellow. The garments of the women are red and green. The style is essentially a plastic Greek style based on line, with some illusionistic additions such as the suppression of the contours on the lighted side. The lively gesticulations add animation.

In addition to these books, we possess a late copy of an illustrated calendar, dating from the Seventeenth Century, but supposedly copying a Ninth Century manuscript which, in turn, is thought to have copied a lost Fourth Century original.[186] The great interest in these calendars lies in the fact that the figures of the months are forerunners of calendar pictures prefixed to Psalters and Books of Hours in the Middle Ages and that they give us some vague idea of the classical examples.

A detailed study of the catacomb paintings would lead us too far afield. Suffice it to say that we have a large body of material from Rome, Sicily, Alexandria, Naples, and other sites illustrating this subject. Some of these have been admirably published.[187] Wilpert's volumes on mosaics deal with Christian Hellenistic art. The church took over the subject matter and technique from pagan decoration and in these works we see the decay of the classical manner. Christian art is the last flowering of the antique. A study of the monuments reveals a steady decline in the paintings, although, as Von Marle points out, there was added a strong human appeal which was foreign to pagan art and which was essentially Christian. In the first place, the artist was far less careful in preparing the ground for his work, so that the whole creation is often technically poor. Feeling for form sinks to a very low level. The use of the impressionistic method tends toward rough sketching, and because no real knowledge of form lay behind this, we get little work that is of artistic merit. In fact, the catacombs have been more extensively studied by historians or by those

---

[185a] The archetype of the group to which the Vatican MS. belongs dated from the Fifth Century but the archetype of all of the extant illustrated Terence MSS. belonged to the Fourth Century.

[186] J. Strzygowski, *Die Calenderbilder des Chronographen vom Jahre 354*, Berlin, 1888, *Jahr. Ergänzungsheft I.*

[187] G. B. de Rossi, *Roma sotterranea cristiana*, 1864-1877; J. Wilpert, *Le Pitture delle catacombe romane*, Roma, 1903; *Die Malereien der Katakomben Roms*, Freiburg, 1903; *Die römischen Mosaïken und Malereien*, 2d ed., Freiburg, 1917; O. Marucchi, *Roma sotterranea cristiana*, Roma, 1909-1914.

interested in the Church than by students of art. For the latter, they are of importance as the continuation of a great tradition. It is especially interesting to follow in these monuments the decline and breaking up of the impressionistic manner. Good examples of this technique may be found in the First Century in the catacombs of Domitilla,[188] in the Third Century in those of SS. Pietro and Marcellino,[189] and in the second half of the Fourth, in the Domitilla monument.[190] In these works, we see a gradual substitution of contour for the rendering of form by color contrast and a general decay in composition.

The word catacomb means "depressions." The name came from the region along the Appian Way not far from San Sebastiano, where the Christians buried their dead. Because of their belief in the resurrection of the body, they did not, like the Romans, burn the bodies of the dead. A very complicated system of underground galleries with *loculi* or niches designed to receive sarcophagi or corpses thus arose. Some six hundred and fifteen acres of these structures exist, often above one another. If the subterranean passages were arranged in a continuous line, they would extend for about five hundred and forty-five miles. These burial places originally belonged to certain prominent Roman families but were afterward taken over by the church and were used as common burial sites.

The ceilings and upper walls of the catacombs were adorned with paintings. These were executed by artisans, who were often Greeks. They were painted hastily and follow the conventions of earlier works. The old scheme used for the ceiling decoration in pagan monuments appears. A circle is found in the center of the roof, with four radiating medallions at the ends of the vertical axes, in each of which is a simple figure. A panel occurs between each pair of these medallions.[191] The oldest ceilings are adorned like Roman tombs with putti, garlands, birds, vineyard scenes, candelabra, etc. The ceiling of the Domitilla Catacomb illustrates this.[192] Even in the Second and Third Centuries, when religious subjects assume prominence, the old pagan motives hold their place. One finds sea animals and monsters, amoretti, Priapus, dolphins with tridents, and Oceanus. In the drawing of the drapery and in the poses and movements of the figures, ancient schemata are followed. In the Catacomb of St. Callixtus of the Fourth Century, there is a room of Oceanus, so called from the head of the god in a panel of the ceiling (Fig. 633). He is symbolic of a renewal of life beyond. The peacock on the walls was the classical symbol for Apotheosis from the days of Antoninus Pius. The socle represents the enclosure of Paradise. Figure 634 from the same catacomb gives a picture of five blessed mortals each in the position of an *orans*, with the hands upheld in prayer. Over the field, birds and branches

[188] J. Wilpert, *Le Pitture*, Pl. 6.          [189] J. Wilpert, *ibid.*, Pl. 94.
[190] J. Wilpert, *ibid.*, Pl. 231.
[191] J. Wilpert, *ibid.*, Pl. 61, Catacomb of SS. Pietro and Marcellino.
[192] J. Wilpert, *ibid.*, Pls. 1-5.

are strewn and the peacock appears again. Below, the old Hellenistic motive of doves drinking from a vase harks back to Sosos of Pergamon. Some examples, such as the Good Shepherd in a mountainous landscape with goats and sheep, point also to Hellenistic prototypes (Fig. 635). The type of background employed here was seen earlier in Roman villa landscapes (Fig. 548). The animals are symbolic. The symbolism of Christian art is a study in itself.[193] In addition to the pagan symbols, there are purely Christian examples, such as the anchor, fish, and cross. The colors employed form a very limited scale—often consisting merely of red, green, and yellow on a white ground. Frequently the plaster alone furnishes the background. Against this, the paintings are placed in the fresco technique with incised preliminary drawing. The older the work, the better the ground, and the more careful the painting, as a rule.

In his illuminating discussion of the sources of Mediæval style, Professor Morey has pointed out the fact that Hellenistic art is not a unit from the First Century B.C., but divides into two distinct currents, one of which centered in Athens and expanded later to Asia Minor; the other arising in Alexandria, took root in Italy.[194] He follows the two styles from their beginnings into Mediæval times. The Neo-Attic style is traced from Athens to the shores of Asia Minor, especially in the Sidamara sarcophagi which date from the Second to the Fourth Centuries A.D. Characteristics of this Neo-Attic style are the two-dimensional figures and a neutral background, or, if a formal background was demanded, an architectural one, *before* which the figures are placed. The style is followed to Cappadocia, Syria, and Mesopotamia. In the latter regions it became the Asiatic style. The illuminated manuscripts of Asia Minor and Syria illustrate this later stage. The Codex Rossanensis, the Matthew fragment from Sinope, and the Vienna Genesis are typical of the Asiatic style, except that the Vienna Genesis has an added touch of illusionism due to the Alexandrian original from which it was copied. In the Asiatic style, which differs from the Neo-Attic in the Oriental influence which emanated from Mesopotamia, natural forms are employed decoratively as to composition, and color is used decoratively and not for modeling. This style passed in the Sixth Century from the East to Coptic Egypt. We find it in Ravenna, in Milan, in the Church of St. Lawrence, in the Basilica of Parenzo. It tended toward abstract representation and decorative design.

In contrast to the Asiatic style is the Alexandrian. It has two tendencies: (a) the Neo-Attic, academic trend, illustrated by works like "Perseus freeing Andromeda"

---

[193] V. Macchioro, "Il Simbolismo nelle figurazioni sepolcrali romane," *Mem. della R. Accad. d. Arch.*, I² (1908), pp. 9-143; *cf.* P. Styger, *Die altchristliche Grabeskunst*, München, 1927. R. Eisler, *op. cit.*, pp. 112 ff., 334 ff., holds that the fish and cross are Dionysiac symbols. *Vs.* this *J.H.S.*, 48 (1928), p. 100.

[194] C. R. Morey, "The Sources of Mediæval Style," *Art Bulletin*, VII (1924-1925), pp. 35-50.

(Fig. 449); and (b), the popular, or Latin style, observable in the Odyssey land-scapes. The characteristic of the popular style was an interest in realistic repre-sentation which turned strongly toward illusionism. Color is employed to gain the illusion of form. This illusionistic style was the prevailing style in Italy for the first three centuries of our era. It probably came from Alexandria, but had more dignity there in the figure style and more limitations in space effects than in Italy. It may be followed from the Fourth Century on in the Joshua Roll and in the Paris Psalter.

An example of the persistence of this tradition in Christian art has been pointed out in Santa Maria Maggiore and other early churches. The problems connected with the decoration of Santa Maria Maggiore are so many and have evoked such voluminous discussion that we are unable to enter into them in detail.[195] Suffice it to say that in the apse are mosaics which represent a river scene with genii which are considered ancient by Ainalov, while others disagree with him. The mosaics of the nave are very old and point to an early date, not later than the Fifth Century. Dis-agreement arises, however, as to whether the arch decorations can be as early as those of the nave because the former are dogmatic in character and introduce versions of early Christian art that are divergent in type from the familiarly known examples. The biblical pictures in the nave seem to many more antique in character. Richter, Ainalov, and Venturi all consider the pictures of the nave and arch con-temporary. Richter would date them in the Second or Third Century, feeling that the work is better in quality than Fifth Century work and must be attributed to the Golden Age of Classic Christian art. He notes the symbolic tendencies of the whole as well. He sees in many details possible inspiration of the Christian East.

Whatever the date of the mosaics—and they probably were not executed before the Fifth Century—the artists were still working in the impressionistic manner. In the "Separation of Lot from Abraham" (Richter, op. cit., Pl. 8, color), the white garments of the patriarchs are shot with yellow, blue, and green. The flesh tones of the faces are of many colors, with white patches for high lights. In the "Marriage of Moses," the head of Jethro has flesh tones modeled in bluish, red, and lilac shades (Richter, op. cit., Pl. 16, color). A very lifelike effect is produced. The landscape backgrounds are purely antique, as is the anatomy of many of the nude figures. The latter remind one at times of the boxers in the mosaic from the Baths of Caracalla (Fig. 640).

Recently Miss Avery has pointed out the continuance of this illusionistic tradition in Santa Maria Antiqua in a Seventh Century painting of an angel which belonged to an Annunciation scene.[196] She shows that the second of the five layers of decora-

---

[195] J. P. Richter and A. Cameron Taylor, *The Golden Age of Classic Christian Art*, London, 1904. J. Wilpert, *Röm. Mosaïken*, I, 412 ff.

[196] M. Avery, "The Alexandrian Style at Santa Maria Antiqua, Rome," *Art Bulletin*, VII (1924-1925), pp. 131 ff., Pls. 89-90. J. Wilpert, *Röm. Mosaïken*, Pls. 133, 135.

tion which are traceable is Greek, and is an intrusion from outside into the normal development of art in Rome from the Sixth to the Eighth Centuries. The style possesses illusionistic qualities and the painting has Greek inscriptions. This and certain other frescoes were the work of Alexandrian artists driven out of Egypt by Arab conquerors. The style was, however, short-lived and was soon replaced by the Italo-Asiatic style of the early Middle Ages.

At the beginning of the Christian era, then, two styles appear which are to become the Greek and Latin styles of the Middle Ages, *viz.:* the Neo-Attic-Asiatic and the Alexandrian-Latin. We have discussed the Latin style in the paintings of the catacombs. It may be traced in manuscripts of the Fourth Century and in mosaics.

The Oriental products of Early Christian art are rare compared with those of Rome and inferior in quality. They appear much like provincial examples of an art whose center was elsewhere. In all probability, the Christians in these regions took their models from their local predecessors. A center like Dura gives an idea of the pagan decoration which was adopted by the early Christians. This older Christian art declined and made way for the art of Byzantium. The elements that united to form the Byzantine style were once more from Hellenistic sources—the Neo-Attic-Asiatic manner of Asia Minor and the illusionism of Alexandria.[197]

[197] D. Ainalov, *Die hellenistischen Grundlagen der byzantinisch. Kunst,* Petrograd (Russian), 1900. *Cf.* O. Wulff, *Repertorium für Kunstwiss.,* XXVI (1903), pp. 34 ff.

# XI

# THE TECHNICAL METHODS AND THE PIGMENTS EMPLOYED IN ANCIENT PAINTING

THE ancients used the fresco, tempera, and encaustic methods of painting. Oil painting was not employed by them. Where modern painters would work in oil, the ancients had recourse to wax and developed the encaustic technique. Two different processes for decorating walls are mentioned by Vitruvius—painting on wet lime, and painting on a dry ground necessarily with some binding medium.[1] The former method was thought to be the more durable. Pliny tells us that the encaustic process was not suitable for painting on walls.

We shall consider first, painting on *wet* lime, or *al fresco*. The term, *fresco*, was unknown in ancient times and seems to have been first used in the Fourteenth Century. It refers to painting *"on the fresh"* plaster. Pliny used the expression, *illinere udo*. The method employed consisted in laying pigments mixed with water on wet lime plaster. These pigments were necessarily limited to those compatible with lime and were mostly earth colors.[2] The walls were usually prepared with great care. As a rule, several layers of plaster were applied which were faced with a fine lime stucco above. Vitruvius advocates at least three layers of sand mortar and three of powdered marble, together with a thorough polishing of the surface. While the plaster ground was still wet, colors mixed in water were put on the wall. No binding medium was necessary. The chemical action of the lime bound the pigments fast. The disadvantage of this method was the necessity for keeping the plaster wet,

[1] Vitr., *De Arch.*, VII, 3, 5 ff.; *cf*. Pliny, *N.H.*, 35, 30-50, esp. 49. *Cf*. 35, 123.
[2] *Cf*. Pliny, *N.H.*, 35, 49; *cf*. A. Eibner, *Entwicklung und Werkstoffe der Wandmalerei vom Altertum bis zur Neuzeit*, München, 1926, pp. 178 ff., 479 ff.

although, as Laurie points out, it was not essential to paint immediately after the application of the last coat of plaster because the thickness of the bed caused the moisture to be held for some time.[3] Furthermore, it was always possible to dampen the wall by sprinkling, or by means of wet cloths. As a result of the action of the lime, the surface presented was not entirely smooth but appears uneven and rough.

The earliest examples of true fresco known today belong to the Cretan-Mycenæan group of paintings. At least the mural decorations in Crete have usually been considered frescoes, in view of the researches of Heaton.[4] Recently, however, some difference of opinion seems to have arisen.[5] As a result of his own investigations and of the work of others, Eibner has concluded that a fresco technique was employed in some paintings from Tiryns and in those from Thebes, but that the paintings from Knossos, Mycenæ, and some from Tiryns show several processes. These processes were: (a) *fresco secco,* or painting with colors mixed with lime water on dry plaster; (b) lime *fresco,* or true fresco painting on wet walls with pigments mixed in water; (c) colors put on with lime or gypsum in a lime-gypsum technique; and (d) a lime and milk process. Eibner finds traces of a sticky, organic substance in most of the fragments examined. This, in his opinion, points to a binding medium and hence to painting *al secco,* usually on a lime ground. The reception of Eibner's results in this field will be awaited with interest.

The presence of organic matter is not proof that an organic medium like glue or egg was used, as Laurie has shown.[6] "Such organic matter may be present accidentally in the original material, may form part of one of the pigments, as, for instance, a pigment prepared from murex or madder, or may have soaked into the buried plaster surface."

With regard to the mixing of colors with lime water, or *fresco secco,* Heaton admits that this was sometimes done, but only as a supplementary device. When colors are placed either on a moist or dry surface by this method, "they are neatly *superposed* on one another and a section shows clean, flat layers. The pigments of the Minoan frescoes are *interfused* and often spread beneath the wet stucco surface."[7] This is characteristic of a pure *fresco* method. Probably the painter often had recourse to the *fresco secco* process when the walls dried before the completion of

---

[3] A. P. Laurie, *Greek and Roman Methods of Painting,* Cambridge, 1910, pp. 83 ff., *cf.* pp. 71 ff.

[4] Noel Heaton, *Tiryns II, Die Ergebnisse der Ausgrabungen des Inst., Kaiserlich Deutsch. Arch. Inst. in Athen,* 1912, pp. 211-217; Sir Arthur J. Evans, *The Palace of Minos,* 1921, I, 528, 534 ff.; G. Rodenwaldt, *Tiryns,* 1912, II, 205 ff.

[5] A. Eibner, *op. cit.,* München, 1926, pp. 58 ff., 107 ff., 289, 109-113, 479. Eibner places the true origins of fresco work in Egypt in the New Kingdom when the gypsum ground was replaced by a lime ground, *op. cit.,* p. 289.

[6] A. P. Laurie, *op. cit.,* p. 94.    [7] Sir Arthur J. Evans, *Palace of Minos,* 1921, I, 535, n. 3.

his task, or, as Eibner suggests, he often finished in *secco* a work begun in *fresco*. On the other hand, Eibner found organic substances, which favor the acceptance of a *tempera* process, at times "in such quantities as have never appeared in Roman-Campanian wall stucco." He denies the possibility of infiltration in the plaster. These substances were found both in the plaster and in the color layer. Eibner grants the presence of the *fresco* method in Crete, but contends that there were several processes and mixed ones. He would probably, from his evidence, consider the *secco* method with a binding medium the most common one.

The Cretan paintings are often executed on a white or a yellow ground. The earliest examples are on red. One of the recently discovered "Partridge" frescoes from Knossos is painted on a black ground. Sometimes two or more colors were combined, and red and blue, red and yellow, and yellow and blue grounds appear, in horizontal stripes separated by wavy black bands. In the late Cretan and early Mycenæan periods, a blue wall-ground becomes the rule. The outline played an important part in early Cretan and in Mycenæan work, always as the boundary of a colored surface, never as an independent line. It is sometimes red, sometimes yellow. The Knossian painters avoided black contour lines in large paintings, even in the case of overlapping arms and hands. Here yellow is found. In some of the late frescoes from Tiryns, however, especially in the deer hunt, there are heavy, black contour lines.[7a]

The Etruscan tomb-paintings are usually held to be true frescoes.[8] They often present this method in a primitive form, the colors being applied directly to the limestone walls without any layer of plaster. This is especially the case at Chiusi. Frequently the walls of Etruscan tombs are wet with moisture and have remained so from Etruscan times until today. The paintings at Corneto are executed for the most part on a thin coat of sand and lime, the nature of the walls demanding a coating and the presence of moisture not calling for a thick plaster bed. The painting layer is scarcely more than one centimeter thick, in contrast to the seven or eight centimeters found at Pompeii. Painting directly on the rock is the exception at Corneto. As a rule, the grounds are painted yellow. Most of the better tombs, if not all, have incisions preceding the preliminary painting. The drawing is usually delineated in red line. The anatomy of all of the figures and the garments were frequently painted

[7a] G. Rodenwaldt, *Tiryns II*, pp. 209, 182.

[8] O. Donner von Richter, in W. Helbig, *Wandgemälde Campaniens*, 1868, *Einl.; Technische Mitth. für Malerei*, Sept., 1903; G. Perrot and C. Chipiez, *Histoire de l'art*, IX, 208; F. Weege, *Etruskische Malerei*, Ch. VII. *Vs.* fresco method, E. Berger, *Maltechnik des Altertums*, 1904; E. Raehlmann, *Über die Maltechnik der Alten*, Berlin, 1910 (Organic substances in plaster). See also, Donner, in *Bullettino dell'Inst. di corrispondenza arch.*, 1869, pp. 201 ff. (Etruria). The above references deal in part with the subject of fresco work in general.

in red. The walls in most of the tombs were thus originally covered with a complete outline decoration in red. The colors applied *en bloc* concealed this preliminary sketching. The last stage in the painting was to outline in black the more important elements of the decoration. This black outline often changed and corrected the preliminary drawing. The plaster was smoothed but not polished.

We have been discussing ancient painting on a *wet* ground. This appears at times in a modified form, colors mixed with lime water being applied to the *dry* plaster. This, as has been said, is termed *fresco secco*. It is quite possible that such a method was used in prehistoric times in the cave-paintings, although no evidence for this has been discovered. The paintings at Altamira lie directly on the natural rock which is of limestone. Limestone is also found in the caves of France, so that the accidental discovery of the possibilities of *fresco secco* may be granted as probable, because of the presence of limestone. The cave man may have found that colors mixed with water would adhere to these walls, especially if the cave walls were damp. Our present evidence, however, points to a *secco* process in the execution of these paintings. We shall consider this problem later.

The fresco method was undoubtedly current at Pompeii, but great variety of opinion prevails among scholars as to the technical processes employed in Campanian painting. Donner has established the fact that fresco was very extensively used there, and that details were often added *al secco, i.e.,* on dry plaster, with the aid of a binding medium. Today there are many advocates of a more general use of *secco* painting in these mural decorations. The great problems are: (1) the possible presence of organic matter in the chemical analyses: Laurie claims that the presence of such matter does not prove the existence of a binding medium or argue for *secco* painting; (2) the problem of the coloring of the upper layer of plaster, which certainly was solidly colored in some cases; this, however, does not necessitate a belief that all Pompeian painting was colored in the uppermost layer in a mass; (3) the problem of the presence of wax: Berger contends that all Pompeian paintings were done with a medium of wax and soda. This, according to Laurie, is not mentioned by ancient writers and is disproved by analysis.

The important thing to be noted is that there was no uniformity in the execution of the Pompeian wall-paintings and several processes were often combined in the same painting, just as we find Cennini ordering work to be painted in *fresco* and finished in *tempera* with a binding medium. It is known that certain organic pigments mentioned by Vitruvius are incompatible with a lime technique. The physical properties of the pigments must therefore, to a great extent, have determined the process employed, although the medium played a certain rôle as well.

The results at which Raehlmann arrived in his miscroscopic and chemical analyses of Pompeian wall-paintings are especially interesting.[8] He found that the upper layer of stucco was always colored in a mass.[8a] This was done so that the optic effects of one color working through another might be taken advantage of. For example, a brownish red wall showed a coat of red paint placed over a layer of black. Sometimes the stucco layer was rose, brown, or gray, with red above, producing different shades of red. By putting these colors in layers above one another the artist avoided the necessity of mixing them on the palette. They were not joined by any binding sections. In the pigments that formed the upper coat Raehlmann found that the green, brown, blue, and, in most instances, the red colors, were not put on *al fresco*. On the other hand, yellow, black, and some reds were executed in the fresco process. This indicates that in the case of brown, green, blue, and certain red pigments the physical properties of the colors were unsuitable for use on lime plaster. Egyptian blue is a case in point and its failure to work well in fresco may explain its absence from the palette of Greece in Polygnotan days. Certain colors like the Egyptian blue did not mix well with earth colors and stood out too much from the ground. They probably did not lend themselves well to the polishing of the fresco wall because of their rough, frit-like character. In Crete, these surfaces were smoothed, not polished. Pigments unsuitable in fresco painting had to be put on by a *secco* or *tempera* process with the aid of a binding medium. In all wall pigments Raehlmann found combustible substances which indicate the presence of organic matter in the colors. When burned, these substances gave forth an odor. This also suggests a binding medium like egg white, glue, etc. The great problem therefore is whether these paintings which reveal organic substances can be frescoes. Raehlmann concludes that the greater part of the Pompeian paintings are not frescoes; most scholars, Eibner among the latest, would accept the view of Donner that the majority are frescoes. Certain colors incompatible with the lime ground in fresco and unsuited by their roughness to wall-smoothing demanded the *tempera* method. This fact was understood in ancient Egypt, where fresco does not seem to have been used, at least, to any extent.[8b] The method was certainly unsuited to a hot country, as the plaster would dry too rapidly. The most interesting discovery of Raehlmann is the presence of

[8a] F. Gerlich, *N.J.*, 21 (1908), p. 140 and Note 4, argues that the upper layer in Pompeian paintings could not have been colored in a mass. He cites as proof the experiment of the painter Böcklin, in which black was mixed with the final layer of the plaster and turned almost white. Modern painters, however, often color the upper layer of stucco in a mass. In order that the color may not turn white, the lime is slaked for some time—even for months.

[8b] A. Eibner, *op. cit.*, pp. 52 ff., 289, 539. The germs of fresco painting are present in Egypt in the New Kingdom when a lime ground was introduced. On this the artist usually painted in a *tempera* process, *i.e.*, on a dry ground with the aid of a binding medium, which was not lime. The upper layer of stucco was often colored in a mass and a coat of another color was placed over it for optic effects. This *secco* painting on a lime ground with a binding medium was further developed in Roman-Campanian painting, according to Eibner.

under-painting in the colored layers. Pliny gives some evidence for painting in layers in his discussion of the way in which to obtain shades of red and purple.[9]

The colored, superposed layers occurred in the more important rooms of Pompeian houses, whereas in the less prominent places the remains of color were on walls of one layer. Here the stucco was poorer, with little admixture of marble and resembled our sand mortar. The process in these cases was *al fresco*. This cheaper and debased stucco is found in the Roman Empire. Above the colored layers in Pompeian paintings was a shining coat which contained no lime and which was not put on by the fresco method. This is the equivalent of a modern varnish. The medium in which the pigments were placed was usually powdered pumice stone. The binding material varied with different colors. Egg white and glue are commonly found. The Pompeian paintings reveal, then, the presence of the combined *fresco* and *tempera* processes. In the opinion of most scholars, fresco predominated.

After the time of the Pompeian-Roman paintings, the next frescoes found are those in the Christian catacombs. The work here was hastily and poorly executed. As a rule, the earlier the paintings, the better the execution. Only one layer of plaster is found in the late catacombs of the Third Century, instead of the six of mortar and marble stucco advocated by Vitruvius. The wall-grounds are white with rare instances of yellow or red (Wilpert, *op. cit.*, Pl. 16). In the early catacombs, the outlines of the figures are often incised; later they were painted with the brush. The impressionistic method employed did not demand contour lines and they are often absent. Eibner states that the walls give the impression of lime painting—either lime *secco,* or lime *fresco,* or the two combined.

In the work of the Egyptian wall-painters, fresco was the exception. Prisse mentions possible instances, but there is little evidence for fresco.[10] The Amarna pavements, earlier considered examples of fresco work, are now, as a result of recent discoveries, thought to be *a tempera*. Eibner discusses the beginnings of fresco.[11] The Egyptian colors were usually applied to a dry wall with a medium which seems to have been size, gum, or glue. These pigments were easily sponged off. On the other hand, certain paintings resisted water. In such cases, wax was probably used.[12]

Egyptian paintings were often applied directly to a ground of Nile mud, especially in the earliest period. In the Old Kingdom, unburned gypsum was used as a ground,

[9] Pliny, *N.H.*, 35, 45; 33, 90-91. I owe the references to Miss Milne.

[10] Prisse d'Avennes, *Histoire de l'art égyptien*, Paris, 1878. *Cf.* Eibner, *op. cit.*, p. 289.

[11] A. Eibner, *op. cit.*, pp. 48 ff., 55 ff., *cf.* p. 577 (Tomb of Tutankhamen). On the technique of the floor-painting at Amarna, see also F. von Bissing, Max Reach; *Annales du Service des Ant. de l'Égypte,* VII (1906), pp. 64-70. Egyptian artists while working with a lime ground, renounced the use of lime hydrate as a natural binding medium. The method used is not lime *secco* or lime *fresco,* according to Eibner.

[12] A. P. Laurie, *op. cit.*, p. 107. *Materials of the Painter's Craft in Europe and Egypt,* London and Edinburgh, 1910, pp. 21 ff.; *Archæologia,* 64 (1913), pp. 315-335.

and the upper surface was smoothed. Some superposed layers occur, as later in Pompeii, *e.g.*, a blue under layer, with a thin gray-green color above, passing into violet. The upper surface here was also smoothed. This painting contained an organic binding medium and was executed in tempera on the dry plaster. Later paintings reveal the presence of gypsum grounds combined with lime.

In the New Kingdom, lime plaster is generally found, but the method employed is not *al fresco*. As late as 1200 B.C. German investigators have traced the optically refined layer technique in Egyptian painting and a continued use of a tempera process, even on lime. Violet is customary for wall-grounds in the New Kingdom— "a bequest of hoary antiquity"—but golden yellow is also found, enriched by a coat of varnish.

Egyptian paintings are our best examples of the tempera process and maintain a long tradition in this technique. The pigments employed have already been mentioned in Ch. II, pp. 40 ff.

In Egypt we also find painting directly on stone without the addition of a stucco layer. This anticipates the later polychrome painting on architecture in Greece.

The cave-paintings of France and Spain are placed for the most part directly on the limestone walls. The binding medium for these so-called "frescoes" is not certainly known, as no adequate chemical investigations seem to have been made. Certain occurrences of a fatty substance on the rough palettes that have been discovered indicate that the binding material was sometimes animal fat. The process is therefore not *fresco*. Balsams, plant saps, milk, and blood serum were doubtless also used as binding mediums. There is no certain evidence as to whether the walls were smoothed or not. Contour lines were very significant in the earlier stages of the paintings. They were often incised. Where color occurs, they are black or red. In the final stage partial contour lines occur, or sometimes none at all, and modeling was achieved by smearing the pigments.

Although many examples of wall-painting existed in the Orient, little is known about them. There is no certainty as to the technical methods employed. Some scholars mention *tempera*. Glazed tiles appear to have played a far greater part in the field of Oriental decoration than actual wall-painting. In Greece, Apelles and the great easel-painters must have painted in a tempera method.

The technical methods employed by the Greek painter, Polygnotos, are much debated and obscure. Several processes were probably used by him. Mention is made of wax painting in connection with his work. It is doubtful whether he used this extensively, as Pausias and later painters developed this method. That Polygnotos painted on walls is a known fact.[13] In these cases, following the practice current

[13] Paus., IX, 4, 2, Temple of Athena Areia at Platæa, *cf*. Pliny, 35, 123. Pausias, the encaustic painter, was unable to restore the paintings at Thespiæ because he was working

earlier in Crete, Mycenæ, and Etruria, the process was probably *al fresco,* although this cannot be proved. Some scholars believe that these works were painted directly on the marble walls, much as grave stelæ were decorated.[14] That panels were used by Polygnotos is obvious from the fact that evidence for the insertion of panels is found in the Pinacotheca of the Propylæa.[14a] We know that these panels must have

in a *method that was not his own.* They were therefore not done in encaustic. *Cf.* Paus., I, 17, 3 (Sanctuary of Theseus, by Mikon). *Cf.* Lucian, *Imag.,* 23; Pliny, *N.H.,* 35, 122.

[14] C. Robert, "Marathonschlacht," p. 104 (XVIII *Hall. Winckelmannsprogr.*); "Nekyia," p. 37 (XVI *Hall. Winckelmannsprogr.*).

[14a] Prof. W. B. Dinsmoor of Columbia University has been kind enough to send me some notes on wooden walls and the painting of Polygnotos, which will later be incorporated into his "Periclean Architects" or "Propylæa":

"We have actual traces of walls lined with wood in the Old Propylon of the Acropolis, where, above the bench, dado, and belt course which line the interior, all constructed in Pentelic marble, the upper part of the wall now shows only backing courses of poros limestone, 0.36 m. behind the face of the wall. The belt course, only 0.086 m. high, runs back into a horizontal groove in the backing wall and is so weak that it could not have carried a heavy superstructure. And in fact the top of the belt course, while unfinished and therefore concealed, is not smoothed sufficiently to form a bed for a stone facing; and on it is a socket 0.028 m. deep and apparently 0.205 m. square, 0.08 m. behind the face of the wall. This socket must have contained the bottom of a vertical timber or stud, of which there would have been a series placed at intervals in the wall, the intervals being filled with mud brick and forming a half-timbered construction. The fact that this vertical studding is recessed 0.08 m. behind the wall face allows room for horizontal planks of this thickness or more probably slightly less, and these in turn would undoubtedly have been painted; the presence of the belt course suggests mural decoration, as in the Pinakotheke of the later Propylæa. And it was probably to these wooden walls of the Old Propylon that the few conservative citizens of Athens applied the ambiguous Delphic utterance concerning wooden walls on the occasion of the Persian invasion of 480 B.C., and it was here that they were slain.

"The Old Propylon, its upper parts destroyed and its lower marble portions calcined and reddened by fire, was restored practically to its original state after 479 B.C. The construction with wooden wall linings must have been reproduced, and these must have been adorned with new paintings, while the dado and belt course, instead of being left in the natural white of the marble, were so injured that they were painted red. It is probable that Polygnotus, now the leading painter at Athens, was responsible for the mural decorations in the restored Propylon; for the wooden panels (*pinakes*) from his hand, later exhibited in the Pinakotheke of the Propylaea, would most appropriately have been sawn out from the walls of the earlier structure on the same spot. It has sometimes been assumed, to be sure, that the paintings seen by Pausanias in the Pinakotheke were actually painted on the marble walls; and the fact that these marble walls with their black belt course were undoubtedly designed for mural paintings (imitating the wooden walls of the Propylon) has further confused the issue, leading even to such absurd theories as that the Pinakotheke, in order to receive wall paintings from the hand of Polygnotus, must have been erected earlier than the rest of the Propylaea. But it is apparent that the walls of the Pinakotheke, while intended for mural paintings, were never so employed, since they still retain their projecting preliminary surface with the open joints which would necessarily have been filled with stucco (of which there are been constructed of wood; marble would be too heavy. Their arrangement is also a complicated problem. Körte thinks that they were placed in rows above one another in frieze fashion; that the composition was like that of the tomb at Gjölbaschi-Trysa[15] (Fig. 366). If they were painted on wooden panels, they were probably easel-pictures and were executed *a tempera*. As far as we are able, then, to form any opinion of the work of Polygnotos, we can probably say that he appears to have painted for the most part *on walls* in the *fresco* method;[16] that, on occasion, he painted on panels, which were probably of wood; the evidence for this method is found in the Pinacotheca. These paintings were probably done in the *tempera* process, with a binding medium like egg or glue. Lastly, he sometimes used encaustic, probably more or less as an experiment.[17]

The third process developed by the ancients was wax painting, which began as early as the middle of the Fifth Century with Polygnotos. This was termed *encaustic,* which means a "burning-in" process.[18] As a matter of fact the method seems to have been rather one of the application of heat to the panels and to the metal instruments used in working the wax than of a "burning-in" process, although the latter may be thought of in the case of painting on marble.

We have cited the passages in which the ancients discuss this method and have shown that there were three methods: (1) painting on panels of wood with the aid of a brush and a heated *cauterium,* or spoonlike instrument for spreading the wax; (2) painting on ivory or marble with a pointed *cestrum* or burin which incised the design before the color was laid on, probably mixed with heated wax; (3) painting on wood, linen, or marble with a brush. The wax process probably arose in Egypt. There the medium could be easily handled, and the wax could be kept soft with ease. The first Greek painter who became famous for the encaustic process was Pausias. His works were small and prove the labored character of the method. The great advantage of the process lay in the richness and depth of color which were obtained by the juxtaposition of various tones and by the relief of the pigments with their pronounced shadows. It was wholly unsuited for extensive surfaces. Pliny tells us that it was not adapted to wall-painting.[19]

no traces) in order to obtain a smooth surface. It is evident, therefore, that the *pinakes* in the Pinakotheke were panel pictures taken from other sources; and with such an explanation we may easily comprehend how it included a collection of 'old masters,' some antedating the building itself."

[15] G. Körte, *Jahr.,* 31 (1916), p. 283.

[16] *Cf.* J. G. Frazer, *Paus.,* 1898, II, 136 ff.; A. P. Laurie, *Greek and Roman Methods of Painting,* p. 49.

[17] Pliny, *N.H.,* 35, 122.

[18] Pliny, *N.H.,* 35, 149; 122; *cf.* 35, 49; 36, 189; Vitr., VII, 9, 3.

[19] Pliny, *N.H.,* 35, 49; Laurie, *Greek and Roman Methods of Painting,* Cambridge, 1910, p. 55.

The process of painting in wax was essentially one in which colors mixed with wax were applied to panels of wood, ivory, marble, or sometimes linen. The question is whether they were applied in a fluid state or were laid on warm and afterwards worked with a hot instrument. Both methods were probably used. Wax was easily kept in a fluid state in southern countries. In the North, it had to be heated and the panel kept warm. In the Egyptian portraits from the Fayûm, backgrounds and garments were often put on with a brush dipped in fluid wax, while facial details were executed by means of a *cauterium* or small branding iron with which the colored sticks of wax were modeled on the panel. A painted sarcophagus from Kertch gives a representation of an encaustic painter, apparently at work on funeral portraits. He is seated before a brazier heating his instruments (Fig. 636).

Extant examples of the encaustic method are to be seen today in the mummy-portraits from Egypt and in the grave stelæ from Pagasæ, in Thessaly. Panel paintings from Sinai indicate that the technique was still in use as late as the Ninth or Tenth Century A.D.[20] Greek painting on marble was sometimes done in the encaustic method with a brush, especially in the case of façades. Sometimes a thin lime layer was used and painting in tempera was employed with glue as a binding medium.[21]

The colors employed in antiquity have been discussed in detail by Pliny and Vitruvius.[22] First of all, the ancients used earth colors, such as red ochers or clays, terre verte, a green earth, and yellow ochers, including sienna—a dirty yellow—and umber. Yellow ochers were roasted to form brown and red. Vitruvius says that the best red earth came from Sinope and the best green from Smyrna. Cinnabar, or vermilion red, the native sulphide of mercury and orpiment, the native sulphide of arsenic, appeared in the painter's palette, the latter forming an unusually beautiful yellow.

Among artificial pigments, white lead, red lead, yellow oxide of lead, verdigris, or copper with vinegar applied, lampblack, black from burnt ivory, charcoal, and bone black were all in use. Blue was a carbonate of copper. It was made by fusing copper, sand, and soda. Vitruvius gives a receipt for making blue.[23] When heated to a certain degree under certain conditions, the carbonate of copper formed green. Malachite green, or raw copper ore, was also employed as early as the predynastic period in Egypt.

In addition to these earth and mineral colors, pigments were made from vegetable and animal dyes, *i.e.*, from the purple dye of the murex and from vegetable coloring matters, such as madder and indigo. Woad and kermes were well-known dyes.

[20] O. M. Dalton, *Byzantine Art and Archæology*, Oxford, 1911, pp. 316-317. Ainalov, *Encaustic Religious Paintings from Sinai*, V.V. 1902, pp. 343 ff.

[21] A. Eibner, *op. cit.*, pp. 69 ff.; cf. pp. 539, 598 ff.

[22] Pliny, *N.H.*, 33, 158-163; 111 (minium); 35, 30-50; 33, 86 ff.; Vitr., VII, 7-14.

[23] Vitr., VII, 11.

Kermes was a red color made from the bodies of insects. Dyes such as kermes were made into lakes, *i.e.*, they were put on a chalk base and were used with a binding medium. Madder, for example, mixed with chalk, gives turkey red, rose, pink, etc. These lakes came in in Hellenistic times. They are not found in early Egypt. Woad was a blue dye. The palette formed by these dyes made from vegetable and animal matter gave the pastel shades so familiar in Hellenistic vases of the Canosa class.

Laurie points out that few modifications have been made in modern times from the very complete palette which the ancient painter possessed. The only one which can be regarded as an improvement is the introduction of ultramarine. When lapis lazuli took the place of Egyptian blue is not certainly known. Egyptian blue was apparently an expensive color and wherever it appears in Greek and Roman times some opulence is evident.

Of the media used by the ancients, such as gum, size, glue, and the white or yolk of egg, the latter probably protected and preserved the pigments best. Where vermilion was exposed to sunlight, they varnished it with wax. Atramentum was apparently a black which was employed as a varnish.[24] Pliny says that it exudes from the earth like the brine of salt pits. This was apparently some form of bitumen and was what Apelles used. Vitruvius confines the word to lampblack and charcoal black.

We have not spoken of the technique of mosaics, which played a secondary rôle in antiquity to paintings executed with pigments. Oftentimes mosaics are of historical importance where paintings fail us: for example, the Alexander mosaic from Pompeii. *Musivum opus*, as mosaic was technically called, from the Greek word, μουσεῖον, an artificial grotto which was often decorated with mosaics, developed in the East.[25] Examples of it are found in ivories from Nineveh and in the capitals of columns and in wall tiles from Egypt. It was extensively employed by the Ptolemies but early examples are known in Greece at Olympia and at Pergamon, as we have seen. In the Orient it was used for pavements and for walls. The mosaic from Delos picturing Dionysos mounted on a tiger is executed in the impressionistic manner, following Alexandrian methods of painting.[26] It illustrates late Hellenistic work. The street scene of Dioskourides (Fig. 445) shows that Pompeian examples were sometimes done in this fashion, following the same tradition.

Examples from 1-100 A.D. are strongly under Egyptian influence and abound in Nilotic motives (*cf.* Fig. 503). We find walls and floors at Pompeii and Rome decorated with mosaic, from the last century of the Republic until the age of the Antonines. Pavements in which the designs were formed of small, regularly shaped

[24] Vitr., VII, 10; Pliny, *N.H.*, 35, 41-43; 97. *Cf.* A. Eibner, *op. cit.*, pp. 174-175. This black demanded an organic binding medium. See Laurie, *op. cit.*, pp. 24, 34.

[25] P. Gauckler, *Musivum opus* in Daremberg and Saglio, *Dict. des Ant.* J. H. Middleton, H. Stuart Jones, *Enc. Brit., s.v. Mosaic.*

[26] M. Bulard, *Mon. Piot*, XIV (1908), Pls. XIII and XV (color).

cubes of marble or stone were known as *opus tessellatum*. If the bed was made of pounded brick and lime, the name *opus signinum* was given to the type. *Opus vermiculatum* implies the employment of "worm-shaped" pieces which were long, narrow, and sinuous. The material used for the *tesseræ* in the First Century was mainly marble from Greece or Luna, less frequently limestone or schist. Brick was almost never used. The range of color thus was limited to red, yellow, olive, black, and white.[26a]

In the age of the Antonines and of the Severi, the art seems to have grown popular and to have spread to the provinces. The glass mosaics are almost all lost. The cubes were probably brought from Egypt. Gold was used as well. Very fine mosaics occur at Timgad. In an example from Tunis (Fig. 637) we have a charming villa scene with the pleasure house of the owner, and trees and birds set into a trim little landscape. The third dimension is badly handled. Other good examples occur in the Marriage of Admetus and Alcestis at Nîmes; in the mosaic of *bestiarii* from Nennig near Trier, and in the better known example from Trier made by Monnus (Fig. 638). Here we see the Muse Euterpe giving instruction in the art of flute-playing. In the center are Calliope and Homer. The months form an outer border in panels. Portraits of Ennius and Hesiod are found, of Livy, Vergil, and Cicero. The mosaic dates from the middle of the Third Century A.D. It bears the inscription *Monnus fecit*. More famous is the portrait of Vergil from Susa in Northern Africa[27] (Fig. 639). Here, the poet is represented seated in the act of composing the Æneid. On his lap is a papyrus roll with the words:

*Musa mihi causas memora quo numine læso*
*Quidve . . .*

The head is strongly individualized. The eyes are dreamy, the cheek bones prominent. He looks the tubercular type that he was. He wears a white toga with a blue stripe. At the left, Clio, the Muse of History, reads from a scroll. She is dressed in a green tunic and yellow mantle. At the right is Melpomene, the Muse of Tragedy, holding a tragic mask. Her theatrical-looking costume is red with gold patterns and she wears a greenish blue mantle. The background of the mosaic is white and the picture is framed in red, white, and brownish black. A second mosaic illustrates the parting of Æneas and Dido. These two monuments date in the First Century A.D. The cubes are of marble and glass paste.[27a]

Other good specimens of mosaics have come from the floor of the Baths of Cara-

[26a] On *opus sectile*, see A. Nesbitt, *Archæologia*, XLV (1880), pp. 267 ff., Pls. XVII-XX (color). On mosaics in Britain, see *Archæologia, Index, s.v. Mosaic, Pavements*.

[27] P. Gauckler, "Les Mosaïques Virgiliennes de Sousse," *Mon. Piot*, IV (1897), pp. 233 ff., Pl. 20 (color).

[27a] A. Schulten, *Arch. Anz.*, 1899, p. 70, dates the Vergil in the middle of the Second Century on the basis of the writing.

calla (Fig. 640). In this period, the figure subjects grow rarer and the panels, which are common, are framed by elaborate ornamental patterns. Here, the guilloche is employed. Twenty-three athletes are represented, of life size; of twenty-six others, the heads alone occur.[27b] Some hold prizes in their hands, such as palms and wreaths. Others, as our example here, are ready for the sport in which they are to engage. The boxer in this case wears the *cestus* bound about his arms. Some hold the discus or spear. Gymnasiarchs, or trainers, also appear. One is seen here wearing a mantle. In the upper panel, *halteres* or jumping weights and the palm of victory are represented. The athletes have a barbarian look. Our artist has faithfully reproduced the types and has emphasized in true Roman fashion the muscular details. The work is rough and not very pleasing from the decorative point of view. The inscriptions prove that the mosaic belongs to the Fourth Century and was laid down after the erection of the building.

Other mosaics have been found in various parts of France and Britain.[28] Some of our finest examples come from Northern Africa as has been shown. The tendency of the latest group is more and more toward abstract pattern. The age of Constantine, however, seems to adhere to the earlier Greek traditions. The mosaics of Santa Costanza very closely resemble works like those found at Uthina, which preserve a Hellenistic tradition. In general, the historical treatment superseded the symbolical. We have discussed the mosaics of Saint Maria Maggiore, which probably date from the Fifth Century and which continued the impressionistic method. The subject may be followed in Dalton.[29] Mosaic technique had a further development in the East where artists preferred to decorate walls and vaults rather than floors. It became one of the dominant interests of Byzantine painters. The gold and blue splendor of much Byzantine work is no inheritance from the West.

The technical processes employed in making a Roman floor were as follows: a rough bed of rubble and lime six or eight inches deep was placed above the ground of earth which had been made firm by ramming. Over this composite layer a second layer of pounded brick and lime was placed—four to six inches deep. Above this was a cement bed of powdered marble and lime. In this lime stucco, the cubes were fastened.[29a] The making of walls, of vaults, and of apses was more complicated. Glass was much used in the later Roman Empire and in Byzantine work.

[27b] This is true of the mosaic in its present state. When it was found, there were forty-five full-length figures and thirty-seven others, including fragmentary ones.

[28] S. Lysons, *Roman Antiquities of Woodchester*, 1797; *Reliquiæ Britannico-Romanæ*, 1813; T. Ashby, *Archæologia*, LVIII (1902), pp. 119 ff., Pls. 10, 11 (Cærwent); cf. Wilmowsky, *Römische Mosaïken aus Trier und dessen Umgegend*, 1888. W. H. St. John Hope, George E. Fox, *Archæologia*, 55 (1896), pp. 215 ff., Pls. X, XI-XV, color (Silchester).

[29] O. M. Dalton, *Byzantine Art and Archæology*, Oxford, 1911, Ch. VI.

[29a] Vitruvius distinguishes: (1) a *statumen* or layer of stones the size of one's hand; (2) a *rudus* of broken stone and lime; (3) a *nucleus* of pounded tile mixed with lime.

## CONCLUSION

THE ancient Greeks and Romans in their experiments with painting grasped most of the secrets of the art known to moderns. Had not their civilization declined, we can believe that they might have attained to the heights achieved by modern painting. Their progress was a long and slow one, with each step carefully and solidly planted in the footprints of experience. Much time was spent in learning to draw and beauty of draughtsmanship was long of more importance than color. When finally problems of chiaroscuro were mastered, the artists became adepts in true painting. Form, however, was always of more interest than color even in the Hellenistic age, so that the artist rarely, if ever, subordinated his figures to his background. He allowed the setting to be a mere "theater drop." It remained for the Romans to take up the illusionism which the Greeks had begun and to develop impressionism in the modern sense; to produce effects of unlimited space and more realistic landscapes. Nature, however, was never caught in her momentary moods; twilights, storms, mists, and clouded skies were not attempted. Landscape remained typical and did not often interpret a fixed locality or a certain hour. In landscape, then, the moderns have far surpassed most things attempted by the Roman. In light effects as well, the ancient painter seems never to have obtained the subtlety of modern work. He did not seek for the delicate transitions found in modern painting. He did not arrive at a complete fusion of various planes, but, by a free arrangement of figures in space and by impressionistic handling of single objects, he was able to give the desired illusion of figures in a tridimensional setting.

Greek painting remained an intellectual art until the Hellenistic age. At that time an emotional element dominated the work. The lofty and ennobled subject matter of the Fifth Century was rejected in favor of the realistic, the trivial, the ugly, the bizarre, or the pretty. The whimsicality of a decadent age held the boards. At this time, the various kinds of paintings were developed which have become the stock in trade of painters today: still-life, genre scenes, animal paintings, landscapes, and portraits. Roman art went even further with these and added historical painting with geographic and topographic details. This was to culminate in works like the column of Trajan.

The decorative style of painting invented in the Augustan age was taken up again before the fall of Pompeii and developed into the fantastic style which Nero's age adopted and turned into arabesque decoration. The influence of this manner on Renaissance artists has been very pronounced. It became the basis of many works of art of the Second and Third Centuries. This style influenced the artists in the catacombs.

The trends of Hellenistic art in the late period form an interesting study. The sources of Mediæval style are to be traced back to it, as has been shown. On one side, it developed from Alexandria into the Latin style with pronounced illusionism. It penetrated the catacombs and illustrated manuscripts. The makers of the mosaics of Saint Maria Maggiore were still working in the impressionistic manner in the Fifth Century A.D. In the separation of Abraham from Lot, the white garments of the patriarchs are cut up into yellow, green, and blue parts. The flesh color of the faces consists of many tones with white patches for high lights. On the other hand, the Neo-Attic style, proceeding East, became the Asiatic style with emphasis on colorism. It reappeared in Byzantine art and in illuminated manuscripts as well. This unbroken tradition lasts from the First Century B.C. to the Ninth and Tenth Centuries A.D. Many studies are now being made to trace the Greek tradition from antiquity into later times. A very interesting one has been undertaken by Friend in his search for the primitive types of the Evangelist portraits in the Gospels.[30] He finds that the standing type of evangelist was current as early as the Fifth Century and goes back to Alexandria. The figures are placed against a neutral background. On the other hand, the seated type, which is placed before an architectural background "that looks like a clumsy attempt to represent the stage front of an ancient theater," originated in Ephesos. They are the poet and philosopher types of antiquity. Other studies dealing with architectural and landscape backgrounds will be welcomed by classical students. The bridge from the Antique to Mediæval times is daily becoming strengthened.

[30] A. M. Friend, *The Portraits of the Evangelists in Greek and Latin Manuscripts, Art Studies*, 1927, pp. 115-147. For a further study of the survival of the antique into later times, see Friend, *Art Studies*, 1929, on the continuance of stage backgrounds in Mediæval MSS.

# BIBLIOGRAPHY

## CAVE-PAINTINGS AND PRIMITIVE ART

FOR a more complete bibliography, see Burkitt, *Prehistory*, pp. 322-332; Osborn, *Men of the Old Stone Age*, 3d edition, 1922, pp. 527-546. More popular works are marked with one star (*), illustrations with two (**). Many standard works such as those of Breuil also have illustrations.

BÉGOUEN, COUNT, The Magic Origin of Prehistoric Art, Antiquity, March, 1929, pp. 5-19.

*BOAS, F., Primitive Art, Oslo, 1927.

**BREUIL, H. (L'Abbé) (with L. Capitan and D. Peyrony), La Caverne de Font-de-Gaume aux Eyzies, Monaco, 1910.

—— **(with E. Cartailhac), La Caverne d'Altamira à Santillane près Santander, Monaco, 1906.

—— (with Alcalde Del Rio and Père Sierra), Les Cavernes de la région cantabrique, Monaco, 1912.

—— Deux roches peintes néolithiques espagnoles, I.P.E.K. (1926), II, pp. 229-235.

—— Gravures rupestres du désert Libyque identiques à celles des anciens Bushmen, L'Anthropol., 36 (1926), pp. 125-127.

—— L'Anthropologie, 1909-1912 (Spanish Paintings).

BREUIL, H., BURKITT, M. C., POLLOCK, SIR MONTAGU, Rock Paintings of Southern Andalusia, Oxford, 1929.

*BROWN, G. BALDWIN, Burlington Magazine, 29 (1916), pp. 66-73, Prehistoric Art; *ib.*, 41 (1922), pp. 91 ff., The Origin and Early History of the Arts in Relation to Æsthetic Theory in General; *ib.*, 41 (1922), p. 134.

—— *The Art of the Cave Dweller, A Study of the Earliest Artistic Activities of Man, London, 1928.

BURKITT, M. C., Prehistory, Cambridge, 1921; 2d ed., 1925.

—— *Our Forerunners, London and N. Y., 1923.

—— Our Early Ancestors, Cambridge, 1926 (Mesolithic, Neolithic, and Copper Ages).

—— Spanish Rock-Shelter Paintings of Æneolithic Age, Antiquaries Journal, IV (1924), No. 2.

CABRÉ, J., El arte rupestre en España, Madrid, 1915.

CAPITAN, L., BREUIL, H., PEYRONY, D., Peintures et gravures murales des cavernes paléolithiques: Les Combarelles aux Eyzies, Paris, 1924, 58 Pls.

CAPITAN, L., PEYRONY, D., L'Humanité primitive dans la région des Eyzies, Paris, 1924 (Guide).

—— La Madeleine, Paris, 1928.

CARTAILHAC, E., see BREUIL.

DÉCHELETTE, J., Manuel d'archéologie préhistorique, 1 (1908), Ch. 10., pp. 239 ff.

EBERT, M., Reallexicon der Vorgeschichte, Berlin, 1924-date.

—— Vorgeschichtliches Jahrbuch, Berlin, 1926-19—— (Begins with Bibliogr. of 1924).

**ELLIOT, G. F. SCOTT, Prehistoric Man and his Story, London, 1925, Ch. 18, pp. 272-297, Prehistoric Art, 4th ed.

FRANCHET, L., Les Couleurs employées aux époques préhistoriques, Prague, 1924; Paris, 1926.

GROSSE, E., Die Anfänge der Kunst, 1894 (Tr. English), The Beginnings of Art, N. Y., 1897; new edition, 1928.

HERNÁNDEZ-PACHECO, E., Las pinturas prehistóricas de las cuevas de la Araña (Valencia), Evolución del arte rupestre de España, Madrid, 1924.

HOERNES, M., Urgeschichte der bildenden Kunst in Europa, 2d ed., Wien, 1915, but esp. pp. 146-191; 581-594. For a later edition see HOERNES, M., MENGHIN, O., op. cit., 3d ed., Wien, 1925.

**KÜHN, H., Die Malerei der Eiszeit, 2d ed., München, 1922.

—— Die Kunst der Primitiven, München, 1923.

—— Die Malereien der Vallortaschlucht, I.P.E.K., Leipzig, 1926, pp. 33 ff.

—— Kunst und Kultur der Vorzeit Europas, Berlin, 1929, I.

LOEWY, E., The Rendering of Nature in Early Greek Art. Trans. by J. Fothergill, London, 1907.

LUQUET, G. H., Les Origines de l'art figuré, I.P.E.K. (1926), I, pp. 3-28.

MACALISTER, R. A. S., A Text-book of European Archæology, Cambridge, 1921.

*MACCURDY, G. G., The Dawn of Art: Cave Paintings, Engravings and Sculptures, Art and Archæology, 4 (1916), pp. 71-90.

—— *Human Origins, N. Y., 1924.

—— *Prehistoric Man, Chicago, 1928.

MORGAN, J. DE, Prehistoric Man, N. Y., 1925, esp. pp. 185-230.

MYRES, J. L., Cambridge Ancient History, 2d ed., 1924, Vol. I.

OBERMAIER, H., Der Mensch der Vorzeit, München, 1912.

—— El Hombre Fósil, Madrid, 1916; 2d ed., 1925.

—— Fossil Man in Spain, New Haven, 1924. Trans. by C. D. Matthew, revised by H. F. Osborn, Ch. VII, pp. 210-264.

*OSBORN, H., Men of the Old Stone Age, 3d ed., N. Y., 1922, Ch. 5; pp. 315-330.

*PARKYN, ERNEST A., Prehistoric Art, London, 1915, pp. 19 ff.

PEAKE, H., and FLEURE, H. J., Hunters and Artists, New Haven, 1927 (The Corridors of Time, Vol. II).

PIETTE, É., L'Art pendant l'âge du renne, Paris, 1907. (Album of plates of drawings and engravings.)

REINACH, S., Répertoire de l'art quaternaire, Paris, 1913.

SCHMIDT, H., Vorgeschichte Europas, Berlin, 1924, Vol. I.

SCHUCHHARDT, C., Alteuropa, Berlin, 1926, pp. 23 ff. Die Kunst.

SOLLAS, W. J., Ancient Hunters, 3d ed., London, 1924.

SPEARING, H. G., The Childhood of Art, N. Y., 1913, pp. 1-133. For a new edition see op. cit., London, 1929.

VERWORN, M., Die Anfänge der Kunst, Jena, 1909, 2d ed., 1920. ——

## PRIMITIVE RACES

BALFOUR, H., Bushman Paintings, Oxford, 1909. (See Tongue.)

BOAS, F., Primitive Art, Oslo, 1927.

BRÜHL, L. LÉVY, The Soul of the Primitive, London, 1928 (tr. by A. Clare).

BURKITT, M. C., South Africa's Past in Stone and Paint, Cambridge, 1928.

FROBENIUS, LEO, OBERMAIER, HUGO, HÁDSCHRA MÁKTUBA, Urzeitliche Felsbilder Klein-Afrikas, München, 1925.

*FRY, ROGER, Burlington Magazine, 16 (1910), pp. 334-338. Bushman Paintings.

HALL, R. N., Bushman Paintings of the Madobo Range, Southern Rhodesia, The Geographical Journal, 39 (1912), pp. 592 ff.

JONES, NEVILLE, The Stone Age in Rhodesia, London, 1926.

MOSZEIK, OTTO, Die Malereien der Buschmänner in S. A., Internat. Arch. für Ethnogr., 18 (1906).

STOW, The Races of South Africa, London, 1905.

**TONGUE, M. H., Bushman Paintings,

### EGYPT

*General Works.*

BISSING, FR. VON, Einführung in die Gesch. der ägypt. Kunst, Berlin, 1908.

—— Denkmäler ägyptischer Sculptur, München, 1906-1914.

BOREUX, C., L'Art égyptien, Paris, 1926.

*BREASTED, J. H., A History of Egypt, 2d ed., N. Y., 1916.

**BUDGE, E. A. W., Wall Decorations of Egyptian Tombs, London, British Museum, 1914.

**CAPART, J., L'Art égyptien, Paris, 1909 (Illustrated).

—— Documents pour servir à l'étude de l'art égyptien, Paris, 1927, I.

—— Leçons sur l'art égyptien, Liege, 1920. Trans. in part into English, W. R. Dawson, Egyptian Art, London, 1923.

—— Lectures on Egyptian Art, Chapel Hill, Univ. of N. Carolina Press, 1928.

CURTIUS, L., Die antike Kunst, 1923, Vol. I. Ägypten und Vorderasien.

Encyclopædia of Color Decoration (Egypt, Assyria, Crete, Greece). London, 1928 (Th. Bossert).

HALL, H. R., Ancient History of the Near East, 4th ed., 1920.

JÉQUIER, G., Décoration égyptienne, Paris, 1911.

—— Les temples Memphites et Thébains, Paris, 1920.

—— Les temples Ramessides et Säites, Paris, 1922.

—— Les temples Ptolémäiques et Romains, Paris, 1924.

KEES, H., Ägyptische Kunst, Breslau, 1926.

—— Studien zur ägyptischen Provinzialkunst, Leipzig, 1921.

LAURIE, A. P., with McCLINTOCK, W.

F. P., and MILES, F. D., Proc. Royal Soc., Vol. 89, pp. 418-429, on Egyptian blue.

LUCAS, A., Ancient Egyptian Materials, London, 1926, Ch. VI, "Pigments and Varnish."

MACKAY, E., The Cutting and Preparation of Tomb-Chapels in the Theban Necropolis, J.E.A., VII (1921), pp. 154 ff.

MARTIN, H., L'art égyptien, l'art assyrien, l'art perse, Paris, 1926, Vol. I.

*MASPERO, G., Art in Egypt, N. Y., 1912. (Ars Una Series.)

—— *Manual of Egyptian Archæology, 6th ed., 1914.

MATZ, F., Zur Komposition ägyptischer Wandgemälde, Jahr., XXXVII (1922), pp. 39 ff.

MERIMÉE, M., Dissertation sur l'emploi des couleurs, des vernis et des émaux dans l'ancienne Égypte.

MEYER, E., Die ältere Chronologie Babyloniens, Assyriens und Ägyptens, Berlin, 1925.

MORET, A., The Nile and Egyptian Civilization, N. Y., 1928.

—— From Tribe to Empire (with G. Davy), N. Y., 1926.

PEET, T. E., The Antiquity of Egyptian Civilization, J.E.A., VIII (1922).

PERROT, G., and CHIPIEZ, C., Histoire de l'art dans l'antiquité, 1882, Vol. I.

—— History of Art in Ancient Egypt, Ch. IV, pp. 331-363, chapters on painting, tr. by W. Armstrong, London, 1883.

*PETRIE, W. M. F., Arts and Crafts of Ancient Egypt, London, 1910, pp. 48 ff.

—— *Egyptian Decorative Art, London, 1895; 2d ed., London, 1920.

PORTER, BERTHA, MOSS, ROSALIND L. B.,

copied and printed in color with a preface by Henry Balfour, Oxford, 1909.

Topographical Bibliography of Ancient Egyptian Hieroglyphic Texts, Reliefs and Paintings, I. The Theban Necropolis, Oxford, 1927.

PRATT, IDA A., Ancient Egypt. Sources of information in the New York Public Library, N. Y., 1925.

PRISSE D'AVENNES, Histoire de l'art égyptien, d'après les monuments, Paris, 1878.

RUSSELL, W. J., in Petrie's Medum, London, 1892, on Egyptian colors.

SCHÄFER, H., Von ägyptischer Kunst, besonders der Zeichenkunst, 2d ed., Leipzig, Hinrichs, 1922, 53 Plates.

—— Einiges über Entstehung und Art der ägyptischen Kunst, Zeitschr. für ägypt. Sprache, 52 (1915), pp. 1-18.

**SCHÄFER, H., and ANDRAE, W., Die Kunst des alten Orients, Berlin, 1925.

SPIEGELBERG, W., Geschichte der ägyptischen Kunst, Leipzig, 1903.

STEINDORFF, G., Die Kunst der Ägypter, Leipzig, 1928.

WRESZINSKI, W., Atlas zur altägyptischen Kulturgeschichte, Leipzig, Series I, 1923.

### Prehistoric (*Thinite*).

BOREUX, C., Les poteries décorées de l'Égypte prédynastique, Rev. des Études ethnogr. et sociol., 1908, Vol. I, pp. 33-52.

BREASTED, J. H., The Origins of Civilization, Scientific Monthly, 1919.

CAPART, J., Les débuts de l'art en Égypte, Brussels, 1904.

—— Primitive Art in Egypt (tr. by A. S. Griffith), London, 1905.

LANGDON, S., The Early Chronology of Sumer and Egypt, J.E.A., VII (1921), pp. 133 ff.

MORGAN, J. DE, Recherches sur les origines de l'Égypte, I, L'âge de la pierre et les métaux, Paris, 1896.

—— Prehistoric Man, N. Y., 1925, pp. 212 ff.

—— La préhistoire orientale, Paris, 1926,

Vol. II, L'Égypte et l'Afrique du Nord.

NAVILLE, É., Les dessins des vases préhistoriques égyptiens (Archives Suisses d'anthropol. générale), Genève, 1916-1921.

PEET, T. E., Art of the Predynastic Period, J.E.A., II (1915), p. 88.

—— Cambridge Ancient History, I (1924),[2] pp. 238-256.

PETRIE, W. M. F., The Royal Tombs of the Earliest Dynasties (Egypt Explor. Fund), Part II, London, 1901, Vol. XXI.

—— Prehistoric Egypt, London, 1920.

—— Diospolis Parva (Egypt Exploration Fund, London, 1901, Vol. XX).

—— Corpus of Prehistoric Pottery and Palettes, London, 1921.

QUIBELL, J. E., and GREEN, F. W., Hierakonpolis, II, Egypt. Research Account, 1902, Vol. V.

SCHARFF, A., Grundzüge der ägyptisch. Vorgeschichte, Leipzig, 1927.

—— Some Prehistoric vases in the British Museum and remarks on Egyptian Prehistory, J.E.A., XIV (1928), pp. 261 ff.

SPEARING, H. G., The Childhood of Art, London, 1929.

### Memphite.

BISSING, F. VON, Das Re-Heiligtum des Königs Ne-Woser-Re, Berlin, 1905; II, Die kleine Festdarstellung, Leipzig, 1923. III (with H. Kees); Die grosse Festdarstellung, Leipzig, 1928.

BORCHARDT, L., Das Grabdenkmal des Königs Ne-user-re, Leipzig, 1907.

—— Das Grabdenkmal des Königs Sahu-re II, 1913.

DAVIES, N. DE G., The Mastaba of Ptahhetep and Akhethetep at Saqqareh, Arch. Survey of Egypt, VIII-IX (1900-1901), London (F. Ll. Griffith).

LYTHGOE, A. M., The Tomb of Perneb, N. Y., 1916, pp. 1-45.

PAGET-PIRIE-GRIFFITH, The Tomb of

Ptah-hetep, Egyptian Research Account, London, 1898, II.

PETRIE, SIR W. M. F., Medum, London, 1892.

QUIBELL, J. E., The Tomb of Hesy, Excavations at Saqqara (1911-1912), Cairo, 1913.

RANSOM, C., The Tomb of Perneb, Metropolitan Museum, N. Y., pp. 47-79; cf. Lythgoe, A. M.

STEINDORFF, G., Das Grab des Ti, Leipzig, 1913.

*Theban, Twelfth Dynasty.*

BLACKMAN, A. M., The Rock Tombs of Meir, London, 1915, Vol. II.

DAVIES, NORMAN DE G., GARDINER, A. H., The Tomb of Antefoker, London, 1920.

GRIFFITH, F. LL., Beni Hasan, London, 1896, 1900, Vols. III-IV.

HALL, H. R., Cambridge Ancient History, I (1924),[2] pp. 299-325; II (1924), pp. 407 ff.

—— Three Hippopotamus Figures of the Middle Kingdom, J.E.A., XIII (1927), pp. 57 ff., Pls. XXII-XXIII.

NEWBERRY, P., Beni Hasan, London, 1893-1894, Vols. I-II.

—— El Bersheh, Arch. Survey of Egypt, London, 1892-1893 (Part II, with F. L. Griffith).

*Theban, Eighteenth Dynasty.*

BAIKIE, REV. JAMES, The Amarna Age, N. Y., 1926.

CAPART, J., Thèbes, Paris, 1925, pp. 254 ff., esp. Ch. XV.

DAVIES, N. DE G., The Rock Tombs of El Amarna, Arch. Survey of Egypt, XIII-XVIII (1903-1908).

—— The Tomb of Nakht at Thebes, N. Y., 1917.

—— The Tomb of Puyemrê at Thebes, 2 vols., N. Y., 1922.

—— The Tomb of Two Sculptors at Thebes, N. Y., 1925.

—— Two Ramesside Tombs at Thebes, N. Y., 1927.

—— Mural Paintings in the City of Akhetaten, J.E.A., VII (1921), pp. 1 ff.

DAVIES, N. DE G., DAVIES, NINA DE G., The Tombs of Two Officials of Tuthmosis the Fourth, London, 1923, 38 Plates.

DAVIES, NINA DE G., GARDINER, A. H., The Tomb of Huy, Viceroy of Nubia in the Reign of Tutankhamūn, London, 1926, 40 Plates.

DAVIS, THEODORE M., MASPERO, SIR GASTON, DARESSY, G., CRANE, L., The Tombs of Harmhabi and Touatânkhamanou (Theodore M. Davis' Excavations), London, 1912.

FRANKFORT, H., J.E.A., XIII (1927), pp. 209 ff., esp. p. 218 and Pls. LI, LIV.

GARDINER, A. H., The Tomb of Amenemhét, London, 1915, 46 Plates (with Nina de Garis Davies).

LEFEVRE, G., Le Tombeau de Petosiris, Cairo, 1923-1924.

MACKAY, E., The Cutting and Preparation of Tomb-Chapels in the Theban Necropolis, J.E.A., VII (1921), pp. 154 ff.

The Mural Painting of Tell el-'Amarneh, Egypt Exploration Society, London, 1929 (H. Frankfort).

PEET, T. E., and WOOLLEY, C. L., The City of Akhenaten, London, Mem. Egypt Explor. Soc., 38 (1923); cf. J.E.A., VIII (1922), pp. 48 ff., Pl. XIII.

PETRIE, W. M. F., Tell El Amarna, London, 1894.

SCHÄFER, H., Kunstwerke aus der Zeit Amenophis IV, Zeitschr. für ägyptische Sprache, 52 (1915), pp. 73-87.

—— Altes und Neues zur Kunst und Religion von Tell el-Amarna, Zeitschr. für ägypt., Sprache, 55 (1918), pp. 1-43, 7 Plates.

—— Die Anfänge der Reformation Amenophis des IV, Sitzb. Preuss. Akad. 1919, pp. 477-484.

—— Die Religion und Kunst von El-Amarna, Berlin, 1923.

—— Kunstwerke aus El-Amarna, Berlin, 1923.

TYTUS, R., A Re-excavation of the Palace of Amenhetep III, N. Y., 1903.

*Ostraka.*

DARESSY, G., Ostraca, Cat. gén. des antiq. Égypt. du Musée du Caire, Le Caire, 1901.

DAVIES, N. DE GARIS, Egyptian Drawings on Limestone Flakes, J.E.A., IV (1917), pp. 234 ff.

SCHÄFER, H., Ägyptische Zeichnungen auf Scherben, Jahr. der Kgl. Preuss. Kunstsamml., 37 (1916), pp. 23 ff.

WILLIAMS, C. RANSOM, Quarterly Bulletin, N. Y. Historical Society, IV (1921), pp. 91 ff.

*Papyri.*

BUDGE, E. A. W., Colored Facsimiles of the Papyri of Hunefer, Anhai, Netchemet, Nu, etc.

—— The Book of the Dead. Facsimile of the Papyrus of Ani in the British Museum, London, 1890. 2d ed., 1894. In 2 vols., 1913.

—— The Book of the Dead, 2d ed., London, 1922.

—— The Gods of the Egyptians, London, 1904.

—— The Greenfield Papyrus in the British Museum, London, 1900.

NAVILLE, E., Papyrus Funéraires de la XXIe Dynastie au Musée du Caire, Paris, 1912.

—— The Funeral Papyrus of Iouiya (Theodore M. Davis' Excavations), London, 1908.

—— Das ägyptische Todtenbuch der XVIII. bis XX. Dynastie, 3 vols., Berlin, 1886.

SPELEERS, LOUIS, Le Papyrus de Nefer Renpet, Brussels, 1917.

*Coffins.*

BUDGE, E. A. W., A Guide to the First, Second and Third Egyptian Rooms, British Museum, London, 1924.

DARESSY, G., Cercueils des cachettes royales, Catalogue gén. des antiq. Égypt., Le Caire, 1909.

EDGAR, C. C., Græco-Egyptian Coffins, Masks and Portraits, Cat. gén. des antiq. Égypt., Le Caire, 1905, 48 Pls.

## THE ORIENT

*General.*

CHILDE, V. GORDON, The Most Ancient East, London, 1928.

CONTENAU, G., Manuel d'archéologie orientale, Paris, 1927, I.

—— Les antiquités orientales: Sumer, Babylonie, Elam, Musée du Louvre, Paris, 1928 (Plates).

—— L'art de l'Asie occidentale ancienne, Paris, 1928 (Bibl. d'hist. de l'art).

CURTIUS, L., Die antike Kunst, Berlin, 1923, I.

DELAPORTE, L., Mesopotamia. The Babylonian and Assyrian Civilization, N. Y., 1925.

EBELING, ER., MEISSNER, B., Reallexicon der Assyriologie, I, Berlin, 1928.

FOUGÈRES, G., CONTENAU, G., GROUSSET, R., JOUGUET, P., LESQUIER, J., Les premières civilisations, Paris, 1926, Vol. I (Egypt, Mesopotamia).

FRANKFORT, H., Studies in Early Pottery of the Near East, London, 1924, Vol. I (Mesopotamia, Syria, Egypt).

HALL, H. R., Cambridge Ancient History, 1924, I², 570-588, Art of Early Egypt and Babylonia; 1924, II, 426 ff., Contemporary Art of Egypt and the Near East.

HALL, H. R., and WOOLLEY, C. L., Ur Excavations, I, Al 'Ubaid, Oxford, 1927.

*HANDCOCK, P., Mesopotamian Archæology, N. Y., 1912.

HEUZEY, L., Origines orientales de l'art, Paris, 1891-1915.

HOGARTH, D. G., The Ancient East, London, 1914.

JASTROW, M., Civilization of Babylonia and Assyria, Phila., 1915.

—— Bildermappe samt Erklärungen zur Religion Babyloniens und Assyriens, Giessen, 1912.

MEISZNER, B., Grundzüge der babylonisch-assyrischen Plastik, Leipzig, 1915.

MORGAN, J. DE, La préhistoire Orientale, Paris, 1927, Vol. III, L'Asie antérieure.

PEAKE, H., and FLEURE, H. J., Priests and Kings, New Haven, 1927 (The Corridors of Time, Vol. IV).

—— Peasants and Potters, New Haven, 1927 (The Corridors of Time, Vol. III).

PERROT, G., and CHIPIEZ, C., Histoire de l'art dans l'antiquité, 1884, Vol. II.

POULSEN, F., Der Orient und die frühgriechische Kunst, Berlin, 1912.

ROGERS, R. W., History of Babylonia and Assyria, N. Y., 1915.

**SCHÄFER, H., ANDRAE, W., Die Kunst des alten Orients, Berlin, 1925.

SEABY, ALLEN W., Art in the Life of Mankind, II: Art in Ancient Times: Prehistoric, Sumerian, Egyptian, Babylonian, Assyrian, and Ægean, London, 1928.

WARD, W. H., Seal Cylinders of Western Asia, Washington, 1910.

—— Cylinders and other ancient Oriental seals in the Library of J. P. Morgan, N. Y., 1909.

### Akkadians.

*CLAY, A. T., The Art of the Akkadians, Art and Arch., V (1917), pp. 69 ff.

KING, L. W., A History of Sumer and Akkad, London, 1910; 2d ed., 1916.

UNGER, E., Sumerische und Akkadische Kunst, Breslau, 1926.

### Sumerians.

*DUNCAN, G. S., The Art of the Sumerians, Art and Arch., V (1917), pp. 93 ff.

FRANKFORT, H., Sumerians, Semites and the Origin of Copper-working, Ant. Journ., VIII (1928), pp. 217-235.

HALL, H. R., WOOLLEY, C. L., Ur Excavations, I. Al 'Ubaid, Oxford, 1927.

HERTZ, A., Rev. Arch., XXVII (1928), pp. 90-104.

KING, L. W., A History of Sumer and Akkad, London, 1910; 2d ed., 1916.

LANGDON, S., Sumerian Origins and Racial Characteristics, Archæologia, 70 (1918-1920).

—— Cambridge Ancient History, I, 356 ff.

—— Excavations at Kish, Paris, 1925, Vol. I.

MEYER, E., Sumerier und Semiten in Babylonien, Abh. der Königl. Preuss. Akad. der Wiss., Berlin, 1906.

PETERS, J. P., Nippur, New York, 1897.

ROSTOVTZEFF, M., The Sumerian Treasure of Astrabad, J.E.A., VI (1920), pp. 4-27.

UNGER, E., Sumerische und akkadische Kunst, Breslau, 1926.

WOOLLEY, C. L., The Sumerians, Oxford, 1928.

—— The Antiquaries Journal, III (1923); IV (1924), Tell El Obeid; V (1925), Ur; VI (1926), Ur; VIII (1928), Ur.

### Elamites.

CHILDE, V. GORDON, The Aryans, London, 1926, pp. 103 ff.

Délégation en Perse, VIII (1905), Mussian (Gautier, Lampre); XV (1914), Bender Bushire (M. Pézard).

FRANKFORT, H., Studies in Early Pottery of the Near East, London, 1924, Vol. I.

—— Sumerians, Semites and the Origin of Copper-Working, Ant. Journ., VIII (1928), pp. 217-235.

KING, L. W., A History of Sumer and Akkad, London, 1910, p. 335.

KING, L. W., and HALL, H. R., Egypt and Western Asia, 1910, pp. 221 ff.

LEGRAIN, L., Mem. de la Mission archéol. de Perse, XVI (1921), Elamite seals. (Délégation en Perse.)

MECQUENEM, R., SCHEIL, V., Mem. de la Mission archéol. de Perse, XX (1928).

MORGAN, J. DE, Revue de l'Art ancien et moderne, Décembre, 1908, pp. 401 ff.

—— Prehistoric Man, N. Y., 1925, pp. 208 ff.

—— La préhistoire Orientale, Paris, 1927, III, 53 ff., Pls. I-III (color).

MYRES, J. L., The Dawn of History, New York, 1911, pp. 120 ff.

PEAKE, H., FLEURE, H. J., Peasants and Potters, New Haven, 1927.

POTTIER, E., Délégation en Perse, XIII (1912), Céramique peinte de Suse.

—— Corpus Vasorum Antiquorum, France, Musée du Louvre, Fasc. I, II, III, IV, Paris, 1923, —.

—— Une théorie nouvelle sur les vases de Suse, Rev. Arch., 23 (1926), pp. 1-39.

WOOLLEY, C. L., The Painted Pottery of Susa, Journ. Roy. Asiatic Soc., London, 1928.

### Kassites.

KING, L. W., Babylonian Boundary-Stones in the British Museum, London, 1912.

SCHEIL, V., Délégation en Perse, IV.

THOMPSON, R. CAMPBELL, Cambridge Ancient History, 1924, I², 552-569.

### Hittites.

CONTENAU, G., La glyptique Syro-Hittite, Paris, 1922.

—— Éléments de Bibliographie Hittite, Paris, 1922.

*COWLEY, A. E., The Hittites, London, 1920.

FRANKFORT, H., Studies in Early Pottery of the Near East, London, 1927, II, 154 ff., Pls. IX-XII.

*GARSTANG, J., Land of the Hittites, London, 1910; The Hittite Empire, 1929.

GENOUILLAC, HENRI DE, Céramique Cappadocienne, Paris, 1926.

**HOGARTH, D. G., WOOLLEY, C. L., LAWRENCE, T. E., Carchemish, London, 1914, Vol. I.

HOGARTH, D. G., Cambridge Ancient History, 1924, II, 252-274; 1925, III, 132-168.

—— Enc. Brit., s.v. Hittites.

—— Hittite Seals, Oxford, 1920.

HROZNY, F., Etruskisch und die "hethitischen" Sprachen, Zeitschr. für Assyriologie, XXXVIII (1928), pp. 171 ff.

LUSCHAN, VON et al., Ausgrabungen in Sendschirli, 1893-1911, Pts. I-IV. (Mitth. aus den oriental. Samml.)

MESSERSCHMIDT, L., Die Hethiter, Der alte Orient (1902).

—— The Ancient Hittites, Washington, 1904 (Smithsonian Institute).

MEYER, E., Reich und Kultur der Chetiter, Berlin, 1914.

—— Geschichte des Altertums, Berlin, II, 1, 1928.

MÜLLER, VAL. K., Die monumentale Architektur der Chatti von Boghaz-köi, Ath. Mitth., 42 (1917), pp. 99-170.

OSTEN, H. H. VON DER, Explorations in Hittite Asia Minor, Oriental Inst. Communications No. 2, Chicago University, 1927. Cf. Amer. Journ. of Semitic Languages, XLIII (1927), pp. 73-176.

PERROT, G., and CHIPIEZ, C., Histoire de l'art, 1887, Vol. IV.

POTTIER, E., L'art Hittite, Syria, I (1920), pp. 169-182; 264-286; II (1921), pp. 6-39; 96-119.

PUCHSTEIN, O., Boghasköi, Die Bauwerke, D.O.G., Leipzig, 1912.

REBER, F. VON, Die Stellung der Hethiter

in der Kunstgeschichte, Sitzungsber. der Königl. Bayer. Akad. der Wiss. Phil. Kl., 13 (1910), München.

SAYCE, A. H., The Hittites, London, 1903.

**WEBER, O., Die Kunst der Hethiter, Orbis Pictus, Band 9, Berlin.

WOOLLEY, C. L., and LAWRENCE, T. E., Carchemish, London, 1921, Vol. II.

*Babylonia.*

ANDRAE, W., Die glasierten Ziegel von der Südburg des Kasr, M.D.O.G., 13 (1902), Berlin.

FRANK, C., Babylon.—Assyr. Kunst. (Kunstgesch. in Bildern, I, 2).

HALL, H. R., Babylonian and Assyrian Sculpture in the British Museum, Paris, 1928.

HARCOURT-SMITH, SIMON, Babylonian Art, N. Y., 1928.

JASTROW, M., The Civilization of Babylonia and Assyria, Philadelphia, 1915.

KING, L. W., A History of Babylon, N. Y., London, 1915.

KOLDEWEY, R., Das wieder erstehende Babylon, Leipzig, 1913. (Tr. by A. Johns, Excavations at Babylon, London, 1914.)

—— Das Ischtar Tor in Babylon, Wiss. Veröff. D.O.G., 32 (1918).

LEGRAIN, L., Culture of the Babylonians, Philadelphia, University Museum, 1925.

MEISSNER, B., Babylonien und Assyrien, Heidelberg, 1920-1924.

MEYER, E., Geschichte des Altertums, Stuttgart, 1928. *Cf.* I,² Pt. 2, 1909.

ROGERS, R. W., History of Babylonia and Assyria, 6th ed., New York, 1915.

ROSTOVTZEFF, M., History of the Ancient World, Oxford, 1926, Vol. I.

*Assyria.*

ANDRAE, W., Die Festungswerke von Assur, Leipzig, 1913.

—— Coloured Ceramics from Ashur and Earlier Ancient Assyrian Wall-Paintings, London, 1925.

BOTTA, E., Monuments de Ninive, Paris, 1849-1850, Vols. I-V (with E. Flandin).

BUDGE, E. A. W., Assyrian Sculptures in the British Museum, London, 1914.

JASTROW, M., The Civilization of Babylonia and Assyria, Philadelphia, 1915.

LAYARD, A. H., Nineveh and its Remains, London, 1849.

—— Second Series of Monuments of Nineveh, London, 1853.

—— Discoveries in the Ruins of Nineveh and Babylon, London, 1853.

OLMSTEAD, A. T., History of Assyria, N. Y., 1923.

PILLET, M., Khorsabad, Paris, 1918.

PLACE, V., Ninive et l'Assyrie, Paris, 1867-1870.

SMITH, SIDNEY, Early History of Assyria to 1000 B.C., London, 1928.

THOMPSON, R. CAMPBELL, Assyria. Cambridge Ancient History, 1924, II, 227 ff.

UNGER, E., Assyrische und babylonische Kunst, Breslau, 1927.

WEBER, O., Assyrische Plastik, Berlin, 1924.

*Phœnicia.*

AUTRAN, C., Phéniciens, Paris, 1920.

BISSING, F. W. VON, Die Kunst der Phoiniker, Leyden, 1925.

CONTENAU, G., La Civilisation phénicienne, Paris, 1926.

WEILL, R., Phéniciens, Égéens et Hellènes dans la Méditerranée primitive, Syria, II (1921), pp. 120 ff.

WOOLLEY, C. L., La Phénicie et les peuples Égéens, Syria, II (1921), pp. 177 ff.

*Persia.*

DIEULAFOY, M., L'art antique de la Perse, 1884-1885.

—— L'acropole de Suse, Paris, 1893.

—— *Les Antiquités de Suse, Paris, 1913.

HUART, C., Ancient Persia and Iranian Civilization, N. Y., 1927.

PERROT, G., and CHIPIEZ, C., Histoire de l'art dans l'antiquité, Vol. V, Paris, 1890.

*PILLET, M., Le Palais de Darius Ier à Suse, Paris, 1914.

SARRE, F., L'art de la Perse ancienne, tr. by P. Budry.

*Pottery.*

GENOUILLAC, H. DE, Céramique Cappadocienne, Paris, 1926.

FRANKFORT, H., Studies in Early Pottery of the Near East, London, 1924, Vol. I, Mesopotamia, Syria, and Egypt; London, 1927, Vol. II, Asia, Europe, and the Ægean.

## CRETE AND THE ÆGEAN

BAIKIE, J., The Sea Kings of Crete, 2d ed., London, 1913.

BLEGEN, C. W., Korakou, A Prehistoric Settlement near Corinth, N. Y., 1921.

—— Zygouries, Cambridge, 1928.

BOSANQUET, R. C., Phylakopi. J.H.S. Suppl. Paper, IV (1904), pp. 70 ff.

—— J.H.S., 24 (1904), pp. 317 ff., Pls. XI-XIV.

**BOSSERT, H. TH., Alt Kreta, Berlin, 1921, Pls. 37-76.

—— Ornament in Applied Art, E. Weyhe, N. Y., 1924.

BOULE, M., Les relations de la Crète minoenne avec l'Égypte et la Libye, l'Anthropologie, XXXVI, 182 ff.

BULLE, H., Orchomenos, Abh. der Kgl. Bayr. Akad. der Wiss., München, 24 (1907).

BURROWS, R., Discoveries in Crete, 2d ed., London, 1908.

CHILDE, V. GORDON, The Aryans, London, 1926, pp. 42 ff.

—— Date and Origin of Minyan Ware, J.H.S., 35 (1915).

—— The Dawn of European Civilization, N. Y., 1925.

*COLLIGNON, M., La peinture préhellénique en Crète, Gazette des Beaux-Arts, 1909, II, 1-35.

DAWKINS, R. M., J.H.S., 23 (1903), 248 ff.

DÖRPFELD, W., Troja und Ilion, Athens, 1902.

DUGAS, C., La Céramique des Cyclades, Paris, 1925.

DUSSAUD, R., Les Civilisations préhelléniques, 2d ed., 1914, pp. 77 ff.

EDGAR, C. C., Phylakopi, J.H.S., Suppl. Paper, IV (1904), pp. 80 ff.

EVANS, SIR ARTHUR, The Palace of Minos, London, 1921, Vol. I; London, 1928, Vol. II (Parts I and II).

—— *The Palace of Minos, Monthly Review, 1901, pp. 115 ff.

—— B.S.A., 1901-date.

—— J.H.S., 21 (1901), Pl. V (color), Mycenæan Tree and Pillar Cult.

—— The Prehistoric Tombs of Knossos, London, 1906.

FIMMEN, D., Die Kretisch-Mykenische Kultur, 2d ed., Leipzig, 1924.

FORSDYKE, E. J., Catalogue of Prehistoric Ægean Pottery, British Museum, London, 1925, Vol. I, Part I.

—— The Pottery called Minyan Ware, J.H.S., 34 (1914).

—— Minoan Pottery from Cyprus and the Origin of the Mycenean Style, J.H.S., 31 (1911), pp. 110-118.

FURTWÄNGLER, A., and LOESCHCKE, G., Mykenische Vasen, Berlin, 1886.

—— Mykenische Thongefässe, Berlin, 1879.

GLOTZ, G., La Civilisation Égéenne, Paris, 1923. (Trans. Eng. The Ægean Civilization, N. Y., 1925.)

GOLDMAN, HETTY, Excavations at Eutresis, Fogg Art Museum, Harvard University, 1927.

HALBHERR, F., Mon. Ant., XIII (1903), p. 58, Pls. VII-X (Hagia Triada).

HALL, E. H., Decorative Art of Crete in the Bronze Age, Philadelphia, 1907.

—— Sphoungaras, Phila., 1912.

—— Excavations in Eastern Crete: Vrokastro, Philadelphia, University Museum, 1914.

*HALL, H. R., Ægean Archæology, London, 1915, pp. 178 ff.

—— The Civilization of Greece in the Bronze Age, London, 1928.

HARLAND, J. PENROSE, The Peloponnesos in the Bronze Age, Harvard Studies in Classical Philology, XXXIV (1923), 1-62.

*HAWES, CHARLES H., and HARRIET BOYD, Crete, the Forerunner of Greece, New York, 1911,² pp. 114 ff.

*HAWES, HARRIET BOYD (with others), Gournia, Philadelphia, 1908.

HAZZIDAKIS, J., Tylissos, Paris, 1921; Eph. Arch., 1912, pp. 197-233, Pls. 18-20.

HEATON, NOEL, Tiryns, Athen, 1912, II, 211-216; J.R.I.B.A., Jan. 7, 1910.

HOGARTH, D. G., and WELCH, F. B., J.H.S., 21 (1901), pp. 78-98.

KARO, G., *Kreta*, in P.W., XI, 1922, pp. 1743 ff.

KERAMOPOULLOS, A. D., Eph. Arch., 1909, pp. 90 ff.; Pls. I-III, Thebes.

LAMB, W., B.S.A., XXIV (1919-1921), pp. 189 ff., Pls. VII-X; XXV (1921-1923), pp. 193 ff., 249 ff.; Pls. XXV-XXIX, XXXIII, XXXV, XLI-XLIII.

LICHTENBERG, R., Die Einflüsse der ägäischen Kultur auf Ägypten und Palästina, Berlin, 1911.

—— Die ägäische Kultur, Leipzig, 1911.

MACKENZIE, D., J.H.S., 23 (1903); 26 (1906).

**MARAGHIANNIS, G., and SEAGER, R., Antiquités Crétoises, Athens, 1915, 3d Series.

MÜLLER, K., Frühmykenische Reliefs aus Kreta und vom griech. Festland, Jahr., 30 (1915), pp. 242 ff.

MURRAY, A. S., SMITH, A. H., WALTERS, H. B., Excavations in Cyprus, London, 1900.

MYLONAS, G. E., L'Époque néolithique en Grèce, Athènes, 1928.

NILSSON, M. P., The Minoan-Mycenæan Religion and its Survivals in Greek Religion, Lund, 1927.

PARIBENI, R., Mon. Ant., 19 (1908), pp. 6 ff.

POTTIER, E., Revue de Paris, 1902, II, 180.

REICHEL, A., Studien zur Kretisch-Mykenischen Kunst, Œst. Jahr., 1908, p. 242.

REINACH, S., Gazette des Beaux-Arts, 62 (1920), pp. 296 ff.

REISINGER, E., Kretische Vasenmalerei, Leipzig, 1911.

RENAUDIN, L., Vases préhelléniques de Thera, à l'École Française d'Athènes, B.C.H., 46 (1922), pp. 113-159.

RIZZO, G. E., Storia dell' Arte, Torino, 1913, Vol. I.

RODENWALDT, G., Der Fries des Megarons von Mykenai, Halle, 1921, fragments from Mycenæ.

—— Fragmente Mykenischer Wandgemälde, Athen. Mitth., 36 (1911), pp. 221-250, Pls. IX-XII.

—— Die Wandgemälde von Tiryns, Athen. Mitth., 36 (1911), pp. 198-206, Pl. VIII.

—— Tiryns, Athen, 1912, Vol. II.

—— Die Kunst der Antike, Berlin, 1927.

—— Mykenische Studien, I, Jahr., 34 (1919), pp. 87-106, Pls. VII-IX.

—— Rekonstruktionen der Stuckreliefs aus Pseira, Arch. Anz., 38-39 (1923-1924), pp. 267-276, Figs. 1-2.

SCHLIEMANN, H., Mycenæ, N. Y., 1878.

—— Tiryns, N. Y., 1885.

SCHUCHHARDT, C., Schliemann's Excavations, London, 1891. (Trans. by Eugénie Sellers.)

SCHWEITZER, B., Altkretische Kunst, Die Antike, II (1926), pp. 291 ff.

SEAGER, R., Excavations on the Island of Pseira, Philadelphia, 1910.

—— Explorations in the Island of Mochlos, N. Y., 1912.

—— Vasiliki, Transactions of the University of Pennsylvania, Philadelphia, 1907, Vols. II-III.

STAÏS, V., Guide illustré du Musée National d'Athènes, 1907-1909.

TSOUNTAS, C., Eph. Arch., 1887, Pls. X-XII (Mycenæ). The Mycenæan Age, N. Y., 1897 (with J. C. Manatt), pp. 239 ff. (Pottery).

WACE, A. J. B., Excavations at Mycenæ, B.S.A., XXV (1921-1923).

—— Cambridge Ancient History, 2d ed., 1924, I, 589 ff.

WACE, A. J. B., BLEGEN, C. W., Pre-Mycenæan Pottery of the Mainland, B.S.A., XXII (1916-1918).

WACE, A. J. B., THOMPSON, M. S., Prehistoric Thessaly, Cambridge, 1912.

**WINTER, F., Kretisch-Mykenische Kunst, Leipzig, 1912 (Kunstgeschichte in Bildern, I, Heft 3).

WOOLLEY, C. L., Asia Minor, Syria and the Ægean, Liverpool A. A., IX (1922), pp. 41-56.

XANTHOUDÍDES, ST., The Vaulted Tombs of Mesará, London, 1924 (trans. by J. P. Droop).

## GREECE: THE PRIMITIVES AND THE ARCHAIC SCHOOLS

### General.

BRUNN, H., Geschichte der Gr. Künstler, Stuttgart, 1889, II, 3 ff.

BUSCHOR, E., Greek Vase-Painting, New York, 1922 (tr. by G. C. Richards).

DEONNA, W., Les origines de la représentation humaine dans l'art grec, B.C.H., 50 (1926), pp. 319-382.

*DEONNA, W., and DE RIDDER, A., Art in Greece, N. Y., 1927.

DUGAS, C., Les vases de l'Héraion, Explor. archéol. de Délos, X, Paris, 1928. (École Française d'Athènes.)

FAIRBANKS, ARTHUR, Catalogue of Greek and Etruscan Vases, I. Early Vases Preceding Athenian Black-Figured Ware, Museum of Fine Arts, Boston, 1928.

FOWLER, H. N., and WHEELER, J. R., Greek Archæology, N. Y., 1909.

FURTWÄNGLER, A., REICHHOLD, K., Griechische Vasenmalerei, Berlin, 1900-date.

GARDNER, P., Principles of Greek Art, 2d ed., N. Y., 1914.

GERHARD, E., Auserlesene Vasenbilder, Berlin, 1840-1858.

—— Trinkschalen und Gefässe, Berlin, 1848.

—— Griech. und Etruskische Trinkschalen, Berlin, 1843.

GIRARD, P., in Daremberg and Saglio, Dict. des Antiq., s.v. Pictura.

—— La Peinture antique, Paris, 1892.

HOURTICQ, L., La Peinture des origines au XVIe Siècle, Paris, 1908.

JARDÉ, A., The Formation of the Greek People, N. Y., 1926.

JEX-BLAKE, SELLERS, The Elder Pliny's Chapters on the History of Art, London, 1896, Translation, introd., and notes.

KLEIN, W., Geschichte der Gr. Kunst, Leipzig, 1904, I, 106 ff. Cf. 1905, Vol. II; 1907, Vol. III.

—— Studien zur Griech. Malergeschichte, in Arch.-Epigr. Mitth. aus Oesterreich, XI (1887), p. 193.

LIPPOLD, G., P.W., XIV, 1, pp. 882 ff., s.v. Malerei.

MORIN-JEAN, Le dessin des animaux en Grèce, Paris, 1911.

MURRAY, A. S., Handbook of Greek Archæology, N. Y., 1892, pp. 348-443.

OVERBECK, J., Die antiken Schriftquellen,

zur Geschichte der bildenden Künste bei den Griechen, Leipzig, 1868.

PERROT, G., and CHIPIEZ, C., Histoire de l'art, Paris, IX, 1911, 214 ff.; X, 1914.

PFUHL, E., Malerei und Zeichnung der Griechen, München, 1923, Vol. I.

POTTIER, E., Revue des Études Grecques (1898), p. 355.

POULSEN, F., Der Orient und die früh-griechische Kunst, Leipzig, 1912.

RAYET, O., and COLLIGNON, M., Histoire de la Céramique Grecque, Paris, 1888.

REINACH, A., Recueil Milliet, Textes grecs et latins relatifs à l'histoire de la peinture ancienne, Paris, 1921.

REINACH, S., Répertoire de Peintures, Grecques et Romaines, Paris, 1922.

ROBERT, C., Die Anfänge der Malerei, Phil. Untersuch., Berlin, X (1886), pp. 121 ff.

RODENWALDT, G., Die Kunst der Antike, Berlin, 1927. (Hellas und Rom.)

ROUSSEL, P., La Grèce et l'Orient, Paris, 1928.

STUDNICZKA, F., Antenor . . . und die Geschichte der archaischen Malerei, Jahr., II (1887), pp. 148 ff.

*TARBELL, F. B., A History of Greek Art, N. Y., 1913, pp. 268 ff.

WALTERS, H. B., Art of the Greeks, 2d ed., N. Y., 1922.

—— History of Ancient Pottery, London, 1905.

WARD, J., History and Methods of Ancient and Modern Painting, N. Y., 1917.

WEIR, I., The Greek Painter's Art, N. Y., 1905.

WOERMANN, K., Geschichte der Kunst, Leipzig, 1915, Vol. I.

WOLTMANN, A., and WOERMANN, K., History of Painting, 1880, Vol. I.

### Geometric.

BRUNN, H., Griech. Kunstgeschichte, München, 1893, I, 52 ff.

BUSCHOR, E., Griechische Vasenmalerei,
2d ed., 1914, pp. 30 ff. (Eng. Tr., G. C. Richards, N. Y., 1922).

CAHEN, É., Sur la représentation de la figure humaine dans la céramique dipylienne, et dans l'art Égéen, Rev. des Études Grecques, 38 (1925), pp. 1-15.

CASKEY, L. D., Two geometric Amphoræ from Thera, A.J.A., XVIII (1914), pp. 297 ff.

CONZE, A., Zur Gesch. der Anfänge gr. Kunst, Wien, 1870, p. 72; Sitzungsb. der Ber. Akad., 1897, p. 98.

DEONNA, W., Les origines de la représentation humaine dans l'art grec, B.C.H., 50, 1926, 319-382.

DRAGENDORFF, H., Thera, 1903, Vol. II.

HEURTLEY, M. A., A Prehistoric site in Western Macedonia and the Dorian Invasion, B.S.A., XXVIII (1926-1927), pp. 158 ff.

KROKER, E., Die Dipylonvasen, Jahr., I (1886), pp. 95-125.

LOEWY, E., The Rendering of Nature in Early Greek Art, trans. by J. Fothergill, London, 1907.

MERLIN, A., Vases grecs du style géometrique au style à figures noires, Paris, 1928.

PERNICE, E., Geometrische Vase aus Athen, Ath. Mitth., XVII (1892), pp. 205 ff., Pl. X; pp. 285 ff.

POTTIER, E., Le Problème de l'art Dorien. (Ann. du Musée Guimet, XXIX (1908), pp. 123 ff.)

POULSEN, F., Die Dipylongräber und die Dipylonvasen, Leipzig, 1905.

RICHARDS, G. C., Greek Vase-Painting, New York, 1922. (See Buschor.)

RICHTER, G. M. A., Two Colossal Athenian Geometric or "Dipylon" Vases in the Metropolitan Museum of Art, A.J.A., XIX (1915), pp. 385-397, Pls. XVII-XXIII.

RIEGL, A., Stilfragen, Berlin, 1893.

SCHWEITZER, B., Untersuchungen zur Chronologie und Geschichte der geometrischen Stile in Griechenland, I, Heidelberg. Diss., Karlsruhe, 1918; II, Ath. Mitth., 43 (1918), pp. 1-188.

SKIAS, A. N., Eph. Arch., 1898, pp. 29 ff., Pls. 2-6.

URE, P. N., Bœotian Pottery of the Geometric and Archaic Styles, London, 1927.

WALDSTEIN, CHARLES, The Argive Heræum, 1905, II, 101 ff. (J. C. Hoppin).

WIDE, S., Geometrische Vasen aus Griechenland, Jahr., XIV (1899), pp. 188 ff.; XV (1900), pp. 49 ff.

—— Nachleben mykenischer Ornamente, Ath. Mitth., XXII (1897), pp. 233 ff.; XXI (1896), pp. 408 ff.

#### Proto-Corinthian Ware.

DUGAS, C., Les vases de l'Héraion, Explor. archéol. de Délos, X, Paris, 1928.

DÜMMLER, F., Jahr., II (1887), p. 19.

GABRICI, E., Cenni sulla origine dello stile geometrica di Cuma, Napoli, 1911.

——Mon. Ant., 22 (1913).

HOPPIN, J. C., A.J.A., IV (1900), pp. 441 ff., Pls. IV-VI.

JOHANSEN, K. F., Les Vases Sicyoniens, Paris, 1923. Cf. Pottier, E., Rev. Arch., 19 (1924), p. 424. Cf. Rev. Arch., 13 (1921), pp. 7-17.

LOESCHCKE, G., Ath. Mitth., 22 (1897), p. 262.

LORIMER, H. L., The Fabrics Called Proto-Corinthian, J.H.S., 32 (1912), pp. 326 ff.

ORSI, P., Not. d. Scavi, 1893, pp. 445 ff.; 1895, pp. 109 ff.

SMITH, C., J.H.S., XI (1890), p. 167, Pls. I-II.

WALDSTEIN (WALSTON), SIR CHARLES, and HOPPIN, J. C., The Argive Heræum, II (1905), pp. 119 ff.

WASHBURN, O., Eine protokorinthische Lekythos in Berlin, Jahr., 21 (1906), pp. 116 ff.

#### Delian-Melian Ware.

CONZE, A., Melische Thongefässe, Leipzig, 1862.

DUGAS, C., B.C.H., 35 (1911), pp. 350 ff.

HOPKINSON, J. H., and BAKER-PENOYRE, J., J.H.S., 22 (1902), pp. 46 ff.

MYLONAS, K. D., Eph. Arch., 1894, pp. 225 ff., Pls. 12-14.

POULSEN, F., and DUGAS, C., Vases archaïques de Délos, B.C.H., 35 (1911), pp. 350-422.

#### Chalkidian Vases.

BUSCHOR, E., Griechische Vasenmalerei, 2d ed., München, 1914, pp. 96 ff.

FURTWÄNGLER, A., and REICHHOLD, K., Griech. Vas., I, 161 ff.; II, 215 ff.; III, 9 f.; 215 ff.

LOESCHCKE, G., Ath. Mitth., XIX (1894), p. 519.

RUMPF, A., Chalkidische Vasen, Berlin, 1927. Text and 2 vols. of Plates.

—— Zur Gruppe der Phineusschale, Ath. Mitth., 46 (1921), pp. 157 ff.

#### Cyrenaic-Laconian Vases.

BUSCHOR, E., Griech. Vasenmalerei, 2d ed., München, 1914, pp. 116 ff.

CHASE, G., A.J.A., 18 (1914), p. 432.

DROOP, J. P., B.S.A., 14 (1907-1908), pp. 30 ff.; XV (1908-1909), pp. 23-39.

—— The Dates of the Vases Called "Cyrenaic," J.H.S., 30 (1910), pp. 1 ff.

DUGAS, C., Rev. Arch., 9 (1907), pp. 377 ff.; 10 (1907), pp. 36 ff. (with R. Laurent); 20 (1912), pp. 88 ff.

—— Les Vases Lacono-Cyrénéens, Rev. Arch., 27 (1928), pp. 50 ff.

STUDNICZKA, F., Kyrene, eine altgriechische Göttin, Leipzig, 1890 (Fig. 10, Vase with Nymph Cyrene).

WALDHAUER, O., Zur Lakonischen Keramik, Jahr., 38-39 (1923-1924), pp. 28-37.

#### Rhodian-Milesian, Naukratite, and Fikellura Ware.

BOEHLAU, J., Aus Ionischen und Italischen Nekropolen, Leipzig, 1898.

Dugas, C., Les vases de l'Héraion, Explor. archéol. de Délos, X, Paris, 1928.

Edgar, C. C., The Inscribed and Painted Pottery (Naukratis), B.S.A., V (1898), pp. 57 ff.

Endt, J., Beiträge zur Ionischen Vasenmalerei, Prag, 1899.

Gardner, E., Naukratis, London, 1888, Vol. II.

—— Two Naucratite Vases, J.H.S., VIII (1887), 119 ff.

—— Early Greek Vases and African Colonies, J.H.S., X (1889), pp. 126-133.

Kinch, K. F., Fouilles de Vroulia, Berlin, 1914.

Longpérier, Musée Napoléon III, Paris, 1880, Pls.

Lorimer, H. L., J.H.S., 25 (1905), pp. 118 ff.

Pfuhl, E., Gött. Gelehrt. Anz., 1915, 313.

—— Malerei und Zeichnung der Griechen, München, 1923, I, 137 ff.

Pottier, E., Vases Antiques du Louvre, Paris, 1897, A-E.

Price, E. R., Pottery of Naucratis, J.H.S., 44 (1924), pp. 180-222.

—— East Greek Pottery, London, 1928.

Prinz, H., Funde aus Naukratis. Klio, Beiheft, 7, Leipzig, 1908.

Reinach, A. J., Les fouilles de Naucratis et l'histoire de la céramique grecque, Journal des Savants, 1909, pp. 354-363.

Salzmann, A., Nécropole de Camiros, Paris, 1875.

Walters, H. B., History of Ancient Pottery, London, 1905, I, 329 ff.

*Pottery from Daphnæ.*

Dümmler, F., Zu den Griech. Vasen von Tell Defenneh, Jahr., X (1895), pp. 35-46.

—— Ant. Denk., II, Pl. 21.

Lorimer, H. L., J.H.S., 25 (1905), pp. 119 ff.

Perrot, G., and Chipiez, C., Histoire de l'art, Paris, IX, 1911, pp. 380 ff.

Petrie, F., Nebesheh and Defenneh, London, 1888, Tanis II, Pls. 25, 29, 30.

Price, E. R., East Greek Pottery (Classification des céramiques antiques), Paris, 1928.

Walters, H. B., History of Ancient Pottery, London, 1905, Vol. I, pp. 349 ff.

*Clazomenian Vases.*

Kjellberg, L., Ant. Denk., II, Pls. 54-57. Text.

Prinz, H., Funde aus Naukratis, Klio, Beiheft, 7 (1908), pp. 44 ff.

Sieveking, J., and Hackl, R., Die Königliche Vasensammlung zu München, 1912, I, 56, Pl. 20.

Zahn, R., Vasenscherben aus Klazomenai, Ath. Mitth., 23 (1898), pp. 38 ff., Pl. VI.

*Proto-Attic Vases.*

Boehlau, J., Frühattische Vasen. Jahr., II (1887), pp. 33-66.

Couve, L., Eph. Arch., 1897, pp. 67-86, Pls. V-VI.

Dumont, A., and Chaplain, J., Les Céramiques de la Grèce propre, Paris, 1888, I, 101-103.

Furtwängler, A., A.Z., 40 (1882), pp. 197-208, Pls. IX-X. Schüssel von Ægina.

Graef, B., Die antiken Vasen von der Akropolis zu Athen, Berlin, 1909-1925 (with P. Hartwig, P. Wolters, and R. Zahn).

Pernice, E., Ath. Mitth., 17 (1892), pp. 205-228, Pl. X; 20 (1895), pp. 116 ff., Pl. III.

Richter, G. M. A., J.H.S., 32 (1912), pp. 370 ff., Pls. X-XII.

Smith, C., A Proto-Attic Vase, J.H.S., 22 (1902), pp. 29-45, Pls. II-IV.

Staïs, V., Ath. Mitth., 15 (1890), pp. 318-329, Pls. IX-XIII (Vourva).

Thiersch, H., "Tyrrenische" Amphoren, Leipzig, 1889.

Wolters, P., and Staïs, V., Ant. Denk., I, Pl. 57, Text. (Nessos amphora.)

*Corinth.*

**Antike Denkmäler, I, Pls. 7, 8; II, Pls. 23, 24, 29, 30, 39, 40.

FURTWÄNGLER, A., Beschreibung der Vasensammlung im Antiquarium, 1885, I, Sec. IX, Nos. 347-955, pp. 49-105; No. 846, p. 92 (Timonidas).

JONES, H. STUART, Chest of Kypselos, J.H.S., XIV (1894), pp. 30 ff.

MASSOW, WILHELM VON, Die Kypseloslade, Ath. Mitth., 41 (1916).

PERNICE, E., Die Korinthischen Pinakes im Antiquarium der Königl. Museen, Jahr., XII (1897), pp. 9-48.

PERROT, G., and CHIPIEZ, C., Histoire de l'art, Paris, IX, 1911, pp. 236 ff.

POTTIER, E., Catalogue des vases antiques de terre cuite, Paris, 1899, II, 448.

RAYET, O., Gazette Archéologique, VI (1880), pp. 101-107.

RAYET, O., and COLLIGNON, M., Histoire de la céramique grecque, Paris, 1888, pp. 143-148.

WILISCH, E., Altkorinthische Thonindustrie, Leipzig, 1892.

*Thermos.*

KLEIN, W., Gesch. der Gr. Kunst, 1904, I, 119.

KOCH, H., Studien zu den Camp. Dachterrakotten, Röm. Mitth., 30 (1915), pp. 51-74.

—— Zu den Metopen von Thermos, Ath. Mitth., 39 (1914), pp. 237-255.

PAYNE, H. G. G., On the Thermon Metopes, B.S.A., XXVII (1925-1926), pp. 124-132.

PERROT, G., and CHIPIEZ, C., Histoire de l'art, Paris, IX, 1911, pp. 260 ff.

SOTIRIADES, G., Eph. Arch., 1900, pp. 161 ff., Pls. 10, 11; 1903, pp. 71 ff. and Pls. 2-6; *Records of the Past, I (1902), p. 173; Ant. Denk., II, Pls. 49-53, A, Text, pp. 5 ff.

VAN BUREN, E. DOUGLAS, Greek Fictile

Revetments in the Archaic Period, London, 1926, pp. 64-71, Pls. 34-38.

*Ionic.*

BÖHLAU, J., Aus Ionischen und Italischen Nekropolen, Leipzig, 1898.

—— Die Ionischen Augenschalen, Ath. Mitth., 25 (1900), pp. 40 ff.

DÜMMLER, F., Vasenscherben aus Kyme in Æolis, Röm. Mitth., 1888, pp. 159 ff., Pl. VI; pp. 165 ff. (Cære).

—— Röm. Mitth., II (1887), pp. 171-192, Pls. VIII-IX.

ENDT, J., Beiträge zur Ionischen Vasenmalerei, Prag, 1899.

FURTWÄNGLER, A., and REICHHOLD, K., Griech. Vas., 1904, I, p. 93 (Italo-Ionic class).

HEINEMANN, M., Landschaftliche Elemente in der griech. Kunst, Bonn, 1910, pp. 40 ff.

HELBIG, W., Vasi di Busiri, Annali, 37 (1865), pp. 296 ff.

JOUBIN, A., De Sarcophagis Clazom., 1901.

MURRAY, A. S., Terracotta Sarcophagi, Greek and Etruscan in the British Museum, London, 1898; Mon. Piot, IV (1897), pp. 27-52, Pls. V-VII.

PERROT, G., and CHIPIEZ, C., Histoire de l'art, Paris, IX, 1911, pp. 377 ff.

PICARD, CH., and PLASSART, A., B.C.H., 37 (1913), pp. 378-417, Pls. X-XVI.

Sarcophagi.**

** Numerous examples of sarcophagi are published in various numbers of the B.C.H. and Jahrbuch. B.C.H., 1890, 1892 (Pottier); 1895 (Joubin); 1910 (Dugas); Jahr., 1904, 1905 (Kjellberg); 1908 (Zahn); 1913 (Hauser, Brants, Von Duhn); 1914 (Pfuhl).

WEBSTER, T. B. L., A Rediscovered Cæretan Hydria, J.H.S., 48 (1928), pp. 196 ff.

WINTER, F., Ant. Denk., I, Pls. 44-46; II, Pls. 25-27.

*Kimon of Kleonai.*

(Pliny, 35, 56; Ælian, V.H., 8, 8.)

BERCHMANS, J., L'esprit décoratif dans la

céramique grecque, 1909 (Extrait des annales de la Société de Bruxelles, 23).

BRUNN, H., Ges. der Gr. Künstler, Stuttgart, 1889, II, 7 ff. (Correct rendering of profile eye.)

DELBRÜCK, R., Beiträge zur Kenntnis der Linienperspektive in der Griech. Kunst, Bonn, 1899.

HARTWIG, P., Kimon von Kleonai und der Euphron. Kreis, Die Griechischen Meisterschalen, Berlin, 1893, pp. 154-166.

HOLWERDA, A. E. J., Jahr., V (1890), p. 258.

KLEIN, W., Euphronios, 2d ed., Wien, 1886, p. 47 (outline drawings).

—— Studien zur griech. Malersgeschichte. Die Sikyonische Schule, Archæologisch-epigraphische Mitth. aus Œsterreich, XI (1887), pp. 193-233.

PFUHL, E., Die Griechische Malerei, Berlin, 1911, pp. 15 ff. (From N.J., XXVII.)

POTTIER, E., Revue des Études grecques, 1898, p. 385.

—— Mon. Piot, II (1895), p. 51.

ROBERT, C., Die Anfänge der Malerei, Philol. Untersuch., Berlin, X (1886), pp. 121-131.

STUDNICZKA, F., Antenor . . . und die Gesch. der archaischen Malerei, Jahr., II (1887), p. 156.

WALTERS, H. B., Art of the Greeks, London, 1906, p. 147. For a new edition see op. cit., 2d ed., 1922.

WINTER, F., A.Z., 1885, p. 201 (outline drawing).

### Attic Plaques.

BENNDORF, O., Griechische und Sicilische Vasenbilder, Berlin, 1869, Pls. I-V.

—— Eph. Arch., 1887, pp. 115 ff., Pl. 6 (color).

CASKEY, L. D., Bulletin of the Boston Museum of Fine Arts, 1927, p. 55.

CASSON, S., Catalogue of the Acropolis Museum, Cambridge, 1921, II, pp. 306 ff.

COLLIGNON, M., Mon. Grec., 1882, pp. 23-52.

—— Gaz. Arch., XIII (1888), p. 225, Pl. 31.

FURTWÄNGLER, A., Beschreibung der Vasensamml. im Antiq., Berlin, 1885, Nos. 1811-1826.

HIRSCHFELD, G., Athenische Pinakes im Berliner Museum, Festschr. für J. Overbeck, Leipzig, 1893, pp. 1-13.

—— Antike Denkmäler, II, Pls. 9-11.

PERROT, G., and CHIPIEZ, C., Histoire de l'art, IX (1911), pp. 248 ff.

WOLTERS, P., Eph. Arch., 1888, p. 181, Pl. XI.

### Grave Stelæ.

CONZE, A., Die Attischen Grabreliefs, Berlin, 1893, Pl. I and text.

DRAGENDORFF, H., Zwei altattische Malereien auf Marmor, Jahr., XII (1897), pp. 1 ff., Pls. I-II.

GIRARD, P., Mon. Grec., I (1880), pp. 11-19.

GURLITT, W., Bemalte Marmorplatten in Athen, Aufsätze E. Curtius gewidmet, 1884, p. 151.

LOESCHCKE, G., Altattische Grabstelen, Ath. Mitth., IV (1879), pp. 36, 289 (Lyseas), Pls. I-II.

—— Arch. Anz., 1913, p. 62.

MILCHHÖFER, A., Gemalte Grabstelen, Ath. Mitth., V (1880), p. 164, Pl. VI.

MÜLLER, K., Die Lyseasstele. Arch. Anz., 37 (1922), pp. 1 ff., Beil. I.

POTTIER, E., B.C.H., VIII (1884), p. 459, Pl. XIV.

RODENWALDT, G., Ant. Denkmäler, III, Pls. 32-33. (Lyseas.)

WOLTERS, P., Bemalte Grabstele aus Athen, Jahr., 24 (1909), p. 53, Pl. V.

### Warrior Tablet, Acropolis.

BENNDORF, O., Eph. Arch. (1887), pp. 115-130, Pl. VI.

CASSON, S., Catalogue of the Acropolis

Museum, Cambridge, 1921, II, pp. 306 ff. (Bibliogr., p. 310).

HOPPIN, J. C., Euthymides and his Fellows, Cambridge, 1917, pp. 90 ff.

PERROT, G., and CHIPIEZ, C., Histoire de l'art, IX, 1911, p. 259, Pl. XIII.

### Polychromy.

BLANCHET, A., La polychromie des bas-reliefs de la Gaule Romaine, Sens, 1924. *Cf.* Rostovtzeff, Mem. Soc. Archéol. de Sens, 1926.

COLLIGNON, M., La polychromie dans la sculpture grecque, Rev. des deux mondes, 127 (1895), p. 823.

DÖRPFELD, W., and BORRMANN, R., 41 Berl. Winckelmannsprogr., Berlin, 1881.

Encyclopædia of Color Decoration (Egypt, Assyria, Crete, Greece, S. Russia, Rome), London, 1928, 120 Pls. (color).

FENGER, L., Dorische Polychromie, Berlin, 1886.

HOMOLLE, TH., B.C.H., 14 (1890), pp. 497 ff.

LECHAT, H., B.C.H., 14 (1890), pp. 552 ff.
—— Note sur la polychromie des statues grecques, Rev. des Études anc., 1908, p. 161.

LOESCHCKE, G., Ath. Mitth., IV (1879), pp. 36, 289 ff.

PERROT, G., and CHIPIEZ, C., La Polychromie artificielle, pp. 211 ff., Histoire de l'art, VIII (1903).

RAYET, O., and COLLIGNON, M., Histoire de la céramique grecque, Paris, 1888, Ch. XXII, La céramique dans l'architecture, pp. 379-391.

RICHTER, G. M. A., Were the Nude Parts in Greek Marble Sculpture Painted? Metropolitan Museum Studies, I (1929), pp. 25 ff.
—— The Sculpture and the Sculptors of the Greeks, New Haven, 1929.

RODENWALDT, G., Fragment eines Votivreliefs in Eleusis, Jahr., 36 (1921), pp. 1 ff., Pl. I.

—— Zur Polychromie der attischen Grabstelen, Arch. Anz., 37 (1922), pp. 170 ff.

SOLON, LEON, Polychromy, N. Y., 1924.

TREU, G., Bemalter Marmorkopf im British Museum, Jahr., IV (1889), pp. 18 ff., Pl. I (color).
—— Olympia, III (1897), Register, *s.v. Bemalung.*

WALLACE, FLORENCE E., Color in Homer and in Ancient Art, Northampton, 1927 (Smith College Classical Studies).

WIEGAND, TH., Die archaische Poros-Architektur der Akropolis zu Athen, Cassel, 1904.

WINTER, F., Das Alexandermosaik, Strassburg, 1909.
—— Gercke-Norden, Einleitung in die Altertumswiss., Berlin, 1910, II, 92 ff.

### Drawing and Design on Greek Vases.

BAUR, P., Centaurs in Ancient Art. The Archaic Period, Berlin, 1912.

BEAZLEY, J. D., Attic Red-Figured Vases in American Museums, Cambridge, 1918.
—— Attische Vasenmaler des rotfigurigen Stils, Tübingen, 1925.
—— Greek Vases in Poland, Oxford, 1928.

BERCHMANS, J., L'esprit décoratif dans la céramique grecque à figures rouges (Extrait des annales de la société d'archéologie de Bruxelles), 23 (1909).

BLAKE, VERNON, The Art and Craft of Drawing, Oxford, 1927.

BRAUCHITSCH, G. VON, Die Panathenäischen Preisamphoren, Berlin, 1910.

BULLE, H., Der schöne Mensch, 2d ed., München, 1912.

BUSCHOR, E., Griechische Vasenmalerei, 2d ed., München, 1914 (tr. by G. C. Richards, Greek Vase-Painting, N. Y., 1922).
—— Attische Lekythen der Parthenonzeit, München, 1925 (Münch. Jahrb. d. bild. Kunst).

CASKEY, L. D., Geometry of Greek Vases, Boston, 1922.

CORNELIUS, H., Elementargesetze der bildenden Kunst, 2d ed., Leipzig, 1911.

Corpus vasorum antiquorum, Paris, 1923-date.

DELBRÜCK, R., Beiträge zur Kenntnis der Linienperspektive in der griech. Kunst, Bonn, 1899.

DEONNA, W., L'expression des sentiments dans l'art grec, Paris, 1914.

—— Ronde bosse et dessin, L'archéologie, 1912, II, pp. 65 ff.

—— Quelques conventions primitives de l'art grec, Rev. des Ét. grecques, 23 (1910), p. 379.

—— Art in Greece, N. Y., 1927 (with De Ridder, A.).

DUCATI, P., Storia della ceramica greca, Firenze, 1922 (2 vols.).

DUGAS, C., Greek Pottery, trans. by W. C. Thorpe, London, 1926.

FOWLER, H. N., and WHEELER, J. R., A Handbook of Greek Archæology, N. Y., 1909.

**FURTWÄNGLER, A., and REICHHOLD, K., Griechische Vasenmalerei, München, 1904- (continued by F. Hauser and E. Buschor).

GARDINER, E. N., J.H.S., 32 (1912), pp. 179 ff.

*GARDNER, P., The Principles of Greek Art, N. Y., 1914.

HAMBIDGE, J., Dynamic Symmetry, The Greek Vase, New Haven, 1920.

HARRISON, J. E., MACCOLL, D. S., Greek Vase Paintings, London, 1894.

HARTWIG, P., Die griechischen Meisterschalen der Blüthezeit des strengen rothfigurigen Stiles, Berlin, 1893.

HAUSER, F., F.R., Griech. Vas., München, 1909, II, 250, 297 ff., Polygnotan Vases.

HEINEMANN, M., Landschaftliche Elemente in der griechischen Kunst bis Polygnot, Bonn, 1910.

*HERFORD, M. A. B., A Handbook of Greek Vase Painting, Manchester, 1919.

**HOPPIN, J. C., A Handbook of Attic Red-Figured Vases, Cambridge, 1919.

—— A Handbook of Greek Black-Figured Vases, Paris, 1924.

—— Euthymides and his Fellows, Cambridge, 1917.

KERCHENSTEINER, G., Die Entwickelung der zeichnerischen Begabung, München, 1908.

KLEIN, W., Die griechischen Vasen mit Lieblingsinschriften, 2d ed., Leipzig, 1898.

—— Die griechischen Vasen mit Meistersignaturen, 2d ed., Wien, 1887.

—— Geschichte der griechischen Kunst, Leipzig, 1904-1907 (3 vols.).

—— Euphronios, 2d ed., Wien, 1886.

LANGE, J., Darstellung des Menschen in der älteren griechischen Kunst, Strassburg, 1899, tr. by M. Mann.

LANGLOTZ, E., Zur Zeitbestimmung der strengrotfigurigen Vasenmalerei und der gleichzeitigen Plastik, Leipzig, 1920.

—— Griechische Vasenbilder, Heidelberg, 1922 (40 Plates).

*LOEWY, E., The Rendering of Nature in Early Greek Art, tr. by J. Fothergill, London, 1907.

LÜCKEN, G. VON, Greek Vase-Paintings. Peintures de Vases grecques, The Hague, 1923.

—— Griechische Vasenbilder, Berlin, 1921.

MORIN-JEAN, Le dessin des animaux en Grèce d'après les vases peints, Paris, 1911.

MURRAY, A. S., Designs from Greek Vases in the British Museum, London, 1894.

NICOLE, G., La peinture des vases grecs, Paris, 1926.

—— Meidias et le style fleuri dans la céramique attique, Genève, 1908.

PERROT, G., and CHIPIEZ, C., Histoire de l'art dans l'antiquité, Paris, IX (1911); X (1914).

PFUHL, E., Malerei und Zeichnung der Griechen, München, 1923.

—— Masterpieces of Greek Drawing and Painting, N. Y., 1926 (trans. by J. D. Beazley).

—— Die Griechische Malerei, Leipzig, 1911.

POTTIER, E., Le dessin par ombre portée chez les Grecs, Revue des études grecques, 11 (1898), pp. 355 ff.

—— Étude sur les lécythes blancs attiques, Paris, 1883.

—— Douris and the Painters of Greek Vases, tr. by B. Kahnweiler, London, 1908.

—— Catalogue des vases antiques, Paris, 1899-1905.

—— Corpus vasorum antiquorum, France, Musée du Louvre, Fasc. I, II, IV, V, Paris, 1923-1928.

—— Vases antiques du Louvre, Paris, 1897-1922 (Album).

RAYET, O., COLLIGNON, M., Histoire de la Céramique grecque, Paris, 1888.

REICHHOLD, K., Skizzenbuch Griechischer Meister, München, 1919.

REINACH, S., Répertoire des vases peints, 2d ed., Paris, 1922.

RICHTER, G. M. A., The Craft of Athenian Pottery, New Haven, 1923.

—— A Handbook of the Classical Collection, Metropolitan Museum, N. Y., 1927.

RIDDER, A. DE, see Deonna, W.

SÉCHAN, L., Études sur la tragédie grecque dans ses rapports avec la céramique, Paris, 1926.

SETA, A. DELLA, La Genesi dello Scorcio nell' Arte Greca, Roma, 1907.

WALTERS, H. B., History of Ancient Pottery, London, 1905.

### Greek Vase-Painting and Monumental Art.

BUSCHOR, E., Attische Lekythen der Parthenonzeit, München, 1925.

LANGLOTZ, E., Zur Zeitbestimmung der strengrotfigurigen Vasenmalerei und der gleichzeitigen Plastik, Leipzig, 1920.

LÜCKEN, G. VON, Archaische griechische Vasenmalerei und Plastik, Ath. Mitth., 44 (1919), pp. 47-174, Pls. I-VI.

PHARMAKOWSKY, B. W., Attic Vase-Painting and its Relation to Monumental Art in the Period directly after the Persian Wars, Petrograd, 1901, 2 (Russian).

WATZINGER, C., Zur jüngeren attischen Vasenmalerei, Œst. Jahr., 16 (1913), 141-177.

WINTER, F., Die jüngeren attischen Vasen und ihr Verhältnis zur grossen Kunst, Berlin, 1885.

### White-Ground Vase-Painting.

BEAZLEY, J. D., Greek Vases in Poland, Oxford, 1928.

BOSANQUET, R. C., J.H.S., 16 (1896), p. 164; 19 (1899), p. 169.

BUSCHOR, E., Attische Lekythen der Parthenonzeit, München, 1925.

COLLIGNON, M., Histoire de la Céramique Grecque, Paris, 1888, pp. 215 ff. (see Rayet).

—— Mon. Piot, XII (1905), p. 29, Pls. 3-5.

DUMONT, A., CHAPLAIN, J., POTTIER, E., Les Céramiques de la Grèce propre, Paris, 1888-1890.

FAIRBANKS, A., Athenian White Lekythoi, New York, 1907 (University of Michigan Studies, Vol. VI); New York, 1914 (University of Michigan Studies, Vol. VII).

FURTWÄNGLER, A., REICHHOLD, K., Griech. Vasenmalerei, I, 249 ff.; II, 24 ff. (Reichhold); III, 302 (Buschor).

HARTWIG, P., Die griechischen Meisterschalen, Berlin, 1893, pp. 499 ff.

LUCE, S. B., The Diphilos-Dromippos Lecythi and their Relation to Mr. Beazley's "Achilles Master," A.J.A., 23 (1919), pp. 19-32.

MCMAHON, ROBERT C., The Technical History of White Lecythi, A.J.A., XI (1907), pp. 7 ff.

MURRAY, A. S., and SMITH, A. H., White Athenian Vases in the British Museum, London, 1896.

PERROT, G., and CHIPIEZ, C., Histoire de

l'art dans l'antiquité, Paris, X (1914), Ch. 28, pp. 683-744.

PHILIPPART, H., Deux coupes attiques à fond blanc, Mon. Piot, 29 (1927-1928).

POTTIER, E., Étude sur les lécythes blancs attiques à représentations funéraires, Paris, 1883.

—— Deux coupes à fond blanc, Mon. Piot, II (1895), pp. 39 ff.

RAYET, O., and COLLIGNON, M., Histoire de la céramique grecque, Paris, 1888, pp. 215 ff.

RIEZLER, W., Weissgrundige attische Lekythen, München, 1914.

WALTERS, H. B., History of Ancient Pottery, London, 1905, I, 454 ff.

WINTER, F., Berlin. Winckelmannsprogr., 55 (1895).

## POLYGNOTOS AND THE PAINTING OF THE FIFTH CENTURY

### General.

BEHN, F., Die Ficoronische Cista, Leipzig, 1907.

BENNDORF, O., Wiener Vorlegeblätter, 1888, Pls. X-XII.

—— Das Heroon von Gjölbaschi-Trysa, Wien, 1889, pp. 150 ff., 245 ff. (with Niemann).

BRUNN, H., Geschichte der Griechischen Künstler, 2d ed., Stuttgart, 1889.

FEIHL, E., Die Ficoronische Cista und Polygnot, Tübingen, 1913 (Diss.).

FURTWÄNGLER, A., and REICHHOLD, K., Griechische Vasenmalerei, München, 1900-date.

JAHN, O., Die Gemälde des Polygnotos in der Lesche zu Delphi, Kiel, 1841.

KLEIN, W., Geschichte der Griech. Kunst, Leipzig, 1904, I, 417 ff.

KOERTE, G., Zu den Friesen von Gjölbaschi, der "Ionischen" Kunst und Polygnot, Jahr., 31 (1916), pp. 257 ff.

LOEWY, E., Polygnot. Ein Buch von griechischer Malerei, Wien, 1929.

PFUHL, E., Malerei und Zeichnung der Griechen, München, 1923.

### Delphi.

Frazer, Pausanias, Vol. V, pp. 356, 360, 372.

JAHN, O., Die Gemälde des Polygnotos in der Lesche zu Delphi, Kiel, 1841.

ROBERT, C., Die Iliupersis des Polygnot, Hallisches Winckelmannsprogr., XVII (1893).

—— Die Nekyia des Polygnot, Hallisches Winckelmannsprogr., XVI (1892).

SCHÖNE, R., Zu Polygnots Delphischen Bildern, Jahr., VIII (1893), p. 187.

SCHREIBER, T., Die Nekyia des Polygnotos in Delphi, Festschr. für J. Overbeck, Leipzig, 1893, p. 184.

—— Die Wandbilder des Polygnotos in der Halle der Knidier zu Delphi, Abh. der Phil.-Hist. Cl. der Kgl. Sächs. Ges. der Wiss., 17 (1897), No. 6.

SCHROEDER, B., Die Polygnotische Malerei und die Parthenongiebel, Jahr., 30 (1915), 95 ff.

WEISZÄCKER, P., Polygnots Gemälde in der Lesche der Knidier in Delphi, Stuttgart, 1895.

### Athens.

HAUSER, F., Nausikaa, Œst. Jahr. VIII (1905), pp. 18 ff., Pl. I (color).

KOEPP, F., Das Gemälde der Schlacht bei Oinoë in der Stoa Poikile zu Athen, Rh. Mus., 69 (1914), pp. 160-169.

ROBERT, C., Die Marathonschlacht in der Poikile, Hall. Winckelmannsprogr., XVIII (1895).

SIX, J., Die Eriphyle des Polygnot, Ath. Mitth., 19 (1894), 335.

### Mikon.

HAUSER, F., Griechische Vasenmalerei, Pl. 108 (Orvieto Krater), and II, pp. 244 ff.

KLEIN, W., Mikon und Panainos, Mikon und Paionios, Jahr., 33 (1918), pp. 1-38.

ROBERT, C., Die Marathonschlacht, Hallisches Winckelmannsprogr., XVIII (1895).

SCHROEDER, B., Mikon und Paionios, Jahr., 29 (1914), pp. 123 ff.

——Zu Mikons Gemälde der Marathonschlacht in der Stoa Poikile, Jahr., 26 (1911), pp. 281 ff.

### Panainos.

BLÜMNER, H., Die Gemälde des Panainos am Throne des Olympischen Zeus, Jahr., 15 (1900), pp. 136 ff.

EVELYN-WHITE, H. G., The Throne of Zeus at Olympia, J.H.S., 28 (1908), pp. 49 ff.

GARDNER, E. A., The Paintings by Panænus on the Throne of Olympian Zeus, J.H.S., 14 (1894), pp. 233-241.

HITZIG-BLÜMNER, Pausanias, Comment., Book V, 11, 6.

MURRAY, A. S., History of Greek Sculpture, 2d ed., pp. 125 ff.

——Ath. Mitth., VII (1882), pp. 274-276, The Barrier of the Throne of Zeus at Olympia.

PELLEGRINI, G., Atti del reale Instituto Veneto di scienze, lettere ed arti, 74 (1915), pp. 1555-1574. Cf. A.J.A., 20 (1916), p. 488.

TYLER, C. H., The Paintings of Panænus at Olympia, J.H.S., 30 (1910), p. 82.

### Apollodoros.

COLLIGNON, M., Mon. Piot, XII (1905), pp. 29 ff.

GARDNER, P., The Scenery of the Greek Stage, J.H.S., 19 (1899), pp. 252 ff. (Agatharchos).

PFUHL, E., Apollodoros, ὁ σκιαγράφος, Jahr., 25 (1910), pp. 12 ff.; 27 (1912), pp. 227-231.

POTTIER, E., Mon. Piot, II (1895), pp. 45 ff.

RIDDER, A. DE, B.C.H., 23 (1899), pp. 317-332.

ROBERT, C., Die Knöchelspielerinnen des Alexandros, Hall. Winckelmannsprogr., 21 (1897).

WINTER, F., 55 Winckelmannsprogr., Berlin, 1895.

### Zeuxis.

BERTRAND, É., Études sur la peinture et la critique d'art dans l'antiquité, Paris, 1893, pp. 70 ff.

BRUNN, H., Gesch. der Griech. Künstler, II, 51.

GUSMAN, P., La Revue de l'art ancien et moderne, 1909, 2, pp. 117 ff.

HAUSER, F., Griech. Vasenmalerei, II, 264.

ROBERT, C., Kentaurenkampf und Tragoedienscene, Hallisches Winckelmannsprogr., 22 (1898).

——Votivgemälde eines Apobaten, Hallisches Winckelmannsprogr., 19 (1895).

### Parrhasios.

BERTRAND, É., Études sur la peinture dans l'antiquité, 1893, pp. 61 ff.

BRUNN, H., Gesch. der Griech. Künstler, II, 66.

PACE, B., Vasi figurati con riflessi della pittura di Parrasio, Mon. Ant., XXVIII (1923), pp. 521 ff.

## ETRUSCAN PAINTING

ADAMS, L. E. W., A Study in the Commerce of Latium, Smith College Studies, II, 1921.

BULLE, H., Der schöne Mensch, 2d ed., München, 1912.

BUONAMICI, G., MODONA, A. Neppi, L'Etruria e gli Etruschi, Firenze, 1926.

CANINA, L., L'antica città di Veii, Roma, 1847, Pls. 28-32.

——L'antica Etruria Marittima, 1846-1849.

CULTRERA, G., Not. degli Scavi, 1920, pp. 244-276.

Curtis, C. Densmore, Mem. Amer. Acad.
Rome, III (1919); V (1925).

Dennis, G., Cities and Cemeteries of
Etruria, London, 1848, 2d ed., 1878;
3d ed., 1883.

Ducati, P., Atene e Roma, 17 (1914), pp.
129 ff.

—— Etruria antica, Torino, 1926, bibliography.

Ducati, P., and Giglioli, G., Arte
Etrusca, Roma, 1927.

Duell, P., The Tomba del Triclinio at
Tarquinia, Mem. Amer. Acad. Rome, VI
(1927), pp. 9-68, Pls. 1-12 C.

Essen, C. C. Van, Did Orphic Influence
on Etruscan Tomb Paintings Exist? Amsterdam, 1927.

Fell, R. A. L., Etruria and Rome, Cambridge, 1924.

Galli, E., Mon. Ant., 24 (1916), pp. 5-
116.

Harmon, A. M., A.J.A., 16 (1912), pp. 1-
10.

Heinemann, M., Landschaftliche Elemente in der griechischen Kunst, Bonn,
1910, pp. 40 ff.

Karo, G., Orient und Hellas in archaischer
Zeit, Ath. Mitth., 45 (1920), pp. 106-
156.

Körte, G., Ein Wandgemälde von Vulci als
Document zur Röm. Königsgeschichte,
Jahr., XII (1897), pp. 57-80.

—— Ant. Denk., II, Pls. 41-43 and text.

—— P. W., s.v. Etrusker.

MacIver, D. Randall, The Etruscans,
Oxford, 1927.

—— Villanovans and Early Etruscans, Oxford, 1924.

Martha, J., L'art étrusque, Paris, 1889,
pp. 377-450.

Messerschmidt, F., Volcenter Malereien,
Die Antike, IV (1928), pp. 103-107, Pls.
12-20.

Micali, G., Antichi Monumenti, Firenze,
1810.

—— Monumenti Inediti, 1844.

Milani, L. A., Studi e Materiali, 1899, I;
1902, II; 1905, III.

—— Italici ed Etruschi, Roma, 1909.

Montelius, O., La civilisation primitive
en Italie, Stockholm, Atlas, I, 1895; II,
1904, Text, 1910.

Müller, K. O., and Deecke, W., Die
Etrusker, Stuttgart, 1877.

Murray, A. S., J.H.S., X (1889), 243-
252.

Petersen, E., Über die älteste Etruskische Wandmalerei (Veii), Röm. Mitth.,
17 (1902), 149-157.

Poulsen, F., Der Orient und die frühgriechische Kunst, Leipzig, 1912, pp.
128 ff.

—— *Etruscan Tomb Paintings, their
Subjects and Significance, Oxford, 1922,
tr. by I. Andersen.

Rumpf, A., Die Wandmalereien in Veii,
Leipzig, 1915 (Dissertation).

Seta, A. della, Religion and Art, tr. by
M. C. Harrison, N. Y., 1914, pp. 245-
265.

—— Italia Antica, Bergamo, 1922, pp.
223 ff.

Stryk, A. von, Studien über die Etruskischen Kammergräber, Dorpat, 1910.

Taylor, L. R., Local Cults in Etruria.
Papers and Monographs of the American
Academy in Rome, II, 1923, pp. 1-27.

Weege, F., Etruskische Gräber mit Gemäl-
den in Corneto, Jahrbuch, 31 (1916),
pp. 105-168, Pls. VI-XVI.

—— **Etruskische Malerei, Halle, 1921
(Corneto).

—— Die Etruskische Malerei, Veii, Chiusi,
Orvieto (in prep., De Gruyter, Berlin).

*Oscan.*

Duhn, F. von, Annali, 50 (1878), pp.
107 ff.

Helbig, W., Annali dell' Instituto, 37
(1865).

Sogliano, A., Mon. Ant., I, 953 ff.

Weege, F., Jahrbuch, 24 (1909), pp. 99-
162, Pls. 7-12.

## PAINTING OF THE FOURTH CENTURY

### Apelles.

BRUNN, H., Geschichte der griechischen Künstler, Stuttgart, II (1889), pp. 136-157.

MEISTER, R., Das Gemälde des Apelles im Asklepieion zu Kos, Festschrift für J. Overbeck, Leipzig, 1893, pp. 109 ff.

SIX, J., Apelles, Jahr., 20 (1905), pp. 169-179; Apelleisches, 25 (1910), pp. 147-159.

WOERMANN, K., Von Apelles zu Böcklin, Eszlingen, 1912.

### Philoxenos.

KÖRTE, G., Das Alexandermosaik aus Pompeii, Röm. Mitth., XXII (1907), pp. 1-24.

PERNICE, E., Bemerkungen zum Alexandermosaik, Röm. Mitth., XXII (1907), pp. 25-34.

SALIS, A. VON, Die Kunst der Griechen, Leipzig, 1919, pp. 221-224, 229.

WINTER, F., Das Alexandermosaik aus Pompeii, Strassburg, 1909.

### South Italian Vases.

DUCATI, P., Storia della ceramica greca, Firenze, 1922. Vol. II, Ch. VIII, 415 ff.

HAUSER, F., in F.R., Griechische Vasenmalerei, 1910, III, 57 ff.

MACCHIORO, V., Per la storia della ceramografia italiota. Röm. Mitth., 27 (1912), pp. 163-188.

PATRONI, G., La ceramica antica nell' Italia meridionale, Napoli, 1897.

WALTERS, H. B., Catalogue of the Greek and Etruscan Vases in the British Museum, London, 1896, IV, Introduction.

### South Russian Painting.

MINNS, E. H., Scythians and Greeks, Cambridge, 1913, pp. 305-358.

ROSTOVTZEFF, M., Ancient Decorative Wall-Painting, J.H.S., 39 (1919), pp. 144-163, Pls. VI-IX.

—— Iranians and Greeks in South Russia, Oxford, 1922, pp. 81, 160-161, Pls. XXVIII-XXIX.

### Tombs.

Delacoulonche, Berceau de la puissance macédonienne, p. 76 (Annales des missions scient., 1858).

FABRICIUS, E., Ein bemaltes Grab aus Tanagra, Ath. Mitth., X (1885), pp. 158-164.

HEUZEY, L., and DAUMET, Mission archéologique de Macédoine, Paris, 1876, pp. 226 ff.; pp. 247 ff.; p. 251.

KINCH, K. F., Macedonian Thracian Tomb, Kopenhagen, 1893 (in Dutch).

VOLLMOELLER, K. G., Über zwei euböische Kammergräber mit Totenbetten, Ath. Mitth., 26 (1901), pp. 333 ff.

### Vases.

DUCATI, P., Saggio di studio sulla ceramica attica figurata del secolo IV av. Cr., Roma, 1916.

### Kabeiric Vases.

PERROT, G., and CHIPIEZ, C., Histoire de l'art, Paris, X (1914), pp. 294-306.

ROMAGNOLI, E., Ausonia, II (1908), pp. 159-163.

WALTERS, H. B., History of Ancient Pottery, 1905, I, 391 ff.

—— Odysseus and Kirke on a Bœotian Vase, J.H.S., XIII (1892), pp. 77-87, Pl. IV (color).

WINNEFELD, H., Ath. Mitth., XIII (1888), pp. 412 ff., Pls. IX-XII.

## HELLENISTIC, GRÆCO-ROMAN, POMPEIAN, AND ROMAN PAINTING

### Antiphilos.

BRUNN, H., Geschichte der griechischen Künstler, Stuttgart, II (1889), pp. 166-169.

KLEIN, W., Geschichte der griechischen Kunst, 1907, III, 22 ff.

PFUHL, E., Malerei und Zeichnung der Griechen, München, 1923, II, 805 ff.

WEISBACH, WERNER, Impressionismus, Berlin, 1910, I, 15, 20, 70.

### Demetrios.

HELBIG, W., Untersuchungen über die Campanische Wandmalerei, Leipzig, 1873, pp. 138, 169, 289, 322.

PFUHL, E., Gött. Gelehrt. Anz., 172 (1910), p. 820.

WOERMANN, K., Die Landschaft in der Kunst der alten Völker, München, 1876.

—— Die Landschaftsmalerei bei Griechen und Römern, Eszlingen, 1912, pp. 24-26. (Von Apelles zu Böcklin.)

### Dioskourides.

BIEBER, M., and RODENWALDT, G., Die Mosaiken des Dioskurides von Samos, Jahr., 26 (1911), pp. 1 ff.

HERRMANN, P., Denkmäler der Malerei, München, 1906-date, pp. 132-138.

### Nealkes.

MÜNZER, F., Hermes, 30 (1895), p. 532, note 2.

PFUHL, E., Gött. Gelehrt. Anz., 172 (1910), p. 821.

### Sosos.

GUSMAN, P., La Villa Impériale de Tibur, Paris, 1904, Pl. 2.

HELBIG, W., Führer, 3d ed., 1912, I, 438; 1913, II, 49.

KELLER, O., Die antike Tierwelt, 1913, II, Fig. 19, p. 46 (color).

NOGARA, B., I mosaici antichi, Milano, 1910, pp. 3-5, Pls. V-VII.

PERNICE, E., Das Taubenmosaik im Kapitolinischen Museum, Arch. Anz., 42 (1927), pp. 247 ff.

SPINAZZOLA, V., Le arti decorative in Pompeii e nel Museo Nazionale di Napoli, Roma, 1928, Pls. 183-184.

### Landscape.

ALTMANN, W., B.P.W., 29 (1909), 1181 (Rec. Rostovtzeff, Die Hellenistisch-Röm. Architekturlandschaft).

DICKINS, G., Hellenistic Sculpture, Oxford, 1920, pp. 14, 29, 73.

FRIEDLÄNDER, L., Darstellung aus der Sittengeschichte Roms, 1910, II,[8] 191 ff., 262 ff. (Plastic character of ancient landscape.)

GOLDSCHMIDT, A., Das Nachleben der antiken Prospektmalerei im Mittelalter, Sitzber. der Kgl. Akad. der Wiss., Berlin, 29 (1916), 611.

HAUSER, F., Die neu-attischen Reliefs, Stuttgart, 1889.

HEINEMANN, M., Landschaftliche Elemente in der griechischen Kunst bis Polygnot, Bonn, 1910.

HELBIG, W., Untersuchungen über die campanische Wandmalerei, Leipzig, 1873, pp. 269 ff.

MATZ, F., Die Naturpersonifikation in der griech. Kunst, Göttingen, 1913 (Diss.).

NOGARA, B., Le Nozze Aldobrandine, Milano, 1907.

PAGENSTECHER, R., Alexandrinische Studien, Sitzungsberichte der Heid. Akad., 1917.

—— Über das landschaftliche Relief bei den Griechen, Sitzungsber. der Heid. Akad., 1919.

—— Die Landschaft in der Malerei des Altertums, N.J., 47-48 (1921), pp. 271 ff.

RODENWALDT, G., Das Relief bei den Griechen, Berlin, 1923, pp. 96 ff.

ROSTOVTZEFF, M., Pompeianische Landschaften und römische Villen, Jahr., XIX (1904), pp. 103 ff.

—— Die hellenistisch-römische Architekturlandschaft, Röm. Mitth., 26 (1911), pp. 1-160.

SCHOBER, A., Der landschaftliche Raum im Hellenistischen Reliefbild, Wien, Jahr., 2, pp. 36-51.

SCHREIBER, T., Die Hellenistischen Reliefbilder und die Augusteische Kunst, Jahr., XI (1896), pp. 78 ff.

SIEVEKING, J., Über hellenistische und römische Relief-Kunst, Taf., 621-630, Schlussbemerkung, Brunn, Bruckmann, Denkmäler Griech. und Röm. Sculptur, München, 1912.

WEISBACH, WERNER, Impressionismus, Berlin, 1910.

WOERMANN, K., Die Landschaft in der Kunst der alten Völker, München, 1876.

—— Über den landschaftlichen Natursinn der Griech. und Römer München, 1871.

—— Die Landschaftsmalerei bei Griechen und Römern, Eszlingen, 1912.

—— Die antiken Odysseelandschaften, München, 1877.

WRIGHT, F. A., The Arts in Greece, London, 1923.

*Pergamon.*

FRÄNKEL, M., Gemälde-Sammlungen und Gemälde-Forschung in Pergamon, Jahr., VI (1891), pp. 49 ff.

HERRMANN, P., Herakles findet Telephos, Denkmäler der Malerei, München, 1906-date, pp. 104 ff.

## FAYÛM PORTRAITS

BUBERL, P., Die griechisch.-ägyptisch. Mummienbildnisse der Sammlung Graf, Wien, 1922.

BULLE, H., Der schöne Mensch, 2d ed., München, 1912, Pl. 320.

CROS, H., et HENRY, CHARLES, L'encaustique chez les anciens, Paris, 1884.

EBERS, GEORG, Die hellenistischen Portraits aus dem Fajjûm, Leipzig, 1893.

—— The Hellenic Portraits from the Fayum, N. Y., 1893.

EDGAR, C. C., On the Dating of the Fayum Portraits, J.H.S., 25 (1905), p. 225.

—— Græco-Egyptian Coffins, Masks, and Portraits, Cat. gén. des ant. égypt., Le Caire, 1905, Vol. 26.

ERMAN, A., Porträt von einer Mumie aus Hawara in den Königl. Mus. zu Berlin, Ant. Denk., II, Pl. 13, text.

GRAF, TH., Catalogue of Th. Graf's Gallery of Antique Portraits, Berlin, 1889.

—— Katalog zu Theodor Graf's Galerie antiker Porträts aus Hellenistischer Zeit, Wien, 1905.

GRAUL, R., Die antiken Porträtgemälde aus den Grabstatten des Faijum, Leipzig, 1888 (Anhang by O. Donner von Richter).

GRÜNEISEN, W. DE, Le Portrait, traditions hellénistiques, et influences orientales, Rome, 1911.

GUIMET, É., Les Portraits d'Antinoé, Paris, 1912.

LYTHGOE, A. M., Bull. Metrop. Museum, March, 1910, 67.

MASNER, K., Mumienmasken und-Busten aus Oberägypten, Arch. Anz., IX (1894), pp. 178 ff.

MÖLLER, G., Das Mumienporträt (Wasmuth's Kunsthefte).

PAGENSTECHER, R., Expedition Ernst von Sieglin, II, Teil I, A, Malerei und Plastik, Leipzig, 1923, pp. 6-17, Pls. VI-VIII, X-XI (color).

PETRIE, W. M. F., Hawara, Biahmu and Arsinoë, London, 1889.

—— Kahun, Gurob, and Hawara, London, 1890.

—— Roman Portraits and Memphis, London, 1911 (IV).

—— Records of the Past, X (1911), pp. 303 ff.

—— The Hawara Portfolio, London, 1913.

REINACH, A., Les Portraits Grèco-Égyptiens, Rev. Arch., 24 (1914), pp. 32 ff.; 1915, pp. 1-36.

RICHTER, O. DONNER VON, Antike Denkmäler, II, Pl. 13, text, 2.

VETH, JAN, Alexandrinische Porträtmalereien, Kunst und Künstler, VII (1909), pp. 441 ff.

WEISBACH, W., Impressionismus, Berlin, 1910.

## DECORATIVE WALL-PAINTING

BULARD, M., Peintures murales et mosaïques de Délos, Mon. Piot, XIV (1908), pp. 116 f., 148, 169.

CUBE, G. VON, Die Römische "Scenæ Frons" in den Pompeianischen Wandbildern 4ten Stils, Beiträge zur Bauwissenschaft, Berlin, 1906, Heft 6.

DELBRÜCK, R., Einteilung und Dekoration der Wände, Hellenistische Bauten in Latium, Strassburg, 1912, II, 128 ff.

HERRMANN, P., Berl. Phil. Woch., 39 (1919), pp. 1227 ff. Rec. Pagenstecher, Alex. Studien, Sitzungsber. der Heid. Akad. der Wiss., 1917.

IPPEL, A., Der dritte Pompeianische Stil, Berlin, 1910.

MAU, A., Geschichte der decorativen Wandmalerei in Pompeii, Berlin, 1882, 20 Pls.

MAU, A., and KELSEY, F. W., Pompeii, its Life and Art, N. Y., 1899, pp. 446-460.

NICCOLINI, Le case ed i monumenti di Pompeii, Napoli, 1854-1862.

PAGENSTECHER, R., Alexandrinische Studien, Sitzungsber. der Heid. Akad., XII (1917), pp. 20 ff.

—— Nekropolis, Leipzig, 1919, Ch. IV, pp. 168 ff.

PFUHL, E., Malerei und Zeichnung der Griechen, München, 1923; I, §§ 17-21; II, 810-812, 868-872, 897-898.

POULSEN, F., Die dekorative Kunst des Altertums, Berlin, 1914, pp. 86-96.

RODENWALDT, G., Röm. Mitth., 32 (1917), pp. 18 ff.

—— Die Komposition der pompeianischen Wandgemälde, Berlin, 1909.

ROSTOVTZEFF, M., Ancient Decorative Wall-Painting, J.H.S., 39 (1919), pp. 144 ff.

STRZYGOWSKI, J., Gött. Gelehrt. Anz. (1906), pp. 910 ff.

THIERSCH, H., Zwei antiken Grabanlagen in Alexandria, Berlin, 1904.

WICKHOFF, F., Roman Art, London, 1900 (tr. by Mrs. S. Arthur Strong), pp. 122 ff.

## HELLENISTIC-ROMAN PAINTING

### Alexandrian Grave Reliefs.

KIESERITSKY, G. VON, WATZINGER, C., Griechische Grabreliefs aus Südrussland, Berlin, 1909.

PFUHL, E., Alexandrinische Grabreliefs, Ath. Mitth., 26 (1901), pp. 258 ff.

### Alexandrian Stelæ and Painted Stelæ of Sidon, etc.

BRECCIA, E., Bulletin de la Société Arch. d'Alexandrie, 1907, p. 43.

—— La necropoli di Sciatbi, Le Caire, 1912. (Cat. gén. des ant. égypt.)

CLERMONT-GANNEAU, CH., Stèles peintes de Sidon, Gaz. archéol., III (1877), pp. 102-115, Pls. 15-16.

MERRIAM, A. C., Painted sepulchral stelai from Alexandria, A.J.A., III (1887), pp. 261 ff.

PAGENSTECHER, R., Nekropolis, Leipzig, 1919, pp. 32 ff.

—— Malerei und Plastik, Ernst von Sieglin Exp., II, Teil I, A, 4-6, Pls. III-V and Beiblatt, Leipzig, 1923.

REINACH, A., Les Galates dans l'art Alexandrin, Mon. Piot, XVIII (1910), pp. 37 ff.

RENAN, E., Mission en Phénicie, Paris, 1864, pp. 209, 395, 408, 411, 661.

SCHIFF, A., Alexandrinische Dipinti, Leipzig, 1905, I.

*Southern Italy.*

GABRICI, E., Tomba Ellenistica di S. Maria la Nuova in Napoli, Röm. Mitth., 27 (1912), pp. 148-161.

—— Mon. Ant., XX (1910), pp. 1 ff. Tombs of Teano.

PAGENSTECHER, R., Grabgemälde aus Gnathia, Röm. Mitth., 27 (1912), pp. 101 ff., Pl. IV.

PETRA, G. DE, Di un antico ipogeo scoperto in Napoli, Mon. Ant., VIII (1898), pp. 217-232, Pls. V-VII (color).

QUAGLIATI, Q., Not. d. Sc., 1906, p. 468, Couch graves, Tarentum.

*Pagasæ Stelæ.*

ARVANITOPOULLOS, A. S., Ephemeris Archaiologike, 1908, pp. 1 ff., Pls. I-IV; 1913, pp. 236 ff.

—— Thessalika Mnemeia, Athens, 1909.

COLLIGNON, M., Revue de l'art ancien et moderne, 1913, I, 81-96.

KARO, G., Arch. Anz., 25 (1910), p. 157; 27 (1912), p. 245; 30 (1915), p. 208.

RODENWALDT, G., Zu den Grabstelen von Pagasæ, Ath. Mitth., 35 (1910), pp. 118 ff.

WALTON, ALICE, Painted Marbles from Thessaly, Art and Archæology, IV (1916), pp. 47-53.

*Grave Stelæ from Chios.*

Beschreibung der antiken Skulpturen, Kgl. Museen zu Berlin, Berlin, 1891, No. 766ᵃ, pp. 288 ff.

BRÜCKNER, A., Ath. Mitth., XIII (1888), pp. 363 ff.

KEKULÉ, R. VON STRADONITZ, Die Griechische Skulptur, Berlin, 1907, pp. 300 ff., and Figure, p. 301.

LAWRENCE, A. W., Later Greek Sculpture, New York, 1927, pp. 23 ff., 115, Pl. 42.

PFUHL, E., Malerei und Zeichnung der Griechen, München, 1923, II, pp. 903 ff.

STUDNICZKA, F., Ath. Mitth., XIII (1888), pp. 195 ff.

TREU, G., Ath. Mitth., XIV (1889), pp. 301 ff.

VOLLGRAFF, W., B.C.H., 26 (1902), pp. 559 f.

*Marissa Tombs.*

PETERS, J. P., and THIERSCH, HERMANN, Painted Tombs in the Necropolis of Marissa, London, 1905. (Palestine Exploration Fund.)

PETERS, J. P., Painted Tombs of Palestine, Art and Archæology, VII (1918), pp. 181 ff.

—— The Painted Tombs at Marissa, Records of the Past, IV (1905), pp. 291-307.

*Hellenistic Vases.*

BEHN, FR., Römische Keramik mit Einschluss der Hellenistischen Vorstufen, Mainz, 1910.

BIARDOT, E. PROSPER, Les terres-cuites grecques funèbres, Paris, 1872, Pl. XLIX, 438. (Polychrome vases of Canosa.) Cf. Pls. XL-L.

BRECCIA, E., Ghirlandomania Alessandrina, Le Musée Égyptien, III (1915), p. 13, Pls. VII-XIX.

——La Necropoli di Sciatbi, Le Caire, 1912, p. 27.

COURBY, F., Vases avec reliefs appliqués du Musée de Délos, B.C.H., 37 (1913), pp. 418 ff.

DUCATI, P., Storia della ceramica greca, Firenze, 1922, II, 476 ff.

JATTA, M., Tombe canosine del Museo Provinciale di Bari, Röm. Mitth., XXIX (1914), pp. 90 ff., Pls. VIII-X (color).

LENORMANT, F., Gaz. Arch., VII (1881-1882), pp. 102 ff.

LEROUX, G., Lagynos, Paris, 1913.

LIBERTINI, G., Centuripe, Catania, 1926.

MACCHIORO, V., Per la cronologia dei vasi Canosini (Messapian Class), Röm. Mitth., 25 (1910), pp. 168 ff.

MAYER, M., Not. d. Sc., 1898, pp. 195 ff.

——Apulien vor und während der Hellenisirung, Leipzig, 1914.

PACE, B., Ceramiche Ellenistiche Siceliote, Ausonia, VIII (1915), pp. 27-34.

PAGENSTECHER, R., Dated Sepulchral Vases from Alexandria, A.J.A., XIII (1909), pp. 387 ff., Pls. IX-XII (Hadra vases). Bibliography, 388.

——Schwarzfigurige Vasen des 4^{ten} und 3^{ten} Jahrhunderts, Bull. de la Soc. Archéol. d'Alex., 14 (1921), III, 229-239.

——Arch. Anz., 1909, pp. 1 ff. (Gnathia Ware).

——Apulien, Leipzig, 1914.

PATRONI, G., La ceramica antica nell' Italia Meridionale, Napoli, 1897.

——Unteritalische Grabdenkmäler, Strassburg, 1912.

PERDRIZET, P., Poterie de l'époque hellénistique, Fouilles de Delphes, V (1908), pp. 171-183.

PHARMAKOWSKY, B., Arch. Anz., 22 (1907), pp. 134 ff.

PICARD, CH., Questions de céramique Hellénistique, Rev. Arch., 22 (1913), pp. 160-192.

——La fin de la céramique peinte en Grande-Grèce, d'après les documents des Musées d'Italie, B.C.H., XXXV (1911), pp. 177-230, Pls. V-IX.

POTTIER, E., Vases Hellénistiques à fond blanc, Mon. Piot, 20 (1913), pp. 163 ff., Pls. XI-XII (color).

RAYET, O., and COLLIGNON, M., Histoire de la céramique grecque, Paris, 1888, 336 (Canosa), pp. 323 ff.

SIEGLIN, E., PAGENSTECHER, R., Beschreibung der griechisch-ägyptisch. Sammlung Ernst von Sieglin, Leipzig, 1913.

SIX, J., Vasen der Sammlung Six zu Amsterdam und des Metrop. Museum of Art zu New York, Ant. Denk., III, Pl. 34, text, 33, Bibliography.

SMITH, A. H., Corpus Vasorum Antiquorum, Great Britain, Fasc. I, British Museum, Fasc. I, London, 1925 (Gnathia).

STERN, E. VON, Ein Beitrag zur Hellenistischen Keramik, 1910.

WATZINGER, C., Vasenfunde aus Athen, Athen. Mitth., 26 (1901), pp. 50-102, Pls. III-IV (color).

——Studien zur unteritalischen Vasenmalerei, Darmstadt, 1899.

ZAHN, R., Hellenistische Reliefgefässe aus Südruszland, Jahr., XXIII (1908), pp. 45-77.

### Glass.

BRECK, J., The Ficoroni Medallion and some other gilded glasses in the Metropolitan Museum of Art, Art Bulletin, IX (1926-1927), pp. 353 ff., Figs. 1-6.

DALTON, O. M., The Gilded Glass of the Catacombs, The Archæological Journal, LVIII (1901).

DELBRÜCK, R., Arch. Anz., XXIX (1914), p. 199, Fig. 9.

GARRUCCI, R., Vetri ornati di figure in oro, Roma, 1858; 2d ed., 1864.

KISA, A., Das Glas im Altertume, Leipzig, 1908, Vols. II, III.

LECLERCQ, DOM. H., Manuel d'archéologie chrétienne, Paris, 1907, pp. 436 ff., Bibliogr., p. 504.

MÉLY, F. DE, La médallion de la croix du Musée chrétien de Brescia, Arethuse, 1926, No. 10, pp. 1-9.

MICHON, E., Verres peints antiques, Bull. de la Soc. Nat. des Ant. de France, 1913.

MORIN-JEAN, Rec. Rostovtzeff, Rev. Arch., (1917), pp. 310 ff.

ROSTOVTZEFF, M., Painted Glass Vases of the Later Hellenistic Times, 1914 (Bull. de la Comm. Imp. Arch.). Russian.

VOPEL, H., Die altchristlichen Goldgläser, Freiburg, 1899.

ZAHN, R., Glaskännchen im Berliner Antiquarium, Die Antike, V (1929), pp. 45 ff., Pl. 6 (color).

*Vases with Plastic Decoration.*

COURBY, F., Les vases grecs à reliefs, Paris, 1922.

—— Vases avec reliefs appliqués du Musée de Délos, B.C.H., 37 (1913), pp. 418 ff.

DUCATI, P., Saggio di studio sulla ceramica attica figurata del sec. IV a.c. Memoria della Real. Accad. dei Lincei, 1916.

—— Storia della ceramica greca, Firenze, 1922, II, 518-539.

GABRICI, E., Cuma, Mon. Ant., 22 (1913), pp. 696 ff., Pls. C-CII.

KÖRTE, G., Gött. gelehrt. Anz., 1913, 153.

MAXIMOVA, M. I., Les vases plastiques dans l'antiquité, époque archaïque, Paris, 1926, tr. by M. Carsow, Vols. I, II.

MINNS, E. H., Scythians and Greeks, Cambridge, 1913, pp. 343-357.

RAYET, O., and COLLIGNON, M., Histoire de la céramique grecque, Paris, 1888, pp. 261-278, 339-378.

TREU, G., Griechische Thongefässe in Statuetten- und Büstenform, 35 Winckelmannsprogr., Berlin, 1875.

ZAHN, R., Hellenistische Reliefgefässe aus Südruszland, Jahr., XXIII (1908), pp. 45-77.

*Aldobrandini Wedding.*

BÖTTIGER, K., Die Aldobrandinische Hochzeit, Dresden, 1810.

BULLE, H., Der schöne Mensch, 2d ed., München, 1912, Pls. 316, 317; 3d ed., München, 1922.

NOGARA, B., Le Nozze Aldobrandine, Milano, 1907.

PFUHL, E., Gött. Gelehrt. Anz., 172 (1910), p. 824.

ROBERT, C., Die Aldobrand. Hochzeit, Hermes, 35 (1900), pp. 657 ff.

RODENWALDT, G., Zur Aldobrandinischen Hochzeit, Arch. Anz., 29 (1914), pp. 447 ff.

WINTER, F., Die Aldobrand. Hochzeit, Das Museum, II, pp. 49 ff.

*Boscoreale Frescoes.*

BARNABEI, F., La Villa Pompeiana di Fannio Sinistore scoperta presso Boscoreale, Roma, 1901.

GIACOMO, S. DI, Les Fresques de Boscoreale, Gaz. des Beaux-Arts, 1901, pp. 15-26.

RICHTER, G. M. A., The Boscoreale Frescoes in the Metropolitan Museum of Art, Art and Archæology, VII (1918), pp. 239-246.

STUDNICZKA, F., Imagines Illustrium, Jahr., 38-39 (1923-1924), pp. 57-128, Pls. II-III.

*Odyssey Landscapes.*

MÜLLER, F., Die antiken Odyssee-Illustrationen in ihrer kunsthistorischen Entwickelung, Berlin, 1913.

NOGARA, B., Le Nozze Aldobrandine, Milano, 1907.

RODENWALDT, G., Die Komposition der Pompeian. Wandgemälde, Berlin, 1909.

WEISBACH, W., Impressionismus, Berlin, 1910.

WOERMANN, K., Die antiken Odysseelandschaften, München, 1877.

## Villa Item.

ENGELMANN, W., New Guide to Pompeii, Leipzig, 1925, pp. 94-109, Figs. 66-75, Plans, 64-65.

HERBIG, R., Zu den Wandgemälden der Villa Item, Arch. Anz., 40 (1925), pp. 262-266.

HERRMANN, P., B.P.W., 31 (1911), pp. 757 ff.

IPPEL, A., Pompeii, Leipzig, 1925, pp. 127-134, Figs. 119-126.

MACCHIORO, V., Zagreus, Bari, 1920.

—— The Villa of the Mysteries in Pompeii (Guide), Naples.

MUDIE COOKE, MISS P. B., The Paintings of the Villa Item at Pompeii, J.R.S., III (1913), pp. 157 ff.

NICOLE, G., Gazette des Beaux-Arts, 1911, pp. 21 ff.

PETRA, G. DE, Notizie degli Scavi, 1910, p. 139, Pls. I-XX.

POTTIER, E., Les fresques de la Villa du Fondo Gargiulo, Rev. Arch., 1915, II, 321.

REINACH, S., Rev. Arch., 1910, II, 430.

RIZZO, E. G., Dionysos Mystes, Mem. Acc. arch. di Napoli, III, 1918.

ROSSBACH, O., B.P.W., 31 (1911), pp. 503 ff.

ROSTOVTZEFF, M., Mystic Italy, N. Y., 1927.

SIEVEKING, J., B.P.W., 31 (1911), pp. 599 ff.

VAN BUREN, E. DOUGLAS, J.R.S., IX (1919), pp. 221-225.

## Farnesina Black Wall.

HELBIG, W., Führer, 3d ed., 1913, II, 151, No. 1356.

LESSING-MAU, Wand- und Deckenschmuck eines Römischen Hauses, Berlin, 1891, Pl. 9.

LOEWY, E., Festschrift zu O. Hirschfeld, Berlin, 1903, p. 419.

ROBERT, C. Illustr. zu einem griech. Roman, Hermes, 36 (1901), pp. 364-368; Mon. XI, Pls. 44-48.

## Stucco.

GUSMAN, P., L'art décoratif de Rome, Paris, 1908-1914, Pls. 72-74, 36.

HELBIG, W., Führer, 3d ed., Leipzig, 1913, II, 117, Nos. 1327-1332.

LESSING-MAU, Wand- und Deckenschmuck, Berlin, 1891, Pl. 8; 15.

—— Mon. XII, Pl. XXXVI.

RONCZEWSKI, K., Gewölbeschmuck im Römischen Altertum, Berlin, 1903.

ROSTOVTZEFF, M., Röm. Mitth., 26 (1911), p. 35, Abb. 11-13.

WICKHOFF, F., Roman Art, London, 1900. (Trans. by Mrs. S. Arthur Strong.)

## Aphrodite and Peitho.

HELBIG, W., Führer, 3d ed., Leipzig, 1913, II, 208, No. 1479.

## House of Livia, Palatine Hill.

Io and Argos, Mon. XI, Pl. 22; Annali, 1880, pp. 136 ff. (Mau).

## Yellow Frieze.

ROSTOVTZEFF, M., Röm. Mitth., 26 (1911).

## Pompeian Wall-Painting.

ALEXANDER, CHRISTINE, Wall Paintings of the Third Style from Boscotrecasse, Metrop. Museum Studies, I, II (1929), pp. 176 ff.

D'AMELIO, P., Dipinti murali di Pompeii, Napoli, 1902.

BARNABEI, F., La Villa Pompeiana di P. Fannio Sinistore scoperta presso Boscoreale, Roma, 1901.

BOISSIER, G., Promenades archéologiques, tr. by D. H. Fisher, Rome and Pompeii, N. Y., 1905, pp. 370 ff.

BRIGGS, R. A., Pompeian Decorations, London, 1911.

CAGNAT, R., CHAPOT, V., Manuel d'archéologie Romaine, 1920, II, Chs. III-IV.

DIEPOLDER, H., Untersuchungen zur Komposition der römisch-campanischen Wandgemälde, Röm. Mitth., 41 (1926), pp. 1-78.

ELY, T., The House of Aulus Vettius, Archæologia, 55 (1897), pp. 301 ff.

GUSMAN, P., La décoration murale à Pompéi, Paris, 1924 (colored plates).

HELBIG, W., Wandgemälde der vom Vesuv verschütteten Städte Campaniens, Leipzig, 1868.

—— Untersuchungen über die Campanische Wandmalerei, Leipzig, 1873.

HERRMANN, P., Denkmäler der Malerei, München, 1906-date.

KLEIN, W., Pompeianische Bilderstudien, Oest. Jahr., XV (1912), pp. 143-167, I; XIX-XX (1919), pp. 268-295, II; XXIII (1926), pp. 71-115, III.

—— Zum Grundproblem der Pompeian. Wandmalerei, Oest. Jahr., XIII (1910), pp. 123-149.

MARCONI, P., La pittura dei Romani, Roma, 1929.

MAU, A., Geschichte der decorativen Wandmalerei in Pompeii, Berlin, 1882.

—— Pompeii in Leben und Kunst, 2d ed., Leipzig, 1908.

—— Röm. Mitth., XI (1896), pp. 6 ff. (House of the Vettii.)

MAU, A., and KELSEY, F. W., Pompeii, its Life and Art, N. Y., 1899.

NICCOLINI, Le case ed i monumenti di Pompeii, Napoli, 1854-1862.

PFUHL, E., Gött. Gelehrt. Anz., 172 (1910), pp. 789-826. Rec. Rodenwaldt, Kompos. der pomp. Wandgemälde.

—— Malerei und Zeichnung der Griechen, München, 1923.

—— Masterpieces of Greek Drawing and Painting, trans. by J. D. Beazley, N. Y., 1926.

PRESUHN, E., Die Pompeianischen Wanddekoration, Leipzig, 1882.

RAOUL-ROCHETTE, Peintures antiques inédites, Paris, 1836.

RODENWALDT, G., Die Komposition der pompeianischen Wandgemälde, Berlin, 1909.

SALIS, A. VON, Die Kunst der Griechen, Leipzig, 1919.

SOGLIANO, A., Le Pitture murale campane, Napoli, 1880.

—— La Casa dei Vettii in Pompeii, Mon. Ant., VIII (1898), pp. 233-388, Pls. VIII-XI.

SPELTZ, A., L'ornement polychrome, I, L'Antiquité, Leipzig, 1915.

SPINAZZOLA, V., Le arti decorative in Pompeii e nel Museo Nazionale di Napoli, Roma, 1928. (Also for glass, stucco.)

TERNITE, W., Wandgemälde aus Pompeii und Herculaneum, Berlin, 1839-1858.

TURNBULL, G., A Treatise on Ancient Paintings, London, 1740.

WATT, J. C., Examples of Greek and Pompeian decorative work, London, 1897 (Very fine drawings).

WICKHOFF, F., Roman Art, London, 1900 (Tr. by Mrs. S. Arthur Strong).

—— Die Wiener Genesis, Wien, 1895 (With W. von Hartel).

WINTER, F., Über Vorlagen pompeianisch. Wandgemälde, Oest. Jahr., V (1902), pp. 96 ff.

WIRTH, F., Der Stil der Kampanischen Wandgemälde im Verhältnis zur Wanddekoration, Röm. Mitth., 42 (1927), pp. 1-83.

ZAHN, W., Die schönsten Ornamente und merkwürdigsten Gemälde aus Pompeii, Berlin, 1828, I; 1842, II; 1852-1853, III.

*Roman National Themes.*

BRIZIO, E., Pitture e sepolcri scoperti sull' Esquilino, Roma, 1876.

CORTE, M. DELLA, Not. d. sc., 1912, 174 ff.

COURBAUD, E., La Peinture d'histoire de l'époque Républicaine. Le Bas-Relief Romain, Paris, 1899, pp. 195 ff.

HELBIG, W., Führer, 3d ed., 1913, II, 190 ff., Nos. 1451-1454.

ROBERT, C., Fregio di pitture riferibili ai miti di Enea e di Romolo scoperte sull' Esquilino, Annali, 50 (1878), pp. 234 ff.; Mon. dell' Inst., X, Pls. 60, 60ª.

URLICHS, L., Die Malerei in Rom vor Caesar's Dictatur, Würzburg, 1876.

*Columbarium of Pomponius Hylas.*

ASHBY, T., B.S.R., V (1910), pp. 463 ff.; Pls. XXVII to XLVII. (Newton.)

*Columbarium of Villa Pamfili.*

JAHN, O., Die Wandgemälde des Columbariums in der Villa Pamfili, Abh. der Kgl. Bayr. Akademie, München, 1857.

ROSTOVTZEFF, M., Die Hellenistisch-Römische Architekturlandschaft, Röm. Mitth., 26 (1911), pp. 26 ff., Figs. 6-8.

SAMTER, E., Le Pitture parietali del Colombario di Villa Pamfili, Röm. Mitth., VIII (1893), pp. 105-144.

—— Arch. Anz., XIII (1898), pp. 47-50.

*Villa Negroni.*

BUTI, C., Pitture antiche della Villa Negroni, Roma, 1778.

KRIEGER, H., Dekorative Wandgemälde aus dem II Jahr. nach Christus, Röm. Mitth., 34 (1919), pp. 24-52.

*Tomb of the Nasonii.*

BELLORI, G., Sepolcro de Nasonii (1680).

—— Picturae antiquae cryptarum Romanarum et sepulchri Nasonum, Romæ 1750. (Drawings by P. Bartoli.)

MICHAELIS, A., and PETERSEN, E., Das Grabmal der Nasonier, Jahr., 25 (1910), pp. 101 ff.

RODENWALDT, G., Gemälde aus dem Grabe der Nasonier, Röm. Mitth., 32 (1917), pp. 1-20.

*Tombs on the Via Latina.*

ALINARI, Photos 2357-2370.

DUHN, F. VON, Arch. Anz., 36 (1921), pp. 113 ff.

EISLER, R., Orphisch-Dionysische Mysteriengedanken in der Christlichen Antike, Berlin, 1925, pp. 123 ff.

GUSMAN, P., L'art décoratif de Rome, Paris, 1908-1914, Pls. 50-51, 45.

PETERSEN, E., Annali, 32 (1860), p. 348; 33 (1861), p. 190, Mon. VI, Pls. XLIII-XLIV, XLIX-LIII.

RONCZEWSKI, K., Gewölbeschmuck im Römischen Altertum, Berlin, 1903, Pls. XVII, XVIII, XX, etc.

STRONG, MRS. ARTHUR, Apotheosis and After Life, London, 1915, pp. 206 ff.

WADSWORTH, E., Stucco reliefs of the First and Second Centuries still extant in Rome, Memoirs of the American Academy in Rome, IV (1924), pp. 69 ff., Pls. XX-XXXV.

*House in the Via de' Cerchi.*

HUELSEN, C., Röm. Mitth., VIII (1893), pp. 289 ff.

MARCHETTI, D., Not. d. Sc., 1892, pp. 44 ff.

STRONG, MRS. ARTHUR, Forgotten fragments of ancient Wall-Paintings in Rome, B.S.R., VIII (1916), pp. 91 ff., Pls. III-IX.

*Ostia.*

CALZA, G., Mon. Ant., 26 (1920), pp. 375 ff.

FORNARI, F., La pittura decorativa di Ostia, Studi Romani, 1913, I, 305 ff., Pls. 29-35.

VAGLIERI, D., Not. d. Sc., 1908, p. 23, Fig. 2.

*SS. Giovanni e Paolo (La Casa Celimontana).*

AMELUNG, W., Atti della Pontificia Academia Romana, 1910, pp. 13 ff.

GATTI, G., La Casa Celimontana dei Valerii, Bull. Comun., 1902, pp. 163 ff.

GERMANO, PADRE, The House of the Martyrs John and Paul, A.J.A., VII (1891), pp. 31 ff.

—— La Casa Celimontana, Roma, 1894.

ROBERT, C., Hermes, 46 (1911), pp. 250 ff.

WULFF, O., Altchristliche und Byzantinische Kunst, 1914, I, 59 ff.

### San Sebastiano.

MANCINI, G., Not. d. Sc., 1923, pp. 53 ff., Pls. X-XVI.

MARUCCHI, O., Notizia sulle recenti scoperte nelle catacombe di San Sebastiano, Bull. Com., 43 (1916), pp. 249-278.

—— Nuovo Bull. di Arch. Crist., 1916, pp. 5 ff., 6 Pls.

STYGER, PAOLO, Il monumento Apostolico della Via Appia secondo gli ultimi scavi della Basilica di San Sebastiano, 1915-1916, Roma, 1917.

### Viale Manzoni Frescoes.

BENDINELLI, G., Ipogeo con pitture scoperto presso il Viale Manzoni, Not. d. Sc., 1920, pp. 123-141, Pls. I-IV.

—— Art and Archæology, XI (1921), pp. 169 ff.

—— Il Monumento sepolcrale degli Aureli al Viale Manzoni in Roma, Mon. Ant., 28 (1923), Pls. I-XVII, pp. 290-478.

MARUCCHI, O., Nuovo Bull. di archeol. Crist., XXVI (1920), pp. 53 ff.; XXVII (1921), pp. 44 ff.; 83 ff.; XXVIII (1922), pp. 128 ff.

PARIBENI, R., Bolletino d'Arte, I (1921), pp. 97-104, Antichissime pitture cristiane a Roma, Milano, 1921.

ROSTOVTZEFF, M., Mystic Italy, New York, 1927, pp. 148 ff.

WILPERT, O., Mem. Accad. Pont., 1924, I, Pt. II, 1-43.

### Illuminated Manuscripts.

BETHE, E., Terentius, Codex Ambrosianus, H 75, phototypice editus, Leyden, 1903 (De Vries, Codices græci et latini, VIII).

—— Die antiken Terenz-Illustrationen, Jahr., 18 (1903), pp. 93-108.

DALTON, O. M., Byzantine Art and Archæology, Oxford, 1911, Ch. VII, pp. 435 ff.

ENGELHARDT, O., Die Illustrationen der Terenzhandschriften, Jena, 1905 (Diss.).

GERSTINGER, H., Die griechische Buchmalerei, Wien, 1926.

HERBERT, J. A., Illuminated Manuscripts, London, 1912, 2d ed.

Homeri Iliadis pictae fragmenta ambrosiana phototypice edita, Milan, 1905.

JACKMANN, G., Die Geschichte des Terenz-Textes im Altertum, Basel, 1924.

JONES, L. WEBBER, The Archetypes of the Terence Miniatures, Art Bulletin, X (1927), pp. 103-120.

NOLHAC, PIERRE DE, Le Virgile du Vatican, Notices et Extraits, XXXV, Pt. II (1897), pp. 683-791.

—— Fragmenta et picturae Virgiliana codicis Vaticani, 3225, Rome, 1899.

—— Les Peintures des Mss. de Vergile, Mel. Arch. Hist., 1884, p. 305 (color).

STRZYGOWSKI, J., Orient oder Rom., Leipzig, 1901.

—— Die Calenderbilder des Chronographen vom Jahre, 354, Berlin, 1888 (Jahr. Ergänzungsheft, I).

WAGENINGEN, J. VAN, Album Terentianum Groningæ, 1907.

WESTON, K. E., The Illustrated Terence Manuscripts, Harvard Studies, XIV (1903), pp. 37-54.

WICKHOFF, F., Roman Art, London, 1900 (tr. by Mrs. S. Arthur Strong). Ch. V, pp. 172 ff.

WICKHOFF, F., and HARTEL, W. R. VON, Die Wiener Genesis, Wien, 1895.

### Byzantine Painting.

AINALOV, D., Die Hellenistischen Grundlagen der Byzantinischen Kunst, Petrograd, 1900 (Russian). Cf. O. Wulff, Repertorium für Kunstwiss. XXVI (1903), p. 35.

BRÉHIER, L., L'art Byzantin, Paris, 1924.

DALTON, O. M., Byzantine Art and Archaeology, Oxford, 1911.

DIEHL, CH., L'art Byzantin, 1894.

—— Manuel d'art Byzantin, Paris, 1910.

—— Choses et gens de Byzance, Paris, 1926, pp. 123 ff.

GERSTINGER, H., Die griechische Buchmalerei, Vienna, 1926 (Byz. Illum.).

JERPHANION, G. DE, Les églises rupestres de Cappadoce, Paris, 1925.

KONDAKOFF, N. P., Histoire de l'art Byzantin, Paris, 1886.

PEIRCE, H. R., and TYLER, R., Byzantine Art, London, 1926 (Kai Khosru Series).

WULFF, O., Repertorium für Kunstwiss. XXVI (1903), p. 35 (Ainalov).

—— Altchristliche und Byzantinische Kunst, 1914, I.

### Tor Marancio.

HELBIG, W., Führer, 3d ed., 1912, I, 265 ff.

NOGARA, B., Ausonia, I (1907), pp. 51 ff., Pl. II.

—— Le Nozze Aldobrandine, Milano, 1907, pp. 55 ff.

### Mosaic.

ASHBY, T., Archæologia, LVIII (1902), pp. 119 ff., Pls. 10-11 (Cærwent).

AURIGEMMA, S., In A Roman Villa at Zliten, Art and Archæology, 23 (1927), pp. 161-169.

—— Mosaico con scene d'anfiteatro in una villa Romana a Zliten in Tripolitania, Dedalo, IV (1923-1924), pp. 333-361, 397-414; V (1924), pp. 197-217.

—— I mosaici di Zliten, 1926.

BIEBER, M., and RODENWALDT, G., Die Mosaiken des Dioskurides von Samos, Jahr., 26 (1911), pp. 1 ff.

BULARD, M., Peintures Murales et Mosaïques de Délos, Mon. Piot, XIV (1908), pp. 185 ff., Pls. X-XV.

CAGNAT, R., CHAPOT, V., Manuel d'archéologie Romaine, II, 1920.

GAUCKLER, P., La mosaïque antique, 1904.

—— Le Domaine des Laberii à Uthina, Mon. Piot, III (1896), pp. 176 ff.

—— Musivum Opus, Daremberg and Saglio, Dict. des antiq.

—— Les Mosaïques Virgiliennes de Sousse, Mon. Piot, IV (1897), pp. 233 ff., Pl. 20 (color).

—— Inventaire des Mosaïques.

GERSPACH, É., La Mosaïque, Paris, 1893, 2d ed.

HETTNER, F., Das Mosaik des Monnus in Trier, Ant. Denk., I, Pls. 47-49.

HOPE, W. H. ST. JOHN, Fox, GEORGE E., Archæologia, 55 (1896), pp. 215 ff. (Silchester.)

—— Inventaire des Mosaïques de la Gaule et de l'Afrique:

I. Gaule, G. L. Lafaye, A. Blanchet.

II. Afrique proconsulaire (Tunisie), P. Gauckler.

III. Afrique proconsulaire, Numidie, Maurétanie (Algérie), F. G. de Pachtère.

LAFAYE, G., Rev. Arch., 1892, I, 322-347.

LEONHARD, W., Mosaikstudien zur Casa del Fauno in Pompeii, Neapel, 1914.

MIDDLETON, J. H., JONES, H. STUART, Encyclopædia Britannica, s.v. Mosaic. (Bibliography of Early Works.)

MORGAN, THOMAS, Romano-British Mosaic Pavements, London, 1886.

MÜNTZ, E., Notes zur les mosaïques Chrétiennes de l'Italie, Rev. Arch., XXXVI (1878), pp. 272 ff.

NOGARA, B., I mosaici antichi, Milano, 1910.

PACE, B., Ricerche Cartaginesi, Mon. Ant., XXX (1925), pp. 190 ff., Figs. 26-30 (Orpheus).

ROBERT, C., Das Mosaik von Portus-Magnus, Jahr., V (1890), p. 215, Pls. IV-VI.

SCHÖNE, R., Das Pompeian. Alexander Mosaik, N. J. (1912), pp. 181-204.

SPINAZZOLA, V., Le arti decorative in Pompeii e nel Museo Nazionale di Napoli, Roma, 1928, Pls. 176-198.

STUDEMUND, W., Zum Mosaik des Monnus, Jahr., V (1890), pp. 1 ff.

WALTERS, H. B., Art of the Romans, N. Y., 1911, pp. 108 ff.

WILMOWSKY, D. VON, Die römisch. Villa zu Nennig und ihr Mosaik, Bonn, I, 1864; II, 1865.

—— Römische Mosaiken aus Trier und dessen Umgegend, Bonn, 1888.

WILPERT, J., Die römische Mosaiken und Malereien, Freiburg, 1917, 2d ed.

WINTER, F., Das Alexandermosaik aus Pompeii, Strassburg, 1909.

WOLTERS, P., Zum Mosaik des Monnus, Jahr., V (1890), pp. 213 ff.


*Catacombs, Christian Art.*

BRÉHIER, L., L'art Chrétien, Paris, 1918.

DALTON, O. M., East Christian Art, Oxford, 1925.

FROTHINGHAM, A. L., The Monuments of Christian Rome, N. Y., 1925.

GARRUCCI, R., Storia della arte Cristiana, Prato, 1873-1881.

GERSTINGER, H., Die griechische Buchmalerei, Wien, 1926.

KAUFMANN, C. M., Handbuch der Christlichen Archäologie, Paderborn, 1905.

KRAUS, F. X., Geschichte der Christlichen Kunst, Freiburg, 1896, I.

LAURENT, M., L'art Chrétien primitif, Paris, 1910.

LECLERCQ, DOM. H., Manuel d'archéolgie Chrétienne, Paris, 1907 (Bibliography).

LEFORT, L., Études sur les monuments primitifs de la peinture chrétienne en Italie, Paris, 1885.

LOWRIE, W., Monuments of the Early Church, N. Y., 1923, pp. 187 ff.

MARUCCHI, O., Roma sotterranea Cristiana, Roma, I, Monumenti del cimitero di Domitilla, 1909.

—— Éléments d'archéologie chrétienne, Paris, 1905.

—— Manuale di archeologia cristiana, Roma, 1923.

MICHEL, A., Histoire de l'art, Paris, 1905, I.

MILLET, G., L'art Byzantin, *in* Michel, Histoire de l'art, 1905, I; 1908, III.

NEUSS, W., Éléments d'archéologie chrétienne, Paris, 2d ed., 1904.

—— Die Kunst der alten Christen, Augsburg, 1926.

RICHTER, J. P., TAYLOR, A. CAMERON, The Golden Age of Classic Christian Art, London, 1904.

ROSSI, G. B. DE, Roma Sotterranea Cristiana, 1864-1867. (Trans. by Northcote and Brownlow, Roma Sotterranea, London, 1879.

SYBEL, L. VON, Christliche Antike, Marburg, 1906, I, 140 ff.; 1909, II, 324 ff.

TOESCA, P., Storia dell' arte Italiana, Torino, I (1927), pp. 17-40.

VENTURI, A., Storia dell' arte Italiana, Milano, 1901, I.

WILPERT, J., Le Pitture delle Catacombe Romane, Roma, 1903.

—— Die Malereien der Katakomben Roms, Freiburg, 1903.

WULFF, O., Altchristliche und Byzantinische Kunst, 1914, I, 50 ff.


*The Technical Methods and Pigments Employed in Ancient Painting.*

BERGER, ERNST, Beiträge zur Entwickelungs-Geschichte der Maltechnik, München, 1901-1912.

—— Die Maltechnik des Altertums, München, 1904.

BREITSCHEDEL, O., Zur Technik der römisch-pompeianischen Wandmalerei, München, 1911.

CROS, H., and HENRY, CH., L'encaustique chez les anciens, Paris, 1884.

DANNENBERG, O., Arch. Anz., 42 (1927), pp. 178-180.

DAVY, H., Philosoph. Trans., 1815, pp. 97 ff.

DONNER, O., see Richter.

EIBNER, A., Entwicklung und Werkstoffe der Wandmalerei vom Altertum bis zur Neuzeit, München, 1926.

GERLICH, F., Die Technik der Römisch-Pompeianischen Wandmalerei, N.J., 21 (1908), pp. 127-147.

HEATON, NOEL, Journal of the Royal Society of Arts, 1910.

—— Tiryns, 1912, II, pp. 211-216.

JOHN, J. F., Die Malerei der Alten nach Vitruv und Plinius, Berlin, 1836.

LAURIE, A. P., Greek and Roman Methods of Painting, Cambridge, 1910.

—— The Materials of the Painter's Craft in Europe and Egypt from the earliest times to the end of the 17th C., London, 1910.

—— Ancient Pigments and their Identification in Works of Art, Archæologia, 64 (1913), pp. 315-335.

MERRIFIELD, MRS., Ancient Practice of Painting.

MONTABERT, PAILLOT DE, Traité complet de la peinture, Paris, 1829-1851, II-III.

MOREAU-VAUTHIER, CHARLES, The Technique of Painting, N. Y., 1923.

Papers of the Society of Mural Decorators and Painters in Tempera, II, 1907-1924, Brighton, 1925 (T. Fyle, N. Heaton).

RAEHLMANN, E., Über die Maltechnik der Alten, Berlin, 1910.

—— Römische Malerfarben, Röm. Mitth., XXIX (1914), pp. 220-239, Pl. XIV (color).

—— Die blaue Farbe in den verschiedenen Perioden der Malerei, Museumskunde, 9, 224-232; Untersuchungen über die gelbe Farbe, Museumskunde, 10, 34-41.

RICHTER, O. DONNER VON, Über die antiken Wandmalereien in technischer Beziehung in Helbig, Wandgemälde Campaniens, Leipzig, 1868, I-CXXVII.

—— Technische Mittheilungen für Malerei, München, 1893.

—— Die encaustische Malerei der Alten, Katalog zu Theod. Graf's Galerie antiker Porträts, Leipzig, 1893.

SARTAIN, JOHN, On the Art of Painting in Encaustic.

SCHMID, HANS, Enkaustik und Fresko auf antiker Grundlage, München, 1926. Ergänzungsschrift zu "Bergers Beiträgen zur Entwicklungsgeschichte der Maltechnik." Rec. O. Dannenberg, Gnomon, IV (1928), pp. 700 ff.

SCHULTZ, W., Das Farbenempfindungssystem der Hellenen, Leipzig, 1904.

SMITH, C., Dictionary of Greek and Roman Antiquities, s.v. Pictura.

TAYLOR, W. B. S., A manual of fresco and encaustic, London, 1843.

VENTURINI, T., La pittura ad encausto al tempo di Augusto, Roma, 1928.

WARD, J., History and Methods of Ancient and Modern Painting, N. Y., 1917, I.

WINTER, F., Über enkaustische Malerei, Arch. Anz., XII (1897), pp. 132 ff.

## LOST PAINTINGS AND COPIES

ASHBY, T., Drawings of Ancient Paintings in English Collections, I, The Eton Drawings, Papers, B.S.R., VII (1914), pp. 1 ff., Pls. I-XXIV.

—— Drawings of Ancient Paintings in English Collections. Part II—The Holkham Drawings. Part III—The Baddely Codex. Part IV—The Chatsworth Sketch-Book, Papers, B.S.R., VIII (1916), pp. 35 ff.

BENDINELLI, G., Le antiche pitture Rospigliosi, Rome, Pallavicini del Museo Naz. 25 Boll. di fil. Class., 33, 2 (1926), pp. 53 ff.

ENGELMANN, R., Antike Bilder aus Röm. Handschr., Leiden, 1909.

LANCIANI, R., Picturae antiquae cryptarum Romanarum (Windsor, Eton, Corsini MS.), Bull. Com., 1895, pp. 165-192.

MICHAELIS, A., and PETERSEN, E., Das Grabmal der Nasonier (Windsor Library), Jahr., 25 (1910), pp. 101 ff.

PONCE, N., Collections des Peintures antiques, qui ornaient les Palais, Thermes, etc., Rome, 1784.

—— Description des Bains de Titus, Paris, 1786.

STRONG, MRS. ARTHUR, Forgotten Fragments of Ancient Wall-Paintings in Rome, B.S.R., VII (1914), pp. 114 ff., Pls. XXV-XXIX, I, the Palatine; II, The House in the Via de' Cerchi, Papers, B.S.R., VIII (1916), 91 ff.

TURNBULL, G., A Treatise on Ancient Paintings, London, 1740.

### Via Salaria.

LEHMANN-HARTLEBEN, K., Arch. Anz., 41 (1926), pp. 98 ff.

PARIBENI, R., Not. d. Sc., 1923, pp. 380 ff., Pls. I-III.

WILPERT, J., Atti d. Pont. Acc. Rom. d. Arch. Rendiconti, 2 (1923), pp. 57-82; cf. 45-56.

### Gargaresh.

CLERMONT-GANNEAU, CH., Compt. Rend. Ac. Iscr., 1903, pp. 357 ff. Cf. pp. 79, 116.

LEHMANN-HARTLEBEN, K., Arch. Anz., 41 (1926), pp. 211 ff.

MARUCCHI, O., Nuovo Bull. di Archeologia Cristiana, 1903, pp. 286 ff.

ROMANELLI, P., Notiziario Archeol., III (1922), pp. 21-32.

### Ravenna.

DALTON, O. M., Byzantine Art and Archæology, Oxford, 1911.

DIEHL, CH., Ravenne, Paris, 1907.

RICCI, C., Ravenna, Bergamo, 1921.

RICHTER, J. P., Die Mosaiken von Ravenna, Vienna, 1878.

# GLOSSARY

*agonistic scenes,* scenes representing athletic contests.

*antefix,* the decorative termination of the covering tiles of a roof.

*anthropoid,* of human form.

*apadana,* name given to the audience chamber of the Persian king.

*ashlar,* masonry of square, hewn stones.

*biga,* a two-horse chariot.

*bucchero,* Etruscan ware, usually of black clay.

*caduceus,* the wand twined with serpents that is carried by Hermes.

*cartonnage,* the layers of linen and plaster composing a mummy-case, carefully moulded to the figure of the deceased.

*chiaroscuro,* treatment or disposition of the light and shade in a picture.

*chiton,* the undergarment worn by the Greeks.

*chlamys,* a short military cloak worn chiefly by horsemen, young men, and Hermes.

*choregos,* the leader of a band of singers and dancers.

*citharœde,* one who plays and sings to the cithara, which was a kind of lyre.

*dromos,* the entrance passage to a chamber tomb.

*ethos,* portrayal or betrayal of habitual individual character.

*ganosis,* the waxing of walls or statues for preservation.

*guilloche,* an ornament in the form of a braid pattern.

*heraldic design,* a composition of two figures balanced on either side of a central axis.

*hetœra,* a female companion as opposed to a wife.

*himation,* a Greek overgarment made of a rectangular piece of cloth.

*hypogœum,* an underground chamber or vault.

*intonaco,* a final coating of plaster placed upon a wall especially for fresco.

*klismos,* a light chair with a curved back and plain, curved legs.

*kolpos,* the fold formed by a loose garment, especially as it fell over the girdle.

*kottabos,* a Sicilian game played at drinking parties. Each person threw the wine left in his cup at a metal basin and called the name of his beloved. If it struck the metal with a distinct sound, it showed his love was returned.

*liknon,* a winnowing fan, *i.e.,* a broad basket in which corn was placed after threshing. It was sacred to Bacchus and was carried in his festival filled with first-fruits and sacrificial implements.

*megaron,* the principal or men's room in the Mycenæan palace. It contained a hearth.

*metope,* one of the square spaces between the triglyphs on the Doric frieze.

*naiskos,* a small shrine.

*omphalos,* the reputed center of the earth at Delphi, marked by a rounded conical stone.

*orthostates,* the upright slabs forming the bottom course of the wall.

*palimpsest,* parchment or other writing-material written upon twice, the original writing having been erased to make way for the second.

*patesi,* the chief ruler, secular and religious, of an early Babylonian city-state.

*peplos,* a woolen garment made of a rectangular piece of cloth.

*peribolos,* an enclosure.

*peristyle,* 1. a covered colonnade surrounding a building; 2. an inner court lined with a colonnade.

*petasos,* a broad-brimmed felt hat.

*pilos,* a conical felt cap shaped somewhat like the modern fez, but pointed.

*pinax,* a board or plank; an object resembling or originally made from a board, such as: 1. a painted board, a picture; 2. a terra cotta plaque; a plate or dish.

*polos,* a headdress of cylindrical form.

*propylon,* a gateway.

*quadriga,* a chariot drawn by four horses harnessed abreast.

*rhyton,* a drinking-horn, often in the form of an animal's head.

*rubble,* a composition made of fragments of stone and waste material.

*schola,* an outdoor stone bench, often of semicircular shape and sometimes topped by columns.

*secco,* painting on dry plaster.

*sima,* a cornice-moulding the outline of which consists of a concave and a convex line.

*situla,* a pail.

*slip,* a semifluid clay for coating earthenware.

*stele,* an upright slab bearing sculptured or painted designs or inscriptions, usually employed as a grave stone.

*stylobate,* the upper step of a temple which formed a platform for the columns.

*tablinum,* an apartment in a Roman house opposite the entrance, commonly used as the reception room.

*temenos,* a sacred enclosure.

*thalassocrat,* a ruler of the sea.

*tholos,* a round building.

*thyrsos,* a staff tipped with an ornament like a pine-cone, carried by followers of Dionysos.

*triclinium,* the dining-room of a Roman house containing three couches.

*triglyph,* a projecting member separating the metopes of the Doric frieze and emphasized by vertical channels.

# INDEX

Achilles discovered by Odysseus at Skyros, 284, 391.

Achilles Painter,
Euphorbos with Œdipus, 187-188;
Mænads, 180;
Painter of white lekythoi, 184, n. 14ᶜ, 186, n. 14ᵉ.

Achilles surrenders Briseis, 286-287.

Achilles Tatius, Perseus freeing Andromeda, 307.

Acrobatic feats, Crete, 80, 84.

Acrobats, women, Crete, 84.

Adaptation of designs to space,
B.-F. artist, Greece, 166-168;
Cave-painter, 6, 8.

Æneas with Anchises and Ascanius, 274.

Aëtion, 273, 274, 314.

Agatharchos, 225, 226, 324, 335, 336.

Aineios, marble disc of, 153.

Aison,
Aryballos. Greeks and Amazons, 171, 180.
Theseus slaying the Minotaur, 189.

Akhenaten, 28, 29, 31.

Akkadian Art,
Hammurabi, reliefs of, 52.
Stele of Naram-Sin, 52.

Akkadians, 47 and n. 3.

Aldobrandini Wedding, 329-330.

Adelricus, 411.

Alexander and Darius at Issus, 280.

Alexander Mosaic, 110, 204, 280-283.

Alexander Sarcophagus, 281, 282.

Alexandria, Helixo Stele, 346.
Origin of impressionism, 275, 336.

Alexandrian grave stelæ, 344-346.

"Alexandrian" reliefs, 337, 338.

Alexandrian style, 414-415.

Aline, Portrait of, 322.

Alkmene on the pyre, Python, 295-296.

Alpera, 9.

Altamira, 3, 4, 5, 6, 7, 8.

Amarna,
Frescoes from, 31;
Reliefs from, 31;
Stucco pavement, 29 ff., 34.

Amasis, 129, 130, 148, 180.

Anakles, 165.

Anapa, painted wooden sarcophagus, 358.

Anau, 46, 54.

Andocides, *see* Andokides.

Andokides, 156.

Andokides Painter,

Athletes, Berlin amphora, 172;
"Ionian" quality of his work, 170;
Paints mannered and precious side of Athenian life, 170.

Animal Paintings, 316.

Animal Paintings, Marissa, 350-351.

Animal Tales, 36.

Anthesterios, Catacomb, 390-391.

Anthropoid mummy-cases, 38.

Antigonos Gonatas, portrait of, 332.

Antinoë, 319.

Antiphilos, 274-277, 306, 336.

Antiphilos, enemy of Apelles, 271.

Antiphilos, originator of impressionism, 274, 275, 276.

Apatourios of Alabanda, 367.

Apelles, 266, 269-272.
Aphrodite of, 270, 290;
Character of painting, 272;
Pupils of, 272-273.

Aphrodite and Eros, 369.

Apollo from Veii, 257.

Apollodoros, 203, 204, 225-228, 236, 299, 335, 336.
Influence on Etruscan painting, 250-251, 252.

Apostles, possible representations of, 401, 402.

Aquarium, 77.

Arabesques, 379, 381.

Arâk, el-Emir, "Palace," 351.

Architectural style, wall-decoration, 326, n. 46ᵃ.

Ardea, Paintings at, 360.

Aregon, Artemis riding on a gryphon, 145.

Ares and Aphrodite, 314.

Ariadne, 71, 82.

Aridikes of Corinth, 135.

Aristeides the Elder, 222, 277, 293, 366.

Aristeides II, 278.

Aristion Stele, 152, n. 52, 157.

Aristonothos, Krater of, 123.

Aristophanes,
Battle of Gods and Giants, 189.

Aristotle, theories of color-contrast, 111, n. 1ᵇ.

Arkesilas cup, Cyrene, 127.

Artemon, 313.
Danaë and pirates marveling at her, 313;
Herakles and Deianeira, 313.

Asiatic influence on Egyptian art, 16, n. 6.

Asiatic style, 414.

Assteas, Hercules Furens, 296.
Scenes from S. I. farces, 296.

Assur, 58.

Assyrian Art,

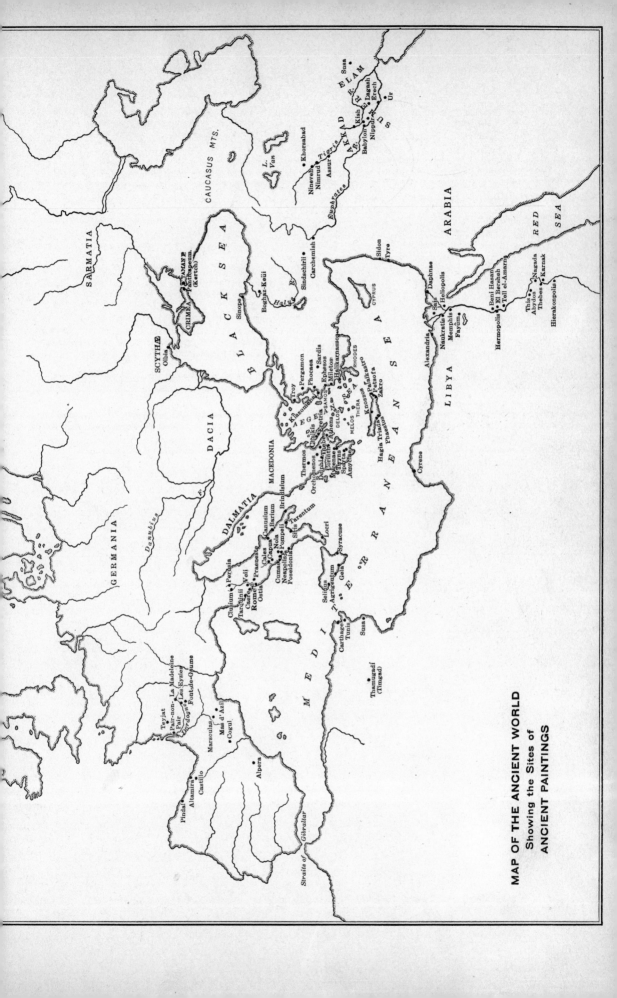

MAP OF THE ANCIENT WORLD
Showing the Sites of
ANCIENT PAINTINGS

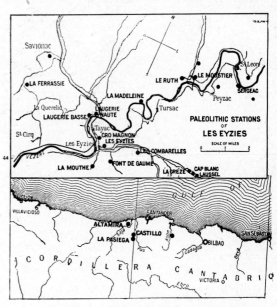

1. Map, Spain and France. Sites of Cave-Paintings.

2. Map, France and Spain. Sites of Cave-Paintings.

3. Castillo. Elephant in red line.

4. La Grèze. Bison, deeply engraved.

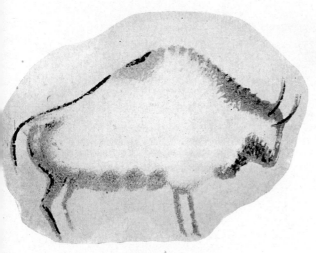

5. Altamira. Black bison.

6. Font-de-Gaume. Ancestral ox.

7. Altamira. Sketch of ceiling-decoration.

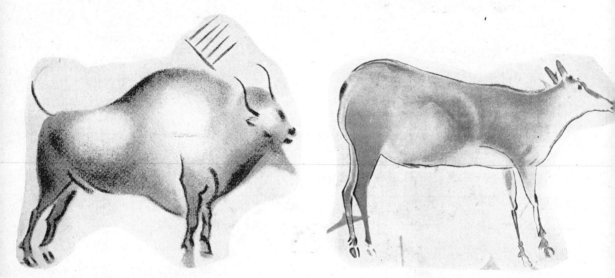

8. Altamira. Black bison.

9. Altamira. Red roe.

10. Altamira. Polychrome bison.

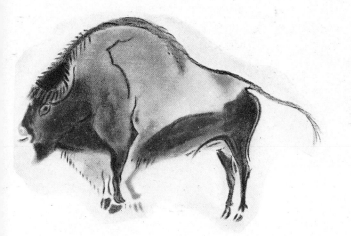

11. Altamira. Bellowing bison.

14. Font-de-Gaume. Engraving of a mammoth.

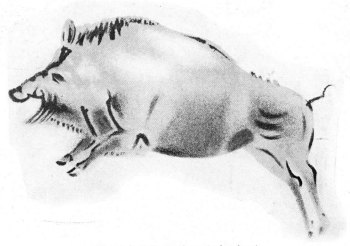

12. Altamira. Galloping boar (5 feet long).

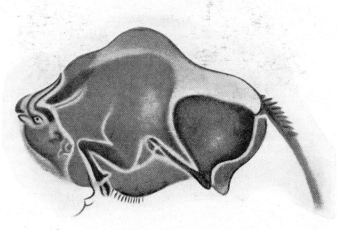

13. Altamira. Recumbent bison.

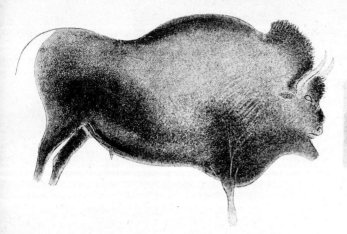

15. Font-de-Gaume. Polychrome bison.

16. Font-de-Gaume. Black wolf on a red ground (1/10).

18. Pair-non-Pair. Rude engravings.

17. Altamira. Horse's head in black outline (1/5).

19. Marsoulas. Engravings. Human heads.

21. Paris, Musée St. Germain.
Engraving on horn. Red deer and fish.

22. Font-de-Gaume. Reindeer facing.

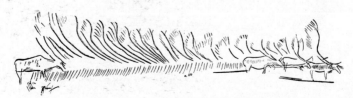

20. La Mairie. Herd of reindeer incised on wing-bone of an eagle.

23. Cogul. Ceremonial dance and hunting scenes.

24. Alpera. Hunting scene.

25. S. Africa, Herschel. Bushman Painting. Decoying ostriches.

26. S. Africa. Bushman Painting. Antelope.

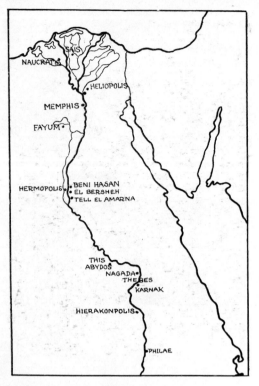

27. Map of Egypt.

28. Cairo. Vases from Gebelein.

29. Petrie Collection.
Vase with fighting warriors.

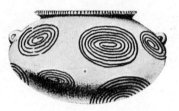

30. Cairo. Vase with spirals.

31. Cairo. Vase with boats, animals and men.

33. Cairo. Vase with goats.

32. Hierakonpolis. Wall-Painting. Trapping and boat scenes.

34. Cairo. Slate Palette of King Narmer.

35. Cairo. Wall-Painting. Geese from Mêdum.

36. Cairo. Princess Nefert.

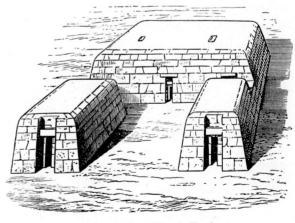

37. Restoration of Mastaba Tombs.

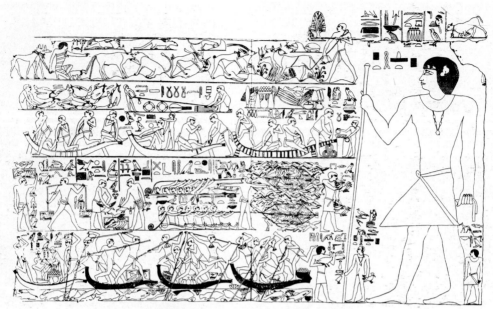

38. Sakkara. Tomb of Ptahhotep. Reliefs.

40. Sakkara. Mastaba of Ti. Relief, Ti and his wife.

39. Cairo. Wooden panel of Hesi-Re.

41. Berlin. Relief. Prisoners of Sahu-Re.

42. Meir. Relief. Lean herdsman.

43 Beni Hasan. Tomb of Ameni. Interior.

44. Beni Hasan. Tomb of Khnemhotep. Fowling and fishing.

45. Beni Hasan. Tomb of Khnemhotep. Cat on papyrus.

46. Beni Hasan. Tomb of Khnemhotep.
Birds in acacia-bush.

47. Beni Hasan. Tomb of Khnemhotep. Caravan of Canaanites.

50. New York. Metropolitan Museum. Hippopotamus in faïence.

48. Beni Hasan. Tomb of Khnemhotep. Feeding oryxes.

51. Berlin. Relief from Dêr el-Bahari. Rowers.

49. Beni Hasan. Tomb of Ameni. Wrestling; siege of a fortress.

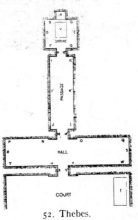

52. Thebes.
Plan of a typical tomb of the XVIIIth Dynasty.

53. Thebes. Tomb of Nakht. Interior.

55. Thebes. Tomb of Nakht. Vintage and fowling scenes.

54. Thebes. Tomb of Nakht. Agricultural pursuits.

56. Thebes. Tomb of Nakht. Cat devouring a fish.

57. Thebes. Tomb of Nakht. Banquet scene with blind harper.

58. London. British Museum. Inspection of cattle.

60. London. British Museum. Banquet scene.

59. London. British Museum. Garden with pond.

61. Turin. Ostrakon. Girl somersaulting.

63. Cairo. Stucco pavement. Bull in a papyrus-swamp.

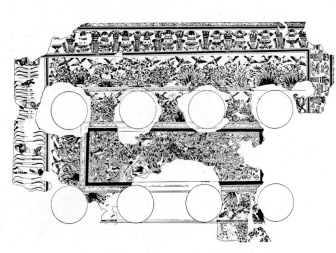

62. Cairo. Stucco pavement.

64. Cairo. Stucco pavement. Calf in marsh grass.

65. Cairo. Stucco pavement. Calves in swamp grass.

66. Cairo. Stucco pavement. Calf bounding into papyrus-clump.

67. Oxford. Ashmolean. Daughters of Akhenaten.

68. Berlin. Relief. Akhenaten and family.

70. Cairo. Relief. Worshiping the Aten.

69. Berlin. Relief. Akhenaten and Queen.

71. Tell el-Amarna. Relief.
Akhenaten and Queen enthroned.

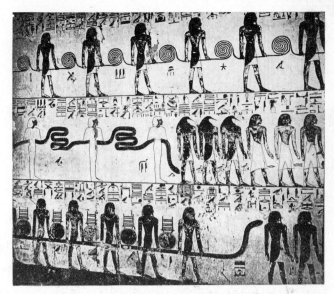

72. Thebes. Tomb of Seti I. Spirits with coiled snakes.

73. Karnak. Relief. Seti I sacking a Palestinian fortress.

74. Thebes. Tomb of Seti I.
Seti I making an offering. Sketch.

75. New York. Metropolitan Museum. Seti I making an offering.

76. Egyptian ornamental patterns.

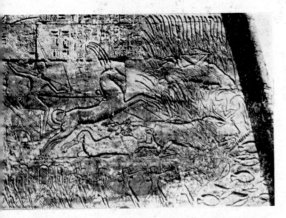

77. Medinet Habu. Relief. Rameses III hunting wild bulls.

78. Cairo. Papyrus. Judgment before Osiris.

80. New York. Historical Society. Ostrakon. Cat and mouse.

79. London. British Museum. Papyrus. "Opening the mouth."

81. Cairo. Stele of Zademonefonukhu.

82. Dêr el-Medineh. Temple of Hathor. Interior, restored.

83a. New York. Historical Society. Coffin of Kami.

84. New York. Metropolitan Museum.
Coffins of Khonsu.

83b. New York. Historical Society. Anthropoid coffin of Teti.

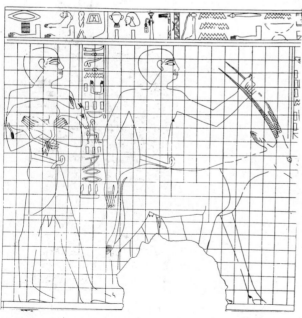

86. Meir. Tomb of Senbi's son. Guiding lines of sketch.

85. New York. Metropolitan Museum.
Coffin of a priest.

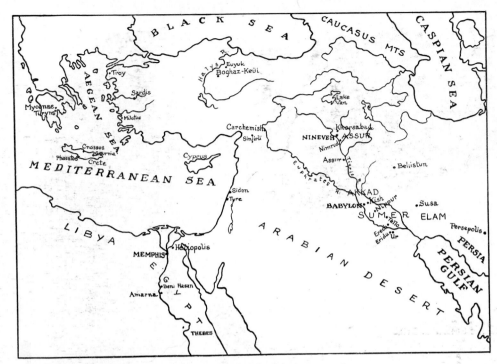

87. Map of the Orient.

88. Paris. Louvre. Ur-Nina preparing to found a temple.

90. Paris. Louvre. Silver vase of Entemena.

89. Paris. Louvre. Stele of the Vultures. Eannatum leading his troops.

92. Paris. Louvre. Bas-relief of Dudu.

91. Paris. Louvre.
Silver vase of Entemena. Detail.

93. Paris. Louvre. Steatite vase of Gudea.

94. Paris. Louvre.
Engraving on a shell cup.
Lion rending a bull.

95. Paris. Louvre.
Goddess worshiped on her mountain throne.

96. Erech (Warka). Terra cotta cone wall.

97. Paris. Louvre. Stele of Naram-Sin.

101. Paris. Louvre. Elamite pottery from Susa. Goblets.

100. Paris. Louvre. Elamite pottery from Susa.

102. Paris. Louvre. Elamite pottery from Susa. Bowls.

98. Paris. De Clercq Coll. Seal Cylinder.

99. Paris. De Clercq Coll. Seal Cylinder

103. Carchemish. Bird-headed demons.

104. London. British Museum.
Kassite boundary-stone. Winged centaur with bow.

106. London. British Museum.
Relief. Assurnasirpal hunting lions.

105. Nimrud. Painted stucco.
Winged bull and ornamental patterns.

107. London. British Museum.
Relief. Assurnasirpal storming a walled town. Prisoners swimming

108. London. British Museum. Relief. Landscape. Trapping deer.

109. London. British Museum. Assyrian demons.

110. Nimrud. Enameled brick from palace of Assurnasirpal.

111. London. British Museum.
Glazed tile. King with eunuch and spear-bearer.

113. Khorsabad. Palace of Sargon. Winged genius.

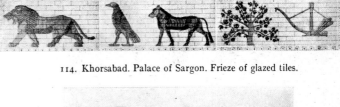

114. Khorsabad. Palace of Sargon. Frieze of glazed tiles.

112. Khorsabad. Palace of Sargon. Restoration.

115. London. British Museum. Relief. Hunting wild horses.

116. London. British Museum.
Alabaster threshold. Palace of Assurbanipal.

117. Babylon. Lion of the Procession Street.

118. Babylon. Ishtar Gate.

124. Babylon. Enameled tiles from Persian building.

119. Babylon. Ishtar Gate. Unenameled bull.

120. Babylon. Ishtar Gate. Enameled wall.

121. Babylon. Ishtar Gate. Dragon.

123. Babylon. Ishtar Gate. Enameled bull.

122. From Nippur. Relief. Dragon.

127. Paris. Louvre. Enameled sphinxes, Palace of Darius, Susa. Restoration.

26. Susa. Palace of Darius. Tribune of Court of Columns. Restoration.

125. Paris. Louvre. Persian Bowmen. Enameled tiles.

128. Paris. Louvre. Winged bull. Palace of Darius and Artaxerxes, Susa.

129. Paris. Louvre. Winged gryphon. Palace of Darius and Artaxerxes, Susa.

130. Persepolis. Apadana of Xerxes. Relief. Lion rending a bull.

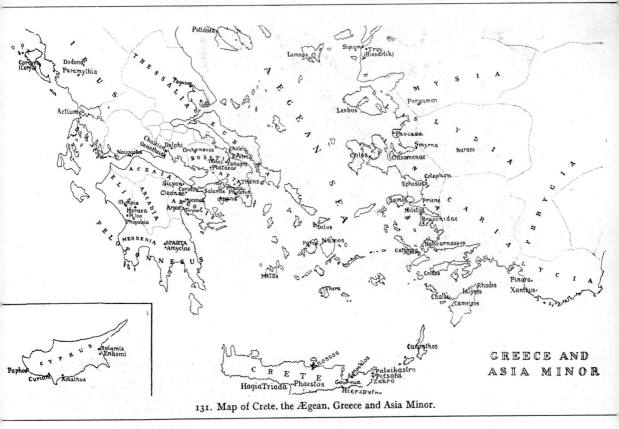

131. Map of Crete, the Ægean, Greece and Asia Minor.

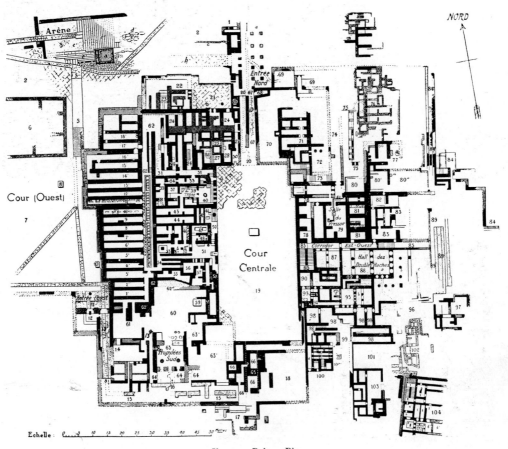

132. Knossos. Palace. Plan.

133. Knossos. Palace. Stepped "Theatral Area."

134. Knossos. Palace. Throne of Minos. Gryphon fresco.

135. Knossos. Palace. Quadruple stairway.

136. Knossos. Palace. Stenciled stucco.

137. Knossos. Palace. Frieze with spiraliform design.

138. Knossos. Palace.
Painted stucco with spiraliform design.

139. Candia. Fresco. "Blue boy" gathering crocuses.

140. Candia. Cat and pheasant fresco.

141. Candia. Fresco. Cretan meadow in flower.

143. Candia. Flying fishes and shells, faïence.

142. Candia. Lily fresco from Knossos.

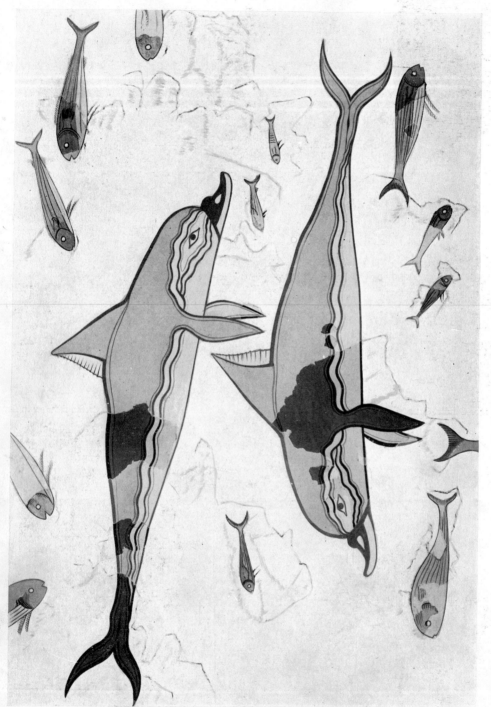

144. Candia. Dolphin fresco from Knossos. Restoration.

145. Candia. Dolphin vase, Pachyammos.

c.

b.

d.

a.

148. Candia. Votive robes and girdles, faïence.

147. Athens. National Museum. Inlaid dagger, Mycenæ.

151. Knossos. Architectural fresco
from Knossos. Restoration.

Knossos. Architectural fresco from Knossos.
Pillar Shrine.

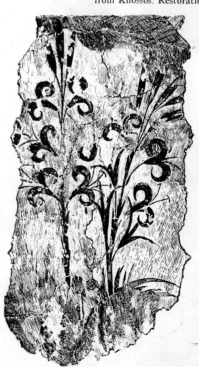

149. Candia. Relief. "Jewel fresco."

146. Candia (?). Lily fresco from Hagia Triada.

152. Candia. Figures. Corridor of the Procession.

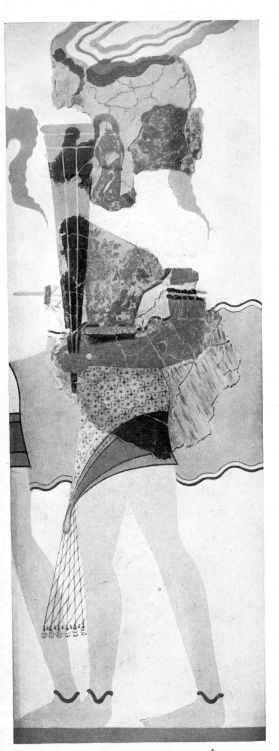

153. Candia. Fresco. "Cup-bearer" from Knossos.

154. Candia. Fresco from Knossos. Young girl.

155. Candia. Fresco from Knossos. "Ariadne."

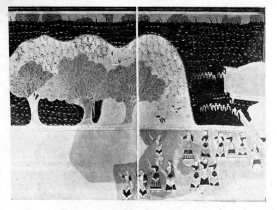

156. Candia. Fresco from Knossos. Festival in Temenos of Goddess.

157. Knossos. Architectural fresco. Pillar Shrine. Restored.

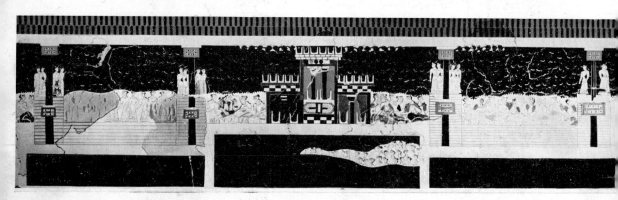

158. Knossos. Restoration of Pillar Shrine.

159. Candia. "Toreador" fresco from Knossos. Restoration.

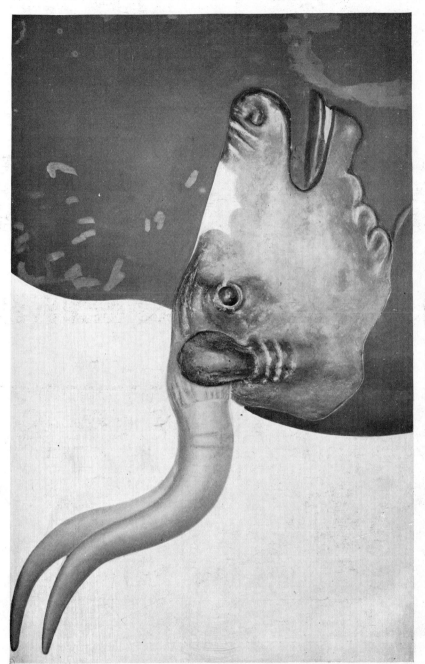

160. Candia. Relief. Bull's head from Knossos. Restored.

161. Knossos. "Chieftain" relief, Knossos. Restoration.

162. Candia. Torso of the "Chieftain."

163. Candia. Painted Sarcophagus from Hagia Triada.

*a.* Candia. Polychrome vase, Phæstos.

*c.* Candia. Polychrome vase.

*i.* Athens. National Museum. Vase from Pylo

*d.* Candia.
Polychrome vase with lilies.

*g.* Athens. National Museum.
Crocus vase, Melos.

*b.* Candia. Polychrome egg-shell vase.

*f.* Candia. Vase from Zakro. Marine life

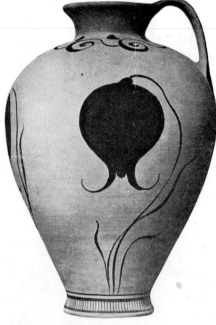

*.* Athens. National Museum. Vase from Pylos.

*j.* Restoration of a Melian Vase in Athens.

*l.* Marseilles. Vase, L. M. I.

*e.* Candia. Lily vase.

164. Cretan Vases.

*k.* Candia. Vase with nymphæa cærulea.

. Athens. National Museum.
Palace" style from Mycenæ.

*a*. Candia. Octopus vase from Gournia.

*d*. Candia. Vase from Isopata.
Architectural motives.

*e*. Candia.
Painted jar with papyrus.

*c*. Candia. Vase from Isopata.
Plant designs.

f. London, British Museum. Mycenæan kylix with octopus.

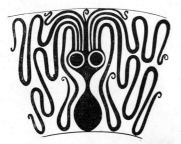

g. Paris. Louvre. Mycenæan octopus.

h. Paris. Louvre. Mycenæan octopus.

165. Cretan-Mycenæan Pottery.

166. Athens. National Museum. Siege of a city. Restored.

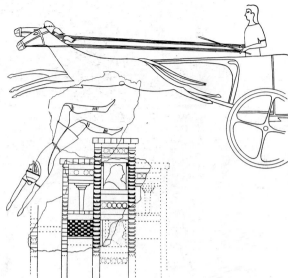

167. Athens. National Museum. Siege of a city. Restored.

168. Athens. Fresco from Mycenæ. Women in loggia.

171. Thebes. Museum.
Woman from a procession. Restoration.

170. Athens. National Museum. Warrior stele.

169. Athens. National Museum.
Fresco. Ass-headed demons.

172. Athens. National Museum. Hunters, Tiryns.

173. Tiryns. Palace. Restoration.

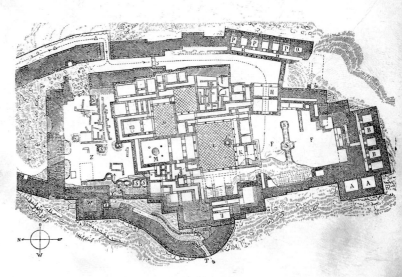

174. Tiryns. Palace. Plan.

175. Athens. National Museum. Departure for a hunt, Tiryns. Restoration.

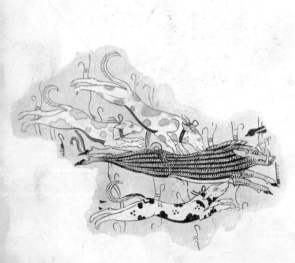

177. Athens. National Museum. Boar-hunt, Tiryns. Restoration.

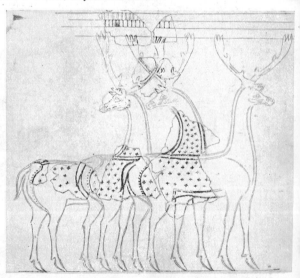

178. Athens. National Museum. Deer from hunt, Tiryns. Restored.

176. Athens. National Museum. Attendant with hound, Tiryns. Restoration.

79. Athens. National Museum. Woman with cista, Tiryns. Restored.

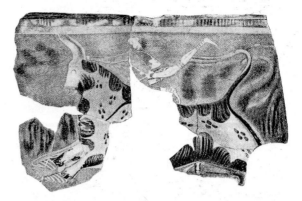

180. Athens. National Museum. Bull fresco, Tiryns.

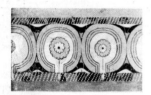

182. Athens. National Museum.
Rosette pattern, Tiryns.

183. Athens. National Museum. Shield pattern, Tiryns.

181. Candia. Limestone frieze, Knossos.

186. Orchomenos. Stone ceiling of a tomb.

184. Athens. National Museum. Spiral pattern, Tiryns.

185. Candia. Ceiling-decoration from Knossos.

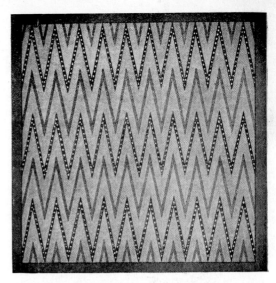

187. Mycenæ. Floor-decoration. Zigzags.

188. Mycenæ.
Floor-decoration.
Scale pattern.

189. Mycenæ.
Floor-decoration.
Circle pattern.

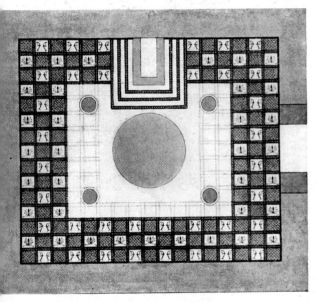

190. Tiryns. Floor-decoration. Megaron.

191. Tiryns. Floor-pattern. Smaller megaron.

192. Tiryns. Floor-patterns. Dolphins, octopods.

193. Athens. National Museum. Warrior vase, Mycenæ.

194. Athens. National Museum.
Vase fragment, Tiryns. Hunt.

195. Athens. National Museum. Fisherman vase, Melos.

196. Candia. Vase from Muliana, Crete.

197. New York. Metropolitan.
Mycenæan vase, Cyprus.

198. Vase from Cyprus. Chariot. Women.

200. Athens. National Museum. Bœotian geometric vase.

99. Athens. National Museum. Geometric vase, Dipylon.

201. Paris. Louvre. Bœotian geometric bowl.

b.    a.    c.    d.

202. Boston. Museum. Corinthian vases.

203. Paris. Louvre. Herakles at the house of Eurytios. Corinthian.

204. Paris. Louvre. Suicide of Ajax. Detail of Fig. 203.

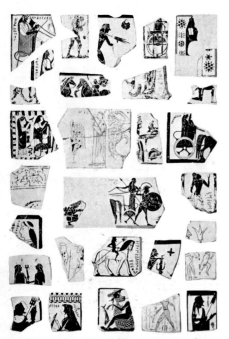

205. Berlin. Museum. Clay plaques from Corinth.

209. Athens. National Museum. Metope from Thermos. Hunter with game

208. Thermos. Temple of Apollo, entablature. Restoration.

207. Athens. National Museum. Clay antefixes and water-spouts. Thermos

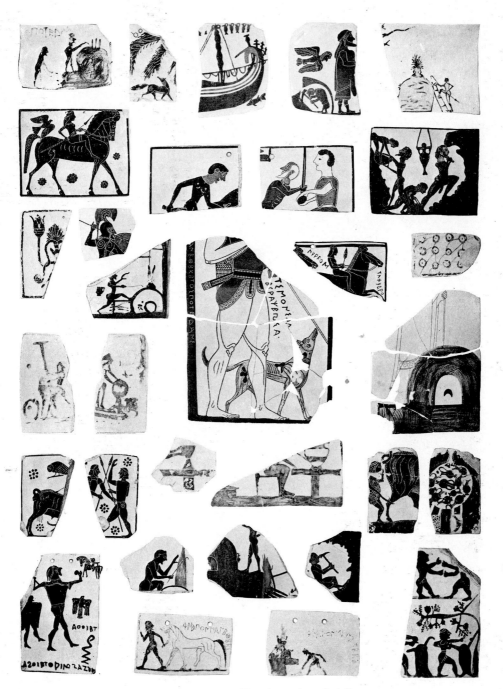

206. Berlin. Museum. Clay plaques from Corinth.

210. Rome. Palazzo dei Conservatori.
Naval battle. Odysseus blinding the Cyclops.

212. London. British Museum. Euphorbos pinax. Rhodes.

211. Paris. Louvre. Rhodian oinochoë.

213. Athens. National Museum. Apollo, Artemis and goddesses.

215. Würzburg. Blind Phineus and Harpies.

214. Vienna. Busiris vase, Cære.

216. Munich. Herakles disemboweling the boar.

219. Athens. National Museum. Odysseus and sirens.

217. Paris. Louvre. Vintage scene.

218. Paris. Louvre. Vineyard scene.

222. Berlin. Sarcophagus from Klazomenai.

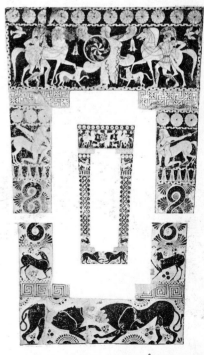

221. Berlin. Sarcophagus from Klazomenai.

220. Berlin. Sarcophagus from Klazomenai.

223. London. British Museum. Sarcophagus from Klazomenai. Cover. Chariot races; battle scenes.

224. London. British Museum. Sarcophagus from Klazomenai. Funeral games.

225. Berlin. Palæstra scene.

226b. Athens. Proto-Attic vase: dance; ornamental patterns.

226a. Athens. Proto-Attic vase.

227b. Athens. National Museum.
Slain Medusa, with her sisters fleeing.

227a. Athens. National Museum: Herakles and Nessos.

228. Florence. Archæological Museum. François vase.

229. London. British Museum.
atyrs and Mænads dancing. Nikosthenes Painter.

230a. Paris. Cabinet des Médailles. Athena and Poseidon. Amasis.

230b. Paris. Cabinet des Médailles. Detail. Shoulder. Amasis.

231. Paris. Cabinet des Médailles.
Dionysos and Mænads. Amasis.

232. Munich. Dionysos sailing over the sea. Exekias.

233. London. British Museum. Burgon Amphora. Athena.

234. Leyden. Canino Collection. Panathenaic Amphora. Athena.

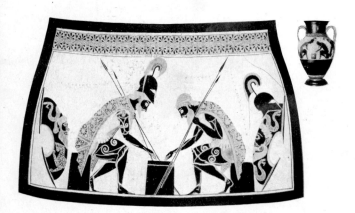

235. Rome. Vatican. Ajax and Achilles at draughts. Exekias.

236. Berlin. Attic funerary plaque.
Procession of mourners; mourning scene.

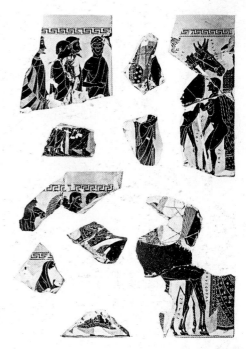

237. Berlin. Attic funerary plaques. Mourning scenes.

238. Berlin. Attic funerary plaques. Funeral procession.

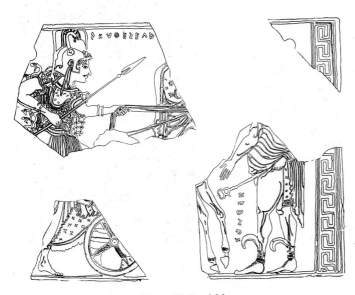

239. Athens. National Museum.
Athena mounting chariot; Hermes. Pinax by Skythes

240. Athens. National Museum. Stele of Lyseas.

241a. Athens. National Museum. Youth on horse.

241b. Athens. National Museum. Base of Lyseas stele.

242. Athens. National Museum. Head of youth. Sunium.

243. Athens. National Museum. Marble disc. Physician Aineios.

244. Athens. Acropolis Museum. Tablet. Warrior, from Acropolis.

246. Munich. Herakles and Geryon. Cup by Euphronios.

245. Paris. Louvre. Herakles and Antaios. Cup by Euphronios.

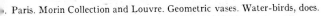

Paris. Morin Collection and Louvre. Geometric vases. Water-birds, does.          252. Paris. Louvre. Geometric vase. Mourning scene.

247. Athens. National Museum. Geometric vase. Mourning scenes. Funeral games.

251. Paris. Louvre.
Dipylon geometric. Warriors, bird, ship.

248. Paris. Louvre. Geometric vase. Charioteer.          250. Paris. Louvre. Geometric vase. Flying bird.

253. Paris. Louvre. Rhodian oinochoë.

254. Paris. Louvre. Rhodian oinochoë. Detail. Goat, gryphon.

255. Munich. Ionic amphora.

257. Vienna. Busiris vase. Negroes on the run.

256. Paris. Louvre. Vase from Cære. Hare running up a mound.

258. Paris. Collignon Collection. Corinthian vase.

263. Paris. Louvre. Corinthian vase. Rider leading another horse.

260. Paris. Louvre. Corinthian vase. Detail. Fantastic animal.

262. Paris. Louvre. Corinthian vase. Detail. Heraldic lions.

264. Paris. Louvre. Corinthian vase. Detail. Herd of oxen.

259. Paris. Louvre. Corinthian vase. Detail. Lion.

261. Paris. Louvre. Corinthian vase. Detail. Sphinx.

269. Paris. Louvre. Horsemen.

268. Rome. Vatican. The Dioscuri at home. Exekias.

270. London. British Museum. Cheiron receiving Achilles from Peleus.

266. Paris. Louvre. Cup by Exekias. Doe.

265. Paris. Louvre. Attic vase with some Corinthian details

267. Bryn Mawr College. Fragment of a cup. Head of a woman.

271. Florence. Archæological Museum. François vase.

272. Munich. Panathenaic vase. Runners.

274. London. British Museum. Scene at a fountain.

273. London. British Museum. Warriors running. Pamphaios.

275. New York. Metropolitan Museum. Black-figured amphora.

276. Paris. Louvre.
R.-F. vase. Cheiron and Achilles. Oltos.

277. London. British Museum.
Young rider. Epiktetos.

279. London. British Museum. Stamnos. Herakles and Acheloös.

280. Paris. Louvre. Stamnos by Hermonax. Revel.

281. Rome. Villa Giulia. Labors of Theseus. Skythes.

0. Munich. Thracian horseman. Euphronios.

278. Panathenaic vases.

287. London. British Museum.
Flute-player and dancer. Epiktetos.

282. Boston. Kylix. Birth of Helen. Three women. Xenotimos.

284. London. British Museum.
Youth chasing a hare. Panaitios Master.

286. London. British Museum. Aphrodite on a goose.

289. Berlin. Selene in her chariot. Brygos Painter.

288. London. British Museum.
Glaukos and Polyeidos. Sotades Painter.

285. Rome. Villa Giulia. Reveler. Skythes.

283. Munich. Running satyr. Phintias.

291. London. British Museum. Hoplitodromos. Pheidippos.

292. Berlin. Youth with horses. Epiktetos.

293. London. British Museum. Symposium. Epiktetos.

294. Berlin. Contest for the Delphic Tripod. Andokides.

295. Munich. The cattle of Geryon. Euphronios.

296. Castle Ashby. Warriors arming. Nikosthenes Painter.

297. Naples. Amazons and Greeks fighting. Aison.

298. London. British Museum. Athletes exercising. Style of Euthymides.

299. Munich. Athletes exercising. Kleophrades Painter.

300. Paris. Louvre. Adventures of Theseus. Panaitios Master.

301. Berlin. Amphora. Wrestling scenes. Andokides.

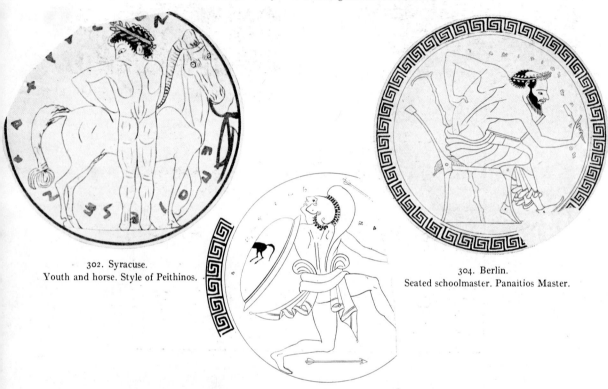

302. Syracuse.
Youth and horse. Style of Peithinos.

304. Berlin.
Seated schoolmaster. Panaitios Master.

303. Berlin. Youthful warrior running. Style of Euthymides.

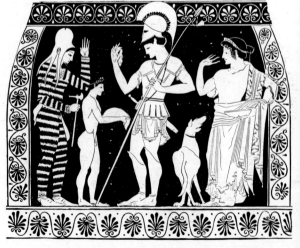

306. London. British Museum.
Warrior leading horse; Amazon. Hypsis.

305. Würzburg. Warrior consulting entrails before departure.
Kleophrades Painter.

307. Paris. Cabinet des Médailles.
Wrestling scene. Panaitios Master.

308. Athens. National Museum. Sculptured bases. Athletes exercising.

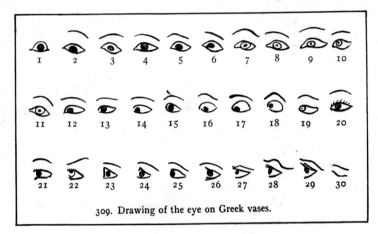

309. Drawing of the eye on Greek vases.

10. Berlin. Achilles binding the arm of Patroklos. Sosias.

311. Paris. Louvre. Sack of Troy. Brygos Painter.

312. Vienna. Contest of Ajax and Odysseus for the armor of Achilles. Douris.

313. Berlin. Mænads dancing. Makron.

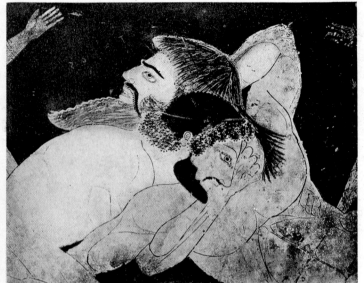

314. Paris. Louvre. Herakles and Antaios. Euphronios.

315. Berlin. Patroklos wounded. Sosias.

316. Munich Mænad. Kleophrades Painter.

1. Munich. Hermes leading a woman to Charon. White-ground vase.

320. Schwerin. Herakles and old woman. Pistoxenos Painter.

317. Munich
Head of Priam. Euthymides.

319. Paris. Louvre. Orvieto Krater. Bearded man.

318. New York. Metropolitan Museum
Head of a warrior. Achilles Master.

323. Rome. Vatican. Æsop and fox.

322. Athens. National Museum.
Mourning scene.

324. Rome. Villa Giulia. Centaur battle.

325. New York. Metropolitan Museum. Amazon Krater.

326. New York. Metropolitan Museum. Amazon battle.

327. Naples. Amazon battle. Aison.

328. Paris. Louvre. Apollo slaying Tityos and Ge.

330. Paris. Cabinet des Médailles. Mænads. Achilles Painter.

329. Paris. Louvre. Apollo slaying Tityos. Detail.

1. Oxford. Ashmolean. Herakles and Deianeira with Hyllos.

332. Naples. Dionysiac celebration. Master of the Berlin Deinos.

34. Boston. Youth beside a tomb.
White-ground vase.

333. Athens. Warrior at home. White-ground vase.

335. Boston.
Girl bringing offerings to a tomb.
White-ground vase.

336. Thebes. Grave stele of Mnason.

337. Petrograd. Hermitage. Drawings on ivory.
Judgment of Paris. Rape of the daughters of Leukippos.

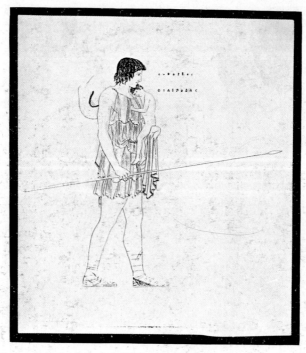

338. Paris. Cabinet des Médailles. Euphorbos with Œdipus.

339. Palermo. Arming scene;
Lecce. Eriphyle legend.

340. London. British Museum.
Musaios, Terpsichore, Melousa.

342. Arezzo. Pelops and Hippodameia. Meidias Painter.

341. Berlin. Satyr and woman;
Satyr swinging a girl. Penelope Painter.

347. London. British Museum. Panathenaic amphora.

343. London. British Museum.
Selene; Eos and Kephalos; Helios.

346. Berlin.
Battle of Gods and Giants. Aristophanes.

345. Madrid.
Theseus and the Minotaur. Aison.

344. London. British Museum. Rape of the daughters of Leukippos. Meidias Painter.

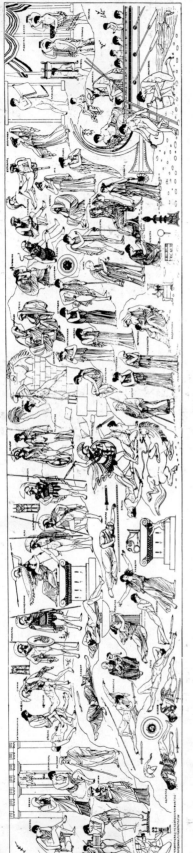

348. Reconstruction. Sack of Troy. Polygnotos.

350. New York. Metropolitan Museum. Amazon battle.

349. Paris. Louvre. Apollo and Artemis slaying the Niobids.

351. Paris. Louvre. Orvieto Krater. Heroes before Marathon.

353. Paris. Louvre. Orvieto Krater. Detail.

352. Paris. Louvre. Orvieto Krater. Detail.

354. Bologna. Theseus in the realms of Poseidon.

355. Syracuse. Amazon vase from Gela. Polygnotos.

357 London. British Museum. Greek attacking an Amazon.

358. Naples. Amazon vase from Ruvo. Niobid Painter.

356. Palermo. Warrior charging.

359. Palermo. Amazon vase. Niobid Painter.

360. Palermo. Greek staying hand of Amazon.
Niobid Painter.

361. London. British Museum. Achilles and Penthesileia. Polygnotos.

362. Reconstruction. Left half. Battle of Marathon. Mikon and Panainos.

363. Munich. Odysseus and Nausikaa.

365. Berlin. Odysseus slaying the suitors. Penelope Painter.

364. Boston. Odysseus and Nausikaa.

366. Vienna. Reliefs from Trysa. Murder of the suitors.

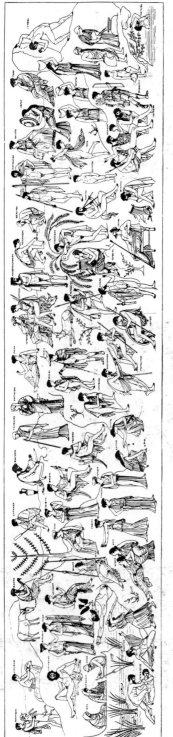

367. Reconstruction. Underworld. Polygnotos.

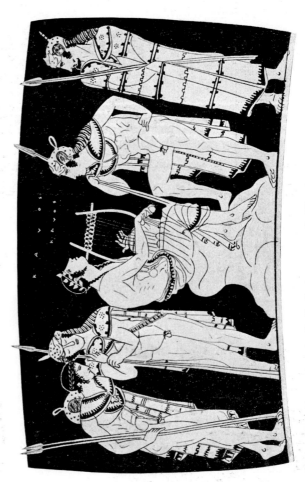

369. Berlin. Orpheus among the Thracians.

368. Paris. Bibliothèque Nationale. Mad Ajax with shepherds (?)

372. Rome. Villa Giulia. Ficoroni Cista. Argonauts among the Bebrykes.

370. Oxford. Ashmolean. Blind Thamyris.

373. Munich. Achilles and Penthesileia. Penthesileia Master.

374. Geneva. Musée Fol. Greeks and Amazons.

371. Naples. Knucklebone-players. Alexandros.

375. Berlin. Mourning scene.

376. Ruvo. Death of the giant, Talos.

377. Berlin. Mosaic. Centaur slaying a tiger.

378. Naples. Peirithoos, Eurytion, Hippodameia.

379. Naples. Greek *apobates*.

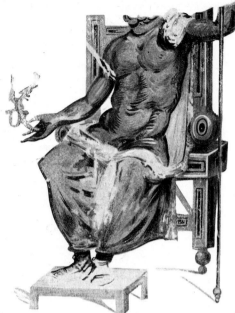

383. Athens. National Museum. Zeus enthroned.

380. London. British Museum. Surprise of Dolon.

381. Boston Museum. Centauress.

384. Naples. Sacrifice of Iphigeneia.

382. Pompeii. House of the Vettii. Herakles strangling the serpents.

385. Map of Etruscan sites.

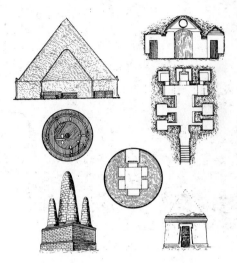

386. Reconstruction. Etruscan tomb forms.

387. Veii. Tomba Campana. Hunting scene (

388. Veii. Tomba Campana. Sphinx, panther, dog.

389. Veii. Tomba Campana. Youth on a winged horse.

390. Corneto  Tomb of the Bulls. Achilles surprising Troilos.

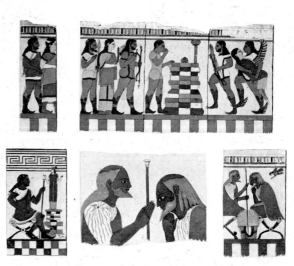

391. Paris  Louvre. Clay plaques from Cære.

392. Corneto. Tomb of the Augurs. Mourning figures.

393. Corneto  Tomb of the Augur  Games. Masked play.

394. Corneto. Tomb of Hunting and Fishing. Hunting scene. Dances.

395. Corneto. Tomb of Hunting and Fishing.
Banquet. Fishing scene.

396. Corneto. Tomb of Hunting and Fishing.

397. Corneto. Tomb of the Lionesses. Reclining youth.

98. Corneto. Tomb of the Lionesses. Decorative border. Dolphins. Birds.

399. Corneto. Tomb of the Painted Vases. Family meal. Dances.

401 London. British Museum. Painted terra cotta sarcophagus.

400. Corneto. Tomb of the Old Man. Banquet.

402 Corneto. Tomb of the Baron. Youths with horses. Greeting.

403. Corneto. Tomb of the Baron. Youths with horses; greeting woman.

406. Corneto. Tomb of the Leopards. Interior. Leopards. Banquet. Musicians.

404b. Corneto. Tomb of the Chariots. Harnessing horses to chariot

404a. Corneto. Tomb of the Chariots. Spectators watching games.

405. Corneto. To⸱⸱⸱ Chariots. Dancers.

407 Corneto. Tomb of the Triclinium. Banquet scene. Restoration.

408. Corneto. Tomb of the Triclinium. Riders. Restoration.

409. Corneto. Tomb of the Triclinium. Dancers. Restoration.

410. Corneto. Tomb of the Triclinium. Flute-player.

411. Corneto. Tomb of the Triclinium. Dancers.

413. Chiusi. Tomb of the Monkey. Funeral games.

412. Corneto. Tomb of the Young Girl. Symposium.

414. Chiusi. Tomb of the Casuccini Hill. Symposium.

416. Chiusi. Tomb of the Monkey.
Giant and dwarf.

419. Corneto Tomb of Hades
Charon. Head of a young woman, Velia.

415. Chiusi. Tomb of the Casuccini Hill. Funeral games.

417. Corneto. Tomb of Hades.
Underworld scene. Odysseus blinding the Cyclops.

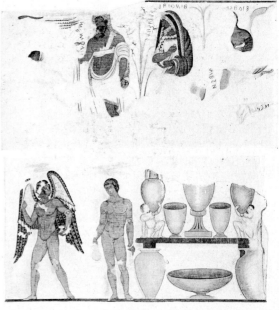

418. Corneto Tomb of Hades. Heroes and demons in underworld.

420. Corneto. Tomb of Hades. Head of Hades.

421. Corneto. Tomb of Hades. Head of Velia, wife of Arnth Velch

423. Orvieto. Golini Tomb. Banquet in Hades.

422. Corneto. Tomb of the Cardinal. The underworld.

424. Orvieto. Golini Tomb Larder and kitchen scenes.

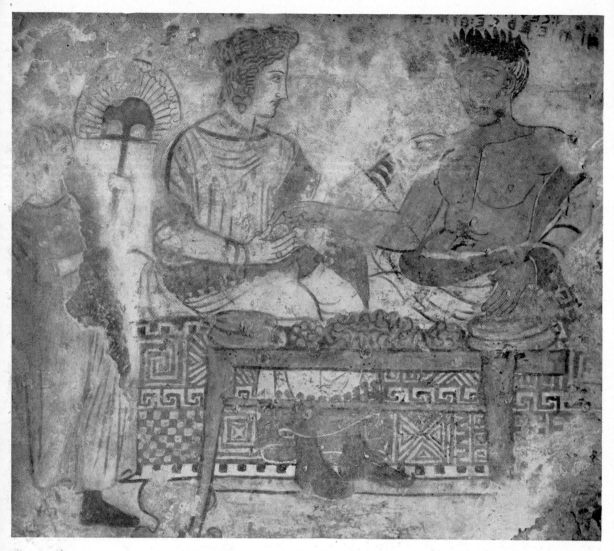

425. Corneto. Tomb of the Shields. Symposium.

426. Rome Torlonia Collection. Servius Tullius frees Cæles Vibenna.

428. Corneto. Tomb of Typhon. Decorative patterns.

427. Corneto Tomb of Typhon Demon.

429. Florence. Archæological Museum. Amazon Sarcophagus.

430. Florence Archæological Museum. Amazon Sarcophagus. End.

431. Orvieto. Painted Sarcophagus from Torre San Severo. Sacrifice of Polyxena.

432. Map of Italy showing Oscan sites.

434. Naples. National Museum. Women engaged in a dance.

435. Lost Painting from Pæstum. Rider bringing home a wounded comrade.

433. Berlin. Tomb-Painting from Nola.
Woman seated on a throne.

436. Naples. National Museum. Returning warriors. Pæstum.

437. Naples. National Museum. Warriors returning home. Pæstum.

438. Capua. Museo Campano. Oscan Horseman.

439a. Capua. Museo Campano. Woman with cista.

439b. Dresden. Woman and servant.

440. Naples. National Museum. Seated woman and servant.

441. Capua. Museo Campano. Gladiators.

442. Rome. Casino Rospigliosi. Victor with palm

444. Naples. Caricature. Æneas with Anchises and Ascaniu

443 Florence. Uffizi. Botticelli. Calumny.

446. Pompeii. House of the Vettii. Cocks.

445 Naples. Mosaic by Dioskourides. Street musicians.

447. Naples. Achilles slaying Trojan captives at the tomb of Patroklos.

450. Athens. National Museum. Grave stele of Tokkes.

448. Rome. Palatine Hill. House of Livia. Io watched by Argo

455. London. British Museum.
Blacas Gem. Victory with a Quadriga.

449. Naples. Perseus freeing Andromeda.

456. Naples. Achilles at Skyros.

457. Pompeii. House of Holconius. Achilles at Skyros.

453 Naples. Alexander Mosaic. Head of Darius. Charioteer. Persians.

451. Naples. Alexander Mosaic.

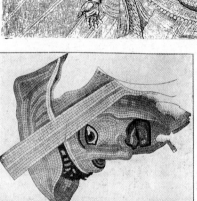

454 Naples Alexander Mosaic
Head of a Persian

452. Naples. Alexander Mosaic. Head of Alexander.

458. Naples  Painting on marble  Niobe protecting her daughters.

460  Pompeii  House of the Vettii. Pentheus torn by Mænads.

462. Pompeii. House of the Vettii  Punishment of Dirce.

461. Naples  Theseus victor over the Minotaur.

463. London. British Museum  Engraved mirror-cover. Pan and Aphrodite at knucklebones.

459. Naples. Achilles surrendering Briseis.

464. Paris. Louvre. Engraved mirror-cover.
Corinth crowned by Leukas.

465. New York. Metropolitan. Engraved mirror-cover. Toilet sce[ne]

466. Thebes. Stele of Rhynchon. Warrior charging.

467. Eleusis. Painted Votive Relief.

469. Petrograd. Zeus and Themis in consultation.

468. Paris. Louvre. Battle of Gods and Giants

470 Naples Orestes and Iphigeneia in Tauris.

472 Paris. Louvre. Expiation of Orestes.

471. Naples. Darius vase.

473. London. British Museum. Alkmene on the pyre. Python.

474 Berlin Stage scene from a South Italian farce. Assteas.

475. London. British Museum Warrior with horse.

476. Petrograd. Contest between Athena and Poseidon.

477. London. British Museum. Kabeiric vase. Odysseus and Circe.

480. Taman Peninsula. Tumulus. Head of Persephone.

478. London. British Museum.
Herakles drawing water at a fountain.

482. Macedonia. Tomb-Painting. Warrior on horse charging an enemy.

479. Kertch. Stele of Apphe.

481. Kertch. Tomb-decoration. Structural style.

484. Naples. Herakles discovers his son Telephos.

483. Naples. National Museum. Man rescuing a donkey from a crocodile.

486. Naples. Head of Arkadia. Detail of Fig. 484.

485. Naples. Head of Herakles. Detail of Fig. 484.

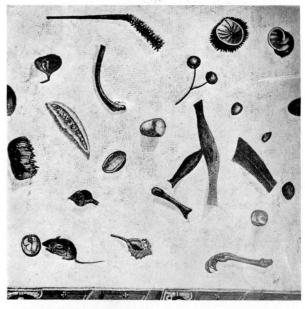

487. Naples. Victorious general decking a trophy.

488. Rome. Lateran. Mosaic of the Unswept Dining-Room.

489. Rome. Capitoline. Drinking Doves. Mosaic.

490 Rome. Vatican. Mosaic Basket of flowers.

494. Naples. Orestes and Pylades among the Taurians.

491. Naples. Still life. Fruit, glass jar.

493. Naples. Medea meditating the murder of her children.

495. Naples. Orestes and Pylades.
Detail of Fig. 494.

492. Naples. Medea meditat
the murder of her children

496. Naples. Herakles and Nessos.

497. Naples. Herakles and Omphale. Detail.

498. Naples. Tired Silenus receiving a drink.

499. Naples. Ares and Aphrodite.

500. Pompeii. Wrestling-match between Pan and Eros.

501. Naples. Mosaic. Lion rending a panther.

502. Naples. African animals.

503. Naples. Mosaic with Nile animals.

504. Naples. Mosaic. Cat, ducks, still-life

507. Rome. Vatican. Mosaic. Goats pasturing.

506. Rome. Vatican. Mosaic Lion rending bull in a rocky landscape.

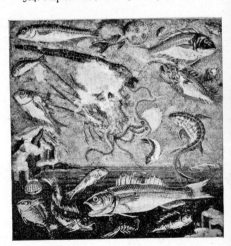

505. Naples. Mosaic with sea-animals.

509. Palestrina. Palazzo Barberini. Nile Mosaic

508. Naples. Landscape with pigmies

510. Palestrina. Palazzo Barberini. Nile scenes.

513. New York. Metropolitan.
Portrait of a Greek youth

512. New York. Metropolitan. Portrait of a woman.

514. Carlsbad. Portrait of a Greek youth

518. Vienna. Graf Collection
Portrait of a young girl

511. New York. Metropolitan. Mummy-case with portrait.

517. London. National Gal
Portrait of a woman.

519. Vienna. Graf Collection.
Portrait of a woman.

516. Vienna. Graf Collection. Portrait of a man.

515. Strassburg. Universi
Portrait of a Greek gir

520. Copenhagen. Ny Carlsberg. Portrait of a Roman.

521. Berlin. "Aline."

522. Vienna. Graf Collection. Invalid woman.

523. New York. Metropolitan. Greek youth.

524. Sidi Gaber (Alexandria). Tomb-Painting. Wall-decoration.

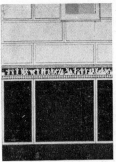

525. Delos. Wall-decoration of houses.

529. Rome. Vatican Library. Odyssey landscapes. Second style.

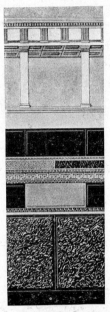

526. Delos. Wall-decoration of house.

528. New York. Metropolitan. Wall-decoration. Villa of Fannius Sinistor.

527. Pompeii. House of Sallust. Wall-decoration. First st

530  Rome. Palatine Hill. House of Livia  Io watched by Argos.

531. Rome Vatican Library  Aldobrandini Wedding.

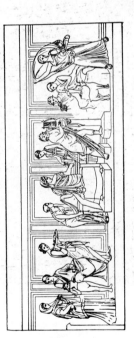

532. Pompeii. Villa Item. "Frescoes." Initiation scenes. Drawing.

534. Pompeii. Villa Item. "Fresco." Fleeing girl and satyrs resting.

535. Pompeii. Villa Item. "Fresco." Girl fleeing at unveiling of phallos.

533. Pompeii. Villa Item. "Fresco." Boy reading ritual of mysteries.

536 Pompeii. Villa Item. Fresco. Dancing satyr.

537. New York. Metropolitan. Woman playing a lyre

539. Rome. National. Aphrodite, Peitho and Eros.

538. Naples. Old man leaning on a staff.

540. Rome. National. Landscape paintings. Scenes of Judgment.

543. Rome. Palatine Hill. House of Livia.
Polyphemos and Galatea.

544. Rome. Palatine Hill. House of Livia. Yellow frieze. Landscapes.

546. Rome. Villa Albani. Inundated landscape.

547. Rome. Prima Porta. Villa of Livia. Garden.

541. Rome. Vatican Library. Odysseus in the Underworld.

542. Rome. Vatican Library. Odysseus in the land of the Cannibals.

545. Naples. Harbor.

549. Naples. Villa landscape.

548. Pompeii. House of M. Lucretius Fronto.
Villa landscapes.

551. New York. Metropolitan. Stele of a Galatian.

552. Alexandria. Warrior. Pompeii. Hunter.

550. Delos. Scenes from the Ludi.

553. Volo. Hediste stele. Pagasæ.

554. Volo. Stele of Stratonikos.

556. Marissa. Tomb I. End wall with decoration.

555. Volo. Stele. Woman and child.

558. Marissa. Tomb I. South wall. Animal frieze. Oryx and gryphon.

557. Marissa. Tomb I. South wall. Hunting scene.

561. Bari. Vase from Canosa.

560. Paris. Louvre. Polychrome Hellenistic vase.

564 Naples. Gnathian ware. Erotes with Quadriga.

565. Kertch. Distemper vase. Greek combating Amazon.

562. New York. Metropolitan. Vases from Hadra.

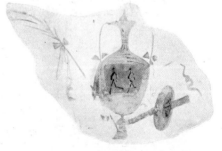

563. New York, Metropolitan, and Amsterdam. Polychrome vase-paintings from Hadra.

559. Marissa. Tomb I North wall.
Animal frieze. Man-headed lion and lynx.

566. Petrograd. Hermitage. Painted Sarcophagus.

568. Rome. Palazzo Conservatori. Scenes of war. Esquiline.

567. Naples. Glass Cinerary Urn. Pompeii.

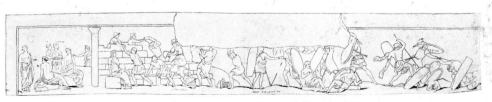

569. Rome. National. Founding of Lavinium, Alba Longa and Rome.

572. Naples. Punishment of Eros.

571. Pompeii. House of Epidius Sabinus. Wall-decoration.

570. Rome. National. Founding of Alba Longa.

573. Naples. Satyr and Mænad.
Satyr and boy with lyre.

574. Pompeii. Stabian Baths. Wall-decoration. Fourth Style. Restoration.

575. Pompeii. House of the Vettii. Cupids as goldsmiths; cupids in chariot-race.

576. Pompeii. House of the Vettii.
Erotes driving crabs and dolphins.

580. Naples. Warships.

577. Naples. Worship of Isis.

579. Naples. Battle between the Pompeians
and their neighbors of Nocera.

578. Naples. Bringing in the Wooden Horse.

581. Naples. Paris on Mount Ida.

582. Naples. Portrait of Terentius Neo.

3. Pompeii. House of the Vettii. Genius and Lares.

584. Pompeii. Street of Abundance. Venus drawn by elephants.

585. Pompeii. Street of Abundance.
Mercury emerging from his temple.

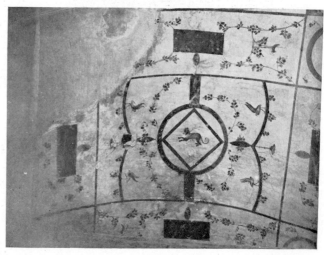

586. Rome. Columbarium of Pomponius Hylas. Ceiling-decoration.

587. Rome. Lateran. Orpheus and Eurydice.

593. Eton College.
Drawings of wall-decorations from Hadrian's Villa.

592. Rome. Villa Negroni. Wall-decoration.

591. London. British Museum. Mosaics. Preparations for sacrifices.

594. Rome. Tomb of the Nasonii.
Drawings of ceiling-decoration.

595. London. British Museum.
Tomb of the Nasonii. Shepherd and maiden.

596. London. British Museum. Tomb of the Nasonii. Rape of Persephone.

597. London. British Museum. Eros.

600. Rome. House in the Via de' Cerchi. Wall-decoration

599. Rome. Via Latina. Tomb of the Pancratii. Vault-decoration.

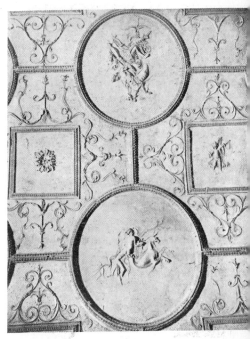

598. Rome. Via Latina. Tomb of the Valerii. Stucco vau

604. Kertch. Catacomb of Anthesterios.

601. Kertch. Vault discovered in 1895. Floral decoration.

603. Kertch. Vault discovered in 1872.
Wall. Incrustation, figure and floral decoration.

602. Kertch. Vault discovered in 1895.
Ceiling-decoration, Demeter, flowers, birds.

605. Palmyra. Tomb-Paintings.

609. Rome. Corsini Codex. Tombs ornamented with floral designs.

608. Dura-Salihiyeh. Wall of Bithnanaia. Chief Priest. Head

607. Dura-Salihiyeh. Wall of Bithnanaia. Priests at the left.

606. Dura-Salihiyeh. Wall with religious rites.

611. Uthina (Oudna) Mosaic. Scene on a farm.

10. Uthina (Oudna). Mosaic. Villa of the Laberii. Vintage scenes.

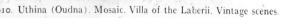

612. Timgad. Mosaic in carpet style. House of Sertius.

613. Timgad. Mosaic in carpet style.

615. Rome. Catacomb of Domitilla. Cupid and Psyche.

614. Timgad. Mosaic. Apollo and Daphne (?).

616. Rome. S. Costanza. Ring vault. Decoration.

618. Rome. S. Costanza. Ceiling-decoration. Floating figures

617. Rome. S. Costanza. Ring vault. Decoration.

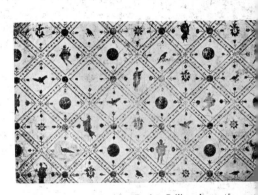

619. Pompeii. Stabian Baths. Ceiling-decoration.

620. Rome. Tomb, Viale Manzoni. Heads, Apostles Peter and Paul.

621. Rome. Tomb, Viale Manzoni.
Christ on the Mount.

622. Rome. Tomb, Viale Manzoni. Landscape.

623. Rome. Tomb of the Gens Octavia.
Hermes leading a child's soul to Hades.

625. Rome. Vatican. Cupids in chariot-race.

626. Rome. Vatican. Pasiphaë. Tor Marancio.

627. Rome. S. S. Giovanni e Paolo. Genii. Putti gathering grapes.

628. Rome. S. Sebastiano. Stucco decoration. Vine pattern.

624. Rome. Vatican. Procession of children, Ostia.

629. Rome. Vatican. Vergil MS. Portrait of Vergil.

630. Rome. Vatican. Vergil MS. Illustration of Georgi

Rome. Vatican. Vergil MS. Shepherds with flocks.

632. Rome. Vatican. Terence MS. Scene from the Adelphi.

634. Rome. Catacomb of St. Callixtus.
Five blessed mortals in Paradise.

633. Rome. Catacomb of St. Callixtus. Cubiculum of Okeanos.

635. Rome. Catacomb of Domitilla. Good Shepherd in landscape.

637 Tunis. Mosaic. Villa in N. Africa.

636. Kertch. Painted Sarcophagus. Encaustic painter at work.

638. Trier. Mosaic. Pavement of Monnus.

639. Tunis. Portrait of Vergil.

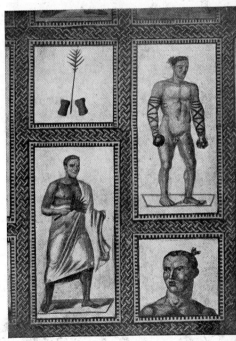

640. Rome. Lateran. Mosaic. Gladiators.